Law Enforcement and the History of Financial Market Manipulation

Law Enforcement and the History of Financial Market Manipulation

Jerry W. Markham

Routledge
Taylor & Francis Group
LONDON AND NEW YORK

First published 2014 by M.E. Sharpe

Published 2015 by Routledge
2 Park Square, Milton Park, Abingdon, Oxon OX14 4RN
711 Third Avenue, New York, NY 10017, USA

Routledge is an imprint of the Taylor & Francis Group, an informa business

Library of Congress Cataloging-in-Publication Data

Markham, Jerry W.
Law enforcement and the history of financial market manipulation / by Jerry W. Markham.
p. cm.
Includes bibliographical references and index.
ISBN 978-0-7656-3673-7 (hardcover)—ISBN 978-0-7656-3674-4 (pbk.)
1. Commodity futures—Law and legislation—United States—History—20th century.
2. Speculation—Law and legislation—United States—History—20th century.
3. Commodity exchanges—Law and legislation—United States—History—20th century.
4. Commodity futures—Law and legislation—United States. 5. Commodity exchanges—Law and legislation—United States. 6. Speculation—United States—History—20th century. I. Title.

KF1085.M378 2013
346.73'092—dc23 2013003419

ISBN 13: 9780765636744 (pbk)
ISBN 13: 9780765636737 (hbk)

Suppose that some rich speculators . . . should, in a cold winter, combine to purchase up all the wood, and refuse to sell it but at an extravagant advance, should we have no law to protect the poor against such oppression?

—*People v. Melvin*, 1 Yates Sel. Cas. 112, 122 (NY Sup. Ct. 1809)

* * *

Speculators look like normal people, except they smoke big fat Cuban cigars. They try to buy something (anything) in anticipation of selling at a profit after the price goes up. Or they sell first and try to buy later at a lower price. Some speculators focus on stocks, others on bonds, and still others on Super Bowl Tickets. (Ticket scalpers are speculators by another name.)

—William L. Silber, *Volcker: The Triumph of Persistence* (2012)

CONTENTS

LIST OF ABBREVIATIONS

33 Act	Securities Act of 1933
34 Act	Securities Exchange Act of 1934
ALJ	administrative law judge
CBOT	Chicago Board of Trade
CEA	Commodity Exchange Authority
CFMA	Commodity Futures Modernization Act of 2000
CFTC	Commodity Futures Trading Commission
CME	Chicago Mercantile Exchange
COL	Cost of Living Council
Commodity Exchange Act	Commodity Exchange Act of 1936
CPUC	California Public Utility Commission
CSE	consolidated supervised entity
Dodd-Frank Act	Dodd-Frank Wall Street Reform and Consumer Protection Act of 2010
ECM	exempt commercial market
EISA	Energy Independence and Security Act
EPAct	Energy Policy Act of 2005
FCM	futures commission merchant
Fed	Board of Governors of the Federal Reserve System
FERC	Federal Energy Regulatory Commission
FINRA	Financial Industry Regulatory Authority
FPA	Federal Power Act
FSA	Financial Services Authority
FTC	Federal Trade Commission
GAO	Government Accountability Office
GFA	Grain Futures Administration
ICE	Intercontinental Exchange
IIF	Institute of International Finance
IPO	initial public offering
NASD	National Association of Securities Dealers Inc.
NBBO	national best bid or offer
NFA	National Futures Association
NYMEX	New York Mercantile Exchange
NYSE	New York Stock Exchange
OTC	over-the-counter
PUMP Act	Prevent Unfair Manipulation of Prices Act
RICO	Racketeer Influenced and Corrupt Organizations Act

SEC	Securities and Exchange Commission
SPDC	significant price discovery contract
SPR	strategic petroleum reserve
SRO	self-regulatory organization
U.S.	United States
USDA	United States Department of Agriculture

INTRODUCTION

The cornerstone for this book was laid in a rather lengthy article that I published some twenty years ago in the *Yale Journal on Regulation*. The title of that article, "Manipulation of Commodity Futures Prices—The Unprosecutable Crime,"[1] reflected its focus on the singular lack of success by the federal government in prosecuting commodity price manipulations. That article was followed over the next several years by two coauthored pieces that tracked the government's continuing unsuccessful efforts to make manipulation a more prosecutable crime.[2]

This book broadens the scope of those now outdated articles by including an examination of government efforts to prevent price manipulations in the stock markets. It also examines more recent commodity price manipulations, including claims that several international banks manipulated the Libor interest rate during the financial crisis in 2008. Those rates affected interest payments on an estimated $300 trillion in loans worldwide. Also addressed are continuing widespread concerns over energy price speculation that have riled consumers and populist politicians for more than a decade. Another topic considered is the ongoing debate over the market effects of high-frequency electronic traders in both the stock and commodity markets.

This book begins by tracing the history of governmental efforts to curb price manipulations back to ancient times. Common law prohibitions on "engrossing," "regrating," and "forestalling—" which sought to prevent middlemen from profiting in commodity markets—proved unworkable and economically undesirable. Nevertheless, the widespread manipulation of agricultural prices after the Civil War resulted in the development of a populist movement, which condemned speculators and sought their regulation.

The populists initially did not gain much traction in Congress, but were able to pass legislation prohibiting commodity market manipulation in the wake of sharp commodity price fluctuations that followed World War I. That statute proved to be ineffective, and commodity price manipulations continued unabated.

The stock market crash of 1929 led to another populist movement that blamed speculators for that crash and the ensuing Great Depression. Those concerns led to the enactment of the Securities Exchange Act of 1934 (34 Act). It prohibited the manipulation of stock prices and created the Securities and Exchange Commission (SEC) to enforce that authority.

The politicians of the New Deal also focused their attention on speculators in the commodity markets, who were blamed for historical low prices in the agriculture sector. Congress responded by replacing the existing antimanipulation legislation covering the commodity markets with the Commodity Exchange Act of 1936.

The Commodity Exchange Authority (CEA), a small bureau in the Department of Agriculture,

1. Jerry W. Markham, *Manipulation of Commodity Futures Prices—The Unprosecutable Crime*, 8 YALE J. ON REG. 281 (1991).

2. Jerry W. Markham & Lawrence H. Hunt Jr., *The California Energy Crisis—Enron's Gaming of Governor Gray's Imperfect Market*, 24 FUT. & DERV. L. REP. 1 (2004); Jerry W. Markham, Lawrence H. Hunt Jr. & Michael S. Sackheim, *Market Manipulation—From Star Chamber to Lone Star*, 23 FUT. & DERV. L. REP. 7 (2003).

initially administered that legislation. However, it proved ineffective and was replaced in 1975 by the Commodity Futures Trading Commission (CFTC). The creation of the CFTC was the result of concerns, which were never proved, that large grain firms had massively manipulated the grain markets, wreaking havoc on consumer grocery prices. The CFTC, however, proved even less successful than its predecessor in stopping price manipulations. Indeed, the CFTC has won only one adjudicated manipulation case in its thirty-eight-year history.

Concern over energy price manipulations in this century led to a change in theory by the CFTC in its prosecutions for manipulation. That change proved to be very successful in obtaining large settlements from energy trading firms. However, it pretty much failed when cases were actually adjudicated in the courts. In response to that frustration, and due to continuing concerns over high gasoline prices, Congress increased the number of law enforcement agencies tasked with attacking energy price manipulations.

The Federal Energy Regulatory Commission (FERC) and the Federal Trade Commission (FTC) were brought into the battle by the grant of new antimanipulation powers that were made applicable to energy traders. In granting that authority to FERC and the FTC, Congress borrowed antimanipulation language from Section 10(b) in the Securities Exchange Act of 1934, which the SEC had long used to attack stock market price manipulations. The Dodd-Frank Wall Street Reform and Consumer Protection Act of 2010 incorporated that same language for use by the CFTC in its future prosecutions of commodity price manipulations. Although Congress believed that this new legislation would ease the burden of the government in proving of manipulation, closer analysis suggests that this probably will not be the case. Even with these expanded powers, there remain several daunting hurdles to successful prosecutions of price manipulators.

Further concerns over manipulation have been raised in recent years with the advent of high-frequency traders that now dominate trading volumes in both the stock and commodity markets. The use of "flash trades" by those traders and other algorithmic trading practices have given rise to concerns that these highly sophisticated traders are taking unfair advantage of more traditional market participants. The SEC and CFTC are now considering rules to curb those traders, although any proof of economic harm from their trading is scarce and is in conflict with other studies.

After addressing that history, this book proposes an alternative to the present, difficult-to-prove "fraud-based" manipulation tests used by the courts in SEC cases and the manipulation tests applied by the courts in CFTC cases. This alternative would take advantage of the ongoing transformation of open outcry stock and commodity markets into electronic trading platforms. Manipulative practices can now be excluded by developing computer algorithms that deny entry of manipulative or other problematic orders from electronic trading platforms. Such rules would provide clear guidelines for traders and avoid the uncertainties of what may constitute price manipulation. This book seeks to provide a road map for such an effort.

ACKNOWLEDGMENTS

I wish to thank Elizabeth Peiffer, who provided much helpful research on historical sources that were difficult to obtain. Rigers Giyshi, a senior research fellow at Florida International University College of Law, also provided valuable assistance. I am also grateful to Norma Ruiz, the librarian at the Commodity Futures Trading Commission, for making that agency's excellent collection on the commodity futures industry available to me.

Law Enforcement and the History of Financial Market Manipulation

1

MANIPULATION

Some History

1:1 MANIPULATION: A PRIMER

Price manipulation over the centuries has been conducted through several stratagems, which because of their complexity and scope, are confusing to the uninitiated. The following is a brief primer that is intended as a guide in understanding how stock and commodity market price manipulations have been carried out historically and how traders seek to profit from such operations. It will also clarify the nomenclature—some say the argot—of the trading practices and instruments used in price manipulations.

In their most extreme form, price manipulations involve the "corner." This is an operation in which the manipulator buys up all available supplies of a commodity in order to dictate prices to would-be purchasers who need the commodity in their operations. Such cornering operations are rarely successful. This is because the purchases needed to carry out the corner drive prices up, but once the corner is completed the manipulator, who usually has no need for them, must sell the supplies. Those sales will drive prices down, undercutting the manipulator's profits.

Corners may also be frustrated when traders on the other side of the market take desperate measures to acquire the commodity needed to satisfy their delivery obligations to the party "running" the corner. Those actions may include shipping supplies from distant points, even though such purchases would not normally be economical. Only in rare cases, and there are some, will the manipulator be able to hold prices at the inflated level caused by the corner. Yet, even if ultimately unsuccessful, these cornering operations are highly disruptive to the efficient operation of the affected markets as prices gyrate back and forth.

A lesser form of the corner is the "squeeze." In such operations, the manipulator gains control of a substantial portion of the available supplies of a particular commodity, but not all. This creates a shortage for other purchasers, and the manipulator is able to squeeze prices higher because of the reduction in supply created by the squeeze operations. A squeeze is considered to have a better chance of success than a corner because the manipulator is not acquiring the entire supply of the commodity. That limitation means that the price change may not be so dramatic as to induce traders on the opposite side of the market to take desperate measures in order to defeat the manipulation.

Of course, the squeezer faces a problem similar to that of a party carrying out a corner—how do you bury the body? The squeezer must get rid of the stocks accumulated in order to carry out the squeeze, which will cause prices to fall and undercut the profits of the operation.

Corners and squeezes are considered "market power" manipulations that generally require substantial resources to carry out. They demand large purchases of the underlying commodity and are usually connected with operations in derivative markets. For example, a particularly popular tool for carrying out commodity price manipulations is the "futures contract," which is a derivative contract traded on licensed contract markets, such as the Chicago Mercantile Exchange.

The parties to a futures contract agree to make and take delivery on a particular date in the future. Historically, most traders did not hold their futures contracts for delivery. Instead, they offset their obligations on the exchange before the delivery date, resulting in a cash settlement of the price difference that occurred between the date of the entry into the futures contract and the date it was offset. The parties to the futures contract will experience a profit or loss depending on the change in price direction and whether they are "long" (the party agreeing to buy the commodity) or "short" (the party agreeing to sell the product). The long will profit when prices go up and lose when prices go down. The converse is true for the short.[1]

Futures contracts provide a great deal of leverage that multiplies gains and losses because payment for the delivery is deferred until the delivery date. The parties are thus required to post only a small amount at the inception of the contract to "margin" or secure their performance on the delivery date.[2]

---

1. In addressing a spectacular manipulation of the potato market, the Supreme Court described the development of the futures contract as follows:

> When buyers and sellers entered into contracts for the future delivery of an agricultural product, they arrived at an agreed price on the basis of their judgment about expected market conditions at the time of delivery. Because the weather and other imponderables affected supply and demand, normally the market price would fluctuate before the contract was performed. A declining market meant that the executory agreement was more valuable to the seller than the commodity covered by the contract; conversely, in a rising market the executory contract had a special value for the buyer, who not only was assured of delivery of the commodity but also could derive a profit from the price increase.
>
> The opportunity to make a profit as a result of fluctuations in the market price of commodities covered by contracts for future delivery motivated speculators to engage in the practice of buying and selling "futures contracts." A speculator who owned no present interest in a commodity but anticipated a price decline might agree to a future sale at the current market price, intending to purchase the commodity at a reduced price on or before the delivery date. A "short" sale of that kind would result in a loss if the price went up instead of down. On the other hand, a price increase would produce a gain for a "long" speculator who had acquired a contract to purchase the same commodity with no intent to take delivery but merely for the purpose of reselling the futures contract at an enhanced price.
>
> In the 19th century the practice of trading in futures contracts led to the development of recognized exchanges or boards of trade. At such exchanges standardized agreements covering specific quantities of graded agricultural commodities to be delivered during specified months in the future were bought and sold pursuant to rules developed by the traders themselves. Necessarily the commodities subject to such contracts were fungible. For an active market in the contracts to develop, it also was essential that the contracts themselves be fungible. The exchanges therefore developed standard terms describing the quantity and quality of the commodity, the time and place of delivery, and the method of payment; the only variable was price. The purchase or sale of a futures contract on an exchange is therefore motivated by a single factor—the opportunity to make a profit (or to minimize the risk of loss) from a change in the market price.

Merrill Lynch, Pierce, Fenner & Smith Inc. v. Curran, 456 U.S. 353, 357-359 (1982) (footnotes omitted).

2. Margin requirements for commodity futures contain two distinctive elements. First, "initial" margin is required for each contract when it is initially executed. This amount is expressed as a small portion of the notional value of the futures contract. Initial margin is set by the exchange based on an assessment of the potential that a commodity price might change before a clearing firm is able to liquidate the account of a defaulting customer. The minimum amount on initial margin that must be posted by a customer is set by exchange rules, but clearing firms may charge more than those minimums when deemed necessary for their own protection. Second, in addition to initial margin, "variation" margin payments are required to be paid

Historically, a corner would be carried out using futures contracts in the following fashion. The manipulator would buy up all or nearly all of the warehouse receipts available for delivery of the commodity on a particular futures contract. At the same time, the trader acquires a dominant long position in the futures contract. For example, in earlier years, a popular corner attempt was for a trader to acquire a dominant long position in the May wheat futures contract on the Chicago Board of Trade (CBOT). The trader would also buy up the stocks of the commodity available for delivery in Chicago, which is where delivery on the futures contracts was required to be made through certificated receipts from local warehouses approved by the CBOT.

As the delivery time approached, the short sellers of May wheat futures contracts would try to liquidate their contracts on the CBOT. They would then discover that the manipulator controlled that market and could dictate the price of their liquidation, at an artificial price set by the manipulator. Alternatively, the shorts could deliver on their futures contracts by buying warehouse receipts covering the actual cash commodity.

The shorts would then discover that the long manipulator controlled those stocks and could still dictate prices to the purchasers. The shorts sometimes resorted to desperate measures to defeat such corners, such as increasing available supplies by shipping wheat into Chicago from Canada. Those efforts were costly, however, and would disrupt the Chicago wheat market because consumers did not need more wheat in Chicago.

Even if the corner were not defeated, the manipulator would be left with large stocks of wheat, which typically would drop in value to their premanipulation price when the manipulator tried to sell the grain. As will be described later in this chapter, the perpetrators of corners came up with various schemes to avoid the problem of burying the corpse of the accumulated commodity in a way that would preserve their profits. Squeezes were carried out in a similar fashion.[3]

Historically, another derivative instrument that has been used for price manipulations in a similar manner is the "option" contract (previously called "privileges"). In the case of an American "call" option, the purchaser is given the right, but not the obligation, to buy a specified amount of a commodity or stock of a corporation from the writer of the option at an agreed-upon price (the "strike" price) for a stated period of time. A "put" option gives the buyer the right to sell the stock to the option writer at an agreed-upon price. In both instances, the purchaser of the option pays the writer a "premium" for these rights.[4]

---

by customers. This is an additional deposit of money required to reflect losses incurred by the customers from adverse price changes on their open commodity futures positions. Variation margin requirements are computed through a "mark to market" system, that is, the market value of the commodity is computed daily to determine if its value has changed. The purchaser or seller experiencing a theoretical loss based on changed market prices is required to post an additional amount equivalent to that loss. Jerry W. Markham, *Federal Regulation of Margin in the Commodity Futures Industry—History and Theory*, 64 Temp. L. Rev. 59, 63-65 (1991). *See also*, V Federal Trade Commission, Report on the Grain Trade 156 (1921) (describing margin requirements for futures contracts).

3. As one court has noted:

> a "squeeze" has been defined as a type of manipulation, generally occurring when the long holder does not have direct control over the cash crop, as in a "corner." A prototypical squeeze occurs when a trader attains a dominant long position and can force shorts facing an inadequate cash supply to cover their positions at unfair prices. The shorts are "squeezed" into settling their holdings with the dominant long at above-market prices as the delivery date approaches.

Frey v. CFTC, 931 F.2d 1171, 1175 (7th Cir. 1990).

4. *See* Jerry W. Markham and David J. Gilberg, *Stock and Commodity Options—Two Regulatory Approaches and Their Conflicts*, 47 Albany L. Rev. 741-791 (1983) (describing option contracts and abuses).

Like the futures contract, the option contract is useful in carrying out a manipulation because it provides leverage to the trader. The option purchaser can make a large profit from price changes affecting the underlying commodity because the purchaser pays only a "premium" for the option right. That premium payment is only a small percentage of the cost that would be required to actually purchase the stock or commodity underlying the option. The premium will be lost if there is no profit on the contract. A profit will be experienced if the underlying commodity increases in value in an amount sufficient to recoup the premium upon the exercise or liquidation of the option.

A relative newcomer to the manipulation arena is the "swap" contract. The simpler form of a swap has been described as follows:

> The "plain-vanilla" interest rate swap, the simplest and most common type of swap contract, obligates one counterparty to make payments equal to the interest which would accrue on an agreed hypothetical principal amount ("notional amount"), during a given period, at a specified fixed interest rate. The other counterparty must pay an amount equal to the interest which would accrue on the same notional amount, during the same period, but at a floating interest rate. If the fixed rate paid by the first counterparty exceeds the floating rate paid by the second counterparty, then the first counter-party must pay an amount equal to the difference between the two rates multiplied by the notional amount, for the specified interval. Conversely, if the floating rate paid by the second counterparty exceeds the fixed rate paid by the first counterparty, the fixed-rate payor receives payment. The agreed hypothetical or "notional" amount provides the basis for calculating payment obligations, but does not change hands.[5]

Other swaps are more complicated. A "total return" swap, for example, calls for exchange of payments based on the value of a particular stock and a specified interest rate.[6] Other swaps may

---

5. Thrifty Oil Co. v. Bank of Am. Nat'l Trust & Sav. Ass'n, 310 F.3d 1188, 1191-1192 (9th Cir. 2002) (footnote omitted). The court gave the following example of such a swap:

> suppose Counterparties A and B enter into a five-year interest rate swap with the following characteristics: (1) Counterparty A agrees to pay a floating interest rate equal to LIBOR, the London Interbank Offered Rate; (2) Counter-party B agrees to pay a 10% fixed interest rate; (3) both counterparties base their payments on a $ 1 million notional amount and agree to make payments semiannually. If LIBOR is 9% upon commencement of the first payment period, Counterparty B must pay A: (10%-9%) * $ 1 million * (.5) = $5,000. These net payments vary as LIBOR fluctuates and continue every six months for the term of the swap. If interest rates rise, the position of Counterparty B, the fixed-rate payor, improves because the payments it receives increase. For example, if LIBOR rises to 11% at the beginning of the next payment period, Counterparty B receives a net payment of $5,000 from A. Conversely, the position of Counterparty A, the floating-rate payor, improves when interest rates fall. The party whose position retains positive value under the swap is considered "in the money" while a party with negative value is considered "out of the money." . . . [T]he $1 million notional amount never changes hands.

Id.

6. As described by one court:

> Cash-settled total-return equity swaps. Total-return swaps are contracts in which parties agree to exchange sums equivalent to the income streams produced by specified assets. Total-return equity swaps involve an exchange of the income stream from: (1) a specified number of shares in a designated company's stock, and (2) a specified interest rate on a specified principal amount. The party that receives the stock-based return is styled the "long" party. The party that receives

exchange a fixed price for a floating market price of a commodity such as crude oil. A credit default swap may be used as credit protection device that exchanges a set value for a debt security upon a default or other credit event.[7]

Swaps provide leverage to traders because only the difference on the notional amount is exchanged. "Synthetic" swaps do not require the participants to have any ownership in the underlying notional. That leverage makes swap contracts a popular tool for speculation, and they may affect prices. For example, a swap trader could acquire a dominant position in the underlying item that is the subject of the swap, allowing the manipulator to squeeze the opposite party in the swap.

A primer on manipulation also needs some consideration of the identity of traders who engage in such operations. For decades, the principal culprits were floor traders on the floors of the commodity futures exchanges in Chicago and New York. However, their role has been much diminished by the evolution of floor trading into electronic trading platforms. The floor traders no longer have time and place advantages that allow them to conspire with, and against, each other to manipulate markets. Another traditional actor was the grain and other commodity firms that had the substantial resources to conduct large-scale market power manipulations. They have been supplanted in recent years by large energy firms, hedge funds, and other professional traders.

Smaller traders should not be written off entirely as manipulators. They can still manipulate prices through various fraudulent practices, even though their market power is limited. For example, false reports and rumors may be used by smaller traders in illiquid markets to create the mistaken belief that market fundamentals are changing. Those rumors are intended to stampede other traders into buying or selling at artificial prices that will benefit the rumormonger's position in the affected stock or commodity. Numerous such schemes were carried out over the Internet by pumping up the value of an illiquid stock through false or misleading claims. The manipulators would then dump their previously purchased stock into the market at the inflated price. Such "pump-and-dump" schemes are simplistic but often effective.

Another form of market manipulation by fraud is rigged trades such as "wash" trades, in which the trader simultaneously buys and sells the same commodity at an artificial price. The trader is at no real risk in such a transaction, and the trade only serves to give a false appearance of bona

---

> the interest-based return is styled the "short" party. These contracts do not transfer title to the underlying assets or require that either party actually own them. Rather, in a total-return equity swap, the long party periodically pays the short party a sum calculated by applying an agreed-upon interest rate to an agreed-upon notional amount of principal, as if the long party had borrowed that amount of money from the short party. Meanwhile, the short party periodically pays the long party a sum equivalent to the return to a shareholder in a specified company—the increased value of the shares, if any, plus income from the shares—as if the long party owned actual shares in that company.
>
> As a result, the financial return to a long party in a total-return equity swap is roughly equivalent to the return when borrowed capital is used to purchase shares in the referenced company. Long swap positions can, therefore, be attractive to parties that seek to increase the leverage of their holdings without actually buying the shares. The short party's financial return, in turn, is equivalent to the return to someone who sold short and then lent out the proceeds from that sale. However, because of the inherent risks in short-equity positions—share value can be more volatile than interest rates—persons holding short positions in total-return equity swaps will usually choose to purchase equivalent numbers of shares to hedge their short exposure.

CSX Corp. v. Children's Inv. Fund Mgmt. (UK) LLP, 654 F.3d 276, 279-280 (2d Cir. 2011).

7. Wachovia Bank, N.A. v. VCG Special Opportunities Master Fund, Ltd., 661 F.3d 164, 167-168 (2d Cir. 2011), *cert. denied*, --- U.S. --- (2012) (describing a credit default swap).

fide market activity. This type of manipulation may not require the manipulator to have strong market power, especially in thinly traded illiquid markets.

Rigged trading manipulations are generally only "minimanipulations" because the trader generally moves prices only in small amounts and these manipulations are usually short in duration. Rigged trading manipulations are carried out for a number of reasons. For example, traders might want to "paint the tape" or "bang the close" in order to set the daily closing or settlement price of a commodity or stock at a lower level. One reason for such a manipulation is that traders are seeking to reduce their margin requirements, which may be set by the exchange based on the closing or settlement price.

Another reason for a rigged trading manipulation is to set the price for a related position in the stock or commodity, a "reference price manipulation." For example, a trader may have entered into a contract with a counterparty that calls for the purchase of a specified amount of crude oil on a future date. The price of that crude oil is to be determined on the date of delivery by reference to the closing price of a futures contract traded on a commodity exchange. Selling parties in such contracts may seek to "bang the close" of the futures contract in order to set a higher price for the crude oil they are selling to the counterparty.

A primer on manipulation also requires a discussion of the "speculator," which is someone who is betting that prices will move in a particular direction and seeks to profit from that change. Speculators are widely viewed with hostility and often blamed for driving prices up or down during periods of market volatility. Although populist politicians claim that all speculators are price manipulators, that is not actually the case. In fact, speculation is not inherently bad and can even be beneficial to firms needing to "hedge" against adverse price changes. As the Supreme Court noted with respect to speculative trading in futures contracts in the context of a manipulation claim:

> The advent of speculation in futures markets produced well-recognized benefits for producers and processors of agricultural commodities. A farmer who takes a "short" position in the futures market is protected against a price decline; a processor who takes a "long" position is protected against a price increase. Such "hedging" is facilitated by the availability of speculators willing to assume the market risk that the hedging farmer or processor wants to avoid. The speculators' participation in the market substantially enlarges the number of potential buyers and sellers of executory contracts and therefore makes it easier for farmers and processors to make firm commitments for future delivery at a fixed price. The liquidity of a futures contract, upon which hedging depends, is directly related to the amount of speculation that takes place.[8]

Nevertheless, hostility toward speculation has long given rise to a tug of war between those who defend it as adding to market efficiency and those who view it as destructive gambling. The compromise reached in Congress between these widely divergent views has been to prohibit "manipulation" and something called "excessive speculation," which is equated with manipulation. History shows that this compromise is unworkable because Congress, the courts, regulators, and commentators have been unable to agree on a definition of what should be condemned under that rubric.

Finally, no primer on manipulation would be complete without a discussion of the long-running and ongoing debates over "short" sales, which many claim are used to manipulate stock or commodity prices downward. These trades involve the sale of a commodity or financial instrument that the seller does not own. The seller hopes that the price of the commodity or stock will decline before delivery to the buyer is required. In the event of a price decline, the short seller can purchase

8. Merrill Lynch, Pierce, Fenner & Smith Inc. v. Curran, 456 U.S. 353, 359 (1982).

the stock or commodity at the lower price, deliver it to the buyer, and profit on the difference between the purchase and sale price. Conversely, of course, if prices increase, the short will have to purchase the stock or commodity at a higher price and sell it for less, thus taking a loss.

Like other forms of speculation, short sales are not inherently manipulative. Indeed, short sales are considered by many economists to be useful in ensuring better price discovery and market efficiency. Short sales may also be used to hedge against price declines on a stock or commodity owned by the trader. Nevertheless, there is much concern that short sales are abusive when they seek to crash a market by continually selling down at lower prices.

Those concerns were expressed most recently during the financial crisis in 2008, when the stock prices of financial services firms plunged and short sales were restricted by the government. A debate arises under such circumstances whether the short seller is simply following the market or whether the short sales drove or intensified the decline. Short sales can be abused when they are coupled with false rumors that are intended to depress prices so that the short can buy in at a lower, more profitable price. Manipulative short sale practices also evidence the fact that traders may try to manipulate market prices both up and down. Indeed, it has not been unusual for a trader to manipulate the market up and then switch positions and try to manipulate it downward through short sales abuses.

1:2 ANCIENT HISTORY

History is strewn with unsuccessful efforts by governments and organized religions to proscribe speculation and price manipulation and to control commodity prices. "In 483 AD, Roman Emperor Zeno issued a decree to the Praetorian Prefect of Constantinople forbidding the manipulation of commodity markets. The Muslim Code also forbade the buying of commodities intended for markets upon the roads outside of towns."[9] "From its beginning in the seventh century, Islam forbade speculative activity (*gharar*) as one of its principles."[10] Hoarding was prohibited under Talmudic law, as were excessive profits by merchants.

A United Nations (UN) report further describes some of these ancient efforts to prevent price manipulations. It notes that around 2350 BC "the rulers of Egypt took control of grain management; by the reign of Ptolemy I in 306 BC, they held ownership of supply, land and granaries, dictating that all [grain] prices were fixed by fiat."[11] This report also notes that the Code of Hammurabi set wages in terms of amounts of grain and that the ancient city-state of Athens fixed grain prices. In 386 BC, a group of Athenian grain merchants was tried for the capital crime of "hoarding and collusion."[12]

As described in the preceding section, the classic concept of manipulation involved a corner or squeeze. Such practices have been traced back to ancient Greece. Aristotle thus notes that around 300 BC one Thales acquired control of all the olive presses in Thios and Miletus through option contracts that gave him the right to control the presses and which he secured with borrowed funds. A large harvest occurred that year and Thales exercised the options and gained control of the presses. He was then able to literally "squeeze" the producers for higher prices in order to gain

9. M. Van Smith, *Preventing the Manipulation of Commodity Futures Markets: To Deliver or Not to Deliver?* 32 HASTINGS L.J. 1569, 1571 (1980-1981) (footnotes and citations omitted).

10. Food and Agriculture Organization of the United Nations (ed. Adam Prakash), *Safeguarding Food Security in Volatile Global Markets* (2011) (citations omitted), http://www.fao.org/docrep/013/i2107e/i2107e13.pdf (accessed September 14, 2011).

11. *Id.*

12. *Id.*

access to his presses.[13] Aristotle also reported on the case of a Sicilian merchant who bought all of the output of an iron mine and was able to corner the market in that ore.[14]

Ancient Rome used *frumentariae leges* (state control of the grain market) to preclude speculation and control grain prices.[15] In China, the Zhou dynasty set grain prices during the first millennium BC. "In fourth century BC India, the *Arthasastra* or 'handbook for princes' instructed that only proper authorities should undertake grain collection and that profit margins charged by merchants be strictly capped."[16] The government of Venice prohibited manipulation by false reports in the fourteenth century.[17]

"The earliest attempts in English Law to regulate trade are also to be found in prohibitions against forestalling, regrating and engrossing."[18] "Regrating" and "forestalling" were also prohibited by Roman law because people who used such speculative practices were believed to interfere with grain supplies, and a check was "put upon their avarice both by imperial instructions and by enactments. . . . The penalties were banishment from trading or relegation to an island for merchants and forced labor for those of the 'lower orders.'"[19]

In England, a *forestaller* was a speculator who sought to profit by purchasing goods on their way to a market, "or who attempted by any means to enhance the price of such goods, or who persuaded persons not to come to the market or not to bring goods to market." A *regrator* was a speculator who bought grain in one market and sold it in another market located within a radius of four miles. An *engrosser* was a speculator who bought up commodities for resale.[20]

Blackstone noted that regrating was viewed as offensive because it enhanced the price of provisions, "as every successive seller must have successive profit." Engrossing also "must of course be injurious to the public, by putting it into the power of one or two rich men to raise the price of provisions at their own discretion."[21]

"[I]n the early 1260s England experienced dramatic fluctuations in the prices of necessities resulting in many deaths from starvation. In response, King Henry III promulgated a statute in 1266 entitled

---

13. I Jerry W. Markham, A Financial History of the United States, From Christopher Columbus to the Robber Barons (1492-1900) 6 (2002).

14. James E. Boyle, Speculation and the Chicago Board of Trade 144 (1920).

15. Food and Agriculture Organization of the United Nations (ed. Adam Prakash), *Safeguarding Food Security in Volatile Global Markets* (2011) (citations omitted), http://www.fao.org/docrep/013/i2107e/i2107e13.pdf (accessed September 14, 2011).

16. *Id.*

17. I Jerry W. Markham, A Financial History of the United States, From Christopher Columbus to the Robber Barons (1492-1900) 13 (2002).

18. Wilson Herbruck, *Forestalling, Regrating and Engrossing*, 257 Mich L. Rev. 365 (1928-1929). *See, e.g.*, Proclamations Against Forestallers and Regraters of Grain (1529); Proclamation Enforcing Statutes Against Regraters, Forestallers, and Engrossers (1551). *See also*, Jerry W. Markham, Lawrence H. Hunt Jr. & Michael S. Sackheim, *Market Manipulation—From Star Chamber to Lone Star*, 23 Fut. & Derv. L. Rep. 7 (2003) (describing these medieval concerns with speculators).

19. Norman T. Braslow, *The Recognition and Enforcement of Common Law Punitive Damages in A Civil Law System: Some Reflections on the Japanese Experience*, 16 Ariz. J. Int'l & Comp. L. 341-342, n. 287 (citations omitted).

20. William S. Holdsworth, A History of English Law 375 (2d ed. 1937).

21. IV William Blackstone, Commentaries on the Law 124 (9th ed.). This meant that

> English merchants were not to forestall wine in Gascony, or buy it up before the vintage, and the time of the common passages; nor were they to charge high for the wine on the pretense that they ran risks. . . . remuneration for risk was obviously regarded as a mere excuse for arbitrary demands on the part of the merchant, and these were not to be permitted at all.

G. Wright Hoffman, *Governmental Regulation of Exchanges*, 155 Annals of the American Academy of Political and Social Science 39, 40 (1931).

'A Statute of the Pillory and Tumbirel, and of the Assize of Bread and Ale,' which fixed the prices of various commodities and subjected forestallers to the town pillory. In 1306 King Edward I oversaw the enactment of a similar law to punish those whose deceptive practices inflated prices to the public."[22]

These "crimes" of speculation were taken seriously in England and were enforced by the infamous Court of the Star Chamber, which operated in secrecy and from which there was no appeal from its sometimes arbitrary decisions.[23] "Indeed, for a ten-year period in the fourteenth century, forestalling was punishable by death, although it appears that no one was ever actually executed."[24] Efforts by the Star Chamber to order corn to be brought to the market at set prices were found to have actually worsened shortages by increasing the temptation to ship grain where higher prices could be obtained.[25]

These prohibitions and price controls proved to be unworkable and unenforceable. As one court later noted: "[t]he Englishmen of the 1400's blindly groping for some means of protecting themselves from unconscionable traders, adopted what now seems the absurd device of prohibiting entirely the buying and selling of certain articles for profit."[26]

The English government gradually awakened to the fact that speculators had an important role to play in pricing commodities.[27] The despised speculators of medieval and more ancient days gave way to recognition that such persons fulfill important economic functions in distributing commodities by more efficiently pricing the commodity and through rationing that results from higher prices. In 1776, Adam Smith wrote in *The Wealth of Nations* that "popular fear of engrossing and forestalling may be compared to the popular terrors and suspicions of witchcraft."[28]

The English prohibition against regrating was repealed in 1772.[29] By 1844, Parliament had repealed its prohibitions on forestalling and engrossing.[30] The repeal did not apply to "to the offence

---

22. Justin Toby McDonald, *Note: An Historical Perspective to the Corporate Bar Provisions of the Securities Enforcement Remedies and Penny Stock Reform Act of 1990*, 49 WASH. & LEE L. REV. 987, 1008 (1992).

23. *Reports of Cases of the Star Chamber and High Commission* 43 (1886). *See also,* XXIII *The Publications of the Selden Society, Court of the Star Chamber* 290 (1908) (regrating of butter and cheese).

24. Herbert Hovenkamp, *The Law of Vertical Integration and the Business Firm: 1880-1960*, 95 IOWA L. REV. 863, 878 (2010) (footnote and citation omitted).

25. II *The Publications of the Selden Society, Select Cases Before the King's Council in the Star Chamber (A.D. 1509-1544)* 290 (1908). *See also,* I *Selden Society, Select Cases Concerning the Law Merchant (A.D. 1270-1638)* 92-93 (1908) (William Kemp of Bury St. Edmunds is accused of being a "forestaller of woolfells, for that he lies in wait and intercepts such wares and merchandise at the end of the vill and elsewhere outside the fair . . .").

26. State v. Duluth Board of Trade, 121 N.W. 395, 403 (Minn. 1909).

27. In France manipulation was linked to speculation. Hubert de Vauplane and Odile Simart, *The Concept of Securities Manipulation and Its Foundations in France and the USA*, 23 BROOL. J. INT'L L. 203, 207 (1997).

28. ADAM SMITH, AN INQUIRY INTO THE NATURE AND CAUSES OF THE WEALTH OF NATIONS 229 (Great Books ed. 1952) (1st ed. 1776).

29. Hebert Hovenkamp, *The Antitrust Movement and the Rise of Industrial Organizations*, 68 TEX. L. REV. 105, 155 (1989).

30. It has been noted with respect to those English laws that

> The ancient common law of this country, and the statutes with reference to the acts known as badgering, forestalling, regrating, and engrossing, indicated the mind of the Legislature and of the judges that certain large operations in goods which interfered with the more ordinary course of trade were injurious to the public; they were held criminal accordingly. But early in the reign of George III the mind of the Legislature showed symptoms of change in this matter, and the penal statutes were repealed (12 Geo. III, c. 71), and the common law was left to its unaided operation. This repealing statute contains, in the preamble, the statement that it had been found by experience that the restraint laid by several statutes upon the dealing in corn, meal, flour,

of knowingly and fraudulently spreading or conspiring to spread any false rumour with intent to enhance or decry the price of any goods or merchandise."[31] This type of offense was exemplified by a ruling issued in 1814 by the English courts in *The King v. De Berenger*.[32] There, the court upheld an indictment charging that defendants manipulated the price of government securities by spreading false rumors that Napoleon Bonaparte had been killed and that a peace treaty would shortly end the war between France and England.

The prohibitions on forestalling, regrating, and engrossing found their way to the American colonies, but were not widely applied. The Carolinas passed a statute in 1669 prohibiting engrossing whereby middlemen bought goods and sold them at unreasonable rates.[33] Selling on commission was viewed as a violation of this statute, but permanent shops were exempted. A little over a century later, Pennsylvania passed "An Act to Prevent Forestalling and Regrating, and to Encourage Fair Dealing."[34]

"Although a few states passed regrating laws that were enforced for a short time, statutes condemning regrating never took hold in the United States."[35] As the Supreme Court noted, as the result of the "development of more accurate economic conceptions and the changes in conditions of society, it came to be recognized that the acts prohibited by the engrossing, forestalling, etc., statutes did not have the harmful tendency which they were presumed to have when the legislation concerning them was enacted, and therefore did not justify the presumption which had previously been deduced from them, but, on the contrary, such acts tended to fructify and develop trade."[36] Nevertheless, a few remnants of these prohibitions remain. Several states passed statutes allowing city councils to prohibit forestalling of agricultural goods sold in city markets. The District of Columbia, for example, passed such a prohibition in 1802.[37] As late as 1908, the Tennessee Supreme Court held that a city council was authorized under such a statute to prohibit hawking farm products from wagons unless the seller was the producer of the goods.[38] Most such ordinances

---

> cattle, and sundry other sorts of victuals, by preventing a free trade in the said commodities, had a tendency to discourage the growth and to enhance the price of the same. This statement is very noteworthy. It contains a confession of failure in the past; the indication of a new policy for the future. This new policy has been more clearly declared and acted upon in the present reign, for the Legislature has by 7 and 8 Vict. c. 24, altered the common law by utterly abolishing the several offenses of badgering, engrossing, forestalling, and regrating. At the same time, this repeal was accompanied by a proviso that nothing in the act contained should apply to the offense of knowingly and fraudulently spreading or conspiring to spread any false rumor with intent to enhance or decry the price of any goods or merchandise, or to the offense of preventing or endeavoring to prevent by force or threats any goods, wares, or merchandise being brought to any fair or market, but that every such offense might be punished as if this act had not been made.

Denver Jobber's Ass'n v. People ex rel. Dickson, 122 P. 404 (Colo. 1912).

31. The Mogul Steamship Ltd. v. McGretor, Gow & Co., 23 Q.B.D. 598 (1889).

32. The King v. De Berenger, 105 Eng. Rep. 536 (1378-1865).

33. 1 William L. Saunders, The Colonial Records of North Carolina 185 (1886).

34. John Dunlap, Laws of Pa. (1778).

35. Hebert Hovenkamp, *The Antitrust Movement and the Rise of Industrial Organization*, 68 Tex. L. Rev. 105, 155 (1989).

36. Standard Oil Company of New Jersey v. United States, 221 U.S. 1, 55 (1910).

37. *See*, Botelor v. Washington, Case No. 1,685, 8 Fed. Cases 962 (D.C. Cir. 1826) (describing that "by-law" of the District of Columbia and holding that "rye-chop" used as feed for horses did not fall within that prohibition). Under the localized economies of the immediate postcolonial period, it was thought that the only real threat to consumers came from efforts to control the local produce markets. Franklin Jones, *Historical Development of the Law of Business Competition*, 36 Yale L. J. 207, 210-211 (1926-1927).

38. Dutton v. Knoxville, 113 S.W. 381 (Tenn. Sup. 1908).

have been repealed, but statutes in Arkansas, Colorado, Montana, and Nebraska still allow city councils to establish markets for vegetables and to prohibit forestalling.[39]

A federal appeals court opined in 1904 that "[i]t may be that the practice of acquiring by a single corporation . . . the power to control the market of a given commodity in a wide area of territory, may become injurious to the public; but, if so, it would seem that the limitations and the means for the restriction and correction required must be supplied by the lawmaking power, since the old law against forestalling the market has become obsolete."[40] Nevertheless, the concept of engrossing did find its way into the antitrust laws.[41] It was thought that conspiracies to fix prices and monopolies should be outlawed in order to ensure correct pricing, which was another medieval concept that was based on a concept of "just" price.

The just price theory is traceable to St. Thomas Aquinas, who preached that raising prices in response to increased demand was a form of theft.[42] Modern economists have shown, however, that raising prices in the face of increased demand is merely rational action that serves the critically important and desirable function of rationing scarce goods. "Prices play a crucial role in determining how much of each resource gets used where and how the resulting products get transferred to millions of people. Yet this role is seldom understood by the public and it is often disregarded entirely by politicians."[43] Consequently, the just price concept still lingers in American politics, especially in recent years in regard to crude oil and other energy product prices.[44]

This just price concept underlies a continuing suspicion and even distaste for speculators (and ticket scalpers) that spurs popular distrust of the commodity and stock traders as gamblers who distort prices. "These views may reflect in part an idea dating back to the middle ages that the middleman is an unproductive parasite who simply makes a profit on the labor of others."[45] Speculation and the middleman were even more vilified in the Soviet Union, where those activities were made serious crimes. However, the Soviet experiment revealed that government, no matter how massive, was incapable of efficiently fulfilling the functions of speculators and middlemen.[46] Yet,

---

39. Arkansas Code § 14-140-101 (2010); Colorado C.R.S. § 31-15-711 (2010); Montana Code Anno. § 7-21-4202; Nebraska R.R.S. § 15-212. New Hampshire still allows its city councils to punish both forestalling and regrating. New Hampshire RSA § 47:17 (2010).

40. Davis v. A. Booth & Co. 131 F. 32, 37 (6th Cir. 1904).

41. *See*, United States v. E.I. du Pont de Nemours & Co., 351 U.S. 377, 391, n. 15 (1956) (discussing the background of The Sherman Act, 15 U.S.C. § 2). *See*, Edward S. Mason, *Monopoly in Law and Economics*, 47 YALE L. J. 34, 38 (1937-1938) (describing differences between engrossing and monopoly).

42. *Just price concept—Aquinas 1225—1274*, http://www.xtimeline.com/evt/view.aspx?id=46396 (accessed August 21, 2011). Of course, such action is now viewed as merely rational and critical to modern society.

43. THOMAS SOWELL, BASIC ECONOMICS 13 (2011).

44. As one author notes:

> One of the earlier theories for which the United States's political system demands respect is that which insists that there exists a 'just' price for goods and services and a 'just' wage for labor. This body of economic thought has its roots in medieval theology, but it contains powerful ideas that are very much alive today. This body of thought does not purport to 'explain' prices, but to specify conditions that prices 'ought' to satisfy.

Charles G. Stalon, *Conference Addendum: Regulating in Pursuit of Efficient and Just Prices*, 8 ADMIN. L. J. 913, 914 (1995).

45. Wendy Collins Perdue, *Manipulation of Futures Markets: Redefining the Offense*, 56 FORDHAM L. REV. 345, 346, n. 7 (1987).

46. A history schoolbook in use in North Carolina high schools as the twentieth century ended, for example, defined a "middleman" as a speculator who "drove up the prices of such luxury items as dyes, silk, perfumes, drugs, gold, jewels, and spices such as pepper, cinnamon, nutmeg, and cloves." JOHN L. BELL AND

despite the horrors that resulted from the Soviet experiment in stamping out markets and speculation, speculators remain unloved in America.[47] Their vilification still fuels populist campaigns against speculation associated with trading scandals and sharp commodity price spikes.

1:3 MANIPULATION ARRIVES IN AMERICA

Concerns over commodity price manipulations appeared early in American history. George Washington blamed inflated commodity prices during the Revolution on "monopolizers, forestallers, and engrossers." He viewed such individuals as "murderers of our cause" who should be "hung in gibbets."[48] Washington also complained that "[v]irtue and patriotism are almost extinct. Stock-jobbing, speculating, engrossing seem to be the great business of the multitude."[49] Forestallers were especially criticized during the Revolution when they withheld goods from the market in Philadelphia in anticipation of higher prices when the French would arrive with hard currency to participate in the war.[50]

Distaste for speculators continued after the Revolution. An effort to corner the market in U.S. government securities in 1792 by William Duer and Alexander Macomb failed and bankrupted Duer. That bankruptcy touched off a debilitating panic in New York[51] and laid the groundwork for the creation of the New York Stock Exchange (NYSE).[52] An early effort to deal with abusive and manipulative trading practices in the stock market is found in the constitution of that exchange. It prohibited "fictitious" sales in 1817. That prohibition was imposed after a nonexistent sale in the stock of the Manufacturing Bank was posted to create a false price.[53]

An indictment brought in the Supreme Court of New York in 1809 charged that a group of cordwainers (shoemakers) had formed a "club" that planned to boycott any master who did not pay the wages they demanded or who employed a shoemaker who was not a member of their union.[54] Prosecuting counsel marched out a parade of horrors in that litigation that he claimed would follow if a corner (in this case a corner on the making of shoes) was beyond indictment: "Suppose all the bakers in N.Y. were to refuse to bake till they received an exorbitant remuneration . . . , and if there be impunity for these, why shall not all other artisans do likewise?"[55] Then, counsel most damningly of all charged, "Suppose that some rich speculators . . . should, in a cold winter, combine to purchase up all the wood, and refuse to sell it but at an extravagant advance,

---

JEFFREY J. CROW, NORTH CAROLINA: THE HISTORY OF AN AMERICAN STATE 17 (1992).

47. More recently, price controls have had severe adverse effects in Venezuela. William Neuman, *Price Controls Keep Venezuela Cupboards Bare*, NEW YORK TIMES, April 21, 2012, at A1. As one author notes:

> Prime Minister Margaret Thatcher in her memoirs said that Mikhail Gorbachev "had little understanding of economics," even though he was at that time the leader of the largest nation on earth. Unfortunately, he was not unique in that regard. The same could be said of many other national leaders around the world, in countries large and small, democratic or undemocratic. In countries where prices coordinate prices automatically, their lack of knowledge does not matter nearly as much as in countries where political leaders try to direct and coordinate economic activities.

THOMAS SOWELL, BASIC ECONOMICS 13 (2011).

48. JAMES T. FLEXNER, GEORGE WASHINGTON: THE FORGE OF EXPERIENCE (1732-1775) 337-338 (1965).

49. CHRISTOPHER HIBBERT, REDCOATS AND REBELS 258 (1990).

50. WILLIAM RANDALL, BENEDICT ARNOLD: PATRIOT AND TRAITOR 478 (1990).

51. FEDERAL RESERVE BANK OF PHILADELPHIA, THE FIRST BANK OF THE UNITED STATES.

52. I JERRY W. MARKHAM, A FINANCIAL HISTORY OF THE UNITED STATES, FROM CHRISTOPHER COLUMBUS TO THE ROBBER BARONS (1492-1900) 109-124 (2002).

53. WALTER WERNER AND STEVEN T. SMITH, WALL STREET 32 (1991).

54. People v. Melvin, 1 Yates Sel. Cas. 112 (N.Y. Sup. Ct. 1809).

55. 1 Yates Sel. Cas. at 121-122.

should we have no law to protect the poor against such oppression?"[56] The court took the matter under advisement.

"Time options" or "time bargains," as they were sometimes called, allowed for the future delivery of securities and were widely used for stock manipulations.[57] Much of the trading on the NYSE involved time bargains for as long as six months. These contracts were secured by a small margin deposit. "Time bargains rarely consisted of a direct exchange of stock; the parties were more likely to settle by paying the difference between contract and market prices."[58] By 1834, time bargains were responsible for 20 percent or more of the trading volume on the NYSE.[59]

In the 1830s, market corners became common on the New York Stock and Exchange Board, the predecessor to the New York Stock Exchange. The Canton Company corner of 1834 and 1835 was remarkable in driving the price of shares from 60, their par value, to 300.[60] During that period, the Morris Canal and Banking Company was the target of a manipulative effort by a pool of traders using time bargains that were settled by paying the difference in price movements in favor of one party or the other. The price of the Morris Canal stock was pushed up to $185 from "almost nothing" and the pool participants realized profits of some 300 percent.[61]

The stock of the United Mexican Mining Co. was also manipulated massively in 1834 and a corner occurred in the stock of the Harlem Railroad in 1835 that employed sales of the stock for future delivery.[62] Speculator Jacob Little was able to make large profits by shorting the market during the stock market panic in 1837, a practice that was considered to be unsavory.[63]

"In 1853, Henry Boardman had complained that gambling in stocks was as much in vogue as card gambling or billiards. 'But the public sentiment tolerates and shelters it.' Even worse, 'it lavishes its respect and its honors upon the men who win the most bets and carry off the largest stakes.'"[64]

Concerns over stock price manipulations and speculations grew after the Panic of 1857. Blame for a speculative bubble preceding that event was placed on the use of time bargains.[65] Nevertheless, speculation continued and became frenzied during the Civil War. Those speculations were often carried out through put and call options on some ten exchanges that were operating in New York during the 1860s.[66]

---

56. The prosecutor then asked what would "become of the poor . . .? The rich will, by their money, find supplies; but what will be the sufferings of the poor classes?" 1 Yates Sel. Cas. at 122.

57. Edmund C. Stedman, The New York Stock Exchange 445 (1905). The origin of time bargains is said to have been a practice employed in the London markets. Stock companies closed their books for six weeks in each quarter to prepare for payments of dividends. Traders would use time bargains during that period to buy the stock, an agreement that would be fulfilled by stock purchased once the books were open again. Gradually time bargains were fulfilled by settlement of price differences. John Francis, Chronicles and Characters of the Stock Exchange 71-72 (1844).

58. Walter Werner and Steven T. Smith, Wall Street 31 (1991).

59. I Jerry W. Markham, A Financial History of the United States, From Christopher Columbus to the Robber Barons (1492-1900) 160 (2002).

60. Walter Werner and Steven T. Smith, Wall Street 72 (1991).

61. *Id.*

62. *Id.* at 162.

63. Jerry W. Markham & Thomas L. Hazen, Broker-Dealer Operations Under Securities and Commodities Law 1-19 (2011).

64. Jonathan Lurie, *Speculation, Risk, and Profits: The Ambivalent Agrarian in the Late Nineteenth Century*, 46 Ag. History 269, 276 (1972).

65. I Jerry W. Markham, A Financial History of the United States, From Christopher Columbus to the Robber Barons (1492-1900) 202 (2002).

66. Jerry W. Markham & Thomas L. Hazen, Broker-Dealer Operations Under Securities and Commodities Law 1-26 (2011).

The manipulations occurring during the Civil War included the stocks of the Michigan Salt Combine; the Chicago & Rock Island Railroad; the Fort Wayne & Chicago Railroad; and the Michigan Southern & Northern Railroad. The stock of the Michigan & Prairie du Chien Railroad was cornered and its price was manipulated from $57 to $275 and then driven down to $110.[67]

The discovery of oil in Pennsylvania gave rise to much speculation.[68] A "petroleum mania" broke out in 1863, and numerous oil companies were formed and their shares sold to the public.[69] The Petroleum and Mining Board in New York became a place where "corners were frequent and large sums exchanged hands in the dexterous manipulation of value."[70] These exchanges dealt in oil company stocks. In one instance, the price of the stock of the Napoleon Oil Company was manipulated upward from $2 to $32 per share.[71] That bubble burst a few years later.[72]

---

67. Edmund C. Stedman, The New York Stock Exchange 184-192 (1905).

68. As one author notes:

> Edwin Drake had drilled the first commercially successful oil well in Pennsylvania in 1859. . . . Prior to that discovery, people had been getting illuminants from sources such as whale oil, grain alcohol, and gas and liquids derived from coal, asphalt, and shale. Then as now, obtaining liquid fuel by these methods was a very expensive proposition, and Drake had no trouble selling his crude for $20 a barrel, which would correspond to $476/barrel in 2009 dollars. Needless to say, the discovery that such precious stuff could be obtained just by drilling into the earth stimulated a frenzy of drilling in the vicinity of Oil Creek, Pennsylvania. Many of these wells also successfully produced oil, and the price had plummeted below 50 cents/barrel (about $12 in 2009 dollars) by 1861.
>
> But it turned out that in each new well, the flow rate dropped fairly quickly as oil was removed, and the drillers also had difficulty figuring out how to prevent water flooding. After an initial phenomenal rate of success, total production from all wells in Pennsylvania declined in 1863 and fell further in 1864.
>
> At the same time, the demand schedule was shifting to the right, due to war spending and most importantly a new tax on alcohol (a competitive source of illuminants) of $2/gallon, which gave a $40/barrel competitive advantage to crude. The result was that the real price of oil quintupled by 1864.

James Hamilton, *The First Oil Shock*, Econbrowser, Analysis of Current Economic Conditions and Policy, http://www.econbrowser.com/archives/2011/01/the_first_oil_s.html (accessed December 25, 2011).

69. I Jerry W. Markham, A Financial History of the United States, From Christopher Columbus to the Robber Barons (1492-1900) 243-244 (2002).

70. *Id.*

71. *Id.* at 244.

72. P.T. Barnum, who was well versed in finance as well as circus performances, complained in 1866:

> Every sham, as has often been said, proves some reality. Petroleum exists, no doubt, and is an important addition to our national wealth. But the Petroleum humbug or mania or superstition, or whatever you choose to call it, is a humbug, just as truly, and a big one, whether we use the word in its milder or its bitterer sense. There are more than six hundred petroleum companies. The capital they call for is certainly not less than five hundred million dollars. The money invested in the notorious South Sea Bubble was less than two-fifths as much—only about $190,000,000. Now, this petroleum business—very much of it is just as thorough a gambling business as any faro bank ever set up in Broadway, or any other stock speculation ever conjured up in Wall Street.

P.T. Barnum, The Humbugs of the World, Ch. XXIV (1866).

1:4 COMMODITY FUTURES MARKETS

The commodity futures contract appeared in America shortly before the Civil War.[73] These contracts, which were first known as "to arrive" contracts, were used for the delivery of grain to terminal markets such as Chicago. By the 1860s, to arrive contracts were themselves traded on exchanges and became the subject of speculation. One merchant warned in 1858 that these contracts were "gambling operations of selling ahead" and that "there is no speculation so dangerous, not even betting on a faro table. . . . Take a fair risk in actual property but never sell a thing which you don't own and don't know the cost."[74]

The to arrive contracts were later replaced by time contracts, which had to be secured by margin deposits.[75] General Ulysses S. Grant wryly observed in his memoirs that, while serving in the Army in San Francisco in the 1850s, plots of land were being sold "'On Change,' much as stocks are now sold on Wall Street. Cash, at time of purchase, was always paid by the broker; but the purchaser had only to put up his margin. He was charged at the rate of two or three percent per month on the difference, besides commissions."[76] During the Civil War, time bargains and forward contracts evolved into futures contracts having standardized terms, which allowed them to be offset and allowed the parties to pocket any gains or pay their losses without having to take delivery of the actual commodity underlying the contract.

The offset feature of the futures contract allowed speculation on grain prices.[77] The use of margin to secure performance also permitted a great deal of leverage for speculators, which proved an inducement for the manipulation of commodity futures prices. Indeed, manipulation became a problem in the commodity markets almost from their inception, disrupting markets and drawing headlines in the process.

The development of the futures contract on the Chicago Board of Trade (CBOT) set the stage for such activities.[78] "During the Civil War futures trading grew to large proportions in connection with supplying grain for the army; and in 1865 the Chicago Board of Trade adopted rules recognizing futures trading as a distinct commercial practice."[79] Trading in "privileges," which were options contracts, was used to wager on grain price changes on the CBOT. The CBOT tried to ban the use of privileges in 1865, but that proved ineffective, and corners and squeezes became widespread in the Chicago market.[80]

---

73. Jerry W. Markham, A History of Commodity Futures Trading and Its Regulation 3-5 (1987) (describing the history of those contracts)

74. 2 Chicago Board of Trade, Proceedings of the History of Futures Seminar, Morton Rothstein, *The Rejection and Acceptance of a Marketing Innovation: Hedging in the Late 19th Century* 11 (Sept. 1982).

75. *Id.* at 12.

76. Ulysses S. Grant, Personal Memoirs 76 (1885).

77. George W. Hoffman, Future Trading Upon Organized Commodity Markets in the United States 29 (1932).

78. Chicago became the center of commodity trading as a result of its role as the principal market for grain. As one court later described that role,

> Most of the grain produced in the United States comes from the west and is transported eastward for consumption in this country or export to foreign countries. Between the time of production and the consumption of a large part of each annual crop of grain, considerable time elapses, during which the grain must be stored. Large facilities for such storage are furnished by elevators and warehouses in Chicago, through which point much of this grain passes.

Armour Grain Co. v. United States Grain Corp., 241 Ill. App. 332, 336 (Ill. App. 1926).

79. J.M. Mehl, *Federal Regulation of Futures Trading*, 4 Fed. Bar Ass'n J. 195 (1940-1942).

80. Jerry W. Markham, The History of Commodity Trading and Its Regulation 8-9 (1987).

The gold market in New York was another hotbed of speculation during and after the Civil War. Gold mining stocks also became the subject of much speculation and manipulation in New York, San Francisco, and Chicago. Gold stocks were traded on exchanges in those cities. Shares on the San Francisco Stock and Exchange Board were often manipulated through trumped-up litigation challenging company-mining claims. The New York Petroleum and Mining Board was "a speculative market where 'corners were frequent, and large sums changed hands in the dexterous manipulation of value.'"[81] Several of those manipulations involved companies with no assets.[82]

The New York Gold Exchange was formed in 1864 and became a popular center for trading in gold and government securities. Market participants engaged in "difference" trading in which they settled their gains and losses through gold certificates issued by the exchange's clearinghouse. "Very often brokers sell 'short' (that is they sell what they haven't got and never had), and make a respectable profit by buying it back at a lower figure than they sold it at. They pay interest for borrowed money, and make a profit."[83]

The value of government securities, as measured by gold prices, rose and fell in value with Union victories and defeats during the Civil War. Telegraph operators were bribed by speculators to provide advance information on those battles.[84] J. Pierpont Morgan made $160,000 in one gold-rigging scheme on the Gold Exchange. The New York Stock Exchange believed that gold trading was disloyal to the Union cause and prohibited gold trading on its floor, as well as short sales of U.S. government bonds.[85]

In order to curb gold speculation, the State of New York prohibited banks from lending on gold in 1863. The federal government also imposed a tax on time sales of gold. Congress went further in 1864 with its first effort to control speculation. Congress prohibited short sales of gold, contracts for deferred delivery of the metal were proscribed, and gold trading could only occur at one's ordinary place of business.[86] Violation of that statute was a crime, and private parties were

81. Jerry W. Markham, A Financial History of the United States, From Christopher Columbus to the Robber Barons (1492-1900) 244 (2002) (citation omitted).

82. *Id.*

83. *Gold as a Commodity*, Harper's Weekly, Feb. 23, 1867, at 114.

84. Jerry W. Markham, A Financial History of the United States, From Christopher Columbus to the Robber Barons (1492-1900) 243-245 (2002).

85. *Id.* at 241.

86. This statute provided

> That it shall be unlawful to make any contract for the purchase or sale and delivery of any gold coin or bullion to be delivered on any day subsequent to the day of making such contract, or for the payment of any sum, either fixed or contingent, in default of the delivery of any gold coin or bullion, or to make such contract upon any other terms than the actual delivery of such gold coin or bullion, and the payment in full of the price thereof, on the day on which such contract is made, in United States notes or national currency, and not otherwise; or to make any contract for the purchase or sale and delivery of any foreign exchange to be delivered at any time beyond ten days subsequent to the making of such contract; or for the payment of any sum, either fixed or contingent, in default of the delivery of any foreign exchange, or upon any other terms than the actual delivery of such foreign exchange within ten days from the making of such contract, and the immediate payment in full of the agreed price thereof on the day of delivery in United States notes or national currency; or to make any contract whatever for the sale and delivery of any gold coin or bullion of which the person making such contract shall not, at the time of making the same, be in actual possession. And it shall be unlawful to make any loan of money or currency not being in coin to be repaid in coin or bullion, or to make any loan of coin or bullion to be repaid in money or currency other than coin.
>
> . . . That it shall be further unlawful for any banker, broker or other person to make any purchase or sale of any gold coin or bullion, or of any foreign exchange, or any contract for any such purchase or sale, at any other place than the ordinary place of business of either the seller

allowed to bring actions to recover penalties assessable under its provisions, one half of such recoveries to go to the government.[87] Gold prices immediately rose 30 percent after the enactment of this legislation, and it was repealed only two weeks after its passage.[88] The resignation of the secretary of the Treasury, Salmon P. Chase, was attributed by some to that failure.[89]

After the war, the government intervened periodically in the gold market to manipulate its value by either selling gold or buying U.S. government securities. This was a haphazard process, and Congress required gold sales and bond purchases to be announced in advance and conducted by public auction. The Treasury Department suspended gold sales in 1869 in order to aid exports of a large grain crop. That suspension set the stage for perhaps the most famous commodity price manipulation attempt of all times. Its mastermind was Jay Gould, the unscrupulous and ingenious robber baron who otherwise devoted his attentions to manipulating railroad stocks. As in several other of his capers, Gould was aided in the gold manipulation by Jim Fisk, another notorious robber baron and colorful society figure.[90]

Fisk and Gould were already infamous for their depredations in the stock market. Along with Daniel Drew, they constantly manipulated the price of Erie Railroad stock and became involved in an epic battle over control of that railroad with Cornelius Vanderbilt in 1868.[91] Among other things, the "Erie gang" printed $10 million in fraudulent Erie stock certificates that were sold to Vanderbilt in an effort to break him. This contest for control led to an armed standoff between the parties before they settled.[92]

Gould purchased $7 million in gold in April 1869, pushing its price up from $130, to $140 per ounce, but his scheme depended on the continuing suspension of government gold sales.[93] To that end, Gould bribed General Daniel Butterfield, the assistant Treasury secretary in New York, and Gould enlisted Abel Corbin, the brother-in-law of President Grant, in the scheme. Gould tried similar tactics with the president's private secretary, Horace Porter, but that effort failed. Becoming suspicious of Corbin's requests that gold sales remain suspended, Grant ordered sales to be resumed. At the time, Gould and Fisk held call options on $100 million in gold, which was more than double the amount of gold held privately in the United States, outside the U.S. Treasury.

Gould was tipped on the president's decision to resume gold sales and began unwinding his position, but Fisk was not similarly informed. Fisk madly bid gold up to $160 per ounce before the market collapsed after news of the government sales was made public. Fisk and Gould artfully maneuvered through the legal system to avoid liability on much of their losses, but several trading firms failed and the entire market was thrown into turmoil.[94]

> or purchaser, owned or hired, and occupied by him individually, or by a partnership of which he is a member.
>
> *And be it further enacted*, That all contracts made in violation of this act shall be absolutely void.

13 Stat. 132 (1864).

87. *Id.*

88. *Id.* at 344.

89. 78 Cong. Rec. 8578 (1934) (remarks of Sen. Gore).

90. Maury Klein, The Life and Legend of Jay Gould 99-115 (1986).

91. Vanderbilt had earlier, in 1863, led a successful corner of stock of the Hudson River Railroad, trapping the bears and earning himself and his pool participants $3 million. John Steele Gordon, The Great Game 106 (1999).

92. *Id.* at 292-295.

93. Kenneth D. Ackerman, The Gold Ring, Jim Fisk, Jay Gould and Black Friday 7 (1988).

94. Jerry W. Markham, A Financial History of the United States, From Christopher Columbus to the Robber Barons (1492-1900) 273-275 (2002).

Benjamin Hutchinson was credited with the first important corner in the wheat market through trading on the CBOT in 1866, and he dominated that trading pit until the late 1880s.[95] By 1868, there was a corner a month on the CBOT.[96] They included three corners in wheat, two in corn, and one in oats, and attempted corners occurred in pork and rye.[97] The year 1868 was also memorable because the CBOT adopted "a rule banning 'corners' (defined as 'making contracts for the purchase of a commodity, and then taking measures to render it impossible for the seller to fill his contract, for the purpose of extorting money from him'). This is the first known regulatory attempt to deter manipulation."[98] In 1869 and 1870, the CBOT adopted rules allowing traders to default on their delivery obligations and seek arbitration for a settlement price in the event of a corner.[99] Nevertheless, manipulations continued year after year.

In 1872, John Lyon, Hugh Maher, and P.J. Diamond combined in an attempt to corner the wheat market after the Chicago fire sharply reduced storage facilities. The conspirators were ruined when the corner failed.[100] Particularly famous was Peyton R. Chandler's attempt to obtain control over the supply of cash oats in the spring of 1872 in order to push up their prices on the CBOT. He was opposed by sellers of options and holders of puts on the CBOT who were trying to push prices down. This battle was "quite generally participated in by members of the board."[101] The corner was broken after oats declined sharply in New York and other markets, and Chandler was bankrupted.

A federal court held in 1874 that the option and put contracts involved in the Chandler corner were unenforceable gambling contracts.[102] In that same year, numerous corners were conducted, including one by "King Jack" Sturges, who cornered the corn market in July 1874. He then changed to the short side of the market and was himself caught in a corner of September corn. Sturges refused to meet his obligations, resulting in his expulsion from the Board of Trade. However, he was later reinstated.[103]

As a result of these abuses, the Illinois legislature passed legislation in 1874 that prohibited options contracts and false rumors designed to manipulate prices.[104] The Supreme Court affirmed

95. Edward J. Dies, The Plunger: A Tale of the Wheat Pit 222-233 (1929). Hutchinson was himself modest about his ability to control markets, stating that

> the market price is the universal price all over the world on any given day, and no man or combination of men can stand up against it. They may take measures to influence it, but they cannot positively control it. It is too mighty, too immense. We can influence the water-power of Niagara; but let us find the man or men who can stop the cataract.

Hutchinson, *Speculation in Wheat*, 153 N. Am. Rev. 414 (1891).

96. Jerry W. Markham, *Manipulation of Commodity Futures Prices—The Unprosecutable Crime*, 8 Yale J. on Reg. 281, 289 (1991).

97. George W. Hoffman, Future Trading Upon Organized Commodity Markets in the United States 31-32 (1932).

98. CFTC, *History of the CFTC*, http://www.cftc.gov/About/HistoryoftheCFTC/history_precftc (accessed October 1, 2011).

99. VII Federal Trade Commission, Report on the Grain Trade 253 (1921).

100. Wojtek Sikorzewski, *A Corner Solution: Commodity Futures, Default Fines, and Unintended Consequences* 3-4, http://www.econ.kuleuven.be/smye/abstracts/p408.pdf (accessed September 5, 2011).

101. V Federal Trade Commission, Report on the Grain Trade 325 (1921), *quoting* Ex parte Young, 6 Biss. (Bissel's U.S. C.C. Rep.) 58 (1874). *See also*, Thomas H. Dewey, A Treatise on Contracts for Future Delivery and Commercial Wagers Including "Options," "Futures," and "Short Sales" 36-40 (1886).

102. In the Matter of Chandler, 13 American L. Reg. 310 (N.D. Ill. 1874).

103. Charles R. Geist, Wheels of Fortune 25 (2002).

104. The statute stated:

a conviction under that statute in 1902.[105] Nevertheless, this legislation and further efforts by the CBOT to prevent options trading were unsuccessful in curbing abuses.[106]

The decade of the 1880s was particularly infamous for manipulations. In 1881, there was, again, nearly a corner a month on the CBOT. Those operations were conducted by wealthy speculators and "pools" of traders who combined to corner a market. The wheat market was cornered four times in 1882, along with corners in lard, ribs, and corn.[107] A wheat corner was also run in the St. Louis market in 1882.[108]

Leopold Bloom was an infamous manipulator. Among other things, he cornered the pork market in 1887. "Probably no corner that has been operated on the board in recent years has created a deeper feeling in the trade against its manipulators. . . . There was a strong advance in lard and ribs on rumors that these articles were to be cornered next."[109] Another famous corner was attempted by "Crazy" E.L. Harper in the wheat market in 1887. He used purloined funds to carry out that unsuccessful operation and was sentenced to ten years in prison.[110]

Benjamin Hutchinson carried out another famous corner of the wheat market in 1888.[111] Among other things, Hutchinson chartered a fleet of ships to move wheat out of the Chicago market. He was said to have made $8 million in the process of carrying out this corner as wheat prices rose from less than a dollar per bushel to more than $2, making many farmers happy.[112]

The CBOT tried to deal with corners by establishing a "Settlement Committee" that would set a price 10 percent above a "fair market price," as determined by the committee, when shorts were caught in a corner and could not deliver.[113] This effort was not successful in stopping corners and was criticized for favoring short sellers who failed to take the necessary steps to ensure that they could meet their delivery obligations.

These manipulations led one senator to remark that "the recent corner in corn, the Harper corner and the Hutchinson corner, each afford abundant proof that [the CBOT] furnishes a market the very reverse of stable, as regard demand or prices; on the contrary, it furnishes a market that is affected by every base rumor, as well as one where fluctuations are abnormally wide, rapid, and frequent, and such as were never dreamed of before."[114]

> Whoever contracts to have or give to himself or another the option to sell or buy, at a future time, any grain, or other commodity, stock of any railroad or other company, or gold, or forestalls the market by spreading false rumors to influence the price of commodities therein, or corners the market, or attempts to do so in relation to any of such commodities, shall be fined not less than $10 nor more than $1,000, or confined in the county jail not exceeding one year, or both; and all contracts made in violation of this section shall be considered gambling contracts, and shall be void.

Ill. Rev. Stat. Crim, Code, § 130 (1874).

105. Booth v. Illinois, 184 U.S. 425 (1902).

106. Jerry W. Markham, The History of Commodity Trading and Its Regulation 8 (1987).

107. James E. Boyle, Speculation and the Chicago Board of Trade 65 (1920).

108. Samuels v. Oliver, 22 N.E. 499 (Sup. Ill. 1889).

109. *Another Boom in Pork*, New York Times, March 5, 1887.

110. Edward J. Dies, Behind the Wall Street Curtain 106 (1952).

111. *Id.* at 71-73.

112. Robert W. Kolb and Pablo T. Spiller, *The Manipulation of Futures Markets: An Overview*, 20-22, Paper presented at conference on Market Manipulation: Law, Economics, and Public Policy sponsored by the Center for Study of Futures and Options Markets and the American Bar Association, Washington, DC (Nov. 8 & 9, 1990).

113. *Id.* at 19.

114. 23 Cong. Rec. 5985 (1882) (remarks of Sen. Washburn).

A corn corner in 1888 found its way into the Illinois courts, which refused to enforce contracts among the parties to that conspiracy. The Illinois Supreme Court found that the trading sought to push corn prices "beyond the natural market by a combination between the parties. . . . All compacts between merchants, speculators or any class of men to elevate or depress the market are injurious to the public interest, and in restraint of trade. When such a purpose is apparent in a contract, it strikes the agreement with nullity." The court asserted that such a combination "is nothing less than a conspiracy against trade, entered into for selfish purposes, and tending to make the poor poorer and the rich richer. Whether the design is to bring the price of any commodity to a point below its value in a fair and open market, or to raise it above its true worth, the illegality of the combination is the same."[115]

Crude oil was also the subject of much speculation on the East Coast, where commodity exchanges trading oil proliferated in New York and Pennsylvania. Trading in futures contracts in which price differences were settled by cash payments, rather than delivery, was used for speculation, "and oil became 'the favorite speculative commodity of the time.'"[116] Trading on the New York Consolidated Stock and Petroleum Exchange ("the Little Board"), under an agreement with the NYSE, became the primary market for mining stocks and oil in petroleum stocks,[117] which at times far exceeded trading in railroad stocks.[118]

In *Commonwealth v. Tack Bros.*,[119] an 1868 decision of a Pennsylvania court addressed a manipulation scheme in which it was claimed that Tack Bros., an oil brokerage firm in Philadelphia, defrauded the plaintiff James O'Connor of $30,000. O'Connor complained that he had been urged by Tack Bros. to short the oil market through time sales of oil deliverable in the future. O'Connor did not own any oil to deliver, but Tack Bros. promised large profits because a claimed lack of oil sales to Europe would push down prices in Philadelphia.

A decline in prices would have allowed O'Connor to cover his short position at a profit before the delivery date. Instead, oil prices rose and O'Connor suffered a loss. The rise in oil prices was attributed to a conspiracy among Tack Bros. and others to raise prices in Antwerp by fraud, which increased prices in the Philadelphia market to O'Connor's detriment. "The object of this combination was to purchase 150,000 bbls. of oil in the Antwerp market, hold it, and thus stimulate the price of oil artificially, both in Antwerp and the oil markets of the world."[120] After considering extensive testimony and argument of counsel, the court allowed a prosecution for conspiracy to proceed.

The Little Board and other petroleum exchanges traded contracts covering millions of barrels of oil and served as oil price setting mechanisms until they were effectively shut down by the Standard Oil trust.[121] Oil futures trading would not resume for another century in the United States, a resumption that was driven by rising oil prices and the OPEC cartel. However, the ability of the Standard Oil Company to set oil prices was curbed by an antitrust action in 1910 that ordered the company to be broken up into thirty-four separate companies.[122] The government had charged that from 1870 to 1882 Standard Oil had engaged in various practices "for the purpose of fixing the price of crude and refined oil and the products thereof, limiting the production thereof, and

115. Foss v. Cummings, 36 N.E. 353, 359-360 (Sup. Ill. 1894).

116. Daniel Yergin, The Prize 33-34 (1991).

117. *The Little Board*, New York Times Dec. 31, 1905.

118. Richard D. Wyckoff, Wall Street Ventures and Adventures 22 (1930).

119. Commonwealth v. Tack Bros., 1 Brewst. 511 (Pa. 1868).

120. *Id.* (court record at page 162).

121. *Id.* at 53-54.

122. Daniel Yergin, The Quest 89 (2011).

controlling the transportation therein, and thereby restraining trade and commerce among the several States, and monopolizing the said commerce."[123]

An iron market manipulation in 1879 resulted in a 100 percent increase in prices. The crude rubber market was another target for manipulation.[124] It was cornered in 1883 by J.O. Goncalves Vianna, Baron de Gondoriz, a Portuguese trader originally from Brazil. The baron pushed rubber prices from 95 cents per pound to $1.20, "up to such an extravagant height as to compel all rubber manufactories in this country to run on short time, and many of them to stop work."[125] That corner ultimately failed.

In the meantime, commodity price manipulations continued in Chicago. Ed Pardridge's "Chicago bear ring" was famous for short side manipulations that created "panic throughout the world" in 1892. Pardridge was reported to have made $500,000 in a single day[126] and sold calls on 4 million bushels of wheat in a single day.[127] Pardridge's short selling was the subject of congressional hearings in 1892. There was much complaint in those hearings over speculators selling commodities they did not own on the commodity exchanges, but no legislation resulted.[128]

B.G. Arnold & Co., a large coffee importer located in New York, failed after it unsuccessfully tried to corner Java coffee. Coffee corners were also attempted in 1887 and 1888, and Edward R. Thomas tried to corner the cotton market.[129] One remarkable corner was conducted in 1893 in "mess pork" on the Chicago market by taking pork out of some 20,000 barrels and cutting the pork ribs in a way that made it nondeliverable on futures contracts. That had the effect of reducing deliverable supplies and driving up pork prices, although the corner failed in the end.[130]

In 1883, the Supreme Court rejected a claim in *Roundtree v. Smith*[131] that contracts traded on the CBOT were illegal gambling transactions because it was not shown that delivery was not intended.[132] A year later, in 1884, the Supreme Court ruled in *Irwin v. Williar*,[133] that, if both parties

---

123. Standard Oil Company of New Jersey v. United States, 221 U.S. 1, 32 (1910).

124. I JERRY W. MARKHAM, A FINANCIAL HISTORY OF THE UNITED STATES, FROM CHRISTOPHER COLUMBUS TO THE ROBBER BARONS (1492-1900) 312 (2002).

125. *Vianna Comes to Grief*, NEW YORK TIMES, Feb. 26, 1883, at 8.

126. Jerry W. Markham, *Manipulation of Commodity Futures Prices—The Unprosecutable Crime*, 8 YALE J. ON REG. 281, 290, N. 37 (1991).

127. *Fictitious Dealing in Agricultural Products, Hearing Before the House Committee on Agriculture*, 52d Cong., 1st Sess. 278 (1892).

128. *Id.*

129. I JERRY W. MARKHAM, A FINANCIAL HISTORY OF THE UNITED STATES, FROM CHRISTOPHER COLUMBUS TO THE ROBBER BARONS (1492-1900) 312 (2002).

130. Wright v. Cudahy, 48 N.E. 39 (Ill. Sup. 1897).

131. Roundtree v. Smith, 108 U.S. 269 (1883).

132. The Court stated:

> Evidence was given that a very large proportion of all the contracts made for the sale of produce at the board of trade of Chicago, were settled by payment of differences, and that nothing else was expected by the parties to them, and the number of these in proportion to the number of bona fide contracts, in which delivery was expected and desired, is said to be so large as to justify the inference that it was so in these cases.
>
> But since the plaintiff testifies that he had no such understanding, since nothing is proved of the intention of the other parties, and since the contracts were always in writing, we do not think the evidence of what other people intended by other contracts of a similar character, however numerous, is sufficient of itself to prove that the parties to these contracts intended to violate the law, or to justify a jury in making such a presumption.

108 U.S. at 276.

133. Irwin v. Williar, 110 U.S. 499, 508 (1884).

to grain futures contracts agreed beforehand that delivery was not to be made, the contract would constitute a gamble and would not be enforceable. Nevertheless, the intent to deliver would be presumed, if the contracts called for delivery, even if delivery was not made and the contract was settled by offset.

Futures trading received another boost from the Supreme Court in 1893 when, in *Bibb v. Allen*,[134] it held that contracts for future delivery traded subject to the rules of the New York Cotton Exchange were not illegal gambling transactions even though the party did not own the cotton at the time it was sold for future delivery. The Court again refused to examine the subjective intent of the parties when the contracts called for actual delivery, even if they might be offset subsequently. The Supreme Court issued still another ruling of the same ilk in 1895 in *Hansen v. Boyd*,[135] with respect to grain futures traded on the CBOT.

Trading in differences on stock prices was common in the over-the-counter market. Such trading was prohibited by many states as gambling transactions.[136] It was, nevertheless, a popular form of speculation. In one famous case, *Justh v. Holiday*,[137] a District of Columbia court held that a broker could not enforce a note against the estate of General George Armstrong Custer because it had been given to cover losses from difference trading on stock prices.

Options contracts were also popular tools for over-the-counter speculations in stocks, which often involved complex strategies, including "straddles."[138] Options were more difficult to classify as gambling contracts. For example, in *Bigelow v. Benedict*,[139] the New York Court of Appeals held in 1877 that an option contract to deliver gold coin at a specified price was not a gambling transaction because it was not shown there was no intent to perform on the contract.[140] The intent test on whether the transaction was intended to be gambling was generally decided on whether the parties could have taken delivery even if they did not do so.[141]

The New York State Senate appointed a special committee in 1882 to investigate the making of corners and dealing in commodity futures contracts. It held extensive hearings and rendered

---

134. Bibb v. Allen, 149 U.S. 481 (1893).

135. Hansen v. Boyd, 161 U.S. 397 (1896).

136. John R. Dos Passos, A Treatise on the Law of Stockbrokers and Stock Exchanges (1882).

137. Justh v. Holiday, 13, D.C. (2 Mackey) 346 (1883).

138. A New York Court described one such transaction as follows:

> The plaintiff bought, through the agency of defendant, a stock option or privilege, known in the language of brokers as a "straddle." The word, if not elegant, is at least expressive. It means the double privilege of a "put" and "call;" and secures to the holder the right to demand of the seller at a certain price within a certain time a certain number of shares of specified stock, or to require him to take, at the same price within the same time, the same shares of stock. . . . The value of a "straddle," it is proven, depends upon the fluctuations of the stock selected. The wider the range of these fluctuations, whether up or down, the greater the amount which may be realized; and of course the longer the option continues the greater the chance of such fluctuations during the period.

Harris v. Tumbridge, 83 N.Y. 92 (1880).

139. Bigelow v. Benedict, 1877 WL 12029 (N.Y. Ct. App. 1877).

140. *See also*, Kirkpatrick & Lyons v. Bonsall, 1872 WL 11515 (Sup. Pa. 1872) (put option on 5,000 barrels of oil was not on its face a gambling transaction); Lehman Brothers v. Strassberger 15 F. Cas. 254 (Cir. N.D. Ala. 1875) (a promissory note given for differences in cotton trading not void as payment for gambling). *See generally*, John R. Dos Passos, A Treatise on the Law of Stockbrokers and Stock Exchanges 411-443 (1882) (describing other cases involving such claims).

141. *See*, Telford Taylor, *Trading in Commodity Futures—A New Standard of Legality*, 43 Yale L. J. 63 (1933-1934) (describing the intent test for such transactions).

a report the following year. The special committee's report on its investigation defended futures trading in general but condemned bucket shops (which were simply parlors for betting on commodity prices) and gambling on commodity prices through margined transactions. It also sought a tax on future transactions where actual delivery is not made.[142]

Among the witnesses before the New York Senate's special committee was Jay Gould. When asked what he thought of the effects of corners on the transportation system, Gould responded that "it rather helps on the whole. . . . The effect of corners is to give the producer a better price on the whole. *They* make the money. It is not the men that make corners generally; they lose."[143] Gould went on to state that "every thing that tends to facilitate speculation really benefits the country—draws capital from all parts of the world."[144] Gould testified that the gold market panic that he had triggered in 1869 was due to "over-trading." He also somewhat proudly explained his role in the cornering of the stock of the Chicago and Northwestern railroad, pushing the price up from $80 to about $250.[145]

Speculator James R. Keene testified in the hearings before the New York special committee. Keene had by then amassed a fortune of some $13 million from his speculations, but lost it all in a commodity market manipulation scheme, which set a pattern for his subsequent trading.[146] Keene rose stoutly to the defense of his profession, saying that without "speculation in futures for the long and for the short account, the business of the country could not be conducted."[147]

Keene rejected criticism that operators on Wall Street were fleecing unsophisticated investors, stating that "I have no doubt that frequently occurs, but there is nothing to compel a lamb to go into Wall Street unless he wishes to go."[148] He also denied that he had attempted to corner the wheat market in 1879 when he bought a reported 30 million bushels of wheat.[149] However, he did admit that he was part of a "combination" that bought "a large amount of wheat" in order to defend the price of wheat previously purchased rather than "submitting ourselves to the tender mercy of the bears."[150]

Still another famous speculator was Henry Clews, who wrote a still popular book in 1908 called *Fifty Years on Wall Street*. Clews testified in the New York special committee hearings that corners were rarely successful because the operator is left holding the property that was purchased to effect the corner.[151] In defense of speculation, he stated that

> Speculation brings into play the best intelligence as to the future of values. It has always two sides. The one that best comprehends the facts and conditions of the situation wins in the end; and the result of the conflicts is the nearest possible approach to the correct valuation. The result of speculation for a fall in prices is based on the presumption of an over supply.

142. *Report of the Special N.Y. Senate Committee Appointed to Investigate the System of Making Corners and Dealing in Futures* 12-13 (1883).

143. *Id.* at 588.

144. *Id.* at 590. Gould also stated, "Supply and demand embrace all speculative transactions; . . . but when it comes down to finally eating up the grain, that is consumption; and those laws will always in the end govern. No legislation can change them unless you will legislate that people shall eat more or less." *Id.* at 591.

145. *Id.* at 599, 589 (1883).

146. Warren F. Hickernell, Manipulation and Market Leadership 19-20 (1921).

147. *Report of the Special N.Y. Senate Committee Appointed to Investigate the System of Making Corners and Dealing in Futures* 787 (1883).

148. *Id.* at 788.

149. *The Wheat Corner Closed*, New York Times, July 20, 1879.

150. *Report of the Special N.Y. Senate Committee Appointed to Investigate the System of Making Corners and Dealing in Futures* 790-791 (1883).

151. *Id.* at 808.

> If it succeeds, the production of the particular article is checked until prices recover, and in the meantime, production is diverted to other articles less abundant. Thus speculation proves a regulator of both values of production. A speculation for a rise in prices is based on a presumption of scarcity or short supply; and its direct effect is to quicken production and thereby restore the equilibrium of prices.
>
> "Corners" usually come from running a speculation to an excessive length, by which the sellers become responsible for deliveries beyond what they can possibly make and thereby place themselves at the mercy of those with whom they have made contracts. These exigencies chiefly affect the speculators, and affect the producing community but little. Extreme prices usually grow out of them; but they are only momentary, and have no effect upon regular or "cash" transactions, which sympathize very remotely with those momentary artificial quotations. Speculation is not to be judged by its occasional excesses, but by its general effects, which the foregoing considerations show to be beneficial.[152]

John D. Rockefeller and Henry Flagler were also hauled before the special committee to be pilloried over the excesses of the Standard Oil companies, but they supplied little useful information. Interestingly, a number of Protestant ministers were called to testify on the evils of futures trading. Henry Ward Beecher was asked whether consumers were "entitled to the possession of all the products of nature at their natural values?" He responded that "[i]f there was anything of that kind labeled on a field of wheat or on other food, what the natural value was, I should feel as though I had a basis to stand on; but I do not understand what natural value is."[153]

Legislation was introduced in the U.S. Congress in 1888 that sought to "punish dealings in futures in agricultural products." The bills were rejected in committee on the grounds that such dealings were contracts over which the states reserved power and were not subject to the commerce power in the Constitution.[154] In the following year, legislation was proposed that sought to impose a tax on options because it was thought that the "result of speculative trading was to reduce the market price to a rate lower than the cost of production and to the lowest point attainable against the resisting force of the actual supply."[155]

A bill introduced in 1889 was titled "A bill to punish dealing in futures in agricultural products" (H.R. 5689) and another was called "A bill (H. R. 7051) to prohibit fictitious and gambling transactions on the price of articles produced by American farm industry."[156] In reporting on those bills, the House Committee on Agriculture stated that the "money of the world, through boards of trade, controls prices through these wicked devices of speculators and gamblers, and the honest farmers are powerless to regulate prices according to the laws of supply and demand."[157]

The committee report stated that experts had estimated that losses to farmers between 1885 and 1887 in the production of wheat, corn, cotton, butter, and cheese amounted to $469 million. The committee report went on to claim that speculators by "shrewd manipulation" were fixing prices. "They break the market by flooding it when the producers would sell, and they force it up by withholding their accumulations from the market after the producers have parted with the great bulk of their crops."[158]

---

152. *Id.* at 808-809.
153. *Id.* at 735.
154. *To Prevent the Sale of Cotton and Grain in Future Markets*, S. Rep. No. 508, 69th Cong., 1st Sess. 71 (1926).
155. *Id.* at 73.
156. H.R. Rep. No. 4141, 50th Cong., 2d Sess. 1 (1889).
157. *Id.*
158. *Id.*

Despite this harsh condemnation, the House Agriculture Committee declined to recommend passage of legislation to bar futures trading because it could find no constitutional power to justify such action. The committee believed that this was a matter for the individual states to address.[159] Nevertheless, one year later, the committee approved a bill that would have imposed a $1,000 special tax on dealers in options and futures, as well as a tax of five cents per pound and twenty cents per bushel on any such contracts in wheat, corn, cotton, oats, pork, and other farm staples.[160] That legislation was not passed.

A depression in agricultural prices in the 1890s occasioned Congress to conduct an investigation to determine its causes, and an extensive report was issued in 1894. Among other things, the investigating committee found that the acreage under cultivation had increased substantially since the Civil War, that big "bonanza" farmers were increasing the efficiency of production, and that grazing on public lands and efficient slaughtering operations had vastly expanded the amount of beef brought to market.[161] This would be one of the few times in U.S. history that Congress examined the fundamental factors affecting commodity prices instead of simply attacking speculators.

Joseph Leiter, a Harvard graduate, attempted unsuccessfully between April 1897 and June 1898 to corner the wheat market. Leiter shipped large quantities of wheat from Chicago to Europe, where there was a crop failure. He built a dominant long position in wheat futures and announced that he was sending the remaining Chicago stocks abroad. Leiter borrowed $7 million from banks to fund his operation, but his corner was broken when a fleet of boats hired by P.D. Armour broke through the ice on Lake Michigan and flooded the Chicago markets with grain from Canada. Leiter lost some $3 million as prices plunged.[162] He was forced to assign his wheat holdings to Armour as a part of a settlement of his debts.[163]

It was said that "the Hutchinsons and the Leiters and the other so-called 'playboys' of speculation, used these public market places as a stage on which to parade their power over prices. They were the market leaders. Their operations churned the markets up and down without regard to fundamental conditions."[164] Leiter also became the model for a popular novel by Frank Norris entitled *The Pit*, while a silent movie called *Corner in Wheat* parodied the wheat manipulators, portraying them as exploiting consumers.[165] However, it was also noted that "[s]ince most corners failed, the greatest loss fell on the promoters of the corner."[166] Commodity price speculations were the target of other novels, including Mark Twain's *The Gilded Age*, which parodied sugar and corn speculations.

Stock prices continued to be the subject of much manipulation in New York. "Prior to 1900 the New York Stock Exchange witnessed many spectacular corners, particularly in railroad stocks."[167] It has been claimed by one modern historian that "[s]peculative manipulation both soured the relationship between directors and shareholders, leading to serious mismanagement, and drove share prices away from their 'intrinsic' or fair value."[168] The famous speculators included "Dia-

159. *Id.* at 2.

160. H.R. Rep. No. 1321, 51st Cong., 1st Sess. 1 (1890).

161. S. Rep. No. 787, 53d Cong, 3d Sess. (1894).

162. Robert W. Kolb and Pablo T. Spiller, *The Manipulation of Futures Markets: An Overview*, at pp. 22-24, Paper presented at a Conference on Market Manipulation: Law, Economics, and Public Policy sponsored by the Center for Study of Futures and Options Markets and the American Bar Association, Washington, DC (Nov. 8 & 9, 1990).

163. *Leiter's Losses Reduced*, New York Times, June 16, 1898.

164. J.M. Mehl, *Federal Regulation of Futures Trading*, 4 Fed. Bar Ass'n J. 195, 197 (1940-1942).

165. Emily Lambert, The Futures 12-13 (2011).

166. James E. Boyle, Speculation and the Chicago Board of Trade 74 (1920).

167. James Edward Meeker, Short Selling 185 (1932).

168. Edward Chancellor, Devil Take the hindmost 188 (1999).

mond" Jim Brady, Thomas Lawson, James Keene, and Edward Stokes.[169] E.H. Harriman was another speculator of note. He made $150,000 in 1874 by shorting the market while "Deacon" S.V. White was trying to corner anthracite coal stocks.[170] Deacon White thereafter switched his activities to the commodity markets and came to grief in an attempted corner of the corn market in September 1891.[171]

Another plague was the "bucket shops," which were gambling dens for betting on commodity or stock prices. The CBOT was able to obtain injunctions that cut off access to its price quotes on which the bucket shops were dependent.[172] The Supreme Court supported that effort in *Board of Trade of the City of Chicago v. Christie Grain & Stock Co.*,[173] giving strong support to the concept of commodity futures trading on organized exchanges.[174] Justice Holmes stated in that case:

> As has appeared, the plaintiff's chamber of commerce is, in the first place, a great market, where, through its eighteen hundred members, is transacted a large part of the grain and provision business of the world. Of course, in a modern market, contracts are not confined to sales for immediate delivery. People will endeavor to forecast the future, and to make agreements according to their prophecy. Speculation of this kind by competent men is the self-adjustment of society to the probable. Its value in well known as a means of avoiding or mitigating catastrophes, equalizing prices, and providing for periods of want. It is true that the success of the strong induces imitation by the weak, and that incompetent persons bring themselves to ruin by undertaking to speculate in their turn. But legislatures and courts generally have recognized that the natural evolutions of a complex society are to be touched only with a very cautious hand, and that such coarse attempts at a remedy for the waste incident to every social function as a simple prohibition and laws to stop its being are harmful and vain.[175]

The Supreme Court also upheld a state tax in Alabama on futures trading through bucket shops, but the Alabama legislation equated bucket shops with the exchanges.[176] Otherwise, state and federal efforts to curb speculation failed. As one author has noted:

---

169. Jerry W. Markham & Thomas L. Hazen, Broker-Dealer Operations Under Securities and Commodities Law 1-45 (2011).

170. Lloyd J. Mercer, E.H. Harriman: Master Railroader 9 (1985).

171. *S.V. White & Co. Suspend*, New York Times, Sept. 23, 1891.

172. Jerry W. Markham & Thomas L. Hazen, Broker-Dealer Operations Under Securities and Commodities Law 1-45 (2011).

173. Board of Trade of the City of Chicago v. Christie Grain & Stock Co., 198 U.S. 236 (1905).

174. *See also*, Browne v. Thorn, 260 U.S. 137 (1922) (cotton transaction on New Orleans Cotton Exchange were prima facie lawful).

175. Board of Trade of the City of Chicago v. Christie Grain & Stock Co., 198 U.S. 236, 247-248 (1905).

176. Ware & Leland v. Mobile County, 209 U.S. 405 (1908). The Alabama statute imposed a license tax as follows:

> For each person engaged in the business of buying and selling futures for speculation or on commission, either for themselves or for other persons, and each place of business commonly known as cotton exchanges, or stock exchanges, and sometimes called "bucket shops," in towns and cities of 20,000 inhabitants or more, $500; in all other towns and cities, $250; but this shall not be held to legalize any contract which would otherwise be invalid.

Id.

> By 1892 thousands of petitions to Congress called for the prohibition of "speculative gambling in grain." And, attacks from state legislatures were seemingly unrelenting. . . . Two nineteenth century challenges to futures trading are particularly noteworthy. The first was the so-called Anti-Option movement . . . [which] was fueled by agrarians and their sympathizers in Congress who wanted to end what they perceived as wanton speculative abuses in futures trading. Although options were (are) not futures contracts, and were nonetheless already outlawed on most exchanges by the 1890s, the legislation did not distinguish between the two instruments and effectively sought to outlaw both. In 1890 the Butterworth Anti-Option Bill was introduced in Congress but never came to a vote. However, in 1892 the Hatch (and Washburn) Anti-Option bills passed both houses of Congress, and failed only on technicalities during reconciliation between the two houses. Had either bill become law, it would have effectively ended options and futures trading in the United States.[177]

The sponsor of the Hatch Act thought that stopping short selling would restore "the functions of the law of supply and demand, now inoperative by reason of the limitless offers of the 'short seller.'"[178] The Washburn Anti-Options bill sought to stop short selling and all other trading in which the participants did not own or were not seeking actual delivery of the underlying commodity. Senator Washburn claimed, in support of this legislation in 1892, that "on the Chicago Board of Trade, at least 95 percent of the sales on that board are of this fictitious character, where no property is actually owned, no property sold or delivered, or expected to be delivered, but simply wagers or bets as to what that property might be worth at a designated time in the future."[179] An effort earlier to include provisions in the Sherman Antitrust Act of 1890 that would have applied to commodity futures trading also failed.[180]

One Senate report found in 1894 that "farm prices of wheat are injuriously affected by the business commonly known as dealing in 'options and futures.'" The Senate committee urged that such trading "be abolished and prohibited under heavy penalties. It ought to be made a felony and punished by imprisonment."[181] These legislative efforts were spurred by the populist movement of the period that blamed volatile commodity price movements on speculative traders.[182]

Silver was another commodity that was targeted for manipulation of the entire economy. The populist (agrarian) movement sought to require that silver be accepted as legal tender and that the money supply be expanded. It was thought that this would inflate the economy and increase farm prices. The Sherman Silver Purchase Act of 1890 required the federal government to purchase large amounts of silver and to issue silver certificates that were redeemable in gold. Silver producers in

177. Joseph Santos, *A History of Futures Trading in the United States*, http://eh.net/encyclopedia/article/Santos.futures (citations omitted) (accessed September 5, 2011). *See also*, John Stassen, *The Commodity Exchange Act in Perspective, A Short and Not-So-Reverent History of Futures Trading Legislation in the United States*, 39 Wash. & Lee L. Rev. 825, 828 (1982) (discussing the Hatch Anti-Option bill's failure).

178. H. Rep. No. 969 52d Cong., 1st sess. 2 (1892). The bill also sought to stop foreign firms from hedging their commercial risks by selling short on American exchanges. *Id.*

179. 23 Cong. Rec. 5982 (1882) (remarks of Sen. Washburn).

180. Jerry W. Markham, *Manipulation of Commodity Futures Prices—The Unprosecutable Crime*, 8 Yale J. on Reg. 281, 291, n. 41 (1991).

181. S. Rep. No. 787, 53d Cong., 3d Sess. 33, 103 (1894).

182. The populist movement was also directed at curbing the power of Wall Street and its financiers. As one author notes, there was a populist "mood, an end-of-days sense that a world was verging on extinction, that if the new order of finance capitalism was allowed to complete its work a whole way of life—small in scale, robustly self-reliant, modest, literate, egalitarian, full of neighborly good fellowship and reassuring routine, intimate with nature, civic-minded and pious—would vanish from the face of the earth." Steve Fraser, Every Man a Speculator 195 (2005).

the Americas and European investors were also reported to have engaged in a massive manipulation scheme to raise the price of silver, but the market collapsed.[183] It was charged that some members of Congress had made $1 million in profits from trading in silver, but nothing was ever proved.[184]

1:5 MANIPULATION ENTERS THE TWENTIETH CENTURY

Stock price manipulations continued into the twentieth century. James Keene was the leader of a pool of investors from the brokerage firm of Moore & Schley that manipulated the stock of the Whiskey Trust in 1900.[185] Keene was employed by J.P. Morgan to assist in the gigantic U.S. Steel stock offering in 1902, the first $1 billion company. Keene was assigned the task of supporting its price during the underwriting.[186]

A spectacular manipulation in 1900 involved an effort by the American Ice Company (AIC) to corner the ice market in New York. AIC raised ice prices in New York City by 100 percent and threatened further increases.[187] In carrying out this corner, New York City dock commissioners were bribed to turn back competitors' supplies, and the ice fields of competitors were smashed by steamships hired by AIC. That corner led to much scandal and even played a role in the presidential campaign of Theodore Roosevelt, who attacked Tammany Hall over the ice monopoly. AIC was indicted at the order of New York governor Charles Evans Hughes. The company was convicted, but the fine was a small one. The company was able to continue its operations for many years.[188]

James J. Hill and J.P. Morgan became involved in a colossal war with E.H. Harriman in 1901 over control of the Chicago, Burlington & Quincy Railroad. Harriman tried to turn the tables by seeking control of the Northern Pacific Railroad, which was controlled by Morgan and Hill. A corner occurred when more shares were sold to Harriman by the shorts than had been issued by that railroad. Its share prices jumped by $650 in one hour after this became known. This corner was "more complete and more disastrous in its result than any of the others that Wall Street had experienced: it was neither expected or desired."[189] James Keene was used by Morgan to conduct this battle.[190]

Commodity price manipulations also continued into the twentieth century. James A. Patten made a $2 million profit from a wheat squeeze in 1902, in which he manipulated prices from $1.00 a bushel to $1.34.[191] In 1904, a bull clique of traders in New Orleans pushed cotton prices to their highest levels in ten years. A group of New York traders cornered the Chicago wheat market in 1905.[192] Herman Sielcken was dubbed the "Coffee King" for his ability to manipulate the coffee market up and down.[193]

---

183. Milton Friedman and Anna Jacobson Schwartz, A Monetary History of the United States (1867-1960) 116, n. 41 (1963).

184. I Jerry W. Markham, A Financial History of the United States, From Christopher Columbus to the Robber Barons (1492-1900) 345 (2002).

185. II Jerry W. Markham, A Financial History of the United States, From J.P. Morgan to the Institutional Investor (1900-1970) 4 (2002).

186. *Id.* at 13.

187. *One Hundred Percent Rise in Price*, New York Times, May 6, 1900, at 18.

188. Jerry W. Markham, A Financial History of Modern U.S. Corporate Scandals, From Enron to Reform 613-615 (2006).

189. *The Northern Pacific Corner Now Broken*, New York Times, May 10, 1901, at 1.

190. II Jerry W. Markham, A Financial History of the United States, From J.P. Morgan to the Institutional Investor (1900-1970) 14 (2002).

191. Paul Sarnoff, Jesse Livermore: Speculator King 77 (1985).

192. II Jerry W. Markham, A Financial History of the United States, From J.P. Morgan to the Institutional Investor (1900-1970) 12 (2002).

193. *Id.* at 40.

A "mining stock craze"[194] led to an unsuccessful corner in the United Copper Co. by Fredrick A. Heinze. That failure touched off a run on the Mercantile National Bank, which was controlled by Heinze. It was saved by the New York Clearing House, but a run then began on the trust companies and the historic Panic of 1907 came into full bloom. J.P. Morgan appeared as a savior of the market and forcefully organized a rescue of the trust companies. The panic then subsided, but not before much damage had been done.[195]

Jesse Livermore cornered the cotton market in 1908 by the purchase of 120,000 bales of cotton. In order to inflate the value of those purchases, Livermore was said to have planted a front-page article in a New York newspaper stating that he had cornered July cotton, causing other speculators to buy cotton. The result was even larger profits for Livermore.[196] Livermore was also known as a stock market operator, a familiar pattern for large speculators who jumped back and forth between the stock and commodity markets in order to profit from price volatility. Among those in that select group was Joseph Leiter, who, after recovering from his wheat market debacle, was sued for a $680,000 loss from an attempt to organize a pool to manipulate the stock of the International Power Company.[197]

Harper's Weekly reported on concerns over the use of "matched" trades, which were prearranged buy and sell orders at the same price by the same person sent to different brokers for execution. Matched orders were permitted by the NYSE.[198] A matched order is similar to a wash sale in that they are orders from the same person to buy and sell a stock at the same price. However, unlike a wash sale, the buy and sell orders are not executed by the same broker. Matched orders are entered through two brokers, one handling the buy side and the other the sell side. This arrangement helps disguise from the market the fact that the orders are intended to offset each other and gives a misleading impression of bona fide market activity.

Such matched orders were used to manipulate prices on the New York Stock Exchange during August 1908. The railroad stocks affected included the Northern Pacific, Great Northern, Rock Island, and New York Central. Massive matched orders on Saturday, August 22, 1908, pushed prices up before they collapsed to their prior level, bankrupting a firm engaged in that operation.[199] *Harper's* asserted that "the fact that prices were practically uninfluenced by transactions of unprecedented magnitude is noteworthy, because it shows that mere manipulation, if it were such, unaccompanied by sound fundamental reasons for a movement of prices either up or down, is one of the most hopelessly ineffective activities in which speculators can engage, and one which brings its own punishment."[200] One senator called the New York Cotton Exchange "one great gambling institution."[201]

"Perhaps the most notorious instance of manipulation in recent years was the 1909 operation in the stock of the Columbus & Hocking Coal & Iron Co., conducted by a pool of which James R. Keene was manager."[202] "A pool is an agreement between named persons of firms

194. *Id.* at 29.

195. *See generally*, ROBERT F. BRUNER AND SEAN D. CAR, THE PANIC OF 1907 (2007).

196. *Id.* at 46-47. Livermore denied that he had planted the article in the *World*. RICHARD SMITTEN, JESSE LIVERMORE 83-84 (2001).

197. *Joseph Leiter Denies New York Is His Home*, NEW YORK TIMES, March 17, 1922.

198. II JERRY W. MARKHAM, A FINANCIAL HISTORY OF THE UNITED STATES, FROM J.P. MORGAN TO THE INSTITUTIONAL INVESTOR (1900-1970) 5 (2002).

199. *See generally*, MARTIN S. FRIDSON, IT WAS A VERY GOOD YEAR 18 (1998) (discussing this trading).

200. Howard Schenck Mott, *Stock Market Manipulation and Its Punishment*, HARPER'S WEEKLY, Sept. 5, 1908, at 28.

201. 43 Cong. Rec. 1403 (Jan. 26, 1909) (remarks of Sen. Davis).

202. *Report of the Committee Appointed Pursuant to House Resolutions 429 and 504 to Investigate the Concentration of Control of Money and Credit*, H. Rep. No. 1593, 62d Cong., 3d Sess. 47 (1913).

to buy or sell within a stated period and in stated proportions, not exceeding a certain number of shares of a particular stock" as designated by the pool manager.[203] This pool was composed of ten NYSE stock exchange firms who entered into a formal written agreement that called for the pool manager to buy up to 20,000 shares of common stock.[204] The pool forced the price of this stock from $24 to $92.5 over the course of about ten months. The pool was broken in January 1910 when a flood of sell orders caused the stock's price to plunge to $25 and later to just $2. Keene, unbeknownst to the other pool participants, some of whom were bankrupted, apparently orchestrated the sell orders.[205] A short-term manipulation occurred in the stock of the Rock Island Co. on December 27, 1909, pushing its price up by $30, before the price fell back to its starting point a few hours later.[206]

James A. Patten continued his manipulations with an attempted corner of the May 1909 CBOT wheat futures contract.[207] *Harper's Weekly* claimed that he had raised the price of bread in America during that operation.[208] That magazine also noted that "[b]ills by the dozens are being introduced into State Legislatures to prohibit trading in grain futures, but Government interference with the business of the country is at a discount these days and not much is likely to be accomplished."[209] It also opined that the government had to bear some blame for the inflated prices of flour by imposing a duty on Canadian wheat that excluded it from the U.S. market. Patten escaped sanctions for the May wheat affair. However, he was later indicted under the Sherman Antitrust Act for cornering cotton in 1909, and the Supreme Court held that his corner could violate that statute.[210] Undaunted, Patten attempted another corner, this time in the December 1913 CBOT futures contract for corn only a few months after the Supreme Court's decision on his earlier cotton corner.[211]

1:6 GOVERNMENTAL REPONSES TO MANIPULATION

The Panic of 1907 resulted in an investigation by New York governor Charles E. Hughes's Committee on Speculation in Securities and Commodities (Hughes Committee), which rendered its report in 1909.[212] The Hughes Committee noted that state gambling laws had been avoided by speculators on the commodity and stock exchanges through "technical delivery" requirements involving offsets of contracts through clearinghouses or "ring settlements." It included among the "patrons" of the NYSE "manipulators" whose corporate connections enabled them "under certain circumstances to move the prices up or down, and who are thus in some degree protected from dangers encountered by other speculators."[213]

---

203. *Id.*

204. WARREN F. HICKERNELL, MANIPULATION AND MARKET LEADERSHIP 16-17 (1921).

205. *Id.* at 48-49.

206. *Id.* at 50.

207. Robert W. Kolb and Pablo T. Spiller, *The Manipulation of Futures Markets: An Overview*, at pp. 25-26, Paper presented at a Conference on Market Manipulation: Law, Economics, and Public Policy sponsored by the Center for Study of Futures and Options Markets and the American Bar Association, Washington, DC (Nov. 8 & 9, 1990).

208. *The Man Who Raised the Price of Bread*, HARPER'S WEEKLY, May 1, 1909, at 1.

209. Franklin Escher, *Finance, The So-Called Corner in Wheat*, HARPER'S WEEKLY, May 1, 1909, at 30.

210. United States v. Patten, 226 U.S. 525 (1913).

211. *See*, WAYNE G. BROEHL, CARGILL: TRADING THE WORLD'S GRAIN 194 (1992) (describing the 1913 attempt).

212. State of New York, *Report of Governor Hughes Committee on Speculation in Securities and Commodities* (June 7, 1909).

213. *Id.* at 4, 5.

The Hughes Committee found that "only a small part" of the trading on the NYSE was of an investment nature and that a substantial part of the trading on that exchange was "virtually gambling."[214] It, nevertheless, rejected calls to curb margin trading and short selling.[215] The Hughes Committee did suggest that doubling margin requirements would reduce speculative losses.[216] It recommended that NYSE margins be increased to 20 percent.[217]

The Hughes Committee had more concern with manipulations to profit from price fluctuations that were planned in advance, especially when accompanied by wash sales.[218] The committee suggested that corners be handled by allowing the NYSE to fix a settlement price where a corner is accomplished.[219] The Hughes Committee concluded that market manipulations used to float initial offerings of securities should be permissible by underwriting syndicates in order to create a market in new securities, as long as this was not accomplished by "matched orders." One of the more famous market operations supporting new offerings considered by the Hughes Committee involved the floatation of the U.S. Steel Co. stock to the public. The price of that massive offering was supported by James Keene. "Under his manipulation Steel common reached 55 in the first months of its appearance on the Stock Exchange, a price which it never touched again" for several years.[220]

The Hughes Committee also found that most business on the three commodity exchanges in New York, which at that time dealt in produce, cotton, and coffee, was "mainly speculative."[221] The New York commodity exchanges prohibited difference trading and wash sales, but allowed futures trading that allowed settlement on the basis of price differences.[222] The Hughes Committee refused to condemn futures trading, noting that an industrial commission created by President William McKinley to study the condition of labor and capital had concluded in 1901 that futures trading was "indispensible" to the global pricing of commodities and that it allowed merchants to hedge against price changes.[223]

The Hughes Committee found that the New York Cotton Exchange was the "most important cotton market in the world" and that it was financing some 80 percent of the crop of the United States.[224] Nevertheless, there had been "instances of excessive speculation upon the Cotton Exchange, notably the Sully speculation of 1904," and "a great deal of speculation of the gambling type."[225] The Coffee Exchange in New York was found to have stabilized coffee prices, but the Hughes Committee noted that the government of Brazil had recently decided to control prices by purchasing excess supplies.[226]

---

214. *Id.*

215. *Id.* at 5-6. The Hughes Committee also rejected demands for a prohibition against naked short selling when the party selling a security has not borrowed or otherwise arranged for the delivery of particular securities. *Id.* at 7. Such restrictions were imposed by the Securities and Exchange Commission in the twenty-first century. *See* Chapter 7.

216. *Id.* at 18-19.

217. Jerry W. Markham, *Federal Regulation of Margin in the Commodity Futures Industry—History and Theory*, 64 TEMP. L. REV. 59, 99 (1991).

218. State of New York, *Report of Governor Hughes Committee on Speculation in Securities and Commodities* 7 (June 7, 1909).

219. *Id.* at 8.

220. *J.R. Keene Called in Exchange Inquiry*, NEW YORK TIMES, March 6, 1909, at 1.

221. State of New York, *Report of Governor Hughes Committee on Speculation in Securities and Commodities* 17-19 (June 7, 1909).

222. *Id.* at 17-19.

223. *Id.* at 18.

224. *Id.* at 19.

225. *Id.* at 20.

226. *Id.*

Another delayed study of the market resulting from the Panic of 1907 was not rendered until 1913 by a committee of the House of Representatives created by House resolutions to investigate the concentration of control of money and credit in the United States.[227] This populist endeavor was headed by Congressman Arsene Pujo from Louisiana, who served as chair of the House Committee on Banking and Currency. The Pujo Committee did, indeed, find a "money trust" that was controlled by a small group of bankers headed by J.P. Morgan, George Baker, and James Stillman.

The Pujo Committee also conducted an investigation of the NYSE and found that a "very important phase of speculation on the New York Stock Exchange is the manipulation of prices up or down, as desired, without regard to the real value of the securities, and the creation of a false appearance of activity in particular stocks."[228] It found that such activity was carried out by wash sales that consisted of "giving of simultaneous or substantially simultaneous orders by the same person or persons to buy and sell the same stock. In this way the market for a stock is given a false appearance of activity, the object being to draw the public into the speculation."[229] Prices were also "artificially raised or lowered through the concentration of buying or selling orders, as the case may be."[230]

The Pujo Committee criticized syndication efforts during initial public offerings of stock issues that sought to stimulate prices in order to sell the issues to the public. It also found that in one instance Salomon & Co. and Lewisohn Bros. had manipulated the aftermarket in a stock issue of the California Petroleum Co. by entering scale up and scale down orders to various brokers over a period of twenty-one days, which created an appearance of activity and overall influenced prices upward. The purpose of those transactions "apparently was to create an appearance of activity in the stock that would enable those to whom it had been sold to resell it to the general public at a profit."[231]

The Pujo Committee's findings were harshly critical of the NYSE. The committee found that some trading on the exchange included investors and some "wholesome speculation." Nevertheless, most of the volume on the NYSE was described as representing "speculation indistinguishable in effect from wagering and more hurtful than lotteries or gambling at the race track or the roulette table." The Pujo Committee concluded "that as an adjunct of such speculation quotations of securities are manipulated without regard to real values and false appearances of demand or supply are created." In even harsher terms, the committee stated that the facilities of the NYSE "are employed largely for transactions producing moral and economic waste and corruption; and it is fair to assume that in lesser and varying degree this is true or may come to be true of other institutions throughout the country similarly organized and conducted."[232]

The Pujo Committee did not seek federal regulation of the NYSE, recommending, instead, state action and greater exchange self-regulation that would include such things as requiring prospectuses on initial public offerings and periodic financial statements by listed companies; margin of at least 20 percent on stock purchases; and prohibition of manipulation by proscribing "simultaneous or substantially simultaneous orders proceeding from the same person or persons to buy and sell the

227. *Report of the Committee Appointed Pursuant to House Resolutions 429 and 504 to Investigate the Concentration of Control of Money and Credit*, H. Rep. No. 1593, 62d Cong., 3d Sess. (1913).

228. *Id.* at 46.

229. *Id.*

230. *Id.*

231. *Id.* at 52. Such practices do not die easily. *See*, Credit Suisse Securities (USA) LLC v. Billing, 551 U.S. 264, 267 (2007) (discussing underwriting practice of requiring purchasers of a popular "hot" issue initial public offering at the initial offering price to buy additional securities in the offering at increasing prices).

232. *Report of the Committee Appointed Pursuant to House Resolutions 429 and 504 to Investigate the Concentration of Control of Money and Credit*, H. Rep. No. 1593, 62d Cong., 3d Sess. 116 (1913).

same security for the purpose of creating an appearance of activity therein, and any orders the purpose of which is to inflate or depress the price of any security."[233]

No commodity or stock manipulation legislation resulted from the Pujo inquiry, but the Federal Trade Commission (FTC) was created in 1914.[234] As described below, the FTC would conduct a massive investigation of the grain trade after World War I that laid the groundwork for regulation of commodity futures trading and proscriptions against commodity price manipulations. Otherwise, except for a brief appearance as a securities regulator before the creation of the Securities and Exchange Commission, the FTC had no significant role in price manipulations until it was given such powers by Congress in 2007.

The Panic of 1907 did result in the passage of a California statute that made it a crime to publish false rumors about the financial condition of banks that could cause runs by depositors and result in a drop in the price of the stock of the bank being attacked. However, that legislation was declared unconstitutional by a California appellate court in 2012. The court held that false statements made on Craigslist, an Internet message board, by a former employee of a bank were protected constitutional speech.[235] As will be seen in later chapters, however, many modern manipulation cases involve claims of manipulation by false statements.

1:7 SPECULATION CONTINUES

In 1908, in response to a House resolution, Herbert Knox Smith, Commissioner of Corporations (which was later replaced by the Federal Trade Commission), submitted a report on the cotton exchanges that addressed pricing problems on the New York Cotton Exchange after a crop failure in 1906. He found that a committee of exchange members had failed to set appropriate standards to measure differences in cotton quality ("fine," good," "fair," "middling," etc.). Several of those exchange committee members were short cotton in 1906 and made large profits from their pricing of contracts on the exchange.[236] The New York Cotton Exchange failed to respond to those concerns and problems continued over the next several years.[237]

---

233. *Id.* at 116-117.

234. 38 Stat. 719 (1914).

235. Summit Bank v. Rogers, 206 Cal. App. 4th 669 (2012). *See also*, Joe Adler, *Law Designed to Prevent Bank Runs Struck Down*, 177 American Banker, June 6, 2012, at 1 (analyzing this case).

236. U.S. Bureau of Corporations, *Report of the Commissioner of Corporations on Cotton Exchanges*, Pt. I at 18 (May 1908).

237. *See*, Newton Hoffman, *The Cotton Futures Act*, 23 J. Pol. Econ. 465 (May 1915) (describing this controversy over grading and its objectionable effects on pricing). This author noted:

> The most serious charge made against the New York Cotton Exchange was that of arbitrarily fixing the differences for the relative values of the various grades of cotton deliverable on contract. Trading is done on the basis of middling, and there have been from 10 to 15 grades above and below this basic grade. The seller of 100 bales, according to the by-laws of the Exchange, had the right to deliver any and all grades of cotton, and the buyer had no option. The prices of the various kinds of cotton within the prescribed range of grades were determined by the so-called "differences" above and below, or "on" and "off" middling. For the last eighteen years the New York Exchange has used the "fixed-difference" system, that is, a committee of the Exchange would meet twice or three times a year, at stated dates, and arbitrarily decide the scale of differences. This body of men, called the Revision Committee, was not bound by any rules of procedure, nor was it restricted to any definite method for arriving at the relative values. It had full discretionary power and could avail itself of any or no information upon which to base its decision. . . . The evil of the system lay in the fact that the fixed differences frequently did not represent the actual relative market values of the different grades of cotton.

The Democratic Party's platform for Woodrow Wilson's presidential campaign in 1912 sought to "suppress the pernicious practice of gambling in agricultural products by organized exchanges and others."[238] A House committee considered some "25 or 30 bills" in 1912 that sought to restrict speculation in cotton futures and other commodities. The committee recommended passage of two bills that would "confine buying and selling to the actual commodity bought and sold, to prevent illegitimate speculation and the creation of fictitious values, to guard the innocent public against the sharp practices of the trained speculator, and to prevent the violent fluctuations in the prices of the necessities of life by eliminating the purely gambling transactions in them."[239]

In 1914, Congress passed the Cotton Futures Act,[240] which sought to impose a penal and prohibitive tax on futures transactions that did not comport with specified grading standards for the quality of cotton to be delivered on the contract. Further, delivery on the contract was required. A federal court, however, struck that legislation because it had been originated in the Senate, rather than the House, as required by the Constitution for revenue measures.[241] New legislation was passed in 1916 that allowed cotton futures trading where the contract prices reflected differences in grade. That act also authorized the Department of Agriculture to create an inspection, grading, and labeling system for cotton.

The New York Mercantile Exchange (NYMEX) was the subject of four separate investigations on whether quotations posted on the exchange for eggs and butter were manipulated and artificial. One such investigation, which was conducted in 1916, was directed by the New York attorney general. He concluded that butter and egg prices on the NYMEX had, since 1903, "been manipulated and misrepresented in the interest of a few members of the Exchange who were very large dealers in those commodities."[242]

The outbreak of World War I caused a closure of the New York Stock Exchange for more than four months, which was only the second such closure in its history.[243] A short wheat crop was accompanied by frenzied speculation and increased prices in that commodity, which again raised animosity toward speculators. Food prices rose by some 50 percent, and critics complained that the "American people are not getting enough to eat" and that "speculators" were "seeking to amass . . . great fortunes at the expense of the health and happiness of the American people."[244] "The Kaiser's Allies in America are the food gamblers" and "[t]hose who undertake to corner the market . . . should be put in the same class with the spy and the traitor and share the same fate . . . !"[245] A London paper charged in 1916 that "wheat gamblers in Chicago" were sending prices "skyward" in a "discreditable spectacle of frenzied speculation."[246]

Speculation also rose in the stock market during World War I. The stock market increased by 50 percent in value in 1915. There were a number of manipulations in "war stocks" during World War

---

Id. at 471.

238. *See*, H.R. Rep. No. 681, 62d Cong., 2d Sess. (1912); II JERRY W. MARKHAM, A FINANCIAL HISTORY OF THE UNITED STATES, FROM J.P. MORGAN TO THE INSTITUTIONAL INVESTOR (1900-1970) 95 (2002) (citation omitted).

239. H.R. Rep. No. 681, 62d Cong., 4 2d Sess. (1912).

240. Pub. L. No. 174, 38 Stat. 693 (Aug. 18, 1914).

241. Hubbard v. Lowe, 226 F. 135 (S.D.N.Y. 1915), *dismissed*, 242 U.S. 654 (1916).

242. *Finds Manipulation in Butter and Eggs*, NEW YORK TIMES, July 24, 1916, at 4.

243. HENRY G.S. NOBLE, THE NEW YORK STOCK EXCHANGE IN THE CRISIS OF 1914 8 (1915).

244. T. KESSNER, FIORELLO H. LAGUARDIA AND THE MAKING OF THE MODERN NEW YORK 45 (1989).

245. *Our War-Profiteers*, LITERARY DIGEST, May 26, 1917, at 1583.

246. *Raps Wheat Speculation*, NEW YORK TIMES, Aug. 14, 1917, at 2.

I of companies that would likely benefit from the production of war materials, such as the Crucible Steel Co.[247] No action was taken to regulate such conduct by the federal government.[248]

A note by President Wilson on December 20, 1916, to the belligerents offering to mediate an armistice caused a sharp drop in the stock market. The note was mistakenly released prematurely to some news services. Charges were made that high government officials had engaged in insider trading before issuance of the note. A congressional investigation found no such trading but did discover that two reporters had leaked the note to some brokerage firms that the reporters were receiving retainers from.[249] The NYSE tried to monitor short selling after a collapse of stock prices in 1917. The NYSE required its member firms to supply the exchange with a list of the stocks they borrowed for short sellers and the names of those customers.[250]

The Chicago Board of Trade restricted trading in wheat futures in 1917 after an "unparalleled rise in prices" that saw May wheat trading at $3.25 per bushel. "[S]peculators who had sold short in trades involving delivery in May were finding it impossible to cover their short sales" due to hoarding and purchases by Allied nations.[251] The CBOT set a settlement price of $3.18 per bushel for May wheat futures and also suspended speculative buying of the July and September contracts, which were settled at $2.75 and $2.45, respectively. That action was taken, in part, as the result of "suggestions from Washington."[252]

The CBOT set a ceiling price on corn and oat futures in 1917. It banned trading in "indemnities" also known as "puts and calls" or "bids and offers," a form of difference trading.[253] The exchange established position limits for traders and set price limits that required the suspension of trading when those limits were met. The U.S. Attorney in Chicago began an investigation of forty large traders on the CBOT. The CBOT then suspended trading in the contracts in which they were trading. The Chicago Butter and Egg Board, which became the Chicago Mercantile Exchange, suspended trading on June 1, 1917. The New York Coffee and Sugar Exchange suspended trading in sugar futures on August 16, 1917, and later coffee futures as well, at the government's request. The New York Cotton Exchange also acceded to a government request that it restrict price movements in cotton futures.[254]

World War I was the first national effort to impose price controls on a national level in the United States.[255] Herbert Hoover was then recalled from Europe, where he chaired the Belgian Relief Commission, to assume the role of the "food czar" in the United States.[256] Hoover sought federal control of wheat prices and predicted a price of $20 per barrel for flour if controls were not implemented.[257] He claimed that there "will be scarcely a bushel of wheat available a year

247. *Id.* at 69.

248. *Id.* at 82-84.

249. Cedric B. Cowing, Populists, Plungers, and Progressives 75-78 (1965).

250. II Jerry W. Markham, A Financial History of the United States, From J.P. Morgan to the Institutional Investor (1900-1970) 81 (2002).

251. William M. Duffus, *Government Control of The Wheat Trade in the United States*, 8 American Econ. Rev. 62, 73 (1918).

252. *Id.* at 75.

253. *Halt Grain Trading; Conference Called*, New York Times, May 15, 1917, at 1.

254. II Jerry W. Markham, A Financial History of the United States, From J.P. Morgan to the Institutional Investor (1900-1970) 97 (2002).

255. The Confederate government experimented unsuccessfully with price controls during the Civil War as a measure for curbing runaway inflation. Those controls failed miserably and the Confederacy was forced to print money in such quantities that it lost all value. I Jerry W. Markham, A Financial History of the United States, From Christopher Columbus to the Robber Barons (1492-1900) 235 (2002).

256. William E. Leuchtenburg, Herbert Hoover 33 (2009).

257. *Hoover Is Alarmed by Wheat Advance,* New York Times, May 11, 1917, at 20.

from now."[258] Hoover also charged that "consumer and producer alike were being exploited by the speculator in wheat."[259]

Hoover testified in congressional hearings that $250 million paid by consumers of flour in a four-month period was in excess of justifiable prices as the result of speculation.[260] Interestingly, even some speculators, including James Patten, supported the legislation because "there isn't wheat enough to go round."[261] However, Senator Reed from Missouri charged that Hoover had used Belgium relief funds to buy wheat and that those purchases had increased prices for American consumers.[262]

The Food and Fuel Control Act of 1917 (also called the Lever Act)[263] was enacted under congressional war powers in order to stabilize prices. It provided fines for hoarding and imposed price controls in order to "prevent scarcity, monopolization, hoarding, and injurious speculation."[264] The Lever Act authorized the president to prescribe regulations "in order to prevent injurious speculation, or in order to prevent unjust market manipulation or unfair and misleading market quotations."[265] The president was authorized to require the commodity exchanges to take such action as he might deem necessary to stop such "evil practices."[266]

This legislation was supported by "[m]any wheat farmers in the United States [who] had for years opposed the activities of the grain exchanges, and particularly trading in futures, and were ready to support any movement designed to stop or restrict operations on exchanges."[267] One economist noted the distaste for "middlemen" by socialists and farm organizations who believed "that a very large proportion of the middlemen now engaged in marketing food products and other necessities can, should, and will be 'eliminated' and replaced by more economical agencies of a cooperative or governmental nature."[268]

H.A. Garfield, the president of Williams College, was appointed as the fuel administrator under the Lever Act legislation, responsible for licensing manufacturers and distributors of fuel oil with gross sales of more than 100,000 barrels annually.[269] Hoover, through the Food Administration, carried out the price control program for wheat and other foodstuffs under the Lever Act. Hoover used patriotic requests for "Meatless Mondays" and "Wheatless" Wednesdays. A gasoline "famine" led to "Gasolineless Sundays."[270]

Incredibly, the Food Administration chose the household of the assistant secretary of the Navy, Franklin Roosevelt, as a model for showing Americans how to conserve food in a "large household." The Roosevelt household was composed of seven family members attended by ten servants. Among other things, the servants were encouraged "to make helpful suggestions in the use of 'left-overs.' . . . Menu rules allow two courses for luncheon and three for dinner."[271] Apparently, the Roosevelt

258. *Halt Grain Trading; Conference Called*, NEW YORK TIMES, May 15, 1917, at 1.
259. *250,000,000,* NEW YORK TIMES, June 20, 1917, at 1.
260. *Sees Peril in Lack of Wheat Control*, NEW YORK TIMES, July 11, 1917, at 1.
261. *Wheat Pit Apathetic*, NEW YORK TIMES, Aug. 14, 1917, at 1.
262. *Attacks Hoover as Arch Gambler*, NEW YORK TIMES, July 17, 1917, at 3.
263. 40 Stat. 276 (1917).
264. *Id.* at § 1.
265. 49 Stat. at 280, § 13.
266. *Id.* at § 1.
267. William M. Duffus, *Government Control of The Wheat Trade in The United States*, 8 AMERICAN ECON. REV. 62, 65 (1918).
268. *Id.* at 68.
269. *Fuel Oil Placed Under License*, NEW YORK TIMES, Feb. 5, 1918, at 1.
270. DANIEL YERGIN, THE QUEST 230 (2011).
271. *How to Save in Big Homes*, NEW YORK TIMES, July 17, 1917, at 3. IV WILLIAM BLACKSTONE, COMMENTARIES ON THE LAW 124 (WAYNE MORRISON, Editor, 2001).

family was unaware of the sixteenth-century sumptuary law of England, 10 Edw. 3 st.3, "which ordains, that no man shall be served, at dinner or supper, with more than two courses; except upon some great holidays there specified, in which case he may be served with three."[272]

Hoover used a program borrowed from ancient Egypt[273] that set "fair" prices for wheat, which were initially set by a committee "representative of all interests and all sections" at $2.20 per bushel in Chicago.[274] That price was later increased to $2.26 per bushel.[275] Hoover's purchasing program for wheat was carried out by the Grain Corporation, a government-owned enterprise that was funded with $50 million in government funds. Wheat prices were set by the Price-Fixing Commission, which was composed of various labor, agricultural, and business interests.[276]

This purchasing program proved to be too successful:

> By mid-September the country's storage facilities were bursting with wheat. Even worse, the money to buy the crop was running out. Under the law, Hoover's Grain Corporation was obligated to purchase every bushel of grain offered it, and at the guaranteed price. In the summer of 1918 it possessed $150,000,000 for this purpose, the maximum possible under the Lever Act. But as the tide of wheat surged off the farms in late summer, even this enormous sum was not enough. By mid-September the Grain Corporation had exhausted its capital and had begun to borrow heavily from banks.[277]

Hoover solved this problem by selling the wheat to the Allies and having the Treasury Department loan funds for their purchases.[278]

The Lever Act became somewhat infamous as a result of Attorney General A. Mitchell Palmer's efforts to enjoin a nationwide coal strike under its provisions.[279] The Lever Act was also dealt a blow by the Supreme Court in *United States v. L. Cohen Grocery Co.*,[280] in which the Court held that the act was unconstitutional insofar as it sought to criminalize the making by any person of "any unjust or unreasonable rate or charge in handling or dealing in or with any necessaries." The Court concluded that such a standard did not adequately inform defendants of the nature of the crime for such a violation. The defendant in that case had been charged with selling sugar at an exorbitant price—in other words, price gouging.

1:8 THE FEDERAL TRADE COMMISSION REPORT

Cotton prices reached a level in April 1918 that had not been seen since the end of the Civil War, but the market plunged as World War I ended. The War Industries Board banned short selling in cotton after a selloff in that market when victory was announced in November 1918, but prices continued to decline. The commodity futures exchanges removed the remaining wartime trading restrictions on grain futures in August 1920.

---

272. IV William Blackstone, Commentaries on the Law 124 (Wayne Morrison, Editor, 2001).

273. See § 1:2.

274. Armour Grain Co. v. United States Grain Corp., 241 Ill. App. 332, 339 (Ill. App. 1926).

275. Food and Agriculture Organization of the United Nations (ed. Adam Prakash), *Safeguarding Food Security in Volatile Global Markets* (2011), http://www.fao.org/docrep/013/i2107e/i2107e13.pdf (accessed September 14, 2011).

276. *Big Corporation to Control Wheat*, New York Times, Aug. 16, 1917, at 1.

277. George H. Nash, The Life of Herbert Hoover: Master of Emergencies (1917-1918) 383 (1996).

278. *Id.* at 384-385.

279. David Alan Corbin, Life, Work, Rebellion in the Coal Fields 197 (1981).

280. United States v. L. Cohen Grocery Co., 255 U.S. 81 (1921).

"Wheat prices began to decline almost immediately and this situation gave rise to the belief in many quarters wheat prices were forced down by short selling of wheat futures by large speculators and grain merchants."[281] The food administration warned that the exchanges would be held accountable for any manipulation in prices.[282] Resumption of futures trading was also accompanied by much price volatility. "The day they began operations we commenced to have the old 10 cents and 20 cents and 30 cents a day fluctuation in the grain market, sometimes up and sometimes down."[283]

The farming sector had ramped up production during the war but demand cooled sharply with the peace, and prices plunged. The price of wheat was slashed between 1919 and 1922, a decline blamed on an "orgy" of speculation and a "great bear raid."[284] The drop in wheat prices was accompanied by a fall in other commodity prices. Corn, for example, dropped from $1.05 per bushel to 41 cents.[285] The decline in wheat prices was blamed on "grain gamblers"[286] and "gave rise to the belief in many quarters that wheat prices were forced down by large speculators and grain merchants."[287]

The Federal Trade Commission (FTC), which was already conducting a food investigation, was asked by the president to investigate the grain markets.[288] The FTC's report on that investigation was published in several volumes between 1920 and 1926.[289] The FTC also published a two-volume report in response to a Senate resolution requesting an investigation of the facts concerning market manipulations in connection with large export transactions.[290]

The FTC's reports examined every aspect of the grain trade, including the role of the commodity exchanges. The agency also analyzed the role of speculation and manipulation on the commodity exchanges. The FTC found that many people were concerned about volatile prices: "The stabilization of prices is generally regarded as of the greatest possible importance to both the consumer and the producer." The report recommended elimination of "useless" price changes. "There is apparently too much speculation for the quick turn."[291]

The FTC found that the delivery requirement on futures contracts made them susceptible to manipulation through corners and squeezes as the delivery time approached.[292] The results of a

---

281. II Federal Trade Commission, Report on Methods and Operations of Grain Exporters XXIII (1923).

282. II Jerry W. Markham, A Financial History of the United States, From J.P. Morgan to the Institutional Investor (1900-1970) 98 (2002).

283. *Futures Trading: Hearings Before the House Committee on Agriculture and Forestry*, 67th Cong., 1st Sess. 5 (1921) (remarks of Rep. Tincher).

284. *Id.* at 100.

285. *Id.* at 99.

286. *Id.* at 100.

287. II Federal Trade Commission, Report on Methods and Operations of Grain Exporters XXIII (1923).

288. *Id.* at 100.

289. I-VII Federal Trade Commission, Report on the Grain Trade (1920-1926).

290. I-II Federal Trade Commission, Report on Methods and Operations of Grain Exporters (1923).

291. VII Federal Trade Commission, Report on the Grain Trade 10-11 (1923).

292. The FTC stated:

> In the true corner some one or more speculators, usually with elevator connections, constitute a concentrated interest on the buying side and accumulate more long contracts than they think it possible for the sellers to make delivery on, thus compelling the latter to settle at a price dictated by the cornering interest. . . . In the process of running a corner the cornerers acquire all or nearly all the wheat (or corn or oats) that is in store in the regular warehouses in Chicago (or at whatever terminal market may be the scene of their operations), either by purchase and storage

corner were that grain prices were artificially increased and short sellers were subjected to undue losses. In addition, supplies of grain were diverted to markets for which there was no economic need from markets where those supplies were needed.[293] The FTC noted that the number of corners had been decreasing: "This may be attributed in part to the development of anti-corner rules, supported by a stronger sentiment against cornering than formerly prevailed in the grain markets."[294]

An aspect of manipulations was "tailing on" by small speculators who sought to profit from increases from a long manipulation and thereby aided the manipulation by their purchases. The FTC found that these speculators often had limited resources and traded on thin margins, making them susceptible to bear attacks. These "lambs" were "incompetent speculators" who were shorn by the more professional traders.[295] Bears could take advantage of these speculators by selling down the market to touch off their stop-loss orders, a practice now known as "gunning the stops." Although a later government case claimed that bear operations had become "one of the main forms of manipulation,"[296] the FTC study found little evidence of this actually occurring at the time. Rather, the bear operators were simply using their market power to push down prices.[297] The CBOT did provide some limited relief to shorts caught in a corner. The CBOT sought "to penalize the short seller who is caught in a corner and compelled to default, but also to prevent his being punished too much."[298] This was done by allowing a defaulting short to seek arbitration before an exchange committee. The committee was authorized to set a settlement price at 10 percent above the "true commercial value" of the commodity.[299]

The FTC found that "squeezes" tended to be more successful than corners because a corner presented the problem of how to "bury the corpse."[300] This was a reference to the fact that the perpetrators of the corner had the problem of selling the supplies acquired during their operation. Such sales would drive down prices and reduce the profits from the corner or even cause a loss. The operators of corners engaged in elaborate schemes to deal with this problem by reducing or diverting stocks that would have to be accepted for delivery in order to complete the corner.[301]

Another phenomenon considered by the FTC was the existence of "congestion," a "natural" corner or squeeze brought about by market conditions that result in a shortage of supplies available for delivery.[302] Congestion may be exacerbated by large traders.[303] In that regard, the FTC

> of the cash grain through earlier deliveries made by sellers of the futures, and thus occupy approximately the position of being the only holders of the actual wheat from whom grain can be bought to meet obligations on the futures contracts by delivery.

V Federal Trade Commission, Report on the Grain Trade 322 (1923).

293. *Id.* at 323.

294. VII Federal Trade Commission, Report on the Grain Trade 9 (1923).

295. II Federal Trade Commission, Report on Methods and Operations of Grain Exporters 49 (1923).

296. In re Henner, 30 Agric. Dec. 1151, 1181, n. 25 (1971).

297. VII Federal Trade Commission, Report on the Grain Trade 255 (1923).

298. V Federal Trade Commission, Report on the Grain Trade 327 (1923).

299. *Id.* at 328.

300. *Id.* at 255.

301. *Id.* at 251.

302. *Id.* at 243.

303. One later government report defined congestion as

> a condition where one or a few traders control such a large percentage of the open contracts that prices may be unduly influenced by the operations of those traders or where, toward the end of the life of a future, delay of liquidation by longs may cause the maturing future to advance in relation to more distant months and relative to prices of the cash commodity.

Report of the Chief of the Commodity Exchange Authority 40 (Sept. 25, 1939).

study asserted that a corner by James A. Patten in 1913 in the December CBOT corn contract was actually an effort to take advantage of natural market conditions that had squeezed supplies.[304] In any event, the price effects of congestion were nearly as bad as those in a corner that deliberately seeks to create such conditions artificially.[305]

The FTC also concluded that a decline from $2.90 per bushel of wheat in Chicago in July 1920 to nearly $1 in September 1922 "was due mainly to the natural factors of supply and demand, while the advance of 60 cents per bushel in May, 1921 wheat was due to a so-called 'natural corner' caused largely by a New York exporter standing for the delivery on his futures contracts for more wheat than could be delivered."[306]

The FTC reviewed several manipulations in the futures markets, including ones in September 1920 corn, May 1921 wheat, and July 1921 rye. A key to those manipulations was the delivery requirement for futures contracts on their termination ("delivery") dates. The fixed time limit on the life of a futures contract "gives the cornerer his opportunity, provided he is able either to foresee or to contrive a conjunction of circumstances that will help him to mulct the shorts."[307] Critics of futures sought to prohibit speculators from standing for delivery, while supporters of the delivery requirement claimed that delivery ensured convergence of futures and cash prices. The FTC study rejected claims that merely standing for delivery was evidence of manipulation, noting that this was a matter of contractual right under the futures contracts.[308]

The FTC study exposed some of the difficulties of proving whether prices were actually artificial as the result of a manipulation. The study cited evidence of a successful manipulation as the existence of price disparities between the delivery point on the futures contract and other market areas.[309] That computation, however, was not a simple one. "Basis" adjustments were needed to reflect the difference in transportation costs between the terminal market and those outside that area. Supply and demand disparities could also exist in remote markets, where an excessive supply or lower demand could account for the difference. Another measure of possible manipulation was price differences between terminal markets such as Kansas City and Chicago that deviated from historical norms, but the FTC noted that prices in both markets could be affected by a manipulation. Still another measurement could be an unusual decline in prices immediately after the taking of large deliveries on a futures contract, but that could be explained by a natural congestion.[310]

The role of intent in manipulations was also considered. The FTC study noted that popular sentiment was concerned only with "who did it" when prices spiked, but the more critical problem was that manipulative intent was often either lacking or could not be proved.[311] The FTC found that high prices could result from large traders who were merely being stubborn and had no intent to create artificial prices. For example, these big "plungers" might merely be "trying out the market" through large transactions. Alternatively, they might be trying to "feel for the bottom" of the market without bad intent even though it appeared to an observer that they were deliberately "hammering" the market.[312] The FTC cited the example of a sale by a large trader of 100,000 bushels of a commodity to see how the market would react. A lack of reaction would signal that

304. VII Federal Trade Commission, Report on the Grain Trade 244 (1923).

305. *Id.* at 243.

306. II Federal Trade Commission, Report on Methods and Operations of Grain Exporters XX (1923).

307. VII Federal Trade Commission, Report on the Grain Trade 251-252 (1923).

308. *Id.* at 269-270.

309. *Id.* at 245.

310. *Id.* at 244-245.

311. *Id.* at 243-244.

312. *Id.* at 259.

the market was experiencing strong demand, and the trader would then switch to the long side and commence a strong purchasing operation. Conversely, the trader might continue selling if the market declined after his large sale.[313]

The FTC suggested that cornering operations by groups would fall under conspiracy prohibitions against controlling prices and that the common-law crime of engrossing could be applied to cornering operations by individuals. The FTC also suggested that application of the Sherman Antitrust Act would be appropriate.[314] The FTC additionally considered whether manipulation was a crime of deceit and fraud:

> The idea of deceit or trickery is in general popularly associated with that of manipulation, although it is probably not essential. The exploitation of shorts by way of a corner, for instance, is primarily a matter of trading advantage of technical conditions of trading to extort money on the basis of values reaching in the pit which do not represent true commercial value. It is not necessary that deceit be involved, although the cornering interest certainly will not take pains to let it be known just how much of a long interest is developing and probably will actually adopt means to conceal the situation until it is too late for the shorts to bring grain in from distant points. Most other instances of manipulation, however, are primarily dependent on deceiving the public, or obtaining information in advance of traders generally, or employing trickery in some other way essential to the project and creating a false impression as to what is happening.[315]

The FTC found, however, that trading on "private information in advance of public knowledge is not an important factor in manipulative speculation in grain."[316]

The FTC found that exchange rules had failed to prevent manipulations and suggested alternative delivery points as a way to ease market congestion.[317] It recommended price limits that would halt trading in volatile market conditions, an action that was taken in 1918 in oat futures with some apparent success.[318] It further recommended limits on the size of trading by individual speculators and restrictions on the ability of short sellers to "bear" the market.[319] The FTC also recommended governmental supervision of the futures markets.[320]

The FTC study did find that low margin levels did have price effects because low margins allowed small speculators to overexpose themselves to the market. They were then forced to liquidate when unexpected market reverses occurred, and those liquidations accentuated market movements. "The exhaustion of margins when the market movement reverses itself, and the selling out of insufficiently margined accounts explains the sharpness of the market reaction when it comes."[321]

The FTC study compared the margining of commodity futures contracts and stocks. Margin for commodities futures is not an extension of credit, as in the case of securities.[322] Rather, it is

---

313. *Id.*

314. V Federal Trade Commission, Report on the Grain Trade 323-325 (1923). For a description of engrossing, see § 1.2.

315. *Id.* at 256-257.

316. *Id.* at 257.

317. *Id.* at 271.

318. *Id.* at 263.

319. *Id.* at 259.

320. *Id.* at 279. For an additional description of the FTC study, see Jerry W. Markham, *Manipulation of Commodity Futures Prices—The Unprosecutable Crime*, 8 Yale J. on Reg. 281, 292-298 (1991).

321. V Federal Trade Commission, Report on the Grain Trade 157 (1923).

322. *See*, Jerry W. Markham, *Federal Regulation of Margin in the Commodity Futures Industry—History and Theory*, 64 Temp. L. Rev. 59 (1991) (describing this distinction and background of margin requirements in both industries).

a good faith deposit of money to ensure that the customer will perform its obligations. The FTC noted that both had credit aspects but that, unlike stocks, delivery on a commodity futures contract is delayed into the future, if taken at all. Also unlike stocks, the volume of futures trading is not "restricted by the necessity of either selling only what one owns or borrowing for delivery what one sells without owning it." Thus, in "this important respect the purchase and sale of futures is a freer form of speculative activity than the purchase and sale of stocks."[323] Margin on futures contracts is also unique because it serves as "both a commercial credit device and a deposit made to secure . . . against loss because of non-performance." Such payments "are not part payments toward the purchase price but are merely deposits made to secure the rights of each of the contracting or interested parties."[324] Margin is used "to bind the bargain."[325]

At the time of the FTC study, the rules of the CBOT allowed members to demand margin from their counterparty of up to 10 percent of the notional value of their contracts. However, the parties could forgo such demands if they trusted each other. Margins for customers trading with a member were then set by the member, but such "credit is rather freely extended to the country in these matters, the member of the Board thus assuming the risks."[326]

1:9 THE FUTURES TRADING ACT OF 1921

Between 1890 and 1920 some 200 bills seeking to regulate futures and options trading were introduced, but none were enacted.[327] That changed with the enactment of the Futures Trading Act of 1921.[328] Congress began holding hearings on legislation to bar commodity price manipulations even before completion of the FTC study. "Many persons had advocated, as a remedy, that all future trading be abolished. Congress took a less extreme position. It set up a system of regulation and prohibited all future trading which did not comply with the regulations prescribed."[329]

In support of this legislation, Senator Arthur Capper (R-KS) claimed that the CBOT was a "gambling hell" and that "Monte Carlo or the Casino at Habana are not to be compared with it."[330] Senator Capper was particularly critical of the fact that the notional value of the contracts traded on the exchanges greatly exceeded that of the available grain in the United States. He attacked the

323. V Federal Trade Commission, Report on the Grain Trade 156 (1923).

324. *Id.* at 20, 17.

325. *Id.* at 156.

326. James E. Boyle, Speculation and the Chicago Board of Trade 85 (1920).

327. *See*, C. Louise Phillips-Corbett, *Statutes and Bills Relating to Futures Trading in Commodities* (available Library of the Commodity Futures Trading Commission) (compilation of bills introduced in Congress between 1883 and 1938).

328. 42 Stat. 187 (1921).

329. Dickson v. Uhlmann Grain Co., 288 U.S. 188, 189 (1932).

330. 61 Cong. Rec. 4763 (1921). Senator Capper charged that this gambling

> is an immoral practice. But we are attempting to correct it in this bill, not merely because of its immoral character and influence but because of its arbitrary interference with economic laws and its disturbance of the balance that demand and supply of commodities when left to itself brings about. This great law of nature has always appealed strongly to the sense of justice in all men. Anything that tends to destroy or frustrate this great democratic law of nature, any combination or any distorted mechanism of trade is offensive to the sense of common justice and fair dealing which all men, and certainly we as Americans, cherish.

Id. at 4761.

"fabulous quantities sold on the exchange that never had any existence, that no grain farmer in the world ever planted, ever toiled over its cultivation and harvest, or offered for sale."[331]

Senator Capper stated that legislation was needed "to eliminate from the exchanges exactly those operations that do not conform to a market place where prices are determined in accordance with the law of demand and supply."[332] He recognized the argument that speculators could not in the long term control prices but stated that speculators often caused "violent and unnatural fluctuations" The senator cited wheat and corn as the target of "an orgy of gambling operations as to drive prices within a period of months far below the coast of production."[333]

A witness testified that large traders openly manipulated the price of wheat, corn, and oat pits on the CBOT, "a piece of audacity having few equals in commercial history." That witness predicted that "doubtless, a few generations hence, the tales of our squeezes and corners and manipulated markets will be read with the same excited interest that we now read of the old buccaneer days."[334]

Another witness claimed that, while the publicity from past corners continued to raise concern, trading on the CBOT had grown so large that future corners were a practical impossibility.[335] Additionally, it was pointed out that corners were already banned by the antitrust laws.[336] Secretary of Commerce Herbert Hoover also testified that the "old-fashioned corner" had "pretty well disappeared." Coming to the defense of the CBOT during the hearings on the Futures Trading Act, Secretary Hoover asserted that the commodity exchanges were the "most economical and efficient agency for the marketing of foodstuffs found anywhere in the world."[337]

Hoover was concerned that short selling was depressing grain prices. His concerns over short selling were echoed by Julius H. Barnes, president of the U.S. Grain Corporation during World War I. Barnes believed that the futures exchanges were being used "for short selling, that by its own volume and weight becomes manipulative in character." Barnes contended that, while "it is also true that even though such a price depression must be temporary in character it may, during its period of effectiveness, do substantial injustice by forcing the liquidation of grain held on margin, or by the price tendency thus displayed, frightening owners otherwise confident of the ultimate value of their goods."[338]

---

331. *Id.* at 4761-4762.

332. *Id.* at 4761-4762.

333. *Id.* at 4761-4762. Senator Capper more colorfully stated on the Senate floor,

> Mr. President, the system of exchange now conducted by the Chicago Board of Trade is an economic monstrosity. In the business of separating men from their money without proper return of goods or service, its market manipulators and gamblers are doing that for which hold-up men are sent to prison. No American industry other than agriculture would tolerate such a joggling of markets for a single minute. No other commodity seesaws up or down every day and every hour, month after month, as does the price of wheat on the Chicago Board of Trade. It is a great injustice to the producers of this country and a great injury to the country's welfare, progress, and stability.

Id. at 4766.

334. *Future Trading in Grain. Hearings Before The Senate Committee on Agriculture and Forestry*, 67th Cong., 1st Sess. 174 (1921).

335. *Id.* at 669; *Futures Trading: Hearings Before the House Committee on Agriculture*, 66th Cong., 3d Sess. 669 (1921).

336. *Futures Trading: Hearings Before the House Committee on Agriculture*, 66th Cong., 3d Sess. 669 (1921).

337. *Id.* at 911, 583.

338. *Id.* at 841-842.

Foreign traders using U.S. futures markets were also accused of forcing prices down so they could buy grain at cheaper prices.[339] Long side manipulations were of lesser concern. As a principal proponent of legislation regulating the futures markets remarked, "I never feared a corner, because that has invariably raised the price."[340] One witness testified that "[t]here is no such manipulation in our market as a downward manipulation that I have ever heard of. . . . We do not have any such condition in our market, and I do not think any market does."[341]

A witness for the CBOT testified that "downward manipulation is impossible" because buyers would "flock to the market" if a short offered at below market prices. This witness further testified that only an upward manipulation could be successful. The CBOT witness also testified that in the "old days" when manipulations were attempted they generally failed.[342] Another witness testified that manipulators "have been inspired by the belief that it would be possible for them to buy a greater quantity of contract grades of grain than could be delivered at the time and place of delivery for which the [futures] contract called."[343]

Another Congressional concern was manipulations by false rumors, including a hoax involving the planting of a rumor that "green bugs" that "work at night" were threatening the wheat harvest, when in fact they were harmless lightning bugs.[344] However, another witness testified that claims of widespread manipulations by "false reports" were "grossly exaggerated."[345]

The Senate Committee on Agriculture and Forestry reported with some exaggeration that

> Every member of a grain exchange who testified before this committee acknowledged that there is at times excessive speculation and undesirable speculation in the futures market. Furthermore, it was brought out that a few big traders at times influence prices—manipulate the market—by the great volume of their operations. Also, it was shown that a continually fluctuating, and not a stable, market is the desire of speculators. Such a market is against the interests of the producer; he must have stable prices in order to market his crops to best advantage. . . .
>
> Furthermore, manipulation on the "short" or selling side of the market by big speculators, and "bear raids" by their followers, such as happen every year shortly before or immediately following harvest, play directly into the hands of European importers, who are enabled to buy millions of bushels of wheat in the futures market at a reduced price, which they later exchange for cash wheat.[346]

The House Committee of Agriculture asserted that "all the witnesses have agreed that the one overshadowing evil that must be eliminated is manipulation. This bill provides, in so far as humanly possible to do so, for the elimination of manipulation upon these grain exchanges."[347]

---

339. *Id.* at 40, 780, 792, 866-69; 61 Cong. Rec. 1372 (1921) (remarks of Rep. Tincher).

340. *Futures Trading: Hearings Before the House Committee on Agriculture and Forestry*, 67th Cong. 1st Sess. 12 (1921) (remarks of Rep. Tincher).

341. *Id.* at 131 (remarks of Mr. Moffitt).

342. *Id.* at 155-157 (remarks of Mr. Griffin).

343. *Future Trading, Hearings Before the House Committee on Agriculture on H.R. 168, H.R. 231, H.R. 2238, H.R. 2331, H.R. 2363, H.R. 5228*, 67th Cong. 1st Sess. 157 (1921).

344. *Future Trading in Grain. Hearings Before The Senate Committee on Agriculture and Fores*try, 67th Cong., 1st Sess. 182 (1921).

345. *Futures Trading: Hearings Before the House Committee on Agriculture and Forestry*, 67th Cong. 1st Sess. 155 (1921) (remarks of Mr. Griffin).

346. Sen. Rep. No. 212, 67th Cong., 1st Sess., 4-5 (1921), *quoted in part in*, Board of Trade v. Olsen, 262 U.S. 1 (1923).

347. 61 Cong. Rec. H1317 (May 11, 1921) (remarks of Rep. Purnell).

Senator Capper, "a leader of the farm bloc in Congress, proposed a solution to the suicides and crimes that he said had resulted from speculation: the Capper-Tincher bill, which Congress passed as The Future Trading Act" of 1921.[348] Senator Capper described the thrust of the legislation as follows:

> Briefly summarized, the evils in the marketing system which this bill undertakes to correct are:
>
> (1) Market manipulation by large operators.
> (2) Promiscuous and unrestricted speculation in foodstuffs.
> (3) Dissemination of false crop information.
> (4) Gambling in indemnities or "puts" and "calls."
> (5) Arbitrary interference with the law of supply and demand.[349]

The Futures Trading Act of 1921[350] limited futures trading in grain to boards of trade designated as "contract markets" by the secretary of agriculture. It was thought that the Futures Trading Act of 1921 would require the futures exchanges to "drive from their midst the man who is prostituting the machinery of grain market for his own selfish purpose by manipulating the price to his own advantage."[351] The Futures Trading Act imposed a prohibitive tax of twenty cents per bushel on all options trades and on grain futures trades that were not executed on a designated contract market. The rules of contract markets were required to "provide for the prevention of manipulation of prices, or the cornering of any grain, by the dealers or operators upon such board."[352] In addition, the governing body of a contract market was required to adopt rules that would prevent "the dissemination by the board or any member thereof of false misleading, or inaccurate report, concerning crop or market information or conditions that affect or tend to affect the price of commodities."[353] This legislation also imposed record-keeping requirements that could be used to identify traders who were manipulating the market.[354]

The Futures Trading Act of 1921 provided that, if the secretary of agriculture had reason to believe that any person was violating any provisions of the act or was attempting to manipulate the market price of grain in violation of contract market rules, he could bring charges against such a person and appoint a referee to take evidence. A commission composed of the secretary of agriculture, the secretary of commerce, and the attorney general was authorized to review the evidence, and upon a finding of guilt, could issue an order requiring all contract markets to refuse such person trading privileges. Such an order was reviewable in the appropriate Circuit Court of Appeals.[355] Missing from this legislation and its legislative history was any meaningful legal definition of what constitutes manipulation. As Professor Wendy Perdue later noted:

> Ironically, the Congress devoting the most time to discussing what manipulation involved ultimately decided that the term was too vague to make criminalization appropriate. As

348. John V. Rainbolt, II, *Regulating the Grain Gambler and his Successors*, 6 HOFSTRA L. REV. 1, 7 (1977).
349. 61 Cong. Rec. 4762 (Aug. 9, 1921).
350. 42 Stat. 187 (1921).
351. 61 Cong. Rec. 4769 (1921) (remarks of Sen. Capper).
352. 42 Stat. 187 (1921).
353. *Id.* at § 5(c).
354. *Id.* at § 5(b) & 10.
355. *Id.* at § 6.

> Senator Norris, then chairman of the Senate Agriculture Committee, stated in explaining why Congress did not make manipulation a crime under the Futures Trading Act: '[T]hese things are various and perhaps impossible of direct definition. I do not know how we would draw a definition to bring it home to the individual.'[356]

The witnesses in congressional hearings agreed that corners turned on market power but gave no other guidance. Asked whether Congress should prohibit manipulation, one witness responded, "It depends on what you call manipulation. I do not know what you mean."[357] One witness described manipulative activity as "the dealing in huge quantities not to cover actual transactions, but to produce unnatural and undue influences either of depression or advance, thus creating a situation which interferes with the free play of prices and introduces into legitimate operations elements of danger, uncertainty, and hazard."[358] A manipulator "is one who suddenly throws upon the market a huge volume of some commodity, and it is an injury to anyone, a hazard to all of us, in the business."[359]

Another witness testified in equally broad terms: "in a general way I think a manipulator is one who attempts to buy or sell more than the market would be able to take care of, and for the purpose of making it impossible to complete contracts, and therefore force a settlement."[360] The witness further defined a manipulator as a speculator who through large quantities of trading attempts "to force artificial conditions or to exaggerate conditions for his own advantage."[361] Still another witness stated that he wanted to "eliminate manipulative speculation; that is, where large money interests can go into a market and temporarily affect the trend of values one way or the other, up or down."[362]

A congressman was also vague in his attempt to define "a manipulator [a]s a speculator or gambler who by reason of his tremendous resources buys or sells grain in such large quantities . . . as to affect the price."[363] Another congressman stated that manipulation occurs when a trader "endeavors to put down the price of wheat temporarily, in order that he may buy cheaper, or endeavors to put up the price of wheat by long buying, when he knows that is not the real value of the wheat, endeavoring to buy in at the lower price, he is engaging in the manipulation of prices."[364]

The lack of a definition raised troubling questions in volatile markets. As a witness noted, "a situation arises frequently in the grain markets where a perfectly legitimate transaction in the beginning develops into a situation before closing of trading that might be considered manipulative."[365] However, this was the crux of the concern of the populists supporting antimanipulation legislation. They wanted price stability and viewed volatility as itself being manipulative.

---

356. Wendy Collins Perdue, *Manipulation of Futures Markets: Redefining the Offense*, 56 FORDHAM L. REV. 345, 353, n. 64 (1987), quoting from *Future Trading in Grain: Hearings on H.R. 5676,* Before the Senate Comm. on Agriculture and Forestry, 67th Cong., 1st Sess. 335 (1921).

357. *Futures Trading: Hearings Before the House Committee on Agriculture and Forestry*, 67th Cong. 1st Sess. 132 (1921) (remarks of Mr. Moffitt).

358. *Futures Trading: Hearings Before the House Committee on Agriculture*, 66th Cong. 3d Sess. 344 (1921).

359. *Id.* at 351.

360. *Id.* at 446.

361. *Id.*

362. *Future Trading in Grain. Hearings Before The Senate Committee on Agriculture and Forestry*, 67th Cong., 1st Sess. 83 (1921) (remarks of Mr. Miller).

363. 61 Cong. Rec. 1323 (1921) (remarks of Rep. Voigt).

364. 61 Cong. Rec. 5560 (1921) (remarks of Rep. Mann).

365. *Future Trading in Grain. Hearings Before The Senate Committee on Agriculture and Forestry*, 67th Cong., 1st Sess. 25 (1921).

Commerce Secretary Hoover had sought to take a practical approach to the issue of manipulation in the hearings on this legislation. He believed that "the wrongful manipulation of the markets is accomplished only by the sale or purchase of very large quantities of grain."[366] The result of such trading is that "grain is brought into the market that would not normally flow there, and thereby such a manipulation has a damaging effect on price and works great injustice."[367] Hoover was questioned on limiting the maximum amount of positions that speculators could hold to, say, 200,000 bushels, but he replied that "it might not be the best way to handle it." He suggested instead that some independent body or commission work with the boards of trade to set limits.[368] Such limits were thought by others as a means to prevent "foreigners" from manipulating the market.[369] However, another witness argued that "because a man does a large volume of trading or is wealthy does not presuppose he has any natural bent toward cornering the market."[370]

The secretary of agriculture, Henry Wallace, testified that "your greatest evil on your boards of trade is the ability of the large operator to dump great quantities of grain at the psychological moment, and thereby beat down the price, and that if you limit the trades by one operator you will have made some real progress in doing away with those evils."[371] Secretary Wallace further testified as to position limits that "if you can give some guide as to how to determine manipulation that is very desirable. And one of the real evidences of manipulation is the dumping of millions of bushels" in a short period. However, he sought to avoid the role of determining what amounts to set as trading limits, preferring that it be delegated to someone else.[372] Position limits were thought by others to be of doubtful value in stopping manipulation.[373]

Another approach suggested in congressional testimony was the disclosure of the positions of large traders on the theory that, if a man "is undertaking to 'bear' the market and the whole world's knowing he is doing it, he is the only loser. Secrecy is absolutely necessary to such efforts

---

366. *Futures Trading: Hearings Before the House Committee on Agriculture*, 66th Cong. 3d Sess. 896 (1921).

367. *Id.* Hoover went on to state:

> We have had two forms of manipulation. . . . One was the old-fashioned corner. . . . The second form of manipulation and the one that I feel does at times take place, is the making of a drive on the price by either the sale or the purchase of such quantities as will affect the price by the volume of material coming to the market at that particular time. I would regard those transactions as an attempt to dislocate the normal flow of the law of supply and demand, and any attempt of any individual to dislocate a free market must be against the public interest. I feel it is also against the interest of the individual producer, because a drive on the market that depresses the price must find a considerable number of farmers who, through the fallen price and their outstanding obligations, are compelled to liquidate, and they have been done an injury. Incidentally, the commodity has been brought in the market and an acceleration of the depression has been created.

Id. at 911-912.

368. *Id.* at 912, 919.

369. 61 Cong. Rec. 1372 (1921) (remarks of Rep. Tincher).

370. *Future Trading, Hearings Before the House Committee on Agriculture on H.R. 168, H.R. 231, H.R. 2238, H.R. 2331, H.R. 2363, H.R. 5228*, 67th Cong. 1st Sess. 186 (1921).

371. *Futures Trading: Hearings Before the House Committee on Agriculture and Forestry*, 67th Cong. 1st Sess. 328 (1921) (remarks of Secretary Wallace).

372. *Id.* at 329 (remarks of Secretary Wallace).

373. *Future Trading, Hearings Before the House Committee on Agriculture on H.R. 168, H.R. 231, H.R. 2238, H.R. 2331, H.R. 2363, H.R. 5228*, 67th Cong. 1st Sess. 13 (1921); *Futures Trading: Hearings Before the House Committee on Agriculture and Forestry*, 67th Cong. 1st Sess. 353 (1921) (remarks of Mr. Dickinson).

and that is the reason why the Chicago Board of Trade keeps no records."[374] One congressman suggested that the manipulators should be hit with a sledge hammer, but it was thought by others that punitive legislation would not be wise and that exchanges should be permitted to clean their own houses.[375]

The conference committee deleted the words "undue" or "unfair" in describing the nature of manipulations that were prohibited, and a prohibition against disseminating "fake" market information was changed to "false" information.[376] The Futures Trading Act did not otherwise define what conduct would constitute manipulation. Rather, a cosponsor of the legislation asserted that, since there was no legal definition of manipulation, the secretary of agriculture would have the power to determine the meaning of the term.[377]

The following colloquy in the House debates on the bill that became the Futures Trading Act also sought to place the onus of preventing manipulation on the secretary of agriculture through limitations on trading. This colloquy evidenced a view that market power—that is, the ability to influence prices—was a prerequisite to manipulation:

> **Mr. Haugen.** It prevents the cornering of grain, and the only way you can prevent cornering is by placing a limit on transactions.
> **Mr. Kelly of Pennsylvania.** What I want to call attention to is the fact that there is no definition as to what manipulation of prices is. Therefore, it cannot be touched unless it is a cornering of grain.
> **Mr. Haugen.** It also prevents the manipulation of prices.
> **Mr. Kelly of Pennsylvania.** That is a grave proposition, and it would take the Supreme Court to decide it.[378]

The Supreme Court did decide, but not on the issue of the lack of a definition of manipulation. In *Hill v. Wallace*,[379] the Supreme Court held that the Futures Trading Act of 1921 was an unconstitutional exercise of the taxing power of Congress in seeking to regulate futures contracts through taxation. The Supreme Court also held, in *Trusler v. Crooks*,[380] that a provision in the Futures Trading Act that sought to tax trading in options on grain out of existence was unconstitutional. Those contracts were variously called "privileges," "bids," "offers," "puts and calls," indemnities," and "ups or downs."[381]

1:10 THE GRAIN FUTURES ACT OF 1922

The price of May futures contracts on the CBOT rose by forty cents in January and February of 1922. That activity was later found to have "resulted chiefly from speculation."[382] One day after the Supreme Court's decision in *Hill v. Wallace*,[383] which was decided in May 1922, the price of wheat rose by forty cents a bushel, but then declined sharply. That price fluctuation was not

---

374. *I Future Trading, Hearings Before the House Committee on Agriculture on H.R. 168, H.R. 231, H.R. 2238, H.R. 2331, H.R. 2363, H.R. 5228*, 67th Cong. 1st Sess. 13 (1921).
375. 61 Cong. Rec. 1336 (1921) (remarks of Rep. Dickinson).
376. 61 Cong. Rec. 5030 (1921).
377. 61 Cong. Rec. 5559 (1921) (remarks of Rep. Tincher).
378. 61 Cong. Rec. 5559 (1921).
379. Hill v. Wallace, 259 U.S. 44 (1922).
380. Trusler v. Crooks, 269 U.S. 475 (1926).
381. *Id.*
382. II FEDERAL TRADE COMMISSION, REPORT ON METHODS AND OPERATIONS OF GRAIN EXPORTERS XX (1923).
383. Hill v. Wallace, 259 U.S. 44 (1922).

readily explainable by market fundamentals and was "evidently a straight-out manipulation of the market."[384]

Henry C. Wallace, the secretary of agriculture, advised Congress that those dramatic price fluctuations had "strengthened the farmer in his belief that prices had been manipulated to his great disadvantage."[385] As the Supreme Court noted "large operators collected cash wheat all over the country and headed it for Chicago for delivery at the attractive prices. This took wheat away from all the other wheat centers of the country where it normally would have remained for consumption and accumulated an almost unsalable quantity in Chicago, greatly disturbing the normal and useful flow of wheat in its ordinary and proper distribution and precipitating a crash in prices.[386]

The manipulation of the May 1922 CBOT wheat contract was carried out by Arthur Cutten, a much reviled speculator. "As a long, he was almost at the point of accomplishing a corner when he was defeated by executives of Armour Grain Company (the biggest shorts), who persuaded the Chicago Board of Trade to allow delivery of wheat in rail cars on track."[387] Cutten had relied on supplies being deliverable only in terminals designated in the contract as the only permissible delivery points, and where he had acquired control of supplies.[388] The CBOT frustrated that plan by expanding the ability of shorts to deliver swiftly and in quantities. Cutten had pushed prices to $1.45 per bushel before the CBOT acted. Wheat then declined to $1.16 per bushel after 8,000 railroad cars of wheat were brought to Chicago for delivery to Cutten.[389]

Congress responded to this market disruption by repackaging the Futures Trading Act of 1921[390] into the Grain Futures Act of 1922.[391] That new legislation was enacted just some four months after the Supreme Court's decision in *Hill v. Wallace*.[392] As the Supreme Court later noted, a "cardinal argument for the passage of the Grain Future Act was the severe decline in prices on the Chicago board of trade subsequent to the decision in Hill v. Wallace."[393] In order to pass constitutional muster, the Grain Futures Act was based on the commerce power of Congress under the Constitution.

The Supreme Court upheld the new statute under that power in *Chicago Board of Trade v. Olsen*.[394] The Supreme Court noted that manipulations by speculators even when "not carried to the extent of a corner or complete monopoly, exert a vicious influence and produce abnormal and disturbing temporary fluctuations of prices that are not responsive to actual supply and demand and discourage not only this justifiable hedging but disturb the normal flow of actual consignments. A futures market lends itself to such manipulation such more readily than a cash market."[395] However, the Supreme Court also noted that "[c]orners in grain through trading in futures have not been so frequent as they were before 1900, . . . though they do seem to have since occurred infrequently."[396]

384. H.R. Rep. No. 1095, 67th Cong., 2d Sess. 2 (1922).

385. S. Rep. No. 871, 67th Cong., 2d Sess. 7-8 (1922).

386. Chicago Board of Trade v. Olsen, 262 U.S. 1 (1923) (footnote omitted) (citing the testimony of Julius H. Barnes before the Federal Trade Commission).

387. Wayne G. Broehl, Cargill: Trading the World's Grain 273 (1992).

388. *Id.*

389. William G. Ferris, The Grain Traders 168-169 (1988).

390. 42 Stat. 187 (1921).

391. 42 Stat. 998 (1922).

392. Hill v. Wallace, 259 U.S. 44 (1922).

393. Dickson v. Uhlmann Grain Co., 288 U.S. 188, 199, n. 4 (1933).

394. Chicago Board of Trade v. Olsen, 262 U.S. 1 (1923).

395. *Id.* at 39.

396. *Id.*

The Court held that the CBOT "conducts a business which is affected with a public interest and is, therefore, subject to reasonable regulation in the public interest."[397] Among the bases for the exercise of its commerce power, the Grain Futures Act contained a recitation that transactions and prices of grain on boards of trade, like the CBOT, were "susceptible to speculation, manipulation, and control, and sudden or unreasonable fluctuations in the prices thereof frequently occur as a result of such speculation, manipulation, or control."[398] Although "[m]any persons had advocated, as a remedy, that all futures trading be abolished,"[399] the Grain Futures Act carried forward the "contract market" licensing scheme of the Futures Trading Act of 1921, which placed the CBOT and other boards of trade under the supervision of the secretary of agriculture.

The Grain Futures Act readopted the antimanipulation provisions of the Futures Trading Act, which required contract markets to prevent the dissemination of misleading prices and manipulation of prices or the cornering of grain.[400] Specifically, the Grain Futures Act allowed registration as a contract market, among other things, only when a board of trade prohibits its members from disseminating "false or misleading or knowingly inaccurate reports concerning crop or market information" and prevents the "manipulation of prices or the cornering of any grain by the dealers or operators upon such board."[401]

Like its predecessor, the Grain Futures Act failed to define what was meant by its proscription of "manipulation." The Seventh Circuit rejected a claim that the Grain Futures Act was unconstitutional on grounds of void for vagueness because it did not contain such a definition.[402] The statute did not, in any event, make actual manipulation a crime. Rather, it prohibited an "attempt" to manipulate.[403] That limitation was not intended to extend the concept beyond cornering attempts. Rather, it was a recognition that many, if not most, corners ended in failure, but the disruptive effects were the same whether the corner was successful or not.[404]

The Court noted in a later case, *Dickson v. Uhlmann Grain Co.*, that the purpose of the Grain Futures Act "was to control the evils of manipulation of prices in grain. Such manipulation, Congress found, was effected through dealings in grain futures."[405] This narrow focus on grain manipulations underscored another limitation of this legislation. Like its predecessor, the Grain Futures Act did not apply to all commodities. Rather, it was limited to wheat, corn, oats, barley, flax, and sorghum.

A small agency in the Department of Agriculture, the Grain Futures Administration, was given the task of determining when such attempts were occurring.[406] The Grain Futures Act carried forward the oversight commission created by the Futures Trading Act that was composed of the secretary of agriculture, the secretary of commerce, and the attorney general of the United States.[407] The secretary of agriculture was authorized to charge persons violating the act or "attempting

397. *Id.* at 40.

398. 42 Stat. 998, § 3 (1922).

399. Dickson v. Uhlmann Grain Co., 288 U.S. 188, 199 (1933), 288 U.S. at 199 (footnote omitted).

400. Chicago Board of Trade v. Olsen, 262 U.S. 1 (1923).

401. 42 Stat. 998, § 5(c) & (d) (1922). For a description of the provisions of the Grain Futures Act, see *Report of the Grain Futures Administration* (1924).

402. Bartlett Frazier Co. v. Hyde, 65 F.2d 350, 354 (7th Cir. 1933), *cert. denied*, 290 U.S. 682 (1933).

403. Chicago Board of Trade v. Olsen, 262 U.S. 1 (1923).

404. A principal proponent of the Futures Trading Act had noted that "only a few men become millionaires" from grain gambling and the vast majority "become paupers." *Futures Trading: Hearings Before the House Committee on Agriculture and Forestry*, 67th Cong. 1st Sess. 173 (1921) (remarks of Rep. Tincher).

405. Dickson v. Uhlmann Grain Co., 288 U.S. at 188, 198-199 (1933).

406. Jerry W. Markham, *Manipulation of Commodity Futures Prices—The Unprosecutable Crime*, 8 YALE J. ON REG. 281, 302-303 (1991).

407. 42 Stat. 998, § 6(a) (1922).

to manipulate the market price of any grain" in violation of the rules of a contract market.[408] A hearing was required, and the commission was authorized to direct contract markets to bar parties found guilty of a violation from trading. That bar was subject to review in a court of appeals.[409] A person found guilty of trading in futures contracts other than on a contract market could be convicted of a misdemeanor under the statute.[410] The same was true for persons who "knowingly or carelessly" made "false or misleading or knowingly inaccurate" reports on crop or market information or conditions that tended to affect prices.[411]

1:11 THE LAW OF STOCK MARKET MANIPULATION

The stock market escaped federal regulation during the 1920s, but there was some jurisprudence on stock market manipulation before the enactment of the federal securities laws in the 1930s. An 1892 English decision in *Scott v. Brown, Doering, McNab & Co.*,[412] considered an agreement for a broker to purchase shares at a premium. The purchases were to have been made in order to deceive the public into believing that there was a real market in the shares and that there were buyers of the shares at a premium. The court held that such an agreement was an illegal and unenforceable contract even though this was a common practice in the London market.

In *McGlynn v. Seymour*,[413] a case decided in 1888, a New York court rejected a claim that wash sales were fraudulent even though they induced other traders in the open market to believe they were bona fide prices.[414] Columbia professor of law Adolf Berle Jr. stated in 1931 that such reasoning was "far away and long ago and would probably find little support today."[415]

The Martin Act that had been passed in New York in 1923 was also sometimes used to attack stock market manipulations.[416] That statute authorized the state attorney general to seek injunctive relief or criminal actions against schemes or artifices to defraud in securities or commodity trading. However, the Martin Act was used only sparingly to attack financial crimes until early in this century. New York attorney general Eliot Spitzer then used that statute to wage war on Wall Street. Those attacks made him a national figure and set the stage for his election to be governor of New York 2007.[417]

---

408. *Id.* at § 6(b).
409. *Id.*
410. *Id.* at § 9.
411. *Id.*
412. Scott v. Brown, Doering, McNab & Co., [1892] 2 QB 724.
413. McGlynn v. Seymour, 14 Daly 420 (N.Y. 1888).
414. The court stated,

> A "wash" sale is, at most, an affirmation that the buyer is paying a certain price for a certain lot of stock. It is not an affirmation that the stock has any intrinsic value, or that the buyer will ever again bid the same price for the stock. It is made on account of persons who are anonymous. If a man buys stock because he is led by "wash" sales, to believe that he can make a fortunate speculation, he cannot have an action of deceit against those who made the "wash" sales. The sales, though fictitious, are not representations of any fact on which a man has a right to rely. They are at most false affirmations of an opinion as to value. Such affirmations are not regarded as statements of fact.

Id.

415. A.A. Berle Jr., *Liability for Stock Market Manipulation*, 31 COLUM. L. REV. 264, 171, n. 13 (1931).
416. *See*, e.g., People v. Rice, 221 App. Div. 443, 223 N.Y. Supp. 566 (1st Dept. 1927).
417. JERRY W. MARKHAM, A FINANCIAL HISTORY OF THE U.S. FROM ENRON ERA SCANDALS TO THE SUBPRIME CRISIS (2004-2006) 327-328 (2011).

New York state law also prohibited fictitious trades that were intended to affect prices in the market,[418] and the New York Stock Exchange proscribed fictitious trades and false reports.[419] The NYSE prohibited corners, and its rules allowed its governing committee to permit the short sellers to postpone delivery on contracts affected by a corner.[420] The NYSE also prohibited options trading on its floor because such trading was viewed as purely speculative and susceptible to manipulation.[421]

In 1927, Charles Dice, a business professor at Ohio State University, wrote that "manipulation is a sort of blanket term that covers many kinds of operations to be found on the commodity market, as well as on the stock market."[422] Dice noted that the press and populist interests were quick to use the term "manipulation" to describe any sudden price change, rather than to examine what underlying fundamentals might have caused it. Dice defined manipulation as

> the creation of an artificial price by planned action, whether by one man or a group of men. A campaign is planned and executed to run the price of a stock up or to hammer it down. Manipulation may take place on the bear side as well as on the bull side. The result is always a price higher or lower than would come into being but for activities of the manipulator. Manipulation always implies the use of special power and ingenious methods in handling the market of the stock manipulated.[423]

Professor Adolf Berle at the Columbia Law School described the state of the law on manipulation in 1931 as follows:

> (1) a false representation made with the intent of affecting the market price was held to give rise to an action to anyone purchasing a security in the open market;
> (2) when false representation was shown to exist, something suspiciously like a presumption of intent to induce purchases was indulged;
> (3) though not definitely recognized by the courts, the mere act of a pretended purchase and sale without actual transfer of interest was generally recognized as such a false representation; and
> (4) the common law test served as a sufficient basis for a preventive statutory action under the New York General Business Law [the Martin Act].[424]

In *Harper v. Crenshaw*,[425] the Court of Appeals for the District of Columbia refused to enforce obligations of a joint venture that was formed in 1928 for the purpose of "the fixing of a fictitious price on the Washington Stock Exchange for the shares of stock in the District National Bank, and to prevent the free and uncontrolled processes of the stock exchange whereby the stock might be

---

418. *Id.* at 691. For a description of the state of the law on market regulation before the enactment of the federal securities laws, *see*, JOHN R. DOS PASSOS, A TREATISE ON THE LAW OF STOCKBROKERS AND STOCK EXCHANGES (1882); RAYMOND VERNON, THE REGULATION OF STOCK EXCHANGE MEMBERS (1941); WILLIAM HARMAN BLACK, THE LAW OF STOCK EXCHANGES, STOCKBROKERS, & CUSTOMERS (1940).

419. CHARLES A. MYER, THE LAW OF STOCKBROKERS AND STOCK EXCHANGES AND OF COMMODITY BROKERS AND COMMODITY EXCHANGES 108 (1931).

420. JAMES EDWARD MEEKER, SHORT SELLING 204 (1932).

421. TWENTIETH CENTURY FUND INC., THE SECURITIES MARKETS 251 (1935).

422. CHARLES A. DICE, THE STOCK MARKET 413 (1927).

423. *Id.* at 414.

424. A.A. Berle Jr., *Stock Market Manipulation*, 38 COLUM. L. REV. 393, 395 (1938).

425. Harper v. Crenshaw, 82 F.2d 845 (D.C. Cir.), *cert. denied*, 298 U.S. 685 (1936).

quoted at a price reflecting the real judgment of the buyers and sellers thereof as to its true market value."[426] The joint venture involved a pool that was formed to support the price of the bank's stock in the event of large blocks being dumped on the market without regard to value. The court concluded that the public would be misled by such stabilizing activities and that such a contract was against public policy.[427]

The mail fraud statute was also used to attack manipulations. In *Harris v. United States*,[428] the Ninth Circuit upheld the convictions of defendants who had manipulated the price of a mining stock on the San Francisco Mining Exchange and the Spokane Mining Stock Exchange in 1929. The defendants reported fictitious wash trades to those exchanges. Those trades were used to push up the price of the stock from $1 to $2.30. That price rise and fictitious reports of trading volume were used to promote the stock to members of the public. In order to prevent purchasers from reselling their stock and undercutting the manipulated price, the defendants promised an even greater price increase to $5 per share and delayed delivery of stock certificates for several weeks in order to frustrate any sales. False reports on the mining company were also prepared and circulated by defendants.

In *United States v. Brown*,[429] a distinguished panel of judges in the federal Second Circuit Court of Appeals upheld the mail fraud convictions of two operators of a stock manipulation. The defendants were found to have manipulated the price of the Manhattan Electrical Supply Co. Inc. (MESCI) through trading on the NYSE. The pool was not successful and one of its participants, a former Texas district attorney, lost $4 million.[430] Defendant Brown was the president of MESCI. He purchased 43,400 of MESCI's 125,000 outstanding shares on margin, with options to purchase as many as 47,500 additional shares. Brown joined with defendant McCarthy in December 1929 to "work off" Brown's shares at constantly rising prices.[431] They carried out that plan by opening ninety-one separate accounts in various names at fifty-two different brokers. Several of the "customers' men" employed by the brokers where the trading accounts were held were bribed to tout the stock.

The defendants also used the brokers to conduct "washing" sales among their numerous accounts in order to increase prices. The defendants additionally issued false statements on MESCI's earnings at a time when the company was incurring losses and claimed falsely that the company was about to sign a large and lucrative contract. These practices attracted much buying interest over a four-month period. The stock price rose from $20 per share to $55 before the market collapsed in May 1930, causing the stock to decline below $20.[432]

The indictment charged that the defendants had acted "for the purpose of artificially manipulating the market in the stock . . . so as to artificially advance and inflate the price thereof without regard to the real value."[433] The Second Circuit decided to ignore a claim that the concept of "real value" was too vague a charge since the fraud charged was more expressly stated elsewhere—that

426. 82 F.2d at 846.

427. *Compare*, Wilcox v. Harriman Securities Corp., 10 F. Supp. 532 (S.D.N.Y. 1933) (cause of action recognized for stock manipulation as a part of a merger plan), *with*, Goess v. Lucinda Shops, Inc., 93 F.2d 449 (2d Cir. 1937) (no rigging of market when defendant touted stock to plaintiff in 1930).

428. Harris v. United States, 48 F.2d 771 (9th Cir. 1931).

429. United States v. Brown, 79 F.2d 321 (2d Cir. 1935) (Learned and Augustus Hand and H. Chase, judges).

430. II Jerry W. Markham, A Financial History of the United States, From J.P. Morgan to the Institutional Investor (1900-1970) 143 (2002).

431. 79 F.2d at 323.

432. 79 F.2d at 323.

433. 79 F.2d at 323.

is, wash sales, bribing the customers' men, and false statements on earnings. Among other things, the court stated that "'[w]ash' sales are a deceit, because they broadcast the fact that a buyer and a seller have agreed to exchange the shares at the published price, when they have not done so."[434] The court declined to rule on whether stock pools were per se illegal, noting that such pools took many forms.[435] The *Harris* and *Brown* cases were viewed as an expansion of the "case law against stock market manipulation."[436]

434. 79 F.2d at 325.

435. 79 F.2d at 323. The New York attorney general also brought an action under the New York Martin Act that sought to enjoin this same pool. People v. Rice, 221 App. Div. 443, 223 N.Y. Supp. 566 (1st Dept. 1927).

436. Rosenberg v. Hano, 121 F.2d 818, 820 (3d Cir. 1941).

2

MARKET MANIPULATION AND THE NEW DEAL LEGISLATION

2:1 THE GRAIN FUTURES ACT

The Grain Futures Act did not stop large speculators or manipulations in the futures markets. Congress directed the secretary of agriculture to investigate a sharp decline in wheat prices that occurred in 1923. The secretary found that several large traders were operating in the market but could find no evidence of manipulation.[1]

Sugar prices exploded in 1923, from $3.65 per hundredweight in February to $5.97 by April. That price increase resulted in an antitrust suit by the Justice Department against the New York Coffee and Sugar Exchange. The government sought to shut down the exchange, charging a conspiracy to create "artificial and unwarranted prices, not governed by the law of supply and demand, but based wholly on speculative dealings not involving the delivery of the quantities of sugar represented thereby, but altogether carried on for the purpose and with the effect of unduly enhancing the price of sugar to the enrichment of said defendants and their principals and to the detriment of the public."[2] The Supreme Court, however, could find no evidence of such a conspiracy and affirmed the dismissal of the case.[3]

Commodity price speculations continued. Arthur Cutten engaged in a corn speculation in 1924 to take advantage of what he correctly predicted would be a crop shortage. He made large profits from the resulting market congestion—that is, a supply shortage in the face of high demand—as prices increased from 40 cents to $1.10 per bushel. Cutten was reported to have made $1.5 mil-

1. Jerry W. Markham, The History of Commodity Trading and Its Regulation 18 (1987).

2. United States v. New York Coffee & Sugar Exchange, 263 U.S. 611, 618 (1924).

3. *Id.* at 611. Justice Taft's opinion in this case set forth a rather impassioned defense of futures trading and commodity exchanges:

> The usefulness and legality of sales for future delivery, and of furnishing an Exchange where under well-defined limitations and rules the business can be carried on, have been fully recognized by this Court. . . . Those who have studied the economic effect of such Exchanges for contracts for future deliveries generally agree that they stabilize prices in the long run instead of promoting their fluctuation. Those who deal in "futures" are divided into three classes: first, those who use them to hedge, i.e., to insure themselves against loss by unfavorable changes in price at the time of actual delivery of what they have to sell or buy in their business; second, legitimate capitalists who, exercising their judgment as to the conditions, purchase or sell for future delivery with a view to profit based on the law of supply and demand; and, third, gamblers or irresponsible speculators who buy or sell as upon the turn of a card. The machinery of such an Exchange has been at times made the means of promoting corners in the commodity dealt in by such manipulators and speculators, thereby restraining and obstructing foreign and interstate trade. In such instances, the manipulators subject themselves to prosecution and indictment under the Anti-Trust Act. . . . But this is not to hold that such an Exchange with the facilities it affords for making contracts for future deliveries is itself a combination and conspiracy thus to restrain interstate and foreign trade.

lion on the July 1924 corn futures contract.[4] He had similar success in a rye speculation in 1924 as prices rose from 72 cents per bushel to $1.50.[5]

More spectacularly, in 1924, Cutten participated in a famous market duel with Jesse Livermore in the May wheat futures market. Cutten was able to force wheat prices upward, resulting in a loss to Livermore. As one report noted:

> One of the shorts in that squeeze was the "Great Bear" himself, Jesse Livermore, who lost $3 million, most of it to Cutten. After that Cutten was perceived by many, including the press, as a sort of swami of futures. And whenever anyone would ask Cutten, the "Great Bull," what direction wheat was heading, the answer would always be "higher," whether he was long or short the market. Two-dollar wheat enticed an entire crop of public speculators, from taxi drivers to upper-crust luminaries, to try their hands at this thing called commodity trading.[6]

Cutten had started buying wheat at $1.05 per bushel and continued to buy as it rose to $2.05. Cutten was said to have made $11 million from his corn and wheat speculations in 1924.[7] It appeared, however, that Cutten misjudged the market after his victory over Livermore.[8] Cutten conceded that "he had overstayed the market. 'I had believed that wheat would go to $2.50, but I was mistaken.'"[9]

Legislation was introduced in 1924 to ban futures trading in grain and cotton unless the parties intended to take delivery on their contracts, but it was not passed.[10] The price increases in wheat and market volatility in early 1925 resulted in "alluring" headlines in front-page articles of newspapers across the country, a signal for large traders to short the market.[11] The Senate passed a resolution in June 1925 requesting an investigation by the secretary of agriculture of trading in wheat futures as their "extreme" price fluctuations were "felt in every grain market in the world" during the early months of 1925.[12]

The price of May wheat increased from $1.19 to $2.05 per bushel between July 1924 and January 1925. Wheat prices then became volatile.[13] A large break occurred on March 13, 1925, when Thomas Howell and Jesse Livermore "loosed an avalanche of wheat and rye that proceeded right through the bottom of the grain market."[14] Arthur Cutten was on the other side of the market.[15]

The volume of grain futures trading between July 1, 1924, and June 30, 1925, was, at the time, the greatest since records had been maintained on trading volume. The Grain Futures Administration (GFA) kept an observer on the floor of the CBOT "in order to obtain a true picture of the trading operations and the influences at work at all times, and more particularly when price fluctuations were unreasonably wide."[16]

---

4. *Cutten a Cool Market Trader*, New York Times, Jan. 2, 1927, at XX8.

5. William G. Ferris, The Grain Traders 176 (1988).

6. Bob Tamarkin, The New Gatsbys: Fortunes and Misfortunes of Commodity Traders 280 (1985).

7. II Jerry W. Markham, A Financial History of the United States, From J.P. Morgan to the Institutional Investor (1900-1970) 103 (2002).

8. William G. Ferris, The Grain Traders 176 (1988).

9. *Id.* at 179.

10. *To Prevent Sale of Cotton and Grain in Future Markets, Hearings Before the Senate Committee on Agriculture and Forestry*, 69th Cong., 1st Sess. 1-3 (1926).

11. U.S. Senate, Fluctuations in *Wheat Futures*, S. Doc. 135 69th Cong., 1st Sess. 11-12 (1926).

12. *Id.* at 1.

13. Jerry W. Markham, The History of Commodity Trading and Its Regulation 19 (1987).

14. *National Affairs: No Proof*, Time, May 25, 1925.

15. *Id.*

16. *Report of the Grain Futures Administration* 1 (Oct. 1, 1925).

The secretary of agriculture recommended that the commodity exchanges adopt "rules limiting the fluctuation of grain futures prices in a single day—rules similar to those found beneficial on the Cotton Exchange."[17] That was done by the CBOT in "Rule 81," which allowed its board of directors to declare an emergency and stop trading when a designated price limit was reached, which would generally be at a level of 5 percent above the average of the prior day's closing prices.[18]

The secretary also conducted an extensive investigation in response to the Senate resolution and concluded, with respect to the May 1925 wheat futures contract, that, on most days with erratic price fluctuations, large traders were buying or selling wheat in the amount of $2 million bushels or more. Eight traders had accumulated long or short positions totaling 2 million bushels or more. "These large speculative operations were important price making factors and the results show the need for the development of some plan of limiting excessive speculative transactions or otherwise preventing sudden and abnormal price fluctuations that have but little, if any, relationship to supply and demand."[19]

The secretary's report broke speculators into two groups: those that were "constructive" in trading on their view of market fundamentals and those that were "destructive" in trading on "mob psychology" and abuse of market power through the trading of large positions. The latter group included traders who rapidly switched from one side of the market to another. "Such operations, while not always profitable, not only cause large price changes but also unbalance the whole market. They can hardly be viewed as other than manipulative and destructive in character."[20]

Language in this report, however, led one commentator to later conclude that the basic position of the Grain Futures Administration "was that to engage in trades that affect price does not constitute manipulation, even if that effect is dramatic or if the trader knows that his transaction is likely to affect price, so long as the reason for entering into the transaction or the profitability of the transaction does not depend on its effect on price." That author believed that the secretary's report indicated that the "motivation behind the transaction forms the critical element in distinguishing manipulation from other transactions. Specifically, manipulation occurs when the trader's expectation of profit derives primarily from his expectation that his transactions will affect the market."[21]

The secretary recommended position limits on both long and short positions, "especially on the buying or selling within a day by speculative traders."[22] The CBOT agreed with the secretary of agriculture that traders should not be allowed to hold more than 5 million bushels of wheat "at any one time, either long or short. This is a 'working agreement' with the U.S. Grain Futures Administration and is strictly enforced, although it does not apply to bona fide hedging. Thus overextension of a trader on a scale which would hurt all other traders is almost impossible."[23] Claims were later made that traders were transferring their positions from the CBOT to the Winnipeg Grain Exchange to avoid such restrictions, but a Royal Canadian Commission concluded that such charges were not true.[24]

17. *National Affairs: No Proof*, TIME, May 25, 1925.

18. Paul Mehl, *Controlling Speculative Activity by Limiting the Size of Lines and the Trading* 5 (USDA, Oct. 9, 1936).

19. U.S. Senate, *Fluctuations in Wheat Futures*, S. Doc. 135 69th Cong., 1st Sess. XI (1926).

20. *Id.* at 5.

21. Wendy Collins Perdue, *Manipulation of Futures Markets: Redefining the Offense*, 56 FORD. L. REV. 345, 358 (1987). Perdue cited for that proposition, among other things, U.S. Senate, *Fluctuations in Wheat Futures*, S. Doc. 135 69th Cong., 1st Sess. 6-7 (1926).

22. U.S. Senate, *Fluctuations in Wheat Futures*, S. Doc. 135 69th Cong., 1st Sess. 6 (1926).

23. *Bear in the Street*, TIME, Oct. 12, 1931.

24. JERRY W. MARKHAM, THE HISTORY OF COMMODITY TRADING AND ITS REGULATION 21 (1987).

Undaunted by concerns over the May wheat futures market, Arthur Cutten "engineered a slight squeeze" in July 1925 wheat futures.[25] The secretary of agriculture found that the "'squeeze'. . . occurred in July wheat (1925), when the price advanced 9 cents on the last day of the month."[26] The secretary recommended that the exchanges counteract such activity by prohibiting the making of new contracts after a specified date during the current delivery month.[27] Legislation was again introduced in 1926 to ban futures trading in grain and cotton unless the parties intended to take delivery on their contracts, but it was not enacted.[28]

Cutten and other speculators started building large positions in the May 1926 wheat futures contract as prices rose. The Grain Futures Administration placed pressure on the CBOT to have Cutten reduce his position in wheat futures, which it did. When word of Cutten's meeting with the CBOT Business Conduct Committee to discuss the reduction of his position leaked, wheat prices fell sharply. Cutten claimed that the meeting cost him a million dollars.[29]

The Grain Futures Administration required daily trading reports to be filed with it by clearing members of each futures exchange. Those reports were required to identify "special accounts," which were the accounts of large traders.[30] It was thought that disclosure would discourage manipulation. These large trader reports became an essential part of the regulatory effort to detect market threats. The Grain Futures Administration protested "propaganda" that claimed this requirement had frightened away bullish traders and caused a drop in wheat prices.[31]

The reporting requirement was suspended by the Grain Futures Administration for eight months in 1927 "wholly and solely on the representation that wheat prices were too low; that a large number of speculators, who otherwise would not trade, would come into the market when the reports were suspended and would buy large quantities of wheat futures, thus raising wheat prices to a level more satisfactory to producers."[32] The U.S. Department of Agriculture (USDA) then conducted an extensive investigation and filed a lengthy report on the reaction of traders to the suspension requirement. It concluded that "[i]nstead of higher prices resulting from the suspension of the reporting requirements, as representatives of the grain exchanges claimed would follow, there were recorded during the period of suspension the lowest prices paid for wheat in Chicago that had been paid in over three years."[33] The secretary's investigation also found that the seven largest speculators in the market were short the market before the suspension and had a short position during six of the eight months of the suspension.[34] Another such suspension was ordered in 1932, but prices only went down after that suspension once again.[35]

The Grain Futures Administration also found that news "flashes" from the trading floors were often misleading in naming parties trading in the markets and amounts being traded. False news reports were another problem, including a spurious telegram claiming that a Canadian wheat

---

25. William G. Ferris, The Grain Traders 180 (1988).

26. U.S. Senate, *Fluctuations in Wheat Futures*, S. Doc. 135 69th Cong., 1st Sess. XI (1926).

27. *Id.*

28. *To Prevent Sale of Cotton and Grain in Future Markets, Hearings Before the Senate Committee on Agriculture and Forestry*, 69th Cong., 1st Sess. 1-3 (1926).

29. II Jerry W. Markham, A Financial History of the United States, From J.P. Morgan to the Institutional Investor (1900-1970) 103 (2002).

30. Jerry W. Markham, The History of Commodity Trading and Its Regulation 15-16 (1987).

31. *Id.* at 16.

32. Letter from the Secretary of Agriculture, *Reports by Members of Grain Futures Exchanges*, Sen. Doc. No. 123, 71st Cong., 4 (1930).

33. *Id.* at 40.

34. *Id.* at 2.

35. *Id.*

pool was experiencing financial difficulties. The Grain Futures Administration sought to have the exchanges censor such reports before their distribution. Reports and rumors on crop conditions were also found to be incomplete and misleading.[36] False crop reports from abroad were found have had market effects in the United States, but such reports were deemed to be outside the jurisdiction of the GFA.[37]

The GFA was successful in pressuring the CBOT to ensure that a firm holding corn futures contracts for eight times the available supply of corn for delivery did not disrupt the market.[38] The GFA also claimed credit in preventing a drop in wheat prices by pressuring the CBOT and large traders to limit large selling orders.[39]

Bills were introduced in Congress in 1926 and 1927 that sought to prohibit or further restrict futures trading.[40] For example, the Senate Committee on Agriculture and Forestry reported out a bill on March 31, 1927, without recommendation, that sought to prevent the sale of grain and cotton on the futures markets. That action was accompanied by a lengthy minority report protesting such legislation.[41] The bill was not passed. A tax was imposed in 1926 on futures transactions at the rate of three cents per trade. That amount was increased to five cents in in 1932, but was repealed in 1938.[42]

Trading in cotton futures, which was not subject to the Grain Futures Act, raised congressional concerns in 1927 and 1928. Members of Congress sought to have cotton futures contracts on the New York Cotton Exchange made deliverable in the south, where the crop was grown.[43] Legislation was also sought "to limit the amount of a single speculative interest in any one delivery month as a measure to guard against price manipulation."[44] The "Rankin bill," sponsored by Representative John Rankin (D-MS), sought to confiscate cotton "withheld from the market with intent to manipulate prices."[45]

The hearings on those proposals again raised the question as to the definition of manipulation. As one witness remarked, "'manipulation' . . . in its use is so broad as to include any operation of the cotton market that does not suit the gentleman who is speaking at the moment."[46] Representative Rankin protested during the hearings on this bill:

> Every time you get to talking about manipulation, some fellow jumps up and reaches for a dictionary and reads a definition of what manipulation is. Of course the dictionary was written by a man who never saw a bale of cotton, possibly, and had never dealt in it. A manipulation is simply any operation that distorts or illogically affects the cotton market in any one month.[47]

---

36. *Id.* at 17-18.
37. Jerry W. Markham, The History of Commodity Trading and Its Regulation 17 (1987).
38. Letter from the Secretary of Agriculture, *Reports by Members of Grain Futures Exchanges*, Sen. Doc. No. 123, 71st Cong., 18 (1930).
39. *Id.* at 19-20.
40. Jerry W. Markham, The History of Commodity Trading and Its Regulation 19 (1987).
41. *To Prevent the Sale of Cotton and Grain in Future Markets*, S. Rep. No. 508, 69th Cong., 1st Sess. (1926).
42. Cedric B. Cowing, Populists, Plungers, and Progressives 255-257 (1965).
43. Julius Baer, Commodity Exchanges 190 (1929).
44. *Id.*
45. *Id.*
46. *Cotton Prices, Hearings Before a Subcomm. of the Senate Comm. on Agriculture and Forestry, Pursuant to S. Res. 142*, 70th Cong., 1st Sess. 154 (1928).
47. *Id.* at 932.

Congressman Rankin concluded that statement by conceding that "I do not know whether I giving you the real definition or not."[48] As for the dictionary definition of manipulation, another witness testified that *Webster's* defined the term as "To work up or down in price by transactions other than those made bona fide or in the ordinary course of business, as by wash sales, cornering the market, spreading fictitious reports, etc., to rig."[49]

Still another witness, Arthur Marsh, rejected that definition and contended that manipulation "is any and every kind of operation or transaction, the purpose of which is not primarily to facilitate the movement of the commodity at prices freely responsive to the forces of supply and demand; but, on the contrary, is calculated to produce a price distortion of any kind in any market either in itself or in relation to other markets." Marsh further stated that manipulators use "devices by which the prices of contracts . . . may be higher than they would be if only the forces of supply and demand were operative; or [use] . . . devices by means of which the price or prices . . . in a given market may be made lower than they would be if they were freely responsive to the forces of supply and demand." Marsh also stated that "[a]ny and every operation, transaction, device, employed to produce those abnormalities of price relationship in the futures markets, is manipulation."[50] Marsh's definition became a touchstone for later efforts to define manipulation, but its vagueness offered little useful guidance.[51]

Arthur Cutten, the speculator, advised Congress that market problems in grain were due to a warehouse monopoly and that "off" grades of wheat should not be allowed for delivery. He would also limit CBOT rules that allowed short sellers to default on delivery and settle their contracts at a designated settlement price.[52] Apparently, such activities interfered with Cutten's speculations. In the event, that legislation did not pass, and attention shifted to the speculative bubble in the stock market during the 1920s.

2:2 THE ROARING TWENTIES

Clarence Saunders, the president of the Piggly Wiggly grocery store chain, tried to corner the available float of that company's stock in 1923, pushing its price from $50 to $124. Saunders was trying to crush a bear raid. The corner failed after the NYSE gave the shorts additional time to deliver.[53] The NYSE then delisted the Piggly Wiggly stock from trading on its facilities.[54] Jesse Livermore and Frank Bliss, both well-known speculators, had participated in the Piggly Wiggly corner attempt. They also manipulated the stock of the Computer Tabulator Company, which later evolved into IBM, from $40 to $80 and reaped over $1 million in profits. Another notable squeeze on short traders involved the Wheeling and Lake Erie Railroad. Its stock was pushed to $100, before falling back to $40.[55]

"The 1920s were the heyday of the investment pool. . . . A pool was nothing more than organized stock rigging, and its intent, to be bullish or bearish, was known only to its members, and often not even to all of them."[56] The purpose of a pool "generally is to raise the price of a security

48. *Id.*
49. *Id.* at 154 (remarks of Mr. Clayton).
50. *Id.* at 201.
51. Jerry W. Markham, *Manipulation of Commodity Futures Prices—The Unprosecutable Crime*, 8 Yale J. on Reg. 281, 312 (1991).
52. *Cutten Offers Rules For Grain Trading*, New York Times, April 9, 1927, at 4.
53. II Jerry W. Markham, A Financial History of the United States, From J.P. Morgan to the Institutional Investor (1900-1970) 134-135 (2002).
54. *Finance: Piggly Wiggly*, Time, March 21, 1923.
55. II Jerry W. Markham, A Financial History of the United States, From J.P. Morgan to the Institutional Investor (1900-1970) 134-135 (2002).
56. Charles R. Geisst, Wall Street: A history 182 (1997).

by concerted activity on the part of the pool members, and thereby to enable them to unload their holdings at a profit upon the public attracted by the activity or by information disseminated about the stock."[57] These pools were often led by some expert market operator, of which there was no shortage.[58] Their number included Jesse Livermore, Michael J. Meehan, Charles Topping, Frank Bliss, and Joseph Kennedy, the father of the future president.

"[T]he services of the specialist in the security marked for manipulation have [also] proved invaluable to the pool managers. The specialist's information regarding the state of the market or its trend was important to persons conducting large operations in the security. The pool manager customarily gave discretionary orders to the specialist, relying on him to exercise those orders at such times and prices as would be best calculated to manipulate the price of the stock in furtherance of the objectives of the pool."[59]

A Senate committee found that trading "fomented by a pool creates a false and deceptive appearance of genuine demand for the security on the part of the purchasing public and attracts persons relying upon this misleading appearance to make purchases. By this means the pool is enabled to unload its holdings upon an unsuspecting public."[60] In 1929, over 100 stocks listed on the NYSE were targets of pool operations. They were funded by numerous banks that loaned the pools over $75 million.[61]

Among the stocks targeted were American Tobacco Company, Archer Daniels Midland, Bendix Aviation, Bethlehem Steel, Borden Co., Chrysler Co., Firestone Tire, Fox Films and Theaters, Gimbel Bros., International Telephone & Telegraph Co., Kroger Grocery, R.H. Macy & Co., May Department Stores, McGraw-Hill, McKesson & Robins, National Cash Register Co., Radio Corporation of America (RCA), R.J. Reynolds Tobacco Co., Standard Oil of California, Studebaker, Yellow Cab Co., and Zenith Radio.[62]

Two of the most famous pools involved RCA and Anaconda Copper. The organizers of the Anaconda Copper pool were Tom Bragg and "Sell-em" Ben Smith, two operators in NYSE stocks.[63] The Anaconda pool operators gathered $30 million to carry out this pool from wealthy financiers and speculators, including Percy Rockefeller and Charles Mitchell, who headed the National City Co., an affiliate of the National City Bank. The National City Co. made profits of $20 million by selling over 1 million shares of Anaconda stock to its customers.[64] The RCA pool was led by Michael J. Meehan, who had been a theater ticket broker before becoming the RCA specialist on the NYSE.[65] The RCA pool pushed the price of RCA from $82 to over $100, providing a profit of some $5 million to pool participants.

A member of the RCA pool was Arthur Cutten,[66] "Chicago's daring speculator" made famous for his manipulations of the commodity futures markets. Cutten was the "heaviest plunger in wheat and corn" before he expanded his operations to include stocks on the NYSE.[67] The government claimed in a brief submitted to the Supreme Court in a case involving his com-

57. S. Rep. No. 1455, 73d Cong. 2d Sess. 31 (1934).

58. Charles R. Geisst, Wall Street: A History 182 (1997).

59. S. Rep. No. 1455, 73d Cong., 2d Sess. 47 (1934).

60. *Id.* at 32.

61. II Jerry W. Markham, A Financial History of the United States, From J.P. Morgan to the Institutional Investor (1900-1970) 149 (2002).

62. S. Rep. No. 1455, 73d Cong., 2d Sess. 33, n. 90 (1934).

63. Charles R. Geisst, Wall Street: A History 183 (1997).

64. II Jerry W. Markham, A Financial History of the United States, From J.P. Morgan to the Institutional Investor (1900-1970) 143-144 (2002).

65. Steve Fraser, Every Man a Speculator 421 (2005).

66. Charles R. Geisst, Wall Street: A History 183 (1997).

67. *Cutten Not Likely to Sell*, New York Times, Dec. 5, 1926, at E15.

modity market activities that Cutten was "the greatest speculator the country ever had."[68] It was reported that Cutten made $10 million from a pool involving the stock of Baldwin Locomotive.[69] He was a large trader in the stocks of United States Steel, Union Carbide, Sears Roebuck and the Radio Corporation.[70] Another stock pool managed by Cutten focused on the Sinclair Consolidated Oil Corp. That pool was financed by the Chase National Bank, and its chair, Albert Wiggin, was a participant in the pool.[71] That pool made some $12 million in profits.[72]

Arthur Cutten's nephew Ruloff E. Cutten, a partner in the stock brokerage firm of E.F. Hutton, was a participant in, as well as promoter of, various pools, including those in American Commercial Alcohol and Sinclair Oil. "If Uncle Cutten is the brain of the combination, Nephew Cutten is certainly its vigorous tongue, its potent legs. There is no more active bustler on the floor of the [NYSE] exchange than Nephew Cutten."[73] An affiliate of the Chase Bank, the Chase Securities Corp. participated in another pool, which was led by Jesse Livermore.[74] Livermore had also risen to fame from commodity market manipulations, but lost badly in a battle with Cutten in the May 1924 wheat futures contract. Livermore was truly a gambler. He declared bankruptcy four times during his career as a speculator, before he committed suicide in 1940.[75] In one great stock market pool in 1927, Livermore was credited with pushing the price of Freeport Texas stock from $19 to $74.25.[76]

The stock pools often used options to obtain leverage and manipulated prices upward by wash sales, false rumors, and market letters published by brokerage firms.[77] One source noted that the touting of stocks was widespread and usually took two forms: "(1) the sending out of circular letters containing market information and advice, allegedly expert and impartial, but which are in reality dedicated to the unloading of certain securities, and (2) the dissemination of the same sort of stuff through financial papers and sheets."[78] A Senate committee stated that the "conclusion is inescapable that members of the organized exchanges who had a participation in or managed pools, while simultaneously acting as brokers for the general public, were representing irreconcilable interests and attempting to discharge conflicting functions."[79]

Professional publicists were employed by pool operators to plant newspaper stories touting particular stocks.[80] One such publicist, A. Newton Plummer, was paid $300,000 to bribe reporters

68. *Cutten Case Ruling Asked in High Court*, New York Times, Feb. 7, 1923, at 35.

69. *Millions in Profits Attributed to Cutten*, New York Times, Sept. 11, 1928, at 29.

70. *Cutten a Cool Market Trader*, New York Times, Jan. 2, 1927, at XX8.

71. S. Rep. No. 1455, 73d Cong., 2d Sess. 64 (1934).

72. II Jerry W. Markham, A Financial History of the United States, From J.P. Morgan to the Institutional Investor (1900-1970) 143 (2002).

73. *Cutten-Sinclair*, Time, Dec. 10, 1928.

74. II Jerry W. Markham, A Financial History of the United States, From J.P. Morgan to the Institutional Investor (1900-1970) 134-135 (2002).

75. *Business: Fourth Down*, Time, March 19, 1934.

76. Paul Sarnoff, Jesse Livermore: Speculator King 81 (1985).

77. For a description of these pool operations *see*, Comment, *Market Operations and the Securities Exchange Act*, 46 Yale L.J. 624, 626-628 (1937).

78. James Wm. Moore and Frank M. Wiseman, *Market Manipulation and the Exchange Act*, 2 U. Chi. L. Rev. 46, 51, n. 23 (1934-1935).

79. S. Rep. No. 1455, 73d Cong., 2d Sess. 36 (1934).

80. One source notes that

> publicity has been one of the most commonly employed manipulative techniques. One of the earliest forms was the spreading of false rumors about political or economic affairs, or the affairs of a single security issuer, leading the public to form erroneous judgments and take market action. Word of mouth rumor-mongering was augmented by the use of fake financial services, tip

to publish some 20,000 articles touting stocks that were carried in over 700 newspapers, including the *Wall Street Journal* and the *New York Times*. Another publicist, David M. Lion, made more than $500,000 from stock options given to him for his efforts in promoting stocks targeted by pools. William J. McMahon was paid by the pools to tout stocks over the radio.[81]

The stock market crash of 1929 did not end pool operations. "Repeal" stocks, which was a reference to companies that would benefit from the repeal of the eighteenth amendment, were among those manipulated. The Libbey-Owens-Ford Glass Co. was the target of a pool that exploited the "popular delusion" that the company made glass bottles that would serve as containers for alcoholic beverages.[82] The pools were assisted by "market letters . . . sent by brokerage firms to their branch offices, which letters are made accessible to the investing and speculating public. Typical of this practice were market letters distributed by E.F. Hutton & Co. with reference to American Commercial Alcohol stock . . . during which period Ruloff E. Cutten, held options on the stock."[83]

Short selling in the stock markets came under attack after the stock market crash of 1929. The Republican Senate floor leader, James Eli Watson, "commonly regarded as a spokesman for the Hoover Administration," stated in October 1931, "It is the belief of many that we shall not recover from our present depression until transactions of this kind [short selling] are either prohibited or greatly curtailed or properly safeguarded. . . . I have no doubt that one or more resolutions of this kind will be passed [by Congress]."[84] "The Scripps-Howard chain papers, professional crusaders, also took up the battle against bears."[85]

In 1931, James W. Gerard, the former U.S. ambassador to Germany, attacked short sellers on the stock markets in a nationwide radio broadcast. President Hoover also expressed concern to NYSE officials that short sellers were hurting the economy. The NYSE suspended short sales unless they were done at the last quoted price, thereby preventing scale-down orders that were much criticized for driving down prices. The NYSE also prohibited short selling for a period of two days in 1931 after England suspended gold payments.[86]

Short sales on the NYSE were also targeted for investigation by the Senate Committee on Banking and Currency after claims that there had been deliberate efforts "to hammer down the price of securities on the stock market."[87] The Senate authorized an investigation into short sales in December 1931. That investigation was later broadened to look at a broad range of market abuses and culminated in the passage of the Securities Exchange Act of 1934.[88]

> sheets, bribed financial writers, and bribed customers' men or brokers who, without disclosing their financial interests, would recommend certain securities. Successful manipulation by publicity techniques was not limited to rumors which were false. If a manipulation by other means than publicity were planned, its success could be promoted by the spreading of advance notice among persons anxious to get in on the ground floor.

Note, *Regulation of Stock Market Manipulation*, 56 YALE L. J. 509, 512 (1946-1947) (footnotes omitted).

81. II JERRY W. MARKHAM, A FINANCIAL HISTORY OF THE UNITED STATES, FROM J.P. MORGAN TO THE INSTITUTIONAL INVESTOR (1900-1970) 144 (2002).

82. S. Rep. No. 1455, 73d Cong., 2d Sess. 36 (1934).

83. *Id.* at 41.

84. *Bear in the Street*, TIME MAGAZINE, Oct. 12, 1931.

85. *Id.*

86. II JERRY W. MARKHAM, A FINANCIAL HISTORY OF THE UNITED STATES, FROM J.P. MORGAN TO THE INSTITUTIONAL INVESTOR (1900-1970) 173 (2002).

87. *Congress Investigates "Short" Selling Practices*, CONG. DIGEST 11, No. 12, at 289 (1932).

88. JOHN C. BURCH AND BRUCE FOERSTER, CAPITAL MARKETS HANDBOOK, App. M at M-9 (2011 Supp.).

The House Committee on the Judiciary held hearings on the short selling of securities in February 1932.[89] It considered bills that included recitations on the dangers of short sales, including the statement that short sales constituted "a constant possible menace to the market value" of stock traded on exchanges and that they were being used for speculation and manipulation.[90] Another bill would have made it a felony to trade in stocks without "intending a bona fide receipt or delivery of the same."[91] Those bills were intended to stop "bear raiding."[92]

Most witnesses were opposed to short selling, but Professor S.S. Huebner from the Wharton School of Finance and Commerce advised the committee that short selling "is a necessary and normal part of an organized market."[93] He then described at length the advantages provided by short sales, including adding liquidity to the market.

2:3 THE NEW DEAL

The 1932 presidential campaign was marked by Franklin Roosevelt's attacks on Wall Street. Among other things he railed against "organized greed and cunning,"[94] and he blamed the Great Depression on "the rulers of the exchange of mankind's goods" who "have failed through their own stubbornness and their own incompetence." Roosevelt proclaimed that the "[p]ractices of the unscrupulous money changers stand indicted in the court of public opinion, rejected by the hearts and mind of men." He asserted that there must be a "strict supervision" of investments and "an end to speculation with other people's money."[95]

President Roosevelt sent a message to Congress on February 9, 1934, that decried "naked speculation" by small traders and "the pool of individuals or corporations with large resources, often not their own, which sought by manipulation to raise or depress market quotations far out of line with reason, all of this resulting in loss to the average investor, who is of necessity personally uninformed."[96] His message to Congress further stated:

> The people of this country are, in an overwhelming majority, fully aware of the fact that unregulated speculation in securities and in commodities was one of the most important contributing factors in the artificial and unwarranted "boom" which had so much to do with the terrible conditions of the years following 1929.[97]

The president sought legislation that would eliminate to the extent possible "unnecessary, unwise, and destructive speculation."[98] Although he wanted legislation that would prevent "purely speculative operations" on both the commodity and securities exchanges,[99] the stock markets were the

---

89. *Short Selling of Securities, Hearing Before the House Committee on the Judiciary*, 72d Cong., 1st Sess. (1932).

90. *Id.* at 2.

91. *Id.* at 5.

92. *Id.* at 7.

93. *Id.* at 68.

94. *See*, Jerry W. Markham, A Financial History of Modern U.S. Corporate Scandals, From Enron to Reform 133 (2006) (describing these denunciations).

95. *Inaugural Speech of Franklin Delano Roosevelt*, Washington, DC, March 4, 1933, http://www.hpol.org/fdr/inaug/ (accessed November 15, 2011).

96. H.R. Rep. No. 1383, 73d Cong., 2d Sess. 1 (1934).

97. H.R. Rep. No. 421, 74th Cong., 1st Sess. 2 (1935).

98. H.R. Rep. No. 1383, 73d Cong., 2d Sess. 2 (1934).

99. *Id.*

first target for his administration. Of significance to the process was the jurisdictional division of labor in Congress. The banking committees assumed jurisdiction over the stock exchanges, while the agriculture committees controlled legislation dealing with agriculture. This made some sense since commodity futures were, at that time, concerned only with pricing agricultural commodities. That congressional division of authority would make less sense, and would lead to much controversy, much later in the century when financial instruments became the dominant subject of futures trading.[100]

At the request of the president, Secretary of Commerce Daniel C. Roper formed a committee to consider what form of regulation was needed for the securities markets. That study resulted in the enactment of the Securities Act of 1933, which required that public stock offerings be registered with the government.[101] The Roper committee issued another report on regulation needed for the stock exchanges, which was transmitted to Congress on January 25, 1934.[102] Among other things, the Roper Committee expressed concern with "pool operations which have artificially influenced the price of shares to the disadvantage of the private shareholder and in the hope of speculative gains to the participants."[103] It recommended that the stock exchanges be issued a federal license "analogous to the system of federal regulation applied to grain exchanges by the Grain Futures Act."[104] The Roper Committee also recommended that devices used by speculative pool operations, such as "wash sales" and "matched orders," be prohibited.[105]

Congress conducted extensive hearings on manipulative practices in its stock market investigations, leading to the enactment of the Securities Exchange Act of 1934 (34 Act).[106] Hearings in the Senate began on April 11, 1932, and totaled some 10,000 pages before they were completed.[107] Those investigations were desultory at first but picked up momentum with the appointment of Ferdinand Pecora as chief counsel for the investigation.[108] His congressional inquiry encountered a storm of "propaganda" orchestrated by the NYSE.[109] Opponents contended that the proposed

---

100. *See*, Jerry W. Markham, *Merging the SEC and CFTC: A Clash of Cultures*, 78 U. Cinn. L. Rev. 537 (2009) and *Super-Regulator: A Comparative Analysis of Securities and Derivatives Regulation in the United States, Great Britain & Japan*, 28 Brooklyn J. Int'l 319 (2003) (describing those disputes).

101. 15 U.S.C. § 77 *et seq.*

102. *Stock Exchange Regulation Letter from the President of the United States to the Chairman of the Committee on Banking and Currency with an Accompanying Report Relative to Stock Exchange Regulation*, Report of the Senate Comm. On Banking and Currency, 73d Cong., 2d Sess. iii (1934).

103. *Id.* at 8.

104. *Id.* at 4.

105. The Roper Committee stated:

> An accompaniment of speculative pool operations is the use of so-called "wash sales" and "matched orders." The effect of this method of using the exchange machinery is most disastrous to the public for it creates the semblance of legitimate activity in securities which does not in fact exist. It is a maxim with speculative pool operators that the best way to advertise a stock to gain a speculative public following is to show increasing turnover in volume of sales with increasing prices. Through the use of "wash sales" and "matched orders" such fictitious market situations are created as to warrant the absolute prohibition of this practice.

Id. at 15.

106. 48 Stat. 881 (1934).

107. 78 Cong. Rec. 2264 (1934) (remarks of Sen. Fletcher).

108. *See*, Ferdinand Pecora, Wall Street Under Oath (1939); Michael Perino, The Hellhound of Wall Street (2010) (describing his investigations).

109. *See, e.g.*, 78 Cong. Rec. 2264, 7689 (1934).

legislation would only further undermine business confidence and impair economic recovery.[110] The Roosevelt administration, nevertheless, prevailed in pushing the 34 Act through Congress.

The debates on the 34 Act contained much in the way of populist attacks on Wall Street that foretell those following the financial crisis of 2008. Brokers on Wall Street were said to have engaged in a "legalized poker game" in the 1920s.[111] The congressman making that remark also chortled that "the idle holders of idle capital . . . are going to get the damnedest licking of their lifetime."[112] Commercial and investment bankers were charged with having made "excessive compensation" from their stock market activities before the 1929 crash.[113] The 513 millionaires living in the United States in 1929 were charged with acquiring wealth that "came from the highway robberies on the stock exchanges."[114]

This concern over pools and wash sales and matched orders also permeated the congressional hearings and committee reports. A Senate subcommittee concluded "that the activity fomented by a pool creates a false and deceptive appearance of genuine demand for the security on the part of the purchasing public and attracts persons relying upon this misleading appearance to make purchases. By this means the pool is enabled to unload its holdings upon an unsuspecting public."[115] The subcommittee rejected claims that some stock pools were "beneficent" in stabilizing market prices. "Although the purpose may be different, the means employed are identical. In all cases fictitious activity is intentionally created and the purchaser is deceived by an appearance of genuine demand for the security. Motive furnishes no justification for the employment of manipulative devices."[116]

Ruloff Cutten, himself adept at stock manipulations, was interrogated on the role of pools in the congressional investigation that led to the enactment of the 34 Act. Cutten stated that "manipulation of a stock is marking a stock up or marking a stock down without a bona fide purchase or a bona fide sale, such as wash sales."[117] He stated that in "broad" public markets it was nearly impossible to conduct a stock price manipulation. "When manipulation starts you have to absorb nearly all the floating supply of the stock before you can manipulate it."[118]

Richard Whitney, representing the NYSE, noted that wash sales were already prohibited by the penal laws of New York and NYSE rules, but he supported a federal nationwide application of such a prohibition.[119] Whitney also supported restrictions on matched orders, which he described as "a form of fictitious transaction whereby two or more persons, by prearrangement, enter orders at about the same time to buy and sell a certain security with the intention or design that these orders will meet and be executed one against the other."[120] Whitney was later sent to prison for fraud.[121] Other witnesses complained about the "pegging" of securities prices during the flotation

---

110. *See, e.g.*, 78 Cong. Rec. 7692 (1934).

111. 78 Cong. Rec. 8089 (1934) (remarks of Mr. Truax).

112. *Id.*

113. S. Rep. No. 1455, 73d Cong., 2d Sess. 114, 186, 205 (1934).

114. 78 Cong. Rec. 8108 (1934) (remarks of Mr. Rankin).

115. S. Rep. No. 1455, 73d Cong., 2d Sess. 32 (1934).

116. S. Rep. No. 1455, 73d Cong., 2d Sess. 32 (1934).

117. *Stock Exchange Practices, Hearing Before the Senate Committee on Banking and Currency on S. Res. 84 and S. Res. 56*, 73d Cong., 1st Sess. 3240 (1934).

118. *Id.*

119. *Stock Exchange Regulation, Hearing Before the House Committee on Interstate and Foreign Commerce on H.R. 7852 and H.R. 8720*, 73d Cong., 2d Sess. 203 (1934).

120. *Id.* at 204.

121. II Jerry W. Markham, A Financial History of the United States, From J.P. Morgan to the Institutional Investor (1900-1970) 206-207 (2002).

of a stock issue by underwriting firms.[122] That practice was intended to stabilize prices until the offering could be completed.[123]

Options were found to have been used in "many fields of manipulative activity. Through the medium of options, manipulators of every sort are enabled to carry on large-scale operations with a minimum of financial risk."[124] During 1929, forty-one stocks listed on the NYSE were the subject of options on at least 10,000 of their shares.[125] Options were also used to hedge short sales in pool operations.[126] One witness expressed concern with stop-loss orders, which

> in a tremendously falling market . . . may have a very unfortunate effect of touching off other stop-loss orders until you get an indefinite number of stop-loss orders in the market and there is nothing to stop the stock from going through air pockets to the very bottom. . . .When a specialist's books are open to his short-selling friends, if they see a big bunch of stop-loss orders of big traders at a certain figure, and can force the market down to the stop-loss orders, they can touch off a huge block of sales which will run the stock way down.[127]

Another witness complained of a manipulation carried out by pushing prices of a stock each day higher by one-eighth by "buying at the close" on the exchange. The manipulator then used those transaction reports to mount a sales campaign and sell the stock to unsuspecting investors.[128] Still another witness asserted that "[s]hort selling, to my mind, is criminal."[129] One witness wanted legislation that would "allow free play to supply and demand in dealing in securities so that the price shall not be artificially made by wash sales and by various other devices that have been used in the past to run up the price, particularly during a period when shares are being sold throughout the country."[130] Another witness expressed concern "with manipulations and, of course, false statements or misleading statements."[131]

Still another witness wanted "to have the fellow on the outside protected from the fellow on the inside who is an officer or director of the corporation or a pool with inside information."[132] A witness argued that "some administrative body" should be endowed "with authority to prevent unfair practices, manipulations, the establishment of false values, or the appearance of values when they do not exist."[133]

One proposed bill, H.R. 7852, contained a section titled "Prohibition Against Manipulation of Security Prices," which sought to proscribe a number of practices deemed manipulative.[134]

---

122. *See, e.g.*, *Stock Exchange Practices, Hearing Before the Senate Committee on Banking and Currency on S. Res. 84, S. Res. 56 and S. Res. 97*, 73d Cong., 2d Sess. 7709, 7736 (1934).

123. *See*, James Wm. Moore and Frank M. Wiseman, *Market Manipulation and the Exchange Act*, 2 U. Chi. L. Rev. 46, 55 (1934-1935) (discusses stabilization activities and why they might be legitimate practices).

124. S. Rep. No. 1455, 73d Cong., 2d Sess. 45 (1934).

125. *Id.*

126. *Id.* at 51.

127. *Stock Exchange Regulation, Hearing Before the House Committee on Interstate and Foreign Commerce on H.R. 7852 and H.R. 8720*, 73d Cong., 2d Sess. 110 (1934).

128. *Stock Exchange Practices, Hearing Before the Senate Committee on Banking and Currency on S. Res. 84 and S. Res. 56, and S. Res. 97*, 73d Cong., 1st Sess. 7019 (1934).

129. *Stock Exchange Regulation, Hearing Before the House Committee on Interstate and Foreign Commerce on H.R. 7852 and H.R. 8720*, 73d Cong., 2d Sess. 826 (1934).

130. *Id.* at 875.

131. *Id.* at 456.

132. *Id.* at 8.

133. *Id.* at 877.

134. *Id.* at 5.

Those proscriptions included "fictitious" trades involving no change in ownership or wash sales. Another target was transactions conducted for "the purpose of raising or depressing the price of such security or securities or for the purpose of creating or with the expectation that there will be created a false or misleading appearance of active trading in such security or securities, or a false or misleading appearance in respect of the market for such security or securities."[135] It was thought that prohibiting such manipulative activities "hits at the practices which are the starting points of manipulation and market activity. They are the practices which fan the flames of public buying."[136]

Counsel for a Senate committee reported that "powerful interests, operating on a large scale in a particular stock, can so manipulate the market and control the price of that stock in normal times as to accomplish almost any desired result."[137] Legislation was sought to prohibit traders from acquiring "substantial control of the floating supply of any security registered on a national securities exchange for the purpose of causing the price of such security to rise on the exchange because of such control of the floating supply."[138] The bill also contained several proscriptions against the touting of stocks through false and misleading statements that are "sufficiently important to influence the judgment of an average investor."[139] However, several states already had prohibitions against fraudulent stock touting.[140]

Another concern expressed in the legislative history was "excessive speculation." As one bill stated, securities traded on the stock exchanges were "susceptible to manipulation and control and the dissemination of such prices gives rise to excessive speculation."[141] "By reason of such manipulation and control and excessive speculation, sudden and unreasonable fluctuations in the prices of securities on such exchanges occur."[142] "Excessive speculation" was equated with manipulation. As representatives from the Roosevelt administration testified, the "underlying principle of the bill is that Federal regulation is necessary in the public interest to control manipulation and excessive speculation in securities and thus to secure and maintain a fair and honest market."[143]

A House committee report tried to strike a balance as to the role of speculation, stating that there was "plenty of room for legitimate speculation in the balancing of investment demand and supply, in the shrewd prognostication of future trends and economic directions; but the accentuation of temporary fluctuations and the deliberate introduction of a mob psychology into the speculative markets by the fanfare of organized manipulation menace the true functioning of the exchanges, upon which the economic well-being of the whole country depends."[144]

Margin trading through broker's loans was thought to have provided "*excessive credit for speculation*."[145] The proposed legislation sought to "discourage the use of credit in the financing

---

135. *Id.*

136. *Stock Exchange Practices, Hearing Before the Senate Committee on Banking and Currency on S. Res. 84, S. Res. 56 and S. Res. 97*, 73d Cong., 1st Sess. 7104 (1934).

137. *Stock Exchange Practices, Letter From the Counsel for the House Committee on Interstate and Foreign Commerce Under S. Res. 84*, 73d Cong., 1st Sess. 632 (1933).

138. *Stock Exchange Regulation, Hearing Before the House Committee on Interstate and Foreign Commerce on H.R. 7852 and H.R. 8720*, 73d Cong., 2d Sess. 6 (1934).

139. *Id.*

140. *See*, James Wm. Moore and Frank M. Wiseman, *Market Manipulation and the Exchange Act*, 2 U. Chi. L. Rev. 46, 66, n. 85 (1934-1935) (compiling those statutes).

141. H.R. 7852, 73d Cong., 2d Sess. (1934).

142. *Stock Exchange Regulation, Hearing Before the House Committee on Interstate and Foreign Commerce on H.R. 7852 and H.R. 8720*, 73d Cong., 2d Sess. 2 (1934).

143. *Id.* at 925.

144. H.R. Rep. No. 1383, 73d Cong., 2d Sess. 11 (1934).

145. S. Rep. No. 1455, 73d Cong., 2d Sess. 12 (1934) (emphasis in original). This Senate committee report stated:

of excessive speculation in securities."[146] One witness objected to the leverage obtained from margin trading: the "manipulative practices you hear so much about become much easier when a terrific volume of margin money can be brought in and, of course, the temptation to engage in manipulative practices becomes stronger the bigger the profit to be made out of it."[147] A congressman asserted that margin requirements limit speculation. "No one denies it can be utilized either as an accelerator or a brake."[148]

A representative from the Federal Reserve Board charged that securities margin "makes necessary rapid sales in the case of a rapid declining market, and therefore adds to the flexibility or the erratic character of the market."[149] He also asserted that large volumes of margin trading by small accounts encouraged market manipulators and made manipulation easier to complete. For example, a manipulator could bid up prices, which would free up margin for small speculators. That excess margin would then be used by the small speculators to take on a larger position, pushing prices up further to the benefit of the manipulator. The manipulator could then take his profits and then short the market and push prices down. This would cause margin calls to be sent to the small speculators who would be forced to liquidate their positions. That liquidation would further push prices down to the benefit of the short manipulator.[150]

The controversial practice of short selling was hotly debated. "Few subjects relating to exchange practices have been characterized by greater differences of opinion than that of short selling."[151] Proponents of short sales argued that "in a crisis short sellers are useful in maintaining an orderly market; and that their activities serve as a cushion to break the force of a decline in the price of stocks. Its opponents assert that short selling unsettles the market, forces liquidation, depresses

---

> When the volume of brokers' loans piles up to the heights reached in recent years, the situation is fraught with peril. In the event of unfavorable developments in the financial world, such loans are promptly called, the borrowers are forced to sell securities on a vast scale, and a decline in security values is precipitated. With the drop in market prices, margin accounts become undermargined, resulting in further involuntary liquidation, which accelerates the decline. The shrinkage in security prices not only demoralizes the margin trader, but impairs the security of collateral loans made by the banks and the value of securities held in their own portfolios.

Id.

146. *Stock Exchange Regulation, Hearing Before the House Committee on Interstate and Foreign Commerce on H.R. 7852 and H.R. 8720*, 73d Cong. 2d Sess. 701 (1934).

147. *Id.* at 108.

148. 78 Cong. Rec. 7865 (1934) (remarks of Rep. Wolverton).

149. *Stock Exchange Regulation, Hearing Before the House Committee on Interstate and Foreign Commerce on H.R. 7852 and H.R. 8720*, 73d Cong., 2d Sess. 6456-6457 (1934). The Federal Reserve Board had created a "Money Committee" during World War I that monitored the "call" loan market, which funded borrowing on stocks. The Money Committee was composed of Benjamin Strong, the governor of the New York Federal Reserve Bank, and several representatives of the banks. The Money Committee was initially concerned that the call market could be impaired by competition from the large government bond issues floated during the war. Later, the Money Committee changed its focus and sought to dampen speculation. The Money Committee requested that NYSE members supply it daily with the amounts of funds on "call" and funds lent on time. The Money Committee also asked that margin requirements on stock loans be increased substantially. The banks agreed to those requests, but the Money Committee came under much criticism from the securities industry for those efforts, and it was disbanded after the war. II JERRY W. MARKHAM, A FINANCIAL HISTORY OF THE UNITED STATES, FROM J.P. MORGAN TO THE INSTITUTIONAL INVESTOR (1900-1970) 80-82 (2002).

150. *See*, Jerry W. Markham, *Federal Regulation of Margin in the Commodity Futures Industry: History and Theory*, 64 TEMP. L. REV. 59, 69, 104 (1991) (describing those concerns).

151. S. Rep. No. 1455, 73d Cong., 2d Sess. 50 (1934).

prices, accelerates declines, and has no economic value or justification."[152] Opponents also pointed to the fact that the NYSE had suspended short sales for two days in 1931 after England announced that it was going off the gold standard. This was viewed as evidence that even the NYSE viewed short sales as a danger.[153]

Still another abuse was insider trading. A Senate committee report stated that "among the most vicious practices" that were unearthed during its extensive hearings on this legislation was "the flagrant betrayal of their fiduciary duties by directors and officers of corporations who used their positions of trust, and the confidential information which came to them in such positions, to aid them in their market activities."[154] Similar concern was expressed about "the unscrupulous employment of inside information by large stockholders who, while not directors and officers, exercised sufficient control over the destinies of their companies to enable them to acquire and profit by information not available to others."[155]

The 34 Act reflected the fact that a "fundamental goal of the federal securities laws is the prevention of manipulation. Manipulation impedes the securities markets from functioning as an independent pricing mechanism and undermines the fairness and integrity of those markets."[156] A House report on this legislation stated that the "most subtle manipulating device employed in the security markets . . . is the conscious marking up of prices to make investors believe that there is a constantly increasing demand for stocks at higher prices."[157] The definition of manipulation, however, otherwise received little attention during the hearings on this legislation. The chief lobbyist for the White House, Tommy "the Cork" Corcoran, did not illuminate this issue when he testified that "you cannot tell at exactly what stage a kitten becomes a cat in determining whether a man bought or sold on the market for the purpose of raising or depressing the price."[158]

Rather than resolve the fights over whether short selling, options, and underwriting stabilizing operations (i.e., "pegging" prices during a distribution) should be prohibited, the regulation of those practices was left to the discretion of the Securities and Exchange Commission (SEC).[159] Restrictions on margin trading, another controversial subject, were left for the Federal Reserve Board to set lending limits and the SEC to enforce.[160] Section 11 of the 34 Act sought to prevent abuses that could be deemed manipulative on the part of specialists by requiring them to maintain a "fair and orderly market."[161] The SEC adopted rules requiring specialists to meet that obligation.[162]

The real thrust of the congressional effort to curb manipulation through the passage of the 34 Act is found in its Sections 9[163] and 10.[164] Section 9 of the 34 Act was intended by Congress to be

---

152. *Id.*

153. *Stock Exchange Practices, Letter From the Counsel for the House Committee on Interstate and Foreign Commerce Under S. Res. 84*, 73d Cong., 1st Sess. 6-7 (1933).

154. S. Rep. No. 1455, 73d Cong., 2d Sess. 55 (1934).

155. *Id.*

156. SEC, *Trading Practices Rules Concerning Securities* Offerings, 61 Fed. Reg. 17108 (April 18, 1996).

157. H.R. Rep. No. 1383, 73d Cong., 2d Sess. 11 (1934).

158. *Stock Exchange Practices, Hearing Before the Senate Committee on Banking and Currency on S. Res. 84, S. Res. 56 and S. Res. 97*, 73d Cong., 1st Sess. 6509 (1934).

159. H.R. Rep. No. 792, 73d Cong., 2d Sess. 8-9 (1934).

160. *Id.* at 7.

161. 48 Stat. 881, 891 (1934).

162. 17 C.F.R. § 240.1111b-1.

163. 78 U.S.C. § 78i.

164. 78 U.S.C. § 78j.

the principal prohibition against manipulation, an intent that is reflected in its title: "Prohibition Against Manipulation of Security Prices."[165] Section 9 was designed "to prevent rigging of the market and to permit operation of the natural law of supply and demand."[166] It sought to prohibit the creation of a price "mirage" rather than the reflection of a genuine demand.[167]

The prohibitions in Section 9(a)(2) were intended to represent the "heart" of the 34 Act.[168] Section 9(a)(2) sought to "perform the wholesome service of outlawing pool operations, as well as every other device used to persuade the public that activity in a security is the reflection of a genuine demand instead of a mirage."[169] The prohibitions in Section 9(a)(2) include the following:

(1) wash sales involving no change in beneficial ownership that are effected "for the purpose" of creating a false or misleading appearance of active trading . . . , or a false or misleading appearance with respect to the market for any such security."[170]
(2) securities transactions effected for the "purpose of creating actual or apparent active trading in such security, or raising or depressing the price of such security, for the purpose of inducing the purchase or sale of such security by others."[171]
(3) the inducement of the purchase or sale of a security "by the circulation or dissemination in the ordinary course of business of information to the effect that the price of any such security will or is likely to rise or fall because of market operations of any one or more persons conducted for the purpose of raising or depressing the price of such security."[172]
(4) to make, for the purpose of inducing the purchase or sale of a security or a security-based swap agreement, "any statement which was at the time and in the light of the circumstances under which it was made, false or misleading with respect to any material fact, and which he [the person making the statement] knew or had reasonable ground to believe was so false or misleading."[173]
(5) for consideration received directly or indirectly from a person offering or selling a security, circulating or disseminating "information to the effect that the price of any such security will or is likely to rise or fall because of the market operations of any one or more persons conducted for the purpose of raising or depressing the price of such security."[174]
(6) to effect alone or with one or more persons "any series of transactions for the purchase and/or sale of any security other than a government security for the purpose of pegging, fixing, or stabilizing the price of such security in contravention of such rules and regulations as the Commission may prescribe."[175]

---

165. 48 Stat. at 889. *See generally*, Lewis D. Lowenfels, *Sections 9(A)(1) and 9(A)(2) of the Securities Exchange Act of 1934: An Analysis of Two Important Anti-Manipulative Provisions Under the Federal Securities Laws*, 85 Nw. U. L. Rev 698 (1991) (describing this statute).

166. United States v. Stein, 456 F.2d 844, 850 (2d Cir. 1972), *cert. denied*, 408 U.S. 922 (1973).

167. United States v. Stein, 456 F.2d 844, 850 (2d Cir. 1969), citing S. Rep. No. 1455, 73d Cong., 2d Sess. 54 (1934).

168. Crane v. Westinghouse Air Brake Co. 419 F.2d 787, 794 (2d Cir. 1969).

169. S. Rep. No. 1455, 73d Cong., 2d Sess. 54 (1934) (footnote omitted).

170. 15 U.S.C. § 78i(a)(1).

171. 15 U.S.C. § 78i(a)(2).

172. 15 U.S.C. § 78i(a)(3).

173. 15 U.S.C. § 78i(a)(4).

174. 15 U.S.C. § 78i(a)(5).

175. 15 U.S.C. § 78i(a)(6).

Sections 9(b) and (c) of the 34 Act gave the SEC plenary authority over the trading of options.[176] This grant of discretionary authority was in lieu of a ban on those contracts. A ban was averted by testimony from the Committee of Put and Call Brokers and Dealers in the City of New York, noting that options had beneficial purposes, such as allowing investors to hedge the risks of holding a security.[177]

Section 9(e) contains an express private right of action for violations of the prohibitions in Section 9.[178] It provides that any person "who willfully participates" in any such transactions "shall be liable to any person who shall purchase or sell any security at a price which was affected by such act or transaction."[179] This sounded promising for plaintiffs seeking damages from manipulations, but the sting for them was in the tail. First, the statute has a short statute of limitations—"one year after the discovery of the facts constituting the violation and within three years after such violation."[180] Second, Section 9 gave the courts discretion to require an undertaking for the payment of the costs and to "assess reasonable costs, including reasonable attorneys' fees, against either party litigant."[181] This is an exception to the "American rule" that does not generally allow the prevailing party, especially defendants, to recover their attorney fees when successful in defeating a claim.[182]

Section 10 of the 34 Act was initially viewed as a more narrow provision that sought to allow the SEC to adopt rules on trading practices over which there had been debate in the congressional hearings on their value in market efficiency. Short sales and stop-loss orders, which were thought by some to "greatly facilitate speculation,"[183] were defended by others.[184] Therefore, instead of being banned, those transactions were subjected to SEC regulation under Subsection 10(a) of the 34 Act.[185]

Subsection 10(b), which was added by a Senate amendment adopted in conference,[186] authorized the SEC "to prohibit or regulate the use of any other manipulative or deceptive practices which it finds detrimental to the interests of investors."[187] Section 10(b) contains

---

176. 48 Stat. at 890.

177. Jerry W. Markham & David J. Gilberg, *Stock and Commodity Options: Two Regulatory Approaches and Their Conflicts*, 47 ALBANY L. REV. 741, 747 (1983).

178. 15 U.S.C. § 78i(e).

179. *Id.*

180. *Id.*

181. *Id.*

182. The Supreme Court has noted:

> By the time the Federal Rules of Civil Procedure were adopted in 1938, federal statutes had authorized and defined awards of costs to prevailing parties for more than 85 years. . . . Unlike in England, such "costs" generally had not included attorney's fees; under the "American Rule," each party had been required to bear its own attorney's fees. The "American Rule" as applied in federal courts, however, had become subject to certain exceptions by the late 1930's. [including 34 Act Section 9(e)]

Marek v. Chesny, 473 U.S. 1, 8 (1985) (citations omitted).

183. H.R. Rep. No. 792, 73d Cong., 2d Sess. 18 (1934).

184. S. Rep. No. 1455, 73d Cong., 2d Sess. (1934); *Stock Exchange Regulation, Hearing Before the House Committee on Interstate and Foreign Commerce on H.R. 7852 and H.R. 8720*, 73d Cong., 2d Sess. 110 (1934).

185. 78 U.S.C. § 78j(a)(1). Securities futures products were later exempted from that provision. 78 U.S.C. § 78j(a)(2).

186. H.R. Rep. No. 1838, 73d Cong., 2d Sess. 32-33 (1934).

187. H.R. Rep. No. 792, 73d Cong., 2d Sess. 18 (1934). Section 10(b) of the 34 Act makes it unlawful

no definition of what the term "manipulation" means.[188] However, the Supreme Court later noted that the term "manipulation" was intended by Congress to refer "generally to practices, such as wash sales, matched orders, or rigged prices, that are intended to mislead investors by artificially affecting market activity," citing Section 9 of the 34 Act.[189] The Supreme Court also noted that Section 10(b) was a "general prohibition of practices deemed by the SEC to be 'manipulative'—in this technical sense of artificially affecting market activity in order to mislead investors."[190]

Section 16 of the 34 Act was an effort by Congress to restrict insider trading by officers and directors of public companies and owners of 10 percent of the stock of such companies.[191] Section 16(a) required such persons to report their transactions in their company's stock.[192] Section 16(b) allowed private suits to recover profits by such persons in the stock of their company within a six-month period.[193] Section 16(c) prohibited short sales by these persons in the stock of their companies.[194]

The purposes of the Securities Exchange Act of 1934, as summarized in a contemporaneous law review article, were "(1) to curb excessive speculation; (2) to give the public adequate financial information concerning the securities traded in; and (3) to prevent illegitimate manipulation of security prices and protect the public against unfair practices."[195] Those authors opined:

> The term "manipulation" may, in short, be applied to any practice which has as its purpose the deliberate raising, lowering or pegging of security prices. Buying and selling in themselves do, of course, affect price, but in a free and open market this is a natural consequence and not their pre-conceived purpose. Manipulation leads to an artificial and controlled price. Such a price, which is broadcast in the form of a market quotation, then, does not reflect an independent appraisal of the security in respect to the floating supply, nor to the immobile holdings throughout the country.[196]

> To use or employ, in connection with the purchase or sale of any security registered on a national securities exchange or any security not so registered, or any securities-based swap agreement (as defined in section 206B of the Gramm-Leach-Bliley Act), any manipulative or deceptive device or contrivance in contravention of such rules and regulations as the Commission may prescribe as necessary or appropriate in the public interest or for the protection of investors.

78 U.S. § 78j(b).

188. Congress granted broad authority to the SEC "to combat manipulative abuses in whatever form they might take, including anti-fraud, prophylactic, and general rulemaking authority." Melissa W. Palombo, *The Short-Changing of Investors: Why a Short Sale Price Test Rule Is Necessary in Today's Markets*, 75 Brooklyn L. Rev. 1447, 1488 (2010) In exercising that authority, the SEC has traditionally concentrated on the activities of participants in securities offerings. Among other things, the SEC has adopted Regulation M to prevent manipulation during public offerings as a part of price "stabilization" efforts during the distribution. 17 C.F.R. §§ 242.100-242.105. *See*, 23A Jerry W. Markham & Thomas Lee Hazen, Broker-Dealer Operations Under Securities and Commodity Laws §§ 9:12 -9:14 (2010) (describing application of Regulation M).

189. Santa Fe v. Green, 430 U.S. 462, 476 (1977).

190. 430 U.S. at 476-477.

191. 48 Stat. at 896.

192. 15 U.S.C. 78p(a).

193. 15 U.S.C. 78p(b).

194. 15 U.S.C. 78p(c).

195. James Wm. Moore and Frank M. Wiseman, *Market Manipulation and the Exchange Act*, 2 U. Chi. L. Rev. 46 (1934-1935).

196. Id. at 46, 50 (footnotes omitted). Another law review article noted that, when Congress enacted the Securities Exchange Act of 1934, speculation was a target but was difficult to identify for regulation:

2:4 THE COMMODITY EXCHANGE ACT OF 1936

The Great Depression had a devastating effect on agricultural prices and became a matter of considerable political and economic concern. President Herbert Hoover sought to raise grain prices through a reprise of the World War I programs. Shortly before the stock market crash of 1929, he created the Federal Farm Board, which sought to increase grain prices that had already been depressed for much of the 1920s. A congressman claimed that grain prices were "hammered down to the extreme low point, but the moment the farmer parts with his grain the speculators start to raise the price and the result is that both the consumers and the farmers are mulcted by a bunch of professional dishonest speculators, . . . [who] sell millions of bushels of wheat, corn, or rye, just for the purpose of artificially lowering the price so that they can buy the grains back at a much lower price."[197]

The Federal Farm Board was created on June 15, 1929, at Hoover's request in order to allow agricultural cooperatives to "sustain orderly markets in various commodities—cotton, wool and pecans, for example—by facilitating voluntary agreements among producers" and by providing for the purchase of surpluses by "stabilization corporations." Congress allocated $500 million to fund this project.[198] After the stock market crash, Hoover also sought to raise grain prices through the Farm Board and the newly created, government-controlled Grain Stabilization Corporation, which was assigned the task of purchasing crop surpluses on the market.

Concern over commodity price declines again focused on the futures exchanges as the Great Depression deepened. At the end of 1930, "the index of prices for 47 farm products was down 29.3% from pre-Crash prices, and publicly traded industrial commodities averaged a price decline of approximately 35%."[199] A spurious telegram claiming financial difficulties at the Canadian wheat pool knocked down wheat prices on September 23, 1930. The Winnipeg Grain Exchange offered a reward of $1,000 for the identity of the culprit, who, however, was not apprehended.[200]

> The difficulty with the functioning of the American markets, the economic observers agreed, was not speculation as such but the fact that the speculators were regularly stampeded into panicky fits of irrational optimism or pessimism, and that they were prone to prefer respectable conformity to independent judgment. Thus the inquiry into speculation as such was inconclusive. Whether the securities market caused the instability of the rest of the economy was not apparent. Even if it was conceded that market crashes disrupted the mechanism of finance, it was not at all clear that we could have a stable securities market in an unstable economy, and no theorist of the securities markets went so far as to contend that speculation in stocks was alone the cause of industrial fluctuations. The draftsmen lost interest in the search for a formula which would eliminate speculation and permit only long-term investment.
>
> Yet the prejudice against speculation left traces in the new system for the control of the securities markets, particularly in the provisions for the control of margin trading and short selling. It is also to be found in the discrimination in the federal income tax law against short-term security transactions in favor of long-term holding. But control of speculation was not to be the central theme of the legislation. Much of the force which might have been directed at speculation itself was spent on the so-called "abuses" of the markets. Fraud in the sale of securities and manipulation in the markets were the twin objects of this drive. It was thought that if the abuses could be corrected, speculation as a whole could successfully perform the functions assigned to it by the classical economic theory.

Note, *Regulation of Stock Market Regulation*, 56 YALE L. J. 509, 510-511 (1947).

197. 78 Cong. Rec. 10451 (1934) (remarks of Rep. Sabath).

198. DAVID M. KENNEDY, FREEDOM FROM FEAR 43-44 (1999).

199. BARRY A. WIGMORE, THE CRASH AND ITS AFTERMATH 133 (1985).

200. *Report of the Chief of the Grain Futures Administration* 6-7 (1931).

Alarm was raised over short sales in 1930 covering 8 million bushels of wheat. Those sales were conducted over a four-day period by the All Russian Textile Syndicate on behalf of the Soviet government. The secretary of agriculture, Arthur M. Hyde, claimed that those sales were part of a communist propaganda campaign. Hyde stated that "'[t]here can be no question that this selling has contributed to the fall of the price of wheat and to the injury of American farmers now engaged in their intensive marketing system.' And he asked the Chicago Board of Trade to do something about it."[201] The CBOT, indeed objecting to this selling, asserted that the sale of futures contracts by foreign governments on U.S. exchanges "is a new development of commerce of seriously objectionable character and it must be brought to an end."[202] Other countries were concerned that Russia was dumping grain on their markets even while Russian citizens were starving.

Denying any effort to push down prices, the All Russian Textile Syndicate claimed that it was merely selling a small quantity of wheat for business reasons and that the sales "were not intended as manipulations for the purpose stated in the press."[203] A House committee later found that the Soviets were hedging their grain sales. The Soviets had been out of the market for several years, and they planned to reenter the market simply by loading ships with grain and seeing what it would fetch upon arrival. They assumed this action would cause prices to fall.[204] The whole affair seemed odd since the Soviet Union abolished all its own commodity exchanges in 1930 and made speculation a crime.[205]

The Grain Stabilization Corp. began purchasing grain in 1930 and pushed U.S. wheat prices to levels between twenty and thirty-five cents per bushel over world prices.[206] The Grain Stabilization Corp. soon owned such a surplus that it posed a threat to the market itself and placed downward price pressures on grain. The corporation also tried to push up prices by buying futures on the commodity exchanges, but that effort failed as well.[207] As *Time* magazine reported, the government jumped "into the wheat pit where it traded in grain like any common speculator. When it closed its week's transactions it was some 25 million bushels long. Because of low prices, its holdings—theoretically the property of all U.S. taxpayers—represented a poor bargain."[208] It was later claimed on the House floor that short sellers on the CBOT had frustrated the Farm Board's efforts to raise commodity prices through those purchases.[209] It was charged that Arthur Cutten had sold short over 70 million bushels of grain on the CBOT while the Grain Stabilization Corp. was conducting its buying operations.[210] However, it was thought by others that an extraordinary surplus of wheat worldwide and other factors were the cause of price breaks.[211]

The Farm Board created a "price-pegging policy for the 1930 wheat crop, which involved buying surpluses totaling some 200 million bushels." That buying pressure pushed wheat prices up to as much as 35 cents per bushel over world prices but then the Farm Board decided not to purchase the 1931 crop surpluses. The Farm Board issued a statement saying that its price-pegging program "'was adopted to meet a most acute emergency. It has made wheat growers many millions. . . . But

201. *When the Russian Bear Is a Wheat Bear*, LITERARY DIGEST, Oct. 4, 1930, at 5.

202. *Report of the Chief of the Grain Futures Administration* 6-7 (1931).

203. *When the Russian Bear Is a Wheat Bear*, LITERARY DIGEST, Oct. 4, 1930, at 5.

204. JERRY W. MARKHAM, THE HISTORY OF COMMODITY TRADING AND ITS REGULATION 21 (1987).

205. Alexander Belozertsev & Jerry W. Markham, *Commodity Exchanges and the Privatization of the Agricultural Sector in the Commonwealth of Independent States: Needed Steps in Creating a Market Economy*, 55 LAW & CONTEMP. PROB. 119, 127 (1992).

206. *Report of the Chief of the Grain Futures Administration* 5 (1931).

207. WILLIAM G. FERRIS, THE GRAIN TRADERS 193 (1988).

208. *Husbandry: Dollar Wheat*, TIME, March 10, 1930.

209. 78 Cong. Rec. 10451 (1934) (remarks of Rep. Sabath).

210. JERRY W. MARKHAM, THE HISTORY OF COMMODITY TRADING AND ITS REGULATION 21 (1987).

211. *Husbandry: Dollar Wheat*, TIME, March 10, 1930.

[the Board] cannot indefinitely buy more than it sells or indefinitely hold what it has bought. It cannot follow a regular policy of buying at prices above the market, paying heavy storage charges and selling below cost.' Wheat prices in the Chicago pit slumped sensationally."[212]

Oversupply was a problem, but Hoover and the Farm Board refused to impose limits on production by the farmers beyond urging them to plow under every third row of cotton. This effort failed and the Grain Stabilization Corp. stopped making cotton purchases in June 1931. It then sold its accumulated inventory of 257 million bushels of grain, placing further pressure on prices and incurring a loss of $345 million. The agriculture situation only worsened with a 1933 bumper crop of cotton that resulted in a presidential order allocating $120 million to destroy 3.5 million bales of cotton. The government also supported the slaughter of 6 million piglets and 200,000 pregnant sows because pork prices were also falling dramatically.[213] Despite those efforts, over one-fourth of American farmers were put out of business during the Great Depression.[214]

Manipulations continued. The Grain Futures Administration concluded that Thomas Howell and others had tried to corner the July 1931 corn futures contract. He and his associates owned some 57 percent of those futures contracts, along with more than 300,000 bushels of cash grain.[215] This enabled these speculators to squeeze corn prices during the last three days of trading from 58 cents to 72 cents per bushel, a rise that was followed by a price collapse.[216] In an action brought under the antitrust laws, Howell was found to have taken delivery on 7 million bushels of corn through futures contracts in Chicago. His holdings then amounted to 90 percent of the deliverable supply of corn in the entire country. This allowed Howell to dictate arbitrarily high prices in settlement of other futures contracts covering 1.5 million bushels of corn.

A federal district court directed a verdict in favor of Howell in an antitrust action for this corner. The evidence showed that Howell had traded through sixteen different accounts and shipped 900,000 bushels of corn to Canada, as well as purchasing 97 percent of the available corn for delivery in Chicago. On appeal, the Circuit Court held such actions would sustain an action under the antitrust laws and remanded the action for a retrial.[217] However, after a retrial, a jury found for the defendant Howell, concluding that the trading was illegal gambling, which left the losses on the participants in the gamble.[218]

President Herbert Hoover publicly attacked domestic short sellers on July 11, 1931:

> It has come to my knowledge that certain persons are selling short in the commodity market, particularly in wheat. These transactions have been continuous over the past month. I do not refer to the ordinary hedging transactions, which are a sound part of our market system. I do not refer to legitimate grain trade. I refer to a limited number of speculators. I am not expressing my view upon the economics of short selling in normal times, but in these times this activity has one purpose and that is to depress prices. It tends to destroy the return of public confidence. The intention is to take a profit from the loss of other people, even though the effect may be directly depriving many farmers of their rightful income. If these gentlemen have that sense of patriotism which outruns immediate profit, and desire to see the

---

212. *Husbandry: No 1931 Pegging*, TIME, March 30, 1931.

213. MICHAEL HILTZIK, THE NEW DEAL 108-109 (2011).

214. WILLIAM LEUCHTENBURG, HERBERT HOOVER 114-115 (2009).

215. *To Amend the Grain Futures Act: Hearings Before the Senate Committee on Agriculture and Forestry*, 74th Cong., 2d Sess. 262 (1936).

216. 80 Cong. Rec. 6161 (1936) (remarks of Sen. Pope).

217. Peto v. Howell, 101 F.2d 353 (7th Cir. 1938).

218. Peto v. Howell, 117 F.2d 249 (7th Cir.), *cert. denied*, 313 U.S. 583 (1941).

> country recover, they will close up these transactions and desist from their manipulations. The confidence imposed upon me by law as a public official does not permit me to expose their names to the public, otherwise I would do so.[219]

"But President Hoover, so often unlucky, picked a bad time in which to flay short wheat speculators as the cause of depressed prices."[220] On that same day, the Department of Agriculture reported an expected increase of several million bushels over the prior year's bumper crop. *Time* magazine charged that "[s]uch harvests stack one surplus on top of another, send prices down correspondingly. Acreage which the Farm Board has been pleading with growers to reduce 20% was cut less than 5%. While flogging short-sellers, President Hoover made no reference to the stubborn refusal of farmers to plant less grain."[221] The *Wall Street Journal* also blamed the lowered grain prices on world conditions and the Farm Board's interference in the market.[222]

The president's message did not, in any event, restore wheat prices, but it did serve to renew interest in Congress over legislation to limit short selling. "It has been said [correctly] that future trading has been made a political football by persons seeking the agriculture vote."[223] The Capper-Dickson bill had previously sought to impose a limit of 2 million bushels of wheat a day on traders on the commodity futures exchanges, and it was reintroduced after Hoover's attack on the shorts.[224]

Hearings were held in January 1932 on short selling grain and cotton on the commodity futures exchanges.[225] Calling the Grain Futures Act "absolutely worthless," Texas congressman Oliver H. Cross sought legislation that would "shut out the thousands and tens of thousands of phantom buyers, short gamblers."[226] The head of the GFA complained that the determination of what constitutes manipulation was "very hard to tell."[227] Another witness was "extremely interested" in how the committee defined manipulation under the Grain Futures Act, asserting that "this is a very important point for serious consideration."[228] The definition of what constituted undesirable short selling was given only passing mention. One witness did propose the following definition that he conceded was not in "proper legal form": "A short sale is a sale for future delivery by a speculator who thinks the market is too high. He takes a gambler's chance to buy lower, later, to make delivery, if necessary."[229]

The GFA advised Congress that it did not have the power to attack short sellers.[230] The head of the GFA, Dr. J.W.T. Duvel, testified before Congress that his agency had not taken action against the traders because "it is practically impossible, merely because a man sells, to prove that he is doing it in order to manipulate the market." Duvel noted that it would have been difficult to have

219. *Commodity Short Selling: Hearing Before the House Committee on Agriculture*, 72d Cong., 1st Sess. 109 (1932).

220. *National Affairs: Hoover on Shorts*, TIME, July 20, 1931.

221. *Id.*

222. See, *The President's "Bear Hunt" in the Wheat Pit*, LITERARY DIGEST, July 25, 1931, at 9 (describing the *Wall Street Journal*'s criticism).

223. Note, *Prevention of Commodity Futures Manipulation Under the Commodity Exchange Act*, 54 HARV. L. REV. 1373, 1374, n. 4 (1941) (citation omitted).

224. *The President's "Bear Hunt" in the Wheat Pit*, LITERARY DIGEST, July 25, 1931, at 9.

225. *Commodity Short Selling: Hearing Before the House Committee on Agriculture*, 72d Cong., 1st Sess. (1932).

226. *Id.* at 10, 12.

227. *Id.* at 220.

228. *Id.* at 341.

229. *Id.* at 248.

230. *Id.* at 180-181.

"produced sufficient evidence to have been able to show that they were intentionally undertaking to manipulate the market. There is no definition in our law of manipulation and it is the hardest thing in the world to get proof of that kind."[231]

The House Committee on Agriculture reported out a bill in June 1932 that would have amended the Grain Futures Act in several ways to stop perceived abuses.[232] It would have authorized the secretary of agriculture to set short-selling limits on futures and even ban short selling.[233] It also sought to stop large sales by the Soviet Union by subjecting "foreign interests" to the secretary's short-sale restrictions, except for hedging purposes.[234] Pointedly excepted from the power to set position limits were buying transactions,[235] an omission undoubtedly tied to the interest of farmers in having crop prices raised by manipulation or otherwise.

The proposed legislation sought to outlaw dealings in privileges, indemnities, bids, offers, puts and calls, and similar transactions because they were "gambling transactions."[236] It sought to prohibit futures commission merchants from defrauding their customers.[237] "All transactions which are or may be used to cause prices to be reported or registered which are not true and bona fide prices are prohibited," including "wash sales," "cross trades," "accommodation trades," "office trades" or "fictitious trades."[238] That legislation was not enacted.

Grain prices reached a 300-year low in November 1932 when Franklin Roosevelt was elected to replace Hoover.[239] "Gross farm income had declined from $12 billion in 1929 to $5 billion in 1932."[240] President Roosevelt assumed office in March 1933 and asserted in his inaugural address that the Great Depression would be fought, among other things, "by definite efforts to raise the values of agricultural products.[241] In a fireside chat, President Roosevelt stated that his administration's policy was to restore commodity prices: "If we cannot do this one way we will do it another. Do it, we will."[242]

Commodity prices had risen following the resumption of trading after the bank holiday declared by Roosevelt when he came into office.[243] The Chicago Board of Trade, however, had to close on July 19–20, 1933, following "what was probably the most sensational collapse in futures prices in the history of the Chicago Board of Trade."[244]

The Grain Futures Administration found that speculative traders controlling fifteen accounts had held large positions of wheat and corn that caused the price collapse when the positions were liquidated in order to take profits.[245] The Grain Futures Administration was under intense political pressure to bring some action against the speculators operating on the CBOT. It chose two of the most infamous members of that group as its targets: Arthur Cutten and Thomas Howell.

---

231. *Id.* at 181, 185.
232. H.R. Rep. No. 1551, 72d Cong., 1st Sess. 1 (1932).
233. *Id.*
234. *Id.*
235. *Id.* at 2.
236. *Id.* at 3.
237. *Id.* at 3.
238. *Id.* at 3.
239. *Wheat Plunges to a 300-Year Low*, Literary Digest, Nov. 12, 1932, at 6.
240. Jean Edward Smith, FDR 289 (2007).
241. *Inaugural Speech of Franklin Delano Roosevelt*, Washington, DC, March 4, 1933, http://www.hpol.org/fdr/inaug/ (accessed November 15, 2011).
242. Michael Hiltzik, The New Deal 112 (2011).
243. *Annual Report of the Chief of the Grain Futures Administration* 5 (1933).
244. 80 Cong. Rec. 6160 (1936) (remarks of Sen. Pope).
245. *Id.* at 6160–61.

Cutten was perhaps the world's most famous speculator at the time, having made a laudatory appearance on the cover of *Time* magazine on December 10, 1928. The *Washington Post* called Cutten the "Croesus of wheat traders," a reference to the legendary golden wealth of the king of Lydia who ruled in 560 BC.[246] "For many years the name of Arthur W. Cutten has been a headliner in grain-market news. When business was lagging in the outlying offices of Chicago commission firms, all they had to do was to whisper that Cutten was buying wheat and the orders would start rolling in from suckers everywhere who believed they were getting in on a bonanza."[247]

Cutten was viewed as "one of the most glamorous figures in speculative history,"[248] but he began losing his luster in the press after the stock market crash of 1929. He also became a target for the government, which was seeking to suppress speculative short selling, which was being blamed for declines in agricultural prices. Hoover's secretary of agriculture, Arthur Hyde, sent a telegraph to Cutten on February 25, 1930, begging Cutten to desist:

> It is reported to me that you have been operating on the bear side of the grain market and that those operations have contributed to the collapse of the market. I have no right or authority to suggest any course to any businessman in his own business but just in the public interest if you could abandon such a course it would help many thousands of people in distress. If the report is not true then disregard my anxiety in the matter.[249]

Cutten responded by insisting that he was not active in the markets and that Secretary Hyde was misinformed. However, it was later claimed that Cutten was actually 4 million bushels short in wheat futures on the CBOT.[250]

After shrugging off Secretary Hyde's concerns, Cutten began a nationwide public relations campaign against government regulation through a series of five articles published in the *Saturday Evening Post* in 1932 and 1933.[251] The *New York Times* also highlighted some of Cutten's vitriolic attacks on the Department of Agriculture and the Farm Board. Among other things, Cutten called them "bureaucratic lapdogs," who were growing "fat at the farmers' expense." More purple prose following in the form of a charge that farmers were being "exploited and the public gouged" by government policies that he called "a steam-roller of ruthless violence, crushing all in its greed for waxing fat on public money."[252]

The Roosevelt administration retaliated by charging Cutten with concealing his trading positions from the GFA.[253] The new agriculture secretary, Henry Wallace, announced the bringing of the case and made specific reference to Cutten's *Saturday Evening Post* articles, noting that Cutten

---

246. *Regulation of Grain Exchanges: Hearing Before the House Committee on Agriculture on H.R. 8829*, 73d Cong. 2d Sess. 138 (1934).

247. *To Amend the Grain Futures Act: Hearings Before the Senate Committee on Agriculture and Forestry*, 74th Cong., 2d Sess. 260 (1936). *See also*, 80 Cong. Rev. 6160 (1936) (remarks of Sen. Pope) (making the same charges).

248. EDWARD J. DIES, STREET OF ADVENTURE 27-28 (1938).

249. WILLIAM G. FERRIS, THE GRAIN TRADERS 192 (1988) (citation omitted).

250. *To Amend the Grain Futures Act: Hearings Before the Senate Committee on Agriculture and Forestry*, 74th Cong., 2d Sess. 261 (1936).

251. Arthur W. Cutten with Boyden Sparkes, SATURDAY EVENING POST, November 19, 26, Dec. 3, 10, 1932 and March 25, 1933.

252. *Cutten Says Bureaus Fatten on Farmers*, NEW YORK TIMES, Jul. 24, 1932, at F4.

253. II JERRY W. MARKHAM, A FINANCIAL HISTORY OF THE UNITED STATES, FROM J.P. MORGAN TO THE INSTITUTIONAL INVESTOR (1900-1970) 103 (2002).

was "vigorously opposing all forms of government regulation of the exchanges" and criticizing the Agriculture Adjustment Administration, which was trying to raise commodity prices.[254]

The government's complaint charged that "Cutten conspired and colluded with various unnamed grain firms to conceal his operations on their books by means of false entries, fictitious and dummy accounts, and false reports."[255] For example, it was charged that Cutten had reported to the GFA that he was short 320,000 bushels of wheat when in fact his total short position was over 2 million bushels.[256] During 1930 and 1931, Cutten sold wheat futures in excess of 100 million bushels. His short positions at times exceeded 7 million bushels and he was short 79 percent of the time in 1930 and 89 percent in 1931.[257] The complaint further charged that Cutten was attempting to manipulate wheat prices.[258]

The GFA waited until 1934 before bringing an action against Cutten for misconduct that occurred in 1931. After holding a hearing on the charges, the Grain Futures Commission entered an order barring Cutten from trading on commodity futures markets for two years. Calling the ruling "outrageous" and "bureaucratic," Cutten vowed to appeal all the way to the Supreme Court.[259] The announcement of the filing of the Cutten case coincided with congressional hearings on commodity market speculation, but the GFA denied Cutten's accusation that there was a connection or political motivation in the filing of the case.[260] Those hearings were held to consider legislation sought by the Department of Agriculture to correct what it perceived as numerous deficiencies in the Grain Futures Act.

The proposed legislation, titled the Commodity Exchange Act,[261] targeted "8 to 16 traders on the Chicago Board of Trade who have been largely responsible for the constant fluctuations in the market that has occurred during the raiding of the market. These violent fluctuations have been caused largely by these big traders, such as Arthur Cutten, who are not interested in any way in the maintenance of the market."[262] It was claimed that the speculation on the commodity exchanges had the "same character of trading" as that on the stock exchanges that had just been regulated by the Securities Exchange Act of 1934.[263]

Cutten was said to be the "J.P. Morgan of the grain exchange in Chicago."[264] Picking up on that theme, another congressman wanted "to place in the same category with Mr. Morgan, Mr. Arthur Cutten of Chicago who has ruined more farmers in this country than any other single man. If you could gather all the bones of the people he has caused to die an economic death, they would form a triumphal arch from Chicago to New York, where he went for bigger gambling operations."[265]

---

254. *Regulation of Grain Exchanges: Hearing Before the House Committee on Agriculture on H.R. 8829*, 73d Cong., 2d Sess. 133 (1934) (quoting *New York Times*).

255. *Id.*

256. *Regulation of Grain Exchanges: Hearing Before the House Committee on Agriculture on H.R. 8829*, 73d Cong., 2d Sess. 132 (1934).

257. *Id.* at 133.

258. *Id.*

259. *Cutten Turns to Courts*, NEW YORK TIMES, Feb. 15, 1935, at 3.

260. *Regulation of Commodity Exchanges: Hearing Before the House Committee on Agriculture*, 74th Cong., 1st Sess. 123, 135 (1935).

261. 78 Cong. Rec. 10449 (1934) (remarks of Rep. Pierce).

262. *Id.* at 10446 (remarks of Rep. Jones). *See also, Regulation of Grain Exchanges: Hearing Before the House Committee on Agriculture on H.R. 8829*, 73d Cong., 2d Sess. 250 (1934) (describing activities of this small group of traders).

263. 78 Cong. Rec. 10446 (1934) (remarks of Rep. Jones).

264. *Id.* at 10447 (remarks of Rep. May).

265. *Id.* at 10448 (remarks of Rep. Truax).

Among other things, the Department of Agriculture sought to require the licensing of futures commission merchants in order to limit "short selling and speculation" on the commodity exchanges.[266] This was an effort to bring the commission merchants who helped conceal Cutten's positions from the department under its heel.[267] The proposed legislation also sought to stop "excessive speculation" by allowing the government to set limits on the amount of trading by any one trader.[268] That power had been sought unsuccessfully by the GFA since 1925.[269]

This focus on "excessive" speculation, as opposed to all speculation, was a recognition that some forms of speculation were beneficial in providing liquidity and price discovery, a fact that was testified to by numerous witnesses in congressional hearings. For example, one witness stated "that speculation stabilizes the price; produces the market and makes grain available as collateral; furnishes a ready-cash market at all times for the farmer and keeps the market in a fluid condition, something that we have got to have."[270] This acceptance of at least some speculation in the commodity futures contrasted with economic views toward the securities markets. "Economists have pointed out that while commodity speculation may be necessary there is no corresponding end served by speculation in securities."[271]

What was meant by "excessive speculation was not defined in the proposed legislation or in the hearings, but it was equated with manipulation: "improper speculation and manipulation,"[272] and activities that "approach manipulative operations, excessive speculation."[273] "It must be remembered that speculation, or even excessive speculation, is not manipulation. But speculation may be a symptom of, or may lead to manipulation."[274]

One congressman lamented the fact that the volume of futures trading on the CBOT was twenty times that of the actual wheat grown in the United States.[275] Another congressman attacked "manipulators" who "toil not neither do they spin, but they invariably take all the profit of the farmer's crop and leave him with bills to pay." He also condemned the "practice of manipulating the exchange so as to drive the price down when the farmer is selling and to raise it after his crop is all gone."[276]

The proposed legislation sought to fill another gap caused by a ruling of the Commodity Exchange Commission, which acted as an oversight body under the Grain Futures Act. That commission ruled in 1933 in *Secretary v. Massey*[277] that the Grain Futures Act did not apply to fraudulent activities that involved the cheating of customers. The commission stated that the purpose of the Grain Futures Act was "to restrain influences which tend, through subversive speculative action, to affect artificially general price levels for a particular kind of grain in some particular market or

---

266. *Regulation of Grain Exchanges: Hearing Before the House Committee on Agriculture on H.R. 8829*, 73d Cong., 2d Sess. 1 (1934).

267. *Id.* at 133.

268. *Id.* at 2.

269. *Id.* at 268.

270. *Id.* at 2129.

271. Note, *Prevention of Commodity Futures Manipulation Under the Commodity Exchange Act*, 54 HARV. L. REV. 1373, 1374, n. 8 (1941) (citations omitted).

272. *Regulation of Grain Exchanges: Hearing Before the House Committee on Agriculture on H.R. 8829*, 73d Cong., 2d Sess. 239 (1934).

273. *Id.* at 279.

274. Note, *Prevention of Commodity Futures Manipulation Under the Commodity Exchange Act*, 54 HARV. L. REV. 1373, 1374, n. 8 (1941) (citations omitted).

275. 78 Cong. Rec. 10447 (1934) (remarks of Rep. Boileau).

276. *Id.* at 10447-10448 (remarks of Rep. Rankin).

277. Secretary v. Massey, slip op. (GFA Dkts. 2-3, Nov. 9, 1933), noted in Jerry W. Markham, *Manipulation of Commodity Futures Prices: The Unprosecutable Crime*, 8 YALE J. ON REG. 281, 304 (1991).

markets." In the case before it, the respondents had committed fraud but it did "not appear that respondents changed or attempted to change the general level of prices."[278] The commission opined in the *Massey* case that the terms "manipulate" and "manipulation" relate to efforts to stimulate or depress the market price of grain, not "to practices between brokers and their principals where the failure of customers to receive the benefit of full market price grows primarily out of acts which in reality amount to breach of duty imposed by a fiduciary relation."[279]

"Such things as 'wash sales', 'puts', 'calls', 'bucketing',[280] and kindred things, are denounced by the bill. Cross trades and accommodation trades are likewise banned. Purely gambling transactions are prohibited, and the bill will prevent transactions which will cause any price to be registered or reported that is not a true and bona fide price." Inexplicably and crudely, the congressman making these remarks likened grain speculators to "the heathen Chinee."[281] Another congressman charged that the Grain Futures Act "has been almost a complete failure. It has no teeth."[282] Indeed, one congressman sought an amendment that would prohibit futures contracts unless actual delivery was made on every contract.[283]

The House report to this proposed legislation was accompanied by a lengthy minority report that among other things noted that cotton had been excluded from the reach of the bill, while members of Congress from the cotton states were the chief advocates of the bill that would regulate only grains.[284] This legislation also met a "great deal of propaganda" by the CBOT,[285] and the bill stalled; it was passed in the House but failed to pass in the Senate before its adjournment.[286]

Congress directed the GFA to investigate what appeared to be a corner in the December 1934 sugar futures contract.[287] It appeared from the secretary's report that the disturbance was due to disruption of world and domestic sugar markets and application of the Cuban sugar quota. The New York Coffee & Sugar Exchange examined the situation and reported that no "so-called corner or squeeze" actually occurred. It did, however, suspend trading in the December 1934 sugar contract, except for liquidation only.[288] Charges were brought by the exchange against several firms for failing to cooperate in liquidating their clients' positions. Those firms, including J. Aron & Co., Hayden, Stone & Co., and Thomson & McKinnon, were censured for that conduct. Other firms, including Lehman Bros., were merely admonished to do better in the future.[289]

This battle in the sugar pit arose after the U.S. government decided to replace tariffs on Cuban sugar with quotas. Two Cuban sugar barons, Julio Lobo and Marcelino Garcia, were on the long side of the market. The principal shorts were Charles Hayden, the leader and founder of Hayden,

---

278. Secretary v. Massey, slip op. at 5-7 (GFA Dkts. 2-3, Nov. 9, 1933).

279. *Id.* at 20.

280. "Bucketing" is a reference to a fraudulent practice in which a broker does not execute a customer's trade on an exchange as directed by its customer. Instead, the broker holds the order, hoping that the market will turn against the customer. In such event, the broker would keep the customer's funds instead of sending them to the exchange to cover the customer's losses. Of course, the broker will incur a loss if the customer's order turned out to be profitable. "Bucket shops" engaging in such trading would simply close shop and move elsewhere when the market went against its bucketing operations. *See*, JERRY W. MARKHAM, THE HISTORY OF COMMODITY TRADING AND ITS REGULATION 24 (1987) (describing bucket shops).

281. 78 Cong. Rec. 10449 (1934) (remarks of Rep. Gilchrist).

282. *Id.* at 10449 (remarks of Rep. Pierce).

283. *Id.* at 10450 (remarks of Rep. Terrell).

284. H.R. Rep. No. 1522 (pt. 2), 73d Cong., 2d Sess. 1-2 (1934).

285. 78 Cong. Rec. 10451 (1934) (remarks of Rep. Hope).

286. 79 Cong. Rec. 8589 (1935) (remarks of Rep. Jones).

287. *Corner in December Sugar Futures*, S. Doc. No. 44, 74th Cong., 1st Sess. (1935).

288. *Id.* at 4-5.

289. *Id.* at 7-9.

Stone & Co., and Punta Alegre, the president of an American company representing the Rockefeller interests that owned large tracts of sugar-producing land in Cuba. Lobo, known as the Cuban "Sugar King," and Garcia took advantage of the new quotas to squeeze the shorts because of the ensuing lack of deliverable supplies. A settlement price was set for the futures contracts that let the shorts off the hook but still provided large profits to Lobo and Garcia. Lobo later boasted that this was the only "perfect squeeze that was ever pulled."[290]

Congress held further hearings in February 1935 to consider legislation that would amend the Grain Futures Act to curb "excessive speculation."[291] Once again, the term "excessive speculation" was not defined in the hearings on the proposed legislation, but one government witness equated it with manipulation, which was also left undefined.[292] Margin requirements were discussed in this hearing, but they were, at the time, subject to an industry code under the National Industrial Recovery Act (NIRA). That code sought "to control excessive speculation by imposing heavier marginal requirements after certain limits in trading are reached."[293] That code set a minimum 10 percent margin requirement for positions up to 2 million bushels and a 25 percent margin for positions above that level. Price limits were imposed on the maximum number of price fluctuations during the trading day, requiring trading to be suspended when those limits were reached. Options and privileges were prohibited.[294]

That code, the result of eight months of negotiation, was approved by the president on March 20, 1934.[295] However, NIRA was declared unconstitutional by the Supreme Court in 1935.[296] The exchanges, nevertheless, continued to impose minimum margin requirements and other restrictions on trading.[297]

The commodity exchanges favored margin requirements as a way of preventing manipulation over position limits.[298] The Grain Futures Administration, however, was skeptical of the value of using margins to control speculation and prevent manipulation. As a witness for the Grain Futures Administration testified,

> on the question of margins, I personally feel that the grain and commodity markets offer different problems in the matter of margins than we find in the stock market. A commodities market is handled in a different way. If large-scale speculative trading is detrimental to the market—and there is no doubt about it—it would seem desirable to provide some means of restricting it. If there is to be a limit, it should be fixed in advance and not changed in the middle of the game, and made the same for all traders. While an increase of margins on large trades, as required under the code, may serve to restrict some speculative operations, it will result in even greater advantage to the trader having sufficient funds to meet such increased margins.[299]

---

290. John Paul Rathbone, The Sugar King of havana 111-113 (2010).

291. *Regulation of Commodity Exchanges: Hearing Before the House Committee on Agriculture*, 74th Cong. 1st Sess. 1 (1935).

292. *Id.* at 128.

293. *Id.* at 112.

294. *Code of Fair Competition for Grain Exchanges and Members Thereof*, March 20, 1934. The code also set minimum wages of $16 per week in large cities. *Id.*

295. Jerry W. Markham, The History of Commodity Trading and Its Regulation 24 (1987).

296. A.L.A. Schechter Poultry Corp. v. United States, 295 U.S. 495 (1935).

297. Jerry W. Markham, *Federal Regulation of Margin in the Commodity Futures Industry: History and Theory*, 64 Temp. L. Rev. 59, 69 (1991).

298. *Id.* at 59, 70, n. 60.

299. *Regulation of Grain Exchanges: Hearings Before the House Comm. on Agriculture on H.R.* 8829,

As will be described in future chapters, the government later changed its position on margin and sought to obtain regulatory authority over its application to futures contracts, while the exchanges resisted that effort and continued to attack speculative position trading limits.

The Commodity Exchange Act legislation was approved by the House in 1935 but was not passed by the Senate.[300] The House report on the bill noted that since "the passage of the Securities Exchange Act of 1934 there has been observed, an increasing tendency on the part of professional speculators to transfer their activities from the security markets to the commodity markets, a tendency which makes the enactment of this bill without further delay of vital importance."[301] More congressional ire was caused by a drop in cotton futures prices in March 1935.[302] A bill sought to stop "'racketeering' by a few large professional traders."[303]

Further frustration was encountered when the government's charges against Cutten eventually reached the Supreme Court in *Wallace v. Cutten*[304] in 1936. The government filed a 147-page brief and charged that Cutten had engaged in a "willful and premeditated course to manipulate prices in defiance of the Grain Futures Act."[305] The government's brief argued that "[i]f the decision of the Circuit Court of Appeals is permitted to stand . . . the Grain Futures Commission will be virtually powerless to prevent manipulation of the price of grain."[306]

The Supreme Court was not impressed, even advising Cutten's counsel that he need not appear for oral argument.[307] The Supreme Court affirmed the Circuit Court ruling that Cutten could not be barred from trading under the Grain Futures Act because the manipulative acts complained of by the government occurred some two years before the filing of the government's complaint. The Supreme Court held the statute applied only to ongoing activities and not to past conduct. This effectively meant that the secretary of agriculture and his GFA were helpless because, as a practical matter, no action could be mounted and completed during the short periods involved in most market manipulations. The action brought against Thomas Howell by the Grain Futures Administration was also dismissed because, like the Cutten case, the charges were filed after the activities in question had ceased.[308]

Further hearings were held in Congress in 1936 on amendments to the Grain Futures Act after the Seventh Circuit Court of Appeals held that Cutten could not be punished for his activities because they were not ongoing.[309] Those hearings were held only a few weeks before that decision was affirmed by the Supreme Court.[310] This legislation again contained the wish list of changes sought by the Grain Futures Administration. The purpose of this legislation was said to

---

73d Cong., 2d Sess. 29 & 280 (1934) (statements of Dr. Duvel, Chief, Grain Futures Administration Dept. of Agriculture).

300. 80 Cong. Rec. 6159 (1936) (remarks of Sen. Pope).

301. H.R. Rep. No. 421, 74th Cong., 1st Sess. 2 (1935).

302. *Id.*

303. *Id.* at 3.

304. Wallace v. Cutten, 298 U.S. 229 (1936).

305. *Opposes Cutten Appeal*, NEW YORK TIMES, Aug. 20, 1935, at 38.

306. *Cutten Case Ruling Asked in High Court*, NEW YORK TIMES, Feb. 7, 1923, at 35.

307. *Cutten Victory Is Hinted*, NEW YORK TIMES, April 28, 1936 at 14.

308. *Report of the Chief of the Grain Futures Administration* 4 (1935). *See*, Note, *Prevention of Commodity Futures Manipulation Under the Commodity Exchange Act*, 54 HARV. L. REV. 1373, 1377-78 (1941).

309. *To Amend the Grain Futures Act: Hearings Before the Senate Committee on Agriculture and Forestry*, 74th Cong., 2d Sess. 260 (1936).

310. *To Amend the Grain Futures Act: Hearings Before the Senate Committee on Agriculture and Forestry on H.R. 6772*, 74th Cong., 2d Sess. (1936). Those hearings were held on April 21, 22 and 23, 1936. *Id.*, while The *Cutten* decision was argued on April 27, 1936, and handed down on May 18, 1936. Wallace v. Cutten, 298 U.S. 229 (1936).

be to reverse the *Cutten* decision[311] and "to limit or abolish short selling, to curb manipulation, and for other purposes."[312] It sought to limit "excessive speculation" because "[i]t is difficult to distinguish between the effects of excessive speculation and the effects of manipulation, corners, and violent fluctuation of market prices."[313]

The House sponsor of the legislation again focused on the activities of a small group of traders: "during the last 15 years about 16 big traders in grain have from time to time taken advantage of unusual conditions to make raids upon the market and to rig the market to the detriment not only of the producer but also all others engaged in legitimate transactions in various farm commodities."[314] Concern was also expressed that the enactment of the Securities Exchange Act of 1934 had led to "a disposition on the part of some of those who had speculated in the other markets to transfer their activities to the commodity markets."[315]

The legislation and the hearings again failed to address the definition of manipulation or "excessive speculation." The definition of the latter appeared to be a moving target that at least one witness thought should be left to an administrative agency.[316] One senator identified excessive speculation as "speculation that brings about unreasonable fluctuations or unwarranted changes in the price level of a commodity."[317] Again this offered no legal certainty as to what was meant by the term, occasioning the following colloquy in the hearings:

> **Mr. Smith.** May I ask, Senator, what would be excessive speculation? How would that be determined?
> **Senator McNary.** You are an expert and I am just a mere Member of Congress. I would rather have your views on that. I have my own.
> **Mr. Smith.** I have asked many millers and many grain men what would be excessive speculation and they don't seem to be able to know themselves.
> **Senator McNary.** The bill itself says "causing sudden or unreasonable fluctuations or unwarranted changes in the price level."
> **Mr. Smith.** Excessive speculation would be pretty much a matter of opinion, that of whoever had the power to regulate it.[318]

Two other senators then chimed in to declare that the bill sought to keep men like Arthur Cutten from controlling the market.[319] The Senate sponsor of the bill vociferously attacked the loophole identified in the *Cutten* case that effectively precluded enforcement of the Grain Futures Act.[320] The Senate supporters also sought to prohibit various manipulative trading practices, such as wash sales, noting that "[s]imilar irregular practices in the securities exchanges of the country have been ruled out by the provisions of the Securities Exchange Act."[321]

311. 80 Cong. Rec. 7858 (May 25, 1936) (remarks of Sen. Murray).
312. *To Amend the Grain Futures Act: Hearings Before the Senate Committee on Agriculture and Forestry*, 74th Cong., 2d Sess. 2 (1936).
313. *Id.* at 68.
314. 79 Cong. Rec. 8589 (1934) (remarks of Rep. Jones).
315. *Id.*
316. *To Amend the Grain Futures Act: Hearings Before the Senate Committee on Agriculture and Forestry*, 74th Cong., 2d Sess. 197 (1936).
317. *Id.* at 15.
318. *Id.* at 16.
319. *Id.* at 16-17.
320. 80 Cong. Rec. 6160 (1936) (remarks of Sen. Pope).
321. *Id.* at 7859 (remarks of Sen. Murray).

Senator Pope defined a "squeeze" or "congestion" as "a condition in maturing futures where sellers (hedgers or speculators), having waited too long to close their trades, find there are no new sellers from whom they can buy."[322] He stated that in a squeeze or congestion "[d]eliverable stocks are low, and it is too late to procure the actual commodity elsewhere to settle by delivery. Under such circumstances, and though the market is not cornered in the ordinary sense, traders who are long hold out for an arbitrary price."[323]

In one bit of back and forth in the hearings, the problem of defining what manipulation is got a rather uncertain airing:

> **Mr. Heffelfinger.** What is a corner on the market?
> **Senator Murphy.** Oh, I guess we all have pretty general ideas about what a corner on the market is, haven't we? . . . Have you known a farmer to benefit from a corner?
> **Mr. Heffelfinger.** Certainly. What year was it we had that situation where the market went up in the spring, 1934, wasn't it? As I say, we have been in business for 40 years and we handled more grain at our country elevators in the month of May than we did in any other month of the year. I think most any country elevator operator would admit that that was a very, very unusual situation.
> **Senator Murphy.** Was there an attempt to run a corner on the commodity at that time?
> **Mr. Heffelfinger.** I presume it might be called that. In other words, the farmer marketed his grain because the prices went up.
> **Senator Norris.** That is probably natural, but I am not interested in having a corner on the market for the benefit of the farmer. It doesn't make any difference to me who benefits. It is a bad thing and it ought to be excluded.
> **Mr. Heffelfinger.** I am not defending a corner or squeeze.
> **Senator Murphy.** I was going to follow that out by asking you if you had ever known the farmer to suffer by reason of a corner?
> **Mr. Heffelfinger.** Have I known the farmer to suffer by reason of a corner?
> **Senator Murphy.** Or an attempt to make a corner?
> **Mr. Heffelfinger.** I can't say that I have in my experience.
> **Senator Murphy.** You asked me what a corner is. Do you know what a corner is? You are arguing against this provision here in relation to a corner. Obviously, you have some knowledge about what a corner is. What is it?
> **Senator Norris.** Mr. Chairman, the American people for many years have been hunting a corner that they could get around [laughter] and find the other side of it.[324]

The legislative history did add some content on what were viewed as disruptive and abusive trading practices. Wash sales were defined by the Senate sponsor of the amendments as "pretended sales made openly in the pit or trading place for the purpose of deceiving other traders. They are employed to give a false appearance of trading and to cause prices to be registered which are not

---

322. *Id.* at 8089 (remarks of Sen. Pope).

323. *Id.* An official in the Department of Agriculture later defined a squeeze as when a trader controls enough of a commodity to create a shortage and thereby squeeze prices. Such a shortage may be intentionally created or it may result from congestion, i.e., a natural shortage that traders seek to exploit. U.S. Dept. of Agric., *Report of the Chief of the Commodity Exchange Administration* 40 (Sept. 25, 1939).

324. *To Amend the Grain Futures Act: Hearings Before the Senate Committee on Agriculture and Forestry*, 74th Cong. 2d Sess. 124 (1936).

true prices. They may be entered and recorded as real trades, but by agreement between the parties privately are either canceled or washed out by other trades."[325]

"Cross trades" were another target, defined as "a device commonly employed by floor brokers for becoming buyers in respect to selling orders of customers, and vice versa. They take the form of a recorded double purchase and sale between two brokers. Each broker is recorded as having bought from and sold to the other the same quantity of the same future at the same price."[326] Cross trades were elsewhere defined as "a fictitious trade, where one broker deals with another broker, and they register the trade as though it were an honest bona fide trade. It is strictly a fictitious trade."[327]

A matter generating considerable debate was how a floor broker should execute two offsetting buy and sell orders that are received simultaneously.[328] A matter of concern was that the broker receiving the orders might execute only the buy order in order to push the market up and then wait and execute the sell order after the increase. A proposed amendment to the bill under consideration would have required such orders to be executed simultaneously.[329]

Still another trading practice sought to be prohibited by this legislation was "accommodation trades," which were defined as "a transaction between two commission houses whereby, one being long with the clearing house and the other being short, the one that is long sells to the one that is short enough of a given future to give each house an even or nearly even position, thus reducing the amount of the margin to be put up with the clearing house."[330] Subsequently, an offsetting trade is made that unwinds the first transaction. In the interim, each house has had free use of the customer margin funds since they need not be transmitted to the clearinghouse.[331]

The proposed legislation also sought to prohibit privileges, indemnities, bids, offers, puts, and calls, which were described as option contracts that required only a small sum to secure the right

---

325. 80 Cong. Rec. 6162 (1936) (remarks of Sen. Pope). Senator Pope further stated,

> For example, Floor Broker A, wishing to buy May wheat when the market is 95 cents per bushel, will offer May Wheat at 94 7/8 or 94 3/4, being sure that his confederate, B, gets the sale. Such sales may induce bona-fide offers at the lower prices, whereupon A turns buyer. In the meantime his fictitious sales are forgotten or washed out by offsetting trades.

Id.

326. 80 Cong. Rec. 6162 (1936) (remarks of Sen. Pope). Senator Pope further stated:

> For example, Broker A is put down as seller to Broker B for 5,000 bushels of May wheat at a dollar a bushel and is also put down as buyer from B of 5,000 bushels at a dollar a bushel. The transaction appears to be without purpose and without effect; but A, having made an actual sale of 5,000 bushels of May wheat for a customer, at, say, $1.01, reports to his commission firm that the customer's order has been executed at a dollar. Thereupon he switches the sold side of his own dollar cross trade for the actual $1.01 sale for the customer, and takes a profit for himself of the 1-cent difference which should have been added to the sale price for the customer. In this example, of course, it is assumed that there is a 1-cent fluctuation in price while the customer's order is in the hands of the floor broker, and before he reports execution. That sort of thing is prohibited by this bill.

Id. See *also*, V Federal Trade Commission, Report on the Grain Trade 251 (1921) (describing cross trades).

327. 80 Cong. Rec. 7871 (1936) (remarks of Sen. Pope).

328. *Id.* at 7865-7870.

329. *Id.* at 7865 (remarks of Sen. Smith).

330. *Id.*at 6162 (remarks of Sen. Pope).

331. *Id.*

to buy or sell a commodity at a stipulated price for a specified period of time, often for only a few days.[332] These contracts were likened to "pure gambling."[333]

Another concern was that commodity futures markets were "extremely sensitive. A false or misleading statement or fictitious trading may in a few minutes turn thousands of dollars into the pocket of some unscrupulous trader. . . . At the same time it may cause millions of dollars in loss to farmers and others affected by a fictitious price movement. Large speculators may temporarily upset the whole price structure."[334]

The focus of this legislation continued to be authority to allow administrative restrictions on the size of speculative positions. The Grain Futures Administration's belief that, while speculative positions in excess of 2 million bushels of wheat were a "threat to market stability," some speculators had held positions in excess of 10 million bushels, multiplying the possibility of market abuse.[335]

The Commodity Exchange Act of 1936 was enacted into law on June 15, 1936,[336] less than a month after the Supreme Court affirmed the dismissal of the Grain Futures Administration's case against Cutten.[337] Cutten did not live to suffer the effects of the Commodity Exchange Act. He died just nine days after the new law was passed.[338] The Commodity Exchange Act replaced the Grain Futures Act and extended jurisdiction to other commodities—that is, cotton, rice, mill feeds, butter, eggs, and potatoes. Wool tops, fats and oils, cottonseed meal, cottonseed, peanuts, soybeans, and soybean meal were added to that list in 1938.[339] Futures commission merchants and floor brokers on the commodity futures exchanges were required to register with the government.[340]

Section 3 of the Commodity Exchange Act concluded that futures exchanges are "affected with a national public interest. . . . The transactions and prices of commodities on such boards of trade are susceptible to excessive speculation and can be manipulated, controlled, cornered or squeezed . . . rendering regulation of such transactions imperative for the protection of such commerce and the national public interest."[341] Section 4(b) of the Commodity Exchange Act prohibited

---

332. It was noted,

> For example, for $6.25 one may, after the market closes one day, buy a bid good the next day entitling him to sell 5,000 bushels of May wheat at, say, 95 cents. The market may have closed at 96 cents. After it opens up the next day at, say, 94 cents, or sells at 94 cents at any time during that day, the buyer of the bid will buy 5,000 bushels of May wheat at 94 cents and exercise his bid option to sell at 95 cents, thus making a profit of $50—less commission—on a $6.25 investment. An offer or call is exactly the reverse of this process.
>
> In advance or decline guaranties, the seller of the contract guarantees to make good the difference between the stipulated price and the price at which some named future sells at any time the buyer may select during the specified period.

80 Cong. Rec. 6162-663 (1936) (remarks of Sen. Pope).

333. 80 Cong. Rec. 6163 (1936) (remarks of Sen. Pope).

334. *Id.* at 6164.

335. *Id.*

336. 49 Stat. 1491 (1936).

337. Wallace v. Cutten, 298 U.S. 229 (1936).

338. *Arthur W. Cutten, Grain Trader, Dies*, NEW YORK TIMES, June 25, 1936, at 21.

339. 52 Stat. 205 (1938).

340. II JERRY W. MARKHAM, A FINANCIAL HISTORY OF THE UNITED STATES, FROM J.P. MORGAN TO THE INSTITUTIONAL INVESTOR (1900-1970) 222-223 (2002).

341. 7 U.S.C. § 5. *See*, John Stassen, *Propaganda As Positive Law: Section 3 of the Commodity Exchange Act (A Case Study of How Economic Facts Can Be Changed by Act of Congress)*, 58 CHI. KENT L. REV. 635 (1982) (discussing the background for this provision).

members of contract markets and their agents from engaging in fraud or deceit or in making false reports to other persons. It also prohibited bucketing customer orders.[342] Section 4(c) prohibited transactions that were of the character of "wash" sales, "cross" trades, "accommodation" trades, or "fictitious" sales.[343] This section further trading in options on the commodities covered by the Commodity Exchange Act and proscribed reports of commodity futures prices that were not "a true and bona fide price."[344]

Section 9(a)(2) of the Commodity Exchange Act[345] made it unlawful for

> [a]ny person to manipulate or attempt to manipulate the price of any commodity in interstate commerce, or for future delivery on or subject to the rules of any registered entity, or to corner or attempt to corner any such commodity or knowingly to deliver or cause to be delivered for transmission through the mails or interstate commerce by telegraph, telephone, wireless, or other means of communication false or misleading or knowingly inaccurate reports concerning crop or market information or conditions that affect or tend to affect the price of any commodity in interstate commerce.

Section 9(a)(4) of the Commodity Exchange Act[346] made it unlawful for any person willfully to falsify, conceal, or cover up by any trick, scheme, or artifice any material fact to a registered contract market.

The effect of the Supreme Court's decision in the *Cutten* case was overturned by additional language in the Commodity Exchange Act that authorized the secretary of agriculture to issue an order directing all contracts markets to refuse trading privileges to any person who "has manipulated or is attempting to manipulate the market price of a commodity."[347] The term "manipulation" was not defined, but a commentator stated a few years after the adoption of the Commodity Exchange Act that the "contention that the word 'manipulate' is not definite enough to constitute a criminal offense would seem to be without merit."[348]

"Sought for many years as a means of coping with the obvious manipulative power of large accounts, the power to limit the amount of daily trading and net commitments of individual operators was finally given the Commodity Exchange Commission in 1936.[349] The use of position limits had been suggested in the Federal Trade Commission's study of the grain markets.[350] Congressional supporters thought position limits would prevent corners and would "prevent upsetting or disturbing the market; in other words . . . prevent manipulation."[351] That power was stated to be necessary in the Commodity Exchange Act as a means of "diminishing, eliminating, or preventing" the burdens of "excessive speculation" that cause "sudden or unreasonable fluctuations or unwarranted changes" in the price of commodities.[352] Those limits did not apply to hedgers.

---

342. 7 U.S.C. 6b (1936).
343. 7 U.S.C. 6c (1936).
344. 7 U.S.C. 6c (1936).
345. 7 U.S.C. § 13(a)(2) (1936).
346. 7 U.S.C. § 13(a)(4) (2006).
347. 49 Stat. at 1498.
348. Note, *Prevention of Commodity Futures Manipulation Under the Commodity Exchange Act*, 54 HARV. L. REV. 1373, 1378 (1941) (footnote and citations omitted).
349. *Id.* at 1373, 1376-1377.
350. Jerry W. Markham, *Manipulation of Commodity Futures Prices: The Unprosecutable Crime*, 8 YALE J. ON REG. 281, 311, N. 207 (1991).
351. 79 Cong. Rec. 8589 (1935) (remarks of Rep. Jones).
352. 7 U.S.C. 6a.

Unlike the Securities Exchange Act of 1934, the Commodity Exchange Act did not regulate margin requirements in order to curb speculation. Rather, the bill that became the Commodity Exchange Act only sought to require margin funds be given special trust fund treatment in order to protect them in the event of a failure of a futures commission merchant handling customer accounts.[353] As noted above, industry advocates had favored margins over position limits as the best measure for curbing manipulation, but the government preferred the latter.[354]

2:5 IMPLEMENTING THE SECURITIES EXCHANGE ACT OF 1934

The enactment of the Securities Act of 1933 (the 33 Act) and the Securities Exchange Act of 1934 (the 34 Act) did nothing to restore confidence in the stock market; a "depression within a depression" appeared in 1937.[355] "From September 1937 to June 1938, industrial production fell by more than a third, profits by 78 percent, and stock prices by more than half."[356] There was much debate over the cause of this market reverse, but most critics focused on actions by the Federal Reserve Board and government policies and taxes.[357]

The Securities and Exchange Commission (SEC) blamed the decline in the stock market in 1937 on short sellers.[358] Under Subsection 10(a) of the 34 Act,[359] the SEC was "empowered to promulgate rules and regulations to purge the markets of the abuses connected with these practices."[360] Section 10(a) of the 34 Act stated that it is unlawful to

> effect a short sale, or to use or employ any stop-loss order in connection with the purchase or sale, of any security registered on a national securities exchange, in contravention of such rules and regulations as the Commission may prescribe as necessary or appropriate in the public interest or for the protection of investors.[361]

---

353. 80 Cong. Rec. 7856 (1936) (remarks of Sen. Pope); 80 Cong. Rec. 7859 (1936) (remarks of Sen. Murray). As Senator Bronson Murray noted, this requirement was added to that legislation because FCM customers were "rank[ed] only as general creditors. Surely they thought their *margins were regarded as trust funds* and would be handled with a reasonable degree of integrity." 80 Cong. Rec. 7858 (May 25, 1936) (emphasis added). Senator Murray further stated:

> The bill . . . seeks to safeguard margins deposited by the public, declaring it to be unlawful for commission merchants to use such funds for their own private operations, or to extend credit to others. This section merely provides that the public's money put up for margins shall be in fact treated as belonging to the customer, and held in trust. Who can object to this?

80 Cong. Rec. 7858 (May 25, 1936). *See also*, Jerry W. Markham, *Federal Regulation of Margin in the Commodity Futures Industry: History and Theory*, 64 TEMP. L. REV. 59, 69-71 (1991) (describing the government's position on using margin to control speculation).

354. II JERRY W. MARKHAM, A FINANCIAL HISTORY OF THE UNITED STATES, FROM J.P. MORGAN TO THE INSTITUTIONAL INVESTOR (1900-1970) 223 (2002).

355. *Id.* at 234.

356. MICHAEL HILTZIK, THE NEW DEAL 378 (2011).

357. II JERRY W. MARKHAM, A FINANCIAL HISTORY OF THE UNITED STATES, FROM J.P. MORGAN TO THE INSTITUTIONAL INVESTOR (1900-1970) 234-235 (2002); MICHAEL HILTZIK, THE NEW DEAL 378 (2011).

358. *Id.*

359. 78 U.S.C. § 78j(a)(1). Securities futures products were later exempted from that provision. 78 U.S.C. § 78j(a)(2).

360. S. Rep. No. 1455, 73d Cong., 2d Sess. 55 (1934).

361. 78 U.S.C. § 78j(a)(1). Securities futures products were later exempted from that provision. 78 U.S.C. § 78j(a)(2).

The SEC studied the market decline in 1937 and concluded that, for leading stocks, short sales constituted a significant part of the declining market's sale side. The study suggested that short selling exacerbated the market's decline. "From this study, and the belief that the existing exchange regulations were ineffective, came the uptick rule."[362] The "uptick rule" established a "tick test," which allowed short sales only after an uptick in a stock's price.[363] This rule would raise much controversy in future years.

In *In the Matter of Meehan*,[364] the SEC brought an administrative action against Michael J. Meehan, the NYSE specialist who had operated many of the famous pools before the stock market crash of 1929. He was charged with manipulating the stock of the Bellanca Corp., an aircraft manufacturer, through matched orders and other trading. The SEC concluded,

> On the face of the record it is not difficult to assay the nature of respondent's activity in Bellanca stock during the period June 19, to October 26 [1935]. We see him active in bringing new buying power into the market, encouraging his friends to buy, inducing persons in the brokerage business to recommend the stock to their customers. We see his associates, such as Wigmore, trading heavily in the stock on narrow price fluctuations. We find a market, when weakness in the stock developed, supported and banked by heavy scale buy orders placed directly by respondent for M.J. Meehan and Company, at other times by respondent for the account of his alter ego, Mrs. Meehan.[365]

The SEC also expressed concern with the investors who bought the stock at Meehan's behest. "The naïveté of all the purchasers is almost beyond belief."[366] The SEC held that Meehan's conduct violated Sections 9(a)(1) and (2) of the 34 Act.[367] The SEC held that such charges "make the motives of the respondent an ingredient of the offense. As to the respondent's motive, there is no direct testimony. The existence or non-existence of the required statutory motive must thus be a matter of inference from the voluminous testimony introduced in the case."[368] The SEC concluded that the evidence established the requisite motive and ordered Meehan to be expelled as a member from all securities exchanges, rejecting a defense that his trading was a permissible effort to stabilize or peg the stock price.

The SEC also brought an administrative proceeding against the principals of White, Weld & Co. and others under Section 9 of the 34 Act, charging a manipulation of the stock of the A.O. Smith Corp. over a period of more than four months.[369] White, Weld was a broker-dealer that acted as an investment banker for A.O. Smith. The stock of A.O. Smith was illiquid and had only a small floating supply available for trading. The SEC charged that respondents manipulated the stock upward in order to make profits on an option contract. A claim that respondents were making sales of stock to "strong hands" that would hold it for investment

---

362. Jonathan R. Macey, Mark Mitchell, and Jeffry Netter, *Symposium on the Regulation of Secondary Trading Markets: Program Trading, Volatility, Portfolio Insurance, and the Role of Specialists and Market Makers: Restrictions on Short Sales: An Analysis of the Uptick Rule and Its Role in View of the October 1987 Stock Market Crash*, 74 CORNELL L. REV. 799, 803 (1989) (footnotes omitted).

363. 17 C.F.R. § 240.10a-1.

364. In the Matter of Meehan, 2 S.E.C. 588 (1937).

365. Securities and Exchange Commission, Securities Exchange Act Release No. 34-1331 (Aug. 2, 1937).

366. *Id.*

367. *Id.*

368. *Id.*

369. In the Matter of White, 3 S.E.C. 466 (1938).

was rejected. The SEC found a violation of Section 9(a)(2) of the 34 Act on the following grounds:

> the combination of circumstances including primarily the 10,000 share option at 55; the timeliness of Russell's purchasing of 500 shares for Stock Account # 2 on April 12 raising the price from 57 to 60, many of the executions being at the offering prices; the continued and likewise timely purchasing of 400 shares on April 13, the last transaction closing the market at 60 1/4, up 3/4 of a point; the 1 1/2 point mark-up of April 20, 100 shares being bought for Stock Account # 2 at 65; the effort, as shown by the execution of scale orders on April 30, May 23, and May 24, to support the market prices which Russell had previously established by his purchases for the firm, and the unmistakable implication in Russell's telegram to Smith on April 23 that White Weld contemplated influencing the market, at least to the extent of "protecting" it, remains irresistible.[370]

The SEC further stated that "the violation of Section 9 (a) (2) and the consequent injury to investors does not hinge upon the existence of criminal intent or a 'bad' purpose. Violation of the statute occurs whenever transactions are effected in a registered security for the purpose of inducing the purchase or sale of that security by others for the purpose of manipulating the market."[371]

The SEC also sought to fight manipulators in court, but only with mixed success. The Second Circuit Court of Appeals dealt the agency a severe setback in one of its first antimanipulation efforts. In that case, *SEC v. Torr*,[372] the Second Circuit reversed a district court's entry of an injunction against defendants who had entered into a secret agreement with various individuals to raise the price of the stock of Trans-Lux Daylight Picture Screen Corporation by recommending it to possible prospects. The salesmen were paid commissions for successful sales but concealed those payments from prospects in order to make it appear that the salesmen were disinterested parties. The defendants had been previously advised by the SEC staff that the secret arrangement was permissible as long as fees were not paid to "customers' men" to solicit prospective customers.

The defendants were unaware that some of the salesmen they were paying were customers' men and stopped their activities when they learned that the SEC was intending to challenge their activities. The SEC claimed that the failure to disclose the payments violated the antifraud provisions of Section 17(a) the Securities Act of 1933[373] and that the sales activities, in supporting the stock price, violated Section 9(a)(2) of the 34 Act.[374] The Second Circuit concluded that the attempt to comply with the law and cessation of activities when the defendants learned of the SEC's concerns evidenced there was no need of an injunction against future violations, citing the Seventh Circuit's decision in *Cutten v. Wallace*.[375]

The SEC was again stymied in an injunctive action brought in federal court charging violations of Section 17(a) of the Securities Act of 1933[376] and Section 9(a)(2) of the 34 Act.[377] In that case, *SEC v. Otis & Co.*,[378] a district court refused to enter an injunction under Section 9(a)(2) against defendants who had acquired a large block of stock of the Murray-Ohio Company. The

370. 3 S.E.C. at 509.
371. 3 S.E.C. at 513.
372. SEC v. Torr, 87 F.2d 446 (2d Cir. 1937).
373. 15 U.S.C. § 77q9(a).
374. 15 U.S.C. § 78i(a)(2).
375. Cutten v. Wallace, 80 F.2d 140 (7th Cir. 1935).
376. 15 U.S.C. § 77q(a).
377. 15 U.S.C. § 78i(a)(2).
378. SEC v. Otis & Co., 18 F. Supp. 100 (N.D. Ohio 1936).

defendants then obtained agreements from vendors that they would withhold their stock from the market for sixty days so that defendant could sell the block. The court found insufficient evidence that manipulation was intended but did enjoin violations of Section 17(a) of the 33 Act in failing to disclose the withholding agreements. The Sixth Circuit affirmed that decision.[379]

The Seventh Circuit approved the entry of an injunction against violations of Section 17(a) of the 33 Act[380] and Section 9 of the 34 Act[381] in *R.J. Koeppe & Co. v. SEC*.[382] There, the defendants were charged with "rigging" the market by employing an individual to "tout" the stock. One defendant told others that his "purpose was to 'put the market up,' to 'get the market up to a dollar or higher.'"[383] The court found that "stock sales reported on the Chicago Curb [Exchange] gave an appearance of activity and an upward trend which made it possible for defendant company's salesmen to sell, at private sales, the large block of stock which it possessed when the so-called campaign was on."[384]

In *Wright v. SEC*,[385] the Second Circuit remanded an administrative sanction of the SEC against respondents charged with manipulating the stock of the Kinner Airplane & Motor Corp. Ltd. That alleged manipulation was carried out on the Los Angles Stock Exchange and the San Francisco Curb Exchange. The defendants boosted the stock price of this illiquid security from 45 cents per share to 75 cents during a six-day period. The defendant's purchases constituted 79 percent of all transactions in the stock on the Los Angles exchange during that period. The trading was conducted through various nominee accounts. This conduct was found to violate Section 9(a)(2) of the 34 Act, but the court held trades in violation of Section 9(a)(1) were not established because the alleged "matched orders" were not of substantially the same size even though the buy and sell orders were entered about the same time. The Second Circuit affirmed the SEC's sanctions after a remand.[386] This case consumed an inordinate amount of time. It was first filed by the SEC in 1936, and hearings were held over the course of the next year, resulting in a transcript of more than 3,500 pages.[387] The Second Circuit did not finally affirm the SEC's sanctions expelling the respondent from membership on the NYSE and other exchanges until 1943, some seven years after the case was filed and nearly eight years after the trading at issue. Such length and complexity became common in manipulation cases.

In *United States v. Minuse*,[388] the defendants were convicted of manipulating Tastyeast Class A stock on the New York Curb Exchange in violation of Section 9 of the 34 Act. Their trading, which occurred in 1935, involved an option obtained "from one Levy on 73,000 shares of the stock and thereafter by means of 'wash sales,' 'matched sales' and 'dummy' accounts they manipulated and inflated the price of the stock above the prices stated in their option so that they could unload the stock upon the public."[389] The defendants were convicted in 1940, but the judgment was reversed on appeal. The appeal after retrial was not completed until 1944, some nine years after the trading in question. An august panel of judges on the Second Circuit Court of Appeals did address the issue of the requisite intent for manipulation, affirming a charge that instructed the jury that

379. Otis & Co. v. SEC, 106 F.2d 579 (6th Cir. 1939).
380. 15 U.S.C. § 77q(a).
381. 15 U.S.C. § 78i.
382. R.J. Koeppe & Co. v. SEC, 95 F.2d 550 (7th Cir. 1938).
383. 95 F.2d at 552.
384. 95 F.2d at 552-553.
385. Wright v. SEC, 112 F.2d 89 (2d Cir. 1940).
386. Wright v. SEC, 134 F.2d 733 (2d Cir. 1943).
387. Wright v. SEC, 112 F.2d 89 (2d Cir. 1940).
388. United States v. Minuse, 142 F.2d 388 (2d Cir.), *cert. denied*, 323 U.S. 716 (1944).
389. 142 F.2d at 389.

"the case comes down to a question of 'good intent or evil intent'; and that for commission of the crime they must 'believe that the defendants entered into an agreement for the manipulation of the stock—that is, an evil intentional manipulation of the stock where the public would be affected and believe this stock would really rise in price.'"[390]

Other problems appeared in Section 9 cases. In *Rosenberg v. Hano*,[391] the Third Circuit dismissed a claim brought under Section 9 of the 34 Act. There, "[p]laintiff-appellant had been told of an 'operation' which would bring about an immediate and pronounced rise in the recommended stock. Instead, he witnessed a prompt and gradual fall."[392] The court held that Section 9 did not apply to such a misrepresentation. Rather the court noted that it was intended to give "statutory sanction and administrative efficiency to the recently expanded case law against stock market manipulation."[393] The court cited *Harris v. United States*[394] and *United States v. Brown*, the mail fraud cases described in Chapter 1, as the basis for that recent expansion.[395]

The court in *Rosenberg* noted that the United States had lagged behind England in attacking stock manipulations. The court concluded that the 34 Act was a recognition that an honest security market depends on more than banning "the cruder form of lying, such as wash sales, matched orders, and the like. The essence of a free market is an appraisal of value. Such appraisal to be trustworthy must be ab initio, so to speak, and must reflect the honest judgment of those whose reason for buying is independent of and uninfluenced by its own probable effect."[396]

The court in *Rosenberg* ruled that to succeed as a claim under Section 9 "the party claiming injury must plead and prove some change in price, because of the prohibited acts. He must either have entered a false market or paid a false price to enter a genuine market."[397] Here, the plaintiff did not engage in such activities. Rather, he "paid the regular list price for a stock which he does not claim had been yet affected by the illegal act; an act, incidentally illegal, irrespective of whether its performance rested in substance or only in the wicked imagination of the defendants."[398]

One early commentator noted in addressing the reach of the 34 Act that "'[m]anipulation' is not a term of legal art having a precise meaning, but is instead a rather general term descriptive of several related types of activity by which the market price or volume of trading in a security is affected." That author believed that the term . . . refers primarily to action upsetting that balance of forces in the market by which prices are determined, and thereby indirectly misleading those who are watching the market, rather than to misrepresentations made directly to an individual or to the public concerning the worth of a security."[399] This commentator also noted that it "now seems to be well established that where a person directly executes transactions raising or lowering the market price, the legal quality of his acts will hinge entirely on his purpose—whether it was a normal one of investment or speculation, or whether it was primarily to change the appearance of the market."[400] This commentator also noted that an open question was whether manipulation

390. 142 F.2d at 389.

391. Rosenberg v. Hano, 121 F.2d 818 (3d Cir. 1941).

392. 121 F.2d at 821.

393. 121 F.2d at 820.

394. Harris v. United States, 48 F.2d 771 (9th Cir. 1931).

395. United States v. Brown, 79 F.2d 321 (2d Cir. 1935).

396. 121 F.2d at 820 (footnote omitted).

397. 121 F.2d at 821 (footnote omitted).

398. 121 F.2d at 821. *See also*, Jolley v. Welch, 904 F.2d 988, 993 (5th Cir. 1990), *cert. denied*, 498 U.S. 1050 (1991) ("a section 9(a) claim requires proof of effect on the purchase price").

399. Arden L. Andresen, *Manipulation of Over-the-Counter Securities Markets*, 10 GEO. WASH. L. REV. 639, 640 (1942).

400. *Id.* at 648.

could be effected by actual transactions rather than wash sales or direct misrepresentations.[401] These issues would also plague future efforts to establish manipulation claims.

2:6 IMPLEMENTING THE COMMODITY EXCHANGE ACT

The Commodity Exchange Act carried forward the Commodity Exchange Commission structure as an oversight body consisting of the secretary of agriculture, the attorney general, and the secretary of commerce. The Grain Futures Administration in the Department of Agriculture was renamed the Commodity Exchange Authority (CEA). The CEA warned early on that the Commodity Exchange Act was "not a guaranty of high prices for agricultural products. . . . It simply provides a measure of restraint over fraudulent and manipulative practices."[402]

The CEA quickly encountered a number of market problems. Congestion arose in the May 1936 corn and rye contracts, and a trader was directed by the CBOT to reduce his position. The CEA issued a call to long traders to report on their positions in the December 1936 corn futures contract. The CEA then found that a trader had an excessively large long position, which he was directed to reduce by the CBOT, and did without incident.[403]

Congestion in the September 1937 corn futures contract caused by a pricing duel between a long trader and two short traders resulted in the suspension of its trading in that contract on the CBOT.[404] The CBOT established a settlement price for traders holding open positions. The CEA found that the principal long trader controlled 74 percent of the market on the long side and that the two shorts held 29 percent of open short positions. The CEA asserted that "the result was a stubborn struggle between the opposing interests. They refused to settle their contracts except on profitable terms."[405]

The CEA brought charges of manipulation against a large grain firm, Cargill Inc., in connection with this affair. The CEA charged that Cargill had tried to corner the September 1937 corn futures contract and that Cargill's short sales of some 10 million bushels in the December 1937 corn futures contract had caused artificial prices. Wash trading was also charged. The CEA suspended the trading privileges of Cargill's president but imposed no sanctions on the firm. Cargill was also expelled from its membership in the CBOT.[406]

Cargill had previously been involved in a spat between the CBOT and CEA over its 1936 long wheat and corn positions, which the CBOT Business Conduct Committee wanted Cargill to reduce. Cargill contended that the CBOT's actions were intended to aid the shorts. Cargill complained that the CBOT wanted "speculative 'shorts' to operate without taking conscientious steps to fulfill their obligations. . . . It even encourages outright gambling by speculative 'shorts' who in many instances . . . have no real intent to deliver."[407] This would become a familiar and much fought over issue. That issue would split the circuit courts as to the duties of shorts and whether they could be exploited by the longs.

---

401. *Id.* at 642.

402. U.S. Dept. Agric., *Report of the Secretary of Agriculture* 75 (1937).

403. Jerry W. Markham, The History of Commodity Trading and Its Regulation 29 (1987).

404. Jerry W. Markham, *Manipulation of Commodity Futures Prices: The Unprosecutable Crime*, 8 Yale J. on Reg. 281, 313-314 (1991).

405. Jerry W. Markham, The History of Commodity Trading and Its Regulation 29 (1987) (citation omitted).

406. Jerry W. Markham, *Manipulation of Commodity Futures Prices: The Unprosecutable Crime*, 8 Yale J. on Reg. 281, 313-314 (1991).

407. Wayne G. Broehl Jr., Cargill 473 (1992) (quoting from internal Cargill memorandum).

Cargill continued its campaign against the shorts into 1937, buying large amounts of cash grain. One Cargill purchasing agent advised that "[i[f I have overlooked a bushel of corn it is surely out in the forks of the creek." A member of the Cargill family stated that after Cargill's purchases "[i]t looks like the country is about out of cash corn."[408] The CBOT, intervening, halted trading in corn futures on September 24, 1937, and set a settlement price.[409] This action set off a classic battle between Cargill on the one hand and the CBOT and the CEA on the other. The incident was the subject of much national publicity and was even said to have inspired a lyric in a Cole Porter song: "Mr. Thorn once cornered corn and that ain't hay."[410]

Cargill instituted an action against the CBOT before the CEA, but it was dismissed by the agency, and the CEA then brought its case against Cargill.[411] Of interest in the proceeding against the CBOT was an exchange between a CBOT lawyer and a Cargill representative over the differences between corners and squeezes. The CBOT lawyer asserted that a squeeze was a tight supply situation in which there was no intention to exploit a shortage, while a corner was a deliberate effort to use market or monopoly power to profit.[412]

An investigation by the CEA of potato trading on the Chicago Mercantile Exchange (CME) found no evidence of short sale manipulations. Instead, the CEA concluded that futures trading in potatoes on that exchange were so small in comparison to the cash market that it had little price effect.[413] An investigation of the egg futures market on the CME in 1939 determined that large traders were concentrated on the short side but were mostly hedgers and their gains from a price decrease were offset by decreases in value of the positions being hedged.[414] Congestion problems occurred three times in 1939 in the cotton market as the result of trading by just a few individuals. Trading privileges of four traders were suspended by the CEA for ten days for manipulation claims involving the March 1940 butter futures contract traded on the Chicago Mercantile Exchange.[415]

The CEA also charged manipulation and attempted manipulation of the October 1940 wool top futures contract traded on the New York Cotton Exchange. An administrative referee found no manipulation or attempted manipulation violations of the Commodity Exchange Act. The referee did find record-keeping violations and improper offsetting of customer orders, but those findings were set aside by the First Circuit Court of Appeals in *Nichols & Co. v. Secretary of Agriculture*.[416]

The CEA elsewhere found evidence of false reports on crop conditions and other misleading information affecting futures prices. These included false claims of a bumper wheat crop and of the development of a black rust in wheat crops.[417] The CEA maintained surveillance over market letters and advisory reports affecting commodity prices issued by futures commission merchants.[418]

408. *Id.* at 481.

409. *Id.* at 488.

410. "Always True to You in My Fashion," by Cole Porter. *See*, Wayne G. Broehl Jr., Cargill 527 (1992).

411. Jerry W. Markham, The History of Commodity Trading and Its Regulation 32 (1987).

412. Wayne G. Broehl Jr., Cargill 451 (1992).

413. Jerry W. Markham, The History of Commodity Trading and Its Regulation 29 (1987).

414. U.S.D.A., *Survey of Egg Futures as of August 31, 1939* (Sept. 1940).

415. In re Great Western Distributors, Inc., CEA Doc. No. 21, noted in Jerry W. Markham, *Manipulation of Commodity Futures Prices: The Unprosecutable Crime*, 8 Yale J. on Reg. 281, 380 (1991).

416. Nichols & Co. v. Secretary of Agriculture, 131 F.2d 651 (1st Cir. 1942), *on rehearing*, 136 F.2d 503 (1st Cir. 1943).

417. Jerry W. Markham, The History of Commodity Trading and Its Regulation 29 (1987).

418. The CBOT had long maintained restrictions on market reports by its members and news services reporting on its prices. James E. Boyle, Speculation and the Chicago Board of Trade 96-97 (1920).

The CEA found that such reports had a substantial effect on prices, albeit only for short periods of time.[419] A CEA study of foreign traders in the commodity futures markets found that their trading was relatively small and posed no threat of manipulation.[420]

The CEA adopted position limits as directed by the Commodity Exchange Act. The CEA explained that the "purpose of such limits is to eliminate drastic price changes brought about by operations of large speculators."[421] The CEA also pressured the commodity futures exchanges to adopt minimum margin requirements in order "to insure fair competition between commission firms" and "to protect customers who, in the absence of substantial margin requirements might be inclined to take a larger position in the market than their means would justify."[422] The CEA further asserted that increased margins could prevent "irresponsible traders and undesirable speculative forces" from entering the market and could "minimize unwarranted switching of speculative accounts from one commodity or market to another."[423]

Paul Mehl, an economist at the Department of Agriculture, prepared a monograph in 1936, after the passage of the Commodity Exchange Act, that considered various ways to control excessive speculation. That paper asserted that excessive speculation could be curbed by five different methods: "through margin requirements, by placing a limitation on the amount the price of futures can fluctuate on a single day, by providing additional days for delivery after the trading in the current month has ceased, by direct action of the Board of Directors or Business Conduct Committee of the Exchange and by placing a limitation on the speculative holdings and trading of individuals."[424]

Mehl stated that progressively higher margins on large positions would tend to restrict speculation. "In order to discourage the accumulation of large dangerous speculative lines, additional margin on a progressive basis could be demanded of an individual as the size of his line increased." However, Mehl warned that "there is the possibility that speculators will accumulate large lines [of credit] if the anticipated profits appear to justify the advancing of large margins."[425]

Notwithstanding the Mehl report, the Department of Agriculture opposed a bill in 1939 that would have allowed the Commodity Exchange Commission to fix margins at not less than 25 percent. The department stated that standards established by the bill were not practical and that such margins would provide an incentive for speculators to switch their trading to commodities that were not regulated by the Commodity Exchange Act.[426] This confirmed the department's position that had been taken before the enactment of the Commodity Exchange Act. When Congress had been considering the bill, the commodity exchanges had urged that margins be used to control speculation instead of position limits. The government argued, however, that positions limits were better tools for limiting excessive speculation "rather than . . . higher margins which are not so readily applicable to commodities as to stocks."[427]

---

419. Jerry W. Markham, The History of Commodity Trading and Its Regulation 31 (1987).

420. *Id.* at 31.

421. *Id.* at 30 (citation omitted).

422. *Id.* (citation omitted).

423. Jerry W. Markham, *Federal Regulation of Margin in the Commodity Futures Industry: History and Theory*, 64 Temp. L. Rev. 59, 71-72 (1991) (citations omitted).

424. Paul Mehl, *Controlling Speculative Activity by Limiting the Size of Lines and the Trading* 1 (Oct. 9, 1936).

425. *Id.* at 1, 4.

426. *Authorize Commodity Exchange Commission to Regulate Margin Requirements, Hearings Before a Subcommittee of the Senate Committee on Agriculture and Forestry*, 76th Cong. 1-2 (1939).

427. II Jerry W. Markham, A Financial History of the United States, From J.P. Morgan to the Institutional Investor (1900-1970) 223 (2002).

A jurisdictional fight arose between the CEA and the SEC. William O. Douglas, the new chair of the SEC and later a Supreme Court justice, sought SEC jurisdiction to curb commodity speculation involving puts and calls. President Franklin Roosevelt ordered the secretary of agriculture, Henry Wallace, to take action. However, Wallace was a rival of Douglas for presidential power, and he refused to allow the SEC to have any role in such regulation. That fight was interrupted by World War II, but this dispute would be the first of many regulatory clashes with the SEC and commodity market regulators over commodity market regulations.[428]

2:7 WORLD WAR II AND THE COMMODITY MARKETS

The outbreak of World War II restored the nation's economy and ended the Great Depression. That conflict caused concerns over volatility in the commodity markets. In May 1940, the Department of Agriculture asked that the commodity exchanges not allow trading in futures to occur below prices then prevailing.[429] The department also sought price stability by asking the commodity exchanges to increase margin requirements and to impose daily trading limits on commodities that would result in a suspension of trading when those limits were reached.[430]

The CEA conducted another investigation to determine if foreign interests were trading in the futures markets, but no dangers appeared.[431] The raw silk market was shut down on the Commodity Exchange Inc. in New York on July 28, 1941, at the request of the federal government. Settlement prices were then set by the exchange. An effort to enjoin that action by Mitsui & Co. Ltd., a large Japanese trading firm that was short in the silk futures market, failed, and it sustained large losses.[432]

The Department of Agriculture conducted investigations of speculative holdings in the commodity futures markets to determine their effect in the event of a national emergency. The government was concerned that small, unsophisticated traders could unduly affect markets by entering in large numbers or cause panic liquidations because of thinly margined accounts. The government found that there had been an unusual amount of in-and-out trading and erratic price movements in soybean futures, which it thought should be curbed by increased margins. On July 11, 1941, after a run-up in commodity prices, the government requested that the exchanges increase margin requirements to 15 percent, an increase of more than 50 percent. The exchanges declined to do so.[433]

On Sunday, December 7, 1941, after the attack on Pearl Harbor, increased margin requirements and trading price limits were imposed by the exchanges at the government's request.[434] Those efforts avoided a disruption of the market, but trading in futures contracts on several commodities, including lard and soybean products, ceased as a result of war needs.[435]

The Emergency Price Control Act of 1942 authorized the Office of Price Administration to control prices. That statute stated that its purposes were to "stabilize prices and to prevent speculative, unwarranted, and abnormal increases in prices and rents; to eliminate and prevent profiteering, hoarding, manipulation, speculation, and other disruptive practices resulting from abnormal mar-

428. *Id.* at 225.

429. Jerry W. Markham, A History of Commodity Futures Trading and Its Regulation 36 (1987).

430. Jerry W. Markham, *Manipulation of Commodity Futures Prices: The Unprosecutable Crime*, 8 Yale J. on Reg. 281, 314-315 (1991).

431. Jerry W. Markham, A History of Commodity Futures Trading and Its Regulation 35 (1987).

432. Crowley v. Commodity Exchange, Inc., 141 F.2d 182 (2d Cir. 1944).

433. *Report of the Chief of the Commodity Exchange Administration* 8 (1941).

434. *See*, Jerry W. Markham, *Federal Regulation of Margin in the Commodity Futures Industry: History and Theory*, 64 Temp. L. Rev. 59, 72 (1991) (describing those investigations and actions).

435. Jerry W. Markham, A History of Commodity Futures Trading and Its Regulation 36 (1987).

ket conditions or scarcities caused by or contributing to the national emergency."[436] Agricultural commodities were subject to a different regimen that set floors on any controls imposed on their prices so that farmers would receive higher prices. The authority to set these controls was relegated to the secretary of agriculture.[437]

Economists have long debated the value of rationing and the effects of the World War II price controls.[438] "Since the time of Adam Smith at least one of the questions that raises the most intense passions among economists is that of Government control over prices."[439] Price controls did seem to have tamped down inflation during the war and concerns over manipulation seemed to have diminished, but one economist claimed they nonetheless had negative effects.[440]

During the closing months of the war, the CEA brought a case charging attempted and actual manipulation of the rye market by the General Foods Corp. and various CBOT members, including Daniel Rice and Philip R. O'Brien, a former CBOT president.[441] This trading was said to be a "national scandal" that was using government contacts to maintain the corner in rye.[442]

A complaint alleging manipulation by those respondents was issued by the War Food Administration.[443] The respondents were charged with attempted and actual manipulation of actual (cash) rye and rye futures from December 1942 through May 1944. This manipulation was carried out by General Food's acquisition of some 9 million bushels of cash rye in Chicago. The CBOT directed that General Foods stop further such purchases. Other respondents then began building long rye futures positions and took deliveries of 2 million bushels of rye in Winnipeg in order to prevent it from being shipped to Chicago.[444]

The complaint charged that these activities were all "speculative and caused an abnormal accumulation of rye in Chicago, which congested the transportation and storage facilities at a time when such facilities were needed for other grain crops for which there was an important demand."[445] The case was tried before an administrative "referee" who ruled in favor of the government. However, after review by an administrative judicial officer, most of the government's claims were rejected, including a charge of cornering the rye market. The judicial officer did, however, find manipulation with respect to a 2 million bushel position in 1944.[446] On appeal, the Seventh Circuit in *General Foods Corp. v. Brannan*[447] rejected the finding of manipulation. The court noted that the government failed to offer any "expert testimony evaluating the data which had been presented, and consequently there is no expert testimony respecting the normalcy or

---

436. 56 Stat. 23-24 (1942).

437. 56 Stat. 23, 27 (1942).

438. For a defense of price controls, *see* John Kenneth Galbraith, A Theory of Price Control (1952). Vestiges of those price controls still linger in the rent-controlled rental market in New York City.

439. *See*, Stephanie LaGuerodie and Francisco Vergara, *The Theory of Price Controls*, 20 Rev. of Political Econ 569 (Oct. 2008) (describing those debates).

440. Paul Evans, *The Effects of General Price Controls in the United States During World War II*, 90 J. of Political Econ. 944 (Oct. 1982).

441. *WFA Charges "Corner" in Rye on Chicago Market in 1944*, New York Times, May 29, 1945, at 17.

442. *"National Scandal" in Rye Is Charged*, New York Times, July 4, 1945, at 18.

443. *WFA Charges "Corner" in Rye on Chicago Market in 1944*, New York Times, May 29, 1945, at 17.

444. General Foods Corp. v. Brannan, 170 F.2d 220, 222 (7th Cir. 1948).

445. *Id.*

446. *Id.* at 220, 223. *See also*, *Trading Penalties Reduced by Flavin*, New York Times, July 16, 1947, at 36; *General Foods Involved in Grain Rigging Charges*, New York Times, April 29, 1947, at 45 (describing that decision).

447. General Foods Corp. v. Brannan, 170 F.2d 220, 222 (7th Cir. 1948).

abnormalcy of rye prices and of market activities. Neither was any testimony offered in proof of, and it is not contended that any short in the Chicago rye market during the relevant period was in need of actual rye for delivery or other purposes or was pressured, coerced or injured by any action taken or contemplated by any of the petitioners."[448] It was later asserted that Rice had in fact tried to corner the rye market and that he buried the "corpse" by using congressional influence to sell the rye abroad.[449]

The Seventh Circuit ruled that "the common criteria usual in manipulation or corner cases are deceit, trickery through the spreading of false rumors, concealment of position, the violation of express anti-manipulation controls, or other forms of fraud. None of these elements are claimed or shown to exist in the instant situation."[450] The court noted that it was "favored with numerous definitions of the word 'manipulation.' Perhaps as good as any is one of the definitions which appears in the government's brief, wherein it is defined as 'the creation of an artificial price by planned action, whether by one man or a group of men.'"[451] The court noted, however, that, according "to the decision of the Judicial Officer, there was not any purpose to create an artificial price but to preserve an existing price resulting from natural forces, and certainly there is no proof that an artificial price was accomplished and we think no sound reason to believe that such was the purpose."[452]

The Seventh Circuit found that the respondents were acting in their own self-interest in protecting the price of their holdings in rye through the 2 million bushel transaction:

> Respondents no doubt were faced with a precarious situation. It may be that they are subject to censure for acquiring such large holdings in cash rye, particularly General Foods who after the transaction under discussion held more than 9,000,000 bushels. There was nothing illegal, however, in these large holdings so far as we are aware. In fact, the Judicial Officer in effect so held as to General Foods. . . .
>
> Self-preservation has oftentimes been referred to as the first law of nature, and we suppose it applies to traders as well as others. We see no reason why the seller respondents as well as General Foods and Metcalf should not under the circumstances made an effort to protect their own interests.[453]

The Seventh Circuit's decision in this case did not sit well with the government, who viewed it as allowing price stabilizing and pegging of prices through futures trades in order to protect the price of a cash position. It was also another signal that manipulation claims under the Commodity Exchange Act would be difficult to prove.

Another CEA case of interest involved a claim of manipulation by false reports. In *In re McGuigan*,[454] the respondent was found by a CEA administrative judicial officer to have manipulated cotton and grain prices by sending telegrams, letters, and circulars throughout the United States from August to December 1945 that promoted the purchase of futures on those commodities. McGuigan "advertised and represented himself to be in the business of selling market advice to traders in grain, cotton, and other commodities . . . for future delivery." He distributed telegrams

448. *Id.* at 220, 223.
449. Jonathan R. Laing, *Still Full of Beans*, BARRONS, April 30, 1990.
450. General Foods Corp. v. Brannan, 170 F.2d 220, 224 (7th Cir. 1948).
451. *Id.* at 220, 231.
452. *Id.*
453. *Id.*
454. In re McGuigan, 5 Agric. Dec. 249 (1946).

and letters to prospective clients and firms urging the purchase and sale of specific commodity futures contracts and "made transactions opposite to those he had advised, thus taking profits from the influenced price change."[455] His promotions allowed him to profit on his purchase of futures contracts on 2.5 million bushels of grain and 50,000 bales of cotton. McGuigan tried to conceal his trading through accounts carried in his wife's maiden name and in fictitious names. The respondent was subjected to a six-year trading suspension for that conduct.

Of a similar ilk was another CEA decision that was appealed to the District of Columbia Court of Appeals in *Moore v. Brannan.*[456] The respondent there prepared a false press release stating that the federal government planned to make large purchases of lard for overseas relief. The press release was intended to increase lard prices and aid the respondent's long position covering 1.8 million pounds of lard. Moore listed four USDA employees as "References" on the release, but they had not agreed to act as references. The release was sent to respondent's Merrill Lynch broker, but a Merrill Lynch employee checked with one of the claimed references and determined that the release was without basis. Moore also left copies of the press release at the National Press Club in Washington, DC, and with the USDA press office, but it was never used in any press report and had no apparent market effect. The District of Columbia Circuit, in a *per curiam* opinion, affirmed the decision of the judicial officer finding attempted manipulation and other violations and barring the respondent from trading for ninety days.

455. In re McGuigan, 5 Agric. Dec. 249 (1946).
456. Moore v. Brannan, 191 F.2d 775 (D.C. Cir.), *cert. denied*, 342 U.S. 860 (1951).

3

POSTWAR MANIPULATION AND SPECULATION

3:1 THE SEC ADOPTS RULE 10B-5

The Securities and Exchange Commission (SEC) was considered a nonessential agency during World War II and was moved to Philadelphia, where it conducted its work out of the Pennsylvania Athletic Club.[1] One momentous event did occur at the SEC during World War II that would become the focal point for antimanipulation efforts in future years. This action was the adoption of SEC Rule 10b-5[2] under Section 10(b) of the Securities Exchange Act of 1934 (the 34 Act).[3] Section 10(b) was of little interest to anyone until Rule 10b-5 was adopted in 1942 to fill a hole in the coverage of the antifraud provisions of Section 17 of the Securities Act of 1933,[4] which applied only to sellers, and not to buyers of securities.[5]

For many years after its adoption, only the cognoscenti knew of the existence of Rule 10b-5, but that rule would, in time, be the focus of thousands of lawsuits and would become the model for amendments to the Commodity Exchange Act of 1936 and other legislation that were designed to provide more effective actions against commodity price manipulations. Oddly, the adoption of Rule 10b-5 was done in an almost casual fashion and without any analysis of its application to price manipulations or how it would meld with the specific prohibitions against manipulation in Section 9 of the 34 Act.[6] Moreover, no consideration was given to what would constitute the elements needed to prove a violation of this new rule.[7]

---

1. The SEC "did not return to Washington until 1948 or so and when it did, it occupied temporary facilities constructed during the war that the staff referred to as the 'tarpaper shack.'" Irving M. Pollack and Stanley Sporkin, co-moderators, *A Brief History of the SEC's Enforcement Program 1934–1981*, SEC Historical Society Oral Histories Committee Roundtable on Enforcement, at 14 (Sept. 25, 2002).

2. 17 C.F.R. § 240.10b-5.

3. 15 U.S.C. § 78i.

4. 15 U.S.C. 77q.

5. Blue Chip Stamps v. Manor Drug Stores, 421 U.S. 723, 767 (1975) (describing the "casual origins" of this rule); Steve Thel, *The Original Conception of Section 10(b) of the Securities Exchange Act*, 42 STAN. L. REV. 385, 408 (1990) (same); ALAN BROMBERG, SECURITIES LAW FRAUD: SEC RULE 10B-5 (1975); Symposium, *Happy Birthday 10b-5: 50 Years of Antifraud Regulation*, 61 FORDHAM L. REV. S1 (1993). In re Cady, Roberts, 40 S.E.C. 907 (1961).

6. 15 U.S.C. § 78i.

7. A subsequent Supreme Court case considering that lack of attention described the background for the adoption of Rule 10b-5 as follows:

> In adopting Rule 10b-5 in 1942, the Securities and Exchange Commission issued a press release stating: "The new rule closes a loophole in the protections against fraud administered by the Commission by prohibiting individuals or companies from buying securities if they engage in fraud in their purchase." SEC Release No. 3230 (May 21, 1942). To say specifically that certain types of fraud are within Rule 10b-5, of course, is not to say that others are necessarily excluded. That this is so is confirmed by the apparently casual origins of the Rule, as recalled by a former SEC staff attorney in remarks made at a conference on federal securities laws several years ago:

The reach of Rule 10b-5 was extended in 1946 by a federal district court in *Kardon v. National Gypsum Co.*,[8] which held that there was an implied private right of action under Rule 10b-5. That decision would lead in future years to a litigation explosion, with Rule 10b-5 being cited in some 15,000 federal court decisions, as well as thousands of arbitrations and SEC administrative proceedings.[9] As "Justice Rehnquist would write several years later in reference to Rule 10b-5, 'we deal with a judicial oak which has grown from little more than a legislative acorn.'"[10]

In finding an implied right of action under Rule 10b-5, the court in *Kardon* followed a tort rule, which holds that a person who violates a legislative enactment is liable in damages to those he injured as the result of such violation. The Supreme Court would later reject that reasoning in determining whether private rights of action should be implied under other federal statutes or agency rules. However, that change in approach came too late to derail the runaway express of Rule 10b-5 actions.

In 1975, the Supreme Court thus took a more restrictive approach to finding implied private rights of action in *Cort v. Ash*,[11] a decision that did not involve Rule 10b-5. The Supreme Court

---

> It was one day in the year 1943, I believe. I was sitting in my office in the S.E.C. building in Philadelphia and I received a call from Jim Treanor who was then the Director of the Trading and Exchange Division. He said, "I have just been on the telephone with Paul Rowen," who was then the S.E.C. Regional Administrator in Boston, "and he has told me about the president of some company in Boston who is going around buying up the stock of his company from his own shareholders at $4.00 a share, and he has been telling them that the company is doing very badly, whereas, in fact, the earnings are going to be quadrupled and will be $2.00 a share for this coming year. Is there anything we can do about it?" So he came upstairs and I called in my secretary and I looked at Section 10(b) and I looked at Section 17, and I put them together, and the only discussion we had there was where "in connection with the purchase or sale" should be, and we decided it should be at the end.
>
> We called the Commission and we got on the calendar, and I don't remember whether we got there that morning or after lunch. We passed a piece of paper around to all the commissioners. All the commissioners read the rule and they tossed it on the table, indicating approval. Nobody said anything except Sumner Pike who said, "Well," he said, "we are against fraud, aren't we?" That is how it happened. Remarks of Milton Freeman, Conference on Codification of the Federal Securities Laws, 22 Bus. Law. 793, 922 (1967).

Blue Chip Stamps v. Manor Drug Stores, 421 U.S. 723, 766-767 (1975) (Blackmun, J., dissenting).

8. 69 F. Supp. 512 (E.D. Pa. 1946).

9. LEXIS search by author conducted on July 12, 2011. Between 1942, when Rule 10b-5 was adopted, and 1968 there were only 284 federal court decisions citing that rule. The SEC became a more activist agency in the 1960s and the courts began to expansively apply Section 10(b), touching off a litigation boom. Between 1968 and 2011, there were more than 14,000 federal court citations to Section 10(b) and Rule 10b-5. Between 2007 and the middle of 2011, more than 2,300 cites were added to that list.

10. Morrison v. National Australian l. Bank Ltd., 561 U.S. ---, --- (2010) (concurring opinion of Stevens and Ginsburg, citations omitted).

11. 422 U.S. 66 (1975). The Court adopted a four part for implying such rights:

> First, is the plaintiff "one of the class for whose especial benefit the statute was enacted," . . . that is, does the statute create a federal right in favor of the plaintiff? Second, is there any indication of legislative intent, explicit or implicit, either to create such a remedy or to deny one? . . . Third, is it consistent with the underlying purposes of the legislative scheme to imply such a remedy for the plaintiff? . . . And finally, is the cause of action one traditionally relegated to state law, in an area basically the concern of the States, so that it would be inappropriate to infer a cause of action based solely on federal law?

422 U.S. at 78 (citations omitted).

subsequently confirmed that it has "abandoned" the approach taken for implying private rights of action under the 34 Act and that it had repeatedly declined to "revert" to "the understanding of private causes of action that held sway 40 years ago."[12]

Four years after the decision in *Cort v. Ash*, the Supreme Court described its acquiescence to an implied private right of action for securities law violations as a deviation from its more current position.[13] The Court, however, allowed private rights of action to continue under Rule 10b-5—by then there was simply too much jurisprudence under the rule in private actions to overrule.

Rule 10b-5 became the favorite choice for class-action plaintiffs, who vied with each other to file such suits immediately upon the report of any setback at a public company. As will be described in a later chapter, the Supreme Court sought, beginning in the 1970s, to slow the growth of litigation under Rule 10b-5 by making Rule 10b-5 claims harder to prove. As the Supreme Court noted in *Janus Capital Group Inc. v. First Derivative Traders*,[14] it had previously held that a private right of action was implied under Section 10(b), but "[c]oncerns with the judicial creation of a private cause of action caution against its expansion," and the Court "must give 'narrow dimensions . . . to a right of action Congress did not authorize when it first enacted the statute and did not expand when it revisited the law.'"[15]

Congress also responded to litigation abuses under Rule 10b-5 by imposing special pleading and other restrictions in such cases.[16] In the meantime Rule 10b-5 became the tool that the SEC would use to greatly expand its jurisdiction in insider trading cases; the rule became its principal focus in manipulation cases. Indeed, the SEC would virtually abandon the use of Section 9 of the 34 Act in attacking manipulation.

Section 9 initially applied only to securities traded on exchanges and not to over-the-counter (OTC) trading.[17] The SEC sought to avoid that limitation by incorporating the prohibitions in Sec-

12. Alexander v. Sandoval, 532 U.S. 275, 287 (2001). In Touche Ross & Co. v. Reddington, 442 U.S. 560 (1979), the Supreme Court held that there was no implied private right of action for damages under Section 17(a) of the 34 Act (15 U.S.C. § 78q(a)) to recover damages for an accountant's misstatements in a brokerage firm's financial reports. *See also*, Transamerica Mortgage Advisors Inc. v. Lewis, 444 U.S. 11, 15-16 (1979) (no implied right of action for violating the antifraud provision in the Investment Advisers Act of 1940, 15 U.S.C. 80b-6); Piper v. Chris-Craft Indus., 430 U.S. 1 (1976) (plaintiffs had no standing to bring a private right of action under § 14(e) of the Securities Exchange Act of 1934, 15 U.S.C. § 78m or under SEC Rule 10b-6, 17 C.F.R. § 240.10b-6).

13. Cannon v. University of Chicago, 441 U.S. 677, 693, n. 13 (1979). The Supreme Court has noted that its creation of this judicial remedy has been acquiesced in by Congress. "We infer from these references an acknowledgment of the 10b-5 action without any further expression of legislative intent to define it." Musick, Peeler & Garrett v. Employers Ins., 508 U.S. 286, 293-294 (1993).

14. Janus Capital Group Inc. v. First Derivative Traders, 564 U.S. ---, --- (2011).

15. 564 U.S. at --- (2011) (citations omitted).

16. Private Securities Litigation Reform Act of 1995, Pub. L. 104-67, 109 Stat. 737.

17. *See, e.g.*, Martin v. Prudential-Bache Securities Inc., 820 F. Supp. 980, 984 (W.D. N.C. 1991) (noting this restriction); Cowen & Co. v. Merriam, 745 F. Supp. 925, 931 (S.D.N.Y. 1990) (same). When originally enacted, the 34 Act applied only to exchange traded securities and not to the OTC market. That omission was corrected in 1938 with the passage of the Maloney Act. Over-the-Counter Market Act, 52 Stat. 1070 (1938), 15 U.S.C. § 78o (1958). That legislation provided for regulation of the OTC market by a national securities association that would be registered with the SEC. This resulted in the creation of the National Association of Securities Dealers Inc. (NASD). *See*, Tamar Hed-Hofmann, *The Maloney Act Experiment*, 6 B. C. L. Rev. 187 (1965) (describing this legislation). The NASD was folded a few years ago into the New York Stock Exchange's self-regulatory organization (SRO) functions, and the combined operation was called the Financial Industry Regulatory Authority (FINRA). *See also*, http://www.finra.org/AboutFINRA/ (accessed August 10, 2011) (describing the role of FINRA).

tion 9 into the definition of "manipulation" under Section 10(b), which applied to both exchange listed and OTC traded stocks. That was done a few years after the SEC adopted Rule 10b-5.[18] The result was that OTC security manipulation claims were pushed under Section 10(b) of the 34 Act, further enhancing the high visibility of that provision and undercutting the safeguards and requirements of Section 9. The SEC also asserted that the "anti-manipulative provisions of Section 9(a) do not operate as a limitation on Section 10(b). The legislative and judicial history of the latter section makes it clear that Section 10(b) and the rules thereunder are to operate independently of other securities laws provisions."[19]

In *SEC v. Resch-Cassin & Co.*,[20] the SEC charged manipulation under both Sections 9 and 10(b) of the 34 Act. The federal district court hearing that case noted that it "is well settled that the manipulative activities expressly prohibited by § 9(a)(2) of the Exchange Act with respect to a listed security are also violations of §17(a) of the Securities Act and §10(b) of the Exchange Act when the same activities are conducted with respect to an over-the-counter security."[21] The court found that the defendants there were seeking to push up the price of a stock that was undergoing its initial public offering. The court found that the "natural consequence of this course of conduct was to artificially stimulate the so-called market price of the stock while making it appear to be the product of the independent forces of supply and demand when, in reality, it was completely a creature of defendants' subterfuge."[22]

Somewhat of an outlier is Section 15(c) of the 34 Act,[23] which was added in 1938 and which applies only to broker-dealers.[24] It prohibits those entities from effecting or inducing any over-the-counter transaction in a security "by means of any manipulative, deceptive, or other fraudulent device or contrivance." The SEC was also granted authority to adopt rules to implement that provision. One such rule is Rule 15c1-2, which states that the "manipulative, deceptive, or other fraudulent device or contrivance," as used in section 15(c)(1), is to be defined "to include any act, practice, or course of business which operates or would operate as a fraud or deceit upon any person" and "any untrue statement of a material fact and any omission to state a material fact necessary in order to make the statements made, in the light of the circumstances under which they are made, not misleading, which statement or omission is made with knowledge or reasonable grounds to believe that it is untrue or misleading."[25] This language tracks SEC Rule 10b-5, and the SEC often combined Section 10(b) and Section 15(c) claims (and Section 17(a) of the 33 Act) when a broker-dealer is involved in a manipulation.[26]

---

18. *Manipulative and Deceptive Devices and Contrivances*, 13 Fed. Reg. 8177, 8183 (Dec. 22, 1948). *See* 17 C.F.R. § 240.10b-1.

19. In the Matter of Podesta, 47 S.E.C. 136, 140 (1979) (footnote and citation omitted).

20. SEC v. Resch-Cassin & Co., 362 F. Supp. 964, 978 (S.D.N.Y. 1973).

21. 362 F. Supp. at 975.

22. 362 F. Supp. at 978. *See also*, In the Matter of Felice, 29 S.E.C. 595, 602 (1949) (respondent was found to have willfully violated Section 9(a)(2) of the act by effecting and aiding and abetting "a series of transactions in Tonopah stock creating actual and apparent trading activity and raising the price of the security, for the purpose of inducing the purchase thereof by others"); In the Matter of Merrill, 8 S.E.C. 620 (1941) (partner in Merrill Lynch consented to finding of Section 9(a)(2) violation during underwriting).

23. 15 U.S.C. § 78o.

24. 49 Stat. 1377 (1938).

25. 17 C.F.R. § 240.15c1-2.

26. *See, e.g.*, In the Matter of In the Matter of Floyd A. Allen & Co., Inc., 35 S.E.C. 176 (1953); In the Matter of Masland, Fernon & Anderson, 9 S.E.C. 338 (1941) (manipulation violations under Section 15(c) of the 34 Act and Rule 15c1-2); In the Matter of Bond & Goodwin Inc., 9 S.E.C. 319 (1941) (same); In the Matter of Kidder Peabody & Co., 18 S.E.C. 559 (1945) (violations of Section 15(c) and Section 9(a)(2)); In the Matter of R.L. Emacio & Co. Inc., 35 S.E.C. 191 (1953) (violations of Sections 10(b) and 15(c) of

In *In the Matter of Halsey, Stuart & Co. Inc.*,[27] the SEC charged the respondent with violations of Section 10(b) of the 34 Act and Sections 15(c)(1) and 17(a) of the 33 Act, but could not charge Section 9 violations because the transactions occurred in the over-the-counter market. The SEC rejected the respondent's contention that "the broad anti-fraud provisions of Section 17(a) of the Securities Act, and Sections 15(c) and 10(b) of the Exchange Act (and the rules thereunder) relating to over-the-counter securities do not cover activity which would be prohibited by Section 9(a)(2) as to listed securities merely because Section 9(a)(2) is, by its terms, limited to listed securities."[28]

The SEC took a broad view of what constitutes manipulation in *In the Matter of Thompson Ross Securities Co.*, stating that "[a]rtificial restraints or stimuli are foreign to the concept of a 'market price.'" The SEC stated in that case it would be materially misleading to claim that a stock was being sold at the "market" when the supply of stock was being artificially limited or where demand is artificially stimulated.[29]

The SEC experienced some litigation setbacks involving the application of Section 9. In *In the Matter of Leroy A. Strasburger & Co.*,[30] the SEC dismissed one of its own administrative proceedings, which had charged a manipulation of the price of Peoria & Eastern income bonds over a four-day period in 1941. The SEC stated that the respondent "in fact created active trading in and raised the price of the bonds in question. This, however, is not in itself sufficient to constitute a violation of Section 9(a)(2). There remains the question whether this series of transactions was effected by respondent for the purpose of inducing other persons to buy or sell the bonds." The SEC found the evidence to be insufficient to sustain a finding of such an unlawful purpose.[31]

In *SEC v. Bennett*,[32] a case filed in the closing months of World War II, a federal district court denied an SEC motion for a preliminary injunction against defendants for allegedly violating Section 9(a)(2) of the 34 Act. The SEC claimed that the president of Bennett & Co. had purchased thousands of shares of its stock while the company's registration statement was pending at the SEC for an additional issuance of shares. The SEC claimed that the purchases were for the purpose of inflating the share price in order to boost the offering. According to the court, the fact that "the 3,800 shares were all bought within an hour, while such registration statement was pending, which registration in itself may have been considered as tending to increase the value of the stock, does not establish that the stock was bought with the intent to create an actual and apparent active

---

the 34 Act and Section 17(a) of the 33 Act); In the Matter of Morrison Bond Co. Ltd., 11 S.E.C. 125 (1942) (violations found of Section 15(c) of the 34 Act and Section 17(a) of the 33 Act). *Compare*, In the Matter of M.S. Wien & Co., 23 S.E.C. 735 (1946) (violations found of Section 10(b) and 15(c) of the 34 Act but not Section 17(a) of the 33 Act); In the Matter of Bressman, Securities Exchange Act Release No. 43188, 2000 WL 1201587 (Aug. 22, 2000) (same).

27. *In the Matter of Halsey, Stuart & Co. Inc.*, 30 S.E.C. 106, 110 (1949). *See also*, In the Matter of Russell Maguire & Co. Inc., 10 S.E.C. 332 (1941) (respondent found to have violated both Section 17(a) of the 33 Act and Section 9 of the 34 Act).

28. *See also*, In the Matter of Barret & Co., 9 S.E.C. 319, 328 (1941) (making a similar ruling); In the Matter of Gob Shops of America Inc., 39 S.E.C. 92, 101 (1959) ("there is no merit in respondents' contention that the principles relating to artificially stimulated activity on an exchange, as set forth in Section 9 of the Securities Exchange Act of 1934, are inapplicable in the case of an unlisted security where trading is done privately and its volume is not made public. We rejected a similar argument in Halsey, Stuart & Co., Inc., 30 S.E.C. 106, at page 127 [1949]").

29. In the Matter of Thompson Ross Securities Co., 6 S.E.C. 1111, 1121 (1940).

30. In the Matter of Leroy A. Strasburger & Co., 14 S.E.C. 397, 403 (1943).

31. *See also*, In the Matter of Edgerton, Wykoff & Co., 36 S.E.C. 583 (1955) (charges of manipulation dismissed where knowledge of manipulation not shown). *Compare*, In the Matter of Adams & Co., 33 S.E.C. 444 (1952) (violations of Section 9(a)(2) found); In the Matter of Chevrier, 42 S.E.C. 583 (1965) (violations of Section 9(a)(2) found by consent).

32. SEC v. Bennett, 62 F. Supp. 609 (S.D.N.Y. 1945).

trading for the purpose of increasing or depressing the prices so as to induce the purchase or sale by others."[33] This case was later settled with a consent injunction.

The SEC refused to follow the ruling by the court in the *Bennett* case. In an administrative proceeding brought against another company, *In the Matter of Federal Corp.*,[34] the SEC rejected the *Bennett* court's views on the intent required for a violation of Section 9. The SEC further stated that the *Bennett* court made an erroneous factual assumption that the registration statement filed with the SEC tended to have increased the value of the stock. The SEC could "see no basis for any general assumption that the mere filing of a registration statement justifies an increase in the market price of outstanding shares of the same class."[35]

The intent question for violations of Section 9(a)(1) and (2) was again raised a few years later in *Thornton v. SEC*.[36] The defendants admitted to making "matched orders and wash sales, but denied the manipulative purpose defined in the statute as that 'of creating a false or misleading appearance of active trading in any security registered on a national securities exchange, or a false or misleading appearance with respect to the market for any such security.'"[37] The defendants claimed that they engaged in those transactions in response to the loan requirements of their bank, which they asserted negated manipulative intent, but the evidence indicated otherwise. Among other things, their firm's financial position was inconsistent with this claim, as were "its purchases and sales to others, including public investors, or for profit, in addition to the wash sales, the sharp inventory changes appearing in its holdings of these stocks pointing to active trading, rather than the maintaining of a definite position as to the particular investment."[38]

In *Norris & Hirshberg v. Securities & Exchange Commission*,[39] the District of Columbia Circuit Court of Appeals affirmed a finding of manipulation in a SEC proceeding. The respondent was a broker-dealer that controlled a large percentage of the "float" (the amount of stock available for trading) in five stocks. It used the margin accounts of naive customers to constantly "whip" these stocks back and forth in those customer accounts with the result that the same customers sold securities to the respondent and then those accounts repurchased the stock within a few days at higher prices.

3:2 POSTWAR SPECULATION

The ending of World War II raised concerns of inflation and the threat of a stock market bubble. The Federal Reserve Board increased margin requirements from 40 percent to 50 percent on February 2, 1945, to 75 percent on July 5, 1946, and to 100 percent on January 21, 1946. The Dow Jones Industrial Average rose to 212.50 before it dropped to 163.12 as those margin requirements were increased. The New York Stock Exchange (NYSE) then, unsuccessfully, sought to have

33. 62 F. Supp. at 609.

34. In the Matter of Federal Corp., 25 S.E.C. 227 (1947).

35. In the Matter of Federal Corp., 25 S.E.C. 227, 230, n.6 (1947).

36. Thornton v. SEC, 171 F.2d 702 (2d Cir. 1948).

37. 171 F.2d at 703.

38. 171 F.2d at 703. *See also*, In the Matter of Batterman, 46 S.E.C. 304 (1976) (in a consent order the SEC stated that "'the finding of manipulative purpose must be based on inferences drawn from circumstantial evidence.' This inference of manipulative purpose is justified where a person with a financial interest in raising or depressing the price of a security engages in the type of market activity proscribed by Sections 9(a) (1) and (2)"); In the Matter of Richards, 4 S.E.C. 743, 745-746 (1939) (actual knowledge is not required to show a violation of Section 9 when respondent had "reason to believe" that a manipulation was underway and claimed that traders were just testing the market when they entered matched orders).

39. *Norris & Hirshberg v. Securities & Exchange Commission*, 177 F.2d 228 (D.C. Cir. 1949).

Congress curb the power of the Federal Reserve Board to set margin limits. The president of the NYSE, Emil Schram, contended that the increase in margins had pushed speculators out of the stock markets into commodity futures and real estate.[40] The commodity exchanges were indeed experiencing record volumes, and wholesale prices rose by some 45 percent between June 1946 and December 1947.[41]

The easing of price controls at the end of World War II caused problems at the Chicago Board of Trade (CBOT) for contracts in grain and other commodities. The government substantially raised ceiling prices on grain in May 1946, and the CBOT acted to control trading and settlement prices in the affected futures contracts. The CBOT's action caused a loss of profits for long positions, which had become quite valuable after the controls were lifted, but the Seventh Circuit rejected challenges to the CBOT's actions.[42]

A large rise in cotton prices after the removal of the price ceilings was followed by a collapse that "constituted one of the most rapid and extensive price movements in the history of the cotton markets."[43] The secretary of agriculture asserted that the price "boom in cotton in the summer of 1946 and the subsequent collapse in October, when prices dropped approximately 8 cents a pound, or $40 a bale just at the height of the cotton-marketing season, . . . was accelerated by the forced liquidation of two large speculative accounts."[44] One of the large traders that was liquidated was Thomas Jordan, "the leading individual cotton trader in the world."[45] Jordan had been up by $10 million as cotton prices rose, but those profits evaporated in the market downturn. Jordan ended up losing $5 million.[46] Commodity markets then crashed worldwide, and the cotton exchanges in the United States in New York, Chicago, and New Orleans were temporarily closed.[47]

The Commodity Exchange Authority (CEA) found that the collapse in cotton prices was accentuated by the liquidation of thinly margined speculative accounts and unwarranted extensions of credit to speculative traders. Some one-third of the traders in the market were liquidated when prices dropped. The CEA asserted that low exchange margin requirements had enticed into the market small speculators that did not have the capital to maintain their positions when the market dropped.[48]

Echoing the concerns of the NYSE, the CEA complained that the increase in speculative activity in the cotton market occurred after the Federal Reserve Board increased margins on securities to 100 percent in January 1946, thereby driving speculators out of the stock markets and into the commodity exchanges. After the collapse of the cotton market, Chester Bowles, the head of the Office of Price Administration, required margins on cotton futures to be increased to $50 per bale, up from the $5 to $15 per bale margin requirements previously required by the commodity exchanges.[49]

---

40. II Jerry W. Markham, A Financial History of the United States, From J.P. Morgan to the Institutional Investor (1900-1970) 270-271 (2002).

41. *Id.*

42. Cargill Inc. v. Board of Trade, 164 F.2d 820 (7th Cir. 1947), *cert. denied*, 333 U.S. 880 (1948); Daniel v. Board of Trade, 164 F.2d 815 (7th Cir. 1947).

43. Commodity Exchange Authority, *Collapse in Cotton Prices*, at 1 (Oct. 1946).

44. *Margin Requirements on Commodity Exchanges, Hearings Before the Senate Comm. on Agriculture and Forestry on 501881.* 80th Cong., 2d Sess. 3 (1948).

45. Frances Frank Marcus, *Thomas Jordan, 90; Was Once Powerful in the Cotton Market*, New York Times, March 31, 1993.

46. *Tom Jordan Starts Panic in Cotton Market*, Life, Nov. 4, 1946, at 42.

47. II Jerry W. Markham, A Financial History of the United States, From J.P. Morgan to the Institutional Investor (1900-1970) 271 (2002).

48. Jerry W. Markham, *Federal Regulation of Margin in the Commodity Futures Industry: History and Theory*, 64 Temp. L. Rev. 59, 73 (1991).

49. II Jerry W. Markham, A Financial History of the United States, From J.P. Morgan to the Institutional Investor (1900-1970) 271 (2002).

The secretary of agriculture stated with respect to the October 1946 break in cotton prices,

> It appears that the only way to prevent a price debacle following advances induced by over speculation is to curb the speculative urge before it reaches the danger point. The only feasible means of doing this is through quick and somewhat arbitrary action in raising margins on speculative positions. It is believed that this could be done without serious loss of market liquidity necessary to facilitate hedging. It is doubtful whether the commodity exchanges can or will exercise margin control in such a manner as to be effective in curbing speculative excesses. Such action necessarily means a loss of commissions and income to brokerage houses. . . . The Federal Reserve Board is authorized to fix margins governing trading in securities and this power has been exercised to curb excessive speculation on the stock exchanges. No such authority is provided for in existing laws applicable to trading in commodities.[50]

The CEA was also concerned with the disparity in margin requirements set by the cotton exchanges. At one point, margin requirements on the CBOT ranged from one-half to one-third of those required by other exchanges, and volume on the CBOT increased tremendously in relation to those other exchanges. The CEA also found that many of the traders attracted to the CBOT by low margins remained with that exchange after margins were equalized among the other cotton exchanges.[51]

The CEA's concerns were extended to the wheat market because speculators had been attracted to that market by margin requirements of only 8 to 12 percent of the notional value of their futures contracts. On March 13, 1947, the secretary of agriculture called for corrective measures to curb speculative excesses. The CEA also asked the exchanges to increase margins on speculative accounts to a minimum of 25 percent. Two exchanges agreed to the CEA's request, and prices declined. However, the CEA found that the effect of the margin increase was largely nullified when the exchanges reduced their margin requirements in May 1947.[52]

A large number of speculators flowed into the Chicago markets as prices began rising in May and June 1947, corn being a particularly attractive speculation. On September 15, 1947, the CEA requested that the commodity exchanges raise their margin requirements to a third of the contract notional values in order to prevent a speculative boom and bust. This would have nearly doubled existing margins, but the exchanges balked and raised their margins only slightly.

The issue was then referred to President Harry Truman. On October 5, 1947, in the first ever televised broadcast from the White House, Truman stated:

> Another factor that contributes to the high prices of food is gambling in grain. Grain prices naturally respond to the law of supply and demand, but they should not be subject to the greed of speculators who gamble on what may lie ahead in our commodity markets.
>
> There is a place for legitimate trading in futures and for hedging transactions. But 90 percent of all accounts in a recent corn futures market were found to be speculative. Trading in wheat futures grew 75 percent in September compared with August. Normal trading in wheat at Chicago should amount to 3 or 4 million bushels a day. In this past September,

---

50. Commodity Exchange Authority, *Report of the Administrator of the Commodity Exchange Authority* 4 (1947) (quoting letter from Clinton P. Anderson, Secretary of Agriculture, to Congress (Mar. 26, 1947).

51. Jerry W. Markham, *Federal Regulation of Margin in the Commodity Futures Industry: History and Theory*, 64 Temp. L. Rev. 59, 74 (1991).

52. *Id.* at 59, 75 (1991).

> however, trading averaged almost 30 million bushels a day. In a single month, on one exchange, almost half the year's crop was traded—bought and sold—just plain gambling.
>
> I am instructing the Commodity Exchange Commission, which consists of the Attorney General and the Secretaries of Agriculture and Commerce, to demand of the grain exchanges that they increase their margin requirements to at least 33 1/3 percent. If the grain exchanges refuse, the Government may find it necessary to limit the amount of trading.
>
> I say this because the cost of living in this country must not be a football to be kicked about by gamblers in grain.[53]

The exchanges backed down and increased their margins.

The Truman administration further attacked commodity speculators by blaming them for inflated commodity prices. "President Truman picked out inflation's villain. The villain was the commodity speculator. Harry Truman said that gamblers in grain were making the cost of living their football. Attorney General Tom Clark said that speculators were 'profiteering in human misery.'"[54] Secretary of Agriculture Clinton P. Anderson asked Congress for legislation that would let him set futures margins and asked that such authority be extended over commodities not then regulated, such as cocoa, coffee, and sugar.[55]

A counterattack was launched by a Truman opponent, Harold Stassen, a former Minnesota governor and perennial presidential candidate. Stassen claimed that Truman administration officials were themselves trading on government inside information about commodities. For example, Stassen charged that Ed Pauley, a Truman adviser and Department of Defense official, had made some $1 million by speculating in commodity prices over the prior three years. Stassen also said that Pauley made a quick profit on a commodity trade while he was entertaining the secretary of agriculture, Clinton Anderson, at Pauley's resort in Hawaii. Robert Hannegan, a politician who had headed the Democratic National Committee for President Truman, was also in attendance.[56]

Pauley resigned from the government as the scandal widened.[57] Pauley later defended his trading in an oral history interview:

> Well, of course, being a grain speculator was not a new role for me. I have been a speculator in real estate, commodities, stocks, bonds, etc. When I took the job with [Secretary of the Army] Royall I told him of my heavy, long position in all kinds of commodities, grains, wools, lard, and most everything, and I had been doing rather well in my activities. Some people call it grain speculation, other people say "your investment in the farmers' future." It all means the same thing, and people who regard speculation as being a horrible thing haven't paid careful attention to the economics of the thing, because you actually do the

---

53. American Presidency Project: *Harry S. Truman: Radio and Television Address Concluding a Program by the Citizens Food Committee,* http://www.presidency.ucsb.edu/ws/index.php?pid=12766#ixzz1gEd50bQZ (accessed December 11, 2011). President Truman had other reasons for disliking the commodity exchanges. His father had become wealthy from trading on the Kansas City Board of Trade but lost big in one speculation in 1901. As a result, President Truman had to forgo college and his piano lessons. Jerry W. Markham, A History of Commodity Futures Trading and Its Regulation 6 (1987).

54. *Investigations: The Good Old American Way*, Time, Dec. 22, 1947.

55. *Anti-Inflation Program as Recommended in the President's Message of November 17, 1947: Hearings Before the Joint Committee on the Economic Report*, 80th Cong. 2-3 (1947).

56. *Speculation in Commodity Markets: Hearings Before a Subcommittee of the Senate Committee on Appropriations*, 80th Cong., 2d Sess. 4 (1948).

57. *Pauley Will Quit Army Post, Graham Tells of Trading Gain,* New York Times, Jan. 14, 1948, at 1, 5.

> farmer, the producer, a great favor when you buy his material today that he won't be able to deliver for a year. You have assured him of his market. He can go out and borrow, do his farming, increase his crops, and so forth. That's the way I describe my activity in the matter. The mere fact that you do this on the open market creates the feeling that you're doing it as a speculator, and that speculation in, say, commodities is wrong. It's not true, otherwise, they should completely outlaw it. It's a major function that serves the farmer and the consumer well.[58]

President Truman's personal physician, General Wallace Graham, was also found to have been speculating in commodities. Graham "was listed as having market commitments covering 50,000 bushels of wheat during September (when Government purchases were heavy and grain prices were zooming)."[59] Graham initially claimed that he was unaware that his broker had purchased the wheat contracts for his account, but his broker said Graham had been kept fully informed of dealings in the account.[60] Graham also claimed that he had "lost his socks" in the investment.[61] However, it was later determined that he had made a profit of more than 100 percent ($6,000) on his speculation.[62]

Graham corrected his earlier story on the trades but still claimed that the trades were made on the advice of his broker and undertaken in order to recoup losses he had experienced in the stock market.[63] Graham admitted that, despite his prior claims otherwise, he continued to speculate in commodities after the president's denunciation of speculators on October 5, 1947. Graham did not close out his trading until the day before President Truman signed a congressional resolution authorizing the disclosure of the names of speculators in the commodity markets.[64]

The Chicago wheat market raised concerns over manipulation in February and March 1948.[65] The secretary of agriculture reported that on February 4, 1948, at a time when a sharp break in wheat prices was occurring, E.T. Maynard, a floor trader in Chicago, sold short approximately 1 million bushels of July wheat and made a profit of as much as $400,000. Maynard had also adroitly ridden the oat market up and down.[66] The secretary rejected speculation that Maynard had traded on inside information.[67] The Senate also exonerated Maynard of wrongdoing and closed an investigation into whether Senator Elmer Thomas (D-OK) had traded in commodities on the basis of inside information.[68]

Secretary of Agriculture Clinton P. Anderson renewed his request for legislation that would let him set futures margins and asked again that such authority be extended over commodities not then regulated, such as cocoa, coffee, and sugar.[69] However, he was under attack by various

58. *Oral Interview with Edwin W. Pauley*, Los Angeles, March 1971, Harry S. Truman Library, pp. 93-94, http://www.trumanlibrary.org/oralhist/pauleye.htm.

59. *Investigations: Target in the White House*, TIME MAGAZINE, Jan. 5, 1948.

60. *The Nation*, NEW YORK TIMES, Jan. 4, 1948, at E2.

61. *$4,000,000 Profits Made by 'Insiders,' Stassen Testifies*, NEW YORK TIMES, Jan. 10, 1948, at 1, 9.

62. II JERRY W. MARKHAM, A FINANCIAL HISTORY OF THE UNITED STATES, FROM J.P. MORGAN TO THE INSTITUTIONAL INVESTOR (1900-1970) 272 (2002).

63. *Graham Admits Making Money in the Market*, ST. PETERSBURG TIMES, Jan. 14, 1948, at 2.

64. *Pauley Will Quit Army Post, Graham Tells of Trading Gain*, NEW YORK TIMES, Jan. 14, 1948, at 1, 5.

65. Jerry W. Markham, *Manipulation of Commodity Futures Prices: The Unprosecutable Crime*, 8 YALE J. ON REG. 281, 316 (1991).

66. *Margin Requirements on Commodity Exchanges: Hearings Before the Senate Comm. on Agriculture and Forestry on 501881.* 80th Cong. 2d Sess. 5-6 (1948).

67. *Big Grain Profit Is Listed*, NEW YORK TIMES, Feb. 12, 1948, at 5.

68. *Maynard Cleared in 'Short' Trading*, NEW YORK TIMES, Feb. 17, 1948, at 15.

69. *Margin Requirements on Commodity Exchanges: Hearings Before the Senate Committee on Agriculture and Forestry*, 80th Cong., 2d Sess. 2 (1948).

members of Congress who blamed the administration for allowing grain prices to fall by curbing government purchases. Senator Wilbert L. ("Pappy") O'Daniel called for Anderson's resignation. He also demanded that "this New Deal gang take its filthy fingers out of the wheat pit," a comment that set off a row in the Senate.[70] In the event, more volatility was introduced into the commodity markets at the end of February 1948 when Secretary Anderson announced that the government would be resuming its buying operations.[71]

The Pauley and Graham commodity trading scandal was swept up into the presidential election in 1948. Republican candidate Thomas E. Dewey insisted that if he were elected "there would be no place in his Administration, 'high or low' for anyone who would speculate in grain or any other commodity 'at the price of human misery'"; he promised to bring to the Capital "men and women of integrity whose first interest is not self-interest; whose aim is not to help themselves but to help America."[72] Truman responded by blaming inflation on speculation; his anti-inflation program included a demand for congressional action to regulate commodities speculation. He also attacked, as noted by one historian, "Republican bloodsuckers on Wall Street who are going to stick a pitch fork in the back of every farmer."[73]

The sharp rise in commodity prices and speculation by government officials and foreign traders resulted in the creation of a select committee of Congress that investigated commodity trading and rendered four reports in 1948.[74] The select committee found that the "export of nearly 1,200,000,000 bushels of wheat and other grains from the United States between July 1, 1946, and June 30, 1948, was the controlling factor which caused scarcity and higher prices for grains and feed for livestock."[75] Virtually, all of those exports were conducted under the Marshall Plan for the relief of Europe.[76]

The select committee could find no conclusive evidence that government employees had traded on inside information concerning the government's commodity purchasing programs, but there was some very suspicious activity. The Department of Agriculture published the names of more than 800 government employees who had speculated in commodity futures.[77] "Considering profits and losses of the 823 employees engaged in speculative commodity trading, a conservative estimate would place the net profit from $10,000,000 to $20,000,000."[78] This activity was at odds with an executive order issued by President Franklin Roosevelt that prohibited federal employees from speculating in stocks and commodities.[79]

Some of the trading by government employees was truly astonishing:

> A female clerk in the Navy Department speculated in 1,785,000 bushels of wheat, 285,000 bushels of corn, 720,000 bushels of oats, 50,000 bushels of rye, 270,000 pounds of lard, 1,500,000 pounds of cottonseed oil, 35,500 bales of cotton, and 48 carloads of eggs. Based

70. William S. White, *Power to Fix Grain Margins Is Asked by the Government*, NEW YORK TIMES, Feb. 12, 1948, at 1, 5.

71. John G. Forrest, *The Financial Week*, NEW YORK TIMES, March 7, 1948, at F1.

72. *Dewy Puts Blame for Soaring Prices on Administration*, NEW YORK TIMES, Sept. 26, 1948, at 1.

73. DAVID PIETRUSZA, 1948, 285, 345 (2011).

74. H.R. Rep. No. 2472, 80th Cong., 2d Sess. (1948); H.R. Rep. No. 2025, 80th Cong., 1st Sess. (1948); H.R. Rep. No. 2449, 80th Cong., 2nd Sess. (1948); H.R. Rep. No. 2462, 80th Cong., 2nd Sess. (1948).

75. H.R. Rep. No. 2462, 80th Cong., 2nd Sess. 2 (1948).

76. *Id.* at 3.

77. H.R. Rep. No. 2449, 80th Cong., 2nd Sess. 3 (1948).

78. H.R. Rep. No. 2472, 80th Cong., 2d Sess. 11 (1948).

79. *Speculation in Commodity Markets: Hearings Before a Subcommittee of the Senate Committee on Appropriations*, 80th Cong., 2d Sess. 12 (1948).

> upon the actual price paid for these commodities, the value of the contracts traded in by this employee, whose salary was about $3,300 per annum was approximately $10,311,990. It is estimated that this employee realized substantial profits.
>
> An appointive official, who served first as Deputy Petroleum Administrator and later as Assistant to the Secretary of the Army, traded in 450,000 bushels of wheat, 700,000 bushels of corn, 1,940,000 bushels of oats, 50,000 bushels of barley, 500,000 pounds of lard, 300,000 pounds of cotton seed oil, and 1,000 bales of cotton. It should be noted here that this official apparently exercised certain control over the separate accounts of at least four members of his family who engaged in comparable extensive speculative operations on commodity markets.
>
> An employee of the Interior Department who served as Petroleum Coordinator traded in 200,000 bushels of wheat, 325,000 bushels of corn, 1,050,000 bushels of oats, 300,000 pounds of cottonseed oil, 5 carloads of eggs, and 1,000 bales of cotton.
>
> The wife of an attorney in the General Accounting Office traded in 110,000 bushels of wheat, 270,000 bushels of corn, 380,000 bushels of oats, 1,050,000 pounds of lard, and 1,800 bales of cotton.
>
> An employee of the Bureau of Internal Revenue of the Treasury Department traded in 73,000 bushels of wheat, 161,000 bushels of corn, 163,000 bushels of oats, and 151,000 bushels of rye.
>
> An officer of the United States Army, together with members of his family traded in 380,000 bushels of wheat, 455,000 bushels of corn, 2,220,000 bushels of oats, 40,000 bushels of rye, 400,000 pounds of lard, 8,100 bales of cotton, and 93 carloads of eggs.[80]

There were separate claims that Senator Joseph McCarthy of Wisconsin was using campaign funds to speculate in soybeans. Senators Albert Chandler of Kentucky, Scott Lucas of Illinois, and Wilbert O'Daniel of Texas were also reported to be speculating in grain.[81]

The select committee found that commodity futures speculation had reached a tremendous volume in 1947. It concluded that speculators had "developed highly complex techniques for concealing the nature of their buying and selling activities and the sources of information upon which they conducted their operations." The select committee urged Congress to monitor the futures exchanges and, if necessary, "enact legislation to eliminate rigging and manipulation on the exchanges."[82]

The president's demand for margin increases was an effort to impose federal control over commodity futures margins, but there was no authority to do so in the Commodity Exchange Act. The CEA considered margin increases more effective than position limits because, as a CEA witness testified before Congress, trading limits could not be made low enough to exclude unwanted small and thinly capitalized speculators without impairing the speculative trading needed to provide liquidity for hedging.[83]

The commodity exchanges raised their margin requirements to satisfy the president, but their action did not have the effect sought by the government. Although the volume of speculative trading in wheat and corn on the exchanges declined sharply, the prices of those commodities continued to climb dramatically.[84] A later economic study of the effect of those increases con-

80. H.R. Rep. No. 2472, 80th Cong., 2d Sess. 11 (1948).

81. II Jerry W. Markham, A Financial History of the United States, From J.P. Morgan to the Institutional Investor (1900-1970) 286 (2002).

82. H.R. Rep. No. 2472, 80th Cong., 2d Sess. 16-17 (1948).

83. *House Banking and Currency Committee Hearings*, 80th Cong., 1st Sess. 324, 325 (1947).

84. Jerry W. Markham, *Federal Regulation of Margin in the Commodity Futures Industry: History and Theory*, 64 Temp. L. Rev. 59, 75 (1991).

cluded that the "results are consistent with a significant decline in market performance" and that "informational efficiency" was "significantly poorer during the entire period of super margins."[85] *Barron's* magazine also questioned the efficacy of the margin increases.[86]

The secretary of agriculture, Clinton P. Anderson, contended that "immediately following establishment of the 33-percent margin rate, the average daily trading in wheat on the Chicago Board of Trade was reduced by 45 percent, from 26,985,000 bushels in the 30 trading days preceding the margin increase to 14,933,000 bushels in the subsequent 30 trading days." He further claimed that volatility in price fluctuations was reduced.[87] With respect to that claim, the CBOT had a different view, which it set forth in a letter to President Truman:

> At your request, the Chicago Board of Trade increased margins to 33 1/3% on new speculative futures transactions. You will recall we stated at that time such action was taken reluctantly believing it would have the effect of accelerating the trend of the market by impairing the volume of trade and in consequence the liquidity of the market to the extent that hedging operations would be handicapped resulting in serious injury to grain farmers, processors, merchandisers, and consumers.
>
> We feel it our duty to call to your attention that these higher margins have caused a contraction of the open interest, consequently the market then as well as now was robbed of much of its liquidity. These factors confirm the feeling of reluctance we expressed when we acceded to your request to increase margins last October, due to the lack of adequate hedging possibilities farmers are being unduly penalized by not being able to sell their grain at country elevators because of the three past successive days markets at various times have dropped the full permissible trading limits, resulting in insufficient buying power to absorb any additional hedges.[88]

The CBOT was of the view that "[m]argins serve no other purpose than to guarantee the sanctity and performance of the contract. They must never be used for any other purpose by anyone."[89]

The Department of Agriculture continued to press for legislation that would authorize the government to set margin requirements. In 1948 Congress held hearings on a bill that would have

---

85. Anne E. Peck and Carlos C. Budge, *The Effects of Extraordinary Speculative Margins in the 1947–48 Grain Futures Markets,* 20 FOOD RESEARCH INSTITUTE STUDIES 179 (1987).

86. Jerry W. Markham, *Federal Regulation of Margin in the Commodity Futures Industry: History and Theory*, 64 TEMP. L. REV. 59, 75 (1991). One author stated:

> The absence of federal margin requirements has to a large extent been made a scapegoat for food and other commodity price increases. Actually, these are chiefly the product of inflationary conditions connected with the present national emergency and crop outlook. Price trends of 1947–1948 under the 33 1/3% margins clearly indicate that increased margin requirements will not nullify the effects of these fundamental supply and demand factors. Efforts to control prices should therefore be aimed directly at these underlying factors, while margin controls should be restricted to their proper function of reducing price fluctuations which do not reflect basic market conditions.

Note, *Federal Regulation of Commodity Futures Trading*, 60 YALE L. J. 846-847 (1951).

87. *Margin Requirements on Commodity Exchanges: Hearings Before the Senate Comm. on Agriculture and Forestry on 501881.* 80th Cong. 2d Sess. 4 (1948).

88. *Id.* at 22.

89. *Id.* at 21.

authorized the secretary to set margin requirements whenever the speculation was threatening "sudden or unreasonable fluctuations or unwarranted changes in the price of any commodities."[90] The government asserted that such legislation would restrain excessive speculation, keep small speculators from entering the market during price booms, and deter massive short selling in periods of falling prices.[91]

Secretary Anderson testified in the hearings on this legislation that speculators were attracted to the futures markets by factors "having little or no connection with the marketing of agricultural commodities. Such bursts of speculative fever make price fluctuations more erratic and unstable. The ultimate end of such speculative booms is sudden collapse and disorderly price movements." Secretary Anderson further stated that it was "the Department's belief that regulation of margin is an effective means of restraining undue speculative activity."[92]

The secretary of agriculture was also concerned that the boom in the commodity prices had drawn small speculators from the real estate and stock markets, with disastrous results. He pointed out that the stock markets had been relatively calm and stable since the imposition of high margin requirements by the Federal Reserve Board.[93] One senator noted, however, that volume on the NYSE on the previous day had been nearly 1.5 million shares despite a margin requirement of 75 percent[94] (trading volume had been about 10 million shares per day in 1928).[95]

The futures industry fought the USDA margin proposal and prevailed. Opponents contended that government control over margins would destroy the commodity markets. This destruction would be caused by the uncertainty created by fears that the government could raise margins, force liquidations, and rob the market of liquidity.[96] An exchange witness also warned that the government actually wanted to use margins to control market prices.[97] Another witness pointed out that margin for stocks was not comparable to those used in the futures industry:

> When you or I buy stock we get the stock. That is, it is delivered to us within 72 hours. If you or I should buy cotton or wheat futures for May delivery, there can be no delivery until May and you in effect are putting up a margin to guarantee that you will take that wheat or cotton during May when it is tendered to you. You have nothing other than a credit established by the depositing of margins on the commodities. . . . A stock or bond in the bank box is good collateral. A contract for cotton or wheat is nothing other than just an agreement to buy or to sell.[98]

Another witness, Darwin S. Fenner, testified as to the importance of speculation to society:

> Speculation is as old as mankind. In essence it is the acceptance of calculated risks in the hope of gain—sometimes material gain, sometimes more intangible rewards such as fame, or glory. Were it not for the courageous individuals who were willing to accept these dangers,

90. *Id.* at 2.
91. *Id.* at 4.
92. *Id.* at 3, 4.
93. *Id.* at 20, 43-44.
94. *Id.* at 53 (remarks of Sen. Lucas).
95. II Jerry W. Markham, A Financial History of the United States, From J.P. Morgan to the Institutional Investor (1900-1970) 149 (2002).
96. *Margin Requirements on Commodity Exchanges: Hearings Before the Senate Comm. on Agriculture and Forestry on 501881.* 80th Cong. 2d Sess. 38 (1948).
97. *Id.* at 104.
98. *Id.* at 53-54.

> the progress of the world might have been delayed for centuries. Columbus was a speculator, willing to hazard life to prove the correctness of his calculations that the earth was round. His reward was eternal fame. Queen Isabella likewise speculated when she financed Columbus's voyage, and history has very properly accorded her a large share of credit for the discovery of the new world. In more recent time the Wright brothers staked their lives and money to prove that man could fly—and a new age of transportation was born. In less spectacular fields, the development of practically all of our modern inventions—the railroads, the telegraph, the telephone, the radio, [was due to] the willingness of speculators to invest their money in new ideas, but because they had the courage to risk their capital their success resulted in substantial rewards. . . . No one can deny that speculators have contributed to the progress of the world and that the credit should be divided between them and the creators of the ideas.
>
> Another class of speculator is one who trades in commodities. It is he who absorbs the surplus of selling during the marketing season when sales by the farmers exceed purchases by the mills, and furnishes the contracts to the trade when mills are fixing prices against their sale of goods. He has a definite place in the economy, for it is he who makes possible the efficient operation of our marketing systems. . . .
>
> If the margin required becomes disproportionately high compared to the potential profit, the small speculators will lose interest and be driven out of the market. Without the constant flow of buying and selling orders, which establish the price of cotton every moment during the day, the market will degenerate into a thin, hollow affair with long intervals and wide variations between quotations.[99]

The chair of the CBOT, Richard F. Uhlmann, testified that speculators are a "blessing" in absorbing market risks.[100] He also pointed out the difference between gambling and speculation:

> A gambler who shakes dice or bets on a horse race creates his own risk voluntarily and he stands to win or lose all on the outcome. He is not performing any economic service since he is not assuming any economic risk which someone else desires to shift. But bear this in mind, speculation has its legitimate place and it is just as common as investments.
>
> Speculation assumes that the economic risk cannot be abolished and through the forecasting of the exchanges assuming the risk involved, the person in the market hopes to derive some benefit therefrom.[101]

The effort to defeat that legislation succeeded, but Congress did pass a resolution requiring the disclosure of the names of large traders (both speculators and hedgers) in the commodity futures markets. Their names were published in the *New York Times* in December 1948.[102]

The CEA reported that a sharp drop in grain prices in February 1949 was accentuated by the liquidations of a large number of small traders whose positions were concentrated on the long side of the market.[103] A study published by the CEA found that most small speculators in grain futures

---

99. *Id.* at 82, 88.

100. *Id.* at. 206.

101. *Id.* at 199.

102. *The List of Major Traders on Commodity Exchanges Made Public by Secretary Anderson*, New York Times, Dec. 23, 1948, at 16.

103. Jerry W. Markham, *Federal Regulation of Margin in the Commodity Futures Industry: History and Theory*, 64 Temp. L. Rev. 59, 76-77 (1991).

were on the long side of the market. Most of those traders lost money at a ratio of losses to profits of 6 to 1, which was attributed to those traders' reluctance to close out losing positions.[104]

Problems continued with a break in grain prices in February 1949, and one in wool tops on March 16 and 17, 1949.[105] A bill was introduced in Congress that would have defined the term "manipulate" in the Commodity Exchange Act to "mean to cause or maintain an artificial price by planned action."[106] That legislation was not passed.

3:3 POSTWAR COMMODITY MANIPULATION CASES

The CEA lost the political battles over margin regulation but was more successful in cases brought against traders believed to be involved in manipulations. The CEA charged in *In re Zenith-Godley Co.*[107] that a broker acting on behalf of the Dairyman's League Cooperative Association Inc. manipulated the price of butter in 1947 on the New York Mercantile Exchange (NYMEX). That manipulation was done in order to support the price of fluid milk, which, under the Agricultural Marketing Act, was based on prices paid for Grade A butter on the NYMEX. The Dairyman's League bought 97 percent of the Grade A butter sold on the NYMEX during a five-day period. The increase in prices in New York during this period caused butter to be diverted from the Chicago market to New York. Proof of manipulation was also offered in the form of a press release by the Dairyman's League boasting of the success of its operation.[108]

An administrative judicial officer found the respondent guilty of manipulation and rejected claims that the Commodity Exchange Act did not apply to cash or spot transactions. It was also found that the respondent acted willfully because it "intended the acts to have results which they in fact did have." However, mitigating circumstances were found in that the president of Zenith-Godley "may have been led to believe by his principals that no irregularity on his part would be involved in making such purchases"; severe sanctions were not imposed. The Dairyman's League and certain of its officers also pleaded guilty to criminal violations of the Commodity Exchange Act for manipulating butter prices and were fined $29,000.[109] A massive manipulation of a similar ilk would occur in the twenty-first century and is described in Chapter 6.

In *Great Western Food Distributors Inc. v. Brannan*,[110] the Seventh Circuit affirmed the decision of a CEA administrative judicial officer, which held that respondents cornered and attempted to manipulate the egg market on the Chicago Mercantile Exchange in December 1947.[111] The trading privileges of three respondents were suspended for a year. On appeal, the Seventh Circuit held that, "[g]enerally speaking, a corner is an executed plan of manipulation of prices of a given

104. Blair Stewart, *An Analysis of Speculative Trading in Grain Futures*, Commodity Exchange Authority Technical Bulletin No. 1001, at 129 (Oct. 1949).

105. Jerry W. Markham, *Manipulation of Commodity Futures Prices: The Unprosecutable Crime*, 8 YALE J. ON REG. 281, 317 (1991).

106. H.R. 4685, 81 1st Cong., Sess. § 1 (1949).

107. In re Zenith-Godley Co., 6 Agric. Dec. 900 (1947).

108. Congress was concerned with manipulation of butter prices during the debates on the bills that became the Commodity Exchange Act of 1936, including a "terrific 1-day smash" that drove butter prices down four cents, "which meant thousands of dollars in lower returns to every dairy farmer in the country on the following day when he was delivering his butterfat to his local creamery." 80 Cong. Rec. 7919 (1936). Land-O-Lakes was also claimed to have used federal funds to manipulate butter prices. 79 Cong. Rec. 8594–95 (1935).

109. *Agriculture Department Accuses Broker of Manipulating Prices of Spot Butter Here*, NEW YORK TIMES, Feb. 11, 1947, at 44.

110. Great Western Food Distributors v. Brannan, 201 F.2d 476 (7th Cir.). *cert. denied*, 345 U.S. 997 (1973).

111. The CEA had charged:

commodity whereby a trader or group of traders gains control of the supply or the future demand of a commodity and requires the shorts to settle their obligations, either by the purchase of deliverable quantities of the supply or offsetting long contracts, at an arbitrary, abnormal and dictated price imposed by the cornerer."[112]

The court further asserted that a corner "may be effected by creation of an artificial demand through purchases of long contracts in excess of the known deliverable supply, or by the purchase of all of the available cash supply; or by a combination of both, as charged in this complaint."[113] The court held that "the intent of the parties during their trading is a determinative element of a punishable corner. Unintentional corners can develop and should not carry the pain of forfeiture of trading privileges."[114]

The court in *Great Western* also evaluated the nature of the expected proof in manipulation cases. It stated that "the technical and complex nature of the charges made necessitated recourse to extensive use of expert testimony, for here, as is often the case in proceedings under regulatory statutes, the evidence is largely of a dual nature: statistical and parol interpretation of the statistics."[115] This conclusion signaled that manipulation cases would be complicated affairs.[116] They would be fought through a battle of the experts over the interpretation of complicated trading data and economic fundamentals and how particular and often equally complex trading strategies fit into those structures.

The facts in *Great Western* underscored this complexity. In order to determine if the respondents cornered the egg market, the amount of deliverable supplies had to be determined and then compared with the amount held by respondents. The CEA wanted to narrow the available supply figures for eggs to aid its proof, while respondents wanted to expand that amount to make its holdings look proportionally smaller. The Seventh Circuit held that fresh eggs were properly excluded from available deliverable supplies because they customarily ranged higher in price

---

> During November and December 1947, the corporate petitioner purchased and held large quantities of December 1947 egg futures on the Chicago Mercantile Exchange, thereby establishing a dominant and controlling "long" position in such futures, which it maintained and strengthened as the close of trading in such futures approached. Coincidentally, it purchased and held large quantities of "cash" eggs, which were deliverable on December futures contracts and, in addition, stood for and received delivery of substantially all of the remaining eggs deliverable in satisfaction of December futures. Thus, by these purchases and deliveries, it was charged that it obtained possession and control of the supply of deliverable eggs in the Chicago and surrounding areas. These eggs were then offered for sale only at prices which made it unduly costly for shorts to purchase them for delivery, with the consequence that the latter were compelled to cover their sales by the purchase of futures at prices fixed by respondent. Thus, the government charged, respondent attained a position whereby it could and did, demand such prices as it saw fit for "cash" eggs and December futures from persons who had sold such futures and were obligated to deliver eggs or purchase futures in order to perform their contracts. The complaint further averred that these transactions were . . . undertaken for the purpose and with the intent of widening the difference between the price of December 1947 and January 1949 egg future contracts, and increasing or preventing a decrease in the price of eggs deliverable in satisfaction of December futures contracts.

201 F.2d at 478.

112. 201 F.2d at 478.

113. 201 F.2d at 478-479 (citations omitted).

114. 201 F.2d at 479 (citation omitted).

115. 201 F.2d at 479.

116. *See,* Comment, *Manipulation of Commodity Futures Prices: The Great Western Case*, 21 U. Chi. L. Rev. 94 (1953-1954) (discussing this case and the definition of manipulation).

than refrigerated eggs and the shorts were given no premium for their delivery. "Consequently, while they were deliverable, fresh eggs were generally not contemplated as part of the supply for these futures transactions. Therefore, we think, they were properly excluded from consideration as part of the available supply."[117] Out-of-town refrigerator eggs were also excluded from available deliverable supplies because the shorts were required by exchange rules to pay a premium of $315 per carload if used for delivery.

The court in *Great Western* found that the respondents were in a position to dictate prices because the shorts were forced to purchase refrigerated eggs from the respondents in order to meet their delivery obligations. The evidence on whether the respondents had in fact dictated abnormal prices required a complicated comparison of trading prices in prior years and among different delivery months for eggs. The court rejected the government's evidence on this issue in part.[118]

The Seventh Circuit did find support for abnormal prices in other evidence offered by the government with respect to the "spread" between December 1947 and January 1948 futures. The government used statistics showing the historical nature of those spreads, but this set off a fight over whether statistics for trading during the war should be excluded because of the effect of price controls on prices and whether prices were unusually affected during the great Depression.[119] The court found that "[t]aking either set of statistics for the years 1932–1948, or employing only the prices during the 1940s, with the proper exclusion of 1944 and 1945, and comparing them with the December–January spread of 1947, it appears that the relationship existent in 1947 was in fact abnormal."[120] The court further found, after another complicated analysis, that price abnormality was established by other evidence on price differences between fresh eggs and refrigerator eggs.[121]

---

117. 201 F.2d at 480.

118. The court found:

> Evidence was introduced by the government tending to show that the supply of refrigerator eggs in December 1947 was higher than it had been in October and November 1947 and in December 1946. Additional proof submitted tended to establish that the real demand, as opposed to technical demand created by a cornering operation, was lower in December 1947 than in the previously mentioned months. Therefore, the government insisted that, by application of the law of supply and demand, the prices of refrigerator eggs in December 1947, and their corresponding futures contracts, should be lower than those in October and November 1947 and December 1946. Next the government asserted that the expected price pattern did not manifest itself in December 1947; that cash refrigerator eggs and futures prices were in fact higher than in the named months; that, if they were not higher, they did not drop to the proper level and thus, were at an abnormal level.
>
> At this point, however, we find what we consider fatal deficiencies in the government's theory. First, we are not provided with the October and November 1947 prices. Thus, nothing exists but the bare assertion that December prices were abnormally high in relation to the preceding months. Secondly, while the record discloses, in quite a different context, that the December 1946 prices were considerably lower than those prevailing in December 1947, this standing alone is inadequate. We are told nothing of the comparative market conditions prevailing in these two years. Certainly a mere dollar and cent comparison, related solely to supply and demand, is not enough. If the market in 1947 was, on the whole, inflated over 1946, surely the 1947 prices could be higher in spite of a decrease in demand and an increase in supply. Therefore, this finding that the prices of refrigerator eggs and their futures were abnormally high in view of the supply and demand situation cannot be said to be sustained by the weight of the evidence.

119. 201 F.2d at 48-483.

120. 201 F.2d at 483.

121. The court found that

Finally, evidence of manipulative intent was found in testimony of a respondent that the trading program at issue was "instituted in hope of a widening spread between December and January prices and that December prices were gradually raised by himself until Great Western was able to liquidate its holdings at an increase in the differential of 4 1/2 to 5 cents. Here then was evidence, from which the inference of intent could be readily drawn."[122]

The CEA prevailed in this case, but the case took almost five years to resolve. It also had little deterrent effect. Great Western Food Distributors was at it again in 1949. Great Western and others pleaded nolo contendere to criminal charges for attempted manipulation and attempted cornering of the October 1949 egg futures contract in violation of the Commodity Exchange Act. This was one of the few criminal cases brought for manipulation under that statute. A separate criminal information charged Sherman Act violations in connection the November 1949 egg futures contract.[123] Great Western was fined $21,200 for this conduct.[124]

3:4 THE KOREAN WAR AND COMMODITY PRICE CONCERNS

The invasion of South Korea on June 25, 1950, led to speculative trading in the commodity markets of an "almost frenzied character."[125] The secretary of agriculture, Charles F. Brannan, charged that speculation in commodity prices after the Korean invasion was "excessive and unrestrained."[126] An investigation by the CEA in August 1950 found that a group of Chinese traders were engaging in large-scale trading in soybeans and causing price increases. A total of forty-nine Chinese accounts were discovered.[127] Fourteen of the traders were operating through a firm in Hong Kong. The positions in each of the accounts were held at one contract below the level required to be reported to the CEA. In total, the Chinese accounts controlled nearly 7 million bushels of soybeans valued at $22 million, and these accounts took delivery on 2 million bushels.[128]

> the prices of December 1947 futures and refrigerator eggs were abnormally high in relation to the price of fresh eggs at the close of December 1947 trading. This was supported by testimony that, normally, fresh eggs sell at a reasonably constant premium of considerable size over cash refrigerator eggs and refrigerator futures, and that, generally, the prices of cash refrigerator eggs and refrigerator futures will reflect precipitous drops in the prices of fresh eggs. This testimony was corroborated by statistics dealing with these relative prices during the years 1932–1947. These statistics established that the average price of fresh eggs over December refrigerator futures at the close of trading in the future was approximately 4 cents per dozen. The fresh egg premium in 1947 was but .5 cent per dozen. This tended to prove price abnormality in December 1947. Furthermore, during these 14 years, (1942 and 1943 were excluded for want of adequate statistics), whenever a precipitous drop in fresh prices occurred, the refrigerator future reflected it in all instances save six. During the last two weeks of December 1947 trading, the fresh egg prices dropped approximately 7.5 cents per dozen. During that same period the refrigerator futures first dropped 2.25 cents per dozen and then rose about 1 cent per dozen to the point of closing, just .5 cent lower than fresh eggs. This, too, was indicative of price abnormality.

122. 201 F.2d at 483.

123. *Report of the Administrator of the Commodity Exchange Authority* 4 (1952).

124. Commodity Exchange Authority, *Summary of Administrative and Judicial Proceedings Under the Commodity Exchange Act (June 15, 1936–June 30, 1972) and Under the Grain Futures Act (Sept. 21, 1922–June 14, 1936)* 95-96 (circa 1973).

125. Jerry W. Markham, *Manipulation of Commodity Futures Prices: The Unprosecutable Crime*, 8 Yale J. on Reg. 281, 317 (1991).

126. *U.S. Pushing Inquiry in Farm Prices: Soybean Market First in Speculator Hunt*, New York Times, Aug. 8, 1950, at 35.

127. II Jerry W. Markham, A Financial History of the United States, From J.P. Morgan to the Institutional Investor (1900-1970) 286-287 (2002).

128. Jerry W. Markham, A History of Commodity Futures Trading and Its Regulation 43 (1987).

Soybean prices rose from $2.20 to $3.45 per bushel as the Chinese positions were accumulated. No evidence of manipulation was found. Rather, Secretary Brannan called it a "speculative splurge." He blamed the ability of those accounts to trade in such amounts on low margin requirements. The secretary said that it was a "sad commentary" on the futures markets that such traders were "permitted to enter the futures markets at bargain rates, giving momentum to an already highly speculative situation."[129]

In his July 19, 1950, radio address on the nation's response to the invasion, President Truman listed as one of the economic measures needed to fight the war legislation "to curb speculation in agricultural commodities."[130] The bill that became the Defense Production Act of 1950 was introduced in Congress on the same day. That bill contained a provision for the regulation of commodity futures margins under the Commodity Exchange Act, which would have authorized the president to prescribe margins for futures contracts whenever he determined that "the nature or extent of speculative trading on boards of trade causes or threatens to cause sudden or unreasonable fluctuations or unwarranted changes in the price of any commodity."[131]

That provision was approved by the House Banking and Currency Committee but was deleted on the floor. Representative Boggs stated that the use of margins to control price increases has "no foundation in fact."[132] Representative Cooley also argued,

> When you reduce the volume of speculation by the lifting of margins, you drive out of the market the little operator and you play into the hands of the big operator. When you reduce the volume of the little traders on the commodity exchanges, one single transaction may be of such magnitude that it might cause gyrations which otherwise would not occur.[133]

Supporters of government authority over margins asked for and obtained a report from the CEA, which stated that "[s]ince the outbreak of hostilities in Korea there have been substantial increases in speculation in most of the more important commodities in which there is futures trading."[134] That speculation was accompanied by "substantial price increases."[135] The CEA report stated that a speculator purchasing just before the North Korean invasion would have made a profit within five weeks of 450 percent on lard, "300 percent on cottonseed oil, 800 percent on soybeans, 150 percent on cotton or wool tops, and a comparatively modest 100 percent on the relatively sluggish wheat market."[136]

A proponent of federal authority over commodity futures margins stated on the House floor that the "stabilizing effect of adequate margin deposits has been tested for more than 15 years in the security markets and this beneficial effect would undoubtedly apply equally to commodity speculation."[137] The measure was, in any event, deleted from the Defense Production Act bill. A substitute provision that would have required the exchanges to limit excessive speculation at the request of the secretary of agriculture was also deleted after the commodity exchanges agreed

---

129. *Runaway Soybean Market Is Laid to Chinese Traders*, New York Times, Aug. 11, 1950, at 27.

130. Truman Address on Korea, July 19, 1950, http://www.learner.org/workshops/primarysources/coldwar/docs/onkorea.html (accessed December 11, 2011).

131. *Defense Production Act of 1950*, Hearings H.R. 9176 Before the House Committee on Banking and Currency, 81st Cong., 2d Sess. 13 (1950).

132. 96 Cong. Rec. 11,759 (1950).

133. *Id.* at 11,754.

134. *Id.* at 11,755.

135. *Id.*

136. *Id.* at 11,756.

137. *Id.* at 11,758 (remarks of Rep. Buchanan).

to increase their speculative margin requirements for most commodities. After passage of the Defense Production Act of 1950, *sans* margin authority, the commodity exchanges reduced their margin requirements down to their prior levels (and lower in some cases), which ranged from 6 to 15 percent for most commodities.[138]

The Defense Production Act imposed wage and price controls, and ceilings were authorized for agricultural commodities.[139] The legislation also contained a provision prohibiting "hoarding,"[140] which had been borrowed from the World War I Lever Act.[141] In an apparent response to the Truman administration scandals, the Defense Production Act also prohibited government employees from speculating in commodities on exchanges and from disclosing confidential information.

The Office of Price Stabilization was used to set price ceilings, and the Wage Stabilization Board was in charge of ensuring that wages were frozen. One of the strongest advocates of price controls during this period was Senator Hubert Humphrey, who complained of "rigging of the market by processors and middlemen." Humphrey also charged that speculators were pushing up defense costs in wool, tin, and lead by buying up large quantities of those commodities and withholding them from the market in order push up prices.[142]

By the time the Defense Production Act was actually enacted, inflationary pressures had decreased. However, another spike occurred when China entered the war. Voluntary price controls were instituted by the Economic Stabilization Agency in December 1950. That action had little effect, and a mandatory and general price freeze was ordered on all prices on January 26, 1951.[143]

"Under the General Ceiling Price Regulation (GCPR) all prices except certain farm commodities and items specifically exempted by statute were frozen at the highest levels they had reached between December 19 and January 25" of 1951.[144] Congress and the administration declined to roll back agricultural price increases. Instead, an inflated "parity" price was set that "retains the congressional intent that parity be used as a measure of the fair share of the national income which the farmer should receive for his contribution to the mobilization program."[145] This was an example of the always conflicted policy views on prices. Consumers complain when prices increase, while producers are pleased. Conversely, producers are unhappy when prices fall, but consumers are pleased.[146]

The Korean War price controls proved ineffective and unpopular. The broad support for price controls during World War II was missing. Price controls were dropped after the Korean War. Political concerns shifted elsewhere until rising energy prices and inflation in the 1970s refocused attention on price controls.

---

138. Jerry W. Markham, *Federal Regulation of Margin in the Commodity Futures Industry: History and Theory*, 64 TEMP. L. REV. 59, 78 (1991).

139. 64 Stat. 798, Pub. L. No. 81-774 (1950).

140. 64 Stat. 798 at § 102.

141. H.R. Rep. No 3042, 81st Cong., 2d Sess. 27-28 (1950) (citing 40 Stat. 276 as the Lever Act).

142. *Speculator "Scandal" Assailed by Senator*, NEW YORK TIMES, Dec. 25, 1950, at 17.

143. Defense Production Act Amendments of 1951, H.R. Rep. No. 639, 82d Cong. 19-20 (1951).

144. *Id.*

145. *Id.* at 27.

146. The price and wage control program during the Korean War also led to a constitutional crisis. A dispute over wages between the steel mills and their labor unions resulted in a call for a national strike that would have shut down virtually all wartime steel production that was needed to wage the fight. The steel producers were unwilling to accede to the wage demands without a steel price increase that could not be implemented under the government controls. President Truman then seized the steel mills and ordered them to be operated under government authority. The Supreme Court held that action to be unconstitutional in Youngstown Sheet & Tube v. Sawyer. Youngstown Sheet & Tube v. Sawyer, 343 U.S. 579 (1962).

3:5 THE STOCK MARKET BOOM: THE 1950S

The Federal Reserve Board (the Fed) was moving stock margin requirements up and down. It reduced stock margins from 75 to 50 percent on March 30, 1949. It increased stock margins back to their 75 percent level in January 1951, but reduced that requirement to 50 percent in February 1953. After some uncertainty, the market surged by 50 percent between September 1953 and January 1955. The Dow Jones Industrial Average exceeded its 1929 high for the first time on November 17, 1954. This market boom caused concerns over speculation and the Fed again increased margin requirements. A congressional inquiry in 1955 that sought to determine whether another speculative bubble was under way revealed little evidence of such a danger.[147]

One important event involving market manipulation concerns arose in *United States v. Morgan*.[148] There, a federal district court judge dismissed an antitrust action brought by the Justice Department against several of the leading securities underwriters. The judge rejected claims that joint underwriting efforts involving the syndication of large offerings violated the antitrust laws. He also held that price maintenance ("stabilization") activities by those investment banks during the distribution of an offering were a necessary and reasonable means to ensure an efficient and quick distribution.

In considering the government's antitrust claims, the judge in the *Morgan* case carefully analyzed Sections 9 and 10 of the 34 Act and concluded that they "have the general effect of providing that stabilization, a well-known species of manipulation, should not be outlawed but should be subject to such rules and regulations as might be formulated by the SEC."[149] The judge also examined SEC actions on stabilization activities in public offerings and concluded that the SEC did not believe that any rules were needed to regulate or prohibit such activities.[150]

The SEC faced staff shortages in the 1950s, and it appeared that the agency was asleep for most of the decade. An extensive investigation of the SEC was conducted by a House committee in 1952.[151] It found that a number of cases had been mishandled.[152] This House committee recommended that the SEC should adopt rules governing stabilization activities during underwritings because of concern over manipulation.[153] The SEC was, in all events, an inactive agency during the 1950s. An electronic search reveals that no federal court cases were brought by the SEC for manipulation under Section 9 of the Securities Exchange Act of 1934 in the 1950s.[154] In addition,

---

147. Sidney Robbins, The Securities Markets: Operations and Issues 128 (1966).

148. United States v. Morgan, 118 F. Supp. 621 (S.D.N.Y. 1953).

149. 118 F. Supp. at 696.

150. 118 F. Supp. at 697.

151. *Study of Securities and Exchange Commission: Hearings Before a Subcommittee of the House Committee on Interstate and Foreign Commerce*, 82d Cong. 2d Sess. (1952).

152. Among other things, the committee's investigation found that the SEC's broker-dealer inspection program failed to uncover that a broker-dealer had embezzled some $650,000 of customer securities. *Study of Securities and Exchange Commission,* H.R. Rep. No. 2508, 82d Cong., 2d Sess. 1-2 (1952). That failure paled in comparison to the embarrassment the SEC experienced in failing to uncover the giant Ponzi scheme by Bernard Madoff in this century.

153. *Study of Securities and Exchange Commission,* H.R. Rep. No. 2508, 82d Cong., 2d Sess. 1-2 (1952).

154. The SEC did bring some administrative proceedings involving manipulation claims. *See,* In the Matter of S.T. Jackson & Co. Inc., 36 S.E.C. 631, 654 (1950) ("respondents controlled and dominated the market for Columbia stock and they sold the common stock to the public at increasing prices which they arbitrarily fixed"); In the Matter of Edgerton, Wykoff & Co., 36 S.E.C. 583 (1955) (charges of manipulation dismissed where knowledge of manipulation not shown); In the Matter of Adams & Co., 33 S.E.C. 444 (1952) (violations of Section 9(a)(2) found); In the Matter of J.A. Latimer, 38 S.E.C. 790 (1958) (registration of broker-dealer revoked where its principals engaged in wash trades and manipulated closing prices on an exchange).

that same search revealed only one criminal indictment under Section 9.[155] This electronic search also found no actions brought by the SEC under Rule 10b-5 charging manipulation.

One action was brought by the SEC under its Rule 10b-6. That rule prohibited transactions by a person participating in a distribution of securities. The district court in that case, *SEC v. Scott Taylor & Co.*,[156] stated:

> Manipulation was one of the basic evils with which Congress was concerned in enacting statutes to regulate the securities market. . . . Manipulation was often accomplished by those about to sell securities or already engaged in selling securities bidding on the market for the same securities, thereby by creating an unjustifiable impression of market activity which would facilitate the sale at artificially high prices. This was one of the practices which the Securities Exchange Act was designed to eradicate, and it is the practice which is covered by Rule X-10B-6.[157]

One notable and complex manipulation case that arose from conduct that occurred in the 1950s involved Gerardo and Gerard Re, a father-son team of specialists on the American Stock Exchange, who joined with a corporate raider, Lowell M. Birrell, to sell unregistered stock of the Swan-Finch Oil Corp. Their conduct very much followed the path of the stock pools in the 1920s that had led to the enactment of the federal securities laws. In affirming their criminal convictions for violations of Section 10(b) of the 34 Act and Rule 10b-5 in *United v. Re*,[158] the Second Circuit Court of Appeals found that the Res distributed over 600,000 shares of Swan-Finch through this scheme with the aid of various brokers who "boiler-roomed" them out to the public.[159] The court rejected a claim that the Res were acting as specialists and that under their duty to maintain a "fair and orderly market"[160] they were inherently authorized to manipulate the market.[161]

155. United States v. Shindler, 13 F.R.D. 292 (S.D.N.Y. 1952).

156. SEC v. Scott Taylor & Co., 183 F. Supp. 904 (S.D.N.Y. 1959).

157. 183 F. Supp. at 907.

158. United States v. Re, 336 F.2d 306 (2d Cir. 1964), *cert. denied*, 379 U.S. 904 (1964).

159. 336 F.2d 310-311 (footnote omitted). The Second Circuit described this scheme as follows:

> Birrell acquired control of Swan-Finch in May, 1954 and immediately committed 10,000 Swan-Finch shares to Re, Sr. and Grande by way of a three-month call. Within two months he had arranged to have the Res appointed specialists. Although it had been long dormant, Swan-Finch stock soon began a rather spectacular market rise. The Government's explanation of this sudden and uncalled for enthusiasm was that as specialists the Res knew exactly how much stock to buy or sell in order to raise or lower the market. With the Res' help, Birrell could control the price at will. There was also evidence that this manipulation extended to other stocks whose market performance was closely tied with that of Swan-Finch.
>
> In June and July, 1956, Sidney Barkley and Charles Rosenthal, undisclosed principals in the over-the-counter brokerage firm of I. F. Stillman & Co., agreed with Birrell to enter the market rigging operation. The Stillman firm, which engaged in so-called "boiler-room" sales tactics, was to support the Swan-Finch market on the Exchange with buy orders and later to sell the stock thus acquired over-the-counter. For this service, Birrell made "under-the-table" cash payments. Since the Stillman sales campaign depended largely on the closing price, Re, Sr. agreed to advise Barkley and Rosenthal of any increased selling so that Stillman could absorb the supply. Re, Sr. was also to tell Barkley and Rosenthal what was "on the book" so that they would know exactly how much to purchase to raise the price on any particular day. If Stillman & Co. was unable to meet the sell orders, it was understood that Re, Sr. would make the purchases required to maintain the desired market level.

160. 15 U.S.C. § 78k.

161. 336 F.2d 314.

3:6 MORE CEA MANIPULATION CASES

A speculative boom and bust occurred in the potato market between 1952 and 1953. In August 1952, potatoes were selling in New York for $4.50 per 100 pounds but dropped to $1 a year later, which was below the cost of their production.[162] The CEA claimed this evidenced "once again, how rapidly increased speculative buying, stimulated by exaggerated rumors of market scarcity and a low margin requirement, can contribute to boom-and-bust conditions in a market."[163] The change in potato prices, however, appeared to be due to fundamentals.[164]

The CEA observed a phenomenon of manipulation through "group technique," which it described in 1953 as involving "closely associated speculators whose combined activities are large enough to manipulate the price, although no one of the group may have holdings large enough to exert an apparent price effect." The CEA noted that proving collusion among group members usually "is difficult, and must be based largely on circumstantial evidence, since the members of the group are not likely to admit collusive action, and the contacts between the various participants are not ordinarily committed to writing."[165] The government continued to seek legislation granting it authority over commodity futures margins, but those efforts were rejected in Congress on eight separate occasions over the next several years.[166]

The CEA was more active than the SEC in pursuing manipulations during the 1950s. The CEA brought over a dozen manipulation cases during that period. One such case, *In re Cargill*,[167] involved actual and attempted manipulation of the oats market in 1951 and 1952. Cargill was charged by the CEA with importing Canadian oats into Chicago, which it sold at a loss in order to profit from a short position in oat futures on the CBOT. Cargill was further charged with falsely reporting that its CBOT positions were hedges rather than speculative.[168]

These imports had also raised concerns on the part of Senator William Jenner (R-IN), and hearings were held in the Senate. CEA officials testified in those hearings that the imports caused oat prices to drop twenty cents per bushel, resulting in a loss in crop value to farmers of $600 million.[169] The CEA referred the matter to the Justice Department for criminal prosecution on grounds of manipulation and making false reports.[170] However, a CEA official testified before Congress that it was "an extremely extensive and complicated problem, Senator, to work up a case that you can present to a jury or grand jury with regard to manipulation. This thing involved some 30 million bushels of oats through a Canadian concern, and its American parent organization."[171] A private antitrust action was also brought against Cargill for its oats trading by two Chicago grain dealers.[172]

---

162. *Potato Growers Are Hit*, New York Times, Aug. 15, 1953, at 16.

163. Jerry W. Markham, *Federal Regulation of Margin in the Commodity Futures Industry: History and Theory*, 64 Temp. L. Rev. 59, 79 (1991) (citation omitted).

164. *Maine's Farmers Wade in Potatoes*, New York Times, May, 17, 1953, at 46; *Suffolk Potatoes Cram Storage Bins*, New York Times, Nov. 15, 1953, at 82.

165. *Report of the Administrator of the Commodity Exchange Authority* 7 (1953).

166. Jerry W. Markham, *Federal Regulation of Margin in the Commodity Futures Industry: History and Theory*, 64 Temp. L. Rev. 59, 79 (1991).

167. In re Cargill, 13 Agric. Dec. 483 (1954).

168. *Cargill Accused in U.S. Complaint*, New York Times, June 16, 1953, at 42.

169. *Cargill, Inc., Sued over Oats Deals*, New York Times, Nov. 6, 1953, at 35.

170. *Manipulation Laid to Grain Concern*, New York Times, May 2, 1953, at 26.

171. *Agricultural Appropriations for 1954: Hearings Before the Senate Committee on Appropriations*, 83d Cong., 1st Sess. 694 (1953).

172. *Cargill, Inc., Sued over Oats Deals*, New York Times, Nov. 6, 1953, at 35.

Cargill claimed that its importation of oats was to remedy an oat shortage and that criticism of its importation was coming from "the speculative and manipulative fraternities,"[173] but it settled the CEA action by consent. The firm's trading privileges were suspended from May 1954 until the end of that year. The government also obtained an injunction in federal court that prohibited Cargill and its affiliates from trading oats during that period.[174] It is unclear what authority was relied on by the government for such an injunction because the CEA had no injunctive powers under the Commodity Exchange Act at that time. Cargill's expulsion from the CBOT in 1940 for cornering the corn market in 1937 remained in effect at the time of its oats manipulation.

The CEA also brought a series of cases involving manipulation of egg prices in the 1950s. Apparently, its actions against Great Western Food Distributors in 1947 and 1949 had not proved much of a deterrent. A case against L. Rudolph Co. Inc. for manipulating July 1952 egg prices through rigged trades on the NYMEX was dismissed.[175] It was charged in that case that the respondents had entered a series of progressively increasing bids near the close of trading on July 8, 1952, but the testimony at an administrative hearing on the charges varied so widely from what the CEA's investigation had found that the case was dismissed by an administrative judicial officer.

In *G.H. Miller & Co. v. United States*,[176] the Seventh Circuit affirmed a finding by a CEA judicial officer that fifteen respondents acted jointly to corner the December 1952 egg futures contract on the Chicago Mercantile Exchange (CME). The court found that the respondents had held all the long positions in December egg futures as delivery approached and 99 percent of deliverable refrigerator eggs. As a result, the shorts were unable to deliver on their contracts without delivering more expensive fresh eggs or out-of-town eggs. The court found that an artificially high price was created that resulted in a profit of nearly $163,000 for the respondents.

The court also credited testimony that the shorts were intentionally "squeezed" by the respondents when one of the long traders demanded a premium from a short trader for the eggs needed for delivery. The short trader testified that he was forced to overpay at least twelve cents per dozen for the eggs. The Seventh Circuit concluded that this was "indicative of the fact that the petitioners had a corner; that they knew it and had the shorts on their knees and at their mercy."[177] The court also held that intent to manipulate could be shown by circumstantial evidence.

> We are fully cognizant of the fact that corners can unintentionally develop and that it is almost impossible to prove by direct evidence that the acts and transactions of the petitioners were undertaken pursuant to an understanding or agreement to act collectively and in a uniform manner. Proof of such concerted action and the intent to so act must generally be circumstantial unless one or more of the participants would so admit. However, the evidence in this record discloses a long chain of circumstances which definitely established prima facie that the petitioners did so act with the intent that their combined acquisitions would cause an artificial price increase and enable them by pressure to unjustly liquidate their holdings at a profit.[178]

---

173. *Company Defends Action*, New York Times, Nov. 6, 1953, at 35.

174. *Cargill Trading in Oats Is Halted*, New York Times, May 5, 1954, at 54.

175. Commodity Exchange Authority, *Summary of Administrative and Judicial Proceedings Under the Commodity Exchange Act (June 15, 1936–June 30, 1972) and Under the Grain Futures Act (Sept. 21, 1922–June 14, 1936)* 27-28 (circa 1973).

176. G.H. Miller & Co. v. United States, 260 F.2d 286 (7th Cir. 1958), *cert. denied*, 359 U.S. 907 (1959).

177. 260 F.2d at 289.

178. 260 F.2d at 290.

Two of the respondents asked the Seventh Circuit to reduce the sanctions imposed by the CEA judicial officer, who revoked their registrations as a futures commission merchant and floor broker and suspended their trading privileges in speculative transactions for one year. The court denied that request, noting that the degree of sanctions was largely vested in the discretion of the executive branch.[179]

The *G.H. Miller* case was a victory for the CEA, but the case took six years to resolve. It was also another failure in deterrence. The CEA found further manipulation of egg prices on the CME in *In re Fox Deluxe Foods Inc.*[180] There a CEA judicial officer found that the respondents manipulated prices in the December 1953 and January 1956 CME egg futures contract through their market power. The respondents held the majority of long futures positions in those contracts, and that holding exceeded available deliverable supplies. Respondents also used recommendations to customers to aid the manipulation.[181] The respondents purchased large amounts of cash eggs on the CME in order to bolster prices and entered into an arrangement with an egg breaking firm, which broke eggs for use in frozen and liquid egg sales, to curtail supplies and create inflated cash egg prices. "There is no doubt that the December 1953 operation was manipulative in purpose, that is, that the respondents sought to use the weight of the corporation's trading and that of its customer accounts to put a 'squeeze' on the shorts and to influence upwards the price of egg futures and cash refrigerator eggs. The 'squeeze' is a well-known manipulative technique and unquestionably constitutes an attempt to manipulate prices within the meaning of the act."[182] The judicial officer in *In re Fox Deluxe Foods* rejected a claim that alternative supplies were available for delivery by the shorts.[183] Sanctions included revocation of registration as a futures commission merchant (FCM) and that of a floor broker. Trading suspensions ranged from six months to one year.

Another case, *In re Berkshire Foods Inc.*,[184] involved the upward manipulation of CME November 1958 egg futures contract. The respondents were charged with actual and attempted manipulation by having acquired a substantial part of the open interest on the exchange shortly before trading concluded in that contract month. That position was in excess of the deliverable supply of cash eggs and allowed the respondents to "squeeze" the shorts.[185] This case was settled by consent and resulted in sanctions against the respondents in that proceeding.

---

179. 260 F.2d at 295-297.

180. In re Fox Deluxe Foods Inc., 18 Agric. Dec. 582 (1959).

181. *Id.*

182. *Id.* (footnote omitted).

183. The judicial officer noted:

> Respondents urge that fresh eggs were deliverable on the December 1953 and January 1956 futures contracts and that therefore there was no attempt to manipulate and no manipulation of futures and cash refrigerator egg prices. Whether or not fresh eggs, a more valuable product than refrigerator eggs, were deliverable on the futures contract seems to us to make little or no difference in adjudication of the issues in these proceedings. True, the availability of fresh eggs might place a ceiling on the extent of manipulation possible just as daily limits on price rises for futures do. And freely available deliverable fresh eggs and declining prices for fresh eggs might make manipulation of futures prices financially unrewarding to the manipulators. But if the prices for futures and for cash refrigerator eggs are artificially enhanced by manipulative means such as a "squeeze" the act is still breached regardless of the deliverability of fresh eggs on the futures contract.

184. In re Berkshire Foods Inc., 19 Agric. Dec. 3 (1960).

185. The CEA's complaint was

> based upon allegations to the effect that the respondents and their customers purchased substantial quantities of November 1958 egg futures and developed concentrated positions in such future near

Other commodity futures were targeted for manipulation in the 1950s. Sanctions were entered by consent in *In re Butler*[186] for the manipulation of four soybean futures contract months in 1954 on the CBOT. The respondent entered into arrangements designed to limit available supplies of deliverable soybeans by, among other things, shipping them out of Chicago on terms that were uneconomic for a normal commercial transaction. The respondent Landon Butler also circulated false reports of other soybean deliveries out of Chicago that were intended to mislead short traders on the amount of deliverable supplies. Butler gained control of substantially all deliverable supplies of soybeans in Chicago in order to benefit his large futures position. Soybean prices reached $4 per bushel before dropping to $3, causing heavy losses to Butler.[187] The trading privileges of the respondent were revoked permanently through a default order.[188] The respondent was also convicted on criminal fraud charges for using fraudulent warehouse receipts.[189] He sold $4.5 million in soybeans he did not own to the Continental Grain Co. and Levalle Inc.[190] Butler was sentenced to three to five years in state prison.[191]

Futures trading in coffee posed problems in 1954. Coffee was not then subject to regulation under the Commodity Exchange Act.[192] The "S" coffee futures contract traded on the New York Coffee and Sugar Exchange was the key speculative medium for coffee. Its restrictive delivery terms made that contract susceptible to manipulation, and coffee prices rose by some 60 percent between December 1953 and April 1954. "It is conservatively estimated that the spiraling prices of coffee cost the American consumer $293 million between January and August 1954, inclusive."[193]

The Federal Trade Commission (FTC) conducted an antitrust investigation of the coffee price rise. The FTC concluded that severe frost damage in Brazil that was the claimed basis for the increase in price was not so severe as to justify such a price rise.[194] A Senate subcommittee considering whether to regulate coffee futures agreed with that conclusion.[195] Poor crop reporting was seen as a basic cause of the price rise, but another factor was "[a]ctivities on the New York

---

> the close of trading in November 1958; that such positions constituted a substantial proportion of the total open interest and exceeded available deliverable supplies; that most of such futures were liquidated during the last two trading days at increased prices; that other traders related to respondent Fox and trading through a registered futures commission merchant other than the respondent corporation made similar purchases and liquidations; that during the same period respondent Berkshire demanded and received excessive prices for cash eggs sold to short traders for delivery against the November 1958 future; that the respondents acted for the purpose and with the intent of raising prices by means of a squeeze, and with the expectation that the firm's customers would be influenced by the respondents and would follow their lead; that such customers were in fact so influenced and did in fact follow the respondents' lead; and that the acts of the respondents brought about a squeeze and caused prices of the November 1958 egg future and prices of cash eggs in Chicago to be at artificial and manipulated levels during November 1958.

In re Berkshire Foods Inc., 19 Agric. Dec. 3 (1960).

186. In re Landon Butler, 14 Agric. Dec. 429 (1955).

187. *Trader Accused in Soybean Deals*, New York Times, March 20, 1955, at 48.

188. *Trader Is Suspended*, New York Times, Jun. 22, 1955, at 39.

189. *Bank Keeps $2.7 Million*, New York Times, May 9, 1958, at 16.

190. *Trader Accused in Soybean Deals*, New York Times, March 20, 1955, at 48.

191. *Commodities Speculator Jailed*, New York Times, March 20, 1956, at 3.

192. *Regulation of Coffee Futures Trading: Hearing Before the Senate Committee on Agriculture and Forestry*, 83d Cong., 2d Sess. (1954).

193. *Study of Coffee Prices*, Report of the Special Subcommittee on Coffee Prices of the Senate Committee on Banking and Currency, 83d Cong., 2d Sess. 1 (1955).

194. Federal Trade Commission, *Economic Report of the Investigation of Coffee Prices* (July 30, 1954).

195. *Study of Coffee Prices*, Report of the Special Subcommittee on Coffee Prices of the Senate Committee on Banking and Currency, 83d Cong., 2d Sess. 25 (1955).

Coffee and Sugar Exchange, including operations of private 'Brazilian speculative interests,' which 'produced an upward price spiral.'"[196] "That bubble burst when the FTC issued its report, leaving in its debris many lost fortunes and millions of dollars of lost consumer purchasing power from 6 months of artificially high retail coffee prices."[197]

The New York Coffee and Sugar Exchange was charged by the FTC with antitrust violations of the Federal Trade Commission Act.[198] The exchange entered into a consent decree that required an expansion of the deliveries that could be made on the contract.[199] The FTC noted in its report on the coffee price bubble that long experience had evidenced that "immunity from market manipulation must be assured by the existence of a broad supply of a competitively traded commodity. More specifically, the contract must be based upon such a large volume of the commodity that no single trader and no single group of traders can likely get control of a sufficient portion of the supply to manipulate prices."[200]

The FTC asked Congress to review the adequacy of margins and various trading practices on the floor of the New York Coffee and Sugar Exchange to determine whether regulation was needed.[201] The Senate Committee on Agriculture recommended an amendment to the Commodity Exchange Act to add coffee as a regulated commodity, but that legislation did not pass.[202]

In a CEA action, *In re Joseph Klein & Co.*, the respondent was sanctioned by consent for manipulating the market in the March 1955 cotton futures contract on the New York Cotton Exchange. This was a price-rigging case charging violations of Section 4(c) of the Commodity Exchange Act as well as actual and attempted manipulation. The respondents entered orders on the New York Cotton Exchange "the purpose of which was to establish a predetermined numeral as the final digit of the low price of the opening or closing range of a previously designated future."[203] That price was sent to India in code twenty-four hours ahead of the execution of the transactions on the New York Cotton Exchange. Apparently, this trading was used to rig a popular but illegal numbers game in India that was based on the closing price on the New York Cotton Exchange.[204] Two respondents had their trading privileges suspended for twenty and sixty days, but this did not stop such schemes. In 1964, Philip H.J. Wag pleaded guilty to a criminal charge of engaging in a wash sale on the New York Cotton Exchange on July 14, 1962, "in connection with a large-scale gambling operation in India and Pakistan."[205]

---

196. *Study of Coffee Prices, Hearings Before a Special Subcommittee of the Senate Committee on Banking and Currency on S. Res. 182 and S. Res. 195*, 83d Cong., 2d Sess. 450 (1955).

197. 120 Cong. Rec. 10627 (1974) (remarks of Rep. Sullivan).

198. 15 U.S.C. § 45 (1952).

199. *See, The Coffee Exchange Debacle: Highlighting the Need for Further Regulation of Futures Trading Through the Sherman and Commodity Exchange Acts*, 64 YALE L. J. 906 (1955) (describing that case).

200. Federal Trade Commission, *Economic Report of the Investigation of Coffee Prices* 386 (July 30, 1954).

201. *Study of Coffee Prices: Hearings Before a Special Subcommittee of the Senate Committee on Banking and Currency on S. Res. 182 and S. Res. 195*, 83d Cong., 2d Sess. 451 (1955).

202. S. Rep. No. 929, 83d Cong., 2d Sess. (1954).

203. In re Joseph Klein & Co., 14 Agric. Dec. 648 (1955).

204. *2 Men Penalized in Cotton Rigging*, NEW YORK TIMES, Sept. 1, 1955, at 35; *Rigging of Cotton Is Laid to Broker*, NEW YORK TIMES, Aug. 27, 1955, at 18. Interestingly, the Eisenhower administration had considered "manipulating" American cotton imports as a way of damaging the Egyptian government. DAVID A. NICHOLS, EISENHOWER 1956 91 (2011).

205. Commodity Exchange Authority, *Summary of Administrative and Judicial Proceedings Under the Commodity Exchange Act (June 15, 1936–June 30, 1972) and Under the Grain Futures Act (Sept. 21, 1922–June 14, 1936)* 96 (circa 1973).

Sanctions were entered in other cases by consent for manipulations of the potato futures market. A short manipulation was charged in the March 1955 futures contract on NYMEX.[206] The respondents had taken delivery of nearly all deliverable supplies of potatoes in February 1955. They then threatened to deliver those supplies in satisfaction of their large short position in the March contract.[207] Short sellers on NYMEX defaulted on 28 million pounds of potato deliveries in June 1955. They were required to pay the longs a fair market price of $4.45 per hundred pounds plus a penalty of 9.25 percent.[208] The CEA charged that the shorts had entered large sell orders in order to push down prices. The orders were entered by the shorts even though they knew they would be unable to deliver on their short position.[209] Several respondents were subject to trading suspensions.[210]

Another manipulation was charged in connection with trading in the May 1955 potato futures contracts on NYMEX.[211] The respondents in that CEA proceeding increased their large short position on the next to last trading day in the contract even though they did not have sufficient potatoes to deliver on the contract. The respondents also disseminated false and misleading statements in order to drive down prices. They falsely claimed they would be making very large deliveries. Still another short manipulation charge was settled by consent by other respondents in connection with the May 1957 NYMEX potatoes futures contract.[212]

Those cases were not the end of potato speculations. A criminal case was brought against four traders for conspiring to evade speculative trading limits in potato futures in 1965 and 1966. One trader was found guilty and fined $140,000, but charges were dismissed as to the others.[213] That conviction was upheld upon appeal by the Second Circuit Court of Appeals in *United States v. Cohen*.[214] The court found that the defendant had "himself placed the orders not only for his own account but also for the accounts of his two sons and his business associate."

Another commodity futures contract of interest to speculators was onions. "Hardly a day passed, it seemed, without somebody trying to corner the onion market or squeeze prices higher or push them lower."[215] The CEA investigated a 1953 attempted corner of the onions market, but advised Congress that the highly perishable nature of onion contracts made their prices so volatile.[216] In 1955 the CEA "investigated a $1.5 million price-rigging scheme in the onion pit that would be one of the most spectacular market-fixing incidents in the history of the Chicago markets."[217] That affair was led by Vincent Kosuga, an onion grower in New York, who joined with Sam S. Siegel, an onion distributor in Chicago, to gain control of 98 percent of all deliverable Chicago onion stocks in November and December 1955. Kosuga, a longtime speculator in onions, was reported to have bribed a weather official in one scheme to issue a false freeze warning in order to push up prices of onion futures.[218]

206. In re Stern, 14 Agric. Dec. 807 (1955).

207. *Stern Faces Quiz on Potato Prices*, NEW YORK TIMES, June 30, 1955, at 37.

208. *6 Potato Traders to be Suspended*, NEW YORK TIMES, July 16, 1955, at 48.

209. *Food Chain Cited in Potato Squeeze*, NEW YORK TIMES, June 8, 1955, at 39.

210. *6 Potato Traders to be Suspended*, NEW YORK TIMES, July 16, 1955, at 48.

211. In re Winn & Lovett Grocery Co., 14 Agric. Dec. 561 (1955).

212. In re Murlas Brothers Commodities Inc., 17 Agric. Dec. 859 (1958).

213. Commodity Exchange Authority, *Summary of Administrative and Judicial Proceedings Under the Commodity Exchange Act (June 15, 1936–June 30, 1972) and Under the Grain Futures Act (Sept. 21, 1922–June 14, 1936)* 74 (circa 1973).

214. United States v. Cohen, 448 F.2d 1224, 1226 (2d Cir. 1971), *cert. denied*, 405 U.S. 954 (1972).

215. BOB TAMARKIN, THE NEW GATSBYS 29 (1985).

216. S. Rep. No. 766, 84th Cong., 1st Sess. 2 (1955).

217. DAVID GREISING & LAURIE MORSE, BROKERS, BAGMEN AND MOLES 81 (1991).

218. EMILY LAMBERT, THE FUTURES 42 (2011).

Kosuga stood for delivery on a large quantity of November futures contracts, causing 28 million pounds of onions to be shipped into Chicago. Kosuga and Siegel then together held some 30 million pounds of onions. Kosuga and Siegel threatened thirteen Michigan onion growers that the onions would be dumped on the market unless they bought a large quantity of the onions, which they did in order to protect the price of their crops.[219] Kosuga and Siegel double-crossed the growers and began shorting onions on the CME. Kosuga had to ship onions out of Chicago for cleaning in order to make them deliverable. As a stratagem, Kosuga used the return of those onions to Chicago to give the appearance of the arrival of new stocks, which drove prices down even further.[220]

Onion prices were $2.75 per fifty-pound bag in August 1955 but were driven down by this scheme to ten cents per bag in March 1956.[221] "At that level, the onions were worth less than the string bags in which they were shipped."[222] The manipulation resulted in "a terrible waste" of onions in Chicago and caused a scarcity of the product in other locales.[223] The Michigan onion growers unsuccessfully tried to escape their obligations to Kosuga by claiming that the agreement was void because it was a part of his illegal manipulation, which the growers claimed violated the Sherman Antitrust Act. The Supreme Court rejected that claim in *Kelly v. Kosuga*.[224]

In *In re Kosuga*,[225] a judicial officer upheld CEA charges that respondents attempted to manipulate the market for cash onions and the CME futures market in 1955 and 1956. The judicial officer asserted that efforts to stabilize or peg prices would constitute manipulation. "It is manipulation of prices to *keep a price from moving* in accordance with free supply and demand conditions just as much as it is to *move* a price to an artificial level. A previously-existing natural price kept from moving by abnormal or artificial means deliberately employed thereby becomes an *artificial* or *manipulated price*."[226]

---

219. The Supreme Court later noted:

> Petitioner, who was a grower of onions, admitted that he bought the onions from the respondent. But he alleged that the respondent and one Sam Siegel had represented to him and to other onion growers that they were the owners of substantial amounts of onions in storage, controlling 600 cars in the Chicago area and 400 more elsewhere throughout the country; that respondent and Siegel further informed the petitioner and other growers, at meetings called for the purpose in November and December 1955, that unless the growers purchased a large quantity of these onions, the respondent and Siegel would deliver them on the futures exchange for the purpose of depressing the futures price and the cash market price of onions. The petitioner and the other growers, who usually sold through trade channels, were fearful that this would cause them considerable loss. It was finally agreed by the petitioner and other growers that they would purchase 287 of the 600 cars of onions stored in the Chicago area, and the respondent and Siegel agreed not to deliver any onions on the futures market for the remainder of the current trading season. The petitioner and the other purchasers themselves agreed not to deliver any of the onions purchased from respondent and Siegel on the futures market for the remainder of the season; this was "for the purpose of creating a false and fictitious market condition," and "to fix the price of onions and limit the amount of onions sold in the State of Illinois."

Kelly v. Kosuga, 358 U.S. 516 (1959).

220. David Greising & Laurie Morse, Brokers, Bagmen and Moles 81-82 (1991).

221. *Commodities: Odorous Onions*, Time Magazine, July 2, 1956.

222. David Greising & Laurie Morse, Brokers, Bagmen and Moles 81 (1991).

223. *Review of Commodity Exchange Act and Discussion of Possible Changes: Hearings Before the House Committee on Agriculture*, 93d Cong., 1st Sess. 5 (1973).

224. Kelly v. Kosuga, 358 U.S. 516 (1959).

225. In re Kosuga, 19 Agric. Dec. 603 (1960).

226. *Id.* (emphasis in original, citations omitted).

An upward manipulation charge was dismissed in the *Kosuga* CEA case. Even though the respondent arranged with onion growers to make their nondeliverable in Chicago in November and December 1955, manipulative intent was not shown. The CEA judicial officer stated that "[d]rawing a line between legitimate trading and trading with manipulative intent is sometimes a very difficult task." The respondents, however, were found to have engaged in a short manipulation in the March 1956 onion futures contract through the sale of futures contracts and onion deliveries in Chicago that were intended to depress prices. Artificial prices were shown by comparing those established by the respondent with prices in prior years.

The onion futures market was not regulated by the CEA until 1955, just in time to encounter the Kosuga manipulation. That regulation was short-lived. Hearings were held in Congress in 1955 and 1956 to consider a ban on futures trading on onions and potatoes, but no action was taken.[227] A subcommittee report did state that it "seems quite clear from testimony at the hearing not only that efforts to manipulate the futures markets in potatoes and onions have taken place from time to time but that these markets as they are presently conducted by the New York and Chicago Mercantile Exchanges not only fail to prevent such activities but provide a fertile ground for efforts at manipulation."[228]

Further hearings were held in 1957 on legislation to ban futures trading on onion futures.[229] Congress imposed such a ban in 1958, the only agricultural commodity on which futures trading has been banned—a ban that remains in place today. The Michigan growers and National Onion Association had pushed that legislation through Congress with the assistance of Congressman Gerald Ford.[230] Potatoes escaped the ban. Secretary of Agriculture E.T. Benson advised Congress when it was considering this ban that because of "perishability, limited storability, and inelastic demand, onions have a record of extreme price volatility that long antedates the advent of futures trading in onions. The prohibition of futures trading in onions could not be expected to eliminate erratic price movements traditional in the marketing of this commodity."[231] Benson also stated that a ban on futures trading would not affect the actual marketing or distribution of onions. A CEA representative testified that a ban would not have any substantial effect on the price received over the season by growers but would eliminate short-term gyrations caused by speculators in futures.[232]

The ban on onion futures was a blow to the CME because onion futures contracts constituted about 20 percent of its trading volume before the ban.[233] As predicted by Benson, this congressional ban did not stop volatility in onion prices. "In a classic 1963 paper, Stanford economics professor Roger Gray examined the historical behavior of onion prices before and after the ban and showed how the futures market had actually served to stabilize prices."[234] Volatility in onions continued into recent years. *Fortune* magazine reported in June 2008 that "[s]ince 2006, oil prices have risen 100%, and corn is up 300%. But onion prices soared 400% between October 2006 and April 2007,

---

227. *Futures Trading: Hearings Before a Special Subcommittee of the House Committee on Agriculture and Forestry*, 84th Cong., 2d Sess., Pts. I-III (1956).

228. *Futures Trading in Onions and Potatoes: Report of the Subcommittee on Futures Trading in Perishable Commodities of the House Committee on Agriculture*, 84th Cong. 3 (1958).

229. *Onion Futures Trading: Hearing Before a Subcommittee of the Senate Committee on Agriculture and Forestry*, 85th Cong., 1st Sess. (1957).

230. Bob Tamarkin, The New Gatsbys 30 (1985).

231. *Onion Futures Trading: Hearing Before a Subcommittee of the Senate Committee on Agriculture and Forestry*, 85th Cong., 1st Sess. 2 (1957).

232. *Id.* at 32.

233. David Greising & Laurie Morse, Brokers, Bagmen and Moles 80 (1991).

234. *The Onion Ringer,* Wall Street Journal, July 8, 2008, at A20.

when weather reduced crops, according to the U.S. Department of Agriculture, only to crash 96% by March 2008 on overproduction and then rebound 300% by this past April."[235]

Manipulation was occurring in other commodities in the 1950s. In *In re Continental Grain Co.*,[236] sanctions were entered by consent in connection with manipulations of the March and December 1955 wheat futures contract on the Kansas City Board of Trade. A separate case brought by the CEA against this respondent also charged manipulation of the September 1957 Kansas City Board of Trade wheat futures contract. In that case, the respondent was charged with entering scale-down orders that sold wheat futures at descending prices in order to push down grain prices and allow Continental to purchase grain for the Commodity Credit Corporation at lower prices. Continental Grain consented to the suspension of registration as a futures commission merchant for ninety days, the floor broker registration of another respondent was suspended for the same period, and ninety-day trading suspensions were imposed on both Continental Grain and the floor broker.

A consent order was entered against E.F. Hutton & Co. in *In re Cate*,[237] in which the CEA had charged that two employees in the E.F. Hutton Kansas City office attempted to and did manipulate the March and May 1959 CBOT wheat futures contract. The two employees solicited orders from customers and entered orders for themselves and others in order to acquire a collectively dominant position in those contract months that exceeded available deliverable supplies. The CEA charged that this position was intended to create a "squeeze" and caused an artificial rise in wheat prices. The CEA further claimed that the employees made unauthorized transactions for customers and ignored customer orders in order to further this squeeze.

Interestingly, Ruloff E. Cutten was then the head of E.F. Hutton. He had been the broker for his uncle Arthur Cutten in pool operations at the center of the stock market manipulations in the 1920s that led to the enactment of the Securities Exchange Act of 1934. Ruloff Cutten denied that the Hutton firm had itself engaged in any trading in wheat for its own account and blamed the entire affair on the two employees. E.F. Hutton agreed to a suspension of registration as futures commission merchant for thirty days if it was found to violate the Commodity Exchange Act within the next year.[238]

A particularly significant decision was rendered in *Volkart Brothers v. Freeman*,[239] which was an appeal of a finding by a CEA judicial officer that the respondent manipulated and attempted to manipulate the price of the October 1957 futures contract on the New York and New Orleans cotton exchanges.[240] The respondent admitted that it had a dominant long position in cotton on

---

235. John Birger, *What Onions Teach Us About Oil Prices*, Fortune, June 30, 2008, http://money.cnn.com/2008/06/27/news/economy/The_onion_conundrum_Birger.fortune/ (accessed December 14, 2011).

236. In re Continental Grain Co., 17 Agric. Dec. 854 (1958).

237. In re Cate, 18 Agric. 884 (1959).

238. *Squeeze Alleged in Wheat Prices*, New York Times, Aug. 6, 1959, at 36.

239. Volkart Brothers v. Freeman, 311 F.2d 52 (5th Cir. 1962).

240. The CEA judicial officer found:

> "At the opening of the trading session October 15, 1957, the total open interest on both exchanges was 13,400 bales, i.e., there were unliquidated futures in that amount held by shorts against the same quantity held by longs. On the long side Volkart had 12,100 bales and other longs had 1300 bales. On the short side the 13,400 bales had to be covered before the end of trading October 15, 1957, by the purchase of futures or the delivery of certificated cotton or cotton which was in the process of certification. There were only about 5000 bales of certificated cotton owned by persons other than Volkart. Consequently there were available, without recourse to Volkart, only about 5000 bales of certificated cotton and 1300 bales of long contracts to meet the demand by the short of 13,400 bales. The remaining demand of 7100 bales had to be met out of Volkart's supply of long contracts and out of whatever cotton was in the process of certification.

October 15, 1957, but denied that it was "controlling" or that it was "intentionally contrived for the purpose of effecting an arbitrary increase in the prices."[241] The respondents in the CEA proceeding further claimed that 1.25 million bales of cotton were available in ports that could have been certificated by the shorts for delivery.

The New York Cotton Exchange argued in an amicus curiae brief that if the opinion of the CEA were to be upheld, "a license will have been given to all traders holding short positions to disregard their obligations to deliver under futures contracts, and holders of long positions will be obligated to protect them against the price increase naturally resulting from the technical situation thus created by them."[242] The respondents presented evidence that there was no artificial price because a control committee on the New York Cotton Exchange did not require liquidations and that prices were only slightly higher than the day before.[243]

The Fifth Circuit stated that the resolution of this case turned on the meaning of the word "manipulate" as used in the Commodity Exchange Act. "There being no statutory definition of 'manipulate,' the term must be construed as used in its known and ordinary signification."[244] The Fifth Circuit noted that the CEA judicial officer had relied for a definition on the testimony of

---

> "Respondents, several of their witnesses and the interveners point to the large stocks of uncertificated cotton in existence October 15, 1957, and seem to take the position that the mere existence of these stocks is proof that there was no artificiality in October cotton futures prices on October 15, 1957, on the New York and New Orleans exchanges. The existence of these large stocks does not negate artificiality in October 15 cotton futures prices. The evidence amply demonstrates that uncertificated cotton was not readily available to the shorts, particularly nonmerchant shorts, on the last day of trading. Every delivery by means of a deliverer's class certificate on the October 1957 future on both exchanges was by a merchant short who had possession of the cotton on or prior to October 14, 1957. There was no practicable alternative for a short on October 15, 1957, who did not have cotton, but to pay the price to get out. This meant for most shorts who did not have cotton to deliver not less than the price fixed by the concentrated controlling long interest with the consequence that prices advanced."
>
> The last day for trading in the October 1957 cotton futures on the New York Cotton Exchange and on the New Orleans Cotton Exchange was October 15, 1957. It was also the "last notice day," i.e., the last day on which a notice of intention to deliver cotton could be issued. October 22, 1957, was the last day on which delivery of cotton on the October futures could be made. A contract was in default if a notice of intention to deliver was not issued by the end of trading on October 15 and was not satisfied by delivery of the commodity on or before October 22.
>
> The rules of each Exchange provide for penalties in the event of a default; e.g., a member found guilty of intentional default may be expelled from the Exchange, and if the default is unintentional the party in default is subject to a penalty of 1/4 cent per pound on the weight of the cotton involved in the default. A defaulting party is liable for any damages caused to the party or parties on the other side of the contract.
>
> The alleged manipulation or attempt to manipulate occurred solely on the last day for trading on the Exchanges, October 15, 1957. Up to that time it is not claimed that the petitioners had committed any illegal act. The respondents claim that on that date the petitioners manipulated the market price of the October 1957 cotton futures by means of (1) their controlling "long" position on the cotton exchanges, (2) the insufficient supply of cotton eligible and available to the shorts for delivery by them on their futures contracts during the period of manipulation, and (3) the establishment of an abnormal or artificially high price by the petitioners in liquidation of their futures contracts.

311 F.2d at 56-57.

241. 311 F.2d at 57.
242. 311 F.2d at 57-58.
243. 311 F.2d at 58.
244. 311 F.2d at 58.

Arthur R. Marsh, the former president of the New York Cotton Exchange, that was given in the 1928 hearings on cotton prices and which is described in Chapter 2.[245] The Fifth Circuit stated that "[c]ertainly the term 'manipulate' means more than the charging of what some may consider to be unreasonably high prices. Otherwise, there would be grave doubt as to the constitutionality of the statutes."[246] The court stated that the Marsh testimony indicated that "there must be a purpose to create prices not responsive to the forces of supply and demand; the conduct must be 'calculated to produce a price distortion.'"[247]

The court further asserted that an unplanned "squeeze" in the market should not result in liability.[248] It cited the post–World War I Federal Trade Commission report on the grain trade as concluding that a squeeze might not necessarily be manipulative.[249] Further, the Fifth Circuit stated that "[e]ven in the case of an unplanned corner, the longs would not be guilty of manipulation."[250] "In brief, before the [CEA] order . . . can be sustained, it must appear not only that they profited from a squeeze, but that they intentionally brought about the squeeze by planned action."[251]

The court also concluded that the respondents did not control the available supply of cotton because the uncertificated cotton had to be considered. The court stated that the CEA respondents "can be held to a purpose to create prices not responsive to the forces of supply and demand only upon the assumption that the shorts should not be held to their contract obligation to deliver the cotton."[252] For the government "to proceed upon the assumption that the shorts should not be required to deliver at maturity would be to put them in the position of regulating a gambling institution rather than a legitimate futures exchange."[253]

The *Volkart* decision imposed a difficult burden of proof on the government. It required a showing that the respondents not only profited from the manipulation but also intentionally caused the manipulation through planned action. Further, the trader would have to be shown to have controlled the actual commodity as well as holding a dominant position in the related futures contract. The *Volkart* court further recognized that natural corners and squeezes may occur, and it stated that traders are free to exploit such situations. The court warned that traders on the opposite side of the market had a duty to protect themselves from corners and squeezes.

3:7 SEC MANIPULATION CASES: THE 1960S

The SEC "faced imposing regulatory challenges in the securities industry in the 1960s. Trading volume reached new heights, with total annual dollar volume of stocks traded on the NYSE increasing nearly fourfold in the 'go-go years' between 1960 and 1968."[254] The SEC conducted

---

245. 311 F.2d at 58 (footnote omitted).
246. 311 F.2d at 58 (footnote omitted).
247. 311 F.2d at 58 (footnote omitted).
248. 311 F.2d at 59, n. 10.
249. 311 F.2d at 59. The court also cited as support for this proposition a treatise that stated,

> "A squeeze is a relatively small corner, occurring in deliveries for some one month or some one grade. Some—or, in fact, most—squeezes are inevitable on both the physical and the exchange markets and are not the result of illegal manipulation."

Julius B. Baer & Olin G. Saxon, Commodity Exchanges and Futures Trading (1949).

250. 311 F.2d at 59.
251. 311 F.2d at 59.
252. 311 F.2d at 60.
253. 311 F.2d at 60.
254. The Bright Image: The SEC, 1961–1973, The "Go-Go" Years, http://www.sechistorical.org/museum/galleries/tbi/gogo_a.php (accessed December 22, 2011).

a *Special Study of the Security Markets* that was sent to Congress in 1963.[255] Among the matters considered was whether the margin requirements implemented under the 34 Act were fulfilling their purposes. The *Special Study* noted that the SEC's principal concern with margins was their use as a tool to prevent speculative excesses that resulted in rapid and extreme changes in securities prices that could affect the entire market. A market break in May 1962 was found to have been moderated by the issuance of margin calls.[256]

The SEC also experienced a great awakening as a regulatory body in the 1960s. Its more activist role was signaled by the appointment in 1961 of William Carey as the agency's new chair. Under his leadership, concerns over manipulation took a back seat to a new crime that he invented out of whole cloth—insider trading. Historically, courts had ruled that insider trading was permitted under common law when the trading was conducted on an exchange. The leading case so holding, *Goodwin v. Agassiz*,[257] was decided in 1933, the same year that the SEC was created.

Congress did not try to supersede the *Goodwin* ruling, except in the limited restriction in Section 16(b) of the 34 Act,[258] requiring forfeiture of short-term insider profits. The SEC did not seek to extend that prohibition until 1961 when Carey wrote an opinion in *Cady, Roberts & Co.*,[259] an administrative proceeding that was settled by consent and never reviewed by a court. Carey wrote in that opinion that SEC Rule 10b-5[260] created a duty to disclose inside information before trading, even on an exchange, or refrain from trading if disclosure is not made. In other words, all investors were to have equal access to material information. He rejected a claim that the defendants did not violate Rule 10b-5 because their trading had not been manipulative. The Second Circuit Court of Appeals adopted the SEC's equal access to information theory in 1968 in *SEC v. Texas Gulf Sulphur Co.*[261] However, as described in a later chapter, the Supreme Court subsequently rejected such a broad approach.

In a 1961 administrative proceeding, *In the Matter of Bruns, Nordeman & Co.*,[262] the SEC stated that the "means most commonly used to create a false appearance of activity in the over-the-counter market is the insertion in the sheets of increasingly higher bids. This device tends to support the price at its inflated level."[263] In another administrative case arising in the 1960s, the

---

255. *Report of Special Study of the Security Markets of the Securities and Exchange Commission*, H.R. Doc. No. 95, 88th Cong., 1st Sess. (1963).

256. *See*, Jerry W. Markham, *Federal Regulation of Margin in the Commodity Futures Industry: History and Theory*, 64 Temp. L. Rev. 59, 107-108 (1991) (describing the *Special Study*'s findings on margin).

257. Goodwin v. Agassiz, 186 N.E. 659 (Sup. Mass. 1933). Disclosure of insider trading could be required in face-to-face transactions involving "special facts." Strong v. Repide, 213 U.S. 419 (1909).

258. 15 U.S.C. § 78p.

259. Cady, Roberts & Co., 40 S.E.C. (1961).

260. 17 C.F.R. § 240.10b-5.

261. SEC v. Texas Gulf Sulphur Co., 401 F.2d 833 (2d Cir. 1968), *cert. denied sub nom.*, Coates v. SEC, 394 U.S. 976 (1969).

262. In the Matter of Bruns, Nordeman & Co., 40 S.E.C. 652, 658-659 (1961) (citations omitted).

263. *See also*, In the Matter of Landau, 40 S.E.C. 1119, 1123 (1962) (bids in published stock market quotations were used to manipulate stock prices); In the Matter of D.H. Blair & Co., 44 S.E.C. 320, 329 (1970 (same); In the Matter of Lewis Wolf Inc., 41 S.E.C. 259 (1962) (market manipulation scheme during public offering); In the Matter of Advanced Research Associates Inc., 41 S.E.C. 579 (1963) (respondents sold stock at increasing prices in a controlled market); In the Matter of F.S. Johns & Co. Inc., 43 S.E.C. 124 (1966) (various dealers entered rapidly increasing quotes in published quotation sheets in order to manipulate stock prices); In the Matter of Salik, 43 S.E.C. 796, 798 (1968) (respondent manipulated closing prices on exchange in order to better the price of an off-exchange block trade); In the Matter of Associated Investors Securities Inc., 41 S.E.C. 160 (1962) (a broker-dealer's representation that it would maintain a market in a security at steadily increasing prices was manipulative even if it had the wherewithal to do so).

SEC rejected a claim that misrepresentation to other dealers concerning a stock was merely market "chatter" that should be ignored. The SEC stated:

> We recognize that it is common for traders to exchange views regarding the present and probable future state of the market in a security and that . . . many firms make markets on the basis of activity in a security rather than on information concerning the issuer's financial condition. It is equally clear, however, that representations and price predictions made by one dealer to another, including those made by one trader to another, may if false or misleading violate the anti-fraud provisions of the federal securities laws just as those made to a customer, whether couched in terms of opinion or fact, and whether or not reliance is placed upon them.[264]

A private action in *Crane Co. v. Westinghouse Air Brake Co.*[265] that found its way up to the Second Circuit in the 1960s focused on what was then a relatively new phenomenon, hostile takeovers and defensive tactics used to defeat them. This case involved a tender offer by Crane Co. of $50 per share for the outstanding stock of Westinghouse Air Brake Co. Westinghouse resisted that offer and, instead, merged with American Standard Inc. Crane charged that American Standard illegally frustrated the tender offer by manipulating the price of Westinghouse Air Brake stock above $50, making the Crane Co. offer unattractive to Westinghouse shareholders. American made a series of trades on the last day of the tender offer. Those trades had an average price of $49.08 per share, and the share purchases totaled some $8.4 million. "The net result of this buying was to represent to the public, whose primary source of information is the tape, that there was a great demand for Air Brake at an increased value. It is reasonable to conclude that many Air Brake stockholders who might otherwise have chosen to tender to Crane chose not to do so because their own holdings in Air Brake looked better as the price went up."[266]

The court considered whether this conduct violated Section 9(a)(2) of the 34 Act,[267] which prohibits transactions that create "actual or apparent active trading in such security or raising or depressing the price of such security, for the purpose of inducing the purchase or sale of such security by others." The court stated that this section "was considered to be 'the very heart of the act' and its purpose was to outlaw every device 'used to persuade the public that activity in a security is the reflection of a genuine demand instead of a mirage.'"[268] The court held that Section 9(a)(2) contains "requirements of both manipulative motive and willfulness. The section does not condemn extensive buying or buying which raises the price of a security in itself."[269] Rather, "Section 9(a)(2) was aimed at preventing an individual from dominating the market in a stock for the purpose of conducting a one-sided market at an artificial level for its own benefit and to the detriment of the investing public."[270]

---

264. In the Matter of Pennaluna & Co. Inc., 43 S.E.C. 298, 307 (1967), *affirmed in relevant part and remanded on other grounds,* Pennaluna & Co. v. SEC, 410 F.2d 861 (9th Cir. 1969), *cert. denied*, 396 U.S. 1007 (1970).

265. Crane Co. v. Westinghouse Air Brake Co., 419 F.2d 787 (2d Cir. 1969), *cert. denied*, 400 U.S. 822 (1970).

266. 419 F.2d at 792-793.

267. 15 U.S.C. § 78i(a)(2).

268. 419 F.2d at 794 (citation omitted). Price mirages have also been of concern under the CEA. *See*, Minpeco S.A. v. ContiCommodity Services Inc., 552 F. Supp. 332, 337, (S.D.N.Y. 1982).

269. 419 F.2d at 794.

270. 419 F.2d at 794.

Section 9 contains specific intent requirements of both "manipulative motive and willfulness."[271] It "does not condemn extensive buying or buying which raises the price of a security in itself. Nor are the requirements of manipulative purpose and willfulness to be interpreted apart from the statute's design to prevent those with a financial interest in a security from manipulating the market therein. The requisite purpose and willfulness is normally inferred from the circumstances of the case."[272] The court further concluded that "Section 9(a)(2) was aimed at preventing an individual from dominating the market in a stock for the purpose of conducting a one-sided market at an artificial level for its own benefit and to the detriment of the investing public."[273] "When a person who has a 'substantial, direct pecuniary interest in the success of a proposed offering takes active steps to effect a rise in the market' in the security, we think that a finding of manipulative purpose is prima facie established."[274] The court found that American Standard had such an interest. Its actions were "not consistent with the normal desire of an investor 'to buy at as low a price as possible.'"[275]

The Second Circuit also held that this conduct violated Section 10(b) of the 34 Act, citing the equal access to information doctrine previously adopted by the court in the *SEC v. Texas Gulf Sulphur* case,[276] which the Supreme Court later rejected.[277] The Second Circuit stated in the *Westinghouse Air Brake* case that "[w]hen securities are subject to trading dominated by an insider such as Standard, there is an obligation to disclose material information to the investing public, and this duty gives rise to liability under 10b-5 to third persons who, as a result of the deception practiced upon the public, are prevented from entering into securities transactions with members of the public."[278] The violation of Rule 10b-5 was held to be the "nondisclosure of the manipulation," rather than the manipulation itself.[279]

In 1966, SEC general counsel Philip A. Loomis Jr. testified before Congress that Rule 10b-5 "has become one of our most important and widely used enforcement provisions and it also has been interpreted by the courts as creating civil remedies for defrauded investors against the person who defrauded them, whether or not such person is a securities broker or dealer."[280] In one such private action, *Carroll v. First National Bank*,[281] the Seventh Circuit held that broker-dealers could obtain damages under Rule 10b-5 from a bank that had participated in a "credit bubble." The complaint charged:

> According to plaintiffs, the scheme originated in January 1966 and involved the purchase of large amounts of securities at different times for speculative purposes. The essence of the scheme was the creation of a "credit bubble" by causing plaintiffs to finance such purchases and, in the expectation of rising market values, "to obtain delay for the participants in payment and settlement of purchases of securities made through and from the plaintiffs so [that]

---

271. Crane v. Westinghouse Air Brake Co. 419 F.2d 787, 794 (2d Cir. 1969), *cert. denied*, 400 U.S. 822 (1970).

272. 419 F.2d at 794.

273. 419 F.2d at 794.

274. 419 F.2d at 795.

275. 419 F.2d at 795 (citation omitted).

276. 401 F.2d at 848.

277. Chiarella v. United States, 445 U.S. 222 (1980).

278. 419 F.2d at 796.

279. 419 F.2d at 797, n. 11.

280. *To Amend the Commodity Exchange Act: Hearings on H.R. 11788 Before the Subcommittee on Domestic Marketing and Consumer Relations of the House Committee on Agriculture*, 89th Cong., 2d Sess. 147 (1966).

281. Carroll v. First National Bank, 413 F.2d 353 (7th Cir. 1969), *cert. denied*, 396 U.S. 1003 (1970).

> the participants [could] hold speculative ownership positions in the securities purchased by use of plaintiffs' funds and resources." The complaint also alleges that purchases beyond the financial capacity of the participants were made for the purpose of manipulating the market price of the purchased securities, thus allowing the participants to unload the securities at inflated prices in order to pay for their original purchases.[282]

The court agreed with the SEC's amicus curiae position that "retaining the Bank in this suit would be entirely consonant with the undisputed goal of the Securities Exchange Act to curb uncontrolled speculation on securities markets."[283] Similarly courts held that "free riding" schemes (entering an order to buy a security with no intent to pay for it unless the price increases) constitutes a form of manipulation in violation of Rule 10b-5. In *A.T. Brod & Co. v. Perlow*,[284] the Second Circuit found such conduct to violate Rule 10b-5 because "the Securities and Exchange Commission, as amicus curiae, has advised us that the artificial demand created by purchasing securities which are not to be paid for unless the market value of the stock rises, can have an unsettling and potentially manipulative effect on the securities market—contrary to the very purpose of the Act."

Inserting quotations in order to create a false appearance of market activity in a stock by an underwriter was held to violate Section 10b-5 in *Tager v. SEC*.[285] In *Associated Securities Corp. v. SEC*,[286] the Tenth Circuit found a violation of Rule 10b-5 when a broker failed to disclose that stock sold to customers was at prices not reasonably related to the prevailing market price. The "classic manipulation" also remained, which one writer defined as a comparatively simple scheme, "involving the raising of the price of a security by a series of purchases designed to (1) restrict the floating supply, (2) create the appearance of activity, (3) cause others to purchase the security as the result of the apparent activity and rising prices."[287]

3:8 CEA MANIPULATION CASES: THE 1960s

The CEA was showing increased concerns in the 1960s over the lack of a definition in the Commodity Exchange Act of what was meant by manipulation. A bill was introduced in Congress in 1960 that would have defined commodity price manipulation as "the causing or maintenance of an artificial price by action intended for that purpose."[288] Another bill was introduced in 1961, and again in 1963, using similar language, except that it sought to make clear that this would not be the only basis for finding manipulation.[289] Those bills were never enacted into law. The CEA also again sought legislation that would have allowed it to set margin levels for futures contracts, but that bill was not passed.[290]

---

282. 413 F.2d at 355.

283. 413 F.2d at 356.

284. A.T. Brod & Co. v. Perlow, 375 F.2d 393, 397 (2d Cir. 1967).

285. Tager v. SEC, 344 F.2d 5 (2d Cir. 1965). *See also*, In the Matter of Halsey, Stuart & Co., 30 S.E.C. 106 (S.E.C. 1949) (similar conduct); In the Matter of Adams & Co., 33 S.E.C. 444 (S.E.C. 1952) (same).

286. Associated Securities Corp. v. SEC, 293 F.2d 738 (10th Cir. 1961).

287. Harold S. Bloomenthal, *The Case of the Subtle Motive and the Delicate Art: Control and Domination in The Counter Securities Markets*, 1960 DUKE L. J. 196, 204-205. *See also*, Note, *Market Manipulation and the Securities Exchange Act*, 624, 46 YALE L. J. 627 (1936-1937) (describing such schemes). *See also, e.g.*, In the Matter of Palombi Securities Co. Inc., 41 S.E.C. 1962) (respondents failed to disclose that they were dominating and controlling the markets they were promoting to investors).

288. S. 2807, 86th Cong., 2d Sess. § 1 (1960).

289. S. 1980, 87th Cong., 1st Sess. § 1 (1961); S. 402, 88th Cong., 1st Sess. § 1 (1963).

290. *See*, Jerry W. Markham, *Federal Regulation of Margin in the Commodity Futures Industry: History and Theory*, 64 TEMP. L. REV. 59, 79 (1991).

Wool futures manipulation cases brought by the CEA for trading that occurred in 1962 and 1963 were settled by consent.[291] Sanctions consisting of suspension of trading privileges for several respondents were ordered for periods ranging from two to ninety days. The 1962 case, *In re Internatio (Wool) Inc.*,[292] involved the May wool future traded on the Wool Associates of the New York Cotton Exchange Inc. The respondents held a long position in that futures contract that was far in excess of available deliverable supplies they did not already control. According to the CEA, the respondents were, therefore, able to demand and receive "prices for the May 1962 future which were in excess of the price justified by supply and demand."[293] The complaint in that case had to be amended to charge that respondents acted "with the purpose and intent of causing prices in the May 1962 wool future which were arbitrary and artificial."[294] *In re Collins*[295] involved charges of attempted and actual manipulation of the May 1963 wool futures contract by gaining a dominant futures position in that contract month and making available supplies of wool unavailable for delivery.

Sugar prices nearly doubled in 1963, and the run-up was blamed on speculators in sugar futures that were, at the time, unregulated.[296] Concerns over a jump in soybean prices in 1963 resulted in a request from the CEA to the CBOT that it raise its margins from 20 cents per bushel to 75 cents. The CBOT agreed to only a five-cent increase.[297] Apparently, however, that was enough to unmask[298] what was then "the biggest commodities scandal in history,"[299] an affair that became known as the "Great Salad Oil Swindle."[300] The perpetrator of that fraud was Anthony DeAngelis.

DeAngelis carried out his scheme through Allied Crude Vegetable Oil Refining Corporation, a company he owned that was located in Bayonne, New Jersey. He tried to profit from the government's Food For Peace Program by purchasing large quantities of edible oils in the United States that he resold abroad. DeAngelis controlled over 50 percent of the export trade in vegetable oil.[301] In order to obtain financing, he forged warehouse receipts on oil that was purportedly held in American Express field warehouses. DeAngelis also purchased nearly 80 percent of the cottonseed oil futures contract on the New York Produce Exchange and 30 percent of the soybean oil futures contracts on the CBOT.[302] He claimed to be hedging anticipated sales of oil to Russia, but those sales were nonexistent.[303]

DeAngelis's fraud was unearthed after Allied was unable to meet margin calls on its futures positions. Among the victims was American Express, which suffered losses of more than $60 million.[304] DeAngelis's broker Ira Haupt & Co., a nationwide broker with some 700 employees and

291. In re Internatio (Wool) Inc., 22 Agric. Dec. 1325 (1962); In re Collins, CEA Doc. No. 121 (1965).

292. In re Internatio (Wool) Inc., 22 Agric. Dec. 1325 (1962).

293. In re Internatio (Wool) Inc., 22 Agric. Dec. 1325 (1962).

294. In re Internatio (Wool) Inc., 22 Agric. Dec. 1325 (1962).

295. In re Collins, CEA Doc. No. 121 (1965).

296. 120 Cong. Rec. 10627 (1974) (remarks of Rep. Sullivan).

297. *To Amend the Commodity Exchange Act: Hearings on H.R. 11788 Before the Subcommittee on Domestic Marketing and Consumer Relations of the House Committee on Agriculture*, 89th Cong., 2d Sess. 30 (1966).

298. *Id.* at 150.

299. Vartanig G. Vartan, *Food Oil Trader Indicted Over $40 Million Receipts*, NEW YORK TIMES, Dec. 24, 1963, at 1.

300. NORMAN C. MILLER, THE GREAT SALAD OIL SWINDLE (1965).

301. H.J. Maidenberg, *Export Dip Seen in Vegetable Oil*, NEW YORK TIMES, Jan. 26, 1964, at F1, F11.

302. *Supervision Lags for Commodities*, NEW YORK TIMES, Feb. 13, 1966, at 119.

303. *Tino DeAngelis: Study in Silence*, NEW YORK TIMES, Dec. 6, 1963, at 63.

304. H. Erich Heinemann, *American Express Is Back From the Brink*, NEW YORK TIMES, April 14, 1968, at F1.

20,000 customers, was bankrupted. That broker had sent DeAngelis a margin call for $18 million on his futures positions that he failed to meet and that Haupt then became responsible for to the exchange clearing house.[305] Another broker, J.R. Williston & Beane, also sustained losses after DeAngelis failed to meet a $610,000 margin call.[306] The New York Stock Exchange advanced nearly $10 million to protect the customers of the bankrupted Ira Haupt.

The CEA won a reputation for inaction and ineffectiveness in its regulatory role as a result of the salad oil scandal. It was compared unfavorably to the SEC, which had become a more active regulator in the 1960s.[307] The CEA defended itself by asserting that there was nothing in its powers that could have prevented the salad oil scandal because the fraud involved warehouse receipts outside its jurisdiction.[308] The CEA was, in all events, a tiny regulator. Its budget was just 7 percent of that of the SEC in 1966. Indeed, the CEA's entire budget was less than the amount the SEC allocated in its budget for just the SEC New York regional office.[309] The CEA, nevertheless, seemed content with its budget. It did not customarily seek budget increases, and it even committed the unusual sin of returning unused funds to the Treasury.[310]

---

305. Haupt's predicament was described by a court as follows:

> A concentration in the long interest like that achieved by Allied is fraught with potential danger to the market, inasmuch as it reduces liquidity, lessens price stability, heightens the risk of a disorderly liquidation of contracts should the demand curve faced by the party holding the interest shift, and in general threatens the maintenance of an orderly market. At the same time, a concentrated long position leaves the person who accumulates it exceedingly vulnerable to declines in the market. And decline the market did, sharply between November 14 and November 19, 1963. During that period Haupt was called upon by the Clearing Association to put up variation margin, and in turn Haupt called upon Allied for reimbursement. By November 19, Allied was unable to respond to Haupt's margin calls, and filed a petition under Chapter XI of the Bankruptcy Act.
>
> Later that day, at a joint meeting of the Exchange's Executive Committee and the Association's Board of Directors, Allied's plight was revealed. Also disclosed was the fact that of the 10,273 futures contracts in which Allied was the buyer, 8,043 were held for it by Haupt. Those present were advised by representatives of Haupt that it would be unable to meet its margin requirements should the market continue to drop. After considerable discussion, and telephonic or personal consultation with approximately two-thirds of the Exchange's Board of Managers, the Executive Committee decided unanimously to recommend to the Exchange Board that trading in cottonseed oil futures be suspended until further notice, and that settlement prices be fixed. On November 20, the Exchange did not reopen, and the Board of Managers formally ratified the decision reached the previous day.
>
> On or about November 22, 1963, Haupt discovered that warehouse receipts, which it received from Allied as collateral for the variation margin it put up during the November 14-19 market decline, were worthless. The receipts were forged, and the salad oil, the presence of which the receipts purported to authenticate, was non-existent. On March 23, 1964, an involuntary petition in bankruptcy was filed against Haupt.

Seligson v. New York Produce Exchange, 378 F. Supp. 1076, 1081-1082 (S.D.N.Y. 1974).

306. Vartanig G. Vartan, *Food Oil Trader Indicted Over $40 Million Receipts*, New York Times, Dec. 24, 1963, at 1.

307. *Supervision Lags for Commodities*, New York Times, Feb. 13, 1966, at 119.

308. *To Amend the Commodity Exchange Act: Hearings on H.R. 11788 Before the Subcommittee on Domestic Marketing and Consumer Relations of the House Committee on Agriculture*, 89th Cong., 2d Sess. 23 (1966).

309. *Id.*

310. *Id.*

More egg manipulations occurred in the 1960s that were the target of CEA charges. *In re Randolph*[311] involved a manipulation of spot eggs on NYMEX on two days in January 1961. The CEA found, by consent, that artificial prices were set in the spot egg market on the NYMEX in order to increase prices on other contracts. Only light sanctions were imposed.[312]

The January 1964 frozen whole egg contract on the CME was the subject of a charge of attempted manipulation in *In re Maduff*. There, two respondents acquired a large long position in that futures contract on the last trading day "in an effort to cause an artificial or arbitrary price in such future."[313] That case was settled by consent with trading and registration suspensions of thirty days.

The manipulation of the CME November 1968 shell egg futures contract that occurred on June 25, 1968, in *In re Henner*[314] resulted in a contested decision by a CEA judicial officer. Once again, only light sanctions were imposed, but this decision would become an important precedent in future years. This was a rigged trading case in which the CEA charged that the respondent paid artificial prices that distorted closing prices.[315] The judicial officer in the *Henner* case conducted an extensive analysis of what constitutes manipulation and concluded that there are many types of manipulation that do not involve control of the market, such as by false reports. "The respondent's trading activities in the present case were similar, in effect, to the issuance of a false press

---

311. In re Randolph, 21 Agric. Dec. 219 (1962).

312. The charges were as follows:

> Prior to January 13, 1961, respondent Randolph Foods, Inc., had sold approximately 4,400 cases of eggs at prices based upon the New York spot quotations for Fancy Heavyweight Mixed eggs on the day of delivery to the purchaser. Respondent Howard Randolph scheduled such eggs for delivery on Friday, January 13, 1961. On January 13, 1961, respondent Howard Randolph initiated and transmitted to respondent Carl A. Bergstrom an order to raise the price of the said grade of eggs on the Exchange spot call on that day by 1/2 to one cent per dozen. The said order was relayed by respondent Carl A. Bergstrom to respondent Robert M. Zadra and the said respondent Zadra, acting pursuant thereto, caused a floor broker on the Exchange to bid for and purchase Fancy Heavyweight Mixed eggs on the spot call of the Exchange on January 13, 1961, at prices which resulted in a New York spot quotation of 37 1/2 cents per dozen for such eggs on that day. Such quotation represented an increase of 3/4 to one cent over the previous day's New York spot quotation for such eggs. The subsequent resale of the eggs so purchased resulted in a loss which was paid by respondent Randolph Foods, Inc.

Id.

313. In re Maduff, 24 Agric. Dec. 1456 (1965).

314. In re Henner, 30 Agric. Dec. 1151 (1971).

315. The CEA charged:

> During the closing period of trading in the November 1968 shell egg future on June 25, 1968, the trading was conducted by means of "board trading." Shortly before the end of such closing period, there were the following offers posted on the "offer board": 600 cases at 40.20 cent per dozen; 600 cases at 40.25 cents per dozen; 600 cases at 40.50 cents per dozen; 1800 cases at 40.75 cents per dozen; 600 cases at 41 cents per dozen; and 600 cases at 41.30 cents per dozen. During the final seconds of such closing period, the respondent, acting for his own account, "bought the board," *i.e.*, he simultaneously accepted all of the posted offers referred to above. The respondent then bid 41.85 cents per dozen for another 600 cases of shell eggs for future delivery. This bid was accepted by another floor broker within the one-minute period after the close of trading, during which the exchange rules permitted the acceptance of a bid made during the closing period of trading at a price higher than the price of the last trade.

In re Henner, 30 Agric. Dec. 1151 (1971).

release because the respondent's trading activities caused interested persons throughout the country to believe, from the press reports of the closing price, that the closing price established on the Exchange by buyers trying to buy as cheaply as they could and sellers trying to sell as high as they could resulted in a price about 155 or 165 points higher than the price actually established in such a manner."[316]

Another case of significance that arose in the 1960s was *Cargill v. Hardin*,[317] in which the respondent in a CEA proceeding was charged with manipulating the May 1963 CBOT wheat futures contract and the Chicago cash market for No. 2 soft red winter wheat. The CEA judicial officer found manipulation of the May 1963 wheat futures contract traded on the CBOT, but rejected a claim that Cargill cornered the cash market for wheat in Chicago. The trading was conducted by Cargill, one of the world's largest grain firms. "In early 1963, Cargill was of the opinion that there would be an ample supply of soft red winter wheat at the end of the crop year, May 1963, and hence hedged its inventory by selling May 1963 wheat futures on the Chicago Board of Trade."[318] That short hedge position reached 8 million bushels, but in March 1963, Cargill revised its view of the market due to unusual market conditions. Cargill thought those conditions would push up prices. It then liquidated its short hedge position and put on a speculative long position of nearly 2 million bushels, which was the speculative limit for such a position.

The Eighth Circuit Court of Appeals noted that the USDA publicly reported just before Cargill assumed its long position that there were 2,804,000 bushels of deliverable grade wheat stored in Chicago warehouses and that, unbeknownst to the market, Cargill owned 2,471,000 bushels. "Cargill was thus in possession of a vital piece of information that other traders and grain dealers in Chicago did not have access to, namely that it owned the bulk of deliverable wheat in Chicago. While all traders of course knew the total quantity of deliverable wheat available in Chicago, only Cargill was in a position to know that it owned the vast majority of this wheat."[319]

In May 1963, Cargill sold wheat from its Chicago warehouse to Spain. "This load out together with other commitments left Cargill with approximately 50,000 bushels of wheat in its warehouse as of Monday afternoon, May 20. This constituted all of the wheat in Chicago warehouses which was available for delivery on the May wheat future."[320] Cargill then had two days to liquidate its long futures position in May 1963 wheat on the CBOT, which would expire on May 21. Cargill entered a liquidating order for 100,000 bushels on May 20 at a price near the CBOT's price limit for the day, but the order was only partially filled. On May 21, the last day of trading, Cargill had a long position of 1,890,000 bushels, which was about 24 percent of the open interest in that contract. At the time, there were only 50,000 bushels of wheat available from any non-Cargill source.[321]

Cargill increased its position in the May wheat future on May 21, increasing its speculative long position to 1,990,000 about one hour before trading would stop in that contract at noon. Prices were declining before that transaction. Fifteen minutes before the noon closing time for the May contract, Cargill entered a series of six scale-up orders, which offered increasing amounts of wheat contracts at increasing prices.[322] At the request of the CBOT, Cargill arranged for the settlement

316. In re Henner, 30 Agric. Dec. 1151 (1971).
317. Cargill v. Hardin, 452 F.2d 1154, 1159 (8th Cir. 1971), *cert. denied*, 406 U.S. 932 (1972).
318. 452 F.2d at 1158.
319. 452 F.2d at 1159.
320. 452 F.2d at 1160.
321. 452 F.2d at 1160.
322. The court describes Cargill's trading as follows:

> At 11:45 the future was trading at $2.20. At this point Cargill transmitted to its broker six orders to sell its futures position as follows:

of the remaining short positions at a price of $2.2825 per bushel. Cargill sold its remaining cash wheat in Chicago at prices at or less than $2.13 per bushel.[323]

The CEA asserted that Cargill had engaged in a squeeze because: "(1) Cargill acquired and held a controlling long position in the May 1963 wheat futures; (2) there was an insufficient supply of wheat available to the shorts for delivery on the futures, and what supply there was controlled by Cargill; (3) Cargill exacted an artificially high price in liquidation of its futures contracts; and (4) the squeeze was intentionally caused by Cargill."[324]

The Seventh Circuit noted that "[m]ost commentators refer to a dominant position in the cash or spot market as a corner, while such position in the futures market is denoted as a squeeze."[325] The court also cited Senator Pope's definition of a squeeze found in the legislative history to the Commodity Exchange Act and which is described in Chapter 2.[326] The court in *Cargill* recognized that there was no definition of the term "manipulation" in the Commodity Exchange Act, but that the Seventh Circuit in *General Foods Corp. v. Brannan* [327] had previously adopted a definition

---

> 200,000 bushels at $2.27
> 200,000 bushels at $2.27 1/4
> 300,000 bushels at $2.27 1/2
> 400,000 bushels at $2.27 3/4
> 500,000 bushels at $2.28
> 390,000 bushels at $2.28 1/4
>
> These orders were limit orders, which meant that the sales could not be made below the prices specified. The maximum price at which the May 1963 future could be sold was $2.28 5/8.
>
> Prices did not reach the limits specified in Cargill's order until 11:53 a.m. At this time Cargill's holdings constituted approximately 62 per cent of the open interest. From this time until the close of trading, Cargill's broker liquidated 1,625,000 bushels for Cargill's account. Prices reached $2.28 5/8, the limit for the day. Confusion and congestion was so great at the close of trading that 420,000 bushels remained open after trading ended, and Cargill had unliquidated holdings of 365,000 bushels.

452 F.2d at 1160.

323. 452 F.2d at 1161.

324. 452 F.2d at 1162.

325. 452 F.2d at 1161 (citation omitted).

326. 452 F.2d at 1161-1162 (footnote omitted). The *Cargill* court went further in distinguishing a corner from a squeeze:

> A squeeze is a less extreme situation than a corner. In this case, there may not be an actual monopoly of the cash commodity itself, but for one reason or another deliverable supplies of the commodity in the delivery month are low, while the open interest on the futures market is considerably in excess of the deliverable supplies. Hence, as a practical matter, most of the shorts cannot satisfy their contracts by delivery of the commodity, and therefore must bid against each other and force the price of the future up in order to offset their contracts. Many squeezes do not involve intentional manipulation of futures prices, but are caused by various natural market forces, such as unusual weather conditions which have caused abnormally low crop production or inadvertent destruction of a substantial volume of the commodity itself. However, given a shortage of deliverable supplies for whatever reason, the futures price can be manipulated by an intentional squeeze where a long acquires contracts substantially in excess of the deliverable supply and so dominates the futures market—i.e., has substantial control of the major portion of the contracts—that he can force the shorts to pay his dictated and artificially high prices in order to settle their contracts.

452 F.2d at 1162.

327. General Foods Corp. v. Brannan, 170 F.2d 220, 231 (7th Cir. 1948).

proposed by the government as "the creation of an artificial price by planned action, whether by one man or a group of men."[328]

The *Cargill* decision also cited a Supreme Court definition of manipulation from *United States v. Socony-Vacuum Oil Co.*,[329] an antitrust case,[330] which stated that "[m]arket manipulation in its various manifestations is implicitly an artificial stimulus applied to (or at times a brake on) market prices, a force which distorts those prices, a factor which prevents the determination of those prices by free competition alone."[331] The Court in the *Socony-Vacuum Oil* case thus stated that "the machinery employed by a combination for price-fixing is immaterial. Under the Sherman Act a combination formed for the purpose and with the effect of raising, depressing, fixing, pegging, or stabilizing the price of a commodity in interstate or foreign commerce is illegal *per se*."[332] However, a different standard applies in antitrust law for monopoly, which is the equivalent of a corner or squeeze in the commodity markets. "The existence or exertion of power to accomplish the desired objective becomes important only in cases where the offense charged is the actual monopolizing of any part of trade or commerce in violation of § 2 of the [Sherman] Act. An intent and a power to produce the result which the law condemns are then necessary."[333]

In any event, the Court in *Cargill* chose to adopt its own definition of manipulation, stating that it "must largely be a practical one if the purposes of the Commodity Exchange Act are to be accomplished. The methods and techniques of manipulation are limited only by the ingenuity of man. The aim must be therefore to discover whether conduct has been intentionally engaged in which has resulted in a price which does not reflect basic forces of supply and demand."[334]

Cargill defended its trading on the ground that its acts were not "uneconomic," which it believed should be the basis for a finding of manipulation. Cargill appeared to be arguing that it was simply a trader seeking to gain from market fundamentals and should not be punished for its success. The *Cargill* court rejected that defense.[335] The court believed that "the question of whether an alleged manipulator has made a profit is largely irrelevant, for the economic harm done by manipulation is just as great whether there has been a profit or a loss in the operation. . . . And it may be pointed out that one of the most common manipulative devices, the floating of false rumors which affects futures prices, does not involve the commission of an 'uneconomic act.'"[336]

The court found that Cargill held a dominant long position in the May wheat futures contract, which the court found to be an important element because "[i]t is evident that a squeeze cannot be successfully executed unless a long has sufficient control of enough futures contracts to force the shorts to come to him to settle their contracts."[337] The court stated that "Cargill's control of 2,000,000 bushels of futures, constituting 62 percent of the long interest, with 15 minutes of trading

328. 452 F.2d at 1163.

329. United States v. Socony-Vacuum Oil Co., 310 U.S. 150, 223 (1940).

330. For a discussion of the differing standards required to prove antitrust and Commodity Exchange Act manipulation claims, *see*, Note, *Price Manipulation in the Commodity Futures Markets: A Reexamination of the Justifications for Simultaneous Causes of Action Under the CEA and the Sherman Act*, 34 UCLA L. Rev. 1305 (1987).

331. 452 F.2d at 1163.

332. United States v. Socony-Vacuum Oil Co., 310 U.S. 150, 223 (1940).

333. 310 U.S. at 224.

334. 452 F.2d at 1163.

335. 452 F.2d at 1163.

336. 452 F.2d at 1163 (citations omitted).

337. 452 F.2d at 1164.

remaining, represents a sufficiently controlling position to warrant consideration of the question whether Cargill actually manipulated prices during this period."[338]

The court further asserted that the "establishment of a dominant long holding is only one aspect of the Government's case; it still must show that the dominant long exacted an artificial price in settlement of his contract."[339] Further, the government was required to show "that there were not adequate supplies of wheat other than those controlled by Cargill from which the shorts could fulfill their delivery requirements on the futures. Obviously, if there were adequate supplies of deliverable grade wheat available to the shorts to deliver to the longs on the future, Cargill would not be able to exact artificial prices in settlement of its contracts, for rather than paying those prices, shorts would instead procure the wheat and deliver it."[340]

Cargill controlled nearly all of the No. 2 soft red winter wheat that was available for delivery in Chicago, but there were sufficient supplies of hard winter wheat that could have been used for delivery without penalty. However, the *Cargill* court excluded the hard winter wheat from the computation of available deliverable supplies because it was a more expensive grade of wheat and no premium was allowed to shorts delivering that grade. The court recognized that there was split in the circuits over whether such exclusion was appropriate, citing *Great Western Food Distributor, Inc. v. Brannan*[341] and *Volkart Brothers v. Freeman*.[342]

In rejecting the *Volkart* requirement that the shorts must take steps to protect themselves, even if that means incurring extra expense, the *Cargill* court stated that the shorts could always settle at a higher price but that this "would not prevent excessive speculation 'causing sudden or unreasonable fluctuations or unwarranted changes' in price condemned" by the Commodity Exchange Act.[343] Instead, the *Cargill* court adopted the definition of the relevant market used for antitrust analysis—that is, products that have "reasonable interchangeability"—and the court did not believe that hard wheat met that definition.[344]

The court also found that the CEA had established the "crucial element" of manipulation—that is, artificial price. The court stated that "if, despite the fact that it had the power and opportunity to do so, Cargill did not in fact cause an artificial price it cannot be guilty of manipulation. Actually, there are two questions involved here—was the price which Cargill received for its futures contracts artificially high, and if so, did Cargill cause it?"[345] The court considered four tests proposed by the government to show artificial price. Three of those tests involved a historical analysis of May wheat futures prices over the prior nine years. The court held those tests established an abnormal movement in the May 1963 contract.[346] The fourth test involved showing that the May 1963 futures price was out of line with cash wheat prices. The parties were in sharp conflict on this issue, but the court resolved the issue in favor of the government.[347]

---

338. 452 F.2d at 1164.

339. 452 F.2d at 1164.

340. 452 F.2d at 1164-1165.

341. Great Western Food Distributors v. Brannan, 201 F.2d 476 (7th Cir.). *cert. denied*, 345 U.S. 997 (1973).

342. Volkart Brothers v. Freeman, 311 F.2d 52 (5th Cir. 1962).

343. 452 F.2d at 1166, *citing* 7 U.S.C. § 6a.

344. 452 F.2d at 1166, *citing* United States v. E.I. Du Pont De Nemours & Co., 351 U.S. 377, 404 (1956).

345. 452 F.2d at 1167.

346. 452 F.2d at 1167.

347. 452 F.2d at 1169.

The court also addressed causation—that is, "whether the artificially high price was caused by Cargill."[348] The court found that it was:

> Throughout the day prior to Cargill's last minute sale the market was resistant to any further increase in the price of the future. Cargill's sell order was at prices 7 and 8 cents over what the future was then selling for, and it was able to get these prices because there was nowhere else for the shorts to go to offset their contracts. It seems clear that the only reason the price advanced so rapidly during the last few minutes of trading was because of Cargill's dominance of the long interest and the high prices it set for liquidation.[349]

The court also compared the actions of other speculators in the market leading up to the liquidation of the contract on May 21 and concluded that Cargill had acted on its market power with its scale-up order in the last fifteen minutes of trading. In contrast, other traders acted in a manner that evidenced they were uncertain as to whether prices would rise.

The court also identified another element required to prove manipulation—that is, that Cargill had acted intentionally in causing the squeeze. Here too Cargill was found guilty:

> Cargill was no novice in futures trading and knew of market conditions which could cause a squeeze. It possessed a very valuable piece of information unknown to the trade at large, namely that it owned practically all the wheat available for delivery on the May future. Furthermore, being a large merchandiser in the Chicago area, it was in a particularly advantageous position to take advantage of the potential squeeze in disposing of its supplies as well as being able to take delivery of whatever wheat might be found by the few shorts able to avoid the squeeze in the futures market. Its behavior in liquidating its contracts was clearly intentional and was highly unusual market behavior; and the method of liquidating the unresolved open interest following the close of trading was also unusual and clearly controlled by Cargill.[350]

The court rejected a claim that Cargill thought that it could market the grain at higher prices if it had to stand for delivery, pointing out to prior sales at lower prices. "The rise of futures to the maximum permissible of $2.28 5/8 was no corrective action to bring futures in line with the cash market, which was substantially lower up to the last day of trading and returned to its previous lows for the month after the squeeze had been effected and the shorts liquidated. It thus appears that Cargill exploited its position in this tight situation, while most of the other longs did not."[351]

The court rejected Cargill's claim that its reliance on the *Volkart* opinion negated an intent to manipulate. The court pointed out that there was contrary authority in the *Great Western Distributors* and *G.H. Miller* cases. The court in Cargill also rejected the premises of Volkart that shorts need to protect themselves by arranging for supplies to deliver:

> Most parties who engage in futures transactions are in no position to either make or take delivery, and if they were required to always make preparations to fulfill their obligations to make or take delivery, the number of persons who could effectively participate in the

348. 452 F.2d at 1169.
349. 452 F.2d at 1169-1170.
350. 452 F.2d at 1170-1171.
351. 452 F.2d at 1172.

futures market would be substantially restricted, thus reducing the liquidity and volume of that market. The main economic functions performed by the futures market are the stabilization of commodity prices, the provision of reliable pricing information, and the insurance against loss from price fluctuation. The functions can be fulfilled only if both longs and shorts can be assured that they can offset their contracts at non-manipulated prices. If in a squeeze situation, the shorts must be forced either to pay manipulated prices to offset their contracts or in the alternative to bring in higher priced outside supplies which are neither wanted nor needed in the local market, then both the cash and the futures markets will be dislocated.[352]

The *Cargill* decision left a split in the circuit courts that the Supreme Court has never resolved. *Cargill* could also be criticized for requiring long traders to avoid harm to short traders, who are trying themselves to exploit market weaknesses at the expense of the longs. The *Cargill* decision was, in any event, a Pyrrhic victory for the CEA. Hidden in its pages was the identification of four elements the court deemed necessary to prove manipulation:

(1) The existence of an "artificial price," a "crucial" element
(2) The ability to cause the artificial price, which meant the creation of a dominant long position in the *Cargill* case
(3) A showing that the party in fact caused the artificial price
(4) An intent to create the artificial price

Establishing those elements proved time-consuming in future cases, as it did in the *Cargill* case. The manipulation in the *Cargill* case involved acts that occurred in May 1963, but the CEA judicial officer did not render an opinion until August 1970. Despite a finding of manipulation, the judicial officer suspended all sanctions "because of the undue protraction of the proceedings, not due to any fault of the petitioners, and because of their apparent reliance on the case of Volkart Bros. as legitimating the conduct in question."[353] Even then the matter was not finally concluded until May 1972 when the Supreme Court declined to review the case, almost nine years after the occurrence of the trading in question.

The CEA became so frustrated by the delay and issues raised in *Cargill* that it asked Congress for legislation in 1965 to overturn the *Volkart* decision. That provision would have defined manipulation as "the exacting, causing or maintaining of an abnormal or artificial price by an action or course of action which raises, depresses, fixes, pegs, or stabilizes the price at or to a level different than that which would otherwise prevail. Any such exacting, causing, or maintaining of an abnormal or artificial price shall constitute manipulation irrespective of any acts or omissions by the holders of futures contracts adversely affected thereby."[354]

This proposed definition sought to relieve the shorts of any obligation to ensure that there were adequate supplies to cover their position. More importantly, it sought to define manipulation to include any act, regardless of intent, that moved market prices to an "abnormal" level.[355] The chair of the CBOT stated with respect to that omission:

352. 452 F.2d at 1173.

353. Cargill v. Hardin, 452 F.2d 1154, 1156 (8th Cir. 1971), *cert. denied*, 406 U.S. 932 (1972).

354. H.R. 11788, 89th Cong., 1st Sess. § 1(d) (1965).

355. *To Amend the Commodity Exchange Act: Hearings on H.R. 11788 Before the Subcommittee on Domestic Marketing and Consumer Relations of the House Committee on Agriculture*, 89th Cong., 2d Sess. 44 (1966).

> I think we could all agree that the very essence of manipulation must be intent. We all know that perfectly legitimate transactions can affect commodity prices. The likelihood of a transaction or series of transactions affecting price increases as the market becomes thinner or, as the quantity bought or sold becomes larger or as the delivery date approaches. Yet under the literal wording of the provision contained in this bill legitimate and unintentional conduct could be subject to prosecution and could be punished by imprisonment and heavy fine.[356]

The CEA responded that its proposed definition would require it to prove a manipulation by showing three elements:

> First, that a price deviation does—or in the case of attempts to manipulate, threatens to—exist between prices, spot or futures, of a regulated commodity and the levels of price that would prevail as a result of the normal determinants of such spot or future prices.
>
> Second, the impact of such deviation does or threatens to impair the effectuation of the declared purposes of the act.
>
> Third, there is a direct and demonstrable relationship between the alleged actions of the accused and the emergence of an artificial or abnormal price.[357]

Included in those elements was the "Government's burden to establish that resultant or threatened price was in fact artificial or abnormal. That is a difficult burden to bear."[358]

A CEA witness testified that a definition of manipulation was needed because the agency's personnel needed guidance from Congress with "regard to due process" and "much more important than that, I think it is the right of an American business person to know as clearly and precisely as is possible what the Congress really had in mind in proscribing or prohibiting acts or relationships."[359] Philip A. Loomis Jr., general counsel for the Securities and Exchange Commission, also testified on the utility of a definition of manipulation: "The Securities Exchange Act does not quite do this, but rather, in section 9, it prohibits various specified types of conduct which, in effect, constitute manipulation. The effect, I think, is very much the same and it is, of course, important in attempting to prevent or punish a manipulation to be able to point to a specific statutory provision which describes the conduct in question."[360] The SEC would later ignore that testimony when it was seeking expansive application of Section 10(b) to manipulation and other conduct.

Professor T.A. Hieronymus, an agricultural economist teaching at the University of Illinois, was critical of the USDA's entire approach to speculation and manipulation:

> The USDA has long been preoccupied with price excesses in futures markets and thus with manipulation and excessive speculation. The underlying concept seems to be that futures markets exist for hedging and that speculation is a necessary evil, that hedging is good and speculation is bad, that speculation should only be tolerated to the degree necessary to absorb the risks shifted hedgers. . . .
>
> Hedging serves useful economic purposes that have long been understood and appreciated. The legislative record is replete with testimonials, the textbooks describe and extoll

356. *Id.* at 51.
357. *Id.* at 16.
358. *Id.* at 24.
359. *Id.* at 23.
360. *Id.* at 33.

> the merits of hedging, and the Commodity Exchange Act has been changed from time to time in the direction of more considerate treatment of hedgers.
>
> In fact, however, hedging is the lesser beauty of futures markets. . . . In addition to absorbing the risks shifted by hedgers, speculators serve the necessary and useful purpose of establishing prices that regulate the flow of stored commodities onto the market and that guide future production.[361]

The professor was also critical of the CEA's proposed definition for manipulation. "As I read this it says that at any time that an artificial price is judged to have existed—that is, if a price declines subsequent to a rise or rises subsequent to a decline—everyone who had a part in the move is guilty of manipulation. Everyone who makes a trade, even the smallest job lot trader, has an effect on price and causes it to be something different than otherwise would have prevailed. Thus every trader would be guilty and those selected by the Secretary would be punished."[362]

Another part of the bill would have allowed the secretary of agriculture to suspend the registration of persons engaging in acts in restraint of trade, which would allow the USDA to attack the equivalent of Sherman Act violations in the commodity markets. This would include a suspension when a person merely had sufficient control of the market even if there was no evidence of an artificial price.[363] The CEA also sought to limit judicial review of the decisions of its administrative hearing officers as a way of further preventing *Volkart*-like decisions. The bill sought to make manipulation a felony and to grant the secretary of agriculture authority to seek injunctive relief against persons engaging in a manipulation of the market.[364]

The CEA also once again sought control over margin for commodity futures contracts as a way to limit speculation. That renewed effort followed a request by the CEA in 1966 that the CBOT increase its margin levels to curb speculation. The CBOT refused that request.[365] Witnesses for the Department of Agriculture asserted in the hearings on this bill that there was a difference between stock and commodity futures margins and that normally exchange set margins were satisfactory. However, the department believed there were "certain situations" in which minimum margins should be set above ordinary levels. "Excessive speculation in the futures market, for example, can seriously disrupt prices and marketing to the detriment of producers, consumers, and users of the market. Control of a large percentage of the futures market by individuals creates the danger of price manipulation, and of unwarranted or unreasonable sudden upward or downward changes in price or otherwise restrains trade."[366] The department again asserted that position limits were effective only in restraining large traders and not the small speculators who flocked to the market during periods of upward movement.[367] That bill met stiff opposition and was not passed.

Additional legislation was introduced in 1967 that would have given the Federal Reserve Board authority to set margins on commodity futures. That bill was portrayed as a consumer protection measure, but was dropped when the Federal Reserve Board expressed opposition. The CEA commissioned a private study by the consulting firm of Robert R. Nathan Associates Inc. on the use of

361. *Id.* at 147.

362. *Id.* at 151.

363. *Id.* at 15.

364. *Id.* at 5-7.

365. Jerry W. Markham, *Federal Regulation of Margin in the Commodity Futures Industry: History and Theory*, 64 TEMP. L. REV. 59, 79 (1991).

366. *To Amend the Commodity Exchange Act: Hearings on H.R. 11788 Before the Subcommittee on Domestic Marketing and Consumer Relations of the House Committee on Agriculture*, 89th Cong., 2d Sess. 11-12 (1966).

367. *Id.* at 12.

margin in controlling speculation. That report, issued in December 1967, found that the increase in initial margin requirements between 1947 and 1948 "probably" helped curb very short-term price fluctuations.[368] The Nathan study report, however, also noted that speculative transactions often moderated rather than accentuated price volatility. It also questioned the ability of the government to determine when and how much margins should be increased to limit volatility.

The secretary of agriculture tried again in 1967 to increase its powers, but eliminated the most controversial provisions of the 1966 bill—that is, those defining manipulation and giving the secretary authority over margins.[369] The secretary still sought to make manipulation a felony and to allow the department to seek injunctive relief. A department witness condemned "massive speculation in which powerful interests slug it out to make the market go the way that will best serve their own speculative positions."[370] He identified various manipulative schemes as establishing a need for the legislation. One such manipulation involved a large trader who, on being advised that he was under investigation, announced that he was closing his large long position, causing prices to fall. Actually, he was short and made a profit from the false announcement. Another trader sold oats short in Chicago and long on the Winnipeg exchange in Canada. The trader then moved cash oats out of Winnipeg to Chicago, causing prices to increase in Winnipeg in aid of its long position and causing prices in Chicago to decline in aid of its short position.[371]

The industry again mounted strong opposition to these proposals. Among other things, the chair of the CBOT asserted that the CEA had not proven that it had any special skill in identifying manipulation, noting that decisions by CEA judicial officers involving manipulation had been reversed three out of six times on appeal to the courts.[372] This opposition was successful. A bill was passed, but its reach was limited to making manipulation a felony and granting the secretary of agriculture power to issue administrative cease and desist orders.[373]

---

368. U.S. Dept. of Ag. Economic Research Service, *Margins, Speculation and Prices in Grain Futures Markets* 1 (Dec. 1967), *noted in*, Jerry W. Markham, *Federal Regulation of Margin in the Commodity Futures Industry: History and Theory*, 64 TEMP. L. REV. 59, 80-81 (1991).

369. Jerry W. Markham, *Manipulation of Commodity Futures Prices: The Unprosecutable Crime*, 8 YALE J. ON REG. 281, 325 (1991).

370. *Amend the Commodity Exchange Act: Hearings Before the House Comm. on Agriculture on H.R. 11930 and H.R. 12317*, 90th Cong., 1st Sess. 43 (1967).

371. *Id.*

372. *Id.* at 110.

373. Pub. L. No. 90-258, 42 Stat. 1003 (1968).

4

MANIPULATION OF COMMODITY PRICES IN A TIME OF INFLATION

4:1 CRUDE OIL PRICE CONCERNS

Historically large increases in crude oil prices were the center of an effort to impose price controls in the 1970s and raised concerns over manipulation that continues today. Crude oil prices began rising after World War II as production sources shifted from the United States to the Middle East. President Eisenhower had imposed import limits on non-U.S. oil as a way of avoiding dependence on foreign oil.[1] Those limits were lifted during the administration of Richard M. Nixon in order to increase supplies in the face of rising oil prices.[2] Nixon was forced to take that and other drastic actions to counter a new national security threat—inflation.

"The Great Inflation of 1965 to the mid-1980s was the central monetary event of the latter half of the 20th century. Its economic cost was large. It destroyed the Bretton Woods system of fixed exchange rates, bankrupted much of the thrift industry, heavily taxed the U.S. capital stock, and arbitrarily redistributed income and wealth."[3] Many people blamed that inflation on speculators and manipulation, but it was more directly the result of fundamental factors that included increased spending on the Johnson-era "Great Society" programs and the Vietnam War.

Nixon sought to deal with this inflation through his New Economic Policy, which was announced on August 15, 1971. It included a ninety-day wage and price freeze, which was extended into three more phases of government control over the economy that went on for more than two years. The reason why price controls administered by bureaucrats provide a poor substitute for the market was soon evident. The Cost of Living Council, which was created to administer these controls, was called on "to respond to 50,000 complaints, 6,000 requests for waivers, and 750,000 requests for interpretation in its first ninety days."[4] Among the compelling issues to be decided by the Cost of Living Council and the Office of Emergency Preparedness was whether the University of Southern California could raise its reserved seat ticket prices by fifty cents for the 1971 football season. A special Temporary Emergency Court of Appeals ruled that it could not.[5]

1. The concern over the country's increasing dependence on oil from the Middle East had been at the center of the Suez Canal crisis in 1956. David A. Nichols, Eisenhower 1956 (2011).

2. Andrew Scott Cooper, Oil Kings 90 (2011).

3. Allan H. Meltzer, *Origins of the Great Inflation*, Federal Reserve Bank of St. Louis Review, 145 (March/April 2005).

4. J. Mashaw, Bureaucratic Justice 10 (1983). Despite strong ideological leanings against price controls, future Defense Department secretary Donald Rumsfeld was appointed as the Cost of Living Council's director, and future U.S. vice president Dick Cheney was its director of operations. Donald Rumsfeld, Known and Unknown: A Memoir 139-140 (2011). Rumsfeld described his assignment as making "sure the new controls were temporary and did as little damage as possible." *Id.* at 140.

5. University of Southern California v. Cost of Living Council, 472 F.2d 1065 (Temp. Ct. Emerg. App. 1972), *cert. denied*, 410 U.S. 928 (1973).

Nixon also shut down the government's gold window to stop a run on U.S. gold stocks. Nixon blamed the gold run on "international gold speculators"[6] and "international money speculators."[7] Nixon's ending of fixed currency rates set by the Bretton Woods agreement at the end of World War II[8] led to the development of massive foreign exchange markets among banks and futures markets where speculators could thrive on foreign currency bets. This change also led to massive fraud in the retail foreign currency market that the Commodity Futures Trading Commission (CFTC) later proved unable to deal with and that required various amendments to the Commodity Exchange Act in order to regulate.[9]

The Nixon wage-price controls were carried out under the Economic Stabilization Act of 1970.[10] That legislation gave the president standby authority to impose regulations to stabilize prices, rents, wages, and salaries. The controls adopted by Nixon under this authority did not apply to raw agricultural commodities. Those price controls were being phased out until the country was hit by a "food supply shock" in 1973. That crisis was spurred by the "great grain robbery" of sales to the Soviet Union, which led to the creation of the CFTC.[11] Wholesale grain prices increased by a shocking 21 percent in a single month.[12] In 1973 grain prices reached a 125-year high and consumer food prices increased by nearly 50 percent.[13]

In a televised speech on July 1, 1973, Nixon addressed the nation's ongoing economic problems and rising energy costs. Among other things, he claimed that the Cost of Living Council had ordered more than 1,000 gas stations to roll back prices that exceeded its price control levels.[14] The Nixon price controls, however, actually ended up "discouraging domestic oil production, while stimulating consumption."[15] International events also intervened in October 1973 to create the country's first "oil shock," which would give rise to futures markets in energy products that became a subsequent target of regulation. That oil shock occurred after the Arab members of the Organization of Petroleum Exporting Countries (OPEC) embargoed exports of crude oil to the United States in protest of U.S. support for Israel during the Yom Kippur War.[16] "Before it was over, the price of oil had rocketed from $3 a barrel to $12 per barrel," an increase of 400 percent.[17]

In another nationwide speech on November 7, 1973, President Nixon declared that his administration would solve the "energy crisis" through "Project Independence," which was supposed to

---

6. ALLEN J. MATUSOW, NIXON ECONOMICS 155 (1998).

7. RICHARD REEVES, PRESIDENT NIXON 362 (2001).

8. III JERRY W. MARKHAM, A FINANCIAL HISTORY OF THE UNITED STATES, FROM THE AGE OF DERIVATIVES TO THE NEW MILLENNIUM 38-39 (2002).

9. *See*, JERRY W. MARKHAM, COMMODITIES REGULATION: FRAUD, MANIPULATION AND OTHER CLAIMS, §§ 14:30 and 14:50 (2010) (describing those problems).

10. 84 Stat. 799 (1970).

11. ALLEN J. MATUSOW, NIXON'S ECONOMY 222, 226-227 (1998).

12. *Id.* at 227.

13. *See*, III JERRY W. MARKHAM, A FINANCIAL HISTORY OF THE UNITED STATES, FROM THE AGE OF DERIVATIVES TO THE NEW MILLENNIUM (1970-2001), at 40-41 (2002) (describing these price increases). The House Committee on Banking and Currency reported out a bill to extend the Economic Stabilization Act that would have included authority for the secretary of agriculture to set margins on commodity futures contracts. That end run around the Agriculture Committee failed. JERRY W. MARKHAM, A HISTORY OF COMMODITY FUTURES TRADING AND ITS REGULATION 65 (1987).

14. STEPHEN E. AMBROSE, NIXON, RUIN AND RECOVERY (1973-1990) 187 (1991).

15. DANIEL YERGIN, THE PRIZE 590 (1991).

16. An oil embargo by Arab countries in 1967 in protest of the Six-Day War with Israel had failed, but the 1973 embargo was devastating. DANIEL YERGIN, THE QUEST 284-285 (2011).

17. DAVID HALBERSTAM, THE RECKONING 19 (1986).

remove U.S. dependence on foreign oil as a major energy source, a goal never achieved. Unfamiliar with the concept of understatement, Nixon likened that program to the Manhattan Project and the NASA moon landing. Project Independence was, in fact, a rather modest rationing program that included fuel-saving restrictions on commercial airline flights, more carpooling and the lowering of thermostats to sixty-five degrees. Nixon also sought the building of the Trans-Alaska pipeline, and an unsuccessful expansion of nuclear energy.[18]

A few weeks later, Nixon announced that he was reducing crude oil supplies to the market, setting quotas on gasoline consumption, reducing heating oil supplies, and imposing a 25 percent reduction in jet fuel for commercial flights. The president also asked gas stations to close voluntarily on Sundays and, somewhat weirdly, sought legislation that would allow him to limit the use of Christmas tree ornaments. Setting an example for the nation, Nixon announced that he had already ordered a reduction in the use of such ornaments at the White House.[19]

Nixon tried to deal with continuing shortages through a new high-level White House energy policy office, and he sought a new Cabinet department for energy and natural resources.[20] Nixon appointed an energy czar, William E. Simon, to head the new White House policy office. "The new office [was] assigned the task of allocating reduced petroleum supplies to refiners and consumers and of controlling the price of oil and gasoline."[21]

The restrictions imposed by Nixon led to a wildcat strike, attended by some violence, by truckers who were suffering from high prices and lack of fuel. "The National Guard was called out to prevent violence, and food and fuel supplies were disrupted in some areas."[22] A national speed limit of fifty-five miles per hour was established by the Emergency Highway Energy Conservation Act, which was enacted into law on January 2, 1974, as a means to conserve gasoline and limit demand for crude oil.[23] Nevertheless, crude oil prices shot up by 400 percent in 1974 and drivers in the United States waited in long lines to buy fuel at gas stations.[24]

After Nixon was driven from office, the new president, Gerald Ford, was faced with continuing energy problems and "galloping" inflation; "[w]holesale prices had spurted up 20.4 percent in the last year alone."[25] In September 1974, Ford warned OPEC, which was controlling prices and production of crude oil, that other nations "cannot allow their policies to be dictated, or their fate decided, by artificial rigging and distortion of world commodity markets." That warning was generally ignored.

"In 1974, inflation reached the highest level since the end of World War I. Within months, unemployment stood at 9.2 percent, two points higher than at any time in the postwar years,"[26] although less than that faced by the Obama administration in 2011. "And there was a growing fear

---

18. Conrad Black, A Life in Full: Richard M. Nixon 941 (2007).

19. Stephen E. Ambrose, Nixon: Ruin and Recovery (1973-1990) 279 (1991).

20. *Id.* at 187.

21. http://energy.gov/management/timeline-events-1971-1980 (accessed March 2, 2011).

22. James R. Healey, *As Oil Prices Rocket, High Diesel Costs Pinch Truckers*, USA Today, Feb. 13, 2003, at 1b.

23. Emergency Highway Conservation Act of 1974, Pub. L. No. 93-239, 87 Stat. 1046. That prohibition was widely ignored and was eased by the 1987 Surface Transportation and Uniform Relocation Assistance Act, Pub. L. No. 100-17, 101 Stat. 264-265, which allowed limits of up to sixty-five miles per hour on interstate highways. All federal limits on automobile speeds were removed in 1995 by the National Highway Designation Act. Pub. L. No. 104-59, 109 Stat. 568.

24. III Jerry W. Markham, A Financial History of the United States, From the Age of Derivatives to the New Millennium 41 (2002).

25. Gerald Ford, A Time to Heal 151 (1979).

26. Daniel Yergin & Joseph Stanislaw, The Commanding Heights: The Battle Between Government and the Marketplace That Is Remaking the World 63 (1997).

that inflation and inflationary expectations were becoming so embedded as to threaten every household, as well as the social order and stability of the nation."[27] Ford responded to those economic concerns with a rather laughable public relations program called WIN (Whip Inflation Now) that involved passing out buttons emblazoned with the WIN logo.[28] Ford approved the Energy Policy and Conservation Act in December 1975,[29] which extended oil price controls until 1979, but did nothing to alleviate a growing concern over energy shortages.

Ford's successor, Jimmy Carter, sought to phase out oil price controls over a two-year period beginning in 1979. Ronald Reagan accelerated the process when he assumed office, eliminating those controls through his very first executive order.[30]

4:2 THE COMMODITY EXCHANGE AUTHORITY FALTERS

The Commodity Exchange Authority (CEA) filed manipulation cases involving trading in the September 1970 shell egg futures contract on the Chicago Mercantile Exchange (CME), the May 1971 wheat futures contract on the Chicago Board of Trade (CBOT), the May 1971 Idaho futures contract on the CME, the December 1971 and March, May, and July 1972 cotton futures contracts on the New York Cotton Exchange, the July 1972 oat futures contract on the CBOT, and the July 1973 corn futures contract on the CBOT.[31] However, most of those cases would have to be resolved by a new federal agency—the Commodity Futures Trading Commission (CFTC)—that was created by Congress to replace the CEA in 1974.[32]

A rare criminal case was brought in 1972 against John P. Bauer and the Bauer International Corp. for false reports concerning market information. Those reports were made as a part of an attempt to manipulate shell egg futures prices on the CME.[33] The individual defendant was sentenced to sixty days in prison.[34] A separate action in *United Egg Producers v. Bauer International Corp.*[35] resulted in a preliminary injunction by a federal district court against defendants prohibiting further false press releases concerning the proposed importation of 425,000 cases (153 million) of Spanish eggs that affected egg futures prices on the CME. Bauer International had used a news service to issue false press releases concerning its importation of Spanish eggs to the news media. Those reports had been carried in the *Journal of Commerce*, the *Chicago Sun Times*, *Barron's*, Reuters News Service, the New York *Daily News*, the *Wall Street Journal*, and the *New York Post*. The court held that it had the authority to issue injunctive relief under the Commodity Exchange Act in order to protect industry participants from such false reports. Actually, there was no such authority until the Commodity Exchange Act was amended in 1974.

27. *Id.* at 65.

28. JULES WITCOVER, MARATHON 46 (1977).

29. Pub. L. No. 94-163.

30. DANIEL YERGIN, THE QUEST 166 (2011).

31. Jerry W. Markham, *Manipulation of Commodity Futures Prices: The Unprosecutable Crime*, 8 YALE J. ON REG. 281, 385-387 (1991). The Supreme Court referred an antitrust action against the CME to the Commodity Exchange Commission for consideration. The suit charged that the CME had manipulated March 1970 egg prices downward. CME v. Deaktor, 414 U.S. 113 (1973).

32. Commodity Futures Trading Commission Act of 1974, Pub. L. No. 93-463, 88 Stat. 1389.

33. Commodity Exchange Authority, *Summary of Administrative and Judicial Proceedings Under the Commodity Exchange Act (June 15, 1936–June 30, 1972) and Under the Grain Futures Act (Sept. 21, 1922–June 14, 1936)* 97-98 (circa 1977).

34. Jerry W. Markham, *Manipulation of Commodity Futures Prices: The Unprosecutable Crime*, 8 YALE J. ON REG. 373, n. 596 (1991).

35. United Egg Producers v. Bauer International Corp., 311 F. Supp. 1375 (S.D.N.Y. 1970).

"The 'Grain Robbery' of 1972 was one of those economic events that, like the OPEC Oil Embargo . . . can truly be said to have changed the world."[36] This saga was touched off after President Nixon announced on June 11, 1971, that restrictions on sales of grain to the Soviet Union were being lifted. Within six months of that announcement, the Soviet Union purchased some 3 million tons of U.S. feed grains.[37] "In July and August 1972 sales of wheat to Russia were made totaling about 440 million bushels and it was sold for a total of about $700 million. In addition, the 1972 grain sales to Russia included barley, corn, sorghum, and soybeans, so that, in all, about 725 million bushels of grain were sold to Russia."[38]

The Soviet purchases totaled nearly 25 percent of the U.S. wheat crop.[39] In the words of Secretary of Agriculture Earl Butz, "[t]his is by all odds the greatest grain transaction in the history of the world."[40] The grain sales to the Soviet Union were made by large grain firms and kept secret while they were being hedged on the grain exchanges. The Soviet sales pushed wheat prices up sharply to $6 from about $1.60 per bushel.[41]

Hearings were held in Congress on the Soviet purchases. There it was charged that "[s]elling 25 percent of our wheat crop created a demand situation and a sympathetic price rise of other grains which in turn created other shortages such as in soybeans."[42] Higher grain costs meant higher livestock and poultry feeding costs and "eventually the large increases were reflected in prices to consumers in higher costs of meats, eggs, poultry, butter, and other commodities."[43]

One congressman attacked the Nixon administration for not imposing price controls on agricultural commodities, but he also charged that "excessive speculation in futures has been a significant part of the problem of food price inflation."[44] The increased commodity prices "resulted in price increases at the retail level which have hurt the American family grievously, and particularly the lower income families and those on fixed incomes. Speculation in non-food futures has contributed significantly to the increases in other living costs."[45]

Another congressman charged that the Soviet wheat sales demonstrated "the disastrous effects that unfair trading practices can have on farmers and consumers alike. Major grain exporting companies speculate freely on the commodities exchanges, and it appears that their manipulation of the trading allowed them to buy wheat cheap and keep it secret from other traders, later they sold it at higher prices to the Russians." He further stated that, "[w]ithout new controls there is nothing to prevent foreign nations from manipulating commodity futures."[46]

Claims were made that a manipulation had occurred on the Kansas City Board of Trade in setting the closing price, which had the effect of increasing subsidy costs to the government by as

---

36. Dan Morgan, Merchants of Grain 121 (1979).

37. *Hearings on Russian Grain Transactions: Hearings Before the Senate Permanent Subcommittee on Investigations of the Committee on Government Operations* (Part 1), 93d Cong., 1st Sess. 8 (1973).

38. *Small Business Problems Involved in the Marketing of Grain and Other Commodities: Hearings Before the Subcommittee on Special Small Business Problems of the House Permanent Select Committee on Small Business*, 93d Cong., 1st Sess. 31 (1973).

39. *See*, Dan Morgan, Merchants of Grain 121 (1979) (describing those purchases).

40. *Id.* at 171.

41. *Grains and Oilseeds*, http://www.crbtrader.com/pubs/enc/grains.pdf (accessed December 28, 2011).

42. *Hearings on Russian Grain Transactions: Hearings Before the Senate Permanent Subcommittee on Investigations of the Committee on Government Operations* (Part 1), 93d Cong., 1st Sess. 3 (1973).

43. *Id.*

44. 120 Cong. Rec. 10627 (1974) (remarks of Rep. Sullivan).

45. *Id.*

46. 120 Cong Rec. 10741 (1974) (remarks of Rep. Adams).

much $300 million.[47] The Justice Department, however, declined prosecution. Alex C. Caldwell, the head of the CEA, testified before Congress that the CEA found no evidence of manipulation of the markets in connection with the Russian wheat purchases.[48] The Commodity Exchange Authority did bring a manipulation case involving corn futures on the CBOT, but that case was later dismissed.[49] The CEA also brought charges against the Continental Grain Co. for filing inaccurate reports on its futures trading and cash positions.

Caldwell testified that the prevention of manipulation and the detection and prosecution of manipulators was the most important activity of the CEA. "It is also the most difficult and most time-consuming."[50] Caldwell's testimony was also instructive on what the CEA believed constituted manipulation and its effects:

> There are various types of price manipulation. The most common involves a corner or a squeeze in the market. In a manipulation of this type, an individual or firm or a group of associated individuals or firms gains control of the futures market and of the supply of the commodity available for delivery on futures contracts.
>
> As a result of this control, the manipulator is able to establish artificially high prices in the futures market. This is possible because the shorts in the market, those who have open sales commitments, are at the mercy of the manipulator.
>
> Since the manipulator has control of the futures market and also of the deliverable cash supply, the shorts have to come to him either to buy futures contracts to cover their short positions or to buy the commodity itself for delivery on their short positions. Since the manipulator is the only source of supply for futures contracts and for the deliverable commodity, he can set an artificially high price which the shorts, having no alternative, must pay.
>
> Manipulation of this type creates the most serious damage to the agricultural marketing structure by causing an unnatural relationship between futures prices and cash prices. This destroys the entire concept of hedging, frequently placing the hedger in a position of greater risk than if he had remained unhedged.
>
> Since futures prices are used as a basis for pricing transactions in the cash market, an upward manipulation of the futures market results in artificially high prices being paid for the cash commodity in various levels of the distribution channel.
>
> In the final analysis, this increases the cost to the ultimate consumer. In addition, manipulation of this type tends to draw the cash commodity to the delivery points in unusual amounts, thus, taking the commodity out of its normal channels of movement from producer to consumer.
>
> This frequently results in an oversupply at the delivery points after the manipulation has been completed, coupled with an undersupply at the normal points of distribution. There are, of course, many variations of this type of price manipulation, but all fall basically into this pattern.[51]

Caldwell also described "bear raids" as another form of manipulation. "In this type of manipulation, the manipulator seeks to force prices downward by heavy and strategically placed sales

47. Jerry W. Markham, *Manipulation of Commodity Futures Prices: The Unprosecutable Crime*, 8 YALE J. ON REG. 281, 331 (1991).

48. *Hearings on Russian Grain Transactions: Hearings Before the Senate Permanent Subcommittee on Investigations of the Committee on Government Operations* (Part 1), 93d Cong., 1st Sess. 167-168 (1973).

49. In re Indiana Farm Bureau Coop. Association, 1982 CFTC LEXIS 25 (C.F.T.C.).

50. *Hearings on Russian Grain Transactions: Hearings Before the Senate Permanent Subcommittee on Investigations of the Committee on Government Operations* (Part 1), 93d Cong., 1st Sess. 165 (1973).

51. *Id.* at 164-165.

and heavy deliveries or the threat of heavy deliveries."[52] A third type of manipulation, which Caldwell described as less damaging and less frequent than other types of manipulation, but more difficult to prove, involved "heavy trading usually concentrated on the opening or closing of the market."[53] Caldwell stated that the purpose of this type of manipulation "is to move futures prices either upward or downward for a brief period to affect the posted opening or closing prices. This type of price manipulation is usually done for some purpose outside the futures market itself. The purposes may be many and varied and in some cases have no relationship at all to the marketing of commodities."[54]

Other commodities were experiencing historic price run-ups, including coffee and sugar, in which there was said to be a price "bubble."[55] The CBOT declared a market emergency in the January 1973 soybean futures contracts and removed daily price limits as delivery approached. Otherwise, short traders would not have been able to cover their positions. "The trading limits having been removed, the price of January 1973 soybean futures contracts rose from $4.69 1/2 per bushel at closing on January 18 to $4.95 per bushel at the opening on January 19. The price at closing that day was $4.98–$5.00 per bushel and on January 22, the last trading day for January 1973 soybean futures, it closed at $4.95–$4.99."[56]

In May 1973, "soybean prices rose by 45 percent, wheat by 22 percent, and corn by 30 percent."[57] Soybean prices increased by more than $8 per bushel over a period of just a few months, nearly reaching $13 per bushel, about four times the price they had sold at a year earlier.[58] At that time, 90 percent of the long side of the CBOT soybean futures contract was concentrated in the hands of just four traders. The CBOT stopped trading in the affected contract months except for liquidation only. "There simply were not enough soybeans available even if transportation had been available, to fulfill long contracts by delivering soybeans in lieu of buying back those long contracts. Therefore, those who had hedged by selling short were at the mercy of those who held the long contracts."[59]

Nixon imposed additional price controls in June 1973. The controls did not apply to raw agricultural products but did freeze meat prices. The result was that "[r]anchers stopped shipping their cattle to the market, farmers drowned their chickens, and consumers emptied the shelves of supermarkets."[60] Cotton prices also rose sharply in the fall of 1973, touching off a "cotton crisis" in which prices doubled in a six-month period. The cotton price spike resulted in more than 500 lawsuits over cotton contracts.[61] At one point a single trader held 67 percent of all long futures contracts on the New York Cotton Exchange, raising concerns of manipulation.[62] Problems were also encountered in the July 1973 corn futures contract on the CBOT, resulting in congestion and

---

52. *Id.* at 166.

53. *Id.*

54. *Id.*

55. 120 Cong. Rec. 10627 (1974) (remarks of Rep. Sullivan).

56. Case & Co. v. Board of Trade of the City of Chicago, 523 F.2d 355, 359 (7th Cir. 1975).

57. Allen J. Matusow, Nixon's Economy 229 (1998).

58. Jerry W. Markham, *Manipulation of Commodity Futures Prices: The Unprosecutable Crime*, 8 Yale J. on Reg. 281, 329 (1991).

59. *Review of Commodity Exchange Act and Discussion of Possible Changes: Hearings Before the House Committee on Agriculture*, 93d Cong., 1st Sess. 4-5 (1973).

60. Daniel Yergin & Joseph Stanislaw, The Commanding Heights: The Battle Between Government and the Marketplace That Is Remaking the World 63 (1997).

61. Jerry W. Markham, *Manipulation of Commodity Futures Prices: The Unprosecutable Crime*, 8 Yale J. on Reg. 281, 330, n. 340 (1991).

62. *Review of Commodity Exchange Act and Discussion of Possible Changes: Hearings Before the House Committee on Agriculture*, 93d Cong., 1st Sess. 5 (1973).

a squeeze when transportation was unavailable for supplies to be sent to Chicago for delivery. This allowed the long traders to demand a premium of $1.30 per bushel from the shorts.[63]

Hearings on grain marketing problems were held in 1973 before a subcommittee of the House Permanent Select Committee on Small Business.[64] Its chair, Neal Smith (D-IA), made recommendations for legislation later that year to the House Committee on Agriculture, which had legislative jurisdiction over the commodity exchanges. Smith noted that in 1972 the commodity exchanges handled $268 billion in notional value in futures contracts on regulated commodities. That figure had been just $60 billion ten years earlier. "And the current $268 billion compares to a total of $200 billion for all stocks handled on the stock exchanges."[65]

Representative Smith pointed out the problems then being encountered in concentrated trading on the commodity exchanges and recommended a number of legislative changes. Smith wanted futures trading on all commodities to be regulated.[66] He sought a new independent agency for regulating the commodity exchanges that would have "the stature and capability comparable to the SEC."[67] The new agency would be given expanded powers, including injunctive authority.[68]

Smith also sought legislation to grant the federal government authority to set margins for futures contracts. Interestingly, he thought that authority was needed because the CBOT had sharply raised margin requirements, increasing costs to market participants.[69] Those increases had been dramatic, with increases of up to 300 percent. This resulted in forced liquidations and disrupted hedging, as well as increasing costs and price volatility.[70]

Alex C. Caldwell, the head of the CEA, testified in opposition to that proposal. This was another reversal of the CEA's views on the need for federal regulatory authority over margins. This latest reversal was apparently the result of the Nathan study conducted for the CEA in 1967 that recommended against CEA control of margins. Caldwell testified that stock and commodity margins were "as different as apples and oranges" and that "[e]xperience has shown that increasing margin requirements on commodity futures transactions is an ineffective means of curbing volatile prices and can increase the extent of a price movement rather than dampen it." He further noted that increased "margin requirements can also interfere with the hedging function performed by futures markets and directly or indirectly result in higher merchandising and processing costs."[71]

The Justice Department questioned Caldwell's views on margin, asking how a "regulatory authority can adequately police undue speculative activity without some input into the margin equation."[72] The comptroller general also recommended a government-dictated formula for increasing margins as prices increase.[73] However, an effort to add margin authority on the House

63. *Id.* at 4.

64. *Small Business Problems Involved in the Marketing of Grain and Other Commodities: Hearings Before the Subcommittee on Special Small Business Problems of the House Permanent Select Committee on Small Business*, 93d Cong., 1st Sess. (1973).

65. *Review of Commodity Exchange Act and Discussion of Possible Changes: Hearings Before the House Committee on Agriculture*, 93d Cong., 1st Sess. 3 (1973).

66. *Id.* at 10-11.

67. *Id.* at 15.

68. *Id.* at 12.

69. *Id.* at 6-7.

70. Jerry W. Markham, *Federal Regulation of Margin in the Commodity Futures Industry: History and Theory*, 64 Temp. L. Rev. 59, 83, n. 151 (1991).

71. *Review of Commodity Exchange Act and Discussion of Possible Changes: Hearings Before the House Committee on Agriculture*, 93d Cong., 1st Sess. 26 (1973).

72. H.R. Rep. No. 975, 93d Cong., 2d Sess. 26-27 (1974).

73. Comptroller General, *Interim Report to the Congress on the CEA and on Commodity Futures Trading* 26 (May 3, 1974).

floor was defeated. The sponsor of the amendment that would have granted such authority unsuccessfully argued that it would otherwise "be impossible to prevent the tremendous speculation that is taking place in commodities."[74]

Caldwell did seek an amendment that would relieve the CEA of investigating cash market manipulations unless they were related to commodity futures trading.[75] He also opposed a proposal to restrict "excessive speculation" when speculative transactions totaled more than 50 percent in outstanding futures contracts. Caldwell thought such a restriction would be impractical and adversely affect hedging.[76] An industry representative also noted that "[n]o analysis of which we are aware has determined what could be meant by 'excessive speculation.' If price manipulations are what is meant, these should be addressed directly. . . . Short of that, 'excessive speculation' appears to be an undefined and indefinable—perhaps because phantom—concept."[77] Nevertheless, similar proposals would emerge in future years.

Representative Smith also recommended the encouragement of computerized trading for matching customer orders instead of sending them to a trading floor for execution.[78] However, Alex Caldwell testified that there was no need to legislate on that subject: "Computerized trading may well be the wave of the future, but many questions of both technological and economic feasibility must be answered before it can or should be implemented."[79] Both were correct: computerized trading was in the future, and when it arrived decades later the trading of futures contracts changed dramatically, although concerns about manipulation would remain.

The House Agriculture Committee took up the legislative task of strengthening the Commodity Exchange Act. It found that speculators were being attracted from the stock markets into commodity futures because the latter offered lower margin requirements, high leverage, and price volatility—the lethal combination sought by speculators.[80] Another concern was the narrow reach of the Commodity Exchange Act, which regulated only a limited number of domestic commodities.

As a witness for the CEA testified, futures markets in unregulated commodities were growing rapidly and becoming increasingly important to the economy. "Manipulation of futures prices and price distortions caused by excessive speculation have serious repercussions on these markets, yet no Federal agency is responsible for preventing price manipulation or curbing excessive speculation in them."[81] It was also stated in the Senate debates on this legislation that futures trading volumes had expanded dramatically in recent years and that this growth and "especially the persistent price increases have cause a wide-felt concern that market abuse and manipulation of prices were occurring."[82] A witness in the hearings on this legislation also complained that "the commodities exchanges have shown themselves to be susceptible to a certain amount of

74. Jerry W. Markham, *Federal Regulation of Margin in the Commodity Futures Industry: History and Theory*, 64 Temp. L. Rev. 59, 86 (1991) (citation omitted).

75. *Review of Commodity Exchange Act and Discussion of Possible Changes: Hearings Before the House Committee on Agriculture*, 93d Cong., 1st Sess. 26 (1973).

76. *Id.* at 29.

77. *Commodity Futures Trading Commission Act: Hearings Before the Senate Committee on Agriculture and Forestry*, 93d Cong., 2d Sess. 852 (1973).

78. *Review of Commodity Exchange Act and Discussion of Possible Changes: Hearings Before the House Committee on Agriculture*, 93d Cong., 1st Sess. 10 (1973).

79. *Id.* at 25.

80. Jerry W. Markham, A History of Commodity Futures Trading and Its Regulation 61 (1987).

81. *Review of Commodity Exchange Act and Discussion of Possible Changes: Hearings Before the House Committee on Agriculture*, 93d Cong., 1st Sess. 26 (1973).

82. 120 Cong. Rec. 30458 (1974) (remarks of Sen. Talmadge).

manipulation and abuse. 'Rigging,' 'cornering,' and 'squeezing' are becoming common terms in the grain industry."[83]

In the end, Congress did pass legislation that massively overhauled the Commodity Exchange Act of 1936. Those amendments were contained in an act titled the Commodity Futures Trading Commission Act of 1974.[84] It was asserted in Congress that these amendments would "significantly strengthen the regulation of commodities trading, protect the investor, and assure the consumer, the farmer, the commodity user, and the public at large that price manipulations and trading abuses on futures exchanges will not be tolerated."[85] Inexplicably, however, the manipulation standard in the Commodity Exchange Act was not changed or defined by the amendments. That omission would have the effect of neutralizing the CFTC's efforts to deal with future manipulations.

The CFTC replaced the CEA as regulator for the commodity futures markets. The application of the Commodity Exchange Act was expanded by the 1974 legislation to include all commodities, not just the previously regulated domestic agricultural markets. That change came at a propitious time because derivatives trading was in the process of expanding from agricultural commodities into a broad array of new financial instruments and "world" commodities like gold, silver, oil, and other energy products. The CFTC was given exclusive jurisdiction over commodity futures trading, and its powers were expanded to include injunctive authority and the imposition of civil penalties.[86]

The CFTC was also given the power to declare a market emergency on a contract market.[87] After making such a declaration, the CFTC was authorized to direct the exchange to take such action as the CFTC might deem necessary "to maintain or restore orderly trading in, or liquidation of, any futures contract." Such emergencies could include "threatened or actual market manipulation and corners," any act of the United States or a foreign government that would affect a commodity, or any "major market disturbance which prevents the market from accurately reflecting the forces of supply and demand for such commodity." The commodity futures exchanges were also authorized to take emergency action. A proposal to regulate margins on commodity futures was rejected.[88]

4:3 THE POTATO DEFAULT

The CFTC had been in existence only about one year when it faced a massive manipulation of Maine potato futures prices. That manipulation was quite a baptism under fire for the SEC because it resulted "in the largest default in the history of commodities futures trading in this country."[89] "The default was virtually unprecedented and, in the words of CFTC officials and members of the industry, shocked the commodity markets and the participants more than any other single event in recent years."[90] The default involved about 1,000 May 1976 Maine futures contracts that were traded on the New York Mercantile Exchange (NYMEX) and 50 million pounds of potatoes that were not delivered.[91]

---

83. *Commodity Futures Trading Commission Act: Hearings Before the Senate Committee on Agriculture and Forestry*, 93d Cong., 2d Sess. 765 (1973).

84. Commodity Futures Trading Commission Act of 1974, Pub. L. No. 93-463, 88 Stat. 1389.

85. 120 Cong. Rec. 34999 (1974) (remarks of Sen. Clark).

86. *See*, Jerry W. Markham, A History of Commodity Futures Trading and Its Regulation 65-72 (1987) (describing the provisions of the CFTC Act of 1974).

87. 7 U.S.C. § 12a(9).

88. 120 Cong. Rec. 10628 (1974) (remarks of Rep. Sullivan).

89. Merrill Lynch, Pierce, Fenner & Smith Inc. v. Curran, 456 U.S. 353, 367 (1982) (citation omitted).

90. H.R. Rep. No. 1181, 95th Cong., 2d Sess. 99 (1978).

91. Strobl v. NYMEX, 768 F.2d 22, 23 (2d Cir. 1985), *cert. denied*, 474 U.S. 1006 (1985).

Potatoes had been the target of several manipulations in prior years. Congress had declined to ban futures trading in potatoes when it was considering legislation that led to the banning of onion futures in 1958. The National Potato Council returned to Congress in 1973 seeking a ban on potato futures. The council sought such a ban because "[p]otatoes are a highly perishable commodity. Because of that perishability and the inability for the product to be carried or held for more than a few months, they should not be included in futures trading."[92] Concern was again expressed in Congress during the debates on the CFTC legislation on the need to prohibit futures trading on potatoes, but no action was taken. Instead, the CFTC was left to deal with future problems.

The default on the May 1976 NYMEX Maine futures contracts was the climax of a classic battle of bulls and bears or, in the words of the first CFTC chair, William Bagley, a fatal game of chicken between the longs and the shorts.[93] The longs were able to corner the market May 1976 Maine futures contract, but the shorts then defaulted. The Department of Agriculture had twice warned before the default that potato stocks were substantially down from the prior year.

> The Supreme Court described the short side manipulation as follows:
>
> To counteract the anticipated price increases, a group of entrepreneurs described in the complaints as the "short sellers" formed a conspiracy to depress the price of the May Maine potato futures contract. The principal participants in this "short conspiracy" were large processors of potatoes who then were negotiating with a large potato growers association on the cash market. The conspirators agreed to accumulate an abnormally large short position in the May contract, to make no offsetting purchases of long contracts at a price in excess of a fixed maximum, and to default, if necessary, on their short commitments. They also agreed to flood the Maine cash markets with unsold potatoes. This multifaceted strategy was designed to give the growers association the impression that the supply of Maine potatoes would be plentiful. On the final trading day the short sellers had accumulated a net short position of almost 1,900 contracts, notwithstanding a Commission regulation limiting their lawful net position to 150 contracts. They did, in fact, default.[94]

This affair was made more colorful by the participation on the short side of the contract by two potato barons—John R. Simplot, who was processing some 50 percent of all Idaho potatoes, and Peter J. Taggares, who was processing about 30 percent of all Washington State potatoes. They sought to depress the price of the Maine May 1976 potato futures contract by shipping potatoes from Idaho to Maine.[95]

This was not the first manipulation of the potato market by Simplot and Taggares. They had been sanctioned, along with several others, in CEA proceedings charging them with manipulating the May 1971 Idaho potato contract on the CME. Taggares and Simplot had established increasingly larger short positions on the 1971 CME potato futures and held large positions through delivery. Those charges were settled by consent before the CFTC came into existence.

---

92. *Review of Commodity Exchange Act and Discussion of Possible Changes: Hearings Before the House Committee on Agriculture*, 93d Cong., 1st Sess. 224 (1973).

93. Jerry W. Markham, A History of Commodity Futures Trading and Its Regulation 83 (1987).

94. Merrill Lynch, Pierce, Fenner & Smith Inc. v. Curran, 456 U.S. 353, 369-370 (1982).

95. *See*, III Jerry W. Markham, A Financial History of the United States, From the Age of Derivatives into the New Millennium (1970-2001) 58-59 (2002) (describing this event).

The CEA sanctions had been the issuance of cease and desist orders and suspension of trading privileges for periods ranging from 90 to 180 days.[96] Those sanctions obviously had no deterrent effect.

The longs retaliated against Taggares, Simplot, and other shorts in the May 1976 Maine futures contract by leasing all railroad cars on the Bangor & Aroostook Railroad in order to prevent the shorts from delivering Maine potatoes on their futures contracts. That long scheme worked and the owners of potatoes in Maine were "unable to deliver warehoused potatoes to persons seeking delivery to fulfill short contracts. As the warm weather set in, the 1,500,000 pounds of potatoes became rotten."[97] "The sellers refusal to deliver brought about the largest default in the history of commodities futures trading."[98]

The CFTC used its new emergency action powers[99] prior to the default to order the NYMEX to increase potato futures margins to 100 percent and to trade for liquidation only. That emergency action did not prevent a default or the manipulation that was under way.[100] The CFTC subsequently brought manipulation charges against both the shorts and longs, but most of the respondents settled with only relatively light sanctions. Taggares and Simplot agreed to a bar from trading on regulated futures markets for periods of four and six years and were assessed with civil penalties of $15,000 and $50,000 respectively. Another trader agreed to a two-year trading bar and a rather mild civil penalty of $2,000, while four traders were permanently barred when they defaulted in the CFTC administrative proceedings.[101]

The CFTC was given a stern lesson in the difficulties of proving manipulation when some potato traders involved in this debacle refused to roll over for a settlement. That litigation dragged on for more than twelve years and resulted in the dismissal of a case against two of the traders. In one instance, a CFTC administrative law judge (ALJ) dismissed a claim that a trader had participated and assisted in the long side of the potato manipulation. The ALJ concluded that the trader had legitimate economic reasons for his trading activities and awarded the trader attorney fees.[102] The Second Circuit also reversed a CFTC finding that another trader in the Maine potato futures contract had engaged in improper trading practices by entering offsetting trades in order to delay receiving a delivery notice.[103]

This default and manipulation attempt was the subject of much private litigation.[104] The Second Circuit Court of Appeals affirmed an award of treble damages under the antitrust laws against the traders involved in the default.[105] The Supreme Court also held in *Merrill Lynch, Pierce, Fenner &*

96. In re P.J. Taggares Co., 32 Agric. Dec. 10 (1973); In re San Jacinto Packing Co., 33 Agric. Dec. 746 (1974).

97. Merrill Lynch, Pierce, Fenner & Smith Inc. v. Curran, 456 U.S. 353, 369, 371, n. 45 (1982).

98. Strobol v. NYMEX, 768 F.2d 22, 23 (2d Cir. 1985), *cert. denied*, 474 U.S. 1006 (1985).

99. 7 U.S.C. § 12a(9).

100. Jerry W. Markham, *Manipulation of Commodity Futures Prices: The Unprosecutable Crime*, 8 YALE J. ON REG. 281, 334-335 (1991).

101. *Id.* at 387. A settlement agreement.

102. In re Stoller, Comm. Fut. L. Rep. (CCH) ¶ 24,356 (C.F.T.C. 1988).

103. Under exchange rules, the oldest long positions received delivery notices first. Here, the trader closed out an old long position and immediately reestablished a new, younger position in order to delay receipt of delivery notices. Stoller v. CFTC, 834 F.2d 262 (2d Cir. 1987). The CFTC refused to accede to the court's decision in future cases, and the Seventh Circuit upheld findings of violations for trading similar to that at issue in the *Stoller* case, *i.e.*, the "freshening" of a position in order to delay receipt of a delivery notice. *See*, Elliott v. CFTC, 202 F.3d 926 (7th Cir.), *cert. denied*, 531 U.S. 1010 (2000).

104. *See*, Jerry W. Markham, *Manipulation of Commodity Futures Prices: The Unprosecutable Crime*, 8 YALE J. ON REG. 281, 336, n. 382 (1991) (listing those cases).

105. Strobl v. NYMEX, 768 F.2d 22 (2d Cir. Cir. 1985), *cert. denied, sub nom.*, Simplot v. Strobl, 474 U.S.

Smith Inc. v. Curran[106] that a private right of action existed for violations of the antimanipulation provisions of the Commodity Exchange Act. The Supreme Court did not specify the parameters of such claims, which created much concern that a flood of consumer claims would be brought whenever commodity prices increased. Congress amended the Commodity Exchange Act in 1982 to restrict such claims to those involved in trading and imposed stricter statute of limitations requirements.[107] Manipulation claims under the amendments were limited to persons who actually engaged in futures trading and who were, therefore, directly affected by the manipulation. Persons only tangentially affected by Commodity Exchange Act violations are not allowed to sue. A House report to this legislation stated that it "included these restrictions on the causes of action to avoid suits for speculative damages to assets that are affected by fluctuations in prices on the commodity market but which are not the subject of transactions on such market."[108] Various courts have held that "excessive speculation" in the form of trading in excess of CFTC-set speculative limits would not provide a basis for a private right of action.[109]

Another effort was mounted in Congress to ban potato futures, but that legislation was not enacted.[110] In order to prevent another default, or perhaps to punish the traders involved in the default, NYMEX increased the margin requirements of the defaulting traders for their positions in the May 1977 Maine potato futures contract from $500 to $5,000 per contract. A federal district court rejected a challenge to that action by Taggares and Simplot, who were forced to liquidate more than 1,000 May 1977 potato contracts.[111] As is not uncustomary, those two speculators would turn on each other within a few years. In 1980, Simplot seized control of the giant (30,000-acre) SimTag farm in Oregon that he operated jointly with Taggares.[112]

More problems arose in the March, April, and May 1979 NYMEX Maine potato futures contracts because potatoes tendered for delivery did not meet delivery requirements set by the exchange. The NYMEX took emergency action and ordered the liquidation of positions at the March 8, 1979, settlement price. The Second Circuit Court of Appeals upheld the dismissal of an antitrust action brought against the NYMEX for taking that action, but allowed discovery on the issue of whether the exchange acted in bad faith for purposes of a damage claim against an exchange under the Commodity Exchange Act.[113] The suits charged that NYMEX should have acted earlier or that it should have changed the delivery terms of the contract in order to avoid the problem. The NYMEX did subsequently change the potato contract terms to allow for cash settlement, but trading in potatoes was discontinued on the NYMEX in 1987. NYMEX then began focusing on energy contracts.[114]

1006 (1985). *See generally*, Note, *The Availability of Antitrust Treble Damages for Commodities Market Manipulation*, 54 FORDHAM L. REV. 853 (1986) (discussing antitrust claims in that action).

106. Merrill Lynch, Pierce, Fenner & Smith Inc. v. Curran, 456 U.S. 353 (1982).

107. 7 U.S.C. § 25. *See* H.R. Rep. No. 565 (Part I), 97th Cong., 2d Sess. 57 (1982). *See*, Don L. Horwitz & Jerry W. Markham, *Sunset on the Commodity Futures Trading Commission: Scene II*, 39 BUS. LAW. 67, 97-98 (1983) (describing this legislation); Cynthia L. Moore, *An Express Private Right of Action for Futures Investors: Does Section 22 of the Commodity Exchange Act Afford Adequate Protection?* 35 CASE W. RES. L. REV. 72 (1985) (same).

108. H.R. Rep. No. 565 (Part I), 97th Cong., 2d Sess. 57 (1982).

109. In re Soybean Futures Litigation, 892 F. Supp. 1025, 1042 (N.D. Ill. 1995); Gunderson v. ADM Investor Services, 2001 U.S. Dist. LEXIS 3383 (N.D. Iowa).

110. EMILY LAMBERT, THE FUTURES 159 (2011).

111. P.J. Taggares Co. Inc. v. NYMEX, 476 F. Supp. 72 (S.D.N.Y. 1979).

112. *Taggares Sues Simplot*, SPOKANE DAILY CHRONICLE, Dec. 13, 1980, at 3.

113. Sam Wong & Son Inc. v. NYMEX, 735 F.2d 653 (2d Cir. 1984).

114. Jerry W. Markham, *Manipulation of Commodity Futures Prices: The Unprosecutable Crime*, 8 YALE J. ON REG. 281, 337 (1991).

4:4 COFFEE EMERGENCY

The CFTC encountered several additional problems caused by large traders in the commodity futures markets after the potato debacle. Coffee was particularly problematic for the CFTC because of a price explosion that followed growing problems in the producing countries beginning in 1975. There was an especially severe frost in the coffee-growing regions of Brazil, Colombia was hit with floods, Angola production was disrupted by a civil war, and Guatemala experienced a damaging earthquake.[115]

Coffee prices skyrocketed from $0.55 per pound in July 1975 to $3.55 in April 1977, leading to a consumer boycott of the product.[116] Elinor Guggenheimer, the New York City commissioner for consumer affairs, asked for a 50 percent reduction in coffee drinking by Americans in order to reduce prices.[117] The high prices also set off a wave of coffee hijackings that stole over $1 million worth of coffee beans.[118]

The price rise caught the attention of large speculators. The CFTC discovered that two long traders controlled 82 percent of the open interest in the September 1976 Coffee "C" futures contract on the New York Coffee and Sugar Exchange Inc. The exchange declared an emergency and ordered trading for liquidation only. In 1977 four more such emergencies were declared in which liquidation-only trading was ordered.[119] Attention was also focused on whether the producing countries were manipulating prices. Those countries had formed a cartel to maintain coffee prices[120] and were also increasing export taxes on coffee.[121] *New York Times* columnist William Safire called the price explosion "Brazil's Coffee Rip-Off."[122] A CFTC representative testified before Congress that the agency was investigating whether traders had sought to inflate coffee prices after a decline resulting from the consumer boycott.[123]

On November 23, 1977, the CFTC declared a market emergency, as did the Coffee and Sugar Exchange, and ordered liquidation of the December 1977 coffee futures contract.[124] "This action was taken amid reports that some coffee producing nations were attempting to drive coffee prices up."[125] The CFTC's emergency order stated that it had "reason to believe that there exists a threat of a market manipulation or corner, and that acts of a foreign government or governments are affecting trade in coffee in a manner which is preventing the market from accurately reflecting the forces of supply and demand."[126] The *New York Times* reported that the governments of Brazil and El Salvador had committed $100 million to a scheme called "Operation Central Park" in an effort to manipulate coffee prices upward.[127] The *New York Times* also reported that the life of a

---

115. *Id.* at 281, 337-338 (1991).

116. *Id.*

117. *Coffee Prices Spur a Boycott to Cut Use by 50%*, NEW YORK TIMES, Dec. 28, 1976, at 26.

118. Judith Cummings, *Soaring Price of Coffee Inspires Protestors and a Wave of Thefts*, NEW YORK TIMES, March 6, 1977, at 36.

119. JERRY W. MARKHAM, A HISTORY OF COMMODITY FUTURES TRADING AND ITS REGULATION 84 (1987).

120. *See* Wayne D. Greenstone, *The Coffee Cartel: Manipulation in the Public Interest*, 1 J. OF FUT. MARKETS 3 (1981) (describing this cartel).

121. Rona Cherry, *From Grower to Table, Coffee Will Cost More*, NEW YORK TIMES, Jan. 12, 1977, at 66.

122. William Safire, *Brazil's Coffee Rip-Off*, NEW YORK TIMES, Jan. 13, 1977, at 34.

123. *Possible Coffee Rigging Is Studied*, NEW YORK TIMES, Feb. 24, 1977, at 52.

124. Jerry W. Markham, *Manipulation of Commodity Futures Prices: The Unprosecutable Crime*, 8 YALE J. ON REG. 281, 337-338 (1991).

125. Compania de Salvadorena de Café, S.A. v. CFTC, 446 F. Supp. 687, 689 (S.D.N.Y. 1978).

126. Equitable Trust Co. v. CFTC, 669 F.2d 269, 271 (5th Cir. 1982).

127. Michael C. Jensen, *U.S. Studying Whether Two Nations Act to Keep Coffee Prices*, NEW YORK TIMES, Dec. 30, 1977, at 1, col. 2.

government regulator had been threatened in connection with the CFTC's investigation of this operation.[128] Several foreign traders challenged the CFTC's emergency action, but the courts dismissed those claims.[129]

The CFTC subsequently brought manipulation charges in *In re Compania Salvadorena de Café S.A.*[130] against traders for the coffee producers in the July 1977 Coffee "C" futures contract traded on the New York Coffee and Sugar Exchange. The CFTC's complaint charged that coffee growers in Colombia, Mexico, and Brazil, and their American brokers, had agreed to manipulate prices on the NYMEX through Compania Salvadorena de Café S.A., a company based in El Salvador. That company agreed to sanctions and was prohibited from speculative trading on U.S. futures markets.[131] This was not a very severe penalty since the company represented large-scale hedging interests that were exempt from speculative position limits as long as they were hedging.

A CFTC administrative law judge held that a defaulting respondent, Ricardo Falla Caceres (the trader for Salvadorena) caused an artificial price. The ALJ found that "[i]n 1974, Salvadorena, the National Federation of Colombian Coffee Growers, the Mexican Coffee Institute and the Brazilian Coffee Institute entered into the 'Punta Arenas' agreement, the purpose of which was to support coffee prices by purchasing coffee in the physical and futures markets." Each party contributed funds for that purpose. The ALJ found that Falla directed his U.S. brokers to "make the market go up" or "make the market strong" and gave discretionary buy orders to counteract selling in the market. He also engaged in wash sales in violation of Section 4(c) of the Commodity Exchange Act.[132] The ALJ further found that Falla's long position constituted 68.6 percent of the total long open interest in the July contract and that he maintained a dominant position from June 15, 1977 through July 25, 1977.

An artificial price was found because the coffee futures price traded in excess of the International Coffee Organization's (ICO) indicator prices for cash coffee that was equivalent to the grade of coffee deliverable on the July futures contract. At one point the disparity amounted to 65 cents per pound, which was ten times higher than had been reached in the prior three years. The July futures contract was also trading at a premium of 33 cents over a dealer's cash quotes for coffee imported into New York from El Salvador and Guatemala.

The artificially high price of the July 1977 futures contract was further evidenced by comparing prices of the September 1977 futures contract, which usually trade at a premium over July. During the period at issue, the closing prices for the July contract exceeded those of the September contract by at least 20 cents per pound each day, and on two days that premium reached 51 cents per pound.[133]

The ALJ found that Falla caused the artificial prices through his dominant position and that he intended to create an artificial price. The ALJ also focused on the fact that Falla ignored a CFTC letter sent on July 8, 1977, expressing concern over the positions he controlled and the limited amount of cash coffee available for delivery.[134] A $200,000 civil penalty was imposed on Falla by default, and he was prohibited from trading on United States contract markets. Charges against several other respondents were dismissed by the CFTC.[135]

---

128. Jerry W. Markham, A History of Commodity Futures Trading and Its Regulation 84 (1987).

129. Compania de Salvadorena de Café, S.A. v. CFTC, 446 F. Supp. 687 (S.D.N.Y. 1978).

130. In re Compania Salvadorena de Café S.A., Comm. Fut. L. Rep. (CCH) ¶ 21,886 (C.F.T.C.

131. *Id.* at 190.

132. 7 U.S.C. § 6c(a).

133. In re Compania Salvadorena de Café S.A., Comm. Fut. L. Rep. (CCH) ¶ 21,886 (C.F.T.C. 1983) (footnotes and citations omitted).

134. *Id.*

135. Jerry W. Markham, *Manipulation of Commodity Futures Prices: The Unprosecutable Crime*, 8 Yale J. on Reg. 281, 339 (1991).

The *Salvadorena* case did not end problems in coffee. Foreign traders acquired a large position in the Coffee "C" futures contract in 1978 by trading through Wiscope S.A., a Swiss financial institution. The CFTC issued a "special call" on Wiscope asking for disclosure of the identity of the traders, but Wiscope refused on grounds that Swiss law prohibited such disclosures. The Second Circuit reversed sanctions imposed by the CFTC on Wiscope for refusing the special call because the CFTC had not given proper notice before demanding the information.[136]

This decision was a severe blow to the CFTC because its reporting system, which was inherited from the CEA, was its "basic tool for market surveillance in the detection and prevention of market congestion and price manipulation and distortion."[137] The CFTC performed that function by administering a market surveillance program which requires market participants with substantial futures positions to file reports regularly with the agency disclosing those positions. "The data provided in these reports enables the CFTC to analyze the markets and detect threats of corners, manipulations, or other market disturbances 'so that reasoned judgments can be made [by] the Commission concerning the likelihood that a manipulation is developing and whether Commission action is warranted.'"[138]

The CFTC's "special call authority" allowed the CFTC to request information that is not routinely supplied to the commission pursuant to the large trader reporting system. "Among possible reasons for such special needs for information may be a particular market situation that warrants unusually close Commission market surveillance."[139] The *Wiscope* decision frustrated that effort.

The coffee manipulation also teed up another important issue for the CFTC. Section 4(a)(1) of the Commodity Exchange Act[140] authorized the CFTC to set trading and position limits for speculators, a power inherited from the CEA. The CEA had concluded in 1952 that position limits restricted large speculators from building positions larger than 2 to 3 percent of open interest before the delivery period, which made it more difficult to achieve a dominant position for purposes of manipulating the market.[141] Position limits had two aspects: one limit curbed the number of intraday transactions and a second limit applied to the number of contracts that could be held overnight. However, bona fide hedging transactions were exempt from those limits.

---

136. Wiscope S.A. v. CFTC, 604 F.2d 764 (2d Cir. 1979).

137. Comm. Fut. L. Rep. (CCH) ¶ 8,001 (1979).

138. William E. McDonnell Jr. & Susan K. Freund, *The CFTC's Large Trader Reporting System: History and Development*, 38 Bus. Law. 917 (1983) (citation omitted). As the CFTC noted, the Commodity Exchange Act

> is intended, among other things, to "deter and prevent price manipulation or any other disruptions to market integrity." To that end, the Commission, through its Division of Market Oversight ("Division"), conducts a comprehensive program of market surveillance. A centerpiece of this program is the large-trader reporting system, under which all large futures and option positions are reported to the Commission. Each day, for every active futures or option market, Division surveillance staff monitors the activities of large traders, key price relationships, and all relevant supply and demand factors in a continuous review for potential market problems. An essential element of the Commission's market surveillance program is the ability to make special calls for information from Commission registrants and other market participants.

Special Calls, 72 F.R. 50209 (Aug. 31, 2007) (footnote omitted).

139. *Special Calls*, 72 F.R. 50210 (Aug. 31, 2007).

140. 7 U.S.C. § 6a(1).

141. Jerry W. Markham, A History of Commodity Futures Trading and Its Regulation 44 (1987).

The CEA took a restrictive or "strict" hedging approach to the bona fide hedging exemption. That approach was upheld in *Corn Products Refining Co. v. Benson*.[142] There, the Second Circuit Court of Appeals upheld a finding by the CEA that the respondent's trading was not bona fide hedging that was exempt from CEA position limits. Since this was a test case, a one-day trading suspension was dropped by the CEA.[143] The legislation creating the CFTC sought to grant more flexibility in determining what would constitute bona fide hedging, allowing it to define that term.[144] The CFTC Advisory Committee on the Role of Contract Markets, which was created to advise the CFTC on the application of position limits and other issues, concluded that position limits "are not a very powerful tool for the CFTC in its futures market regulatory role, nor can they be made to be."[145]

That advisory committee also asserted:

> The idea of controlling speculators as though they were less important or more dangerous than hedgers is basically unsound. Speculative position limits, by their nature, point the finger of suspicion at speculators. In fact, however, five of the eight market manipulation cases brought under the Commodity Exchange Act between 1972 and 1975 were against commercial operators with hedging exemptions for at least part of their trading.[146]

The coffee manipulation confirmed the fact that hedgers have enormous commercial resources and have an incentive to manipulate the market. Commercial traders would continue to be principal players in manipulations.

The CFTC advisory committee recommended elimination of limits on the number of contracts that could be traded during a single trading day. The committee asserted that such daily limits "may actually cut back participation of speculators at the very time when they are most needed. On active trading days some speculators are forced out of the pit during the later hours of daily trading—reducing liquidity."[147] The CFTC followed that recommendation and eliminated daily trading limits.[148]

The CFTC advisory committee viewed price limits, as opposed to position limits, more favorably. Price limits halt trading when price movements reach certain preestablished limits. The committee believed that

> the purpose underlying price limits was to protect the financial integrity of member firms and clearinghouses; that is, price limits place a ceiling on the risk confronted by member firms and clearinghouses and provide member firms and clearinghouses with an opportunity to collect additional funds in an orderly and unburdensome manner prior to the next day's trading. To the extent that price limits permit persons to commit funds to the futures markets in a more orderly manner and prevent sudden, excessive payments

---

142. *Corn Products Refining Co. v. Benson*, 232 F.2d 554 (2d Cir. 1956).

143. Commodity Exchange Authority, *Summary of Administrative and Judicial Proceedings Under the Commodity Exchange Act (June 15, 1936–June 30, 1972) and Under the Grain Futures Act (Sept. 21, 1922–June 14, 1936)* 26-27 (circa 1973).

144. Jerry W. Markham, A History of Commodity Futures Trading and Its Regulation 71 (1987).

145. *Report of the CFTC Advisory Committee on the Economic Role of Contract Markets*, Comm. Fut. L. Rep. (CCH) ¶ 20,187 (July 19, 1976).

146. *Id.*

147. *Report of the CFTC Advisory Committee on the Economic Role of Contract Markets*, Comm. Fut. L. Rep. (CCH) ¶ 20,187 (July 19, 1976).

148. Comm. Fut. L. Rep. (CCH) ¶ 20,756 (C.F.T.C. 1979).

of maintenance margin or payouts of excess margin over short periods of time, they may reduce the risks borne by clearing members and clearinghouses and thereby benefit the public and the industry.[149]

The CFTC advisory committee further noted that fixed speculative limits were not effective. "A flat limit that is not overly restrictive in non-delivery months is 'no limit' during the delivery month."[150] In recognition of that concern, the CFTC proposed a new rule in 1978 that would have required futures exchanges to limit positions of traders in maturing futures contracts to no more than 25 percent of the open interest in that future, unless the exchange affirmatively determined that the position was not a threat to orderly trading.[151] The proposal would have applied to all traders, regardless of whether their positions constituted bona fide hedging positions or speculation. The proposed rule would not have required automatic divestiture of a position in excess of 25 percent. Instead, the exchanges would have been required to analyze the probable effects of a large position on the futures market. Only if an exchange determined that the position could result in price manipulation or market congestion would it then notify and direct the holder to take whatever action was necessary to prevent congestion or manipulation.

The 1978 proposal was called "Charlie's rule," after its principal proponent, Charles Robinson, a long-time CEA employee who had joined the CFTC as an adviser to one of the commissioners.[152] The proposal proved highly controversial and was not adopted because of uncertainty over what was expected of the exchanges under its provisions.[153] An internal CFTC staff memorandum also expressed concern that the proposed rule presented some intractable problems such as the assumption that the exchanges could determine "what are orderly markets and what is orderly trading. In that connection, there are definitional problems with the terms 'price manipulation' and 'market congestion.'"[154] As described in Chapter 7, a form of this proposal was adopted by the CFTC after the Financial Crisis in 2008 and was challenged successfully in court by the industry.

4:5 SPECULATIVE LIMITS AND THE SOYBEAN AFFAIR

Another power denied to the CEA, and given to the CFTC, was the authority to seek injunctive relief against violators of the Commodity Exchange Act.[155] However, this new authority proved ineffective in stopping a massive soybean speculation in a case brought against Bunker and Herbert Hunt and their family members. The Hunts lived in Dallas, Texas, and were then the wealthiest family in the world. Their wealth was due chiefly to the somewhat eccentric family patriarch, H.L. Hunt, who had started his fortune by winning some East Texas oil leases in a poker game. H.L. had also been a speculator in the futures markets, not always with success.[156]

---

149. 45 Fed. Reg. 55469v (Aug. 20, 1980). (footnote omitted).

150. *Report of the CFTC Advisory Committee on the Economic Role of Contract Markets*, Comm. Fut. L. Rep. (CCH) ¶ 20,187 (July 19, 1976).

151. 43 Fed. Reg. 15438 (Apr. 13, 1978).

152. *See, Price Volatility in the Silver Futures Market: Hearings Before the Senate Subcommittee on Agricultural Research and General Legislation of the Committee on Agriculture, Nutrition, and Forestry*, 96th Cong. 56 (1980) (describing Charlie's rule).

153. 43 Fed. Reg. 15438 (Apr. 13, 1978).

154. Jerry W. Markham, *Manipulation of Commodity Futures Prices: The Unprosecutable Crime*, 8 Yale J. on Reg. 371 (1991) (citation omitted).

155. 15 U.S.C. § 13a-1 (1974).

156. II Jerry W. Markham, A Financial History of the United States, From J.P. Morgan to the Institutional Investor (1900-1970) 97 (2002).

Soybeans increased in price by some $4 per bushel in 1977 as a result of export restrictions in Brazil and an announcement of large purchases by China. Corn and wheat prices were also rising. Soybeans were trading in early April 1977 at more than $10 per bushel when the Hunts entered the market.

Bunker and Herbert Hunt controlled long positions on about 4,500 soybean futures contracts on the CBOT that called for delivery of some 23 million bushels of soybeans for their own accounts and for those of their five children and a family corporation. The Hunts' profits were estimated to be nearly $100 million from their combined positions as soybean prices increased. Those contracts required the delivery of about one-third of the entire U.S. soybean crop and nearly all of the deliverable supply of soybeans in Chicago. The Hunts' futures contracts for the approaching May delivery month totaled 8 million bushels while there were only 10 million bushels available for delivery under those contracts.[157]

The CFTC did not charge manipulation even though the Hunts collectively had a dominant position in the market that was placing strong pressure on prices. Rather, the CFTC charged violations of its speculative limits on soybean traders. This was not a novel theory. The CEA had previously brought numerous administrative disciplinary actions against traders filing false reports or breaching speculative position limits.[158] For example, in *In re Goodman*,[159] charges of

---

157. JERRY W. MARKHAM, A HISTORY OF COMMODITY FUTURES TRADING AND ITS REGULATION 94 (1987).

158. Those cases are summarized in Commodity Exchange Authority, *Summary of Administrative and Judicial Proceedings Under the Commodity Exchange Act (June 15, 1936–June 30, 1972) and Under the Grain Futures Act (Sept. 21, 1922–June 14, 1936)* 97-98 (circa 1973). *See, e.g., Id.*: In re Martin, CEA Doc. No. 35, at 15 (respondent found to have exceeded daily trading limit for rye futures on the CBOT in June 1945); In re Feldstein, CEA Doc. No. 36, at 16 (violations of reporting requirement for CME egg futures in Oct. 1945); In re Brown, CEA Doc. No. 40 at 18 (reporting violations in CME futures); In re Cotton Products Co., CEA Doc. No. 53, at 25 (failed to file trading reports for cottonseed futures in 1949); In re Sirota, CEA Doc. No. 54, at 25 (failure to file cottonseed oil futures reports); In re Codoy, CEA Doc. No. 56, at 27 (failure to report lard and other futures positions); In re Byer, CEA Doc. No. 62, at 31 (filing false reports to conceal positions trading above speculative limits); In re Albert, CEA Doc. No. 64, at 32 (incomplete reports on potato futures on NYMEX); In re Ludwig, CEA Doc. No. 66, at 33 (filing false reports and exceeding daily and net position limits on CME egg futures); In re General Commerce Corp., CEA Doc. No. 76, at 39 (failed to file large trading reports for lard futures on the CBOT in 1957); In re Awad, CEA Doc. No. 79, at 40 (failure to file lard futures reports in 1958); In re H. Sacks & Sons, CEA Doc. No. 80, at 40-41(failure to file reports for potato futures on NYMEX in 1958); In re Goodman, CEA Doc. No. 81, at 41 (exceeded speculative position limits in rye futures on CBOT in 1957-1958); In re Feldstein Produce Co., CEA Doc. No. 83, at 42 (failed to file reports and exceeded speculative position limits for egg futures on CME); In re Strohmeier, CEA Doc. No. 88, at 45 (failed to file large trader reports for CME egg futures in 1956 and 1958); In re Ludwig, CEA Doc. No. 94, at 49 (exceeded speculative limits for egg futures on CME); In re Schmidt, CEA Doc. No. 107, at 55 (reporting and speculative limit violations for egg futures in 1962); In re Simmons, CEA Doc. No. 108, at 56 (reporting and speculative limit violations for egg futures in 1962); In re Cashman, CEA Doc. No. 114, at 59 (exceeded speculative position limits in rye futures); In re Haag, CEA Doc. No. 116, at 60 (exceeded speculative limits and failed to file large trader reports for CME egg futures in 1962 and 1963); In re Phelan, CEA Doc. No. 119, at 62 (failed to file large trader reports in 1963-1964); In re Decatur Cotton Oil Co., CEA Doc. No. 123, at 64 (failed to file cottonseed reports in 1964); In re Jordan, CEA Doc. No. 124, at 64 (failed to file reports and exceeded position limits through controlled accounts in wheat futures); In re Tabbara, CEA Doc. No. 132, at 70 (failed to file large trader reports for wheat futures); In re Jones, CEA Doc. No. 138, at 73 (failed to file reports for trading in potato futures in 1966); In re Hills, CEA Doc. No. 140, at 74 (exceeded daily trading limits and position limits in soybean futures in 1965); In re Collins, CEA Doc. No. 142, at 75 (failed to file reports on wool futures); In re Endico, CEA Doc. No. 146, at 77 (exceeded position limits for potato futures in 1966-1967); In re Simmons, CEA Doc. No. 149, at 79 (exceeded speculative position limits in potato futures in 1967); In re Kerrigan, CEA Doc. No. 162, at 84 (exceeded position limits and submitted false reports for corn futures on CBOT in 1966); In re Kaminga, CEA Doc. No. 172, at 89 (failed to file reports for cattle futures in 1970).

159. In re Goodman, CEA Doc. No. 105, noted in Commodity Exchange Authority, *Summary of Admin-*

speculative position limit violations and reporting failures for soybeans in 1958 and 1959 were settled by consent. A one-year trading suspension was imposed.

The courts had also upheld CEA disciplinary actions for speculative limit violations. In *Kent v. Hardin*,[160] the Fifth Circuit Court of Appeals affirmed a ninety-day trading suspension of a trader and his son-in-law whose combined positions exceeded CEA speculative limits for wheat, soybeans, and potato futures. The court found that the trader had financed the trading of the son-in-law. In *Goodman v. Benson*,[161] the Seventh Circuit Court of Appeals upheld a twenty-day trading suspension for a trader who failed to file trading reports and exceeded speculative position limits for rye futures. The respondent had been trading through seven different futures commission merchants and ignored a previous warning from the CEA for exceeding position limits in rye.

A criminal conviction for exceeding CEA speculative limits for potato futures was upheld *in United States v. Cohen*[162] by the Second Circuit Court of Appeals. There the defendants were a father, his two sons, and a business associate. The father was convicted after a bench trial in the district court, but the other defendants were acquitted. The Second Circuit noted that when the father reached his speculative limit trading, trading would commence on his son's account until it reached the speculative limit and the same pattern occurred in the other two defendants' accounts. The father was found to have controlled, financed, and taken the profits from the trading.

Although not novel, the charges against the Hunts seemed a bit ironical since the CFTC had previously decided to adopt the recommendations of its Advisory Committee on the Role of Contract Markets that the agency deemphasize the use of speculative limits as a tool to control speculation.[163] The absence of manipulation charges against the Hunts also seemed to signal timidity since the CFTC charged that the Hunts' "excessive holdings threaten disruption of the market and could cause serious injury to the American public."[164] However, the CFTC would have had a difficult time proving that the Hunts were actually manipulating the market because fundamental economic factors were also driving soybean prices.[165] Manipulative intent of an artificial price would have been difficult to establish because the Hunts had hired a climatologist to advise them on the fundamental effects of weather patterns on soybean production.[166] That made it appear that, rather than seeking an artificial price, the Hunts were seeking to predict actual market prices based on fundamentals.

At the time of the CFTC's case against the Hunts, an individual speculator was limited to a net long or short position of no more than 3 million bushels of soybeans in any one future or in all futures months combined. In applying that limit, the Commodity Exchange Act requires the aggregation of speculative positions of traders acting together pursuant to an express or implied agreement or understanding.[167] "Congress concluded that excessive speculation in commodity contracts for future delivery can cause adverse fluctuations in the price of a commodity, and au-

---

istrative and Judicial Proceedings Under the Commodity Exchange Act (June 15, 1936–June 30, 1972) and Under the Grain Futures Act (Sept. 21, 1922–June 14, 1936) 55 (circa 1973).

160. Kent v. Hardin, 425 F.2d 1346 (5th Cir. 1970).

161. Goodman v. Benson, 286 F.2d 896 (7th Cir. 1961).

162. United States v. Cohen, 448 F.2d 1224 (2d Cir. 1971), *cert. denied*, 405 U.S. 954 (1972).

163. *Report of the CFTC Advisory Committee on the Economic Role of Contract Markets*, Comm. Fut. L. Rep. (CCH) ¶ 20,187 July 19, 1976).

164. H.J. Maidenberg, *U.S. Fights Effort by Hunts to Corner Soybean Market*, New York Times, April 29, 1977, at NJ1.

165. Seth S. King, *Soybean Prices Up on Demand, Not Hunt Case*, New York Times, April 30, 1977, at 44.

166. Jerry W. Markham, A History of Commodity Futures Trading and Its Regulation 96(1987).

167. 7 U.S.C. § 6a(1).

thorized the Commission to restrict the positions held or trading done by any individual person or by certain groups of people acting in concert."[168]

The CFTC examined the Hunts' positions and concluded that they were acting in concert. The CFTC sued the Hunts, claiming violations of its speculative limit of 3 million bushels that a speculator could own singly or in concert with others.[169] The Hunts counterclaimed, seeking an injunction and damages for the public disclosure of their trading positions by the CFTC. The district court enjoined the CFTC from further such disclosures and held a hearing on the CFTC's charges against the Hunts.[170]

The evidence presented by the CFTC established that Nelson Bunker Hunt and William Herbert Hunt each consistently held a long position at the 3 million bushel limit in soybean futures contracts, usually in the delivery month. After reaching that limit, Bunker Hunt ordered the purchase of May 1977 futures contracts covering 750,000 bushels of soybeans for his son Houston. He then ordered the same amount that was spread among the accounts of his three daughters.

The children of Bunker Hunt had never traded futures contracts before this affair. Houston was a freshman at the University of Tulsa, where he lived in a fraternity house. One daughter was living in a sorority house at the University of Alabama. The daughters testified that they decided to invest in soybean futures after discussing it among themselves at a luncheon at the Neiman Marcus Zodiac Room, a tea room popular with the matrons of Dallas society.[171] Herbert Hunt took similar actions for his son Douglas.

"As of April 14, 1977 the Hunt family's collective position involved over twenty-three million bushels of old crop soybeans: over 10.8 million in May futures, 7.7 million in July futures, and 5.2 million in August futures. These collective figures, of course, put the Hunt family well over the speculative limits in soybeans."[172] Although the federal district court in Chicago found that the Hunts had violated this requirement, he refused to enjoin them from further such violations on the ground they could be expected to obey the law in the future.[173]

The district court judge found no evidence that the Hunts were trying to corner the market and said that the only issue was whether they should be enjoined for speculative limit violations.[174] However, the Seventh Circuit Court of Appeals reversed that decision in *CFTC v. Hunt*,[175] with one judge on the three-member panel dissenting.[176] Although the Hunts had been freed by the district court to take

168. CFTC v. Hunt, 591 F.2d 1211, 1215 (7th Cir.), *cert. denied*, 442 U.S. 921 (1979).
169. 17 C.F.R. § 150.4 (1975).
170. CFTC v. Hunt, 591 F.2d 1211, 1214 (7th Cir.), *cert. denied*, 442 U.S. 921 (1979).
171. Jerry W. Markham, A History of Commodity Futures Trading and Its Regulation 96(1987).
172. CFTC v. Hunt, 591 F.2d 1211, 1218-1219 (7th Cir.), *cert. denied*, 442 U.S. 921 (1979).
173. CFTC v. Hunt, Comm. Fut. L. Rep. (CCH) ¶ 20,496 (N.D. Ill. 1977).
174. *No Evidence Found That Hunts Sought Corner in Soybeans*, New York Times, May 7, 1977, at 11.
175. CFTC v. Hunt, 591 F.2d 1211 (7th Cir.), *cert. denied*, 442 U.S. 921 (1979).
176. In reversing the district court's denial of an injunction, the Seventh Circuit found that the Hunts'

> misconduct was systematic and carefully preconceived. Their soybean positions which were challenged by the Commission were maintained throughout the enforcement proceedings until the futures contracts came to their natural conclusion. Further, the Hunts consistently maintained that their conduct was blameless. And finally, the prominent place of the Hunt family in the commodity markets generally, suggests that it is not unlikely that they will be regular participants in the soybean markets in the future. Thus, they will be in a position in which they are capable of committing future violations. Given the presence of all these factors, injunctive relief should have been granted.

CFTC v. Hunt, 591 F.2d 1211, 1220-1221 (7th Cir.), *cert. denied*, 442 U.S. 921 (1979).

delivery on their positions,[177] the Seventh Circuit directed the district court to consider the CFTC's demand that the Hunts disgorge any profits they made from their illegal trading. The Seventh Circuit also dismissed the Hunts' counterclaims against the CFTC and its officials.[178]

A private action seeking damages for the Hunts' violation of CFTC position limits was dismissed by a federal court.[179] The CFTC subsequently settled an administrative proceeding with the Hunts by requiring them to pay a somewhat paltry civil penalty of $500,000. That sanction failed to serve as a deterrent to the Hunts. Indeed, they seem to have been emboldened by the event and went on to try and corner the world silver market not long after the Seventh Circuit's decision on their soybean speculation.[180]

4:6 THE MARCH 1979 WHEAT EMERGENCY

A shortage of the 1978 wheat crop raised more concerns about manipulation, and problems were encountered in the December 1978 CBOT futures contract. Two traders from the same firm controlled more than 60 percent of the long side of the market in that contract as it approached the delivery date, and prices rose by twenty-five cents per bushel in the last days of trading. The CFTC contacted the traders and warned them against manipulation. One trader liquidated his position, but the other trader took delivery of a substantial part of his position.[181]

The CFTC then shifted its focus to the March 1979 CBOT wheat futures contracts because of a continued concentration of long traders. On Wednesday, March 14, about a week before the March 1979 wheat futures contract expired, the CBOT advised the CFTC that the major long traders would be liquidating their positions. However, one of the four remaining large longs obtained a temporary restraining order from a Chicago court that prohibited the CBOT from requiring him to liquidate his position.

The next morning, Thursday, March 15, 1979, the March futures price rose nine cents, and the March-May wheat contract spread widened to more than eighty-seven cents, the largest it had been all year. By the end of the trading day on Thursday, "the four major longs still held positions totaling about 9 million bushels—87 percent of the long open interest and more than 8 times the total deliverable supply of wheat in Chicago."[182] On the evening of Thursday, March 15, the CFTC declared a market emergency and issued an order to the CBOT directing the suspension of all trading in the March 1979 wheat futures contract on the following day, Friday, March 16.[183]

The CFTC's order stated that an emergency existed because significant transportation and warehouse shortages had caused a major market disturbance, which prevented the market from accurately reflecting the forces of supply and demand. The CFTC asserted that it had reason to believe that a manipulation or corner in wheat was threatened from the combined long open positions in the March contract of a small number of speculative traders.[184]

---

177. *Court Frees Hunts to Act on May Soybean Delivery*, NEW YORK TIMES, May 13, 1977, at 84.

178. CFTC v. Hunt, 591 F.2d 1211, 1221-1225 (7th Cir.), *cert. denied*, 442 U.S. 921 (1979).

179. Liang v. Hunt, 477 F. Supp. 891 (N.D. Ill. 1979).

180. Soybean prices remained a concern, but the CFTC was able to pressure a large trader holding a substantial portion of the March 1978 soybean oil stocks to liquidate his futures position on the last day of trading. JERRY W. MARKHAM, A HISTORY OF COMMODITY FUTURES TRADING AND ITS REGULATION 134 (1987).

181. *March Wheat Futures Trading on the Chicago Board of Trade: Hearing Before the Subcommittee on Conservation and Credit of the House Committee on Agriculture*, 96th Cong., 2d Sess. 6 (1979).

182. *Id.* at 8.

183. Board of Trade of the City of Chicago v. CFTC, 605 F.2d 1016, 1018 (7th Cir. 1979), *cert. denied*, 446 U.S. 928 (1980).

184. The CFTC's emergency order stated that

After the issuance of that emergency order, the CFTC and the CBOT became involved in a quarrel over whether trading should be suspended entirely in March wheat or just for liquidation only. The CFTC issued a supplemental order on Friday evening, March 16, that required the suspension of all trading and the settlement of outstanding contracts at the closing price on March 15. The CBOT went to the federal district court in Chicago on the next day, Saturday, March 17, seeking to enjoin the CFTC's emergency action.[185]

At a hearing held by the district court on Sunday, March 18, five witnesses for the CBOT testified there was no emergency. The CFTC refused to submit any evidence, contending that its emergency orders were not reviewable by a court. The federal district court enjoined the CFTC's emergency action order at the conclusion of the hearing on that Sunday. On the following day, Monday, March 19, the CFTC sought an emergency stay of the District court's order, but a three-judge panel on the Seventh Circuit Court of Appeals denied that request,[186] and the March contract was settled in the normal fashion without mishap.[187]

The Seventh Circuit Court later held that the district court had erred in enjoining the CFTC's emergency order for the March 1979 contract and that the decision to declare an emergency was left to the discretion of the CFTC.[188] That decision was hardly a victory for the CFTC, since the March 1979 contract had long since expired. Moreover, the Seventh Circuit's decision raised concerns in Congress that the CFTC might abuse its discretion to declare an emergency, and the statute was subsequently amended to allow judicial review of such declarations.[189]

---

(1) a small number of speculative traders has established and as of this date, is continuing to maintain large, potentially dominant, long open positions in the Contract;
(2) although only four trading days remained before expiration of trading in the Contract on March 21, 1979, this small number of speculative traders is continuing to maintain large long open positions in the Contract while at the same time other traders in the Contract are reducing their long open positions; as a result, the combined long positions of this small number of traders are comprising an increasingly large portion of the total open interest in the Contract as the last day of trading approaches, with that combined interest representing as of this date more than eighty percent of the total open interest in the Contract;
(3) the combined long open positions presently maintained in the contract by the small number of traders substantially exceed the total quantity of wheat currently available in positions from which delivery can be made in fulfillment of the Contract;
(4) even as to wheat currently in deliverable position pursuant to the Contract, not all is acceptable or available for delivery on the Contract in that a portion of this wheat is of undeliverable variety or grade, or is owned by or committed to commercial users;
(5) there is a significant shortage of transportation facilities by which additional wheat may be moved into deliverable position during March 1979, the period allowed for deliveries to be made pursuant to the Contract;
(6) there is a significant shortage of warehouse facilities to accommodate any such additional wheat;
(7) there is a perceived distortion of the price relationships between the Contract and other values of wheat.

Board of Trade of the City of Chicago v. CFTC, 605 F.2d 1016, 1018-1019 (7th Cir. 1979), *cert. denied*, 446 U.S. 928 (1980).

185. Board of Trade of the City of Chicago v. CFTC, 605 F.2d 1016, 1019 (7th Cir. 1979), *cert. denied*, 446 U.S. 928 (1980).

186. *Id.*

187. Jerry W. Markham, *Manipulation of Commodity Futures Prices: The Unprosecutable Crime*, 8 YALE J. ON REG. 281, 341 (1991).

188. Board of Trade of the City of Chicago v. CFTC, 605 F.2d 1016 (7th Cir. 1979), *cert. denied*, 446 U.S. 928 (1980).

189. For a description of the events in the March 1979 CBOT wheat futures contract, see Richard G. Heifner,

It was claimed in congressional hearings held on this amendment that the CFTC's declaration of an emergency could have "serious long-term implications for the viability of the market" because government action "introduces a type of uncertainty that traders are ill-equipped to handle."[190] It was further claimed that halting trading by the CFTC was "fraught with dangers. It can impose great inconvenience and unexpected losses upon the innocent as well as the guilty. It introduces difficult problems in determining fair settlements and tends over the long run to undermine confidence in and usefulness of the market."[191]

The statute as amended in 1982 defined emergencies to include, as well as "threatened or actual market manipulations and corners, any act of the United States or a foreign government affecting a commodity or any other major market disturbance which prevents the market from accurately reflecting the forces of supply and demand for such commodity."[192]

The CFTC virtually abandoned the use of its emergency powers after the March 1979 wheat debacle. It did declare an emergency when President Jimmy Carter imposed a grain embargo on the Soviet Union after it invaded Afghanistan in January 1980. The CFTC suspended trading for two days in futures contracts on wheat, corn, oats, soybeans, soybean meal, and soybean oil in order to allow the market to assess the effects of that action.[193] The embargo was not popular. Ronald Reagan lifted it when he assumed office. Congress also passed legislation allowing future such embargoes to operate only prospectively, absent war or a national emergency.[194]

4:7 FEEDER CATTLE

Several private actions charged that Thomas Dittmer and his futures commission merchant, Refco Inc., manipulated the price of feeder cattle contracts in 1979. That litigation turned into a debacle for plaintiffs.[195] As described in Chapter 3, the Eighth Circuit had taken an expansive view of what constitutes manipulation in *Cargill v. Hardin*.[196] That court had no such inclination for the 1979 feeder cattle futures trading by Dittmer. The Eight Circuit held in five separate cases that plaintiffs had failed to prove that defendants had engaged in manipulation or other actionable trading misconduct.[197]

Report on a Study of the March 1979 Chicago Wheat Futures Contract, reprinted, CFTC Reauthorization, Hearings Before a House Subcommittee on Conservation, Credit, and Rural Development of the Committee on Agriculture, 97th Cong., 2d Sess. 716 (1982).

190. *CFTC Reauthorization, Hearings on H.R. 5447 Before the Subcomm. on Conservation, Credit, and Rural Development of the House Comm. on Agriculture*, 97th Cong., 2d Sess. 727(1982).

191. *Id.*

192. Futures Trading Act of 1982, Pub. L. No. 97-444, § 225, 96 Stat. 2294, 2315 (1982).

193. *See*, H.R. Rep. No. 565, 97th Cong., 2d Sess. 59-60 (1982) (describing the use of the CFTC emergency powers).

194. III Jerry W. Markham, A Financial History of the United States, From the Age of Derivatives into the New Millennium (1970-2001) 85 (2002).

195. This litigation was accompanied by a scandal involving the first lady and later senator and secretary of state Hillary Clinton. She had an account at Refco that returned her a profit of $100,000 on a $1,000 investment in a very short period of time without making a required margin deposit. Her broker, Robert Bone, was disciplined by the Chicago Mercantile Exchange for various improprieties in allocating profits among his customers' accounts. Stephen Engelberg, *New Records Outline Favor for Hillary Clinton on Trades*, New York Times, May 27, 1994, at A20.

196. Cargill v. Hardin, 452 F.2d 1154, 1159 (8th Cir. 1971), *cert. denied*, 406 U.S. 932 (1972).

197. Dudley v. Dittmer, 795 F.2d 669 (8th Cir. 1986); Greenwood v. Dittmer, 776 F.2d 785 (8th Cir. 1985); Horn v. Ray E. Friedman & Co., 776 F.2d 277 (8th Cir. 1985); Bone v. Refco Inc., 774 F.2d 235 (8th Cir. 1985); McIlroy v. Dittmer, 732 F.2d 98 (8th Cir. 1984).

In one of those cases, *Dudley v. Dittmer*,[198] the Eighth Circuit ordered a retrial of a jury verdict in favor of the plaintiffs that had been tried on fraud and manipulation theories. The court ruled there was insufficient evidence to sustain a fraud claim and remanded for a new trial based only a claim of manipulation. After a trial on remand, a jury found that the defendants had manipulated the market in violation of the Commodity Exchange Act, the antitrust laws, and the Racketeer Influenced and Corrupt Organizations Act (RICO), but the Eighth Circuit set side that verdict in *Utesch v. Dittmer*.[199] The court noted,

> The scheme, according to the plaintiffs, had three stages. First, Dittmer and Refco established long positions in the May 1979 feeder cattle contract and the June and August 1979 live cattle contracts, thereby acquiring the right to obtain a large number of cattle that would be ready for delivery in the October 1979 market. Second, in order to increase the price of the October futures contract, Dittmer urged Refco brokers and customers to take long positions in the October and December 1979 live cattle contracts by representing that there would be significant price increases in the cash price of cattle for those months. Third, in the first week of October 1979, Dittmer and Refco closed out their long positions, took short positions, began to make massive deliveries of their cattle in the market, and tendered notices of intent to deliver even larger amounts of cattle.[200]

The court held that to "establish manipulation that injured them, the plaintiffs were required to show that the post–October 2 prices in the October 1979 futures market were artificially low, i.e., lower than they would have been under the operation of normal supply and demand market forces, and that the decline in the futures price was a proximate cause of the decline in cash prices."[201] The Eighth Circuit further held that, even if the defendants had the power to affect prices, the evidence failed to show that the defendants were responsible for the fall in feeder cattle or feeder cattle futures prices. In addition, the evidence was "insufficient to show that Dittmer's investment recommendations and other statements he made regarding the October futures cattle market were false, misleading or inaccurate, or that he knew or believed them to be so when he made them."[202]

4:8 THE SILVER CRISIS

The silver crisis that arose in 1980 was a truly historical event that can best be compared to the attempt by Jay Gould and Jim Fisk to corner the gold market after the Civil War. Nelson Bunker

---

198. Dudley v. Dittmer, 795 F.2d 669 (8th Cir. 1986).

199. Utesch v. Dittmer, 947 F.2d 321 (8th Cir. 1991), *cert. denied*, 503 U.S. 1006 (1992).

200. 947 F.2d at 324.

201. 947 F.2d at 329.

202. 947 F.2d at 327-328. Dittmer later gave up his interest in Refco and that firm went on to become one of the largest futures commission merchants in the world. However, it was forced to declare bankruptcy in 2005 after a massive fraud in which it concealed trading losses of $1 billion from its public shareholders when the firm went public. The Refco CEO, Philip Bennett, pleaded guilty to criminal charges, and Refco president Tone Grant was convicted of fraud after a trial. *Ex-Refco Boss Guilty of Fraud in Losses Scam; Former President of Bankrupt Derivatives Firm Faces Life in Prison*, New York Times, April 18, 2008, at B03. The remnants of Refco were sold to MF Global Inc., which in turn failed spectacularly in 2011 after its CEO, Jon Corzine, the former governor and senator from New Jersey, made a massive losing bet on Greece's sovereign debt. Some $1.2 billion in customer funds went missing as the company was failing. Ben Protess & Azam Ahmed, *U.S. Inquiry of MF Global Gains Speed*, New York Times, Jan. 10, 2012, at B1.

Hunt and his brother Herbert began their acquisitions that led to the silver crisis not long after the Seventh Circuit ordered them to be enjoined from future speculative limit violations after their soybean speculation. Indeed, the Hunts were reported to be amassing a large position in the silver market at the time the CFTC filed its soybean case.[203] The default by the Hunts in March 1980 on their margin calls for their silver positions touched off the crisis. As an SEC staff report found, "For six days late in March 1980 it appeared to government officials, Wall Street and the public at large that a default by a single family on its obligations in the plummeting silver market might seriously disrupt the U.S. financial system."[204]

The Hunts had begun their silver speculations in 1973 and took delivery on 55 million ounces of silver on their December 1973 futures contracts at a cost of $160 million. That silver was purchased at about $3 per ounce.[205] They shipped 40 million ounces of that silver to Switzerland for storage on three specially chartered cargo jets guarded by a group of cowboys who normally worked the Giant Circle K Ranch owned by the Hunts. The Hunts continued to pursue silver investments and ramped up their acquisitions in mid-1979.[206]

The silver crisis that occurred in 1980 had its beginnings in 1979 when silver was trading at about $6 per ounce. Silver prices climbed to nearly $50 an ounce between mid-1979 and January 1980. There were no CFTC speculative limits on silver futures, and the Hunts were able to amass a giant position in silver futures and cash silver. By August 1, 1979, Bunker Hunt owned 21 million ounces of silver bullion and 9,000 silver futures contracts, each for 5,000 ounces of silver on the CBOT and the Commodity Exchange Inc. (COMEX) in New York. Herbert Hunt then owned 21 million ounces of silver bullion and 4,000 silver futures contracts.

The Hunts augmented this massive position by additional acquisitions made through International Metals Investment Co. (IMIC), a company the Hunts owned jointly with two Saudi Arabian sheikhs, Sheikh Ali bin Mussalem and Sheikh Mohammed Aboud Al-Amoudi.[207] IMIC had accumulated 8,400 silver futures contracts by August 1979 and took delivery on, or exchanged futures for, a total of 68 million ounces of silver in October 1979.[208] By the end of 1979, the Hunts and IMIC owned more than 130 million ounces of silver bullion and futures contracts on another 90 million ounces that were due for delivery in March 1980. The Hunts also enrolled a group of foreign speculators to buy silver futures contracts on the U.S. exchanges. This group of speculators included Naji Nahas, a Brazilian who had made millions of dollars in coffee speculations. Collectively, those speculators built a silver futures position of 42 million ounces on U.S. exchanges.[209]

At the behest of the CFTC, the COMEX and CBOT took measures that punctured the silver bubble. "Three major actions intended to protect the financial integrity of the silver futures market and mitigate the threat of manipulation were taken by the exchanges. First, margin requirements on silver futures contracts were raised several times during late 1979 to a point where the initial margin on non-spot futures, $50,000, represented from 20 to 60 percent of the value of a silver contract when silver was between $16.35 and $48.70 per ounce. Second, limits on speculative

203. *U.S. Opposes Hunts on Soybean Holdings*, NEW YORK TIMES, May 1, 1977, at F 19.

204. Staff of the Securities and Exchange Commission, *Report on the Silver Crisis of 1980* 3-4 (Oct. 1982).

205. JEROME TUCCILLE, KINGDOM 314 (1984).

206. Harry Hurt III, *Silver Finger*, PLAYBOY, Sept. 1980, at 116.

207. III JERRY W. MARKHAM, A FINANCIAL HISTORY OF THE UNITED STATES, FROM THE AGE OF DERIVATIVES TO THE NEW MILLENNIUM 61 (2002).

208. Harry Hurt III, *Silver Finger*, PLAYBOY MAGAZINE (Sept. 1980).

209. *Id.*

positions in the silver futures market were imposed. Third, trading for liquidation only was instituted in late January" of 1980.[210]

"After a series of exchange actions prompted in part by the concerns of the CFTC, the price of silver peaked at $50 per ounce in late January 1980. It then fell quickly throughout the remainder of the first quarter of 1980."[211] When silver prices peaked at $50 per ounce, the Hunts' silver holdings were valued at about $10 billion. On March 18, 1980, silver prices dropped by a third, from $39.50 to $10.80. On "Silver Thursday, March 27, 1980, the Hunts' game of checkers came to an end. . . . Unable to meet their margin calls, the Hunt brothers had triggered the first great panic since October 1929."[212]

"For several days in March 1980 there was considerable uncertainty in the financial marketplace concerning the solvency of several major brokerage firms and the impact that the failure of one or more of these firms might have on financial markets in general."[213] "There were rumors that the brothers' principal broker, Bache, Halsey Stuart Shields, was going under, and the Dow plunged in "wild selling."[214] The CFTC chair, James M. Stone, famously claimed that the entire "financial fabric of the United States was endangered" by the Hunts.[215]

The Hunts had financed this position through massive loans from their banks and brokers. A syndicate of thirty banks loaned the Hunts $450 million that was used for their silver trading; Bache & Co., a Hunt broker, loaned them $230 million; Citicorp loaned about $100 million; First National of Chicago loaned $70 million; and First National of Dallas loaned $35 million. The Hunts also owed Engelhard Minerals and Chemicals Corp. $665 million in a silver purchase agreement for some 19 million ounces of silver.[216]

Trading in the stock of Bache, Dean Witter Reynolds and Shearson Loeb Rhoades was suspended by the SEC after the Hunts' margin defaults.[217] The banks and brokerage firms were bailed out by a $1.1 billion syndicated loan from a group of banks that was blessed by the Federal Reserve Board chair, Paul Volcker.[218]

Bunker Hunt, his brother Herbert, and several other traders were charged with manipulation by the CFTC after an investigation lasting some five years. Some nine years after the crisis, the two Hunt brothers agreed to sanctions that permanently barred them from futures trading and imposed a $10 million civil penalty for each brother.[219] The Hunts and others were also the subject of several private actions. A district court held in *Minpeco S.A. v. ContiCommodity Services Inc.*[220] that

---

210. *Report to the Congress in Response to Section 21 of the Commodity Exchange Act*, Pub. L. No. 96-276, 96th Cong., 2d Sess. § 7, 94 Stat. 542 (June 1, 1980) (footnote omitted).

211. *Id.*

212. L.J. Davis, *Silver Thursday*, HARPER'S MAGAZINE (May 1981). *See generally*, STEPHEN FAY, BEYOND GREED (1983) (describing the silver crisis).

213. *Report to the Congress in Response to Section 21 of the Commodity Exchange Act*, Pub. L. No. 96-276, 96th Cong., 2d Sess. § 7, 94 Stat. 542 (June 1, 1980) (footnote omitted).

214. L.J. Davis, *Silver Thursday*, HARPER'S MAGAZINE (May 1981).

215. *Silver Prices and the Adequacy of Federal Actions in the Marketplace, 1979-80*, H. Rep. No. 395, 97th Cong., 1st Sess. 24 (1981).

216. III JERRY W. MARKHAM, A FINANCIAL HISTORY OF THE UNITED STATES, FROM THE AGE OF DERIVATIVES TO THE NEW MILLENNIUM 62-63 (2002).

217. *Silver Prices and the Adequacy of Federal Actions in the Marketplace, 1979-80*, H. Rep. No. 395, 97th Cong., 1st Sess. 1 (1981).

218. HARRY HURT III, TEXAS RICH 415 (1981).

219. In re Hunt, COMM. FUT. L. REP. (CCH) ¶ 23,296 (C.F.T.C. 1996) & ¶ 23,244 (C.F.T.C. 1987). Before the settlement, the CFTC had been enjoined from continuing its case against the Hunts by a Texas bankruptcy court. *See*, CFTC, 1988 ANNUAL REP. 68 (1989).

220. Minpeco S.A. v. ContiCommodity Services Inc., 552 F. Supp. 332, 337 (S.D.N.Y. 1982). Similarly,

silver price manipulation claims under the Commodity Exchange Act could go forward where the defendants created a "price mirage" that lured others into the market. The court noted that, while normally a trader does not have to disclose its trading activities to others, a duty to disclose could arise under such circumstances. That case went to trial more than eight years after the crisis.

The *Minpeco* trial witnessed a battle of prominent economic experts. They variously estimated that, in the absence of the Hunts' trading, the silver market would at its peak have reached from $8 to $45 per troy ounce, which was a rather large spread that demonstrates how difficult it is to prove price effects.[221] The *Minpeco* jury was instructed that in order to find manipulation under the Commodity Exchange Act, they must find specific intent to produce an artificial price and that such a price was achieved as a result of defendants' actions and those actions were the proximate cause of plaintiffs' injuries. Specific intent was defined by the court as "the conspirators knew what they were doing and that they did it with a purpose or conscious object of creating an inflated and artificial price."[222] The jury was also instructed that, in order to prevail on the Commodity Exchange Act claims, "the plaintiff had to prove that the conspiracy played a *substantial* part in bringing about or actually causing the artificial price."[223]

The *Minpeco* jury awarded damages totaling $132 million for violations of the antimanipulation provisions of the Commodity Exchange Act, the antitrust laws, RICO, and common law fraud.[224] That victory was considerably tarnished when the Hunts then declared bankruptcy with claims of some $2 billion against their estates.[225] All in all, the whole affair proved that the antimanipulation provisions in the Commodity Exchange Act were not a deterrent to speculative attacks on the commodity markets.[226]

The silver crisis, not surprisingly, raised concerns in Congress over the efficacy of the CFTC. It was noted that "[t]here has been a major market disruption in every year since 1975, when the

in *Cargill v. Hardin*, 452 F.2d 1154, 1159 (8th Cir. 1971), the court noted that the defendant's knowledge of its dominant position in the cash market aided its futures price manipulation:

> It is important to note here that Cargill was thus in possession of a vital piece of information that other traders and grain dealers in Chicago did not have access to, namely that it owned the bulk of deliverable wheat in Chicago. While all traders of course knew the total quantity of deliverable wheat available in Chicago, only Cargill was in a position to know that it owned the vast majority of this wheat.

221. Jeffrey Williams, Manipulation on Trial 14 (1995).

222. Dennis Klejna & Stephen H. Meyer, *The Prohibition Against Commodity Manipulation: Review of Enforcement and Civil Actions*, at 19, Conference on Market Manipulation: Law, Economics, and Public Policy, sponsored by the Center for Study of Futures and Options Markets and the American Bar Association, Washington, DC (Nov. 8–9, 1990).

223. Minpeco, S.A. v. Hunt, 718 F. Supp. 168, 174, n. 6 (S.D.N.Y. 1987). The Hunts' silver trading spawned much litigation with only mixed results for the plaintiffs. *See, e.g.*, Korwek v. Hunt, 827 F.2d 874 (2d Cir. 1987); Gordon v. Hunt, 98 F.R.D. 573 (S.D.N.Y. 1983); Grosser v. Commodity Exchange Inc., 639 F. Supp. 1293 (S.D.N.Y. 1986), *aff'd per curiam*, 859 F.2d 148 (2d Cir. 1988); De Autcha v. Commodity Exchange Inc., 608 F. Supp. 510 (S.D.N.Y. 1985); Bishop v. Commodity Exchange Inc., 564 F. Supp. 1557 (S.D.N.Y. 1983); Strax v. Commodity Exchange Inc., 524 F. Supp. 936 (S.D.N.Y. 1981); Goldschmidt v. Hunt, 556 F. Supp. 123 (N.D. Tex. 1983); Zeltser v. Hunt, 90 F.R.D. 65 (S.D.N.Y. 1981).

224. Minpeco, S.A. v. Hunt, 718 F. Supp. 168 (S.D.N.Y. 1987).

225. Nina Andrews, *Hunts Make Progress on Bankruptcy*, New York Times, Nov. 6, 1989.

226. The silver market was the subject of other manipulation claims. *See*, In re Clayton Brokerage Co., CFTC Doc. No. 80-19 (C.F.T.C. 1980) (settlement of claims involving silver futures contracts in 1978); In the Matter of Dial, Comm. Fut. L. Rep (CCH) ¶ 23,772 (C.F.T.C. 1987) (CFTC administrative law judge dismisses claims of manipulation of silver).

CFTC was first established"[227]—that is, a crisis in potatoes, coffee, soybeans, wheat, and silver. A Senate committee report also found that in the run-up to the silver crisis, "[f]aced with dramatic and disorderly market conditions, the CFTC took none of the specific preventive or emergency actions allowed under the Commodity Exchange Act, although it had both the statutory duty to act and the requisite information."[228]

Concerns were also raised over coordination among federal regulators during the silver crisis. A joint study conducted by the CFTC, SEC, the Federal Reserve Board, and the Treasury Department concluded that the "enormous resources available to a wealthy speculator or a foreign government pose special threats to futures markets."[229] However, the SEC refused to join in on the findings of the CFTC on the effect of the exchanges' decision to impose position limits on existing positions, an action that effectively crashed the market.[230] The SEC also filed its own extensive report on the silver crisis.[231]

In a report to Congress on the silver crisis, the CFTC stated that its surveillance staff "considers the elements of manipulation to be (a) a trader or group of traders who act in concert and have the capacity to affect the price of a commodity, (b) the exercise by that trader or group of traders of their capacity to affect the price, (c) an artificial price, and (d) intent." The report went on to describe how each of these elements was assessed by the staff to determine if a possible manipulation was under way. For example, price artificiality required "an evaluation of changes in cash and futures price levels, futures price differentials between contract months (spreads), cash and futures price differentials (basis), and intermarket price differentials, particularly between delivery points and other locations."[232] A CFTC commissioner also testified before Congress that the "classic concept of manipulation is a distortion of the future against the cash."[233]

One witness sought to give authority to the CFTC to adopt a form of Charlie's rule that would allow the CFTC to impose position limits in maturing futures contracts.[234] Congress adopted such a provision in 1982 that allowed the CFTC to set different trading or position limits for different numbers of days remaining until the last day of trading in a contract.[235] In the meantime, the CFTC promulgated rules requiring the exchanges to set speculative limits for contracts they trade.[236] The CFTC rules required "every contract market to adopt speculative position limits for all futures contracts and related commodity options that were not already subject to such limits. Those limits must be set at levels acceptable to the Commission."[237] The CFTC thus required the exchanges, as opposed to the agency itself, to adopt speculative position limits.[238] The Commodity Exchange Act was amended to allow the CFTC to enforce those exchange rules.[239]

---

227. *Joint Agency Reports on Silver Markets: Hearing Before the House Subcommittee on Conservation, Credit, and Rural Development of the Committee on Agriculture*, 97th Cong., 1st Sess. 2 (1981).

228. *Silver Prices and the Adequacy of Federal Actions in the Marketplace, 1979-80*, H. Rep. No. 395, 97th Cong., 1st Sess. 5 (1981).

229. Robert D. Hershey Jr., *Silver Study Warns of Repeat of Chaos*, New York Times, June 2, 1981.

230. Jerry Knight, *SEC Disavows Silver Study*, Washington Post, June 1, 1981.

231. *Report of the Staff of the Securities and Exchange Commission: The Silver Crisis of 1980* (1982).

232. *Report of the Commodity Futures Trading Commission on Recent Developments in the Silver Futures Market to the Senate Committee on Agriculture, Nutrition, and Forestry*, 96th Cong., 2d Sess. 15, 18-19 (1980).

233. *Silver Prices and the Adequacy of Federal Actions in the Marketplace, 1979-80*, H. Rep. No. 395, 97th Cong., 1st Sess. 11 (1981).

234. H.R. Rep. No. 565, 97th Cong., 2d Sess. 73 (1982).

235. Futures Trading Act of 1982, Pub. L. No. 97-444 (1982).

236. H.R. Rep. No. 565, 97th Cong., 2d Sess. 66 (1982).

237. *Joint Agency Reports on Silver Markets: Hearing Before the House Subcommittee on Conservation, Credit, and Rural Development of the Committee on Agriculture*, 97th Cong., 1st Sess. 9 (1981).

238. 17 C.R.F. § 1.61.

239. 7 U.S.C. § 6a, as amended by Futures Trading Act of 1982, Pub. L. No. 97-444, § 204, 96 Stat.

Federal Reserve Board (Fed) chairman Paul Volcker testified before Congress that low margin requirements for futures aided hedging but also attracted unwanted speculators like the Hunts.[240] A Treasury Department official testified that higher margin requirements could screen out speculators who did not have sufficient capital to be suitable for such leveraged trading.[241]

Legislation was introduced that would have given the CFTC limited authority to set margins. Another bill would have allowed the Federal Reserve Board to set margins for futures on financial instruments and loans used to finance the purchase of financial instruments in either the cash or futures markets. That legislation was strongly opposed by the industry. Opponents argued, among other things, that the government was ill-suited to make margin changes for short-lived futures contracts in volatile markets without destroying them for hedging purposes.[242] A CFTC commissioner noted that high margin levels, even if imposed over an extended period, had not proved to be an effective means to control prices.[243] Economists also pointed out that higher margin requirements would not have prevented the silver crisis. Indeed, the futures exchanges had raised margins to unheard-of levels. Those increases caused a drop in the level of trading, but prices continued to increase and become more volatile as the market thinned and before it collapsed and brought on the crisis.[244]

A unilateral effort by the Fed to regulate margins on stock index futures was also opposed by the industry and the CFTC.[245] In the end, Congress amended the Commodity Exchange Act to expand the CFTC's power by authorizing it to direct the futures exchanges to increase margin levels in the event of a market emergency.[246] However, the CFTC had already assumed that it had such power when it ordered margins to be increased to 100 percent during the 1976 potato futures debacle.[247]

SEC chair Harold Williams was the proponent of margin rules for commodity futures trading that would be set by the Federal Reserve Board.[248] A study by the Fed on that issue was completed in 1984.[249] Its findings were a surprise. The Fed recommended that stock margins be reduced and equalized with futures and that security exchanges should be allowed to set stock margins. Fed chair Paul Volcker did suggest that margins set by the stock and commodity futures exchanges should be monitored by a council of federal agencies. This proposal was opposed by the CFTC, which noted

---

2294. *See, e.g.*, Saberi v. CFTC, 488 F.3d 1207 (9th Cir. 2007) (upholding CFTC sanctions for violations of exchange position limits).

240. *Silver Prices and the Adequacy of Federal Actions in the Marketplace, 1979-80: Hearings Before a Subcommittee of the House Committee on Government Operations,* 96th Cong., 2d Sess. 238, 242-244 (1980).

241. *Id.* at 407-408.

242. *See*, Jerry W. Markham, *Federal Regulation of Margin in the Commodity Futures Industry: History and Theory*, 64 TEMP. L. REV. 59, 92 (1991) (describing the arguments over margin controls in the wake of the silver crisis).

243. *Price Volatility in the Silver Futures Market: Hearings Before the Subcommittee on Agricultural Research and General Legislation of the Senate Committee on Agriculture, Nutrition and Forestry,* 96th Cong., 2d Sess. 45 (1980).

244. *Id.* at 46.

245. Jerry W. Markham, *Federal Regulation of Margin in the Commodity Futures Industry: History and Theory*, 64 TEMP. L. REV. 59, 94-96 (1991).

246. Futures Trading Act of 1982, Pub. L. No. 97-444. § 225, 96 Stat. 2315.

247. Jerry W. Markham, *Federal Regulation of Margin in the Commodity Futures Industry: History and Theory*, 64 TEMP. L. REV. 59, 94, n. 32 (1991).

248. *Silver Prices and the Adequacy of Federal Actions in the Marketplace, 1979-80: Hearings Before a Subcommittee of the House Committee on Government Operations,* 96th Cong., 2d Sess. 58 (1980).

249. *A Study by the Staff of the Board of Governors of the Federal Reserve: A Review and Evaluation of Federal Margin Regulations* (Dec. 1984).

that Congress had on prior occasions rejected federal control over futures margins. Volcker's recommendation was supported by Treasury and the SEC, but was not adopted.[250]

There was a subtext to the SEC's effort to inject the government into margin setting for futures. The development of futures contracts on securities products in the 1970s that were in the exclusive jurisdiction of the CFTC had touched off a long-running battle between the two agencies.[251] The CFTC and SEC reached a démarche in 1982 that allocated jurisdictional boundaries, and that agreement was enacted into law. This did little to dampen hostilities between the two agencies and the next great market crisis—the stock market crash of 1987—would renew concerns over commodity futures speculation.[252] The CFTC, however, would have to face other speculation and manipulation concerns before that event.

Cotton futures were a problem in 1981 because long futures positions in that commodity exceeded available stocks. The November 1981 feeder cattle futures contract had concentrated positions and the CME declared a market emergency, ordering trading for liquidation only. Futures positions in pork bellies and live hogs were another problem. Pork bellies were the subject of an emergency action in 1983 by the CME, which required forced liquidations and increased margin requirements. The July 1983 corn futures contract came under pressure but serious problems were avoided. The cocoa market was of concern in 1985 as the result of some large commercial positions.[253]

4:9 THE CFTC DEFINES MANIPULATION

When the CFTC was created, it inherited some unresolved manipulation cases that had been brought by the Commodity Exchange Authority (CEA). Those cases allowed the CFTC to place its own mark on defining what is needed to prove manipulation. In doing so, the CFTC created standards that are very difficult to prove, going even further than the *Volkart* court in their burdens.[254] The CFTC's leniency on manipulation was first signaled in *In re Hugh P. King*.[255] That case arose when the CEA became concerned about the large position of a trader in the July 1972 oat future. The CEA had no injunctive authority and could only warn the trader against any manipulative activity. The trader responded that he would liquidate his long position but only at a premium of four cents over the September future. The trader placed orders to sell at a price just over that four-cent premium and was able to sell out his position.

The CEA charged King with manipulation. The CFTC took over the litigation when it was created and approved a settlement of the charges in 1976. The CFTC stated in its settlement order that this was one of several cases it had inherited from the CEA that were contributing to a burdensome caseload and straining CFTC resources. The CFTC order warned that, when manipulation is found after adjudication, the most severe sanctions would be imposed. In view of the long delay in

250. *See*, Jerry W. Markham, *Federal Regulation of Margin in the Commodity Futures Industry: History and Theory*, 64 TEMP. L. REV. 59, 97-98 (1991) (describing the Fed study and CFTC and SEC responses to the Volcker recommendations).

251. *Silver Prices and the Adequacy of Federal Actions in the Marketplace, 1979-80: Hearings Before a Subcommittee of the House Committee on Government Operations,* 96th Cong., 2d Sess. 67-83 (1980).

252. *See*, Jerry W. Markham, *Super-Regulator: A Comparative Analysis of Securities and Derivatives Regulation in the United States, Great Britain and Japan*, 28 BROOKLYN J. OF INT'L L. 319, 356-364 (2003) (describing this regulatory competition).

253. JERRY W. MARKHAM, A HISTORY OF COMMODITY FUTURES TRADING AND ITS REGULATION 135-136 (1987).

254. *See*, In re Indiana Farm Bureau Coop. Ass'n, COMM. FUT. L. REP. (CCH) ¶ 21,796 (C.F.T.C. 1982).

255. In re Hugh P. King, Comm. Ft. L. Rep. (CCH) ¶ 20,211 (1976).

resolving the *King* case, however, much lighter sanctions were imposed, which the CFTC stated would not have precedential value in future cases. A cease and desist order and a forty-five-day suspension of trading privileges and floor broker registration for the respondent were imposed.

Similar action was taken with another case brought by the CEA in *In the Matter of Tyson Foods Inc.*[256] There, it was charged that respondents attempted to manipulate and did manipulate the price of the September 1970 shell egg futures on the CME by buying up available deliverable supplies while accumulating a long position that was in excess of the reduced deliverable supply. "[I]t was therefore impossible for all holders of short contracts to satisfy such short contracts without purchasing futures or deliverable cash eggs from said Respondents." The CFTC found in the settlement agreement that on September 21, 1970, the last day of trading, respondents placed sale orders to offset their long position. "These orders set price limits, below which sales could not be made, ranging to 48.55 cents per dozen. Said Respondents sold future contracts on that day at prices ranging to 48.20 cents per dozen. Such prices were abnormally and artificially high."[257] Some of the orders could not be executed at the prices demanded, and respondents were left with a total long position of 231 contracts at the close of trading, constituting 99.1 percent of the open interest. Those contracts were settled after the close of trading by cash deliveries. The sanctions agreed to included trading suspensions ranging from sixty days to one year, cease and desist orders, and a civil penalty on one respondent in the amount of $10,000.[258]

Those settlements were followed by some cases that were adjudicated by the CFTC after an adversary hearing. In *In the Matter of Hohenberg Brothers*,[259] the CEA had brought an attempted manipulation charge with respect to the December 1971 cotton futures contract traded on the New York Cotton Exchange. Hohenberg Brothers Co., a large cotton merchandising firm, had partially hedged its long position of some 294,000 bales of cotton through short positions in futures on the New York Cotton Exchange. The price for that futures contract declined by some four cents a pound, causing Hohenberg Brothers to begin an "aggressive sales campaign" for its cash cotton. Hohenberg Brothers also increased the number of its short futures contracts until its position constituted about 46 percent of the short open interest in that contract on November 23, 1971, the first delivery notice date. The company had some 65,000 bales of cotton certified as deliverable on the futures exchange. The CEA had charged that the company was attempting a short manipulation by driving the prices of cotton down.

An administrative law judge at the CFTC dismissed the claim after a hearing and the CFTC's Division of Enforcement appealed to the CFTC, seeking a reversal. Instead, the CFTC affirmed the decision. The CFTC noted that an attempted short manipulation was a case of the first impression for the new agency. Prior litigated manipulation cases under the Commodity Exchange Act had all involved allegations of actual manipulation even when attempted manipulation was also charged, with the exception of *Moore v. Brandon*,[260] which involved only attempted manipulation by a long trader. "However, since in that case the respondent offered no evidence in his defense, neither the Judicial Officer nor the court had occasion to discuss the elements of attempted manipulation."[261]

256. In the Matter of Tyson Foods Inc., 1977 CFTC LEXIS 67.

257. *Id.*

258. The CFTC later amended the settlement order to allow Tyson Foods to hedge its hog positions as well as its other activities that were for hedges. In the Matter of Tyson Foods Inc., Comm. Fut. L. Rep. (CCH) ¶ 20, 608 (C.F.T.C. 1978).

259. In the Matter of Hohenberg Bros., Comm. Fut. L. Rep. (CCH) ¶ 20, 271 (C.F.T.C. 1977).

260. Moore v. Brandon, 191 F.2d 775 (D.C. Cir., *cert. denied*, 342 U.S. 860 (1951).

261. In the Matter of Hohenberg Bros., Comm. Fut. L. Rep. (CCH) ¶ 20, 271, n. 39 (C.F.T.C. 1977).

The CFTC held that an "attempted manipulation requires an intent to affect market prices artificially and some overt act in furtherance of that intent."[262] The CFTC further stated that it could "discern no difference in the intent required to accomplish a manipulation and that required by an attempted manipulation, which is simply the performance of an act or conduct which was intended to effect an artificial price."[263] The CFTC further stated that "a profit motive was not a necessary element of manipulation. . . . A dominant or controlling position in the market is [also] not a requisite element to either manipulation or attempted manipulation and is not essential to altering successfully the forces of supply and demand."[264]

The CFTC could not find evidence that Hohenberg Brothers was attempting to depress prices artificially. The company had tendered 35,700 bales of cotton for delivery against its short futures position, but it did so because it could not economically roll over its December futures position into more distant months and that delivery on the December contracts was its best option.[265] Hohenberg Brothers also knew that there were "strong hands" that would accept its delivery notices without undue effect on market prices.

"Even though respondents' activities may have involved a 'profit motive,' absent a finding of manipulative intent, trading with the purpose of obtaining the best price for one's cotton does not constitute, in itself, a violation of the Commodity Exchange Act. It is clear that respondents intended to obtain the best price available for their stocks of certified cotton by tendering notices of delivery against their short position in the December future."[266] A phone call from the head of Hohenberg Brothers to Plains Cotton Cooperative alerting that cotton dealer to Hohenberg's plans to tender for delivery was also not found to have been designed to depress prices.[267]

The Plains Cotton Cooperative had been the subject of another Commodity Exchange Authority manipulation case that was inherited by the CFTC.[268] In that case, Plains Cotton was charged with an actual and attempted manipulation of the May and July 1972 cotton futures contract and the price of spot cotton. It had maintained large long positions in various cotton futures months and began accepting large deliveries starting in November 1971, including deliveries from Hohenberg Brothers. Plains Cotton made most of the spot cotton undeliverable that it received on the December 1971, March 1972, and May 1972 futures, thereby reducing cotton stocks. Plains Cotton settled with the CFTC, without admitting or denying the allegations of the complaint. Cease and desist orders were entered, along with one-year trading suspensions.

In *In re Indiana Farm Bureau Coop. Association*,[269] the CFTC dismissed another CEA-instituted manipulation case. This one involved the July 1973 corn futures contract on the Chicago Board of Trade. This alleged manipulation occurred when the grain markets were under pressure from wheat sales to the Soviet Union and prices rose dramatically. The respondent was charged with manipulating corn prices by standing for delivery on corn futures contracts in an amount that the CFTC enforcement staff claimed amounted to four times the amount of available deliverable supplies. The CFTC, however, rejected that claim. It concluded that, while corn prices were

---

262. *Id.*

263. *Id.* at 271.

264. *Id.* at 271, n. 39.

265. "The Company's tender of notices of delivery on first notice day was large in light of previous tenders by a single account on the No. 2 cotton contract on the New York Cotton Exchange, but nevertheless amounted to less than 18% of the total open interest." In the Matter of Hohenberg Bros., Comm. Fut. L. Rep. (CCH) ¶ 20, 271 (C.F.T.C. 1977).

266. *Id.*

267. *Id.*

268. In the Matter of Plains Cotton Cooperative, 1977 CFTC LEXIS 84 (C.F.T.C.).

269. In re Indiana Farm Bureau Coop. Association, 1982 CFTC LEXIS 25 (C.F.T.C.).

artificially high, it was not shown that the respondent was the cause of those prices or that they intended an artificial price.

The CFTC enforcement staff had further claimed that manipulation had occurred because of scale-up orders entered by the respondent at increasingly higher prices. The CFTC, however, found that the entry of such orders was consistent with hedging activities.[270] Liquidation orders entered in the last twenty minutes of trading were also not shown to be accompanied by manipulative intent.

The CFTC conducted an intensive analysis of the concept of manipulation in its decision in *In re Indiana Farm Bureau*, reviewing prior definitions of manipulation adopted in court opinions in *Cargill v. Hardin*,[271] *General Foods Corp. v. Brannan*,[272] and *Volkart Brothers v. Freeman*.[273] The CFTC stated:

> Thus, to determine whether an artificial price has occurred, one must look at the aggregate forces of supply and demand and search for those factors which are extraneous to the pricing system, are not a legitimate part of the economic pricing of the commodity, or are extrinsic to that commodity market. When the aggregate forces of supply and demand bearing on a particular market are all legitimate, it follows that the price will not be artificial. On the other hand, when a price is affected by a factor which is not legitimate, the resulting price is necessarily artificial. Thus, the focus should not be as much on the ultimate price, as on the nature of the factors causing it.[274]

The CFTC also reconsidered its interpretation of the intent element in the *Hohenberg Brothers*,[275] concluding that some "refinement" was in order. The CFTC stated that "intent is the essence of manipulation." Here the complaint had charged "specific intent" as it is understood in the criminal law, but the CFTC enforcement staff argued that a less stringent "general intent" standard should be applied. The CFTC staff argued that it should be "sufficient, for purposes of manipulative intent, that the necessary consequence of their action was an unlawful result," which was a "'reasonable foreseeability' alternative formulation of intent" involving "intentional conduct which results in a manipulated price where that result was reasonably foreseeable."[276]

The CFTC rejected that formulation, holding that "the requisite level of mens rea required to prove manipulation or attempted manipulation under the Commodity Exchange Act is that of 'specific intent,' or as that term is also commonly understood to mean today, 'purposeful conduct.'"[277] However, the CFTC also noted that "[i]ntent is a subjective factor and since it is impossible to discover an attempted manipulator's state of mind, intent must of necessity be inferred from the objective facts and may, of course, be inferred by a person's actions and the totality of the circumstances."[278]

The CFTC then went on at some length to express the importance of the intent element and how it can be proved:

---

270. Compare, SEC v. Haase, SEC Litg. Rel. No. 10268, 1984 SEC LEXIS 2330 (D.D.C.) (SEC manipulation charges settled by consent where defendant placed sixteen separate purchase orders and where all but one of these purchases were "on an 'uptick', that is, at a price higher than the previous order").

271. Cargill v. Hardin, 452 F.2d 1154, 1163 (8th Cir. 1971), *cert. denied*, 406 U.S. 932 (1972).

272. General Foods Corp. v. Brannan, 170 F.2d 220, 221 (7th Cir. 1948).

273. Volkart Brothers v. Freeman, 311 F.2d 52, 58 (5th Cir. 1962).

274. In re Indiana Farm Bureau Coop. Association, 1982 CFTC LEXIS 25.

275. In the Matter of Hohenberg Bros., Comm. Fut. L. Rep. (CCH) ¶ 20, 271 (C.F.T.C. 1977).

276. In re Indiana Farm Bureau Coop. Association, 1982 CFTC LEXIS 25.

277. *Id.*

278. *Id.* The CFTC stated in this regard:

> We are unable to discern any justification for a weakening of the manipulative intent standard which does not wreak havoc with the market place. It is the intent of the parties which separates otherwise lawful business conduct from unlawful manipulative activity. This being so, a clear line between lawful and unlawful activity is required in order to ensure that innocent trading activity not be regarded with the advantage of hindsight as unlawful manipulation. . . . [M]arket participants have a right to trade in their own best interests without regard to the positions of others as long as their trading activity does not have as its purpose the creation of "artificial" or "distorted" prices. Indeed, it is this very motivation which gives lifeblood to the forces of supply and demand, and makes the price discovery function of the marketplace viable. Moreover, since the self-interest of every market participant plays a legitimate part in the price setting process, it is not enough to prove simply that the accused intended to influence price.
>
> Accordingly, we hold that in order to prove the intent element of a manipulation or attempted manipulation of a futures contract price under §§ 6(b) and 6(c) of the Commodity Exchange Act, as amended, it must be proven that the accused acted (or failed to act) with the purpose or conscious object of causing or effecting a price or price trend in the market that did not reflect the legitimate forces of supply and demand influencing futures prices in the particular market at the time of the alleged manipulative activity.[279]

The CFTC considered what constituted a "squeeze" and what trader conduct was inappropriate in a "congested" market. The CFTC reviewed various definitions of a squeeze, noting that prices could be squeezed without manipulative conduct in a congested market where deliverable supplies are in shortage. The CFTC stated that "[h]olding out for high prices is normally rational and lawful market behavior. Such activity only becomes unlawful when it is accompanied by manipulative intent as generally manifested by conduct other than simply seeking the best price in a pit in which there may be supply shortages."[280] The CFTC stated that "seeking the best price for one's commodity is a legitimate, indeed critical, price-creating force in the futures markets that in-and-of-itself cannot be the basis for an inference of manipulative intent. It is imperative that each side of the market seek the best price in order for price discovery to occur and that 'best' price is, of necessity, at the expense of the other side."[281]

The CFTC believed that the "acquisition of market dominance is the hallmark of a long manipulative squeeze. For without the ability to force shorts to deal with him either in the cash or futures market, the manipulator is not able to successfully dictate prices because a short may buy grain from other sources and deliver against his commitments."[282] Further, "where a long does not intentionally

---

> Since proof of intent will most often be circumstantial in nature, manipulative intent must normally be shown inferentially from the conduct of the accused. But once it is demonstrated that the alleged manipulator sought, by act or omission, to move the market away from the equilibrium or efficient price—the price which reflects the market forces of supply and demand—the mental element of manipulation may be inferred. Further, while knowledge of relevant market conditions is probative of intent, it is not necessary to prove that the accused knew to any particular degree of certainty that his actions would create an artificial price. It is enough to present evidence from which it may reasonably be inferred that the accused "consciously desire[d] that result, whatever the likelihood of that result happening from his conduct."

Id. (footnote and citations omitted).

279. In re Indiana Farm Bureau Coop. Association, 1982 CFTC LEXIS 25.

280. *Id.* (citation omitted).

281. *Id.* (footnotes and citations omitted).

282. *Id.* (footnotes and citations omitted).

create the conditions for a squeeze, and a congested futures market arises from other causes, often a 'natural' corner or low deliverable supply, manipulative intent may not be inferred where a long does not exacerbate the congestion itself, but simply seeks the best price from the existing situation."[283]

In a footnote, the CFTC elaborated on what is and is not permissible conduct. "Seeking the optimum price from the futures market (risking, of course, the possibility of delivery) is not unlawful. Manipulative intent may be inferred, however, where, once the congested situation becomes known to him, the long exacerbates the situation by, for example, intentionally decreasing the cash supply or increasing his long position in the futures market."[284]

The CFTC then went on to try and reconcile the *Cargill* and *Volkart* holdings by asserting that the results in those cases were controlled by their particular facts. After reviewing the facts in the *Indiana Farm Bureau* case, the CFTC concluded that the evidence did not support a finding that respondents intended to create an artificial price.[285] "The decision to stand for delivery was respondents' contractual right" and that decision "was motivated by pre-existing commercial needs and the uncertainty of prices in the inactive cash market." The respondent did not reduce local cash supplies of the commodity and it did not increase its long position in the last day of trading when it could have squeezed the market.[286]

The CFTC also found that the shorts had not acted responsibly by making sure there were sufficient available supplies. The CFTC asserted that, even when there is a shortage of deliverable supplies, the shorts have a contractual duty to deliver. "A short who, for whatever reason, enters the delivery month unprepared or unable to deliver runs the risk that he will have to offset at the long's price. Where a long has not intentionally created or exploited a congested situation, the long has a contractual right to stand for delivery or exact whatever price for its long position which a short is willing to pay in order to avoid having to make delivery."[287] This holding appeared to signal that the CFTC was adopting, and even extending, the *Volkart* decision that the CEA had sought to overturn by legislation.

Another case inherited from the CEA involved the May wheat contract on the CBOT. That contract had been the target of squeezes since the 1920s and before ("the same thing happens year after year at almost exactly the same time, becoming so familiar that the 'May squeeze' is marked on Chicago's calendar as methodically as Easter or Decoration Day") because May is a transitional period when the old wheat crop is nearly consumed and new wheat is not yet available.[288] In *In re Frey*,[289] the CFTC dismissed a charge that two floor brokers manipulated and attempted to manipulate the price of May 1971 wheat futures contracts on the CBOT. The two respondents in that case held 97.1 percent of the long open interest in the May wheat contract. On the last day of trading, the May futures contract opened at $1.615 per bushel, but the respondents sought to and did liquidate their positions near the exchange's daily price limit of $1.70.

The CFTC reversed a finding of manipulation by an administrative law judge (ALJ). In doing so, the CFTC conducted an extensive analysis of the cash market and available deliverable supplies in the *Frey* case. It held that premium grades of a commodity that is available for delivery are not necessarily excludable from the supply calculus if such supplies are considered to be deliverable under exchange rules. This decision appeared to be somewhat inconsistent with the decision of the Seventh Circuit in

283. *Id.* (footnotes and citations omitted).
284. *Id.* at n. 12.
285. *Id.* at 25.
286. *Id.*
287. *Id.*
288. In re Frey, Comm. Fut. L. Rep. (CCH) ¶ 24,578 (C.F.T.C. 1990).
289. In re Frey, Comm. Fut. L. Rep. (CCH) ¶ 23,786 (C.F.T.C. 1987).

Great Western Food Distributors v. Brannan,[290] which had excluded from the calculation of deliverable supplies fresh eggs as being undeliverable and premium refrigerated eggs because a premium of $315 per car was required for delivery. Similarly, in *Cargill v. Hardin*,[291] the Eighth Circuit had excluded hard winter wheat from the deliverable supply calculation because, while the shorts could have delivered that grade, they would receive no premium for delivering that expensive grade.

The CFTC found in *Frey* that there were some 26 million bushels that the shorts could have made deliverable with "prudent planning." "In these circumstances, Cox and Frey could not foreclose the shorts' delivery option and thus lacked the ability to influence market prices. Their conduct in the futures market (i.e., evidence suggesting that their trading activity created or exploited market congestion) is not dispositive, because market congestion cannot exist when deliverable supplies are adequate."[292]

The CFTC considered a finding by the ALJ that the respondents had created an artificial price. The CFTC stated that this analysis requires that "the focus should not be as much on the ultimate price, as on the nature of the factors causing it."[293] The CFTC also considered whether the respondent caused an artificial price, noting that its *Indiana Farm Bureau* decision had caused confusion over what was needed to prove causation. The CFTC held that an artificial price is proximately caused by an act, or a failure to act, that plays "a substantial part in bringing about or actually causing the artificial price; and that the artificial price was either a direct result or a reasonably probable consequence of the act or omission."[294]

The respondents in the *Frey* case contended that a large grain firm was the true culprit because it was acting as a short speculator, pushing down prices and failing to ensure it had supplies to deliver on its contracts when the contract expired. The CFTC accepted at least part of that argument: "[w]e emphasize that futures market participants who remain in the market late into the delivery month must be prepared to perform all of their obligations in the delivery process, *i.e.*, making or taking delivery of the underlying commodity. Participants who are not so prepared cannot assume they will be able to offset in the futures market without experiencing the prospect of an adverse price movement."[295]

Holding that its enforcement staff had failed to prove a completed price manipulation or the ability to influence market prices, the CFTC questioned whether manipulative intent was present. A respondent in the *Frey* case demanded that the CFTC pay his attorney fees after that action, which is allowed by the Equal Access to Justice Act if a governmental disciplinary action was not "substantially justified."[296] In the course of denying that petition, the CFTC stated that the developing nature of the law of price manipulation was a significant factor weighing against an award of attorney fees, noting that "[p]rice manipulation is not defined in the Commodity Exchange Act. In half a century, there have been only five appellate court opinions analyzing the elements of the offense."[297]

The Seventh Circuit Court of Appeals upheld the denial of attorney fees, in the course of which it conducted an analysis of what constituted manipulation under the Commodity Exchange Act. The court stated that such manipulations involve the "intentional exaction of a price determined by forces other than supply and demand," but "sophisticated economic justification for the distinc-

290. Great Western Food Distributors v. Brannan, 201 F.2d 476 (7th Cir.). *cert. denied*, 345 U.S. 997 (1973).
291. Cargill v. Hardin, 452 F.2d 1154, 1159 (8th Cir. 1971), *cert. denied*, 406 U.S. 932 (1972).
292. In re Frey, Comm. Fut. L. Rep. (CCH) ¶ 23,786 (C.F.T.C. 1987).
293. *Id.* (citations omitted).
294. *Id.* at n. 8 (citation omitted).
295. *Id.* at 786 (footnote omitted).
296. 5 U.S.C. § 504(a)(1).
297. In re Frey, Comm. Fut. L. Rep. (CCH) ¶ 24,578 (C.F.T.C. 1990).

tions made in this area of the law may at times seem questionable. Sometimes the 'know it when you see it' test may appear most useful."[298]

The Seventh Circuit noted that courts generally require four elements to prove manipulation: (1) intent; (2) the ability to influence prices; (3) existence of an artificial price; and (4) causation of the artificial price.[299] That became the generally accepted formula for determining whether a manipulation that was prohibited by the Commodity Exchange Act had occurred. The respondents in *Frey* did not control the cash supply of the commodity, but the Seventh Circuit stated that the CFTC staff claim that such proof was unnecessary was "a plausible proposition; to force a squeeze there is no logical necessity for the dominant long to control the cash crop, only that he put the shorts in the unsavory position of dealing with him in the face of a known shortage of cash commodities."[300]

The CFTC prevailed on the attorney fee claim in the *Frey* case, but the case was otherwise a regulatory disaster. It took twenty years to resolve at an enormous expenditure of government and private resources and raised the hurdle again for proving manipulation.

4:10 ENERGY FUTURES ARRIVE

Rising energy prices in the 1970s gave rise to more concerns over manipulation as consumers faced unprecedented increases in gasoline and heating oil. President Jimmy Carter sought to gradually decontrol domestic oil prices, which were then controlled at below world market prices, and imposed an excess profits tax on domestic oil producers. The Carter oil decontrol program actually involved maintaining price controls over "old" oil, which was oil from production areas in operation in 1972 that was controlled at a price well below its actual market value, and "new" oil from properties brought into production after that year that was not subject to price controls.[301]

These price controls led to a massive gaming of the crude oil market by Marc Rich, an infamous commodity speculator. Rich used a series of "daisy chain" transactions to convert "old" oil, controlled at a price of $6 per barrel, into "new" oil that could be sold for a much higher world oil price of $30 per barrel. He then used a tax evasion scheme to avoid paying taxes on the massive profits he received from this operation.[302] Rich fled in 1983 to Switzerland where he became a fugitive from U.S. justice over tax evasion charges and illegal sales involving Iran. He was pardoned in 2001 by outgoing President William Clinton, setting off a furor in the press.[303]

In the event, Carter's efforts on energy did nothing to cushion the country from a second "oil shock" in 1979.[304] That shock was even more severe than the one experienced in 1973 under President Nixon. The Carter oil shock led to a "Great Panic" in the United States among consumers, as gas shortages caused more than 50 percent of gas stations to shut down periodically during the

298. Frey v. CFTC, 931 F.2d 1171, 1175 (7th Cir. 1991). The court discussed the concept of a squeeze:

> a "squeeze" has been defined as a type of manipulation, generally occurring when the long holder does not have direct control over the cash crop, as in a "corner." A prototypical squeeze occurs when a trader attains a dominant long position and can force shorts facing an inadequate cash supply to cover their positions at unfair prices. The shorts are "squeezed" into settling their holdings with the dominant long at above-market prices as the delivery date approaches.

299. *Id.*

300. *Id.*

301. *See*, W. Carl Biven, Jimmy Carter's Economy 193 (2002).

302. *See*, A Craig Copetas, Metal Men (1985) (describing Rich's trading operations and schemes).

303. Louise Radnofsky, *U.S. News: For Holder, Rich Pardon Resurfaces*, Wall Street Journal, Nov. 24, 2008, at A6.

304. W. Carl Biven, Jimmy Carter's Economy 193 (2002).

summer of 1979, the season of highest road use for vacationing Americans. On the July 4 holiday some 90 percent of all gas stations in the New York City area were closed.[305] Gas rationing among the states was ordered in May 1979 by the still new Department of Energy. Long lines became common at gas stations, at least at those that remained open.[306]

The conservative economist Milton Friedman was one of the strongest critics of price controls. He contended that the gas lines that formed in 1974 after the OPEC oil embargo and again in the spring and summer of 1979 after the revolution in Iran were "striking" examples of why price controls do not work. He pointed out that, unlike the United States, European and other countries did not experience lines at gas stations during those oil shocks because price controls here did not allow the market to function. "The smooth operation of the price system—which for many decades had assured every consumer that he could buy gasoline at any of a large number of service stations at his convenience and with a minimal wait—was replaced by bureaucratic improvisation."[307]

Energy futures contracts were introduced as the result of price spikes in the 1970s that had threatened the economy of the country on two separate occasions and led to price controls that proved unworkable. NYMEX energy contracts soon became the worldwide benchmark for crude oil prices, which provided market-made rationing guides and provided an impetus for alternative energy sources as prices rose. Heating oil futures began trading on the NYMEX in 1978.[308] Crude oil futures contracts began trading in 1983 on the NYMEX and CBOT.[309]

Initially, the crude oil futures markets were thinly traded and became the center of much contrived trading that was used to create artificial tax losses or to defer gains for tax purposes from year to year. Instead of charging market power manipulation to attack those abuses, the CFTC sought to treat this as a special class of manipulation—that is, "rigged trading"—that could also be charged under Section 4(c) of the Commodity Exchange Act. Section 4(c) prohibits any trade that "is of the character of, or is commonly known to the trade as, a 'wash sale' or 'accommodation trade,' or a trade that is a 'fictitious sale,'" or that "is used to cause any price to be reported, registered, or recorded that is not a true and bona fide price."[310] This statute is the analogue of Section 9 under the 34 Act, which is discussed in Chapter 2.[311]

The CFTC spent considerable time and resources defining the trading practices that are prohibited by Section 4(c).[312] In one early case, *CFTC v. Savage*,[313] the Ninth Circuit Court of Appeals held that Section 4(c) requires the same scienter requirement, "knowledge," that is required to prove violations of the general antifraud provision in the Commodity Exchange Act.[314] The scienter requirement for Section 4(b) has been interpreted as requiring "knowing" conduct.[315]

---

305. III Jerry W. Markham, A Financial History of the United States, From the Age of Derivatives into the New Millennium (1970-2001) 41 (2002).

306. Saundra Saperstein and Molly Sinclair, *Federal Judge Rejects Request by Maryland for Extra Gasoline*, Washington Post, July 7, 1979, at A1.

307. Milton Friedman and Rose Friedman, Free to Choose: A Personal Statement 14 (1980).

308. Emily Lambert, The Futures 158 (2011).

309. H.J. Maidenberg, *Commodities, Trading Crude Oil Futures*, New York Times, March 28, 1983, at D8.

310. 7 U.S.C. § 6c.

311. 15 U.S.C. § 78i.

312. See, Jerry W. Markham, Commodities Regulation: Fraud, Manipulation and Other Claims Chs. 13-14 (2011) (setting forth cases decided under Section 4(c)).

313. *CFTC v. Savage*, 611 F.2d 270, 284 (9th Cir. 1979).

314. 7 U.S.C. § 6b.

315. *See, e.g.*, Reddy v. CFTC, 191 F.3d 109, 119 (2d Cir. 1999); Piasio v. CFTC, 2002 U.S. App. LEXIS 27222 (respondent "knew that they would be executed or attempted to be executed as wash sales"); Wilson v. CFTC, 322 F.3d 555, 560 (8th Cir. 2003) (respondent "knowingly participated in wash sales").

"One cannot have an 'accommodation' sale or a 'fictitious' transaction if one in fact believes he is bargaining faithfully and intends to effect a bona fide trade." This suggests that so-called "open market" trades (which are discussed in Chapter 8 and are bona fide trades openly executed in the market but with the intent to affect prices) would not be prohibited by Section 4(c).

The CFTC used Section 4(c) to attack wash sale and fictitious trading charges that were used for tax evasion through so-called tax straddles.[316] These tax straddles were prearranged fictitious trading that created a trading loss in one year for tax purposes and then reversed the loss in the next year, both without economic risk to the participants.[317] The Commodity Exchange Authority had studied such trading practices in 1947,[318] and it also brought a case against a trader in 1948 for engaging in such tax trading.[319] Nevertheless, tax straddles remained widespread when the CFTC was created in 1974. The CFTC then broadly attacked tax straddles and referred several cases to the Justice Department for criminal prosecutions.[320] The IRS also attacked this trading, including the bringing of an action that bankrupted singer Willie Nelson.[321]

In one criminal case, *United States v. Turkish*,[322] the Second Circuit upheld convictions of tax law violations that involved a fraudulent manipulation of commodity futures prices in crude oil futures in order to gain advantages for tax liability.[323] Turkish was able to avoid the normal risks of adverse price fluctuations that could have impaired the ability to acquire tax benefits for a client

---

316. Tax trading and wash sales have also been a problem in the securities industry. *See, e.g.*, In the Matter of Rathi, 2003 WL 21757255 (S.E.C.) (wash trades conducted on electronic trading platform in illiquid stocks).

317. Jerry W. Markham, *Prohibited Floor Trading Activities Under the Commodity Exchange Act*, 58 FORDHAM L. REV. 1 (1989) (describing these abuses).

318. Commodity Exchange Authority, *Futures Trading and Income Tax* (Dec. 1947).

319. In re Goldwurm, 7 Agric. Dec. 265 (1948). The Commodity Exchange Authority had also held that the reporting of false or nonexistent trades violated Section 4(c). In the Matter of Ritten, 23 AG. DEC. 747 (1964); In the Matter of Gerstenberg, 26 AG. DEC. 816 (1967).

320. *See, e.g.*, United States v. Winograd, 656 F.2d 279 (7th Cir. 1981), *cert. denied*, 455 U.S. 989 (1982) (convictions on criminal charges of violations of Section 4(c) of the Commodity Exchange Act and other federal statutes involving Mexican peso futures contracts upheld).

321. Todd Mason, *Mamma, Don't Let Your Babies Grow Up to Work for the Tax Boys*, WALL STREET JOURNAL, Jan. 29, 1991, at C1. For a partial list of tax cases involving this practice, see Jerry W. Markham, *Prohibited Floor Trading Activities Under the Commodity Exchange Act*, 58 FORDHAM L. REV. 1, 24, n. 132 (1989).

322. United States v. Turkish, 623 F.2d 769 (2d Cir. 1980), *cert. denied*, 449 U.S. 1077 (1981).

323. The court described this activity as follows:

> Turkish was a principal participant in a scheme that used fraudulent means to enable C.R. Rittenberry & Associates, Inc., an oil company, to create artificial tax losses in one year, offset by equally artificial taxable gains in a subsequent year, thereby postponing for a year the taxes on millions of dollars of corporate income. The scheme involved the use of tax "straddles," the simultaneous purchase and sale at different prices of equal numbers of commodity futures contracts to be performed in different months. In the normal use of tax straddles, opportunities for arguably lawful tax avoidance are created when the market price varies from the prices at which the original contracts were both bought and sold. If the market declines, the trader offsets his purchase with an equivalent sale, thereby locking in a tax loss on his original purchase. He then offsets his original sale contract with an equivalent purchase, thereby locking in an approximately equal profit on his original sale contract. He benefits when the profit is taxable in the year following realization of the loss. In normal transactions the trader takes the risk that market price movements will be too narrow to create much opportunity for tax postponement and also the more serious risk that prices will not move uniformly with respect to both his original contracts. In the latter event the profit available to be locked in may be less than the locked-in loss.

623 F.2d at 770.

through a tax straddle "by fraudulently manipulating virtually the entire business of one trading ring on the New York Cotton Exchange, the Crude Oil Futures Market."[324]

Turkish and his associates moved prices up and down at will, so that clients "could take short-term capital losses during one tax year and defer an equal amount of off-setting capital gain to a subsequent year, all with no risk and a considerable saving in the postponement of taxes."[325] In a related case, the Second Circuit noted that "[t]estimony given at Turkish's criminal trial . . . indicated that 'tens of thousands' of crude oil futures transactions were rigged during the criminal conspiracy and that 'less than ten' were not. . . . Under the circumstances, it is highly unlikely that there ever was a real market for crude oil futures during the period in question; the whole basis of the rigging conspiracy was the ability of certain brokers to move futures prices at their 'whim.'"[326]

The CFTC also took a stab at using rigged trading charges as the basis for a manipulation claim in the context of tax straddles.[327] In *In re Sundheimer*,[328] the CFTC revoked the registration of a respondent who pleaded guilty to criminal charges that he "fixed, rigged and fraudulently prearranged trades and manipulated the movement of prices on the Crude Oil Market of the New York Cotton Exchange for the purpose of creating predetermined losses for an oil company."[329] The CFTC held that the guilty plea to those charges was an admission of a violation of Section 4(c) of the Commodity Exchange Act. However, the CFTC was "not persuaded that a guilty plea to a criminal information charging merely that respondent 'manipulated the movement of prices on the Crude Oil Market' in the context of a false tax return case prosecuted by the Department of Justice necessarily establishes all the elements of a market manipulation as proscribed by the Commodity Exchange Act." This clearly signaled that the latter form of manipulation had special elements that not even a criminal charge could satisfy.[330]

The Second Circuit Court of Appeals upheld the CFTC's finding of an "accommodation" trade in *Sundheimer* that violated Section 4(c). The court stated that "[i]t is this intent, the absence of good-faith, arms-length trading, and the undisclosed prearrangement for losses and gains, that

---

324. 623 F.2d at 770-771.

325. 623 F.2d at 770-771.

326. Lasker v. Bear Stearns & Co., 757 F.2d 15, 18 (2d Cir. 1985).

327. A rigged trading case, *In re Perlmutter*, 1979 CFTC LEXIS 19 (C.F.T.C. 1979) arose from wash sales in crude oil futures contracts traded on the Petroleum Associates of the New York Cotton Exchange Inc. This case involved fictitious trades that were done to create tax losses without risk to the trader. The respondent here had been found guilty of tax fraud, and the CFTC brought a case charging that he was unfit for registration as a floor broker on a commodity exchange. The respondent consented to a finding that he engaged in wash sales in violation of Section 4(c) of the Commodity Exchange Act and manipulation and attempted manipulation in violation of that statute.

328. In re Sundheimer, Comm. Fut. L. Rep. (CCH) ¶ 21,245 (C.F.T.C. 1981), *aff'd on other grounds*, Sundheimer v. CFTC, 688 F.2d 150 (2d Cir. 1982), *cert. denied*, 460 U.S. 112 (1983).

329. Sundheimer v. CFTC, 688 F.2d 150, 152 (2d Cir. 1982), *cert. denied*, 460 U.S. 112 (1983).

330. In *In the Matter of Dial*, Comm. Fut. L. Rep (CCH) ¶ 23,772 (C.F.T.C. 1987), a CFTC administrative law judge dismissed claims of manipulation of the silver futures market in 1978 on similar grounds. The respondents had been convicted of fraud in "front-running" customer orders, but, as the ALJ stated,

> As essential elements in a manipulation case under the CEA Act the alleged manipulator must be shown to have a degree of monopoly power or dominant market position, and manipulative intent, and that there be the existence of an artificial market price caused by the perpetrator. The indictment against Defendant Donald D. Dial does not directly address these matters, particularly, the requisite market economics and statistical factors are absent. A number of inferences and interpolations would be required to supplement the facts contained in the indictment to justify findings and conclusions that this Defendant manipulated or attempted to manipulate the market price of silver in November 1978 and that there was an attendant artificial market price.

demonstrates the 'accommodation' nature of the transactions in the instant case."[331] The court held that, even if real sales were contemplated, rather than fictitious ones, this would not change the artificial character of the arrangement.[332]

Proving the existence of any of the short list of prohibited practices in Section 4(c) (wash sales, fictitious trades, and accommodation or cross trades) would have appeared to many to be an easy way to attack abusive trading practices, but the CFTC would have none of that in the *Sundheimer* case. The CFTC ruled that, while the trades at issue were "accommodation" trades, they were not "fictitious" trades because they resulted in an actual change in market position.[333] This was a contentious issue because defendants in manipulation cases often argue that their trading cannot be manipulative if the trades are "real" ones that are executed in the market with an unrelated counterparty. These types of trading activities are sometimes referred to as "open market" operations.

Evidencing the CFTC's propensity to change its legal theories when needed, the CFTC later modified the view expressed in *Sundheimer* on fictitious trades and held, in a case involving the Maine 1976 potato futures contract, that even open trades would violate Section 4(c) as fictitious trades if they were prearranged wash trades that did expose the participants to market risk.[334] The CFTC tried to back off that decision after the CME challenged it as imposing liability simply for trying to reduce market risk. The Second Circuit then ruled in *Stoller v. CFTC*[335] that such a change in interpretation was without notice and was improper.[336]

In the event, the need for fictitious trading for tax purposes was ameliorated by a change in the tax laws under the Economic Tax Recovery Act of 1981, which granted favorable treatment to futures trading profits.[337] NYMEX was also able to gain traction as a liquid market in energy contracts. As 1984 ended, NYMEX became "a primary force in the pricing of the millions of barrels of oil that change hands daily around the world," as OPEC lost its ability to dictate prices.[338] Those contracts also became targets for speculators and manipulation and were blamed for the massive increase in gasoline prices in the United States in the current century.[339]

In one early energy futures manipulation case, the Second Circuit Court of Appeals in *Apex Oil Co. v. Di Mauro*[340] considered antitrust and Commodity Exchange Act manipulation claims

331. 688 F.2d at 152.

332. 688 F.2d at 153.

333. That was the traditional interpretation of Section 4(c). *See*, Nichols & Co. v. Secretary of Agriculture, 136 F.2d 503 (1st Cir. 1943) (prearranged orders were permissible because they were executed on the floor by open outcry).

334. In the Matter of Collins, Comm. Fut. L. Rep. (CCH) ¶ 22,982 (C.F.T.C. 1986), *modified*, Comm. Fut. L. Rep. (CCH) ¶ 23,401 (C.F.T.C. 1986), *rev'd sub nom.*, Stoller v. CFTC, 834 F.2d 262 (2d Cir, 1987). The CFTC made this statement as guidance because a district court had held in another case that the term "fictitious" trades was unconstitutionally vague. United States v. LaMantia, Comm. Fut. L. Rep. (CCH) ¶ 20,6667 (N.D. Ill. 1978). That decision has been largely ignored. *See also*, U.S. v. Siegel, COMM. FUT. L. REP. (CCH) ¶ 20,844 (N.D. Ill. 1979) (the term "wash sales" in Section 4(c) was not unconstitutionally vague).

335. Stoller v. CFTC, 834 F.2d 262 (2d Cir, 1987).

336. The CFTC, nonetheless, continued to apply its revised position on whether actual trades were prohibited by Section 4(c) if they were prearranged. In re Gimbel, COMM. FUT. L. REP. (CCH) ¶ 24,213 (C.F.T.C. 1988), *aff'd*, 872 F.2d 196 (7th Cir. 1989); In re Elliot, COMM. FUT. L. REP. (CCH) ¶ 27,243 (C.F.T.C. 1998).

337. Pub. L. No. 97-34, 95 Stat. 172, §§ 501-509 (1981).

338. Stuart Diamond, *Setting Crude Prices in the Pit*, NEW YORK TIMES, Dec. 9, 1984, at F4.

339. The derivative market for energy contracts suffered another blow in 1994 when a large complex of German companies suffered a loss of $1 billion from trading by what it claimed was a rogue trader. Jerry W. Markham, *Guarding the Kraal: On the Trail of the Rogue Trader*, 21 J. CORP. L.131 (1995). The CFTC also brought and settled a case against the group that charged it had been selling illegal off-exchange futures contracts. In the Matter of MG Refining and Marketing Inc., 1995 CFTC LEXIS 190 (C.F.T.C.).

340. Apex Oil Co. v. Di Mauro, 822 F.2d 246 (2d Cir. 1987), *cert. denied, sub nom.*, Coastal Corp. v.

involving the February 1982 futures contracts for No. 2 home heating oil traded on the NYMEX. The plaintiff Apex Oil Company charged that competing oil companies, a broker, and the NYMEX conspired to force Apex to deliver oil on its February 1982 contracts in the first three delivery days of that month at one delivery site. Apex claimed that this made it impractical for Apex to deliver on time and forced it to pay premium prices to defendant and other oil companies for delivery in order to avoid a default. The Second Circuit upheld dismissal of those claims against all but one defendant. The court found sufficient evidence to present to a jury that the remaining defendant engaged in a prohibited antitrust conspiracy and that such participation would support a manipulation claim under the Commodity Exchange Act.[341]

After remand, the district court in *Apex Oil Co. v. Di Mauro*[342] allowed certain antitrust claims to go forward but dismissed in large part the manipulation claims under the Commodity Exchange Act. The district court stated that, "where a long squeeze is alleged, it must be pleaded and proved 'that the respondent accumulated a position in the futures market that exceeded the available deliverable supply.' . . . It is well recognized that a long squeeze cannot be effected unless the defendants have market dominance. . . . Without market dominance, the longs have no ability to force a short to deal with them, since the short can go elsewhere to obtain the commodity and deliver."[343] The district court noted that there was "compelling reason" for the requirement of market dominance in Commodity Exchange Act manipulation claims because "many, if not most, market squeezes occur naturally and without unlawful activity."[344] The "shorts could even trigger a squeeze by not arranging for delivery on their contracts." "Where the squeeze is caused by market forces unrelated to long activity, the market dominance requirement will quite properly insulate the long from liability as it is not prevented from acting in its own self-interest to obtain the highest price."[345] Here, the defendants were found to lack market dominance in both the cash and futures markets.

The district court on remand in *Apex* further held that there is no liability under the Commodity Exchange Act for a "conspiracy to manipulate." A party will be liable as an aider and abettor but such liability requires that the secondary actor actually participate in the manipulation.[346] The district court did allow an attempted manipulation claim to go forward because "[w]hile the long defendants did not have the market dominance necessary to actually corner the oil market and to effect a long manipulative squeeze, the Court cannot conclusively determine at this stage of the litigation that they might not have attempted to do so or otherwise taken steps resulting in an artificial price increase."[347]

4:11 OTHER RIGGED TRADING ISSUES

In *In re Rosenberg*,[348] the CFTC ruled that something more than suspicious circumstances is required to prove noncompetitive trading for purposes of Section 4(c). In that case, the respondent had made trades that resulted in money being transferred among accounts in "suspiciously narrow time frames." The CFTC faced other controversies over whether so-called Ginzi trades used for

Apex Oil Co., 484 U.S. 977 (1987).

341. 822 F.2d at 260-261.

342. Apex Oil Co. v. Di Mauro, 713 F. Supp. 587 (S.D.N.Y. 1989).

343. 713 F. Supp. at 601 (citations omitted).

344. 713 F. Supp. at 602 (citations omitted).

345. 713 F. Supp. at 602.

346. 713 F. Supp. at 603.

347. 713 F. Supp. at 603. This litigation continued to be the subject of motions limiting its scope. *See*, Apex Oil Co. v. Di Mauro, 744 F. Supp. 53 (S.D.N.Y. 1990) and 1990 U.S. Dist. LEXIS 10867 (S.D.N.Y. 1990).

348. Comm. Fut. L. Rep. (CCH) ¶ 24,992 (C.F.T.C. 1987).

split tick trading were a violation of Section 4(c)[349] and whether U.S. brokers had a duty to prevent Japanese trading houses from using wash trades to avoid taxes in Japan.[350]

The use of Section 4(c) presented other problems because the CFTC adopted the view that any preexecution discussion over a trade would result in a charge of prearranged fictitious trading. For example, in *In the Matter of BlackRock Institutional Trust Co. NA*,[351] the CFTC found by consent that an employee of the respondent entered into prearranged fictitious trades on the floor of the Chicago Board of Trade. The trades involved Treasury note futures spreads. The orders were entered through different brokerage firms about one minute apart and were intended to match. The orders were large orders and one was an "all or none" order that further ensured matching. The CFTC stated that a "prearranged trade is a textbook example of a fictitious sale."[352]

The CFTC thought that trading purity would best be achieved by requiring all futures trading to be executed in the exchange trading pits through open outcry that would allow all participants to participate equally.[353] There were, however, several flaws in that theory. Foremost was the fact that the commodity exchanges do not compete with each other. Rather, for the most part, exchanges have a monopoly on the contracts they trade. That monopoly is aided by the fact that futures trades and commodity options can only be traded on those regulated "contract" markets.[354]

Floor traders on those exchange monopolies who traded for their own account also had a time and place advantage over all traders who did not have direct floor access. That advantage was said to be offset by the liquidity those traders provided to the marketplace. However, traders off the exchange provided liquidity for which they were not similarly compensated.[355] The floor community also sometimes used its time and place advantage to engage in prearranged, fictitious, and after-hours trading in order to cheat customers.

Those rigged trading practices were exposed in a spectacular FBI sting operation on the Chicago exchanges in 1989.[356] Undercover FBI agents, wired for sound, took on the role of traders

---

349. In re Murphy, Comm. Fut. L. Rep. (CCH) ¶ 23,798 (C.F.T.C. 1985). A split-tick trade involves prearranged trades that allow traders to trade in price increments smaller than those permitted by exchange rules.

350. In re Three Eight Corp., Comm. Fut. L. Rep. (CCH) ¶ 25,749 (C.F.T.C. 1993). *See also,* In the Matter of LFG, LLC, Comm. Fut. L. Rep. (CCH) ¶ 28,629 (C.F.T.C. 2001) (same). In re Trillion Japan Co., Comm. Fut. L. Rep. (CCH) ¶ 26,082 (C.F.T.C. 1994) (dismissing similar charges).

351. In the Matter of BlackRock Institutional Trust Co. NA, Comm. Fut. L. Rep. (CCH) ¶ 32,143 (C.F.T.C. 2012).

352. *See also,* In the Matter of J.P. Morgan Securities LLC, Comm. Fut. L. Rep. (CCH) ¶ 32,144 (C.F.T.C. 2012) (same conduct).

353. Supporting that requirement was an old Commodity Exchange Authority rule, Rule 1.38, which states:

> All purchases and sales of any commodity for future delivery, and of any commodity option, on or subject to the rules of a contract market shall be executed openly and competitively by open outcry or posting of bids and offers or by other equally open and competitive methods, in the trading pit or ring or similar place provided by the contract market, during the regular hours prescribed by the contract market for trading in such commodity or commodity option.

17 C.F.R § 1.38.

354. *See*, Jerry W. Markham, *The Commodity Exchange Monopoly: Reform Is Needed*, 48 Wash. & Lee. L. Rev. 977 (1991).

355. *See generally*, Jerry W. Markham & Daniel J. Harty, *For Whom the Bell Tolls: The Demise of Exchange Trading Floors and the Growth of ECNs*, 33 J. Corp. L. 865 (2008) (describing these advantages).

356. *See*, David Greising & Laurie Morse, Brokers, Bagmen and Moles: Fraud and Corruption in the Chicago Futures Markets (1991) (describing these scandals); Jerry W. Markham, *The Commodity Exchange Monopoly: Reform Is Needed*, 48 Wash. & Lee L. Rev. 977 (1991) (same).

on the floors of the CME and CBOT. Forty-six traders were indicted for various abusive trading practices, including "edges," "leads," "matches," and "trading off" an order, all of which sought to avoid or reduce competition for orders in the pit or allow for petty theft from orders. Illegal after-hours trading was also occurring. This law enforcement operation was widely publicized and it appeared that the government had finally carried out an effective operation against trading abuses. That glory was not long-lived. The government's success in the trials on criminal charges stemming from this operation was only mixed, but clearly these abuses were widespread.[357]

Another concern was that the floor traders did not have the capacity to handle large size institutional "block" trades. Such trades were negotiated "upstairs" in the offices of broker-dealers in the securities industry and reported on the floor of the exchange after their terms had been agreed to by the parties. If required to be executed on the floor, those institutional orders, and their ultimate customers, would have received unfavorable prices that did not reflect the actual value of the security (or commodity) being bought or sold.[358]

The CFTC eventually allowed block trading through so-called sunshine trades, but only after much industry protest over restriction on block trades.[359] "Bunch" orders for executing and allocating a single order for multiple accounts also fell prey to the prearranged trading prohibition. Such orders needed an average pricing mechanism to permit an even allocation of differing prices in the executed bunched order. The CFTC tried to alleviate these problems by allowing limited order allocations.[360]

4:12 THE ORANGE JUICE "ATTEMPTED MANIPULATION"

Finding it nearly impossible to prove an actual manipulation of commodity futures prices, the CFTC enforcement staff tried to reduce its burden of proof in a case involving trading in orange juice futures. The CFTC charged in *In the Matter of Abrams*[361] that, rather than an actual manipulation, an individual speculator "attempted" to manipulate the September 1984 orange juice futures contract on the Citrus Associates of the New York Cotton Exchange.[362]

Attempted manipulation had often been charged in CEA cases, but it normally was simply a throwaway claim, with actual manipulation being the focus of the cases. Little attention was paid to what were the elements of an attempted manipulation claim until the CFTC's decision in *In*

---

357. *See*, Jerry W. Markham, *The Commodity Exchange Monopoly: Reform Is Needed*, 48 WASH. & LEE. L. REV. 977, 987-992 (1991) (describing these trading practices and the FBI sting operation).

358. II JERRY W. MARKHAM, A FINANCIAL HISTORY OF THE UNITED STATES, FROM J.P. MORGAN TO THE INSTITUTIONAL INVESTOR (1900-1970) 360 (2002).

359. *See*, JERRY W. MARKHAM, COMMODITIES REGULATION: FRAUD, MANIPULATION AND OTHER CLAIMS, §14:2 (2010) (describing this controversy). The CFTC reopened this debate after the passage of the Dodd-Frank Act by proposing rules that would require further reporting on block trades for swap trades. See Scott D. O'Malia, *Re-Proposed Procedures to Establish Appropriate Minimum Block Sizes for Large Notional Off-Facility Swaps and Block Trades; Further Measures to Protect the Identities of Parties to Swap Transactions* (Feb. 23, 2012), available at http://www.cftc.gov/ PressRoom/Speeches Testimony/omaliastatement022312b (accessed April 22, 2012).

360. *See*, JERRY W. MARKHAM, COMMODITIES REGULATION: FRAUD, MANIPULATION AND OTHER CLAIMS, § 14:6 (2010) § 14:6 (describing this controversy).

361. In re Abrams, COMM. FUT. L. REP. (CCH) ¶ 24,408 (C.F.T.C. 1989). The CFTC denied interlocutory review because there were remaining counts to be decided on record-keeping issues. *Id.* at 577.

362. This was not the first claim of manipulation of orange futures. A district court denied class action status to a claim that ContiCommodity Services Inc., a futures commission merchant, and one of its brokers, Norton Waltuch, both of which were heavily involved in the silver crisis, manipulated the November 1977 orange futures contract. Pollock v. Citrus Associates of the New York Cotton Exchange, 1981 U.S. Dist. LEXIS 15878 (S.D.N.Y. 1981).

the Matter of Hohenberg Brothers,[363] described above. There, the CFTC held that an "attempted manipulation requires an intent to affect market prices artificially and some overt act in furtherance of that intent."[364] This meant that the CFTC enforcement staff would not have to prove that a respondent had the ability to and did cause an artificial price.

The CFTC enforcement staff took some time to take advantage of the reduced requirements for attempted manipulation but tried to do so in the *Abrams* case.[365] This case arose after the respondent Abrams, a speculator, concluded that a hard freeze in December 1983 had substantially damaged Florida citrus crops. He believed there would be a shortage of orange juice in 1984, and he took a large futures position in the September month that reached 36 percent of open interest in August 1984. Abrams began "stopping" delivery notices in September, indicating that he would accept delivery. This alarmed the exchange and CFTC because available deliverable supplies were limited by the fact that the industry had shifted from delivery of orange juice in drums to bulk delivery. Abrams was taking delivery even though he had no commercial use for the product.

As other traders liquidated their positions, the percentage of the open interest held by Abrams increased to 98 percent. Abrams refused to accept delivery of uncertified orange juice because it would be delayed in delivery and because it raised quality problems. Abrams also began entering scale-up orders to liquidate his short position in the last five trading days of the futures contract. Those orders were unfilled because of the high price demanded by Abrams. Abrams then took delivery on 699 futures contracts. "By accepting delivery rather than liquidating at prevailing prices, Abrams not only sacrificed a profit of approximately $50,000 but also incurred additional costs of over $900,000."[366] Abrams was charged with attempted manipulation and his futures commission merchant, Drexel Burnham, Lambert Inc., was charged with aiding and abetting his attempted manipulation by loaning him funds to take delivery on his position.

The CFTC staff filed this case in 1988, more than three years after the event. In 1989, an administrative law judge at the CFTC dismissed the attempted manipulation claim.[367] The CFTC, thereafter, settled the case against the brokerage firm respondent, dropping the manipulation charges and imposing sanctions by consent over minor record-keeping issues.[368] However, in 1993, the CFTC reversed the administrative law judge's grant of summary disposition that had dismissed the charges brought against the individual respondent, finding that the dismissal was premature.[369]

---

363. In the Matter of Hohenberg Bros., Comm. Fut. L. Rep. (CCH) ¶ 20, 271 (C.F.T.C. 1977).

364. In the Matter of Hohenberg Bros., Comm. Fut. L. Rep. (CCH) ¶ 20, 271, n. 39 (C.F.T.C. 1977).

365.This effort was presaged in 1982 by a witness in congressional hearings on the emergency action taken by the CFTC on the March 1979 wheat affair. He noted in a paper submitted to a House Agriculture subcommittee,

> The Commodity Exchange Act does not define manipulation or threatened manipulation, but the distinction between the two is important. Actual manipulation involves: (1) dominant or controlling positions in both the futures and cash markets; (2) intent to manipulate; and (3) price distortion. Threatened manipulation does not require that any of the above three conditions actually hold, but only that we have forewarning of their occurrence.

Richard G. Heifner, Report on a Study of the March 1979 Chicago Wheat Futures Contract, reprinted, CFTC Reauthorization, Hearings Before a House Subcommittee on Conservation, Credit, and Rural Development of the Committee on Agriculture, 97th Cong., 2d Sess. 767 (1982).

366. In re Abrams, Comm. Fut. L. Rep. (CCH) ¶ 26,479 (C.F.T.C. 1995).

367. In re Abrams, Comm. Fut. L. Rep. (CCH) ¶ 24,408 (C.F.T.C. 1989). The CFTC denied interlocutory review because there were remaining counts to be decided on recordkeeping issues. In re Abrams, COMM. FUT. L. REP. (CCH) ¶ 24,577 (C.F.T.C. 1989).

368. In re Abrams, Comm. Fut. L. Rep. (CCH) ¶ 26,479, n. 7 (C.F.T.C. 1995).

369. In re Abrams, Comm. Fut. L. Rep. (CCH) ¶ 25,684 (C.F.T.C. 1993).

On remand, the ALJ held an evidentiary hearing and, once again, dismissed the case. The ALJ found that the evidence did not establish that the trader had attempted to create an artificial price or that he had attempted to squeeze the market.[370] The CFTC affirmed that dismissal in 1995, almost eleven years after the occurrence of the conduct at issue. Nevertheless, in dicta, the CFTC asserted that an attempted manipulation claim was viable under the Commodity Exchange Act.[371] That proved to be enough encouragement for the CFTC staff to focus on attempted manipulation claims, rather than actual manipulation.

Private actions claiming actual manipulation violations under the Commodity Exchange Act continued, but they too encountered difficulties. In *Grossman v. Citrus Associates of the New York Cotton Exchange*,[372] a district court dismissed a claim that a weather service manipulated December 1985 orange futures prices through a false weather report. "Plaintiffs allege that Freese-Notis issued an intentionally misleading weather forecast on December 17, 1985 while privately telling its favored clients that Freese-Notis would later publish a report that would 'eliminate all mention of a freeze.'"[373] The plaintiffs charged that the correction would cause prices to drop and allow the favored clients to profit from their short positions. The court found, however, that this claim was not supported by the facts. Manipulation charges against other defendants were dismissed for failing to plead the claims with sufficient particularity.[374] A related action against the New York Cotton Exchange, which claimed that it should have taken emergency action after weather reports about a freeze proved false, was also dismissed.[375]

4:13 THE FERRUZZI AFFAIR

Soybean price manipulation concerns arose in 1989 after the United States experienced one of the most severe droughts in more than fifty years. The Gruppo Ferruzzi S.p.A., one of Europe's largest grain firms, sought to exploit a resulting shortage of soybeans. Ferruzzi acquired a substantial portion of the deliverable supply of cash market soybeans in Chicago, as well as a large position in the July 1989 soybean futures contract on the CBOT. That contract was under pressure because it called for delivery of "old crop" soybeans—that is, those harvested in 1988, which were in shortage due to the drought. Alternative supplies from Brazil and Argentina also appeared to be in danger because of drought conditions in those countries.[376]

By mid-May of 1989, the Ferruzzi Group held long positions of more than 16 million bushels in May 1989 soybean futures on the CBOT, which constituted about 90 percent of the open interest and exceeded available deliverable supplies. The CFTC, becoming concerned over this position, revoked Ferruzzi's hedging exemption and ordered it to liquidate its soybean future holdings down under the 3 million speculative limit for soybeans in the May futures. Instead of liquidating, Ferruzzi rolled its May futures position into the July futures where it already had a substantial position. After that roll and further purchases in the August delivery month, Ferruzzi held July and August futures for more than 39 million bushels of soybeans. The CFTC again revoked Fer-

370. In re Abrams, Comm. Fut. L. Rep. (CCH) ¶ 26,237 (C.F.T.C. 1994).

371. In re Abrams, Comm. Fut. L. Rep. (CCH) ¶ 26,479 (C.F.T.C. 1995).

372. Grossman v. Citrus Associates of the New York Cotton Exchange, Comm. Fut. L. Rep. (CCH) ¶ 24,480 (S.D.N.Y. 1989).

373. Comm. Fut. L. Rep. (CCH) ¶ 24,480.

374. Grossman v. Citrus Associates of the New York Cotton Exchange Inc., 706 F. Supp. 221 (S.D.N.Y. 1989).

375. Grossman v. Citrus Associates of the New York Cotton Exchange Inc., 742 F. Supp. 843 (S.D.N.Y. 1990).

376. In re Soybean Futures Litigation, 892 F. Supp. 1025, 1034 (N.D. Ill. 1995).

ruzzi's hedging exemption and ordered Ferruzzi to cut its July and August futures positions to levels under those set for speculators.

The CBOT also became concerned over the size of the Ferruzzi position in the July futures contract. Declaring a rare emergency, the CBOT ordered Ferruzzi to liquidate 20 percent of its position daily until it was below 3 million bushels. The CBOT's action caused chaos in the market, causing prices to plunge and setting off claims that it was favoring local short traders by ordering such action.[377] Specifically, some critics thought that the CBOT was acting to protect Cargill Inc., its once archenemy (see Chapters 2–3) from losses caused by increased soybean prices, but such charges were never proven.[378] Ferruzzi brought a $30 million lawsuit against the CBOT, charging that it was manipulating the market in order to force prices lower.[379] A report by the General Accounting Office, however, found that all CBOT members serving on the exchange's board or Business Conduct Committee had recused themselves from the decision to take emergency action against Ferruzzi.[380]

The CBOT later settled disciplinary charges it brought against Ferruzzi as a member of the CBOT by imposing a $2 million fine. Ferruzzi also agreed to transfer its CBOT membership to Central Soya, an affiliated grain operation. No findings of manipulation were made, and Ferruzzi agreed to drop its claims against the CBOT.[381] A group of farmers sued the CBOT under the antitrust laws for taking the emergency action against Ferruzzi, claiming that this caused an unnecessary drop in soybean prices to the detriment of farmers. It was claimed that this action was taken to rescue Cargill, a competitor of Ferruzzi. The Seventh Circuit allowed a portion of that claim to proceed.[382] However, the case was subsequently taken away from a jury and dismissed, some ten years after the trading at issue.[383]

Despite widespread concern that Ferruzzi was attempting to manipulate the soybean market, and despite the fact that the CFTC had asked Ferruzzi thirteen times to seek a reduction of its position, the CFTC brought no disciplinary action against the firm.[384] Critics of that inaction pointed out that the CFTC had brought only a few manipulation cases in its then fifteen-year history. They also noted that the CFTC's requirements for price manipulation made such claims extremely difficult to prove. As one CFTC commissioner stated, "Hell, it's virtually impossible."[385]

A private class action suit was brought that charged manipulation and violation of speculative position limits by Ferruzzi, which was ostensibly a hedger that was excepted from such restrictions. The plaintiffs contended, however, that Ferruzzi was speculating rather than hedging, which would require the application of the speculative limits. A federal magistrate in Chicago recommended dismissal of the speculative limit claim because the "Commodity Exchange Act does not recognize a private right of action for excessive speculation."[386]

With respect to the manipulation claim in the class action against Ferruzzi, the magistrate recognized "that manipulation cases generally have not fared well with either the CFTC or the courts" and that "there is a 'dearth of settled case law' on price manipulation; as a result, the courts

377. Eric N. Berg, *Curb on Soybean Trading Puts Market in Turmoil*, New York Times, July 13, 1989, at A1.

378. Eric N. Berg, *Court Upholds Soybean Ruling*, New York Times, July 14, 1989, at D1.

379. *Ferruzzi Loses Court Request*, New York Times, Sept. 15, 1990, at 32.

380. General Accounting Office, *Chicago Futures Market, Emergency Action Procedures* 6 (April 1990).

381. *Ferruzzi Leaves CBOT Over '89 Soybean Fray*, Chicago Tribune, Aug. 23, 1993, at C3.

382. Sanner v. Board of Trade of the City of Chicago, 62 F.3d 918 (7th Cir. 1995).

383. Zimmerman v. CBOT, 360 F.3d 612 (7th Cir. 2005).

384. General Accounting Office, *Chicago Futures Market, Emergency Action Procedures* 4 (April 1990).

385. *Id.* at 352.

386. 892 F. Supp. at 1061.

and the CFTC are still struggling to define the basic elements of the claim and to differentiate between fair means and foul in futures trading."[387] That ambiguity remained despite the fact that the antimanipulation provisions in the Commodity Exchange Act had been in existence for nearly sixty years.

The plaintiffs in the class action sought to expand the reach of manipulation under the Commodity Exchange Act through a "[m]anipulation-by-false-reports theory" in which it was claimed that Ferruzzi "was able to inflate prices by misleading regulators about their processing and export requirements, thus exaggerating the market's demand for cash soybeans and thereby artificially inflating prices."[388] Such a claim would reduce or avoid the necessity of proving that the defendant created an artificial price by controlling both the futures and cash markets. The magistrate ruled that such a theory could constitute part of a manipulative scheme.

The magistrate also denied a motion for summary judgment on the issues of whether Ferruzzi controlled the cash and futures markets in soybeans, whether there was an artificial price that was caused by Ferruzzi, and whether there was manipulative intent, finding material issues of facts over the claims made by the plaintiffs and Ferruzzi.[389] That class action lawsuit was later settled for $21.5 million.[390]

Ferruzzi reported losses of $100 million from its grain trading during this affair.[391] The firm then teetered toward bankruptcy and collapsed in 1993, owing some $17 billion to creditors. Criminal investigations and charges followed over bribes to politicians by Ferruzzi, creating an immense political scandal in Italy.[392] Adding drama to the affair, a former Ferruzzi president committed suicide just before his arrest, and his wealthy widow then became a nun.[393]

4:14 THE SUMITOMO AFFAIR

Yasuo Hamanaka, a rogue trader for the Sumitomo Corp., a Japanese trading company, engaged in a massive manipulation of the copper market in 1995–1996. Hamanaka was called "Mr. 5 percent" because that was supposedly the amount of the worldwide copper market that he controlled for Sumitomo. Hamanaka's scheme collapsed when copper prices fell sharply in 1996, causing losses of $2.6 billion to Sumitomo.[394] After a year-long trial in Japan for forgery and fraud, Hamanaka was sentenced to eight years in prison.[395]

Although Hamanaka's manipulation was directed at metal prices on the London Metals Exchange, his trading had price effects in the United States. In a negotiated settlement with the Sumitomo Corp., the CFTC found violations of the antimanipulation provisions of the Commodity Exchange Act and Sumitomo was fined $150 million. That was, at the time, the largest fine ever levied by a government agency.[396]

387. 892 F. Supp. at 1043.

388. 892 F. Supp. at 1045.

389. 892 F. Supp. at 1051-1058.

390. *Former Ferruzzi Settles Lawsuit on Soybeans Market,* WALL STREET JOURNAL, Oct. 4. 1996, at C13.

391. *Ferruzzi Expects Big Loss*, NEW YORK TIMES, Sept. 25, 1989, at D5.

392. John Tagliabue, *In a Courtroom in Milan, Italian Society Is on Trial*, NEW YORK TIMES, Feb. 6, 1994, at 3.

393. *Magnate's Widow to Become Nun*, CHICAGO TRIBUNE, June 9, 1994 at D18; *For Italian Billionaires, Riches to Rags*, CHICAGO TRIBUNE, Jan. 11, 1992 at C1.

394. Floyd Norris, *A Record Penalty for Sumitomo, A Lesson on Market Volatility*, NEW YORK TIMES, May 12, 1998, at D13.

395. *Rogues Gallery*, CHICAGO TRIBUNE, Sept. 16, 2001 at C3.

396. Melody Petersen, *Merrill Charged With 2d Firm in Copper Case*, NEW YORK TIMES, May 21, 1999, at C1.

The CFTC's settlement order found that Hamanaka created a scheme to recover large speculative losses incurred in his trading on behalf of Sumitomo by creating a dominant position in copper futures on the London Metals Exchange in 1995 and 1996. He stood for delivery on that position, which caused an artificial spike in copper prices.[397] Hamanaka's trading in London was found by the CFTC to have affected domestic copper because there was a correlation between copper prices on the London market and those in the United States. The Japanese trader's activities in America were tenuous, but the CFTC charged that he was acting in concert with a U.S.-based copper merchant to increase prices in London. The Sumitomo trader also entered into agreements with an American firm that called for copper deliveries on a monthly basis for three years.

In another consent judgment arising from the Sumitomo case, *In re Global Minerals & Metals Corp.*,[398] the CFTC found that affiliates of Merrill Lynch, the giant brokerage firm, had aided and abetted the manipulation of the copper market by Hamanaka. It was charged that the Merrill Lynch entities assisted the manipulation by providing financing and accepting scale-up price orders on the London Metals Exchange. A Merrill Lynch affiliate was also engaging in "buy–sell back" and other financing that provided more than $500 million to Sumitomo. Similar charges against Drexel Burnham, another futures commission merchant, had been rejected in the orange juice case.[399] Merrill Lynch agreed to pay a fine to the CFTC in the amount of $15 million and another $10 million to London authorities to settle the charges over its role. The CFTC fine was, at the time, the largest ever imposed on a futures commission merchant.[400] Sumitomo sued its banks, UBS and J.P. Morgan Chase, for lending money that allowed Hamanaka to carry out his scheme, and collected $210 million in settlements.[401] It obtained another $275 million from its broker, Merrill Lynch.[402]

Private class action lawsuits involving the Sumitomo trading were settled,[403] including one for $134 million, which was then the largest class action settlement in the history of the Commodity Exchange Act. In approving that settlement, and "lodestar" attorney fees of $32 million, a judge in the Southern District of New York gave weight to the fact that "generally, price manipulation cases are notoriously risky and are more difficult and risky than securities fraud cases."[404]

The Sumitomo manipulation claims under the Commodity Exchange Act were accompanied by antitrust claims, which is not unusual.[405] In *Metallgesellschaft AG v. Sumitomo Corp.*,[406] the

---

397. In re Sumitomo Corp., COMM. FUT. L. REP. (CCH) ¶ 27,327 (C.F.T.C. 1998).

398. COMM. FUT. L. REP. (CCH) ¶ 27,686 (C.F.T.C. 1999).

399. In re Abrams, COMM. FUT. L. REP. (CCH) ¶ 24,577 (C.F.T.C. 1989).

400. Felicity Barringer, *Merrill Lynch Is Settling Copper Trading Complaints*, NEW YORK TIMES, July 1, 1999, at C5.

401. *UBS Will Pay $85 Million to Resolve Copper Suit*, NEW YORK TIMES, April 8, 2006, at C7.

402. Kenneth N. Gilpin, *Final Lawsuit Is Settled in Copper Loss*, NEW YORK TIMES, April 2, 2002, at C5.

403. *Suitomo Settles Copper Lawsuit*, NEW YORK TIMES, Sept. 19, 1998, at C2.

404. In re Sumitomo Copper Litigation, 74 F. Supp. 2d 393, 397 (S.D.N.Y. 1999). The district court dismissed antitrust claims because the conduct of the defendant in the United States did not cause plaintiffs' injuries. In re Sumitomo Copper Litigation, Comm. Fut. L. Rep. (CCH) ¶ 28,404 (S.D.N.Y. 2000).

405. *See, e.g.*, Utesch v. Dittmer, 947 F.2d 321; In re Copper Litigation (8th Cir. 1991); Minpeco S.A. v. Hunt, 718 F. Supp. 168 (S.D.N.Y. 1989). *See also*, United States v. Patten, 226 U.S. 141 (1913) (holding that cornering a market could violate antitrust laws). Such antitrust claims are described in JERRY W. MARKHAM, 13 COMMODITIES REGULATION: FRAUD, MANIPULATION & OTHER CLAIMS, Ch. 17 (2009). *But see, e.g.*, Credit Suisse Sec. (USA) LLC. v. Billing, 51 U.S. 264 (2007) (finding implied repeal of the antitrust laws by the federal securities laws). The "primary jurisdiction" doctrine for first referring antitrust claims to matters within an agency's expertise has also been applied to claims involving Commodity Exchange Act jurisdiction. FRAUD, MANIPULATION & OTHER CLAIMS, *supra*, § 17:7.

406. Metallgesellschaft AG v. Sumitomo Corp., 325 F.3d 836 (7th Cir. 2003).

Seventh Circuit held that the Foreign Trade Antitrust Improvement Act of 1982[407] granted jurisdiction with respect to claims by foreign short traders that Sumitomo had manipulated world copper prices.[408] The case was remanded to determine whether the plaintiffs had standing to recover damages. That litigation then dragged on for years.[409]

Antitrust issues also found their way into other CFTC manipulation claims involving the Sumitomo affair. In *In the Matter of Global Minerals & Metals Corp.*,[410] a CFTC administrative law judge considered claims against respondents who, unlike the Merrill Lynch affiliates, did not settle charges over their assistance in Hamanaka's trading. The ALJ likened price manipulations prohibited by the CEA to an illegal restraint of trade under the antitrust laws. In a later opinion, the ALJ noted that the CFTC staff was advancing an antitrust-based "leverage" theory in the *Global Minerals & Metals* case as proof of manipulation under the Commodity Exchange Act.[411] Under this leverage theory, antitrust liability will lie if a firm dominating one market is able to project its power into a second market, thereby monopolizing both. The CFTC dismissed this case before this antitrust theory could be tested in litigation.[412]

4:15 ACADEMIC VIEWS

The reason for this dismissal in the *Global Minerals* case was telling. The CFTC concluded that the amount of time being spent by its staff on this case was too burdensome and that the cost of pursuing the case would outweigh any benefits from its prosecution. This once again highlighted the fact that manipulation under the Commodity Exchange Act had become an unprosecutable crime. As one law review article noted in the wake of the Sumitomo affair, "'the courts and the CFTC are still struggling to define the basic elements of the claim and to differentiate between fair means and foul in futures trading.' . . . Importantly, though, the Division of Enforcement of the CFTC has never succeeded in adjudicating a manipulation claim."[413]

As the twentieth century ended, the scorecard for the CFTC in its antimanipulation efforts was that, of the six cases inherited from the Commodity Exchange Authority, three were contested and all three of them were dismissed. The other three CEA-initiated cases were settled with mostly mild penalties. The CFTC brought twelve manipulation cases on its own in the first twenty-five years of its existence. Three of those cases were contested, and the charges were dismissed in all three. The remaining cases were settled or resulted in default judgments with, except for Sumitomo, mostly mild sanctions.[414] This was not an impressive record.

The inability to prosecute antimanipulation claims has been the subject of much academic comment. One law review article lamented in 1979 that "the law governing manipulations has become an embarrassment—confusing, contradictory, complex, and unsophisticated.[415] Legal commentary

407. 15 U.S.C. § 6a.

408. *See also*, Loeb Industries v. Sumitomo Corp., 306 F.3d 469 (7th Cir. 2002) (dismissing some claims where injury was not direct).

409. *See, e.g.*, In re Copper Antitrust Litigation, 436 F.3d 782 (7th Cir. 2006).

410. Comm. Fut. L. Rep. (CCH) ¶ 27,914 (C.F.T.C. 1999).

411. In the Matter of Global Minerals & Metals Corp., Comm. Fut. L. Rep. (CCH) ¶ 28,635 (C.F.T.C. 2001).

412. In the Matter of Global Minerals & Metals Corp., Comm. Fut. L. Rep. (CCH) ¶ 29,793 (C.F.T.C. 2004).

413. Benjamin E. Kozinn, *Note: The Great Copper Caper: Is Market Manipulation Really a Problem In the Wake of the Sumitomo Debacle?* 69 Fordham L. Rev. 243, 263-264 (2000) (footnotes omitted).

414. Jerry W. Markham, *Manipulation of Commodity Futures Prices: The Unprosecutable Crime*, 8 Yale J. on Reg. 281, 356 (1991).

415. Edward T. McDermott, *Defining Manipulation in Commodities Futures Trading: The Futures "Squeeze,"* 74 Nw. L. Rev. 202, 205 (1979).

placed much of the blame for this failure on the lack of a definition in the Commodity Exchange Act and the little guidance provided by the legislative history of that statute. "Consequently, the task of interpreting manipulation has been left in the hands of the courts, administrative agencies such as the CFTC, and academic commentators. Accordingly, any student of commodity manipulation law will discover a body of law that is 'a murky miasma of questionable analysis and unclear effect."[416]

"Although manipulation is defined nowhere in regulatory statutes, courts and commentators have suggested various formulations."[417] Academic commentators took a variety of approaches. Some sought to narrow the definition, some sought to provide clarity, and others advocated the avoidance of a clear definition in order to prevent evasion.[418] Still others urged abandonment of the field entirely. Professor James Boyle, an agricultural economist, for example, opined in 1920 that the "underlying idea of manipulation is the deliberate and conscious influencing of price through dissimulation. A vigorous campaign of advertising may bear or bull a stock or grain. Is this advertising manipulation? Not so long as it is free from deception or fraud. There must be some deceit."[419] He believed that merely influencing price without deceit did not constitute manipulation.

The late Professor Thomas A. Hieronymus, another well-known agricultural economist, also argued in favor of a high level of tolerance for traders.[420] He believed that the marketplace would punish anyone creating a distorted price. Such traders would make themselves targets for other market participants who would be quite happy to "shoot" at them. In other words, anyone creating an artificial price must suffer as other market traders attack that indefensible, artificial position. As Professor Hieronymus argued,

> Manipulation is its own best cure. To manipulate a price is to put it where it doesn't belong. The over-priced inventory or the underpriced commitment invariably leads to losses. . . . In the actively speculated markets the forces of countervailing power effectively prevent manipulation. It is only in the thin markets that power plays cause minor distortions which are profitable. A speculator of moderate scale commented, "Show me a market that someone has distorted and I will show you a way to make money, both with him and against him." The greater the level of speculation, the less is the amount of hanky-panky. Let them trade out.[421]

The so-called Chicago school of law and economics, which promotes market discipline over government regulation, split over the issue of what constitutes manipulation and how it should be regulated. Daniel Fischel, former professor and dean of the University of Chicago Law School, and his coauthor, David J. Ross, argued that the concept of manipulation should be abandoned altogether.[422] They noted with respect to market power manipulations that

---

416. Benjamin E. Kozinn, *Note: The Great Copper Caper: Is Market Manipulation Really a Problem In the Wake of the Sunitomo Debacle?* 69 FORDHAM L. REV. 243, 248 (2000).

417. Daniel R. Fischel & David J. Ross, *Should the Law Prohibit "Manipulation" in Financial Markets?* 105 HARV. L. REV. 503 (1991).

418. William P. Harrington, *The Manipulation of Commodity Futures Prices*, 55 ST. JOHN'S L. REV. 240 (1981).

419. JAMES E. BOYLE, SPECULATION AND THE CHICAGO BOARD OF TRADE 152 (1920).

420. Thomas A Hieronymus, *Manipulation and Commodity Futures Trading: Toward a Definition*, 6 HOFSTRA L. REV. 41 (1977).

421. THOMAS HIERONYMUS, ECONOMICS OF FUTURES TRADING FOR COMMERCIAL AND PERSONAL PROFIT 327-328 (1977).

422. Daniel R. Fischel & David J. Ross, *Should the Law Prohibit "Manipulation" in Financial Markets?* 105 HARV. L. REV. 503 (1991).

> market power can arise from legitimate trading activity. Presumably, any long trader wants to make as much money as he can. Of course, a long trader who finds himself with market power, whether or not he obtained it intentionally, will probably take advantage of the opportunity to charge prices above the competitive price. Thus, unlike making a false statement, noncompetitive pricing at expiration is not a bad act that provides an objective test for identifying manipulative trading in futures markets. There is no objective test that distinguishes the manipulative trades from other trades that may or may not lead to the exercise of market power.[423]

Fischel and Ross contended that fictitious trades should be analyzed as a species of fraud and that actual trades should not be prohibited as manipulative regardless of the intent of the trader.[424]

Seventh Circuit judge Frank Easterbrook, also from the Chicago school of law and economics, took a different approach. He asserted that "'[m]onopoly' in a futures market . . . turns out to be a species of fraud."[425] Judge Easterbrook identified two types of such manipulation fraud: one in which the trader has a dominant position in the open interest in a future contract (what he calls "Position Fraud"), the other in which the trader has control of most of the open interest in a futures contract and the underlying commodity (what he calls "Ownership Fraud").[426] Judge Easterbrook attributed secrecy as the basis for Position Fraud—he believed that the market is deceived by the concealment of the large position. However, traders almost universally go to great lengths to try to conceal their position from the market, lest other traders take advantage of their situation. Judge Easterbrook conceded the point that merely holding a large position does not establish Position Fraud but confusingly stated,

> Concealment by itself may be beneficial. Concealing one's position may be useful in obtaining the profit from one's ability to predict actual conditions of supply and demand, and hedgers need secrecy to avoid revealing their positions in the cash commodity. Secrecy is a valuable commercial strategy, which increases the value of searching for new information. The essential distinction is between secret strategies necessary to capture the value of new information about underlying conditions and secrecy designed to cause prices to diverge from those that reflect the underlying conditions. So a reasonable economic definition of manipulation is conduct in which the profit flows solely from the trader's ability to conceal his position from other traders and the trades do not move price more quickly in the direction that reflects long-run conditions of supply and demand.[427]

Judge Easterbrook's definition of manipulation drew criticism from Professor Fischel, who charged that such a definition is "unsatisfactory. . . . [W]hat happens if the trades move prices in one direction because the trader genuinely believes that prices will move in this direction, but the trader turns out to be wrong and prices ultimately move in the opposite direction? Trading based on a genuine belief that prices will ultimately move in the direction of the trades is the essence of non-manipulative trading."[428] It was meaningful that Easterbrook and Fischel, who often col-

---

423. *Id.* at 544.

424. *Id.* at 507.

425. Frank H. Easterbrook, *Monopoly, Manipulation, and the Regulation of Futures Markets*, 59 J. Bus. S103, S106 (1986).

426. *Id.* at S106.

427. *Id.* at S118.

428. Daniel R. Fischel & David J. Ross, *Should the Law Prohibit "Manipulation" in Financial Markets?* 105 Harv. L. Rev. 503, 509 (1991).

laborated in their writings,[429] were unable to agree in their very public academic debate on what constitutes manipulation. They are both from the same school of legal thought.

Professor Fischel's views were the subject of a lengthy rebuttal by Stephen Thel, a professor of law at Fordham. Professor Thel conceded that defining manipulation is complicated, but he urged deference to the regulatory agencies and their ability to control the markets. He cautioned that the uncertainty of what constitutes manipulation made it hard to find a solution and counseled against "incautious legal intervention." He was "not sure exactly how the law should respond to manipulation, but the complexity of the problem indicates that the response should not be guided by the flights of legal imagination that the subject of manipulation sometimes inspires."[430]

The Chicago school of thought was also under attack from the behavioral school of economic thought, which posits that markets are not inherently efficient and are often influenced by inefficient activities.[431] The behavioralists too have entered the debate on identifying market manipulation. Among other things they have suggested application of "enterprise liability," which would impute joint liability for actions taken by separate actors but as a part of a joint activity, a doctrine that stems from tort law.[432] This doctrine would presumably allow a lesser showing of intent in manipulation cases, but it remains highly controversial.

A number of other law school professors have attempted to formulate less theoretical definitions and methodologies for dealing with manipulation under the Commodity Exchange Act. For example, Georgetown professor Wendy Perdue published an intensive analysis of the manipulation prohibitions in the Commodity Exchange Act. She concluded that, "[d]espite the ease and frequency with which critics have leveled the charge of manipulation and the fact that federal law has prohibited 'manipulation' for over 65 years, a satisfactory definition of manipulation has yet to emerge."[433]

Professor Perdue noted that, while courts and commentators have tried to define the term, "none of their definitions is satisfactory" because "they focus on whether the resulting price is 'artificial.'"[434] Rather than seeking to determine whether a price is "artificial," Perdue focused on whether the trader's conduct was reasonable and proposed a definition focused on that concept. Under this definition, manipulation would be defined as conduct that is "uneconomical or irrational" whatever its effect on market price.[435]

Professor Perdue was critical of approaches taken by other commentators. For example, she criticized Judge Easterbrook's article as suffering "from many . . . practical problems . . . , including the problems of determining 'conditions of supply and demand' and defining the 'long-run.'

---

429. *See, e.g.*, Frank H. Easterbrook & Daniel Fischel, *The Economic Structure of Corporate Law* (1991) & *Mandatory Disclosure and the Protection of Investors*, 70 Va. L. Rev. 669 (1984).

430. Stephen Thel, *$850,000 in Six Minutes: The Mechanics of Securities Manipulation*, 79 Cornell L. Rev. 219, 280 (1994).

431. *See generally*, Christine Jolls, Cass R. Sunstein, and Richard Thaler, *A Behavioral Approach to Law and Economics*, 50 Stan. L. Rev. 1471 (1998) (describing this school of thought); Donald C. Langevoort, *Taming the Animal Spirits of the Stock Markets: A Behavioral Approach to Securities Regulation*, 97 Nw. L. Rev. 135 (2002) (describing the application of this theory to securities regulation).

432. John D. Hanson & Douglas A. Kysar, *Taking Behavioralism Seriously: The Problem of Market Manipulation*, 74 N.Y.U.L. Rev. 630 (1999); John D. Hanson & Douglas A. Kysar, *Taking Behavioralism Seriously: Some Evidence of Market Manipulation*, 112 Harv. L. Rev. 1422 (1999).

433. Wendy Collins Perdue, *Manipulation of Futures Markets: Redefining the Offense*, 56 Fordham L. Rev. 345, 346 (1987).

434. *Id.* at 347 (footnotes omitted).

435. *Id.* at 348 (footnote omitted).

Moreover, in attempting to ascertain the motivation for a trader's desire for secrecy, many courts likely will find themselves lost in a standardless examination of intent."[436]

The author of this book took issue with the efforts by Professor Perdue and other academicians who sought to create a definition as a cure for the difficulties of proving manipulation. This author asserted that manipulation under the Commodity Exchange Act had proved to be an "unprosecutable" crime, which was the subtitle of the article. The article argued that, whatever the definition of manipulation adopted by the courts or regulators, the same issues and concerns would be present. This is because of the desire to avoid stifling trading and the competitiveness of the markets by punishing traders who may unintentionally affect market prices in some adverse manner.[437]

The author's unprosecutable crime article proposed that specific abusive market practices should be defined as manipulative in order to provide guidance and certainty to traders and regulators alike. The article advocated that existing regulatory approaches should be modified in order to create a "fair and orderly" market structure that would prevent and deter conduct that might be manipulative or disruptive.[438] As described in Chapter 8, however, those suggested reforms have been overtaken by the revolutionary changes in both the securities and commodity exchanges, from open outcry auction markets to electronic trading platforms, in the twenty years since publication of that article.

Robert C. Lower, a practitioning attorney, was critical of the approach advocated by the unprosecutable crime article for regulation of particular trading activities.[439] Instead, Lower advocated better contract terms and self-regulatory rules as the best means for preventing manipulation. Richard D. Freidman, professor of law at the University of Michigan, also criticized the positions advocated in the unprosecutable crime article.[440] As did others, Professor Freidman noted that "Congress has been intent on preventing manipulation since the beginning of federal commodities regulation in the 1920s, yet courts, administrators, and academic commentators have failed to agree on a sensible approach to the basic question: What is manipulation?"[441]

Professor Freidman offered a "substantially different test" for determining whether manipulation has occurred. He called this a "modified-sanctions approach," which recognizes that the "essence of a squeeze is exploitation of the shorts' vulnerability to default. The only way to test for that is to determine what the price would be if the sanctions for default were limited to the ordinary

---

436. *Id.* at 388.

437. Jerry W. Markham, *Manipulation of Commodity Futures Prices: The Unprosecutable Crime*, 8 Yale J. on Reg. 281, 359-360 (1991).

438. *Id.* at 360-361. *See also*, Arnold Levinson, *Abuses in the Commodity Markets: The Need for Change in the Regulatory Structure*, 63 Geo. L.J. 751 (1975) (suggesting regulatory changes as a way to meet market abuses).

439. Robert C. Lower, *Disruptions of the Futures Market: A Comment on Dealing With Market Manipulation*, 8 Yale J. on Reg. 391 (1991).

440. Freidman wrote,

> Perhaps, though, Jerry Markham is correct in arguing that manipulation will remain an "unprosecutable crime" so long as adjudicators must determine after the fact just why the market price jumped, and that it is better to rely on more comprehensive preventive regulation. I am reluctant to reach that conclusion, however, because, as Markham recognizes, such regulation carries its own costs. I prefer to hope, until hope appears vain, that the apparent intractability in manipulation litigation does not inhere in the subject but results from a failure to understand it.

Richard D. Freidman, *Stalking the Squeeze: Understanding Commodities Market Manipulation*, 89 Mich. L. Rev. 30, 60 (1990).

441. *Id.* at 31.

measure of contract damages."[442] Professor Freidman explained at length how this formula would be applied, but his formula and its distillation still remain somewhat inscrutable.

Professor Craig Pirrong, a leading economist in the field of futures trading, attacked the author's unprosecutable crime article on the grounds that it would inhibit useful economic activity. Professor Pirrong also criticized Wendy Perdue and other legal commentators because of their concern with determining the subjective intent of the actor as a precondition for liability. Instead, Professor Pirrong advocated quantifying manipulation through econometric analysis because it is an "economic offense."[443]

Pirrong sought an ex post facto analysis of the trading to determine if the actor had market power during the delivery period. Apparently, he would presume intent from the use of such power and would look to economic analysis to determine if there were any nonmanipulative explanations for the conduct. That approach was faulty, however, because hindsight evaluations are always perfect, while a trader seeking to predict a market does not have such a perfect 20/20 hindsight advantage. It would appear that a wrong or even a stupid guess on the part of a trader with a large position would, under Professor Pirrong's analysis, inevitably result in a finding of manipulation and a felony conviction.

More recently, Professor Pirrong has stated that in "its efforts to draft statutes that conceivably cover any possible type of manipulative conduct, Congress has instead created laws that do not reliably reach any kind of manipulative conduct, especially the types that are quite common and quite costly."[444] Pirrong further stated, "[i]n some respects (though not completely) following the recommendations of Markham, I would suggest language that (a) specifically identifies conduct that is likely to be (market power) manipulative, and (b) sets out standards for determining whether this conduct, in fact, distorted prices."[445] Professor Pirrong then proposed legislation that would focus on an econometric analysis of whether a trader took "excessive" deliveries or purchases and sales of a commodity that result in a price "distortion."[446] Manipulative intent would be proven by Pirrong's proposal through an econometric analysis of whether the trader's actions were commercially reasonable, but for the trader's effects on prices.

A lawyer and former CFTC chair, Philip McBride Johnson made an extensive examination of manipulation law under the Commodity Exchange Act. His article describes the traditional elements of manipulation and analyzes the case law in order to provide a "much needed survey of the murky legal boundaries of manipulative behavior."[447] The Johnson article critiques the case law, noting its difficulties and varying interpretations, and takes issue with using manipulation charges under the Commodity Exchange Act to address rigged trading.[448] In a treatise he coauthored, Johnson further stated that commodity "[p]rice manipulation is akin to the exercise of monopoly power to dictate prices that would be unachievable in a truly competitive market."[449]

442. *Id.* at 34.

443. Craig Pirrong, *Commodity Market Manipulation Law: A (Very) Critical Analysis and a Proposed Alternative*, 51 Wash. & Lee L. Rev. 945, 947 (1994).

444. Craig Pirrong, *Energy Market Manipulation: Definition, Diagnosis, and Deterrence*, 31 Energy L. J. 1, 13-14 (2010).

445. *Id.* at 14. Pirrong stated that "[b]y identifying particular forms of conduct that are most likely to be manipulative, and by setting out rigorous methods for quantifying price distortions and evaluating intent, this approach also reduces the likelihood that innocent (although perhaps aggressive) traders are accused of, and perhaps found liable for, market power manipulation. *Id.*

446. *Id.*

447. Philip McBride Johnson, *Commodity Market Manipulation*, 38 Wash. L. Rev. 725 (1981).

448. *Id.* at 778.

449. Philip McBride Johnson, and Thomas Lee Hazen, Derivatives Regulation § 5.02[3] (4th ed. 2002).

Another practitioner, George A. Davidson, stated that the problem of defining manipulation "has bedeviled courts and administrative tribunals for decades. Tribunals have wavered back and forth between under inclusive rules, which find liability only in the obvious case and do not reach the entire problem, and over inclusive formulations, which risk punishing the innocent along with the guilty."[450] Davidson asserted that the academic effort to formulate a workable definition of manipulation should be abandoned in favor of confronting "directly the characteristics of the futures markets that permit squeezes to develop. Since the problem with the futures market is the secret delivery market concealed within a larger market consisting almost entirely of offset traders, the solution is to eliminate that secret delivery market."[451]

This seems to be an approach similar to that proposed by Judge Easterbrook and may have been rendered impractical by subsequent market changes. Delivery as an option has been eliminated on many futures contracts and the cash market in many commodities is virtually limitless in size, obviating the importance of the delivery requirement. Moreover, no rational trader would want its position disclosed to the market. Such disclosure would, as a practical manner, proscribe large positions by institutional traders and undermine the utility of the markets for hedging and pricing.

Still another practitioner, Edward T. McDermott, noted that the Commodity Exchange Act leaves the task of defining manipulation to the courts and the CFTC, but they "have made little progress toward defining manipulation."[452] McDermott, apparently taking a lead from the Federal Trade Commission study described in Chapter 1, suggested that the common law principal of "prevention or hindrance" should be applied to preclude manipulation.[453] This common law doctrine prohibits someone from preventing or hindering other parties from fulfilling their contractual obligations. McDermott believed that a trader buying up the cash commodity and preventing the shorts from delivering would be engaging in such an act. Another commentator criticized that approach.[454]

A recently graduated law school student has noted that "[s]ince definition has been left to judicial and administrative construction, it was inevitable that conflicting standards and tests for manipulation would emerge. The lack of a coherent definition leaves an aggressive, large-scale trader guessing at what point financial self-interest violates the act."[455] That author advocated a set of rules that would force cash settled liquidations during periods of empirically determined market congestion. The market seems to have accepted that approach, since most derivatives are now cash settled, but manipulation concerns remain.

More recently, Professor Emilios Avgouleas advocated a more nuanced definition of manipulation that would contain five objective elements and two subjective ones. He would define manipulation as behavior involving misrepresentations, concealments, artificial transactions, and "trading schemes" that seek to induce trading by others. Such prohibited trading "must be effected

450. George A. Davidson, *Squeezes and Corners: A Structural Approach*, 40 Bus. Law. 1283 (1985). Mr. Davidson further stated, "The problem is that it is very hard to distinguish the unlawful conduct of the squeezer from conduct undertaken for the entirely lawful purpose for which traders enter the futures market: to make money. As one commentator has observed, a manipulative squeeze is 'like ordinary market behavior in many of its manifestations.'" *Id.* at 1287 (footnote omitted).

451. *Id.* at 1297.

452. Edward T. McDermott, *Defining Manipulation and Commodity Futures Trading: The Futures 'Squeeze,'* 74 Nw L. Rev. 202 (1979) (footnote omitted).

453. 74 Nw L. Rev. at 204.

454. *See*, William P. Harrington, *The Manipulation of Commodity Futures Prices*, 55 St. John's L. Rev. 240, 266-271 (1981).

455. Ralph T. Byrd, *No Squeezing, No Cornering: Rules for Commodity Exchanges*, 7 Hofstra L. Rev. 923, 932 (1979).

in a way, as to lead the price of these investments to an artificial level," so that the manipulator could realize financial gains that would not have been possible in the absence of such behavior.[456] This definition still leaves unanswered the problem of proving that the price is artificial and that it was caused by the trader. The level of intent required is also omitted.

From this survey of academic thought, it is clear that no technical "legal" definition can be constructed that will allow for broad agreement on what is or is not prohibited. "Much of the confusion is inherent in the concept of manipulation. It is extraordinarily difficult—some would say impossible—to formulate a test that will easily or consistently distinguish between legitimate self-interested market behavior and illegitimate and unfair tactics motivated by greed. . . . To date, no-one has been able to establish a 'smoking-gun,' 'conduct based test' for manipulation."[457]

As the Seventh Circuit stated in *Frey v. CFTC*,[458] "[s]ophisticated economic justification for the distinctions made in this area of the law may at times seem questionable. Sometimes the 'know it when you see it' test may appear most useful. Nonetheless, the relevant distinctions have been authoritatively articulated, and we rely on them here but with appropriate recognition of their limitations."[459] The "know it when you see it" approach, however, allows the government to pick and choose what trading practices it might or might not like at any given time. Such an approach gives little guidance to traders and opens the door to "political" actions to suppress speculation in times of rising prices.

456. Emilios Avgouleas, The Mechanics and Regulation of Market Abuse 116 (2005).

457. *U.S. Strategic Petroleum Reserve: Recent Policy Has Increased Costs to Consumers But Not Overall U.S. Energy Security, Report by the Minority Staff of the Senate Permanent Subcommittee on Investigations of the Committee on Governmental Affairs*, 108th Cong., 1st Sess. 127 (2003).

458. Frey v. CFTC, 931 F.2d 1171 (7th Cir. 1991).

459. 931 F.2d at 1175.

5

MANIPULATION SETBACKS UNDER THE FEDERAL SECURITIES LAWS

5:1 RULE 10B-5 UNDER ATTACK

The Securities and Exchange Commission (SEC) rode a wave of judicial support in the 1960s that turned it into a powerhouse agency through the broad application of Section 10(b) of the Securities Exchange Act of 1934 (34 Act)[1] and Rule 10b-5 thereunder.[2] Judicial deference also encouraged the SEC to place more reliance on Section 10(b), rather than Section 9 of the 34 Act,[3] in its manipulation cases.[4] This expansive judicial view on the reach or Rule 10b-5 was personified by the opinion of Justice William O. Douglas (a former SEC chair) in *Superintendent of Insurance v. Bankers Life & Casualty Co*. There, in an opinion that he wrote for the Supreme Court, Douglas stated that Section 10(b) must be read "flexibly, not technically and restrictively. Since there was a 'sale' of a security and since fraud was used 'in connection with' it, there is redress under §10(b) whatever might be available as a remedy under state law."[5]

The *Superintendent of Insurance* decision was a high-water mark for the SEC. The Supreme Court's jurisprudence on Rule 10b-5 subsequently became schizophrenic, sometimes restrictive, sometimes liberal, when the ideology of the majority of the justices on the Court changed over time. In recent years, restrictiveness has prevailed, making claims brought under Section 10(b) much more difficult to prove. As law professor Thomas Hazen notes, "[s]tarting in 1975 a new conservative majority on the Supreme Court sharply reversed this trend, in a series of decisions

1. 15 U.S.C.78j(b).

2. 17 C.F.R. § 240.10b-5. As noted by Professor Thomas Hazen:

> In the 1960s and early 1970s, many federal appellate courts and district courts developed expansive interpretations of Rule 10b-5 (and other antifraud provisions of the securities laws). They applied it to impose liability for negligent as well as deliberate misrepresentations, for breaches of fiduciary duty by corporate management, and for failure by directors, underwriters, accountants and lawyers to prevent wrongdoing by others. In private actions for damages, the courts were willing to imply a private right of action in anyone whose losses were even remotely connected with the alleged wrongdoing, or even in someone who had suffered no loss if her suit would help to encourage compliance with the law. The Supreme Court aided and abetted this development, giving an expansive reading to the terms "fraud" and "purchase or sale" and to the "connection" that had to be found between them.

Thomas L. Hazen, *The Jurisprudence of SEC Rule 10b-5: Securities Law for Nonsecurities Lawyers*, San Diego, CA (July 28–29, 2005), http://files.ali-aba.org/thumbs/datastorage/skoobesruoc/pdf/Cl001-ch36_thumb.pdf (accessed July 6, 2011).

3. 15 U.S.C. § 78i.

4. *See, e.g.*, SEC v. Sayegh, 906 F. Supp. 939 (S.D.N.Y. 1995), *aff'd sub. nom.*, SEC v. Militano, 101 F.3d 685 (2d Cir. 1996) (Section 10(b) violations charged where broker was using third party "beards" to disguise his manipulation of a stock in order to prevent the impairment of a brokerage firm's net capital).

5. Superintendent of Ins. v. Bankers Life & Casualty Co., 404 U.S. 6, 12 (1971).

giving a narrow reading to the terms of Rule 10b-5 and other antifraud provisions. . . . The tone of these later Supreme Court decisions is even more important than their actual holdings. They cast doubt on the continued vitality of many of the expansive decisions of the preceding 15 years, even those that have not been specifically overruled."[6] This chapter describes the advancement of this more conservative approach.

5:2 THE *BIRNBAUM* DOCTRINE

In 1952, in *Birnbaum v. Newport Steel Corp.*,[7] an eminent panel of jurists in the Second Circuit held that Rule 10b-5 imposed a requirement that plaintiffs be a purchaser or seller of securities as a condition for bringing suit under that provision. Acting as amicus curiae in several private actions, the SEC made a concerted effort in the 1970s to overturn the "*Birnbaum* rule." The SEC finally carried the day in the Ninth Circuit on that issue, but the Supreme Court reversed that decision in 1975 in *Blue Chip Stamps v. Manor Drug Stores*[8] and reaffirmed the *Birnbaum* rule. The Supreme Court held that "Section 10(b) does not punish deceptive conduct, but only deceptive conduct 'in connection with the purchase or sale of any security registered on a national securities exchange or any security not so registered.'"[9] However, the Court noted in *Blue Chip Stamps* and other cases that the purchaser or seller doctrine would not apply to SEC injunctive actions.[10]

The Supreme Court's affirmance of the *Birnbaum* rule in *Blue Chip Stamps* was based on a policy concern that it was needed to curb abusive litigation under Rule 10b-5. "Cabining the private cause of action by means of the purchaser-seller limitation would, in the Court's view, minimize these ill effects."[11] The purchaser or seller rule was applied in *Blue Chip Stamps* to an investor who did not buy a security because of a fraudulent act—that is, it involved "a person who did not actually buy securities, but who might have done so had the seller told the truth."[12]

---

6. Thomas L. Hazen, *The Jurisprudence of SEC Rule 10b-5: Securities Law for Nonsecurities Lawyers*, San Diego, CA (July 28-29, 2005), http://files.ali-aba.org/thumbs/datastorage/skoobesruoc/pdf/CI001-ch36_thumb.pdf (accessed July 6, 2011).

7. Birnbaum v. Newport Steel Corp., 193 F.2d 461 (2d Cir.), *cert. denied*, 343 U.S. 956 (1952) (Swan, L. Hand & A. Hand, jj.).

8. Blue Chip Stamps v. Manor Drug Stores, 421 U.S. 723 (1975).

9. Morrison v. National Australia Bank Ltd., 561 U.S. ---, --- (2010) (citations omitted).

10. 421 U.S. at 752, n. 14. *See also*, SEC v. National Securities Inc., 339 U.S. 453, 468, n. 9 (1969) (SEC not subject to *Birnbaum* rule); Merrill Lynch, Pierce, Fenner & Smith Inc. v. Dabit, 547 U.S. 71, 80-91 (2006) (same). In *SEC v. Zandford*, 535 U.S. 813 (2002), the Supreme Court held that the purchaser or seller requirement was met where a securities broker looted the discretionary account of an elderly customer and his mentally retarded daughter. In another decision, *The Wharf (Holdings) Ltd. v. United Int'l Holding, Inc.*, 532 U.S. 588 (2001), the Supreme Court considered whether the purchaser or seller requirement would apply to an option on stock. There, it was claimed that the defendant violated Rule 10b-5 by selling the plaintiff an option to buy stock while secretly maintaining an intention never to honor the option. "In deciding whether the Rule covers the circumstances present here, we must assume that the 'security' at issue is not the cable system stock, but the option to purchase that stock." 532 U.S. at 593. The Supreme Court held that the purchaser or seller doctrine did not bar this claim.

11. Merrill Lynch, Pierce, Fenner & Smith Inc. v. Dabit, 547 U.S. 71, 80-91 (2006).

12. The Wharf (Holdings) Ltd. v. United Int'l Holdings Inc., 532 U.S. 588, 594 (2001). The Supreme Court noted in *Blue Chips Stamps*:

> Three principal classes of potential plaintiffs are presently barred by the *Birnbaum* rule. First are potential purchasers of shares, either in a new offering or on the Nation's post-distribution trading markets, who allege that they decided not to purchase because of an unduly gloomy representation or the omission of favorable material which made the issuer appear to be a less favorable investment vehicle than it actually was. Second are actual shareholders in the issuer

Later, in *Virginia Bankshares v. Sandberg*,[13] the Supreme Court noted that the purchaser or seller rule would affect those who hold onto a security because of the manipulative activities of a defendant. Nevertheless, the *Blue Chip Stamps* case had "held against expanding the class from actual buyers and sellers to include those who rely on deceptive sales practices by taking no action, either to sell what they own or to buy what they do not."[14] That ruling severely limits the class of persons who may bring Rule 10b-5 claims for manipulative activities. Even if the value of a security is severely affected by a price manipulation, only those who bought and sold during the manipulation will have standing to sue under Rule 10b-5.

5:3 THE SCIENTER REQUIREMENT

Another example of the Supreme Court's more restrictive approach to Rule 10b-5 is found in *Ernst & Ernst v. Hochfelder*,[15] in which, in 1976, the Court rejected a claim that negligence would be sufficient for proof of a violation of Rule 10b-5. The negligence standard is much easier to prove than a specific intent or scienter standard. Under a negligence standard, it need only been shown that a defendant was not sufficiently careful, while scienter requires a showing of specific intent to commit a wrongful act.

Various circuit courts of appeal had divided over which standard was applicable under Section 10(b) of the 34 Act and Rule 10b-5. The Supreme Court was called upon to resolve that split in the circuits in the *Hochfelder* case. The Supreme Court held that scienter was required and that plaintiffs bringing actions under Section 10(b) and Rule 10b-5 must plead and prove that the defendant acted with a mental state embracing intent to deceive, manipulate, or defraud.[16]

The various courts of appeal subsequently considering the scienter issue held that this requirement could be met by showing that "the defendant acted intentionally or recklessly, though the Circuits differ on the degree of recklessness."[17] For example, the Eleventh and Fifth Circuits have held that Rule 10b-5 requires showing either intent to deceive, manipulate, or defraud, or "severe recklessness."[18] The Eleventh Circuit defined "severe reckless" as a "demanding standard" that is "limited to those highly unreasonable omissions or misrepresentations that involve not merely simple or even inexcusable negligence, but an extreme departure from the standards of ordinary care, and that present a danger of misleading buyers or sellers which is either known to the defendant or so obvious that the defendant must have been aware of it."[19]

> who allege that they decided not to sell their shares because of unduly rosy representation or a failure to disclose unfavorable material. Third are shareholders, creditors, and perhaps others related to an issuer who suffered loss in the value of their investment due to corporate or insider activities in connection with the purchase or sale of securities which violate Rule 10b-5. It has been held that shareholder members of the second and third of these classes may frequently be able to circumvent the Birnbaum limitation through bringing a derivative action on behalf of the corporate issuer if the latter is itself a purchaser or seller of securities. . . . But the first of these classes, of which respondent is a member, cannot claim the benefit of such a rule.

421 U.S. at 737-738 (citation omitted).

13. Virginia Bankshares v. Sandberg, 501 U.S. 1083, 1091-1092 (1991).

14. Virginia Bankshares v. Sandberg, 501 U.S. 1083, 1091-1092 (1991).

15. Ernst & Ernst v. Hochfelder, 425 U.S. 185 (1976).

16. *See*, Tellabs Inc. v. Makor Issues & Rights, 551 U.S. 308, 319 (2007) (quoting *Ernst & Ernst* v. *Hochfelder*, 425 U.S. 185, 193-194, n. 12 (1976)); Herman & Maclean v. Huddleston, 459 U.S. 375, 382 (1983) (same).

17. Tellabs Inc. v. Makor Issues & Rights, 551 U.S. 308, 319 n.3 (2007).

18. Thompson v. RelationServe Media Inc., 610 F.3d 628, 634 (11th Cir. 2010); Lormand v. US Unwired Inc., 565 F.3d 228, 251 (5th Cir. 2009).

19. Thompson v. RelationServe Media, Inc., 610 F.3d 628, 634 (11th Cir. 2010).

The Seventh Circuit also took a restrictive approach to recklessness as scienter. It defined reckless conduct as a "highly unreasonable [act or] omission, involving not merely simple, or even inexcusable negligence, but an extreme departure from the standards of ordinary care, and which presents a danger of misleading buyers or sellers that is either known to the defendant or is so obvious that the actor must have been aware of it."[20] The D.C. Circuit adopted that standard, calling it "extreme recklessness."[21] The Sixth Circuit also followed the Seventh Circuit formula, but added the fillip that "recklessness, as a mental state, 'falls somewhere between intent and negligence.'"[22]

Other circuits have used different formulations. For example, the Ninth Circuit requires that it must be shown that the defendant "possessed actual knowledge or acted with deliberate recklessness."[23] The First Circuit held that a plaintiff can establish scienter by showing that defendants "either consciously intended to defraud, or that they acted with a high degree of recklessness."[24] The Second Circuit adopted a "reckless disregard for the truth" scienter standard by which "we mean 'conscious recklessness—*i.e.*, a state of mind *approximating actual intent*, and *not merely a heightened form of negligence*.'"[25] The Second Circuit elaborated further on this standard, stating that the idea of recklessness is applied to

> conduct that "at the least is highly unreasonable and which represents an extreme departure from the standards of ordinary care to the extent that *the danger was either known to the defendant or so obvious that the defendant must have been aware of it*" [emphasis by the court]; or to evidence that the "defendants failed to review or check *information that they had a duty to monitor*, or ignored *obvious* signs of fraud," and hence "should have known that they were misrepresenting material facts" [emphasis added]. An "*egregious* refusal to see the *obvious*, or to *investigate the doubtful*, may in some cases give rise to an inference of . . . recklessness" (internal quotation marks omitted) [emphases added].[26]

The Second Circuit noted that a defendant corporate officer who prepared and proceeded to file documents with the SEC containing statements whose veracity he himself had questioned had had an obvious duty to verify the suspicious information.

The Third Circuit adopted the Second Circuit's approach to defining recklessness, concluding that it was the "most restrictive" approach among the various circuits considering the issue.[27]

The Supreme Court has not acted to clarify the exact standard for scienter. Indeed, it has repeatedly reserved deciding on "whether recklessness suffices to fulfill the scienter requirement."[28]

20. Sundstrand Corp. v. Sun Chemical Corp., 553 F. 2d 1033, 1045 (7th Cir. 1977), *cert. denied*, 434 U.S. 875 (1977).

21. *SEC v. Steadman*, 967 F.2d 636, 641-642 (D.C. Cir. 1992) (*citing Sundstrand Corp.*, 553 F.2d at 1045).

22. Robert N. Clemens Trust v. Morgan Stanley DW Inc., 485 F.3d 840, 847 (6th Cir. 2007) (citations omitted).

23. N.M. State Inv. Council v. Ernst & Young LLP, 2011 U.S. App. LEXIS 7680 (9th Cir. 2011) (citation omitted).

24. Miss. Public Employees' Ret. Sys. v. Boston Scientific Corp., 523 F.3d 75, 85 (1st Cir. 2008) (citation omitted).

25. South Cherry St., LLC v. Hennessee Group LLC, 573 F.3d 98, 109-110 (2d Cir. 2009) (citation omitted, emphasis in original).

26. 573 F.3d at 109-110 (citations omitted, emphasis supplied by the court).

27. In re Advanta Corp. Sec. Litig., 180 F.3d 525, 534 (3d Cir. 1999).

28. Tellabs Inc. v. Makor Issues & Rights, 551 U.S. 308, 319 (2007) (quoting). *See also*, Herman & Maclean v. Huddleston, 459 U.S. 375, 379, n. 4 (1983) (same); SEC v. Aaron, 446 U.S. 680 (1980) (same).

However, although the issue is not without doubt,[29] the Supreme Court seems content to apply the reckless standard to Rule 10b-5 when an issue concerning its application arises. Thus, in *Matrixx Initiatives Inc. v. Siracusano*,[30] the Supreme Court held that, since the petitioner did not "challenge the Court of Appeals' holding that the scienter requirement may be satisfied by a showing of 'deliberate recklessness' we assume, without deciding, that the standard applied by the Court of Appeals is sufficient to establish scienter."[31]

The SEC tried to avoid imposition of the scienter requirement in its own injunctive actions despite the decision of the Supreme Court in *Hochfelder*.[32] The SEC claimed that, since the government was acting in the public interest, it should be relieved of the heavy burden of proof required to establish scienter. The SEC was allowed to prove the lesser negligence standard by various courts of appeal[33] before the issue reached the Supreme Court in *Aaron v. SEC*.[34] Although it had stated that the *Birnbaum* rule does not apply to SEC enforcement actions, the Supreme Court held in the *Aaron* case that the SEC must establish scienter, even in SEC-initiated injunctive actions under Rule 10b-5 and Section 10(b) of the 34 Act.

The Court in *Aaron* was also called upon to determine whether the provisions of Section 17(a)(1), (2) and (3) of the Securities Act of 1933 (33 Act) impose a scienter requirement.[35] Like Rule 10b-5,[36] Section 17(a)(1) of the 33 Act proscribes employment of any "device," "scheme," or "artifice to defraud."[37] However, neither Rule 10b-5 nor Section 17(a) of the 33 Act contains the "any manipulative or deceptive device or contrivance" language on which Section 10(b) of the 34 Act is premised.[38] Conversely, Section 10(b) of the 34 Act does not contain the "device," "scheme," or "artifice to defraud" language found in Rule 10b-5 and Section 17(a)(1) of the 33 Act.

---

29. In *Safeco Insurance Company of America v. Burr*, 551 U.S. 47 (2007) the Supreme Court considered a provision in the Fair Credit Reporting Act (15 U.S.C. § 1681) that requires notice to any consumer subject to adverse action based in whole or in part on any information contained in a consumer credit report. Anyone who willfully fails to provide such notice is civilly liable to the consumer. The Supreme Court held in that case that "reckless" conduct would constitute a willful violation of that provision. The Court considered common law definitions of what constitutes reckless conduct but refused to draw a distinct line between negligence and reckless conduct because the facts in the case before it did not reach the level of either standard—the defendant's conduct was "objectively reasonable." 551 U.S. at 69.

30. Matrixx Initiatives Inc. v. Siracusano , --- U.S. --- (2011).

31. *Id.*

32. Ernst & Ernst v. Hochfelder, 425 U.S. 185 (1976).

33. *See, e.g.*, SEC v. Universal Major Industries Corp., 546 F.2d 1044 (2d Cir. 1976); SEC v. World Radio Mission, Inc., 544 F.2d 535 (1st Cir. 1976).

34. Aaron v. SEC, 446 U.S. 680 (1980).

35. 15 U.S.C. § 77q(a).

36. 17 C.F.R. § 240.10b-5.

37. Section 17(a) contains three subsections that include the following prohibitions:

> (1) to employ any device, scheme, or artifice to defraud, or
> (2) to obtain money or property by means of any untrue statement of a material fact or any omission to state a material fact necessary in order to make the statements made, in light of the circumstances under which they were made, not misleading; or
> (3) to engage in any transaction, practice, or course of business which operates or would operate as a fraud or deceit upon the purchaser.

15 U.S.C. § 77q(a).

38. 15 U.S.C. § 78j(b). The 34 Act was designed to protect investors against manipulation of stock prices. S. Rep. No. 792, 73d Cong., 2d Sess., 1-5 (1934).

The Supreme Court in *Aaron* held that Section 17(a)(1) of the 33 Act contains a scienter requirement because it uses the same language as Rule 10b-5. The Court drew a different conclusion with respect to the prohibitions in Section 17(a)(2). The Court held that certain provisions in Section 17(a)(2) of the 33 Act did not contain language that would evidence that Congress intended a specific intent requirement.[39] That language makes it unlawful "to obtain money or property by means of any untrue statement of a material fact or any omission to state a material fact necessary in order to make the statements made, in light of the circumstances under which they were made, not misleading."[40]

Section 17(a)(3) of the 33 Act raised another issue in determining whether it required scienter. The Supreme Court had previously held in *SEC v. Capital Gains Research Bureau Inc.*[41] that intent to deceive was not required to establish a violation of Section 206(2) of the Investment Advisers Act of 1940 (40 Act). That section contained proscriptive language like that in Section 17(a)(3) of the Securities Act.[42] The Court in *Aaron* drew a precarious line for determining the level of intent in these various provisions by focusing on the common language in Section 206(2) of the 40 Act and Section 17(a)(3) of the 33 Act. That language makes it unlawful for any person "to engage in any transaction, practice, or course of business which *operates* or *would operate* as a fraud or deceit."[43] The Court in *Aaron* held that this language "quite plainly focuses upon the *effect* of particular conduct on members of the investing public, rather than upon the culpability of the person responsible."[44]

---

39. 446 U.S. at 696.
40. 15 U.S.C. § 77q(a)(2).
41. 375 U.S. 353 (1963).
42. Section 206 provides in pertinent part that it

> shall be unlawful for any investment adviser, by use of the mails or any means or instrumentality of interstate commerce, directly or indirectly—
>
> (1) to employ any device, scheme, or artifice to defraud any client or prospective client;
> (2) to engage in any transaction, practice, or course of business which operates as a fraud or deceit upon any client or prospective client;
> (3) . . .
> (4) to engage in any act, practice, or course of business which is fraudulent, deceptive, or manipulative.

15 U.S.C. § 80b-6.

43. 446 U.S. at 697 (emphasis supplied by the Court).
44. 446 U.S. at 697. The SEC has described the Supreme Court's parsing of the provisions of Section 17(a) for scienter purposes as follows:

> Actions pursuant to Securities Act Sections 17(a)(2) and 17(a)(3) do not require a showing of scienter. . . . In *Aaron,* the Supreme Court sought to determine whether scienter was required in a Commission injunctive proceeding pursuant to the antifraud provisions of Exchange Act Section 10(b) and Securities Act Section 17(a). The Court examined the language of both sections and determined that scienter was required under Section 10(b) because the words "manipulative," "device," and "contrivance," which are used in the statute, evidenced a Congressional intent to proscribe only knowing or intentional misconduct. Similarly, the Court concluded that subsection (1) of Section 17(a) required proof of scienter because Congress used such words as "device," "scheme," and "artifice to defraud." In contrast, the Court concluded that the absence of such words under subsections (2) and (3) of Section 17(a) demonstrated that no scienter was required. Section 17(a)(2) prohibits any person from obtaining money or property "by means of any untrue statement of a material fact or omission to state a material fact," which the Court found to be "devoid of any suggestion whatsoever of a scienter requirement." Similarly, the Court found, in

The holding in *Aaron*[45] raised the profile on the little used Section 17 of the 33 Act, but that section is still limited to sell side transactions and would not apply to a party buying up a security.[46] The decision in *Aaron* also raises some perplexing questions in the manipulation context. If the focus is on the effect of conduct, plaintiffs claiming under Sections 17(a)(2) and (3) of the 33 Act will have to prove that conduct had an "effect." This would require proof of actual manipulation or fraud in order to gain advantage of the negligence standard. This suggests that proof of price artificiality will be required in actions under these provisions.

The *Aaron* decision was, in any event, no boon to private plaintiffs. The courts have held that there is no private right of action implied in Section 17(a) of the 33 Act.[47] There are express private rights of action in the 33 Act, but private litigants have preferred Rule 10b-5 because the 33 Act also has several restrictions on damages and permits defenses that often thwart plaintiffs.[48] This preference was aided by the Supreme Court in *Herman & Maclean v. Huddleston*,[49] which held that an implied private right of action could be brought under Section 10(b) of the 34 Act even if the charge was subject to the express private rights under the 33 Act.

Section 17(a)(1) of the 33 Act still has teeth in SEC actions. Criminal actions may also be brought under that section where scienter is present. In *United States v. Naftalin*,[50] the Supreme Court upheld a criminal conviction under Section 17(a)(1) of the 33 Act where the defendant had engaged in a short selling scheme in which he defrauded his brokers by selling short stock that he falsely claimed he owned. The defendant was gambling that the stocks would decline but they went higher, requiring the brokers to buy in the stock at a loss. Nevertheless, the government otherwise generally favored Section 10(b) of the 34 Act in bringing criminal prosecutions of stock manipulations. For example, in *United States v. Charnay*,[51] the Ninth Circuit Court of Appeals reversed the dismissal of an indictment under Section 10(b) against Howard Hughes and others for a short sale manipulation scheme that was designed to depress the stock price of a company Hughes Tool Company was trying to take over.[52]

5:4 MANIPULATION AS FRAUD

The Supreme Court held in *Ernst & Ernst v. Hochfelder* that the use of the word "manipulative" in Section 10(b) of the 34 Act was "especially significant. It is and was virtually a term of art when

---

> construing Section 17(a)(3), under which it is unlawful for any person "to engage in any transaction, practice, or course of business which operates or would operate as a fraud or deceit," that scienter was not required because it "quite plainly focuses upon the effect of particular conduct on members of the investing public, rather than upon the culpability of the person responsible."

Prohibition Against Fraud, Manipulation, and Deception in Connection With Security-Based Swaps, 75 Fed. Reg. 68560, 68563 (Nov. 10, 2008).

45. 446 U.S. 680 (1980).

46. *See generally*, United States v. Naftalin, 441 U.S. 768, 778 (1979) (Section 17(a) of the 33 Act "was intended to cover any fraudulent scheme in an offer or sale of securities, whether in the course of an initial distribution or in the course of ordinary market trading").

47. *See, e.g.*, Sears v. Likens, 912 F.2d 889, 893 (7th Cir. 1990); Newcome v. Esrey, 862 F.2d 1099, 1102 (4th Cir. 1988); Finkel v. The Stratton Corp. 962 F.2d 169, 175, (2d Cir. 1992).

48. *See*, 15 U.S.C. §§ 77k and 77l.

49. Herman & Maclean v. Huddleston, 459 U.S. 375 (1983).

50. United States v. Naftalin, 441 U.S. 768 (1979).

51. United States v. Charnay, 537 F.2d 341 (9th Cir.), *cert. denied*, 429 U.S. 1000 (1976).

52. The case was later dismissed after a key witness for the government made himself unavailable for trial. United States v. Charnay, 577 F.2d 81 (9th Cir. 1978).

used in connection with securities markets. It connotes intentional or willful conduct designed to deceive or defraud investors by controlling or artificially affecting the price of securities."[53] In reaching that conclusion, the Court cited a *Webster's* dictionary definition of manipulation as trading by matched orders, wash sales, and fictitious reports designed to rig the market. This seemed to downplay market power as manipulation absent some fraudulent conduct. In contrast, "[i]t has long been recognized that manipulation is the consequence of an exercise of market power in futures markets."[54]

One year after the *Hochfelder* decision, the Supreme Court spoke again on the scope of manipulation prohibitions in Section 10(b) of the 34 Act in *Santa Fe v. Green*.[55] There, the Supreme Court held that Section 10(b) was a "general prohibition of practices deemed by the SEC to be 'manipulative'—in this technical sense of artificially affecting market activity in order to mislead investors."[56] The *Santa Fe* decision rejected the assertion that Section 10(b) of the 34 Act applied to breaches of fiduciary duties. Rather, it is limited to fraud-based conduct, in contrast to the market power approach to manipulation under the Commodity Exchange Act of 1936. The Supreme Court went further in *Chiarella v. United States*,[57] stating that "Section 10 (b) is aptly described as a catchall provision, but what it catches must be fraud."[58]

The Court in *Santa Fe*, as it did in *Hochfelder*, also defined the term "manipulation" to refer "generally to practices, such as wash sales, matched orders, or rigged prices, that are intended to mislead investors by artificially affecting market activity." In reaching that conclusion the Court cited Section 9 of the 34 Act,[59] which was specifically directed at prohibiting the "[m]anipulation of security prices."[60] By referencing Section 9, the *Santa Fe* Court seemed to be treating that provision and Section 10(b) as coextensive.

Section 9 of the 34 Act provides broad powers to the SEC and was explicitly addressed to manipulation, a subject that seems to be an afterthought in Rule 10b-5.[61] Section 9 was specifically designed "to prevent rigging of the market and to permit operation of the natural law of supply

---

53. Ernst & Ernst v. Hochfelder, 425 U.S. 185, 199 (1976).

54. S. Craig Pirrong, David Haddock, & Roger Kormendi, *Maintaining the Integrity of Grain Futures Contracts: The Economics of Manipulation and Its* Prevention, at p. 80, Conference on Market Manipulation: Law, Economics, and Public Policy, sponsored by the Center for Study of Futures and Options Markets and the American Bar Association, Washington, DC (Nov. 8–9, 1990).

55. Santa Fe v. Green, 430 U.S. 462 (1977).

56. 430 U.S. at 476-477. *See also*, Schreiber v. Burlington Northern Inc., 472 U.S., 12 (1985) (the term "manipulative" as used in § 14(e) of the 34 Act, 15 U.S.C. § 78n(e), the antifraud provision for tender offers, "requires misrepresentation or nondisclosure. It connotes 'conduct designed to deceive or defraud investors by controlling or artificially affecting the price of securities,'" citing *Hochfelder*). *See also*, Norman S. Poser, *Stock Market Manipulation and Corporate Control Transactions*, 40 U. MIAMI L. REV. 6, 715-720 (1986) (describing differences between deceptive and manipulative conduct); THOMAS LEE HAZEN, TREATISE ON THE LAW OF SECURITIES REGULATION § 12.1[1][B] (4th ed. 2002) (arguing that *Schreiber* should not be extended to Section 10(b) of the 34 Act).

57. Chiarella v. United States, 445 U.S. 222, 234-235 (1980).

58. *See generally*, O'Neill v. Maytag, 339 F.2d 764, 768 (2d Cir. 1964) (Rule 10b-5 is not a "mandate to inquire into every allegation of breach of fiduciary duty respecting the issuance or sale of corporate securities").

59. 430 U.S. at 476.

60. 15 U.S.C. § 78i. *See generally*, Crane v. Westinghouse Air Brake Co. 419 F.2d 787, 794 (2d Cir. 1969), *cert. denied*, 400 U.S. 822 (1970) (discussing application of Section 9 of the 34 Act); United States v. Stein, 456 F.2d 844, 850-851 (2d Cir. 1969) (same); SEC v. Resch-Cassin & Co., 362 F. Supp. 964, 976 (S.D.N.Y. 1973) (same).

61. For a discussion of the elements needed to prove a claim of manipulation under Section 9 of the Securities Exchange Act of 1934, see Chemetron Corp. v. Business Funds Inc., 682 F.2d 1149, 1164 (5th Cir. 1982), *vacated on other grounds*, 460 U.S. 1007 (1983).

and demand."[62] Section 9 sought to prevent the creation of a price "mirage" rather than the reflection of a genuine demand.[63] The same has been said to be true of Section 10(b). "This prohibition with respect to manipulative activity is not confined to any particular kind of manipulation, but as more specifically defined in Rule 10b-5 is necessarily designed to outlaw every device 'used to persuade the public that activity in a security is the reflection of a genuine demand instead of a mirage."[64] Nevertheless, as noted by a leading treatise, the concept of manipulation under the 34 Act "is a narrow one and does not extend to many acts and practices which have the effect of manipulating the price of a security but are not so intended."[65]

In *Alabama Farm Bureau Mutual Casualty Co. v. American Fidelity Life Insurance Co.*,[66] the Fifth Circuit held that the *Santa* Fe decision did not preclude application of Rule 10b-5 to a claim that defendant corporate officers had engaged in a share buyback scheme in order to preserve their corporate positions. The court held that even if this conduct was not a "manipulative" device within the meaning of Rule 10b-5, there was "deception" in the defendants' misrepresentation and omissions concerning the fact that the repurchases would be conducted in a manner that would artificially inflate the price of the stock in order to benefit the defendants personally.[67] This decision seemed to suggest that a failure to disclose would be substituted for defining manipulation as a "term of art."

The SEC also subsequently gave a vaguer and broader definition of manipulation under Section 10(b) than that described in the *Santa Fe* decision. The SEC defined manipulation as the "'intentional interference with the free forces of supply and demand.' In determining whether a manipulation has occurred, we have 'depended on inferences drawn from a mass of factual detail' including 'patterns of behavior,' 'apparent irregularities, and from trading data.' We also have noted that the 'earmarks' of a manipulation often include 'a rapid price surge dictated by the firm that controlled the security's market, little investor interest, an abundant supply, and the absence of any known prospects for the issuer or favorable developments affecting it.'"[68]

In another case, *In the Matter of J.A.B. Securities Co. Inc.*,[69] which involved a short selling scheme, the SEC further confused manipulation with fraud. The SEC noted that "[m]anipulation strikes at the integrity of the pricing process on which all investors rely. Hence it runs counter to the basic objectives of the securities laws."[70] The SEC quoted a Senate committee report on the 34 Act that stated that its purpose was "to purge the securities exchanges of those practices which have prevented them from fulfilling their primary function of furnishing open markets for securities where supply and demand may freely meet at prices uninfluenced by manipulation or control." The

62. United States v. Stein, 456 F.2d 844, 850 (2d Cir. 1972), *cert. denied*, 408 U.S. 922 (1973).

63. United States v. Stein, 456 F.2d 844, 850 (2d Cir. 1972), citing S. Rep. No. 1455, 73d Cong., 2d Sess. 54 (1934).

64. SEC v. Resch-Cassin & Co., 362 F. Supp. 964, 975 (S.D.N.Y. 1973) (quoting 3 Louis Loss, Securities Regulation, 1549-1555 (2d ed. 1961)). Accord, SEC v. Kimmes, 799 F. Supp. 852, 859 N.D. Ill. 1992), *aff'd sub nom. on other grounds*, SEC v. Quinn, 997 F.2d 287 (7th Cir. 1993). Price mirages have also been of concern under the Commodity Exchange Act. *See*, Minpeco S.A. v. ContiCommodity Services Inc., 552 F. Supp. 332, 337, (S.D.N.Y. 1982).

65. Thomas Lee Hazen, Treatise on the Law of Securities Regulation § 12.1[1][2][A] at p. 334 (4th ed. 2002).

66. Alabama Farm Bureau Mutual Casualty Co. v. American Fidelity Life Insurance Co., 606 F.2d 602 (5th Cir. 1979), *cert. denied*, 449 U.S. 820 (1980).

67. 606 F.2d at 613.

68. Brooklyn Capital & Securities Trading Inc., 52 S.E.C. 1286, 1290 (1997) (footnotes and citations omitted).

69. In the Matter of J.A.B. Securities Co. Inc., 47 S.E.C. 86, 91 (1979) (citations omitted).

70. 47 S.E.C. at 93.

SEC also stated that "Rule 10b-5 prohibits market manipulations as well as the failure to disclose them . . . [and] that the '[f]ailure to disclose that market prices are being artificially depressed operates as a deceit on the market place and is an omission of a material fact.'"[71]

In *Pagel Inc. v. SEC*,[72] the Eighth Circuit expressed agreement with the SEC's view that when "individuals occupying a dominant market position engage in a scheme to distort the price of a security for their own benefit, they violate the securities laws by perpetrating a fraud on all public investors."[73] However, the Second Circuit in *Frigitemp Corp. v. Financial Dynamics Fund*[74] stated that it "need not accept the legal conclusion of the complaint that the appellees 'manipulated' the stock, for massive buying for investment need not be synonymous with unlawful manipulation. Since the appellees apparently bought almost all the shares that were theoretically available, they were presumably the only major buyers. When they decided to sell at the high price they themselves had created, they simply came up against the proverbial question: 'Sell to whom?'"

Despite the limitations imposed by *Hochfelder* and other restrictive decisions by the Supreme Court on Section 10(b), the government continued to eschew prosecutions under Section 9, in favor of Section 10(b) of the 34 Act and Section 17(a) of the 33 Act.[75] An electronic search finds only five SEC injunctive actions brought under Section 9 in the decade beginning in 1970, and all five were combined with charges under Section 10(b) of the 34 Act and Section 17(a) of the 33 Act.[76] A criminal case was also brought in the 1970s under Section 9 of the 34 Act and Section 17(a) of the 33 Act and convictions were upheld on charges of a long manipulation.[77] Apparently, only three reported court cases were brought by the SEC in the 1980s under Section 9.[78]

---

71. 47 S.E.C. at 93, *quoting* S. Rep. No. 1455, 73d Cong., 2d Sess. 81 (1934). *See also*, In the Matter of Patten Securities Corp., 51 S.E.C. 568, 572 (1993) ("Manipulation is the deceptive movement of a security's price, accomplished by an intentional interference with the forces of supply and demand" (citations and footnotes omitted)); In the Matter of Pace, 51 S.E.C. 361, 363 (1993) ("The effect of the scheme was to suspend the normal interplay of market forces, and to cause a misleading appearance that there was sufficient market interest in the security to sustain a price that was, in fact, not an accurate reflection of the security's worth" (footnote and citation omitted); Guarny v. Winehouse, 190 F.3d 37, 45 (2d Cir. 1999) ("The gravamen of manipulation is deception of investors into believing that prices at which they purchase and sell securities are determined by the natural interplay of supply and demand, not rigged by manipulators").

72. Pagel Inc. v. SEC, 803 F.2d 942, 946 (8th Cir. 1986).

73. *See also*, In the Matter of Rooney, Pace Inc., 48 S.E.C. 891 (1987) (distorting market prices through domination and creation of an "in-house market" in new stock issue violated Section 10(b) of the 34 Act and Section 17(a) of the 33 Act).

74. Frigitemp Corp. v. Financial Dynamics Fund, 524 F.2d 275, 277, n. 1 (2d Cir. 1975).

75. *See, e.g.*, Pagel Inc. v. SEC, 803 F.2d 942 (8th Cir. 1986) (affirming SEC finding of manipulation violations under those statutes); SEC v. Cooper, 402 F. Supp. 516 (S.D.N.Y. 1975) (finding manipulation in violation of those statutes); SEC v. Electronics Warehouse Inc., 689 F. Supp. 53 (D. Conn. 1988), *aff'd per curiam sub nom.*, SEC v. Calvo, 891 F.2d 457 (2d Cir. 1989), *cert. denied*, 496 U.S. 942 (1990) (same); SEC v. Charles A. Morris & Associates Inc., 386 F. Supp. 1327 (W.D. Tenn. 1973) (same).

76. SEC v. General Host Corp., 483 F. Supp. 105 (S.D.N.Y. 1977); SEC v. Lummis, 1977 U.S. Dist. LEXIS 12783 (N.D. Cal. 1977); SEC v. Rega, 1975 U.S. Dist. LEXIS 11581 (S.D.N.Y. 1975); SEC v. D'Onofrio, 1975 U.S. Dist. LEXIS 12081 (S.D.N.Y. 1975); SEC v. Resch-Cassin & Co., 362 F. Supp. 964, 978 (S.D.N.Y. 1973).

77. United States v. Projansky, 465 F.2d 123 (2d Cir.), *cert. denied*, 409 U.S. 1006 (1972). *See also*, United States v. Quinn, 445 F.2d 940 (2d Cir.), *cert. denied*, 404 U.S. 850 (1971) (convictions affirmed for violations of Section 17(a) of the 33 Act and Section 9 of the 34 Act for manipulation scheme to sell unregistered stock of a company traded on the Salt Lake Stock Exchange).

78. SEC v. Drexel Burnham Lambert Inc., 1989 U.S. Dist. LEXIS 10414 (S.D.N.Y. 1989); SEC v. Manus, 1981 U.S. Dist. LEXIS 15317 (S.D.N.Y. 1981); SEC v. Pattiz, 1981 U.S. Dist. LEXIS 11626 (S.D.N.Y. 1981). *See also*, In the Matter of Baterman, 46 S.E.C. 304 (1976) (consent to findings of violations of Section 9 and 10(b) of the 34 Act in connection with put and call wash trades and matched orders).

The courts have only lightly considered the interplay between Sections 9 and 10(b) of the 34 Act. This is because there have been only a few challenges to the SEC's ability to apply Section 10(b) and Rule 10b-5 to activities that are clearly within the ambit of Section 9.[79] In *Schaefer v. First National Bank*,[80] the Seventh Circuit held that a plaintiff could bring a private right of action under Section 10(b) of the 34 Act even though Section 9 specifically prohibited the conduct at issue. The Second Circuit later stated in *Ross v. A. H. Robins Co.*[81] that, notwithstanding such authority, "we believe that this position is overly broad in light of more recent Supreme Court decisions which have cast considerable doubt on the continuing vitality of the view that the remedies in the securities acts were meant to freely overlap." However, the Supreme Court in *Herman & Maclean v. Huddleston*[82] ruled that a cause of action could be brought under Section 10(b) of the 34 Act even though the conduct at issue was covered by Section 11 of the 33 Act, which provides for private remedies for misrepresentations made in registration statements.[83]

In *Chemetron Corp. v. Business Funds Inc.*,[84] the Fifth Circuit held that a Rule 10b-5 claim would not be permitted where it would nullify the limitations of Section 9 for an express right of action. However, the Supreme Court vacated that decision for reconsideration in light of the *Huddleston* decision.[85] On remand, the Fifth Circuit held that rights under Section 9 and Rule 10b-5 could be cumulative.[86] The *Chemetron* court also held that the following elements are required to prove a Section 9 claim by a private litigant: "(1) a series of transactions in a security creating actual or apparent trading in that security or raising or depressing the price of that security, (2) carried out with scienter (3) for the purpose of inducing the security's sale or purchase by others, (4) was relied on by the plaintiff, (5) and affected the plaintiff's purchase or selling price."[87]

A more serious hurdle was addressed in *The Rockies Fund Inc. v. SEC*.[88] The D.C. Circuit held in that case that Section 9 of the 34 Act imposed a specific intent requirement, while the prohibitions in Rule 10b-5 imposed a lesser standard of extreme recklessness. "In other words, extreme recklessness requires a stronger showing than simple recklessness but does not rise to the level of specific intent . . . , [which] could potentially have significant effects on the interplay between Section 10(b) and Section 9(a)(1) and SEC actions under each provision."[89] The defendant argued

---

79. For examples of manipulation schemes addressed by the SEC, *see, e.g.*, SEC v. U.S. Environmental Inc., 155 F.3d 107 (2d Cir. 1998) (wash sales and matched orders); Graham v. SEC, 222 F.3d 994 (D.C. Cir. 2000) (wash sale manipulation scheme); SEC v. Duchesne, 2007 WL 2349907 (D.D.C. 2007) (manipulation involving matched trades and false public statements); United States v. Downing, 297 F.3d 52 (3d Cir. 2002) (upholding convictions under a pump-and-dump scheme); Emergent Capital Investment Management LLC v. Stonepath Group Inc., 2003 WL 22053957 (2d Cir. 2003) (upholding allegations of loss causation in pump-and-dump scheme). *See also*, Tager V. SEC, 344 F.2d 5 (2d Cir. 1965) (fictitious quotations in the pink sheets in order to assist the selling of a securities issue). *See generally*, Judith R. Starr & David Herman, *The Same Old Wine in a Brand New Bottle: Applying Traditional Market Manipulation Principles to Internet Stock Scams*, 29 Sec. Reg. L. J. 236 (2001).

80. Schaefer v. First National Bank, 509 F.2d 1287, 1292-1293 (7th Cir. 1975), *cert. denied*, 425 U.S. 943 (1976).

81. Ross v. A. H. Robins Co., 607 F.2d 545, 554 (2d Cir. 1979), *cert. denied*, 446 U.S. 946 (1980).

82. Herman & Maclean v. Huddleston, 459 U.S. 375, 387 (1983).

83. 15 U.S.C. § 77k.

84. Chemetron Corp. v. Business Funds Inc., 682 F.2d 1149, 1169 (5th Cir. 1982).

85. Chemetron Corp. v. Business Funds Inc., 460 U.S. 1007 (1983).

86. Chemetron Corp. v. Business Funds Inc., 718 F.2d 725 (5th Cir. 1983).

87. 682 F.2d at 1164. *Accord*: Ray v. Lehman Brothers Kuhn Loeb Inc. 624 F. Supp. 16, 23 (N.D. Ga. 1984).

88. 428 F.3d 1088 (D.C. Cir. 2005).

89. 428 F.3d at 1093.

that to apply the lower extreme recklessness standard to practices prohibited specifically by Section 9 would undermine the specific intent standard in that section.

The court in *The Rockies Fund* case found it unnecessary to determine which standard applied because the SEC failed to prove intent under either standard. This left that issue open for consideration in future actions by the SEC—that is, should the SEC or private plaintiffs be allowed to bring an action under Section 10(b) that should have been more appropriately brought under Section 9 in order to obtain a lesser burden of proof? In other words, does the SEC have the power to amend, and effectively delete, the scienter requirements of Section 9 by bringing actions under Rule 10b-5 over conduct, such as wash trades, that is specifically addressed in Section 9?

5:5 THE MATERIALITY REQUIREMENT

Another requirement imposed by the Supreme Court on Rule 10b-5 actions is that of "materiality," which is frequently, and often successfully, raised as a defense in actions under the federal securities laws.[90] As the Supreme Court held in *Basic Inc. v. Levinson*,[91] the materiality element requires the plaintiff to show that there "was a substantial likelihood that a reasonable shareholder would consider it [disclosure of the deceptive conduct] important in deciding how to vote."[92] This requirement may bring market power back into the equation for proving manipulation, since false reports or trades that had an immaterial effect on the market would not rise to the level of fraud.

Materiality means that "there must be a substantial likelihood that the disclosure of the omitted fact would have been viewed by the reasonable investor as having significantly altered the 'total mix' of information made available."[93] "It is not enough that a statement is false or incomplete, if the misrepresented fact is otherwise insignificant."[94] The materiality requirement has significance for manipulation claims. For example, an act or misrepresentation that is claimed to be manipulative must be material. This requires a determination of whether a reasonable investor would find the information to be significant.

It has been asserted that "the amorphous legal standard of materiality lies at the heart of securities law."[95] The materiality element excludes information of "dubious significance" and seeks not to set too low a standard that "might bring an overabundance of information within its reach."[96] In *United States v. Gaudin*,[97] the Supreme Court stated that determining the existence of materiality requires an "application-of-legal-standard-to-fact" solution, "commonly called a 'mixed question of law and fact,' [that] has typically been resolved by juries." Its resolution requires "delicate assessments of the inferences a 'reasonable [decision maker]' would draw from a given set of facts and the significance of those inferences to him, . . . [is] peculiarly one for the trier of fact."[98]

90. David A. Hoffman, *The "Duty" to Be a Rational Shareholder*, 90 Minn. L. Rev. 537, 563-564 (2006); Stephen M. Bainbridge & G. Mitu Gulati, *How Do Judges Maximize? (The Same Way Everybody Else Does—Boundedly): Rules of Thumb in Securities Fraud Opinions*, 51 Emory L.J. 83, 116 n. 94 (2002).

91. Basic Inc. v. Levinson, 485 U.S. 224 (1988).

92. 485 U.S. at 231, quoting from TSC Industries Inc. v. Northway Inc., 426 U.S. 438 (1976), which adopted a materiality standard for other provisions of the 34 Act.

93. 485 U.S. at 231-231.

94. 485 U.S. at 238.

95. Erik F. Gerding, *The Next Epidemic: Bubbles and the Growth and Decay of Securities Regulation*, 38 Conn. L. Rev. 393 438 (2006).

96. Basic Inc. v. Levinson, 485 U.S. 224, 231 (1988).

97. United States v. Gaudin, 515 U.S. 506, 512 (1995).

98. 515 U.S. at 512, quoting TSC Industries Inc. v. Northway Inc., 426 U.S. 438, 450 (1976).

The Supreme Court added further uncertainty by rejecting any "bright line" tests for establishing materiality under Rule 10b-5.[99]

The Supreme Court further held in *Virginia Bankshares Inc. v. Sandberg*[100] that, in order to avoid psychological examinations, disbelief or undisclosed motivation is not considered material. Nevertheless, conclusory, qualitative opinions may be material. In another case, *Matrixx Initiatives Inc. v. Siracusano*,[101] the Supreme Court held that even unproven reports of adverse facts or reports that have not been shown to be statistically significant may be material.

The materiality requirement is most often raised in private actions, but is also applicable to SEC enforcement actions. As the Supreme Court has stated, "[w]e find no authority in the statute, the legislative history, or our previous decisions, for varying the standard of materiality depending on who brings the action."[102] Consequently, "[i]t is not enough . . . for the SEC to point to a false statement—the misrepresentation must concern a material fact."[103] The materiality requirement has also been applied to a criminal action under Rule 10b-5.[104]

5:6 THE RELIANCE ELEMENT

Another element required for a private plaintiff to prove a Rule 10b-5 claim is reliance upon the misrepresentation or omission. "Reliance by the plaintiff upon the defendant's deceptive acts is an essential element of the § 10(b) private cause of action. It ensures that, for liability to arise, the 'requisite causal connection between a defendant's misrepresentation and a plaintiff's injury' exists as a predicate for liability."[105] Such reliance must be reasonable.[106]

Reliance arises in two contexts: affirmative misrepresentations and failures to disclose a material fact. The "traditional (and most direct) way a plaintiff can demonstrate reliance is by showing that he was aware of a company's statement and engaged in a relevant transaction—*e.g.*, purchasing common stock—based on that specific misrepresentation."[107]

Failures to disclose raise more complex issues in proving reliance on such a nonaffirmative act. The Supreme Court has sought to ease that burden by finding a rebuttable presumption of reliance in two circumstances where omissions are involved. "First, if there is an omission of a material fact by one with a duty to disclose, the investor to whom the duty was owed need not provide specific proof of reliance."[108] In *Affiliated Ute Citizens v. United States*,[109] the Supreme

---

99. Basic Inc. v. Levinson, 485 U.S. 224, 236 (1988); Matrixx Initiatives Inc. v. Siracusano, 563 U.S. ---, --- (2011).

100. Virginia Bankshares Inc. v. Sandberg, 501 U.S. 1083 (1991).

101. Matrixx Initiatives Inc. v. Siracusano, 563 U.S. --- (2011).

102. Basic Inc. v. Levinson, 485 U.S. 224, 241, n. 18 (1988).

103. United States SEC v. Pirate Investor LLC, 580 F.3d 233, 240 (4th Cir. 2009), *cert. denied*, ---U.S. --- (2010); SEC v. Phan, 500 F.3d 895, 908 (9th Cir.2007); SEC v. Ginsburg, 362 F.3d 1292, 1302 (11th Cir. 2004); SEC v. First Jersey Sec. Inc., 101 F.3d 1450, 1467 (2d Cir. 1996), *cert. denied*, 522 U.S. 812 (1997).

104. United States v. Bingham, 992 F.2d 975, 976-977 (9th Cir. 1993) (per curiam) (reversing a criminal conviction under Rule 10b-5 because the government's expert testimony was "far too abstract to satisfy the materiality requirement" given other information about the stock at issue that was available to investors).

105. Stoneridge Inv. Partners LLC v. Scientific-Atlanta Inc., 552 U.S. 148, 159 (2008) (citation omitted). *Accord*: Erica P. John Fund Inc. v. Halliburton Co., --- U.S. ---, --- (2011).

106. *See, e.g.*, Banca Cremi, S.A. v. Alex Brown & Sons Inc., 132 F.3d 1017 (4th Cir. 1997) (reliance by sophisticated investor was not reasonable); Schlesinger v. Herzog, 2 F.3d 135 (5th Cir. 1993) (plaintiff did not use due diligence).

107. Erica P. John Fund Inc. v. Halliburton Co., 563 U.S. ---, --- (2011).

108. Stoneridge Inv. Partners LLC v. Scientific-Atlanta Inc., 552 U.S. 148, 159 (2008) (citation omitted).

109. 406 U.S. 128 (1972).

Court thus held that cases under Rule 10b-5 "involving primarily a failure to disclose, positive proof of reliance is not a prerequisite to recovery. All that is necessary is that the facts withheld be material . . . . This obligation to disclose and this withholding of a material fact establish the requisite element of causation in fact."[110]

The reliance standard was considerably weakened by something called the "fraud-on-the-market doctrine," in which reliance is presumed when the statements at issue become public because that information will be "reflected in the market price of the security."[111] On the vote of four of its nine members, the Supreme Court in *Basic Inc. v. Levinson*[112] adopted the fraud-on-the-market theory to establish a rebuttable presumption of reliance. This theory was based on what appeared to be a sophisticated economic analysis of market efficiency.[113]

The Supreme Court stated in *Basic* that an "investor who buys or sells stock at the price set by the market does so in reliance on the integrity of that price. Because most publicly available information is reflected in market price, an investor's reliance on any public material misrepresentations, therefore, may be presumed for purposes of a Rule 10b-5 action."[114] However, even the justices in the majority in *Basic* that supported this theory conceded that the market efficiency theory might have some shortcomings. The majority opinion noted that there "may be a certain incongruity between the assumption that Basic shares are traded on a well-developed, efficient, and information-hungry market, and the allegation that such a market could remain misinformed, and its valuation of Basic shares depressed, for 14 months, on the basis of the three public statements."[115]

The *Basic* majority blew that concern off as a matter to be sorted out at trial,[116] but Justice White, in dissent, was less forgiving in the flaws that might be concealed in this untried theory. He pointed out that "the fraud-on-the-market theory was a mere babe" in economic thought.[117] Justice White stated that, "while the economists' theories which underpin the fraud-on-the-market presumption may have the appeal of mathematical exactitude and scientific certainty, they are—in the end—nothing more than theories which may or may not prove accurate upon further consideration. Even the most earnest advocates of economic analysis of the law recognize this."[118] Justice White also noted that, ironically, the advocates of the fraud-on-the-market theory had used it as an

---

110. 406 U.S. at 153-154.

111. Stoneridge Inv. Partners LLC v. Scientific-Atlanta Inc., 552 U.S. 148, 159 (2008) (citation omitted).

112. 485 U.S. 224 (1988).

113. The Supreme Court stated in justification of the adoption of this theory:

> The modern securities markets, literally involving millions of shares changing hands daily, differ from the face-to-face transactions contemplated by early fraud cases, and our understanding of Rule 10b-5's reliance requirement must encompass these differences. "In face-to-face transactions, the inquiry into an investor's reliance upon information is into the subjective pricing of that information by that investor. With the presence of a market, the market is interposed between seller and buyer and, ideally, transmits information to the investor in the processed form of a market price. Thus the market is performing a substantial part of the valuation process performed by the investor in a face-to-face transaction. The market is acting as the unpaid agent of the investor, informing him that given all the information available to it, the value of the stock is worth the market price."

485 U.S. at 243-244.

114. 485 U.S. at 247.

115. 485 U.S. at 249, n. 29.

116. 485 U.S. at 249, n. 29.

117. 485 U.S. at 250.

118. 485 U.S. at 254.

argument for displacing government. Those proponents argued that markets were more efficient than government in punishing wrongdoers because an efficient market would expose their conduct and undercut their fraudulent schemes. However, the majority in *Basic* turned that theory on its head to broaden the reach of Rule 10b-5.[119]

The Supreme Court granted *certiorari* in *Amgen Inc. v. Connecticut Retirement Plans & Trust Funds*,[120] to determine whether class action plaintiffs must prove materiality before the claims they make can be certified for adjudication. This case provided the Court with an opportunity to revisit the fraud-on-the-market theory. The Supreme Court subsequently ruled that direct proof of reliance was not needed in order to have a class-action certified. The court held that the fraud-on-the-market theory "facilitates class certification by recognizing a rebuttable presumption of classwide reliance on public, material misrepresentations when shares are traded in an efficient market."[121] This decision was accompanied by a concurring opinion from Justice Samuel Alito, which stated that recent evidence suggested that the fraud-on-the-market theory may rest on faulty economic grounds. He thought that reconsideration of that theory might, therefore, be appropriate in a future case.

The fraud-on-the-market theory, in all events, has proved to be controversial. Among other things, it was blamed for an explosion in class action litigation abuses.[122] Questions have also been raised over whether particular markets are sufficiently efficient to reflect misstatements or omissions that are not made directly to a purchaser or seller.[123] On a broader front, critics have questioned whether securities markets as an overall matter are as efficient as claimed by the Supreme Court in *Basic Inc*. The fraud-on-the-market theory evolved from the so-called Chicago school of law and economics, which posited that markets are more efficient regulators than government. Market discipline, it was urged, would force rational action on market participants. The emergence of the Chicago school of thought set off a decades-long debate in legal academia between its adherents and its critics who preferred government regulation and judge-made fiduciary duties over market discipline.[124] The Chicago school was gaining ascendance until economists and scientists began questioning its premises. An "efficient" market assumes that its prices reflect all available information. In contrast, an "inefficient market, by definition, does not incorporate into its price all the available information about the value of a security."[125] Critics argue that securities markets are, at best, only semistrong in efficiency because they do not reflect inside information.[126]

---

119. 485 U.S. at 259.

120. *Amgen Inc. v. Connecticut Retirement Plans & Trust Funds*, 132 S. Ct. 2742 (2012).

121. *Amgen Inc. v. Connecticut Retirement Plans & Trust Funds*, --- U.S. --- (2013).

122. Barbara Black, *Eliminating Securities Fraud Class Actions Under the Radar*, 2009 COLUM. BUS. L. REV. 802, 809.

123. *See, e.g.*, Unger v. Amedisys Inc., 401 F.3d 316 (5th Cir. 2005) (discussing the factors to consider in determining whether the market for a stock is efficient). *See also*, Eckstein v. Balcor, Film Investors, 8 F.3d 1121 (7th Cir.1993) (discussing the split among the circuits over a "fraud-created-the-market" theory premising that fraud permitted an issue of securities to trade in the market and that, but for the fraud, the securities would have been "unmarketable" and that the investor relied on their existence).

124. One of the controversial issues raised by the Chicago school adherents was their criticism of the SEC's insider trading prohibition. HENRY MANNE, INSIDER TRADING AND THE STOCK MARKET (1966); Jonathan Macey, *Getting the Word Out About Fraud: A Theoretical Analysis of Whistleblowing and Insider Trading*, 105 MICH. L. REV. 1899 (2007). For a rebuttal of those views, *see, e.g.*, Robert A. Prentice & Dain C. Donelson, *Insider Trading as a Signaling Device*, 47 AM. BUS. L.J. 1 (2010).

125. Freeman v. Laventhol & Horwath, 915 F.2d 193, 198 (6th Cir. 1990).

126. *See generally*, Eugene F. Fama, *Efficient Capital Markets: A Review of Theory and Empirical Work*, 25 J. OF FIN. 383, 388 (1970) (describing three forms of market efficiency determined by the amount of information available: strong, semistrong, and weak).

Economists also began attacking the premises of the fraud-on-the-market-theory. Those critics pointed out that rational actors, as erroneously premised by efficient market theorists, are not the only ones that determine market prices. Rather, markets are skewed by, among other things, "noise" traders, who are uninformed individuals making sometimes irrational decisions.[127]As described in Chapter 4, flaws in the efficient market theory led to the behavioral theory school of thought. Behavioral finance adherents argue, based on cognitive psychology and decision-making theories, that market prices are affected by human behavior that, at times, is irrational and exploitive.[128]

The fraud-on-the-market theory raises other issues.[129] Securities law fraud plaintiffs must prove certain things in order to invoke the rebuttable presumption of reliance laid down in *Basic*. "It is common ground, for example, that plaintiffs must demonstrate that the alleged misrepresentations were publicly known (else how would the market take them into account?), that the stock traded in an efficient market, and that the relevant transaction took place 'between the time the misrepresentations were made and the time the truth was revealed.'"[130] "To invoke this presumption, the plaintiffs seeking . . . [class action] certification must prove that their shares were traded on an efficient market, . . . , an issue they will surely have to prove *again* at trial in order to make out their case on the merits."[131]

In addition, the courts have also long held that there is no duty to disclose information to one who should reasonably be aware of it.[132] Rule 10b-5 does not protect nondisclosed facts equally available to both parties.[133] This would include taking cognizance of information printed in newspapers that negates omitted or misleading information.[134] These rules have played into the

---

127. *See generally, e.g.*, J. Bradford De Long et al., *Noise Trader Risk in Financial Markets*, 98 J. POLIT. ECON 703 (1990). *But see*, Daniel R. Fischel, *Program Trading, Volatility, Portfolio Insurance, and the Role of Specialists and Market Makers: Efficient Capital Markets, the Crash, and the Fraud on the Market Theory*, 74 CORNELL L. REV. 907 (1989) (rebutting critics of efficient market theories who claimed "noise" traders interfere with market efficiency).

128. It has been noted:

> During the last three decades, while law faculties across the nation were succumbing to the brilliant simplicity of the Coase theorem and the analytical force of the law and economics movement, social scientists in other departments were discovering evidence that should have given pause to even the most ardent legal positivist. Those scientists—cognitive psychologists, behavioral researchers, probability theorists, and others—were discovering powerful evidence that the rational actor model, upon which the law and economics model depends, is significantly flawed. In place of the rational actor model, those scientists were developing a human decision maker model replete with heuristics and biases, unwarranted self-confidence, a notable ineptitude for probability, and a host of other nonrational cognitive features.

John D. Hanson & Douglas A. Kysar, *Taking Behavioralism Seriously: The Problem of Market Manipulation*, 74 N.Y.U.L. REV. 630, 640 (1999). *See also*, Frederick C. Dunbar & Dana Heller, *Fraud on the Market Meets Behavioral Finance*, 31 DEL. J. CORP. L. 455 (2006) (describing effects of behavioral finance on the fraud-on-the-market theory).

129. *See generally*, Donald C. Langevoort, *Theories, Assumptions, and Securities Regulation: Market Efficiency Revisited*, 140 U. PA. L. REV. 851(1992) (discussing concerns about overcompensation of plaintiffs under the fraud-on-the-market theory).

130. Erica P. John Fund Inc. v. Halliburton Co., 563 U.S. ---, --- (2011) (citation omitted).

131. Wal-Mart Stores Inc. v. Dukes, 564 U.S. ---, n. 6 (2011), citing Erica P. John Fund Inc. v. Halliburton Co., --- U.S. ---, --- (2011).

132. *See, e.g.*, Selbert v. Sperry Rand Corp., 586 F.2d 949, 952 (2d Cir. 1978) (citing numerous cases).

133. Sailor v. Northern States Power Co., 4 F.3d 610, 612 (8th Cir. 1993).

134. Heliotrope Gen. Inc. v. Ford Motor Co., 189 F.3d 971, 981, n. 18 (9th Cir. 1999) (taking judicial notice of newspaper articles in finding disclosure).

fraud-on-the-market theory. For example, the Ninth Circuit held in *In re Apple Securities Litigation*[135] that "the defendant's failure to disclose material information may be excused where that information has been made credibly available to the market by other sources" such as widely circulated newspapers or magazines.

The defendants in the *Apple Securities Litigation* were charged with making overly optimistic statements about the performance of computer products that were to be introduced to the market. The defendants contended that newspaper articles had widely questioned those claims, and that this publicity negated materiality and reliance. The Ninth Circuit agreed, at least to certain claims, holding that such publicly available information had to be included in the total mix of information. Once it was included, the fraud-on-the-market theory created a rebuttable presumption that the negative news reports were reflected in the stock price.

This is called the "truth-on-the-market" defense.[136] "Under this corollary, a misrepresentation is immaterial if the information is already known to the market because the misrepresentation cannot then defraud the market."[137] For example, the Second Circuit has ruled that a manipulation claim under Rule 10b-5 cannot be sustained where there is disclosure in the publicly available documents and the website of the issuer and in SEC and newspaper reports. Those disclosures stated that an underwriter of auction rate securities could intervene and artificially support the auction process when interest rates were periodically reset for those securities. In that case, the underwriter had the market power to set an artificial price.[138] Nevertheless, the Supreme Court has noted that not every mixture of true and false information will negate the false statements: "[N]ot every mixture with the true will neutralize the deceptive. If it would take a financial analyst to spot the tension between the one and the other, whatever is misleading will remain materially so, and liability should follow."[139]

The reliance and materiality elements have implications for fraud-based manipulation claims under Rule 10b-5. For example, widespread newspaper reports that short sellers are manipulating the price of a stock downward or that a particular individual (later a defendant) was attacking the market could negate reliance on actions by the defendant. Similarly, false statistics given to a publication may be rendered immaterial if this was a widely known practice or if the market had received hard information that the price was artificial.

On a different note, the government seeks to avoid the burden of proving the reliance element under Rule 10b-5 on the grounds that it is acting in the public interest and should not have to

---

135. 886 F.2d 1109 (9th Cir. 1989), *cert. denied sub nom.*, Schneider v. Apple Computer Inc., 496 U.S. 942 (1990). *See also*, Rubke v. Capitol Bancorp. Ltd., 551 F.3d 1156, 1162-63 (9th Cir 2009).

136. As one article notes:

> The Second, Fourth, Fifth, Seventh, and Ninth Circuits have expressly recognized the truth on the market defense. This defense recognizes that if the market has become aware of concealed information, the facts omitted by defendant would already be reflected in the stock's price and the market will not be misled. Some courts have held that a defendant may rebut fraud on the market by proof that information challenging the misrepresentation was readily available. However, to ensure that the challenging information was entered "credibly" into the market, the defendant may have to show that the withheld or misrepresented information was "transmitted to the public with a degree of intensity and credibility sufficient to effectively counterbalance any misleading impression created by [the defendant's] one-sided representations."

Palmer T. Heenan et al., *Securities Fraud*, 47 Am. Crim. L. Rev. 1015, 1063 (2010).

137. Ganino v. Citizens Utils. Co., 228 F.3d 154, 167 (2d Cir. 2000).

138. Finn v. Smith Barney, 2012 U.S. App. LEXIS 6185 (2d Cir.) (unpublished decision).

139. Virginia Bankshares Inc. v. Sandberg, 501 U.S. 1083, 1097 (1991).

prove reliance and other elements in its injunctive and administrative proceedings.[140] As the Ninth Circuit noted in *Kramas V. Sec. Gas & Oil Inc.*,[141] "[p]rosecutions and enforcement actions involve interests and procedures different from those involved in private damage suits."[142] Therefore, the Ninth Circuit asserted, the "Government is not 'required to prove that anyone was defrauded or that any investor sustained a loss, but such proof is essential to recovery by a private investor.'"[143]

The viewpoint expressed in *Kramas* might not quite square with the Supreme Court's decision in *Aaron v. SEC*,[144] in which the Supreme Court refused to apply a scienter standard in SEC enforcement actions that would have been less burdensome than that imposed on private plaintiffs. The Court held that the statute reads alike for all plaintiffs, public and private. The Supreme Court noted in *Aaron* that the 34 Act allows the SEC to seek injunctive relief against any person who "is engaged in or *about to engage* in" a violation of the act or regulations and that, "upon a proper showing," a district court shall grant the injunction.[145] The *Aaron* Court held that a "proper showing" includes, "at a minimum, proof that a person is engaged in or is about to engage in a substantive violation of either one of the Acts or of the regulations promulgated thereunder."[146] "Accordingly," this means that, at least "when scienter is an element of the substantive violation sought to be enjoined, it must be proved before an injunction may issue."[147]

5:7 CAUSATION ELEMENTS

The Supreme Court has further limited Section 10(b) of the 34 Act and Rule 10b-5 by imposing causation requirements in private actions.[148] These requirements flow from traditional legal principles that limit recovery of damages to those proximately caused by a wrongdoer's conduct. "It is an instance of the common law's universal requirement that the tort plaintiff prove causation. . . . No hurt, no tort."[149]

---

140. The debate over whether the SEC should be subject to less restrictive standards in its injunctive actions than private plaintiffs is a long-running one. *See, e.g.*, Harvey L. Pitt & Jerry W. Markham, *SEC Civil Injunctive Actions: A Reply*, 6 REV. OF SEC. REG. 955 (1973) (advocating a more lenient standard).

141. 672 F.2d 766 (9th Cir. 1982), *cert. denied*, 495 U.S. 1035 (1982).

142. 672 F.2d at 770 (citation omitted).

143. 672 F.2d at 770 (citation omitted). *See also e.g.*, SEC v. Fife 311 F.3d 1, 9 (1st Cir. 2002), *cert. denied*, 538 U.S. 1031 (2003) (government not required to show reliance in an action brought under Section 17(a) of the 33 Act).

144. 446 U.S. 680, 700-701 (1980).

145. 446 U. S. at 700, citing 15 U.S.C. § 78u(d) (emphasis supplied).

146. 446 U.S. at 700-701.

147. 446 U.S. 701. The CFTC has asserted that reliance is not a requirement in its enforcement actions under Section 4(b) of the Commodity Exchange Act, 7 U.S.C. § 6b, which is the principal antifraud provision in that statute. *See, e.g.*, In the Matter of Global Telecom, Comm. Fut. L. Rep. (CCH) ¶ 30,143 (C.F.T.C. 1991). A district court held, however, that the CFTC was required to prove reliance. CFTC v. American Metals Exchange Corp., 775 F. Supp. 767, 775 (N.J. 1991), *aff'd*, 991 F.2d 1993 (3d Cir. 1993). *But see, e.g.*, CFTC v. R.J. Fitzgerald & Co., 310 F.3d 1321, 1328, n.6 (11th Cir. 2002), *cert. denied*, 543 U.S. 1034 (2004); CFTC v. Commonwealth Financial Group, 874 F. Supp. 1345, 1355 (S.D. Fl. 1994), *vacated and remanded without opinion*, 79 F.3d 1159 (11th Cir. 1996) (district court held reliance not required); CFTC v. AVCO Financial Corp., 28 F. Supp. 2d 104, 115 (S.D.N.Y. 1998), *aff'd in part and remanded sub nom.*, CFTC v. Vartuli, 228 F.3d 94 (2d Cir. 2000) (same); CFTC v. Rosenberg, 85 F. Supp. 2d 424, 446 (D. N.J. 2000) (same); CFTC v. Wilkshire Investment Management Corp., 407 F. Supp. 2d 1304, 1309 (S.D. Fl. 2005) (same).

148. Stoneridge Investment Partners LLC v. Scientific-Atlanta Inc., 552 U. S. 148, 157 (2008); Dura Pharms. Inc. v. Broudo, 544 U.S. 336, 341-342 (2005).

149. Bastian v. Petren Resources Corp., 892 F.2d 680, 683-684 (7th Cir.), *cert. denied*, 496 U.S. 906 (1990) (citations omitted).

The inclusion of a proximate cause standard in Rule 10b-5 actions had been presaged by a Supreme Court decision in *Holmes v. Securities Investor Protection Corp* (SIPC).[150] There, the defendant was a conspirator in a stock-manipulation scheme that resulted in the insolvency of two broker-dealers that, in turn, caused losses to the SIPC insurance fund. SIPC sought damages under the Racketeer Influenced and Corrupt Organizations Act (RICO)[151] The Supreme Court concluded that the conspirators' conduct had not proximately caused injury to customers not trading in the stock being manipulated. The link was too remote between the stock manipulation and the customers' harm, which was purely contingent on the harm suffered by the broker-dealers.

The Supreme Court directly addressed the causation elements of Section 10(b) in *Dura Pharmaceuticals Inc. v. Broudo*,[152] holding that plaintiffs must plead and prove "proximate causation and economic loss" in order to prove a violation.[153] The *Dura* Court rejected a decision by the Ninth Circuit, which held that plaintiffs could establish loss causation merely by proving that the price of the stock on the date of purchase was inflated because of a misrepresentation. The Supreme Court noted that a loss will not be sustained until the shares are sold, and many factors could intervene to prevent a loss.[154] The causation elements require proof that the plaintiff sustained an "economic loss" from a transaction and that there was "loss causation" that is attributable to the defendant's misconduct.[155]

---

150. Holmes v. Securities Investor Protection Corp., 503 U.S. 258 (1992).
151. 18 U.S.C. §§ 1961-1968.
152. 544 U.S. 336 (2005).
153. 544 U.S. at 346.
154. The Court stated:

> Shares are normally purchased with an eye toward a later sale. But if, say, the purchaser sells the shares quickly before the relevant truth begins to leak out, the misrepresentation will not have led to any loss. If the purchaser sells later after the truth makes its way into the marketplace, an initially inflated purchase price *might* mean a later loss. But that is far from inevitably so. When the purchaser subsequently resells such shares, even at a lower price, that lower price may reflect, not the earlier misrepresentation, but changed economic circumstances, changed investor expectations, new industry-specific or firm-specific facts, conditions, or other events, which taken separately or together account for some or all of that lower price. (The same is true in respect to a claim that a share's higher price is lower than it would otherwise have been—a claim we do not consider here.) Other things being equal, the longer the time between purchase and sale, the more likely that this is so, *i.e.*, the more likely that other factors caused the loss.

544 U.S. at 342-343.

155. *See, e.g.*, Stoneridge Investment Partners LLC v. Scientific-Atlanta Inc., 552 U. S. 148, 157 (2008). More specifically, these elements have been described as follows:

> Economic loss. The plaintiff must have suffered measurable monetary damages for which he seeks recovery. As with the common law tort of fraud, such damages must constitute an actual economic loss, and not merely nominal or trivial damages. This element also requires the plaintiff to have already suffered the economic loss; he cannot merely expect a loss in the future.
>
> Loss causation. There must be a causal connection between the defendant's material misrepresentation or omission and the plaintiff's economic loss. That is, the plaintiff's loss must not only be related to the defendant's fraudulent misrepresentation or omission, but actually caused by it. . . . Therefore, the loss causation element requires the plaintiffs to allege and prove that, for example, they bought the stock at a price that was artificially inflated as a result of the defendant's misstatement or omission. This means that the plaintiffs must allege and prove that there is a strong relationship between the defendant's conduct and the plaintiffs' subsequent loss.

Government Accountability Office, GAO-11-664 *Securities Fraud Liability of Secondary Actors* 10, 21 (July 21, 2011) (footnotes omitted). *See also*, Thomas L. Hazen, Securities Regulation § 12:11 (4th ed. 2002).

The injection of these elements by the *Dura Pharmaceuticals* decision into the law of manipulation has been resisted by the lower courts. In *Rosado v. China North East Petroleum Holdings Ltd.*,[156] the Second Circuit held that the fact that a stock's share price recovered soon after a fraud became known does not itself defeat an inference of economic loss in a securities fraud suit under Section 10(b) of the 34 Act. A decision in the Southern District of New York in *In re Initial Public Offering Securities Litigation* declined to apply the *Dura* standard in a market manipulation case under Rule 10b-5:

> [m]anipulative conduct is different. A market manipulation is a discrete act that influences stock price. Once the manipulation ceases, however, the information available to the market is the same as before, and the stock price gradually returns to its true value. For example, suppose that a bank manipulates the market for a stock by engaging in "wash sales," fictitious trading for the purpose of creating a false appearance of activity. By creating an appearance of increased trading volume, wash sales may drive up the price of a security. Once the wash sales cease, ordinary trading resumes. The spectre of wash sales may continue to affect the stock price for some time as investors recall the recent increased activity and observe the higher price; over time, however, the security will fall back to its true investment value.
>
> In market manipulation cases, therefore, it may be permissible to infer that the artificial inflation will inevitably dissipate. . . . It is that dissipation—and not the inflation itself—that [may] cause plaintiffs' loss.[157]

The court in the *Initial Public Offerings* case noted that the "gravamen of plaintiffs' complaint is that the Underwriters manipulated the IPO market to drive up the price of securities, knowing that they were causing the securities to be overvalued and that the stock prices would eventually recede to reflect the actual value of the securities, thereby injuring innocent investors. That is loss causation."[158] In another decision, *In re Platinum and Palladium Commodities Litigation*,[159] the Southern District of New York refused to apply the *Dura* decision to a manipulation claim under the Commodity Exchange Act involving trades made in an illiquid market that were intended to affect the closing price.

The Supreme Court rejected an effort to conflate the reliance and causation elements in *Erica P. John Fund Inc. v. Halliburton Co.*[160] There, the Supreme Court considered the effect of the causation requirement on the rebuttable presumption of reliance under the fraud-on-the-market theory it had previously announced in *Basic Inc. v. Levinson*.[161] The Court held in *Halliburton* that securities fraud plaintiffs need not prove loss causation in order to obtain class certification in a fraud-on-the-market case where reliance is presumed. The Court defined the difference between loss causation and reliance as follows: "[l]oss causation addresses a matter different from whether an investor relied on a misrepresentation, presumptively or otherwise, when buying or selling a stock."[162]

The Court held that the element of reliance in a Rule 10b-5 action is "'transaction causation,' not loss causation."[163] Transaction causation focuses on the investor's decision to

156. Rosado v. China North East Petroleum Holdings Ltd., Fed. Sec. L. Rep. (CCH) ¶ 96,953 (2d Cir. 2012).

157. In re Initial Public Offering Securities Litigation, 297 F. Supp. 2d 668, 674-675 (S.D.N.Y. 2003) (footnote omitted).

158. 297 F. Supp. 2d at 674.

159. In re Platinum and Palladium Commodities Litigation, 2011 WL 4048780 (S.D.N.Y. 2011).

160. Erica P. John Fund Inc. v. Halliburton Co., 563 U.S. --- (2011).

161. 485 U.S. 224 (1988).

162. Erica P. John Fund Inc. v. Halliburton Co., 563 U.S. ---, --- (2011).

163. 563 U.S. at --- (citation omitted).

engage in the transaction. "Loss causation, by contrast, requires a plaintiff to show that a misrepresentation that affected the integrity of the market price *also* caused a subsequent economic loss."[164] The Supreme Court explained in *Halliburton* that a plaintiff might be found to have presumptively relied on an omission under the fraud-on-the-market theory, thereby establishing transaction causation, but loss causation might still prevent recovery, as when the omission is not the cause of a later decline in the value of the stock that causes the loss. The Supreme Court elsewhere noted that the fraud-on-the-market theory involves "transaction causation."[165]

If other factors "were responsible for the loss or part of it, a plaintiff would not be able to prove loss causation to that extent. This is true even if the investor purchased the stock at a distorted price, and thereby presumptively relied on the misrepresentation reflected in that price."[166] Nevertheless, those factors have "nothing to do with whether an investor relied on the misrepresentation in the first place, either directly or presumptively through the fraud-on-the-market theory. Loss causation has no logical connection to the facts necessary to establish the efficient market predicate to the fraud-on-the-market theory."[167]

The Court in *Halliburton* declined to equate loss causation with "price impact," which "simply refers to the effect of a misrepresentation on a stock price";[168] that is, Halliburton claimed that, if a misrepresentation does not affect market price, an investor cannot be said to have relied on the misrepresentation merely because he purchased stock. The Court held that it would not consider that claim because it was not the basis of the ruling of the lower court. That confusing bit of sidebar, unfortunately, avoided the issue of what is the proper role of price impact analysis in Rule 10b-5 litigation. Typically, fraud-on-the-market cases will, if litigated, turn into a battle of the experts in which each side presents price "event reports" by renowned economists. Those reports contain econometric regression, Monte Carlo, and other quantitative theoretical analyses that purport to prove the effect, or lack thereof, of a trader's conduct.[169]

The price impact issue raises other concerns. A leading treatise states that "a successful government prosecution does not depend on a showing that the price was actually driven above or below the security's fair value. It is sufficient to establish that the manipulator engaged in conduct calculated to artificially affect the security's price. However, in the context of a private suit, an actual effect on price must be shown."[170]

The SEC took a similar position in *In the Matter of Edward J. Mawod & Co. Inc.*,[171] in which it was claimed that there was no upward manipulation of a stock price to aid a merger because the merger turned out to be very successful—no harm, no foul. The SEC stated that such a claim confused private actions for damages with governmental proceedings brought in the public interest. Manipulation was prohibited and '[no] exception was made for victimless manipulation."[172] The SEC asserted that manipulations "substitute fiction for fact. Once in a great while the fiction

164. 563 U.S. at --- (emphasis in original).

165. Dura Pharms. Inc. v. Broudo, 544 U.S. 336, 341 (2005).

166. Erica P. John Fund Inc. v. Halliburton Co., 563 U.S. ---, --- (2011).

167. 563 U.S. at ---.

168. 563 U.S. at ---.

169. Michael J. Kaufman and John M. Wunderlich, *Regressing: The Troubling Dispositive Role of Event Studies in Securities Fraud Litigation*, 15 Stan. J. L. Bus. & Fin. 183 (2009) (describing the nature and use of such event studies).

170. Thomas Lee Hazen, Treatise on the Law of Securities Regulation 12.1 (5th ed. 2005).

171. In the Matter of Edward J. Mawod & Co Inc., 46 S.E.C. 865 (1977), *aff'd* Edward J. Mawod & Co. Inc. v. SEC, 591 F.2d 588 (10th Cir. 1979).

172. 46 S.E.C. at 871.

turns out to have been benign when viewed in light of hindsight. Even then it is still fiction. The vice is that the market has been distorted and made into a 'stage-managed performance.'"[173]

Such a carve-out for the government once again raises issues of whether, and when, the government should be relieved of proving the elements of a Rule 10b-5 violation. The fact that a defendant's conduct has no price impact might, for example, be strong evidence that it was not manipulative. On the one hand, should the government bear the burden that it was in fact manipulative, since that is the nature of the violation? On the other hand, should the defendant bear that burden as an affirmative defense in order to lighten the government's load?

5:8 SECONDARY LIABILITY

An important part of Rule 10b-5 litigation has been the search for a theory under which deep pockets, like large accounting and law firms and banks, can be held liable for the actions of their clients. Those actors are rarely involved directly in the fraud or manipulation, so plaintiffs have sought to impose fiduciary duties or theories of secondary liability, such as aiding and abetting, in order to establish liability on such parties. The Supreme Court has steadily beat back those efforts.

In *Santa Fe v. Green*,[174] the Supreme Court held that the mere breach of a fiduciary duty created by state law would not itself constitute a Rule 10b-5 violation. There must be some fraud or deceit to rise to that level. The scienter requirement imposed by the Court in *Ernst & Ernst v. Hochfelder*[175] also took an accounting firm off the hook because it was guilty, at best, of only negligence, not intentional fraud.

It would be a rare case where a large accounting firm's audit failures are due to something other than negligence. The same is true of legal representation by large deep-pocket law firms representing companies or individuals that are engaging in fraud or manipulation. Any assistance given by the law firms in preparing documents or legal advice to a manipulator is typically peripheral to a fraud scheme and does not normally involve intent or anything more than negligence, if that.

A government entity, the Securities Investor Protection Corporation, sought a way around the *Hochfelder* decision by claiming that an accounting firm was responsible for losses from the improper audit of a broker-dealer under the provisions of Section 17(a) of the 34 Act, which requires broker-dealers to keep certain accounting records and to have their financial reports audited. The Supreme Court rejected that search for a deep pocket in *Touche Ross & Co. v. Reddington*.[176] Retreating from its once liberal application of implied rights of private action, the Supreme Court held there was no such implied right under this section of the 34 Act.

Another blow was dealt to Rule 10b-5 plaintiffs in search of a deep pocket by the Supreme Court's decision in *Central Bank of Denver v. First Interstate Bank of Denver*.[177] There, the plaintiff claimed that a bank acting as an indenture trustee for municipal bond issues was secondarily liable for losses stemming from a municipal bond default. The bank had allowed the underwriting of those bond issues to go forward even though it had been advised that the appraisal used to value the properties that were securing the bonds was out of date and overly optimistic. The Supreme Court rejected that claim of secondary liability, holding that private litigants under Rule 10b-5 cannot obtain damages from defendants for aiding and abetting the violation of a principal actor.

173. 46 S.E.C. at 872.
174. Santa Fe v. Green, 430 U.S. 462 (1977).
175. Ernst & Ernst v. Hochfelder, 425 U.S. 185 (1976).
176. Touche Ross & Co. v. Reddington, 442 U.S. 560 (1979).
177. Central Bank of Denver v. First Interstate Bank of Denver, 511 U.S. 164 (1994).

The Court in *Central Bank* ruled that as in "earlier cases considering conduct prohibited by § 10(b), we again conclude that the statute prohibits only the making of a material misstatement (or omission) or the commission of a manipulative act."[178] The Court stated that it would not "amend the statute to create liability for acts that are not themselves manipulative or deceptive within the meaning of the statute."[179] The Court believed that its reasoning on this issue was confirmed by the fact that aiding and abetting liability would undercut an "element critical for recovery under 10b-5 . . . : reliance. . . . Were we to allow the aiding and abetting action proposed in this case, the defendant could be liable without any showing that the plaintiff relied upon the aider and abettor's statements or actions."[180] This meant that, in a private action under Rule 10b-5, "the conduct of a secondary actor must . . . satisfy each of the elements or preconditions for §10(b) liability, . . . [including] reliance upon a material misrepresentation or omission by the defendant."[181]

The *Central Bank* decision was a severe blow to the plaintiffs' bar in cutting off access to many deep-pocket defendants, and relief was sought in Congress. That effort was not successful. As the Supreme Court later noted, "although *Central Bank* prompted calls for creation of an express cause of action for aiding and abetting, Congress did not follow this course."[182] Instead, the Private Securities Litigation Reform Act of 1995 ("PSLRA") allowed only the SEC to bring civil actions against aiders and abettors.[183] The Dodd-Frank Act went further in 2010 and reduced the scienter burden for the SEC in proving aiding and abetting liability. Dodd-Frank now allows "recklessness"[184] instead of the actual knowledge requirement previously imposed by courts.[185]

After the decision of the Supreme Court in *Central Bank*, class action plaintiffs sought to avoid the barrier posed by the *Central Bank* decision by charging that secondary actors were liable as principals, rather than aiders and abettors, because they were participants in a fraud scheme. This gambit became known as "scheme liability."[186]

That theory resulted in some massive settlements from banks financing Enron's fraudulent accounting and derivative activities, but that bonanza was cut short by the Supreme Court in *Stoneridge Investment Partners LLC v. Scientific-Atlanta Inc.*[187] The plaintiffs in *Stoneridge*

---

178. 511 U.S. at 177.
179. *Id.*
180. 511 U.S. at 180.
181. 552 U. S. at 158.
182. *Stoneridge Investment Partners LLC v. Scientific-Atlanta Inc.*, 552 U.S. 148, 158 (2008).
183. *See*, Section 104 of the PSLRA, 109 Stat. 757, codified at 15 U.S.C. § 78t(e).
184. Dodd-Frank Wall Street Reform and Consumer Protection Act of 2010 § 929O.
185. *See, e.g.*, Howard v. SEC, 376 F.3d 1136 (D.C. Cir. 2004) (discussing this requirement).
186. As one article noted:

> Central Bank has caused plaintiffs to reexamine section 10(b) and Rule 10b-5 in an effort to identify alternative theories of liability for those traditionally charged as aiders and abettors. With the loss of aiding and abetting, private plaintiffs have most often alleged that secondary actors should be held liable as primary violators on one or more of the following grounds: (1) participation in a conspiracy to violate section 10(b), (2) issuance of a material misstatement or omission, and (3) participation in a 'scheme to defraud' under Rule 10b-5.

Richard H. Walker & David M. Levine, *The Limits of Central Bank's Textualist Approach: Attempts to Overdraw the Bank Prove Unsuccessful*, 26 HOFSTRA L. REV 1, 41 (1997). *See generally*, James D. Cox, *Securities Litigation: The Fundamental Issues: Participants: Just Deserts for Accountants and Attorneys After Bank of Denver*, 38 ARIZ. L. REV. 519 (1996) (discussing working around *Central Bank*).

187. Stoneridge Investment Partners LLC v. Scientific-Atlanta Inc., 552 U. S. 148 (2008). Some of Enron's banks settled Enron-related class actions in amounts totaling over $6.6 billion. Merrill Lynch and other

claimed that they suffered losses after purchasing stock of Charter Communications Inc. that was selling at an inflated price due to some fraudulent accounting machinations. The defendants were customers and suppliers of Charter who agreed to engage in fictitious transactions that allowed Charter to claim inflated profits in its misleading financial statements that were filed with the SEC and which pushed up its stock price. However, the defendants played no role in preparing or disseminating the financial statements. "It was Charter, not respondents, that misled its auditor and filed fraudulent financial statements; nothing respondents did made it necessary or inevitable for Charter to record the transactions as it did."[188]

The Supreme Court held in *Stoneridge* that "reliance is tied to causation, leading to the inquiry whether respondents' acts were immediate or remote to the injury."[189] The Court held that the defendants had no duty to disclose; and their deceptive acts were not communicated to the public market. Since no member of the investing public had knowledge, either actual or presumed, of defendants' deceptive acts, the plaintiffs could not show reliance on any of defendants' actions. The indirect chain to the defendants' acts were too remote for liability.

Stoneridge rejected plaintiffs' "concept of reliance—i.e., that in an efficient market investors rely not only upon the public statements relating to a security but also upon the transactions those statements reflect—the implied cause of action would reach the whole marketplace in which the issuing company does business."[190] The Court further pushed back efforts to expand Rule 10b-5 by asserting that its "precedents counsel against petitioner's attempt to extend the §10(b) private cause of action beyond the securities markets into the realm of ordinary business operations, which are governed, for the most part, by state law."[191]

The Supreme Court, in *Janus Capital Group Inc. v. First Derivative Traders*,[192] dealt another setback to proponents of secondary liability in private litigation under Rule 10b-5. There, in a 5–4 decision, the Court refused to extend "controlling person" liability under section 20(a) of the 34 Act to an investment adviser.[193] The defendant was an investment adviser to a group of mutual funds that were alleged to have issued prospectuses containing false statements relating to its restrictions on market timing practices by fund participants.[194] The majority held that, even

financial institutions refused to settle and moved to dismiss the scheme liability claims. Those motions were granted and affirmed by the Supreme Court in light of its decision in *Stoneridge Investment Partners*. *See*, Jerry W. Markham, A Financial History of the U.S. From Enron Era Scandals to The Subprime Crisis (2004-2006) 35 (2011) (describing those settlements).

188. Stoneridge Investment Partners LLC v. Scientific-Atlanta Inc., 552 U.S. at 148.

189. 552 U.S. at 160.

190. 552 U.S. at 148.

191. *Id.* The Court further stated that the "argument that there could be a reliance finding if this were a common-law fraud action is answered by the fact that § 10(b) does not incorporate common-law fraud into federal law . . . and should not be interpreted to provide a private cause of action against the entire marketplace in which the issuing company operates." *Id.* Interestingly, the *Stoneridge* defendants agreed before the Supreme Court's decision to pay $45 million to settle SEC charges of aiding and abetting over this conduct. Government Accountability Office, GAO-11-664 *Securities Fraud Liability of Secondary Actors* 27 (July 21, 2011).

192. Janus Capital Group Inc. v. First Derivative Traders, 564 U.S. --- (2011).

193. Section 20(a) states that "[e]very person who, directly or indirectly, controls any person liable under any provision of this chapter or of any rule or regulation thereunder shall also be liable jointly and severally with and to the same extent as such controlled person." Such liability is excused if "the controlling person acted in good faith and did not directly or indirectly induce the acts constituting the violation or cause of action."15 U.S.C. § 78t(a). The SEC has defined "control" under the 33 Act as "the possession, direct or indirect, of the power to direct or cause the direction of the management and policies of a person, whether through the ownership of voting securities, by contract, or otherwise." 17 C.F.R. § 230.405.

194. *See generally*, Jerry W. Markham, *Mutual Fund Scandals: A Comparative Analysis of the Role of Corporate Governance in the Regulation of Collective Investments*, 3 Hastings Bus. L.J. 67 (2006).

though the adviser may have assisted in preparing the funds' prospectus, the adviser itself did not "make" the statements in the prospectus that were at issue for purposes of Rule 10b-5. "Absent liability by the advisor, the creator was not liable as a control person."[195]

The majority in *Janus Capital* also narrowly interpreted the provision in Rule 10b-5 that applies to "any person, directly or indirectly, . . . [who] make[s] any untrue statement of a material fact." The majority in *Janus* held that the investment adviser did not "make" the statement contained in the prospectuses because it did not have "ultimate authority over the statement, including its content and whether and how to communicate it."[196] "For purposes of Rule 10b-5, the maker of a statement is the person or entity with ultimate authority over the statement, including its content and whether and how to communicate it. Without control, a person or entity can merely suggest what to say, not 'make' a statement in its own right."[197]

The SEC staff asserted that *Janus Capital* made a "major change" and a "radical narrowing" of primary liability under Section 10(b) of the 34 Act, but the SEC staff said it was not clear whether the decision applied to SEC enforcement actions.[198]

The effects of *Stoneridge* were soon apparent. The Second Circuit held in *United States v. Finnerty*[199] that a violation of Rule 10b-5 requires that the defendant must convey some impression that is misleading to investors. In that case a New York Stock Exchange specialist had interpositioned his account between customers so that he was able to profit at their expense. The court held that merely communicating a trade order, without more, did not constitute a deceptive misrepresentation or omission under Rule 10b-5. Citing and quoting from *Stoneridge*, the Second Circuit held:

> Like a thieving bank teller, the government argued, Finnerty had the motive and the means to profit from interpositioning. But there is no evidence that Finnerty conveyed an impression that was misleading, whether or not it could have a bearing on a victim's investment decision in connection with a security. We need not decide whether some form of communication by the defendant is always required to prove deception (although that is the template of virtually every case). To impose securities fraud liability here, absent proof that Finnerty conveyed a misleading impression to customers, would pose "a risk that the federal power would be used to invite litigation beyond the immediate sphere of securities litigation and in areas already governed by functioning and effective state-law guarantees."[200]

195. Janus Capital Group Inc. v. First Derivative Traders, 564 U.S. at ---. The Supreme Court further held in *Morrison v. Australian Bank*, 561 U.S. ---, --- (2010), that liability under § 20(a) of the 34 Act is obviously derivative of liability under some other provision of the Exchange Act. This means that, in the case of Rule 10b-5, there must be an underlying violation of § 10(b) by a person under the control of the defendant before controlling liability will attach. The Dodd-Frank Act authorized the SEC to bring an enforcement action for control person liability under section 20(a). This provision was intended to resolve a conflict among the circuits on whether the SEC had such authority or whether it was limited to private actions. Government Accountability Office, GAO-11-664 *Securities Fraud Liability of Secondary Actors* 30 (July 21, 2011).

196. 564 U.S. at ---.

197. 564 U.S. at ---.

198. *Extent to Which Janus Applies to SEC Actions Not Clear; Official Says*, 44 Sec. Reg. & L. Rep. (BNA) 463 (March 5, 2012). The SEC staff was considering the use of aiding and abetting liability claims as a way to avoid the ruling in *Janus*. *SEC Looking to Aiding/Abetting Claims in Wake of Janus Decision, Official Says*, 44 Sec. Reg. & L. Rep. (BNA) 457 (March 5, 2012).

199. United States v. Finnerty, 533 F.3d 143 (2d Cir. 2008).

200. 533 F.3d at 149 (citation and footnote omitted).

Subsequently, however, the Second Circuit held in *VanCook v. SEC*,[201] that a broker-dealer that fostered a late trading scheme like the one at issue in *Janus Capital* did violate Rule 10b-5 because, among other things, he ignored a directive in his customer's prospectuses that trades be executed by 4:00 p.m. The court in *VanCook* did not distinguish or even cite the Supreme Court's decision in *Janus Capital*.

5:9 EXTRATERRITORIAL LIMITATIONS

The Supreme Court has also limited the extraterritorial application of Section 10(b) of the 34 Act. The parameters of that limitation evolved over time, chiefly through decisions rendered by the Second Circuit Court of Appeals in applying the "conduct" and "effects" tests for transnational jurisdiction.[202] An expansive extraterritorial application of the rule was generally applied under those two tests. In the case of conduct taking place in the United States that defrauded only foreigners, the courts were "reluctant to conclude that Congress intended to allow the United States to become a 'Barbary Coast,' as it were, harboring international securities 'pirates.'"[203]

The Courts were also chary of ignoring fraudulent conduct emanating from abroad that had the effect of defrauding U.S. citizens. The Second Circuit broadly held that "the anti-fraud provisions of the federal securities laws . . . apply to losses from sales of securities to Americans resident in the United States whether or not acts (or culpable failures to act) of material importance occurred in this country."[204]

The courts did seek to avoid application of Rule 10b-5 to mere transient acts that might have occurred in the United States, say a casual meeting by two foreigners in New York to discuss development of a foreign fraud. To limit application of extraterritorial jurisdiction in such cases, mere "preparatory acts" of fraud were excluded from jurisdiction.[205]

---

201. VanCook v. SEC, 653 F.3d 130 (2d Cir. 2011), *cert. denied*, --- U.S. --- (2012).

202. The Second Circuit stated:

> To provide guidance on this topic, we have stated that, where "a court is confronted with transactions that on any view are predominantly foreign, it must seek to determine whether Congress would have wished the precious resources of United States courts and law enforcement agencies to be devoted to them rather than [to] leave the problem to foreign countries." . . . In applying this standard, we have consistently looked at two factors: (1) whether the wrongful conduct occurred in the United States, and (2) whether the wrongful conduct had a substantial effect in the United States or upon United States citizens. . . . In evaluating these two factors, we apply what are known respectively as the "conduct test" and the "effects test."

SEC v. Berger, 322 F.3d 187 (2d Cir. 2003). *See also*, Daniel S. Kahn, *The Collapsing Jurisdictional Boundaries of the Antifraud Provisions of the U.S. Securities Laws: The Supreme Court and Congress Ready to Redress Forty Years of Ambiguity*, 6 N.Y.U.J.L. & Bus. 365 (2010) (describing these tests and the evolution of their application).

203. SEC v. Kasser, 548 F.2d 109, 116 (3d Cir. 1977).

204. Bersch v. Drexel Firestone Inc., 519 F.2d 974 (2d Cir. 1975). *See also*, ITT v. Cornfeld, 619 F.2d 909, 918 (2d Cir. 1980) (describing this standard). The D.C. Circuit had expressed some reluctance in applying such a broad standard. *See*, SEC v. Banner Fund Int'l, 211 F.3d 602 (D.C. Cir. 2000); Zoelsch v. Arthur Andersen & Co., 824 F.2d 27 (D.C. Cir. 1987).

205. As the Second Circuit stated:

> We do not think Congress intended to allow the United States to be used as a base for manufacturing fraudulent security devices for export, even when these are peddled only to foreigners. This country would surely look askance if one of our neighbors stood by silently and permitted misrepresented securities to be poured into the United States. By the same token it is hard to

The issue of the extraterritorial application of Rule 10b-5 reached the Supreme Court in 2010, some forty years after the lower courts began struggling with its contours. In that decision, *Morrison v. National Australia Bank Ltd.*,[206] the Supreme Court considered a fraud claim under Section 10(b) of the 34 Act that presented a "foreign-cubed" jurisdictional issue. Foreign-cubed meant that (1) foreign plaintiffs were suing (2) a foreign issuer in an American court for violations of America securities laws based on (3) securities transactions in a foreign country.

The plaintiffs in *Morrison* were a class of Australian "ordinary" shareholders of the defendant National Australia Bank, which was not listed on any U.S. exchange, except that there was a market for its shares in American depository receipts (ADRs).[207] The plaintiffs claimed that the National Australia Bank misrepresented the profitability of a Florida-based mortgaging business that it had acquired in 1998. The value of that business had to be written down in 2001, causing a drop in the value of the bank's ordinary shares in Australia and its ADRs traded in the United States.

The Supreme Court held in *Morrison* that the Second Circuit erred in dismissing the case as an issue of subject-matter jurisdiction (the power to hear a case) instead of a "merits" issue on the reach of Rule 10b-5.[208] The Court then applied a long-standing canon of statutory construction, which assumes that, unless a contrary intent appears, Congress intends statutes it enacts to apply only within the territorial jurisdiction of the United States. The Supreme Court also found confusing the conduct and effects tests crafted by the Second Circuit to measure jurisdiction. Instead, the Supreme Court applied a "transactional" test that will apply the federal securities laws only to securities listed on domestic exchanges and to domestic transactions in foreign securities.[209]

The *Morrison* case was decided only a few days before enactment of the Dodd-Frank Act, but its holding was quickly made a target for that legislation. Dodd-Frank amended both the 34 and 33 Acts to extend the SEC's jurisdiction to "(1) conduct within the United States that constitutes significant steps in furtherance of a violation, even if the securities transaction occurs outside the United States and involves only foreign investors; or (2) conduct occurring outside the United States that has a foreseeable substantial effect within the United States."[210] Dodd-Frank directed the SEC to conduct a study to determine whether private rights of action should be allowed for claims falling under such a broadened jurisdictional umbrella.[211] As it stands now, however, the Dodd-Frank foreign jurisdiction standard will apply to SEC actions in the future and the *Morrison*

> believe Congress meant to prohibit the SEC from policing similar activities within this country; . . . Our ruling on this basis of jurisdiction is limited to the perpetration of fraudulent acts themselves and does not extend to mere preparatory activities or the failure to prevent fraudulent acts where the bulk of the activity was performed in foreign countries. . . . Admittedly the distinction is a fine one. But the position we are taking here itself extends the application of the securities laws to transnational transactions beyond prior decisions and the line has to be drawn somewhere if the securities laws are not to apply in every instance where something has happened in the United States, however large the gap between the something and a consummated fraud and however negligible the effect in the United States or on its citizens.

IIT v. Vencap, Ltd., 519 F.2d 1001, 1017-1018 (2d Cir. 1975).

206. Morrison v. National Australia Bank Ltd., 561 U.S. --- (2010).

207. *See,* City of Monroe Employees Ret. Sys. v. Bridgestone Corp., 399 F.3d 651, 656 n. 2 (6th Cir. 2005) (describing ADRs).

208. 561 U.S. at ---.

209. 561 U.S. at ---.

210. Dodd-Frank Act § 929P (amending 15 U.S.C. § 77v (a) and15 U.S.C. § 78aa). *See also,* 15 U.S.C. § 80b-14 (amending the Investment Advisers Act of 1940 by adding the same language).

211. Dodd-Frank § 929Y. That study was due eighteen months after the date of the enactment of Dodd-Frank. *Id.* The SEC sought public comment on this issue. *See,* Securities Exchange Act Release 34- 63174 (S.E.C. Oct. 25, 2010).

standard will continue to apply to private rights of action, at least until Congress takes some action in response to the SEC report.[212]

One of the cases affected by the *Morrison* decision was an action brought against Goldman Sachs & Co. and Fabrice Tourre, one of its salesmen, that the Obama administration used to justify enactment of the Dodd-Frank provisions that closed the Enron loophole and regulated OTC swaps.[213] Goldman Sachs settled the case,[214] but Tourre moved to dismiss the charges against him on *Morrison* grounds. That motion was granted in part and denied in part by the district court.[215]

The district court dismissed SEC charges under Rule 10b-5 insofar as the SEC alleged that a synthetic collateralized debt obligation was fraudently sold to a German commercial bank and that a European bank engaged in a related credit default swap. The court concluded that those entities engaged in no purchase or sale of those interests in the United States. The court concluded that, without a purchase or sale, those parties did not engage in a "domestic transaction" within the *Morrison* test.[216] The district court, however, found jurisdiction with respect to claims made by the SEC under Section 17(a) of the 33 Act because, unlike Section 10(b), Section 17(a) applies not only to the "sale" but also to the "offer . . . of any securities or any security-based swap agreement."[217] The court held that an offer from the United States was a domestic transaction even if made to a foreign party for purposes of Section 17(a).[218]

The new Dodd-Frank Act provisions may affect the analysis of the court in the *Goldman* case in future SEC actions, but the *Goldman* decision will continue to raise issues in private actions. Thus, in *Basis Yield Alpha Fund v. Goldman Sachs Group Inc.*,[219] the district court dismissed on jurisdictional grounds a private action brought by an Australian hedge fund, Basis Yield Alpha Fund, against Goldman Sachs over another credit default transaction called Timberwolf 2007-1. The hedge fund claimed that it was misled because Goldman had not disclosed that it was shorting the deal.[220] However, the court found a lack of jurisdiction under *Morrison* because the deal was consummated

212. *See*, Richard W. Painter, *The Dodd-Frank Extraterritorial Provision: Was It Effective, Needed or Sufficient?* 1 Harv. Bus. L. Rev. 195 (2011) (discussing the effects of Section 929P of Dodd-Frank on Rule 10b-5 claims).

213. One author has noted that this provision in the Dodd-Frank Act will raise jurisdictional questions concerning OTC security-based swap agreements. Richard W. Painter, *The Dodd-Frank Extraterritorial Provision: Was It Effective, Needed or Sufficient?* 1 Harv. Bus. L. Rev. 195 (2011).

214. Goldman Sachs agreed to pay $550 million in settlement, the largest ever SEC settlement. Nevertheless, the settlement was, ironically, considered a victory for Goldman because many thought that the settlement would cost Goldman twice that amount. Jerry W. Markham, A Financial History of the U.S. From the Subprime Crisis to the Great Recession (2006-2009) 735 (2011).

215. The SEC accused Tourre of fraudulently arranging a synthetic collateralized debt obligation (CDO) called ABACUS 2007-AC1 that was sold to institutional investors in Europe. The SEC charges that Goldman did not tell those investors that the subprime mortgages in ABACUS were selected by hedge fund manager John Paulson, who had become famous for having made $5.7 billion personally during 2007 and 2008 by betting against subprime mortgages. That omission was deemed important by the SEC because Paulson was taking a short position against the ABACUS CDOs through credit default swaps. SEC v. Goldman Sachs & Co., 2011 WL 2305988 (S.D.N.Y.). *See*, Jerry W. Markham, *SEC v. Goldman Sachs & Co.: Serious Fraud or Just More Banker Bashing?* 30 Fut. & Derv. L. Rep. 7, 8 (2010) (discussing the SEC case and its weaknesses).

216. Certain domestic parties were found to have been involved in domestic transactions.

217. 15 U.S.C. § 77q(a).

218. In *SEC v. Ficeto*, 2011 WL 7445580 (C.D. Cal.), a district court denied a motion to dismiss an SEC manipulation charge involving thinly traded OTC securities that were manipulated by marking the close. The court also held that *Morrison* did not apply to bar charges against a foreign trader manipulating OTC stock in the United States.

219. Basis Yield Alpha Fund v. Goldman Sachs Group Inc., 2011 U.S. Dist. LEXIS 80298 (S.D.N.Y.).

220. That transaction had been described as "one shitty deal" in an internal Goldman email that was made public and sensationalized in Senate hearings over Goldman's role in the financial crisis. Liz Rappaport, *Mortgage Win for Goldman*, Wall St. J., July 22, 2011, at C2.

abroad with a foreign entity—that is, the Australian hedge fund. Nevertheless, the Second Circuit stated in another case that securities transactions would be domestic and subject to the 34 Act even if not executed on a U.S. exchange if title or irrevocable liability is incurred here.[221]

It is unclear what will be the effect of *Morrison* on claims under the Commodity Exchange Act.[222] In earlier cases, the courts had applied analysis similar to those under the 34 Act prior conduct and effects tests in determining the parameters of foreign jurisdiction. For example, in *Psimenos v. E.F. Hutton & Co.*,[223] the Second Circuit held that subject matter jurisdiction was available under Section 4b of the Commodity Exchange Act in an action brought by a Greek resident. The plaintiff claimed that the Greek agent of a broker located in the United States had defrauded him through trading on U.S. commodity markets. The court based its ruling on earlier decisions under the federal securities laws, asserting that "[t]rading activities on United States commodities markets were significant acts without which Psimenos' losses could not have occurred, and are sufficient to establish jurisdiction."[224] Interestingly, the decision in *Psimenos* was cited with approval by the Second Circuit in finding a lack of jurisdiction in the *Morrison* case.[225]

In *Tamari v. Bache & Co. (Lebanon) S.A.L.*,[226] the Seventh Circuit accepted the effects and conduct test used in the securities industry and found jurisdiction in circumstances similar to those in *Psimenos*.[227] However, in *Mak v. Wocom Commodities Ltd.*,[228] the Seventh Circuit rejected jurisdiction over a claim involving a Hong Kong plaintiff defrauded by other Hong Kong residents who were falsely claiming to be executing the plaintiff's orders on U.S. markets. Instead, the orders were "bucketed." The court held the effect of such fraud on U.S. markets was too vague and indefinite to sustain jurisdiction.

Subsequently, in *SDN BHD v. Sternberg*,[229] the Seventh Circuit equated jurisdictional issues under the Commodity Exchange Act with those under the 34 Act. The Supreme Court in *Morrison* specifically cited and discussed *SDN BHD v. Sternberg* in its opinion, describing it as a "leading" case before rejecting its assertion that the 34 Act applied extraterritorially.[230] Rather, "the focus of the Exchange Act is not upon the place where the deception originated, but upon purchases and sales of securities in the United States. Section 10(b) does not punish deceptive conduct, but only deceptive conduct 'in connection with the purchase or sale of any security registered on a national securities exchange or any security not so registered.'"[231]

---

221. Absolute Activist Value Master Fund v. Ficeto 672 F.3d 143 (2d Cir. 2012).

222. The CFTC issued a statement of policy in 1984 on its jurisdiction over transnational claims in its reparations proceedings. Comm. Fut. L. Rep. (CCH) ¶ 22,075 (April 13, 1984). *See generally*, Jerry W. Markham, *The Seventh Amendment and CFTC Reparation Proceedings*, 68 Iowa L. Rev. 87 (1982) (describing CFTC reparations proceedings). The CFTC stated that it would not adjudicate reparations claims that involve predominantly foreign conduct, but that broader jurisdiction might be claimed in enforcement actions for policy reasons. The CFTC later claimed such broader jurisdiction in an enforcement case against the Sumitomo Corp. that largely involved trading in the London market that had price effects in the United States. In re Sumitomo Corp., Comm. Fut. L. Rep. (CCH) ¶ 27,327 (C.F.T.C. 1998).

223. Psimenos v. E.F. Hutton & Co., 722 F.2d 1041 (2d Cir. 1983).

224. 722 F.2d at 1048.

225. Morrison v. National Australian Bank Ltd., 547 F.3d 167, 171 (2d Cir. 2008*), aff'd*, 561 U.S. --- (2010).

226. Tamari v. Bache & Co. (Lebanon) S.A.L., 730 F.2d 1103 (7th Cir.), *cert. denied*, 469 U.S. 871 (1984).

227. *See,* Gassner v. Stoller & Co., 671 F. Supp. 1187 (N.D. Ill. 1987) (following *Tamari*).

228. Mak v. Wocom Commodities Ltd., 112 F.3d 287 (7th Cir. 1997).

229. SDN BHD v. Sternberg, 149 F.3d 659 (7th Cir. 1998), *cert. denied*, 525 U.S. 1114 (1999).

230. 561 U.S. at ---.

231. 561 U.S. at ---.

Courts have previously held that the Commodity Exchange Act does not apply to transactions on foreign exchanges.[232] Start In *Mormels v. Girofinance S.A.*,[233] the district court dismissed fraud claims under the Commodity Exchange Act and the federal securities laws where the plaintiffs, residing in Costa Rica, opened a commodity trading account for U.S. futures contracts with a Costa Rican corporation, which held itself out as an agent of a U.S. brokerage firm. Various activity was alleged to have occurred in the United States, but the core of the fraud was committed in Costa Rica.[234] However, the CFTC adopted an antifraud rule that prohibited fraud in the United States in connection with trading of commodity futures contracts on foreign exchanges.[235] Congress also amended Section 4b of the Commodity Exchange Act in 1982 to confirm that the CFTC had authority to regulate trading by U.S. customers on foreign futures exchanges.[236]

5:10 INSIDER TRADING LIMITATIONS

The Supreme Court cut back on the broad-based insider trading concept of "equal access to information" posited by the SEC decision in *Cady, Roberts & Co.*[237] As described in Chapter 3, that action was an administrative proceeding that was settled by consent and never reviewed by a court. The expansive application of Rule 10b-5 in the *Cady, Roberts* case was adopted by the Second Circuit in *SEC v. Texas Gulf Sulphur Co.*[238] The Supreme Court rejected the "equal access to information" doctrine in *Chiarella v. United States*.[239] In that case, a printer obtained and traded on nonpublic information about a corporate takeover bid from confidential financial reports being printed at the company where he worked. He was convicted of violating Section 10(b) of the 34 Act.[240] The Court in *Chiarella* held that the printer had no general duty under Rule 10b-5

---

232. Palmer Trading Co. v. Shearson Hayden Stone Inc., Comm. Fut. L. Rep. (CCH) ¶ 20,900 (N.D. Ill. 1979); deAtucha v. Commodity Exch. Inc., 608 F. Supp. 510 (S.D.N.Y. 1985); Kleinberg v. Bear, Stearns & Co., Comm. Fut. L. Rep. (CCH) ¶ 22,613 (S.D.N.Y. 1985).

233. Mormels v. Girofinance, S. A., 544 F. Supp. 815 (S.D.N.Y. 1982).

234. *Compare*, Cresswell v. Prudential-Bache Securities Inc., 580 F. Supp. 55 (S.D.N.Y. 1984) (trading scheme defrauding non-U.S. investors, which was originated in European offices, but reviewed and approved by U.S. broker in New York and where trades occurred on U.S. exchanges, was sufficient for jurisdiction under Commodity Exchange Act). *See generally*, Jerry W. Markham, Commodities Regulation: Fraud, Manipulation and Other Claims, § 1:13 (2010) (describing other cases on Commodity Exchange Act foreign jurisdiction).

235. 17 C.F.R. § 30.2.

236. 7 U.S.C. § 6(b). *See, Foreign Options and Foreign Futures Transactions*, 51 Fed. Reg. 12104 (April 8, 1986) (discussing this amendment).

237. Cady, Roberts & Co., 40 S.E.C. (1961).

238. SEC v. Texas Gulf Sulphur Co., 401 F.2d 833 (2d Cir. 1968), *cert. denied sub nom.*, Coates v. SEC, 394 U.S. 976 (1969). One aspect of the *Texas Gulf Sulphur* opinion that did survive Supreme Court scrutiny was based on the concept of false reporting in the press release that misleadingly downplayed the value of a mineral find by the company. The Supreme Court held in *Basic Inc. v. Levinson*, 485 U.S. 224 (1988), that misleading press releases are actionable under Rule 10b-5.

239. Chiarella v. United States, 445 U.S. 222 (1980).

240. As the Supreme Court noted:

> In this case, the petitioner was convicted of violating § 10(b) although he was not a corporate insider and he received no confidential information from the target company. Moreover, the "market information" upon which he relied did not concern the earning power or operations of the target company, but only the plans of the acquiring company. Petitioner's use of that information was not a fraud under § 10(b) unless he was subject to an affirmative duty to disclose it before trading.

445 U.S. at 231 (footnote omitted).

to disclose the information at issue before trading. The Court stated, "[a] duty to disclose under section 10(b) does not arise from the mere possession of nonpublic market information."[241]

Such a duty to disclose would arise only where there existed a fiduciary relationship between the trader and the source of the information. This meant that an investor having no fiduciary relationship could trade upon nonpublic market information. "Moreover, neither the Congress nor the Commission ever has adopted a parity-of-information rule. Instead, the problems caused by misuse of market information have been addressed by detailed and sophisticated regulation that recognizes when use of market information may not harm operation of the securities markets."[242]

The requirement in *Chiarella* requiring a breach of a fiduciary duty to establish an insider trading fraud under Section 10(b) seems at odds with the holding in *Santa Fe v. Green*[243] that the breach of a fiduciary duty will not amount to a Section 10(b) violation in other contexts. In any event, as the First Circuit Court of Appeals has noted, the "issue . . . is whether the securities law imposes on defendants a 'specific obligation' to disclose information of the type that plaintiffs claim was omitted."[244] Consequently, a party need not disclose its trading strategies or positions to the market before trading, even if that information would have a material effect on the market. This is because "[s]ilence, absent a duty to disclose, is not misleading under Rule 10b-5."[245]

Disclosure is required, however, where a party chooses to speak. "[E]ven a voluntary disclosure of information that a reasonable investor would consider material must be complete and accurate."[246] This requirement is important in the manipulation context because it allows the government to attack so-called pump-and-dump schemes in which widespread false publicity is used to manipulate a stock price to the actor's advantage.[247] Related to these schemes is the concept of "scalping" (not to be confused with "scalping" in the futures industry, which involves legitimate quick in-and-out trades).[248] Scalping in the securities industry involves an actor who publishes market-moving information about a security and trades in front of that publication, knowing that it will have market effect.[249]

---

241. 445 U.S. at 235.

242. 445 U.S. at 233.

243. Santa Fe v. Green, 430 U.S. 462 (1977).

244. Hill v. Gozani, 638 F.3d 40, 57 (1st Cir. 2011) (citation omitted).

245. Basic Inc. v. Levinson, 485 U.S. 224, 239, n. 17 (1988).

246. Hill v. Gozani, 638 F.3d 40, 54 (1st Cir. 2011) (citation omitted). The First Circuit has also noted, "Nevertheless, this obligation has its limits: It 'does not mean that by revealing one fact about a product, one must reveal all others that, too, would be interesting, market-wise'; a company must reveal only those facts 'that are needed so that what was revealed would not be so incomplete as to mislead.'" *Id.* (citation omitted) *See also*, Helwig v. Vencor Inc., 251 F.3d 540, 564 (6th Cir. 2001), *cert denied*, 536 U.S. 935 (2002) ("This is entirely consistent with our requirement that an actor speak fully and truthfully when making a voluntary disclosure."). In *Last Atlantis Capital LLC v. AGS Specialist Partners*, 2010 WL 4365549 (N.D. Ill.), a district court held that options exchange specialists generally would not fall under the SEC's shingle theory requiring best execution of customer orders. The court stated, however, that the broker-dealer defendants could be liable for best execution obligations where they had made public statements asserting they would ensure best execution. *But see*, In the Matter of Albert Fried & Co., 47 S.E.C. 1 (1978) (specialist failed to meet his obligations to investors by failing to disclose an agreement to keep a stock above the current market).

247. *See generally, e.g.*, United States v. Laurienti, 611 F.3d 530 (9th Cir. 2010), *cert. denied*, --- U.S. --- (2011) (describing pump-and-dump scheme); LaSala v. Bordier Et Cie, 519 F.3d 121 (3d Cir. 2008 (same); Dlugash v. SEC, 373 F.2d 107, 109 (2d Cir. 1967) ("rapidly rising prices in the absence of any demand are well-known symptoms of such unlawful market operations").

248. Jerry W. Markham, *Front-Running: Insider Trading Under the Commodity Exchange Act*, 38 CATH. L. REV. 69, 127, n. 91 (1988).

249. Zweig v. Hearst Corp., 594 F.2d 1261 (9 Cir. 1979); SEC v. Blavin, 760 F.2d 706 (6th Cir. 1985).

The SEC had argued as an alternative theory in *Chiarella* that Rule 10b-5 was violated because the printer had committed fraud by stealing or "misappropriating" the nonpublic information that his employer required him to hold in confidence. The Supreme Court, however, refused to consider that argument in *Chiarella* because it had not been raised before the jury in the district court, a condition precedent for appellate review.[250] The government later tried again to raise the misappropriation theory in another criminal case, *Carpenter v. United States*.[251] There, a financial columnist for the *Wall Street Journal* and a stock broker traded on nonpublic market information that was to appear in the reporter's columns, which would have market effect after publication. The Supreme Court was equally divided on the application of the misappropriation theory, which under the rules meant that the decision of the Second Circuit, which affirmed the convictions under Section 10(b) of the 34 Act, were not disturbed. The Supreme Court in *Carpenter* did unanimously uphold convictions of the defendants for this same conduct under the mail and wire fraud statutes. The Supreme Court held that their actions constituted a fraud upon the *Wall Street Journal* because that newspaper had been deprived of its property right of making exclusive use of the confidential business information in its columns before publication. After changes in its membership, the Supreme Court accepted the "misappropriation" theory as well as a "classical" doctrine for insider trading liability under Rule 10b-5 in *United States v. O'Hagan*.[252]

In *Dirks v. SEC*,[253] the Supreme Court rejected the SEC's expansive demand for liability of "tippees" who traded on nonpublic information received from an insider at Equity Funding of

---

See generally, David B. Levant, *Financial Columnists as Investment Advisers: After Lowe and Carpenter*, 74 Cal. L. Rev. 2061(discussing regulation of scalping).

250. 445 U.S. at 235-236. The SEC later adopted rule 14e-3 [17 C.F.R. § 240.14e-3] under the Williams Act [82 Stat. 454] to prohibit anyone from using information to trade on nonpublic information concerning a merger. The Supreme Court upheld the SEC's power to enact that rule. United States v. O'Hagan, 521 U.S. 642, 651-652 (1997).

251. Carpenter v. United States, 484 U.S. 19 (1987).

252. United States v. O'Hagan, 521 U.S. 642, 667-677 (1997). The Supreme Court defined classical insider trading:

> Under the "traditional" or "classical theory" of insider trading liability, § 10(b) and Rule 10b-5 are violated when a corporate insider trades in the securities of his corporation on the basis of material, nonpublic information. Trading on such information qualifies as a "deceptive device" under § 10(b), we have affirmed, because "a relationship of trust and confidence [exists] between the shareholders of a corporation and those insiders who have obtained confidential information by reason of their position with that corporation." That relationship, we recognized, "gives rise to a duty to disclose [or to abstain from trading] because of the "necessity of preventing a corporate insider from . . . taking unfair advantage of . . . uninformed . . . stockholders." The classical theory applies not only to officers, directors, and other permanent insiders of a corporation, but also to attorneys, accountants, consultants, and others who temporarily become fiduciaries of a corporation. The "misappropriation theory" holds that a person commits fraud "in connection with" a securities transaction, and thereby violates § 10(b) and Rule 10b-5, when he misappropriates confidential information for securities trading purposes, in breach of a duty owed to the source of the information. Under this theory, a fiduciary's undisclosed, self-serving use of a principal's information to purchase or sell securities, in breach of a duty of loyalty and confidentiality, defrauds the principal of the exclusive use of that information. In lieu of premising liability on a fiduciary relationship between company insider and purchaser or seller of the company's stock, the misappropriation theory premises liability on a fiduciary-turned-trader's deception of those who entrusted him with access to confidential information.

521 U.S. at 651-652 (citations omitted).

253. Dirks v. SEC, 463 U.S. 646 (1983).

America. In that case, an investment analyst, Raymond Dirks, was tipped by an insider that Equity Funding officers were engaged in a massive fraud. The analyst was following the company for clients, and he had them liquidate their holdings, which totaled $16 million, before Equity Funding declared bankruptcy. The SEC censured Dirks for aiding and abetting violations of Rule 10b-5 by clients and investors who sold their holdings based on the tip passed on by Dirks. The Supreme Court reversed that sanction.

The Supreme Court noted that the "tippers received no monetary or personal benefit for revealing Equity Funding's secrets, nor was their purpose to make a gift of valuable information to Dirks. As the facts of this case clearly indicate, the tippers were motivated by a desire to expose the fraud. In the absence of a breach of duty to shareholders by the insiders, there was no derivative breach by Dirks."[254] The Supreme Court held that "there is no general duty to forgo market transactions 'based on material, nonpublic information.' Such a duty would '[depart] radically from the established doctrine that duty arises from a specific relationship between two parties.'"[255]

The approach taken by the SEC for insider trading should be contrasted with that of the CFTC. In enacting the CFTC Act of 1974, Congress had considered various insider trading prohibitions,[256] but only prohibited CFTC commissioners or employees from trading futures contracts or tipping others on nonpublic information.[257] That prohibition was extended to employees of commodity exchanges and self-regulatory bodies in the Futures Trading Practices Act of 1992.[258]

A false reporting prohibition is contained in Section 4(b) of the Commodity Exchange Act, which is the principal antifraud provision in that statute.[259] Section 4b(a)(2)(ii) states that it is illegal "willfully to make or cause to be made" to another person "any false report or statement thereof, or willfully to enter or cause to be entered for such person any false record thereof."[260] Traditionally, Section 4b was used to attack fraud by brokers (futures commission merchants) on their customers.[261] The CFTC, however, in *In the Matter of Moster*,[262] held, in a consent order in one of its administrative proceedings, that a proprietary trader for the Bank of America violated Section 4b(a)(2)(ii) of the CEA in 2004 when he booked fictitious trades that inflated the value of his trading book. Although that decision had little effect on market manipulation issues, it signaled that the CFTC was seeking to expand false reporting charges.[263]

---

254. 463 U.S. at 667 (citations omitted).

255. 463 U.S. at 667 (citations omitted).

256. CFTC, *A Study of the Nature, Extent and Effects of Futures Trading by Persons Possessing Material, Nonpublic Information*, submitted to the Committee on Agriculture of the House of Representatives and the Committee on Agriculture, Nutrition and Forestry of the Senate pursuant to Sec. 23(b) of the Commodity Exchange Act, as amended, at App. I-B (Sept. 1984).

257. 7 U.S.C. § 13(d) & (e).

258. Pub. L. No. 102-546, 106 Stat. 3590 (1992). The SEC had experienced a scandal in the 1960s when one of its employees provided nonpublic information on a SEC investigation of the Georgia Pacific Co. to a trader who shorted the stock. United States v. Peltz, 433 F.2d 48 (2d Cir. 1970), *cert. denied*, 401 U.S. 955 (1971).

259. 7 U.S.C. § 6b. The Supreme Court has stated that the language of Section 4(b) in the CEA is "similar" to Section 10(b) in the 34 Act. Merrill Lynch, Pierce, Fenner & Smith Inc. v. Curran, 456 U.S. 353, 389, n. 88 (1982).

260. 7 U.S.C. ¶ 6b(a)(2)(ii).

261. In *Darrah v. First American Investment Services Inc.*, 2010 WL 5582903 (C.F.T.C. 2010), the CFTC held that the elements of a fraudulent inducement claim are as follows: (1) a material misleading statement and/or omission; (2) made with scienter; (3) on which complainant reasonably relied; and (4) which proximately caused complainant's damages.

262. In the Matter of Moster, COMM. FUT. L. REP. (CCH) ¶ 31,314 (C.F.T.C. 2009).

263. *See also*, CFTC v. Doyle, COMM. FUT. L. REP. (CCH) ¶ 30,577 (S.D.N.Y. 2007) (violation of Section 4(b) for fraudulent customer trade allocations, but not reporting fraud); CFTC v. Bursztyn, COMM. FUT. L.

Section 4(b) raises other issues in the context of manipulation. The SEC attacked manipulative trading as a form of fraud under the federal securities laws. However, the SEC's broadest application of that concept has been its insider trading cases, which are based on a theory of equal access to information that the CFTC has refused to accept. In a 1984 study ordered by Congress in the Futures Trading Act of 1982,[264] the CFTC decided that it would not adopt the SEC's broad prohibition on trading on the basis of nonpublic information in the futures markets. The CFTC noted that many commodity market participants, particularly hedgers, had unequal access to market-moving information that was proprietary to their businesses.[265]

The CFTC's approach to that issue was much the same as that taken in *Laidlaw v. Organ*,[266] a Supreme Court decision that was handed down in 1817. There, a purchaser of tobacco failed to disclose to the seller the buyer's prior knowledge of the signing of the Treaty of Ghent, which resulted in a substantial increase in tobacco prices when its existence became publicly known. The Supreme Court, in an opinion written by Justice John Marshall, held there was no duty to disclose that information. Nevertheless, Justice Marshall cautioned that affirmative deceptive statements denying knowledge of such information could be actionable if the seller was misled.

In 2008, Congress added a proviso to Section 4(b) of the Commodity Exchange Act that adopted the approach taken by the Supreme Court in *Laidlaw*. This amendment states that Section 4(b) does not require disclosure of "nonpublic information that may be material to the market price, rate, or level of the commodity or transaction, except as necessary to make any statement made to the other person in or in connection with the transaction not misleading in any material respect."[267] This may have the effect of circumscribing claims such as the one raised in *Cargill v. Hardin*,[268] where the Eighth Circuit had noted that the defendant's knowledge of its dominant position in the cash market had aided its futures price manipulation.[269]

Rep. (CCH) ¶ 30,390 (S.D.N.Y. 2006) (foreign currency fraud under CFTC Regulation 1.17(b), 17 C.F.R. § 1.1(b)). The CFTC had brought other fictitious trading charges by traders under its authority in Section 4(c). *See, e.g.*, In the Matter of Lui, Comm. Fut. L. Rep. (CCH) ¶ 30,491 (C.F.T.C. 2007).

264. 96 Stat. 2294, § 236 (1982).

265. The CFTC study found,

> Numerous futures market participants may have legitimate access to what some may perceive as superior information. For example, hedgers, who comprise a substantial portion of the markets, also participate in the production, processing, distribution and/or consumption of the cash commodity underlying the futures market. By the nature of their businesses, many hedgers are privy to nonpublic information that may prove to be material in futures markets. Alternatively, speculators have knowledge of their own futures or cash market positions and some traders may have superior resources with which to purchase or develop research information. Moreover, traders on the floor of an exchange may have advantages of time and place over others. Such access to superior or more timely information is inherent in the markets, and futures market participants voluntarily accept this situation if they choose to trade.

CFTC, *A Study of the Nature, Extent and Effects of Futures Trading by Persons Possessing Material, Nonpublic Information*, submitted to the Committee on Agriculture of the House of Representatives and the Committee on Agriculture, Nutrition and Forestry of the Senate pursuant to Sec. 23(b) of the Commodity Exchange Act, as amended (Sept. 1984).

266. Laidlaw v. Organ, 15 U.S. 178 (1817).

267. 7 U.S.C. 6b(b). *See also*, Basic Inc. v. Levenson, 485 U.S. 224 (1988) (issuer of securities need not disclose merger talks, but would commit fraud on the market under the federal securities laws by making affirmative misrepresentations of such talks).

268. *Cargill v. Hardin*, 452 F.2d 1154, 1159 (8th Cir. 1971).

269. The court stated in *Cargill*:

The CFTC's 1984 study on insider trading also considered manipulation concerns raised by the Federal Trade Commission over trading in front of private analyst reports that could have market effects. For example, a bullish market report published by a large firm could, predictably, push prices upward. This would allow the firm to profit by trading in advance of the report. One such instance arose from claims that Phibro-Salomon, a large financial services firm, profited from trading in interest rate futures. That trading occurred just before the publication of a market-moving forecast by Henry Kaufman, the firm's chief economist, in August 17, 1982, which predicted that interest rates would fall. The CFTC found no basis for action because it could find no relationship between Phibro-Salomon's trading and the timing of Kaufman's report.

The CFTC also opposed a bill introduced in Congress in 1991 that would have prohibited the use by principals and employees of nonpublic information about cash market positions of their employer.[270] The CFTC offered an alternative to this legislation that would have allowed it to attack such practices through its rule-making powers. That legislation was not passed. Nevertheless, the CFTC subsequently adopted a misappropriation theory for information stolen from an employer like that used by the SEC. A consent order of injunction was entered in *CFTC v. Kelly*[271] in response to charges that the respondents misappropriated market-moving information from John W. Henry & Co., a trading firm located in Boca Raton, Florida. One of the respondents, Thomas E. Kelly, was a trader at J. Henry. He passed the firm's trading plans on to another respondent, Andrew D. Rhee, who traded ahead of ("front-runned") J. Henry's trades. They made about $4.7 million from this scheme. The respondents were accused of violating the cheating and defrauding provision in subsections 4(b)(a)(i) and (iii) of the Commodity Exchange Act, as opposed to the false reporting provision in Section 4(b)(a)(ii). The traders also pleaded guilty to criminal charges under the Commodity Exchange Act.[272]

> It is important to note here that Cargill was thus in possession of a vital piece of information that other traders and grain dealers in Chicago did not have access to, namely that it owned the bulk of deliverable wheat in Chicago. While all traders of course knew the total quantity of deliverable wheat available in Chicago, only Cargill was in a position to know that it owned the vast majority of this wheat.

452 F.2d at 1159.

270. The language in that bill is set forth in H.R. Rep. No. 6, 101st Cong., 2d Sess. 11 (1991). The CFTC stated in opposition to that measure,

> The prohibition against insider trading based on material nonpublic information originated in the securities markets. It is well recognized, however, that there are significant differences between the securities markets and the futures markets. It is possible that making insider trading a felony, without more information on what problems might exist, could have an unintended chilling effect on the normal flow of information in the futures markets. In this regard, we have not found problems associated with the misuse of proprietary information . . . by employees of reportable traders. And while as a general matter we agree that employees should not misuse their firms' information for personal gain in the futures or options markets, we believe more information regarding the nature and magnitude of this problem is needed in order to justify statutory solutions like those in the bill.

H.R. Rep. No. 6, 101st Cong., 2d Sess. 59 (1991).

271. CFTC v. Kelly, COMM. FUT. L. REP. (CCH) ¶ 27,465 (S.D.N.Y. 1998). For a discussion of issues under the CEA raised by brokers trading in front of customer orders with market-moving effects, see Jerry W. Markham, *"Front-Running": Insider Trading Under the Commodity Exchange Act*, 38 CATH. U. L. REV. 69 (1988).

272. Benjamin Weiser, *2 Commodities Brokers Plead Guilty to Insider Trading Worth $4.7 Million*, NEW YORK TIMES, July 24, 1998, at B3.

The Seventh Circuit in *United States v. Dial*[273] also upheld criminal charges of mail and wire fraud where a broker traded ahead of (front-runned) his customers' silver futures trades.[274] Interestingly, the customers being front-runned made money because prices in the silver market were increasing, but the court noted they would have made even more in the market if the broker had not traded ahead of their order.[275]

5:11 DERIVATIVE AND STOCK MARKET MANIPULATION CONCERNS

Concerns over speculation and manipulation of commodity futures prices spilled over into the securities markets after the stock market crash of 1987, an event that witnessed the worst stock market decline since the stock market crash of 1929. New York Stock Exchange (NYSE) listings lost $1 trillion in value during the 1987 crash. On October 19, 1987, a trading day that became known as "Black Monday," the Dow Jones Industrial Average dropped 508 points. On October 23, 1987, the NYSE and commodity exchanges trading stock index futures took emergency action, imposing daily price limits on those contracts.[276]

The NYSE blamed the futures exchanges for the trading that exacerbated the 1987 crash. The NYSE focused specifically on algorithmic "program trading" that tried to anticipate market movements based on prior trading data, but could accelerate a market decline by generating increasing volumes of sell orders as the market falls.[277] This was called the "cascade scenario" by the SEC.[278] Also of concern was "portfolio insurance," which was a hedge on offsetting market positions. The NYSE reported that on Black Monday three portfolio insurers bought and sold $2 billion of stocks and $2.8 billion in futures.[279]

---

273. United States v. Dial, 757 F.2d 163 (7th Cir.), *cert. denied*, 474 U.S. 838 (1985).

274. In that case Judge Posner asserted,

> Traders on a commodity futures exchange will . . . want some assurance that there are no people in the market who have preferential access to information. If there are known to be such people, the other traders will tend to leave the exchange for other exchanges that do not have such people—and several commodity exchanges besides the Board of Trade offer trading in silver futures contracts. If trading is "rigged" on all commodity futures exchanges, there will be less commodity futures trading, period, and the social benefits of such trading . . . will be reduced. . . . So if "trading ahead"—as the practice of a broker's putting in his own orders for execution ahead of his customers' orders is called—became widespread, customers would realize that the market was rigged against them. And trading ahead serves no social function at all. The broker obtains a profit from information that he has not invested in producing but that comes to him automatically in his capacity as a broker. It is like a lawyer's discovering that his client is about to make a takeover bid for another company and rushing out and buying some of that company's stock before the bid is made public.

757 F.2d at 165-166.

275. For a description of cases raising insider trading issues in commodity-related transactions, *see* JERRY W. MARKHAM, COMMODITIES REGULATION: FRAUD, MANIPULATION AND OTHER CLAIMS, § 18:8 (2010) (describing that legislation).

276. CFTC Division of Economic Analysis and Division Trading and Markets, *Final Report on Stock Index and Cash Market Activity During October 1987 to the Commodity Futures Trading Commission* 182-185 (1988).

277. *See generally*, Lawrence Damian Mccabe, *Puppet Masters or Marionettes: Is Program Trading Manipulative as Defined by the Securities Exchange Act of 1934?* 61 FORDHAM L. REV. S207 (1993) (describing program trading and potential abuses).

278. SEC Division of Market Regulation, *The October 1987 Market Break* 1-9 (1988).

279. Jerry W. Markham & Rita McCloy Stephanz, *The Stock Market Crash of 1987: The United States Looks at New Recommendations*, 76 GEO. L. J. 1993-1995 (1988).

Concerns were raised that a stock index futures contract traded on the Chicago Board of Trade (CBOT) had been manipulated during the crash.[280] After investigating that claim, the CFTC and SEC staffs reported that they found no evidence of manipulation.[281] That conclusion set off a controversy over whether the CBOT had provided bad data to the CFTC. Standing by its staff findings, the CFTC rejected claims that it had reached its conclusion that there was no manipulation before it even began a formal investigation.[282]

Concerns were raised in Congress over short sales that were made during the crash.[283] The SEC voiced criticism over the CFTC's lack of restrictions on short sales, such as the "tick test" used by the SEC, the absence of which could "arguably" encourage speculation. However, the SEC concluded in the end that such a restriction was impracticable in the futures markets.[284] The SEC had itself come under "bitter criticism" for allowing Merrill Lynch and other index arbitrage traders to engage in short sales in unwinding positions without complying with the tick test.[285]

The CFTC and SEC and other interested parties, such as the Chicago Mercantile Exchange, filed competing reports on the cause of the stock market crash of 1987.[286] President Reagan appointed Nicholas Brady to head the independent and more objective Presidential Task Force on Market Mechanisms, known as the Brady Commission, to investigate and report independently on the crash. The Brady Commission found that a precipitating factor was the fact that the stock and commodity markets had become inextricably intertwined as a result of the growth of stock index futures contracts.[287]

---

280. James B. Stewart & Daniel Hertzberg, *How the Stock Market Almost Disintegrated a Day After the Crash,* WALL STREET JOURNAL, Nov. 20, 1987, at 1, col. 6.

281. CFTC Division of Trading and Markets, *Analysis of Trading in the Chicago Board of Trade's Major Market Index Futures Contract on October 20, 1987* (1988); SEC Division of Market Regulation, *The October 1987 Market Break* 3-30 (1988).

282. *CBOT Denies Giving False Data for CFTC Inquiry,* WALL STREET JOURNAL, Jan. 8, 1988, at 3; James B. Stewart & Bruce Ingersoll, *CFTC Report on Major Market Index Spurs New Questions on Its Oct. 20 Surge,* WALL STREET JOURNAL, Jan. 7, 1988, at 3.

283. Jonathan R. Macey, Mark Mitchell, & Jeffry Netter, *Symposium on the Regulation of Secondary Trading Markets: Program Trading, Volatility, Portfolio Insurance, and the Role of Specialists and Market Makers: Restrictions on Short Sales: An Analysis of the Uptick Rule and Its Role in View of the October 1987 Stock Market Crash,* 74 CORNELL L. REV. 799 (1989).

284. SEC Division of Market Regulation, *The October 1987 Market Break* 3-26 (1988).

285. Jonathan R. Macey, Mark Mitchell, & Jeffry Netter, *Symposium on the Regulation of Secondary Trading Markets: Program Trading, Volatility, Portfolio Insurance, and the Role of Specialists and Market Makers: Restrictions on Short Sales: An Analysis of the Uptick Rule and Its Role in View of the October 1987 Stock Market Crash,* 74 CORNELL L. REV. 799, 803, 811 (1989) (footnotes omitted).

286. *See, e.g.,* CFTC Division of Economic Analysis and Division Trading and Markets, *Final Report on Stock Index and Cash Market Activity During October 1987 to the Commodity Futures Trading Commission* (1988); SEC Division of Market Regulation, *The October 1987 Market Break* (1988); Nicholas Katzenbach, An Overview of Program Trading and Its Impact on Current Market Practices (NYSE 1987); *Preliminary Report of the Committee of Inquiry Appointed by the Chicago Mercantile Exchange* 45 (1987).

287. The Brady Commission concluded,

> Analysis of market behavior during the mid-October break makes clear an important conclusion. From an economic viewpoint, what have been traditionally seen as separate markets—the markets for stocks, stock index futures, and stock options—are in fact one market. Under ordinary circumstances, these marketplaces move sympathetically, linked by financial instruments, trading strategies, market participants and clearing and credit mechanisms.
>
> To a large extent, the problems of mid-October can be traced to the failure of these market segments to act as one. Confronted with the massive selling demands of a limited number of institutions, regulatory and institutional structures designed for separate marketplaces were incapable of effectively responding to "intermarket" pressures. The New York Stock Exchange's

The Brady Commission concluded that there was a need for coordinated regulation among federal financial regulators with an interest in futures trading or the financial instruments underlying futures contracts. It recommended that a single federal agency should be authorized to adopt intermarket regulations for futures and stocks in certain critical matters.[288] The Brady Report recommended that the Federal Reserve Board (the Fed) be given the role of single regulator.[289] That recommendation proved to be a nonstarter. Instead, a presidential working group (PWG) was created under an executive order issued by President Ronald Reagan. The PWG was supposed to act as a coordinating body among financial regulators. It was chaired by the secretary of the Treasury and its members included the Fed, SEC, and CFTC.[290]

The Brady Commission further recommended federal margin regulation for futures contracts as a means to control speculation and leverage. The PWG split over the issue of margin regulation. Congress later granted the Federal Reserve Board authority to set stock index futures margins, but the Fed delegated that authority to the CFTC, which subdelegated it to the exchanges, so nothing changed.[291] Trading halts ("circuit breakers") were recommended by the PWG and were imposed on trading on the stock markets when certain price parameters were exceeded.[292] However, the

---

> ("NYSE") automated transaction system ("DOT") [Designated Order Turnaround], used by index arbitrageurs to link the two marketplaces, ceased to be useful for arbitrage after midday on October 19. The concern that some clearinghouses and major market participants might fail inhibited intermarket activities of other investors. The futures and stock markets became disengaged, both nearly going into free fall.
>
> The ability of the equity market to absorb the huge selling pressure to which it was subjected in mid-October depended on its liquidity. But liquidity sufficient to absorb the limited selling demands of investors became an illusion of liquidity when confronted by massive selling, as everyone showed up on the same side of the market at once. Ironically, it was this illusion of liquidity which led certain similarly motivated investors, such as portfolio insurers, to adopt strategies which call for liquidity far in excess of what the market could supply.

Report of the Presidential Task Force on Market Mechanisms iv (Jan. 8, 1988).

288. The Brady Commission report recommended,

> - One agency should coordinate the few, but critical, regulatory issues which have an impact across the related market segments and throughout the financial system.
> - Clearing systems should be unified across marketplaces to reduce financial risk.
> - Margins should be made consistent across marketplaces to control speculation and financial leverage.
> - Circuit breaker mechanisms (such as price limits and coordinated trading halts) should be formulated and implemented to protect the market system.
> - Information systems should be established to monitor transactions and conditions in related markets.
>
> The single agency must have expertise in the interaction of markets—not simply experience in regulating distinct market segments. It must have a broad perspective on the financial system as a whole, both domestic and foreign, as well as independence and responsiveness.

Report of the Presidential Task Force on Market Mechanisms vi (Jan. 8, 1988).

289. *Report of the Presidential Task Force on Market Mechanisms* 61-63 (Jan. 8, 1988).

290. *See*, Jerry W. Markham & Rita McCloy Stephanz, *The Stock Market Crash of 1987: The United States Looks at New Recommendations,* 76 Geo. L.J. 1993, 2028 (1988) (describing background of formation of the PWG).

291. Jerry W. Markham, *Merging the SEC and CFTC: A Clash of Cultures*, 78 U. Cinn. L. Rev. 537, 573 (2009).

292. *Interim Report of the Working Group on Financial Markets* 4-5 (1988).

circuit breakers seemed to have little positive effect and were discarded in 2007, almost twenty years after they were first proposed.[293] As described in Chapter 7, the SEC subsequently required trading halts during periods of high volatility.

The net result of the inquiries and concerns that followed the stock market crash of 1987 and a market break in October 1989[294] was that little was done to curb speculative abuses or manipulation. The Market Reform Act of 1990[295] did seek to provide the SEC additional powers in dealing with market emergencies in the wake of those market breaks. It granted the SEC broader powers in the event of a market emergency, including the authority to halt all securities market trading, subject to presidential review.[296] An emergency was defined as a sudden and excessive fluctuation of securities prices generally or threats to fair and orderly markets, or a substantial disruption of the safe or efficient operation of the national system for clearance and settlement of securities transactions.

The Market Reform Act of 1990[297] authorized the SEC to "promulgate rules to address manipulative trading practices and market volatility. . . . It is a fairly controversial grant of authority to the agency that will be exercised only with extreme care."[298] This authority was not sought by the SEC, but was intended to be used to limit "practices that affect market volatility."[299]

The stock market crash of 1987 was followed by a series of insider trading scandals involving Ivan Boesky, Michael Milken, the "Junk Bond King," and his brokerage firm, Drexel Burnham Lambert Inc.[300] They were accused of engineering two complicated stock manipulation schemes.[301]

---

293. Jerry W. Markham & Daniel J. Harty, *For Whom the Bell Tolls: The Demise of Exchange Trading Floors and the Growth of ECNs*, 33 J. Corp. L. 865, 882 (2008),

294. The Dow Jones Industrial Average dropped by more than 190 points on October 13, 1989. The trading was the result of extraordinary price volatility in which $160 billion in stock values was lost in ninety minutes. A SEC staff report concluded that speculative trading and large institutional activity fueled this market break, while a CFTC report found no large trader activity or manipulation to have caused price volatility. Jerry W. Markham, *Federal Regulation of Margin in the Commodity Futures Industry: History and Theory*, 64 Temp. L. Rev. 59, 121 (1991).

295. Pub. L. No. 101-432, 104 Stat. 963 (1990).

296. 15 U.S.C. § 78l(k).

297. Pub. L. No. 101-432, 104 Stat. 963 (1990).

298. Remarks Before the Securities Transfer Association by SEC Commissioner Mary L. Schapiro, Boca Raton, Florida, Nov. 2, 1990.

299. It authorized the SEC

> (1) to prescribe means reasonably designed to prevent manipulation of price levels of the equity securities market or a substantial segment thereof; and
> (2) to prohibit or constrain, during periods of extraordinary market volatility, any trading practice in connection with the purchase or sale of equity securities that the Commission determines (A) has previously contributed significantly to extraordinary levels of volatility that have threatened the maintenance of fair and orderly markets; and (B) is reasonably certain to engender such levels of volatility if not prohibited or constrained.

15 U.S.C. § 78i(i).

300. These scandals are described in David A. Vise & Steve Coll, Eagle on the Street (1991).

301. The SEC described the first scheme as follows:

> In April 1985, Drexel underwrote an offering of Wickes convertible preferred stock which Wickes could cause to be converted into common stock if the closing price of Wickes common stock equaled or exceeded $6.08 per share for at least 20 of any 30 consecutive trading days. From the date of the public offering, Wickes management wanted to call the preferred stock for conversion as soon as practicable. By the close of the market on April 22, 1986, Wickes common stock had closed at or above the threshold price on 19 of 27 consecutive trading days. By the afternoon

Milken settled the SEC case and pleaded guilty to criminal charges. He agreed to pay a fine of $600 million and was initially sentenced to ten years in prison, later reduced by several years.[302] Drexel Burnham, Lambert also pleaded guilty to criminal charges and paid a fine of $650 million, which crippled the firm, and it later failed.[303] Boesky also pleaded guilty to criminal charges and was sent to prison and fined $100 million.[304]

In another high-profile manipulation case of this era, the SEC charged that Boyd Jefferies and his brokerage firm manipulated a security by pegging its closing price at the request of a third party. Jefferies & Co. made purchases of the stock on the NYSE and the Pacific Stock Exchange

---

> of April 23, 1986, the price of Wickes common stock had dropped below the threshold price. [Cary] Maultasch contacted the [Ivan] Boesky organization and instructed it to purchase, in its own name but for the benefit of Drexel and Milken, sufficient quantities of Wickes common stock to cause the closing price to equal or exceed $6.125. During the last half hour of trading, the Boesky organization purchased 1.9 million shares of Wickes common stock, at prices ranging between $6 and $6.125. Wickes common stock closed at $6.125 on April 23, 1986. As a result, Wickes was able to initiate the mandatory redemption of the preferred stock. Drexel received a $2.3 million fee for agreeing to be standby underwriter for the redemption.

SEC v. Drexel Burnham Lambert Inc., SEC Litig. Rel. No. 11859, 1988 SEC LEXIS 1865 (S.D.N.Y.). The SEC also charged another manipulation it described as follows:

> In March 1986, Stone's board of directors approved a public offering of securities to be underwritten and managed by Drexel which were to be convertible into common stock at a specified price fixed at a premium over the closing price of Stone common stock on the day the offering was priced. Stone informed Drexel that it did not want to proceed with the offering until Stone common stock reached a price of $46 to $48 per share so that the conversion price would approximate $60 per share. From early April to April 14, the price of Stone common stock remained below $46 per share. On April 14, Maultasch, under the supervision of Milken and pursuant to the Arrangement, instructed the Boesky organization to purchase Stone common stock for the benefit of Drexel and Milken in the name of the Boesky organization and told the trader that he could bid above the price at which Stone common stock was then trading. The Boesky organization's purchases were over 37 percent of the total volume of Stone common stock traded that day. Stone common stock closed at $46.75 per share on April 14, 1986. After the close of trading, Stone told Drexel to go forward with the offering. On April 15, 1985, on instructions received from [Pamela] Monzert throughout the day, and for Drexel's and Milken's benefit, the Boesky organization purchased additional shares of Stone common stock. The series of transactions in Stone common stock were effected for the purpose of, and with the effect of, creating actual or apparent active trading in, raising the price of, and inducing the purchase and sale of Stone common stock and convertible securities.

Id.

302. The criminal charges were controversial; accusations were made by a prominent law professor that the charges were politically motivated, and others charged that the government had extorted Milken's guilty plea by threats to his relatives. DANIEL FISCHEL, PAYBACK: THE CONSPIRACY TO DESTROY MICHAEL MILKEN AND HIS FINANCIAL REVOLUTION (1995).

303. JERRY W. MARKHAM, A FINANCIAL HISTORY OF MODERN U.S. CORPORATE SCANDALS, FROM ENRON TO REFORM 636 (2005).

304. JESSE KORNBLUTH, HIGHLY CONFIDENT 105 (1992). Boesky was involved in several other manipulations, including one that rocked the City of London. Boesky revealed as a part of a plea bargain that in 1986 Guinness had massively manipulated its share price in order to prevail in a takeover battle with the Argyll Group PLC. over the acquisition of the Distillers Company. Steve Lohr, *Guinness Scandal Roils Britain*, NEW YORK TIMES, Jan. 30, 1987. Guinness had pumped $100 million into a fund managed by Boesky, which Boesky used to help manipulate the Guinness stock. Ernest Saunders, the Guinness CEO, and other Guinness executives were jailed over their role in this debacle. *The Guinness Affair: Bitter End*, THE ECONOMIST, Nov. 27, 1997.

at or on the close of trading in amounts totaling approximately 66 percent of the trading volume that day, pegging the stock at least one-eighth of one point in order to have it close at the requested price. The SEC complaint alleged "that Jefferies & Co. subsequently sold the securities at a loss and was recompensed for such loss pursuant to a false invoice it created for purported 'investment banking services' rendered. As a result of such conduct, the Complaint alleges that the defendants violated Section 10(b) of the Exchange Act and Rule 10b-5 thereunder."[305] That case was settled by consent.

5:12 TREASURY SECURITIES MANIPULATION CONCERNS

By 1990, over 60 percent of futures contracts being traded were financial futures, rather than agricultural or other "hard" commodities.[306] That number would grow to 75 percent in 2011.[307] Even more startling was a finding by the SEC staff in its report on the stock market crash of 1987 that, due to market efficiency, futures contracts traded on commodity exchanges were leading the stock exchanges in setting stock prices. This had the effect of creating a "synthetic" stock market.[308] The securities and futures markets were becoming intertwined in other ways. Futures trading on Treasury securities was a leader in exchange volume. By 1994, the second most actively traded futures contract was the U.S. Treasury bond contract on the CBOT, being bested only by euro futures on the CME.[309]

Problems appeared early on in the Treasury pit. The Treasury futures market on the CBOT had been targeted for fraud in 1988 by a gang of thieves who used wigs and other disguises, as well as fake trading credentials, to gain access to the Treasury bond pit on the CBOT for a one-year period.[310] That debacle was followed by a more serious affair involving a large government prime dealer, Salomon Brothers, now a part of Citigroup. That firm was caught up in a massive scandal in 1991 resulting from efforts by one of its traders to squeeze Treasury securities.[311] The trader, Paul Mozer, carried out that squeeze by evading a 35 percent restriction imposed by the Treasury on the amount of notes or bonds that any one dealer could purchase at a Treasury auction for two-year notes.

Mozer used customer accounts without their permission to buy 86 percent of the May 1992 two-year Treasury note auction.[312] In one instance Mozer entered an unauthorized order for $1 billion for the account of Mercury Asset Management.[313] It was claimed that Mozer was able to

305. SEC v. Jefferies, SEC Litig. Rel. No. 2314, 1987 SEC LEXIS 2314 (S.D.N.Y.).

306. III JERRY W. MARKHAM, A FINANCIAL HISTORY OF THE UNITED STATES, FROM THE AGE OF DERIVATIVES TO THE NEW MILLENNIUM 162 (2002).

307. *History of Financial Futures*, http://cmz-trading.com/education/financial-futures/history-of-financial-futures/ (accessed January 31, 2011).

308. SEC Division of Market Regulation, *The October 1987 Market Break* 3-6 (1988).

309. III JERRY W. MARKHAM, A FINANCIAL HISTORY OF THE UNITED STATES, FROM THE AGE OF DERIVATIVES TO THE NEW MILLENNIUM 135 (2002).

310. The scheme involved riskless trading in which the trader would keep profitable trades and fail to report to the clearinghouse unprofitable ones, leading to profits of some $200,000. DAVID GREISING & LAURIE MORSE, BROKERS, BAGMEN AND MOLES 71 (1991). The leader of the gang, Thompson Sanders, was a member of the CBOT and was sentenced to six years in prison. He was also fined $1,125,000 by the CBOT. *Trader Fined $1,125,000*, NEW YORK TIMES, Feb. 28, 1989, at D6.

311. This scandal was the subject of a book: MARTIN MAYER, NIGHTMARE ON WALL STREET: SALOMON BROTHERS AND THE CORRUPTION OF THE MARKETPLACE (1993).

312. Jonathan Fuerbringer, *Salomon Brothers Admits Violations at Treasury Sales*, NEW YORK TIMES, Aug. 10, 1991.

313. III JERRY W. MARKHAM, A FINANCIAL HISTORY OF THE UNITED STATES, FROM THE AGE OF DERIVATIVES TO THE NEW MILLENNIUM 215 (2002).

squeeze Treasury note prices by over $20 million.[314] Mozer was convicted of criminal charges for his role in this squeeze and was sentenced to four months in prison. Salomon Brothers was fined $290 million for this infraction and for failing to report it in a timely fashion to regulators. The head of the firm, John Gutfreund, was fined $100,000 by the SEC and barred from serving as the head of any brokerage firm.[315]

In *Three Crown Ltd. Partnership v. Salomon Brothers*,[316] a district court considered a claim that the defendants manipulated the market for April and May 1991 two-year Treasury note futures. The defendants were Salomon Brothers, Paul Mozer, and several hedge funds and their managers, including George Soros and his Quantum Fund and Michael Steinhardt. The plaintiffs were commodity pools that traded in Treasury securities and futures. They claimed violations of the antitrust laws, SEC Rule 10b-5, RICO, and common law fraud. Apparently, no claim of manipulation was made under the Commodity Exchange Act.

The complaint charged that the defendants took a large long position in the Treasury notes through direct purchases and repurchase agreement (repo) agreements, which caused Treasury notes to be held off the market. It was claimed that this was done in order to squeeze prices to an artificial level. The defendants were claimed to have concealed their position by purchases through several primary dealers. The court initially denied dismissal of a claim that the defendants had caused damages to short note sellers.[317] The court, however, later granted partial summary judgment, holding that the plaintiffs had shown no proof that this activity prevented the plaintiffs from trading at unmanipulated prices or that this activity prevented the plaintiffs from engaging in a "butterfly" strategy through which it sought to profit. The plaintiffs were seeking damages for trades they did not make because of the alleged manipulation. However, the court held that the Supreme Court's decision in *Blue Chip Stamps v. Manor Drug Stores*[318] denied recovery under Rule 10b-5 because the plaintiffs were neither purchasers nor sellers. Damages were also found to be unavailable under the antitrust and other laws relied upon by plaintiffs.

A case brought by the SEC with respect to these activities resulted in a settlement in which Steinhardt Management Co. and the Caxton Corp. jointly agreed to pay $76 million in fines and disgorgement of profits.[319] The SEC complaint charged that Steinhardt and Caxton bought large leveraged long positions in April two-year cash Treasury notes in mid-April 1991. Their combined positions eventually rose to over 158 percent of the approximately $12 billion of April two-year notes auctioned by the U.S. Treasury. Steinhardt and Caxton held amounts totaling from $12 billion to $19 billion of April two-year notes from May 1991 to September 1991.

The short sellers to Steinhardt and Caxton had to make delivery by borrowing notes in the repo market or by buying notes in the cash market. Many short sellers in both markets were dependent upon Caxton and Steinhardt, the holders of controlling positions, as major sources of the notes, but the defendants withheld their notes from the cash and repo markets. The result was a short squeeze in which short sellers were forced to either borrow notes at unfavorable repo rates or cover their short positions in the cash market at inflated prices, resulting in large profits to Caxton and Steinhardt.[320]

---

314. Bradford D. Jordan & Susan D Jordan, *Salomon Brothers and the May 1991 Treasury Auction: Analysis of a Market Corner*, 20 J. OF BANK. & FIN. 25 (1996).

315. Salomon Brothers became the subject of much ridicule for the high-risk bets taken by management on almost anything. *See*, MICHAEL LEWIS, LIAR'S POKER (1989).

316. Three Crown Ltd. Partnership v. Salomon Brothers, 906 F. Supp. 876 (S.D.N.Y. 1995).

317. Three Crown Ltd. Partnership v. Salomon Brothers, 1995 U.S. Dist. LEXIS 9961 (S.D.N.Y. 1995).

318. Blue Chip Stamps v. Manor Drug Stores, 421 U.S. 723 (1975).

319. JEFF MADRICK, AGE OF GREED 263 (2011).

320. SEC Litigation Release No. 14358, 1994 SEC LEXIS 3961.

The Treasury Department changed the way in which it handled Treasury auctions after this affair. The Government Securities Act Amendments of 1993[321] also allowed the Treasury to demand reports from "specified persons holding, maintaining, or controlling large positions in to-be-issued or recently issued Treasury securities." The Treasury Department adopted an "on demand" reporting system for these reports. It began testing that system in 1997. In 1998, the Treasury required reports from traders holding $2.5 billion or more of the 5½ percent ten-year Treasury note due February 2008.[322]

An attempted manipulation of the Treasury market occurred in 1992 through trading in futures and options on the CBOT. This scheme involved the purchase by Anthony Catalfo and Donald Zimmerman of Treasury bond puts and the sale of Treasury bond futures contracts in massive quantities. "They reasoned, in line with elementary principles of mass psychology, that such large-scale investment in a downward-looking position would cause other traders to think the market was going down and to act accordingly."[323] They planned to close their positions after the market declined.

Catalfo began trading by using a worthless check in the amount of $50,000 that he posted with his clearing firm, Lee B. Stern & Co., as margin for their trading. In the first nine minutes of trading in the Treasury bond option pit on October 22, 1992, the conspirators purchased over 4,100 put options with a premium cost of $2.1 million. They quickly made a profit of over $1 million from that massive position.[324] The scheme soon unraveled after CBOT staff began examining these unusual trades. "Other traders, who had watched the massive purchases, realized what was happening and moved in for the kill. By the time Stern had disentangled itself from those trades, it had lost $8.5 million, which was $2 million more than the company's net worth."[325] Catalfo was convicted of wire fraud in federal court and was sentenced to forty-two months in prison. Zimmerman fled to Canada to avoid prosecution.

The CFTC tried to stretch the reach of its antimanipulation authority through a negotiated settlement in another case involving Treasury trading. In that settlement, *In re Fenchurch Capital Management Ltd.*,[326] the CFTC found manipulation where the respondent stood for delivery on the June 1993 ten-year U.S. Treasury note futures contract that was traded on the CBOT. After the close of trading in that contract month, the respondent gained control over a dominant portion of the available supply of the cheapest delivery Treasury notes on that contract. It increased its position in the issue through repo transactions at a time when the notes were in tight supply. It also intentionally withheld the notes from the market. This required the shorts to deliver more valuable Treasury securities without offsetting compensation. The decision was novel in that the alleged manipulation did not commence until after trading had expired in the futures contracts, and affected only a portion of the supply that was available for delivery.

Another Treasury bond scandal arose after Peter J. Davis, a consultant to Goldman Sachs & Co., leaked an embargoed Treasury Department conference report on October 31, 2001. The embargoed announcement advised that the Treasury was planning to discontinue the issuance of the thirty-year bond. Davis leaked the information to John M. Youngdahl, a vice president and senior economist at Goldman Sachs. Goldman traders then purchased $84 million in thirty-year bonds and established

---

321. 103 Pub. L. No. 202, 107 Stat. 2344 (1993).

322. *Treasury, in Test, Says Biggest Noteholders Must File Reports*, WALL STREET JOURNAL, June 9, 1998, at C24.

323. United States v. Catalfo, 64 F.3d 1070, 1072 (7th Cir. 1995), *cert. denied*, 517 U.S. 1192 (1996).

324. 64 F.3d at 1075.

325. 64 F.3d at 1075-1076.

326. In re Fenchurch Capital Management Ltd., COMM. FUT. L. REP. (CCH) ¶ 26,747 (C.F.T.C. 1996).

a large long futures position in the bond in anticipation of a price rise once this information became public. Goldman Sachs made about $4.3 million from those trades. Massachusetts Financial Services Company was also tipped by Davis, and it purchased $65 million in Treasury bonds.

Youngdahl and Davis were sued by the SEC for insider trading, and Youngdahl pleaded guilty to criminal charges of fraud for misappropriating the information. He was sentenced to thirty-three months in prison. Davis was not indicted but was barred from the securities industry.[327] Goldman Sachs paid $9.3 million to settle SEC charges over its failure to properly supervise Youngdahl. Massachusetts Financial agreed to pay almost $1 million to settle charges over its trading.[328]

A plaintiff in *Premium Plus Partners LP v. Davis* charged that when news of the suspension of the thirty-year Treasury bond became public, "the ask price for 30-Year Treasury Bonds increased, triggering the largest one-day rally in the price of 30-Year Treasury Bonds since 1987. In the wake of the public release of the information on October 31, 2001, the price of 30-Year Bonds increased by some 6%."[329] The federal district court in that case held that the Treasury bond trades were not subject to the antimanipulation provisions of the Commodity Exchange Act because they were exempted from its reach by the so-called Treasury amendment that was added to the statute in 1975.[330] The Treasury amendment, among other things, exempted transactions in government securities from CFTC regulation unless the transactions involved futures on Treasury securities.[331] The court did allow discovery on the issue of whether Goldman Sachs manipulated the market by using the leaked information to trade. The claims in that case were later settled for $200,000. A class action claim over this conduct was also dismissed.

Private litigants charged that Pacific Investment Management Co. (PIMCO) manipulated the Treasury futures market for ten-year notes on the CBOT in May and June 2005. The Seventh Circuit Court of Appeals in *Kohen v. Pacific Investment Management Co. LLC*[332] upheld a class action certification of that claim under the antimanipulation provisions of the Commodity Exchange Act. The plaintiffs claimed that PIMCO increased the percentage of a Treasury note issue that it owned from 12 to 42 percent over a two-week period. The plaintiffs charged that PIMCO used this dominant position to artificially increase prices at a cost of $600 million to investors.[333] The Seventh Circuit noted that "a buyer may be able to force up the price by 'cornering' the market . . . [so] that sellers can fulfill their contractual obligations only by dealing with that buyer."[334] The class action claims over this charge were settled for $92 million.[335]

---

327. Premium Plus Partners LP v. Goldman, Sachs & Co., 648 F.3d 533 (7th Cir. 2010).

328. *Goldman Settles Insider Trading Charges*, Los Angeles Times, Sept. 5, 2003, http://articles.latimes.com/2003/sep/05/business/fi-goldman5 (accessed February 12, 2012).

329. Premium Plus Partners LP v. Davis, 2005 U.S. Dist. LEXIS 6158 (N.D. Ill. 2005) (citations omitted).

330. Premium Plus Partners LP v. Davis, 2008 U.S. Dist. LEXIS 60597 (N.D. Ill.).

331. 7 U.S.C. § 2(c)(1) (1974). For a description of the Treasury amendment, see Jerry W. Markham, *Regulation of Hybrid Instruments Under the Commodity Exchange Act: Alternatives Are Needed*, 1990 Columbia Bus. L. Rev. 1, 8 (1990). The CFTC had tried to narrow the Treasury amendment to allow the CFTC to attack boiler rooms that were fraudulently selling OTC derivatives to unsophisticated investors. The Supreme Court rejected that effort. Dunn v. CFTC, 519 U.S. 465 (1997). However, the Commodity Exchange Act was amended in 2000 and 2008 to give the CFTC authority to regulate OTC retail foreign currency transactions. *See*, Jerry W. Markham, Commodities Regulation: Fraud, Manipulation and Other Claims, § 27:14.50 (2010) (describing that legislation).

332. Kohen v. Pacific Investment Management Co., LLC, 571 F.3d 672 (7th Cir. 2009), *cert. denied*, --- U.S. --- (2010).

333. 571 F.3d at 675-676.

334. 571 F.3d at 675.

335. The suit claimed $600 million in damages but was settled for $92 million after some adverse evi-

The government successfully prosecuted David G. Sklena, a trader on the Chicago Board of Trade, in 2010.[336] He had made $1.65 million in profits through trading in the five-year Treasury note futures pit on April 2, 2004. That trading occurred immediately after the release of a government report that employment numbers were better than expected. Sklena and another trader, who died before trial, used the volatility in the market caused by that report to reap profits from customer orders through noncompetitive trades.[337] Sklena was convicted after a bench trial on wire fraud counts and on what the court characterized as "commodity fraud" under Section 4(b) of the Commodity Exchange Act[338] as well as price manipulation under that statute[339] and for noncompetitive trading in violation of a catchall provision under the Commodity Exchange Act involving violations of other provisions of the statute or CFTC regulations.[340] Interestingly, in a related action that was settled by consent, the CFTC charges over the same conduct did not include manipulation claims. Rather, it focused on fraud under Section 4(b)[341] and improper trading practices under Section 4(c)[342] of the Commodity Exchange Act.[343]

In March 2012, the CFTC charged subsidiaries of JPMorgan Chase & Co. and BlackRock Inc. with engaging in prearranged trading in U.S. Treasury futures in violation of Section (4c) of the Commodity Exchange Act. The two companies were fined a total of $390,000.[344] The CFTC charged that employees of respondents had engaged in preexecution communications with a customer. The result was a matching of the customer's own orders with each other, placing the customer on both sides of the transaction. The CFTC concluded that this activity resulted in a prearranged fictitious sale. In one transaction, a BlackRock employee engaged in preexecution communications with an account executive at the selling futures commission merchant in order to pair the customer orders with BlackRock. The Chicago Mercantile Exchange (CME) was investigating whether Glenn Hadden, a high-profile trader for Goldman Sachs, manipulated the closing prices of Treasury futures on that exchange in 2008 in order to benefit other positions.[345]

On a grander scale was the fear being raised by the foreign holdings of U.S. debt by international investors. Those traders held 47 percent of U.S. debt and agency securities on June 30, 2010.[346] This amount included large holdings by China, which raised concern that the Chinese government

---

dentiary rulings against the plaintifffs. *Pimco to Pay $92 Million to Settle Bond Market Manipulation Suit*, Lost Angeles Times, Dec. 30, 2010; *Pimco to Pay $92 Million to Settle Market Manipulation Lawsuit*, Bloomberg, http://www.bloomberg.com/news/2010-12-30/pimco-to-pay-92-million-to-settle-futures-lawsuit.html (accessed February 12, 2012).

336. *See*, United States v. Sklena, No. 09 CR 302 Memorandum Opinion (May 9, 2011), http://il.findacase.com/research/wfrmDocViewer.aspx/xq/fac.20110509_0001204.NIL.htm/qx (accessed August 16, 2011).

337. CFTC Press Release No. 5434 (Jan. 10, 2008), http://www.cftc.gov/PressRoom/PressReleases/pr5434-08.html (accessed August 16, 2011).

338. 7 U.S.C. § 6b(a)(1)(i).

339. 7 U.S.C. § 13(a)(2).

340. 7 U.S.C. § 13(a)(5).

341. 7 U.S.C. § 6b.

342. 7 U.S.C. § 6c.

343. In the Matter of Sklena, CFTC Doc. No. SD 09-01 (C.F.T.C. Aug. 7, 2009), http://www.cftc.gov/ucm/groups/public/@lrenforcementactions/documents/legalpleading/enfsklenanotice08072009.pdf (accessed August 16, 2011).

344. *CFTC: BlackRock, JP Morgan Units to Pay Penalties for Prearranged Trades*, Wall Street Journal, March 8, 2012.

345. Susanne Craig, *Trader at Morgan Stanley Faces Inquiry on Manipulation*, New York Times, Dec. 3, 2012 at A1.

346. Government Accountability Office, *Ownership of Federal Debt*, http://www.gao.gov/special.pubs/longterm/debt/ownership.html (accessed February 22, 2012).

might try to manipulate the Treasury market and attack the dollar as part of economic warfare on the United States.[347] That seems unlikely, since the United States is a major market for China, but rationality does not always drive international relations or market manipulations.

5:13 PUMP-AND-DUMP SCHEMES

The SEC faced a challenge from a plague of "pump-and-dump" stock manipulation schemes that arose during the dot.com stock market bubble at the end of the twentieth century. These frauds took many forms but generally involved the buying up of a large number of shares of the stock of a particular company by the promoter of the scheme. The price of that stock was then pumped up by the promoter through a fraudulent sales campaign, which falsely touted the prospects of the company, which often had none. The stock acquired by the managers of the fraud was then dumped into the market at its inflated price.[348]

Such schemes were by no means new to the stock market. "As far back as the 1700s, con artists on London's Exchange Alley were using a 'pump and dump' scheme to defraud investors" during the "South Sea Bubble." The stock price of the South Sea Company was "inflated by false rumors of profitability spread about the company by owners of the shares, who then sold the shares at a substantial profit after the price of the shares increased."[349]

The pool operations that are described in Chapter 2, which the federal securities laws had tried to eliminate, often employed pump-and-dump tactics. The SEC also had to contend over the years with numerous boiler room operations that used high-pressure cold calls to solicit investors and thereby artificially inflate a stock's price.[350] The 1980s also witnessed numerous fraudulent and manipulative schemes involving low-priced "penny" stocks.[351] These schemes included "blind pool" and "blank check" offerings in which investor funds are solicited in stock offerings without any stated purpose for their use. "A common method of perpetrating penny stock fraud is through the marketing of 'shell' corporations, or 'blank check companies' with no operating history, few employees, few or no discernible assets, and no legitimate likelihood of success in the future. Often the only legally stated purpose of such companies is to seek investment opportunities through mergers and acquisitions."[352]

---

347. James Rickards, Currency Wars: The Making of the Next Global Crisis (2011).

348. *See*, Joseph I. Goldstein, Sarah B. Ackerson & Laura A. Novack, *An Overview of Market Manipulation: Legal and Practical Aspects*, at pp. 28-37, Conference on Market Manipulation: Law, Economics, and Public Policy sponsored by the Center for Study of Futures and Options Markets and the American Bar Association, Washington, DC (Nov. 8–9, 1990) (describing the elements of such "hype-and-dump manipulations").

349. Kevin C. Bartels, *"Click Here to Buy the Next Microsoft": The Penny Stock Rules, Online Microcap Fraud, and the Unwary Investor*, 75 Ind. L. J. 353 (2000) (footnotes omitted). The share price of the South Sea Company reached £1,050 before dropping to £150 a few months later and causing much scandal. I Jerry W. Markham, A Financial History of the United States, From Christopher Columbus to the Robber Barons (1492-1900) 97-99 (2002).

350. *See, e.g.*, Coplin v. United States, 88 F.2d 652 (9th Cir.), *cert. denied*, 301 U.S. 703 (1937) (violations of Section 17(a) of the 33 Act); In the Matter of Landau Co., 40 S.E.C. 1119 (1962) (violations of Section 17(a) of the 33 Act and Sections 10(b) and 15(c) of the 34 Act); In the Matter of F.S. Johns & Co. Inc., 43 S.E.C. 124 (1966) (same). For a description of these boiler room operations, see 3 Thomas Lee Hazen, The Law of Securities Regulation of § 14:18 (4th ed. 2002).

351. "Penny stocks are low-priced, highly speculative stocks generally sold in the over-the-counter (OTC) market and generally not listed on an exchange. Often, they do not qualify for listing on the National Association of Securities Dealers Automated Quotation system (NASDAQ)." H.R. Rep. No. 617, 101st Cong., 2d Sess. 8 (1990).

352. H.R. Rep. No. 617, 101st Cong., 2d Sess. 5 (1990).

In a three-year period at the end of the 1980s, the National Association of Securities Dealers, Inc., (now FINRA) brought disciplinary actions against 250 penny stock dealers.[353] Criminal actions were brought against the worst of those penny stock firms, including Blinder Robinson, F.D. Roberts Securities, and Monarch Funding. The head of Blinder Robinson, Meyer Blinder, was convicted of stock fraud and RICO violations for rigging the market of two companies through a blind pool. He was sentenced to nearly four years in prison.[354] The SEC also waged war over an extended period on First Jersey Securities Inc. and its owner Robert Brennan over penny stock sales. First Jersey and Brennan were ordered to pay some $75 million in fines and damages and both declared bankruptcy. Brennan was ultimately convicted of bankruptcy fraud.[355]

Congress passed the Securities Enforcement Remedies and Penny Stock Reform Act of 1990[356] in response to these scandals. It gave the SEC power to sanction officers of public companies and provided for penalties ascending in severity according to the degree of the offense.[357] It also regulated blank check offerings through enhanced disclosure requirements.[358] This legislation did not, however, forestall a wave of pump-and-dump manipulation schemes in the late 1990s that were carried out through the Internet in the stock of thinly traded small-cap companies.[359]

These pump-and-dump operations involved such colorful characters as Tokyo Joe's Societe Anonyme Corp., which charged Internet subscribers up to $2,400 per year for Tokyo Joe's stock tips. The company, operated from the home of its owner, Yun Soo Oh Park, collected more than $1.1 million in fees. The SEC charged that through his advice to the thousands of members on his website, "Park was essentially able to manipulate and affect the price of stocks he would buy and sell. For example, he would purportedly encourage members to buy shares of certain stocks, which he also already owned, in order to inflate the price, and then he would reap the benefit by selling his shares profitably, a practice known as scalping."[360]

---

353. III JERRY W. MARKHAM, A FINANCIAL HISTORY OF THE UNITED STATES, FROM THE AGE OF DERIVATIVES TO THE NEW MILLENNIUM 148-149 (2002). *See also*, H.R. Rep. No. 617, 101st Cong., 2d Sess. 10-16 (1990) (further describing these abuses).

354. United States v. Blinder, 10 F.3d 1468 (9th Cir. 1993).

355. United States v. Brennan, 326 F.2d 176 (3d Cir.), *cert. denied*, 540 U.S. 898 (2003).

356. Pub. L. No. 101-429, 104 Stat. 931.

357. Matthew Scott Morris, *The Securities Enforcement Remedies and Penny Stock Reform Act of 1990: By Keeping Up With the Joneses, the SEC's Enforcement Arsenal Is Modernized*, 7 ADM. L.J. AM. U. 151 (1993).

358. *See generally*, O. Dennis Hernand, *Broker-Dealer Regulation Under the New Penny Stock Rules*, 1993 COLUM. BUS. L. REV. 27.

359. These pump-and-dump schemes have been described as follows:

> The new "cyber" boiler rooms allow scam artists to conduct sophisticated market manipulations at almost no cost over the Internet from the comfort of their own homes. In four easy steps, a manipulator can consummate the entire fraud. The first step is to set up a site or home page where potential investors can find out about the issuer. In step two, the manipulator, using bulk e-mail or a spamming program, personally contacts potential investors regarding an investment opportunity. In step three, the manipulator begins a 'buzz' about the issuer and its shares by posting false information to bulletin boards, newsgroups, and discussion forums. Finally, in step four, the manipulator strengthens the buzz by employing an Internet investment newsletter. It is that easy to hype the stock, and easier still to sell the stock back into the exchanges or over-the-counter markets at a profit and reap the financial rewards of having inflated the stock price.

Nancy Toross, *Double-Click on This: Keeping Pace With On-Line Market Manipulation*, 32 LOY. L.A.L. REV. 1399, 1420-1421 (1999) (footnotes omitted).

360. SEC v. Park, 99 F. Supp. 2d 889, 892 (N.D. Ill. 2000).

The SEC created an Office of Internet Enforcement, and 200 lawyers were assigned to this "cyber-force" in order to combat these manipulative Internet practices. Among the schemes it dealt with was one carried out by a group of Georgetown law students, and one of their mothers, through a website called FastTrades.com, which had some 9,000 subscribers. The students made $350,000 from trading in four stocks promoted on their website. A fifteen-year-old boy was charged with defrauding investors of $285,000 in an Internet pump-and-dump scheme. In another case, a seventeen-year-old high school student defrauded over 1,000 investors and was ordered to pay a $1.2 million civil penalty as a result of an Internet pump-and-dump scheme.[361] More recently, twin sixteen-year-old brothers from England were charged by the SEC with running a pump-and-dump scheme that they promoted with false claims of a "stock picking robot" that would pick penny stocks that were about to jump in price.[362]

Numerous regulatory actions were brought against pump-and-dump firms using old-fashioned telephone sales as well as the Internet to commit fraud.[363] Those cases included actions against A.R. Baron, H.J. Meyers & Co. Inc., Biltmore Securities, A.S. Goldman, Duke & Co., and DMN Capital Investments.[364] The shoe designer Steve Madden was found guilty of manipulating the stock prices of twenty-three public offerings through two brokerage firms, Stratton Oakmont and Monroe Parker Securities. Madden was sentenced to forty-one months in prison.[365]

Some schemes involved hiding or misrepresenting the identity of someone sending an email in order to deceive the recipient. "For example, by pretending to be a company insider when in actuality the user is a short term investor in the company's stock, the user can disguise his or her identity and post false or inaccurate information on the Internet to artificially hype the stock."[366] A variation on such schemes is the "free-riding" fraud that has been common in the stock market for years. This involves a trader who opens an account at a firm, purchases stock, but refuses to pay for it if the stock price does not immediately rise. One court characterized such a scheme as "heads I win, tails you lose."[367] Free-riding schemes also involve naked short sales where the trader falsely claims to own stock that he asks a broker to sell. The trader will close out the short position at a profit if the stock price declines or simply walk away if it rises. These schemes,

---

361. JERRY W. MARKHAM, A FINANCIAL HISTORY OF MODERN U.S. CORPORATE SCANDALS, FROM ENRON TO REFORM 25, 27 (2005).

362. Susanne Craig, *S.E.C. Files Charges Against Father and Son, and Twin Brothers*, http://dealbook.nytimes.com/2012/04/20/the-s-e-c-keeps-it-in-the-family/.

363. *See generally*, *e.g.*, SEC v. Whittemore, 659 F.3d 1 (D.C. Cir. 2011) (pump and dump scheme); SEC v. Poirier, 140 F. Supp. 2d 1033, 1037 (D. Ariz. 2001) (defendants found to have "participated in a classic 'pump and dump' scheme by forming Garcis U.S.A. Inc. ('Garcis'), acquiring shares of Garcis and then pumping false information into the market about Garcis to inflate share prices intending to sell off their shares at the inflated value before the false information was discovered"); SEC v. Omnigene Development Inc., 105 F. Supp. 2d 1316, 1317 (S.D. Fl. 2000) (defendant found to have "participated in a 'scalping' or 'pump and dump' scheme—that is, a scheme to invest in a stock and cause a rise in its value by disseminating false or misleading promotions and thereby create a profit for himself"); SEC v. Ampudia, 2007 WL 1051425 (S.D.N.Y. 2007) (emergency order to stop a pump-and-dump scheme in several stocks); SEC v. Luskco, 2007 WL 1260777 (C.D. Cal. 2007) (pump-and-dump scheme in low-priced stocks using spam emails); SEC v. One or More Unknown Traders, 530 F. Supp. 2d 192 (D.D.C. 2008) (pump-and-dump scheme); In the Matter of Terrell, 2000 WL 248549 (S.E.C.) (Internet pump-and-dump scheme); In the Matter of Scacci, 1999 WL 710848 (S.E.C.) ("classic" pump-and-dump scheme); SEC v. McCaskey, Fed. Sec. L. Rep. (CCH) ¶ 91533, 2001 WL 102905 (S.D. N.Y. 2001) (pump-and-dump scheme).

364. JERRY W. MARKHAM, A FINANCIAL HISTORY OF MODERN U.S. CORPORATE SCANDALS, FROM ENRON TO REFORM 27-28 (2005).

365. Robert F. Worth, *Shoe Company Chief Sentenced in Fraud Case*, NEW YORK TIMES, April 5, 2002.

366. Nancy Toross, *Double-Click on This: Keeping Pace With On-Line Market Manipulation*, 32 LOY. L.A.L. REV. 1399, 1418 (1999) (footnote omitted).

367. Rooney Pace Inc. v. Reid, 605 F. Supp. 158, 161 (S.D.N.Y. 1985).

which have been the subject of numerous disciplinary proceedings, usually involve violations of Regulation T restrictions on margin trading.[368]

In *United States v. Corr*,[369] the defendants were convicted of a manipulation scheme involving "wooden tickets," which the Second Circuit identified "as an order to purchase securities for which the purchaser does not pay whether or not the intention not to pay existed at the time of the order." The defendants were also "parking" stock as part of their scheme, which "is an artificial device to avoid depressing the market price and it occurs when a broker, unable to keep securities in his trading account, ostensibly sells the same to another broker, with the understanding that the same securities will be purchased back by the ostensible seller before the settlement date. In this manner the shares are not sold into the market."[370]

In *SEC v. Berliner*,[371] the defendant was enjoined by consent after being charged with manipulating the price of a stock through a false rumor sent by text messages to brokers and hedge funds, which were reported in the press. The text messages stated that a Blackstone Group acquisition of the Alliance Data Systems Corp. was being negotiated at a much lower price than previously reported. The news reports of this false claim caused the Alliance stock price to fall by 17 percent before the rumor could be corrected. The defendant had shorted the Alliance stock and made a large profit.[372]

In *In the Matter of Setteducati*,[373] the SEC dismissed a manipulation claim because bid quotations in the wake of an initial public offering were not shown to have been based on anything other than market fundamentals. The SEC noted that manipulations are often associated with a rapid price surge in a stock that has little investor interest because of an absence of any known prospects. The SEC also noted that typically the manipulation of a stock price is followed by a price collapse.[374]

---

368. *See*, 23A JERRY W. MARKHAM & THOMAS LEE HAZEN, BROKER-DEALER OPERATIONS UNDER SECURITIES AND COMMODITY LAWS § 8:9 (2012) (describing these schemes and prosecutions).

369. United States v. Corr, 543 F.2d 1042, 1045, n. 4 (2d Cir. 1976).

370. 543 F.2d at 1045, n. 5. *See also*, United States v. Russo, 74 F.3d 1383 (2d Cir. 1996), *cert. denied*, 519 U.S. 927 (1996) (parking manipulation scheme). Parking schemes are also used in order to evade SEC net capital requirements for broker-dealers. *See*, 23 JERRY W. MARKHAM & THOMAS LEE HAZEN, BROKER-DEALER OPERATIONS UNDER SECURITIES AND COMMODITY LAWS § 4:20 (2012) (describing these schemes); Lewis D. Lowenfels and Alan R. Bromberg, *Securities Market Manipulations: An Examination and Analysis of Domination and Control, Frontrunning, and Parking*, 55 ALB. L. REV. 293 (1991) (same).

371. SEC v. Berliner, 2008 WL 1827759 (S.D.N.Y. 2008) (SEC press release describing settlement).

372. *See also, e.g.*, In the Matter of Pagliarini, 2011 WL 674086 (S.E.C. 2011) (consent order finding failure to supervise in connection with sales used to manipulate the prices of several micro-cap stocks); SEC v. Badian, 2010 WL 4840063 (S.D. N.Y. 2010) (action involving failure to supervise proprietary account used to manipulate a stock); In the Matter of Wolfe & Hurst Bond Brokers Inc., 2009 WL 1323408 (S.E.C.) (manipulation of municipal bond market auctions by arrangements that artificially narrowed spreads); In the Matter of Regional Brokers Inc., 2007 WL 2803985 (S.E.C.) (similar findings): In the Matter of Kirlin Securities Inc., 2009 WL 4731652 (S.E.C.) (SEC upholds FINRA finding that share price was manipulated in order to avoid delisting from NASDAQ); In the Matter of Pozner, 2003 WL 22935774 (S.E.C.) (bid quotes used to manipulate a stock); In the Matter of Winkler, 2003 WL 22971038 (S.E.C.) (manipulation by broker improperly using customer accounts); In the Matter of Ingardia, 2003 WL 1738888 (S.E.C.) (similar charges); In the Matter of Benedetto, 2003 WL 22303270 (S.E.C.) (broker bribed to recommend stock to customers as part of a manipulation scheme); In the Matter of Myler, 2003 WL 21276164 (S.E.C.) (payments made to brokers to induce recommendations as part of a manipulation scheme); In the Matter of Debois, 2003 WL 21946858 (S.E.C.) (similar charges); In the Matter of Perles, 2002 SEC LEXIS 847 (S.E.C.) (manipulation by matched and prearranged trades); In the Matter of Romano, Securities Exchange Act Release No. 44241, 74 S.E.C. Docket 1888, 2001 WL 456374 (2001) (defendants manipulated the price of a stock from five cents to over five dollars); In the Matter of Nordvik, 2000 WL 1775285 (S.E.C.) (manipulation by matched trades).

373. In the Matter of Setteducati, 2003 WL 22570689 (S.E.C.).

374. *See also*, In the Matter of Fertman, 51 S.E.C. 943. 948 (1994) ("classic factors" in a manipulation

In *United States. v. Manas*,[375] the Second Circuit upheld the sentencing of defendants who had engaged in a manipulation of the stock of Spaceplex International Amusement Centers Ltd. They used a market maker to place bids and make trades to give the appearance that the stock had an active market. The defendants planned to use a broker to sell Spaceplex shares to investors in a private placement when the price rose to $3 per share, allowing them to profit. They also planned to conduct a secondary public offering when the share price reached $8, but the scheme was caught out in a government sting operation.

A private action in *Stephenson v. Deutsche Bank AG*.[376] raised some novel claims of manipulation. The complaint alleged that the defendants manipulated the price of three thinly traded securities while the securities were loaned to several broker-dealers, including plaintiffs. "Because the securities were marked to the market, the rise in market price required the borrowing broker-dealers to send hundreds of millions of cash collateral upstream to the architects of the scheme. In the end, the broker-dealers were left with essentially worthless securities—causing the collapse of MJK Clearing, Inc. a Minnesota-based broker-dealer—while the scheme's planners ran off with the money."[377] The complaint also alleged involvement in this scheme by a "headline grabbing cast of characters including the notorious Saudi arms dealer Adnan Khashoggi."[378]

5:14 THE PRIVATE SECURITIES LITIGATION REFORM ACT OF 1995

Newt Gingrich's Contract With America, which became the centerpiece of the Republican platform in 1994, contained provisions for tort reform that would require that losing plaintiffs in federal lawsuits pay the attorney fees of their opponents, the so-called English rule for allocating attorney fees.[379] The Republicans lost that fight in enacting the Private Securities Litigation Reform Act of 1995 (PSLRA).[380] That effort was defeated because it would have spelled the doom for such actions. Instead, the PSLRA allows sanctions only for abusive actions that violate Rule 11 of the Federal Rules of Civil Procedure. The PSLRA creates a rebuttable presumption that the appropriate sanction for the substantial failure of a complaint to comply with Rule 11 is an award to the opposing party of the reasonable attorney fees and other expenses incurred in the action.[381] However, that modest reform has proved to be no real deterrent to filing Rule 10b-5 class action lawsuits.[382]

Nevertheless, the PSLRA, which was the only bill passed over a presidential veto during the Clinton administration, did impose some restrictions on class actions under the federal securities laws that have had some effects on Rule 10b-5 cases.[383] Specifically, the PSLRA heightened the

---

include "a rapid surge in a security's price that is driven by control of the security's supply and that occurs despite scant investor interest in the security and in the absence of any known prospects for or favorable developments affecting the issuer").

375. United States. v. Manas, 272 F.3d 159 (2d Cir. 2001), *cert. denied sub nom.*, Fasano v. United States, 573 U.S. 1023 (2002).

376. Stephenson v. Deutsche Bank AG., 282 F. Supp. 2d 1032 (D. Minn. 2003).

377. 543 F. Supp. 2d at 1042.

378. 534 F. Supp. 2d at 1041.

379. *See*, Jerry W. Markham, A Financial History of Modern U.S. Corporate Scandals, From Enron to Reform 636 (2005) (describing this background). Manipulation schemes also included efforts to reduce the stock float in order to make it easier to manipulate a security's price. *See, e.g.*, In the Matter of Charles M. Blair & Co. Inc., 48 S.E.C. 65 (1984).

380. Pub. L. No. 104-67, 109 Stat. 737 (1995).

381.15 U.S.C. § 78u-4(c)(3).

382. *See generally*, James D. Cox, *Making Securities Fraud Class Actions Virtuous*, 39 Ariz. L. Rev. 497, 523 (1997) (describing these "modest" reforms).

383. President Clinton claimed in his memoirs that this veto override was responsible for the Enron-era

burden for pleading a claim under Rule 10b-5 for private plaintiffs.[384] That statute requires, among other things, particularized pleadings that evidence the basis of the fraud claim. The pleadings must further establish a "strong inference" of scienter as a condition for bringing a class action under Rule 10b-5.[385]

As the Supreme Court has noted, the PSLRA requires that "securities fraud complaints 'specify' each misleading statement; that they set forth the facts 'on which [a] belief' that a statement is misleading was 'formed'; and that they 'state with particularity facts giving rise to a strong inference that the defendant acted with the required state of mind.'"[386] The PSLRA did not define what it meant by "strong inference" of scienter, and the courts of appeal were divided on how to define the term. That split was resolved by the Supreme Court in *Tellabs Inc. v. Makor Issues & Rights Ltd.*[387] There, the Supreme Court held that, in order to qualify as a strong inference of scienter, there must be pleaded facts that are "more than merely plausible or reasonable—it must be cogent and at least as compelling as any opposing inference of non-fraudulent intent."

The PSLRA addressed causation required in private actions under Rule 10b-5. The PSLRA now requires plaintiffs to prove that the act or omission of the defendant alleged to violate Rule 10b-5 "caused the loss for which the plaintiff seeks to recover damages."[388] The PSLRA also created special standards for proving damages in a Rule 10b-5 class action involving fraud or manipulation. The PSLRA applies when the plaintiff seeks to establish damages by reference to the market price of a security.[389] Such damages may not exceed the difference between the price paid or received by the plaintiff and the mean trading price of the security during a ninety-day look-back period. That look-back period begins on the date on which the information correcting the misstatement or omission that is the basis for the action was disseminated to the market.[390] The purpose of this provision is to prevent "windfall" damages arising from market fluctuations unrelated to the fraud, "thereby limiting damages to those losses caused by the fraud and not by other market conditions."[391]

Class action lawyers sought to avoid the restrictions in the PSLRA by filing their cases in state courts. Congress responded to that evasion with the Securities Litigation Uniform Standards Act of 1998. (SLUSA).[392] That legislation preempted state class actions with more than fifty class

---

financial scandals that arose after he left office. BILL CLINTON, MY LIFE 689 (2005).

384. *See*, Damian Moos, *Pleading Around the Private Securities Litigation Reform Act: Reevaluating the Pleading Requirements for Market Manipulation Claims*, 78 CAL. L. REV 763 (2004) (discussing this requirement in the context of manipulation claims)

385. Pub. L. No. 104-67, 109 Stat. 737 (1995).

386. Dura Pharms. Inc. v. Broudo, 544 U.S. 336, 345-3426 (2005). The PSLRA imposed "stricter pleading requirements in private securities fraud actions that, among other things, require that a complaint 'state with particularity facts giving rise to a strong inference that the defendant acted with the required [fraudulent] state of mind." The Wharf (Holdings) Ltd. v. United Int'l Holdings Inc., 532 U.S. 588, 597 (2001) (quoting from the PSLRA but inserting the word "fraudulent"),

387. 551 U.S. 308, 314 (2007).

388. 15 U.S.C. § 78u-4(b)(4).

389. 15 U.S.C. § 78u-4(e)(1).

390. This period is shortened when the plaintiff sells the security before the expiration of ninety days. 15 U.S.C. § 78u-4(e)(2).

391. THOMAS L. HAZEN & JERRY W. MARKHAM, CORPORATIONS AND OTHER BUSINESS ORGANIZATIONS: CASES AND MATERIALS 782 (3d unabridged ed. 2009), citing and quoting PSLRA Conference Report. It has also been asserted that the purpose of this provision is "to prevent 'excessive' recoveries in situations where stock prices overreact to the disclosure of fraud." Robert Allen, *Comment: Securities Litigation as a Coordination Problem*, 11 U. PA. J. BUS. L. 475 (2009)

392. 15 U.S.C. § 78bb(f)(1)(A).

members involving publicly traded securities that raised claims of state securities laws or common-law fraud claims. In *Merrill Lynch, Pierce, Fenner & Smith Inc. v. Dabit*,[393] the plaintiffs sought to bring a class action raising state law claims over an alleged stock price manipulation. The plaintiffs claimed they were fraudulently induced not to sell or purchase their securities as a result of that manipulation. However, the Supreme Court held in that case that SLUSA barred such an action. SLUSA prohibited class actions based on state law and which claim a misrepresentation or omission of a material fact "in connection with the purchase or sale" of a security.

The plaintiffs in *Dabit* contended that they were not subject to that bar because they were not purchasers or sellers of a security. The Supreme Court ruled that such a distinction was irrelevant because "the identity of the plaintiffs does not determine whether the complaint alleges fraud 'in connection with the purchase or sale' of securities. The misconduct of which respondent complains here—fraudulent manipulation of stock prices—unquestionably qualifies as fraud 'in connection with the purchase or sale' of securities."[394] The *Dabit* decision means that persons sustaining damage from a manipulation will not be able to sue under Rule 10b-5 unless they purchased or sold a security into the manipulated market.

Congress acted again in 2005 to limit class action abuses with the Class Action Fairness Act,[395] which conferred original federal jurisdiction over class actions with at least 100 claimants, with at least some diversity and an aggregate amount in controversy of at least $5 million. "According to the sponsors of the Class Action Fairness Act, the purpose of the sections expanding federal subject matter jurisdiction was to prevent the practice used by some lawyers of manipulating the citizenship of the named parties and/or the amount in controversy, which made it impossible for the defendants to remove the cases from state to federal court."[396]

5:15 MORE DEFINITIONAL PROBLEMS

An American Bar Association conference held in Washington, DC, in 1990 focused on manipulation in both the securities and commodity futures markets.[397] This was another indicator that these markets were becoming intertwined and that manipulation was a common problem for both. Several participants at the Washington conference lamented the lack of a definition of manipulation in the Commodity Exchange Act.[398] Securities industry participants pointed to the explicit identification of manipulative practices in Section 9 of the 34 Act as providing guidance for manipulation claims under that act. They also pointed to numerous successful manipulation cases under Section 10(b) of the 34 Act that seemed to evidence superiority in approach over those brought under the Commodity Exchange Act.[399]

---

393. Merrill Lynch, Pierce, Fenner & Smith Inc. v. Dabit, 547 U.S. 71 (2006).

394. 547 U.S. at 89.

395. Pub. L. No. 109-2, 119 Stat. 4 (2005) codified at 28 U.S.C. §§ 1332(d), 1453 & 1711-1715.

396. Stephen J. Shapiro, *Applying the Jurisdictional Provisions of the Class Action Fairness Act of 2005: In Search of A Sensible Judicial Approach*, 59 Baylor L. Rev. 77, 80 (2007).

397. Conference on Market Manipulation: Law, Economics, and Public Policy sponsored by the Center for Study of Futures and Options Markets and the American Bar Association, Washington, DC (Nov. 8–9, 1990).

398. *See*, Robert W. Kolb & Pablo T. Spiller, *The Manipulation of Futures Markets: An Overview*, at 1 ("The Courts, Congress, and regulators have yet to agree on the legal definition of a futures market manipulation"); Jerrold E. Salzman, *Manipulation vs Exploitation*, at p. 1 ("Thirty years of judicial and administrative decisions, exchange actions, and scholarly writing have failed to produce a workable definition of manipulation under the Commodity Exchange Act"); Barry J. Mandel, *Manipulation in Commodities Markets: Law and Public Policy*, at pp. 18-19 ("despite the admirable intentions behind these provisions of the CEA, to this day the area of commodity manipulation remains unclear at best").

399. Joseph I. Goldstein, Sarah B. Ackerson & Laura A. Novack, *An Overview of Market Manipulation:*

Barry J. Mandel, a private attorney, presented a paper at the Washington conference in which he noted that the discussions of manipulation under the Commodity Exchange Act in *Minpeco S.A. v. ContiCommodity Services Inc.*[400] and *Strobl v. NYMEX*[401] "concerning fraud on the market strike very close to the types of discussions courts have used in describing manipulation under the securities laws." He suggested that Section 9 of the 34 Act could "be used as a guide to define futures manipulation."[402]

Another conference participant, Jerrold E. Salzman, an attorney for the CME, raised an issue that would become a centerpiece for future government prosecutions—that is, engaging in cash market practices that were intended to aid the pricing of a futures market position. Salzman asserted that "a wide range of cash market activities are 'legitimate' alone or in conjunction with futures trading. Defining cash market practices that tend to enhance the value of a futures position held by the actor is destructive."[403] Regulators, nevertheless, regard such conduct as manipulative and conversely believe that futures trading designed to aid the pricing of a cash market position is also manipulative.

Legal and Practical Aspects; Harvey L. Pitt, Mark J. Dorsey & Marwan S. Kaddoura, *Manipulation of Market Mechanisms Under the Securities Laws.*

400. Minpeco S.A. v. ContiCommodity Services Inc. 552 F. Supp. 332, 337 (S.D.N.Y. 1982).

401. Strobl v. NYMEX, 582 F. Supp. 770 (S.D.N.Y 1984), *later aff'd*, 768 F.2d 22 (2d Cir. 1985), *cert. denied, sub nom.*, Simplot v. Strobl, 474 U.S. 1006 (1985).

402. Barry J. Mandel, *Manipulation in Commodities Markets: Law and Public Policy*, at pp. 18-19, Conference on Market Manipulation: Law, Economics, and Public Policy sponsored by the Center for Study of Futures and Options Markets and the American Bar Association, Washington, DC (Nov. 8–9, 1990). However, a law professor had noted before the Washington conference,

> It may seem surprising that, more than fifty years after the inception of federal securities regulation, the meaning of so basic a concept as manipulation should require clarification. The eradication of manipulation was, after all, one of the main purposes of the Securities Exchange Act of 1934 . . . and Congress designed several of its provisions to accomplish this result. Yet the Act nowhere defines the term "manipulation" or "manipulative."
>
> For many years, the absence of a definition did not seem to create major interpretive problems. By and large, courts, regulators, and commentators agreed on what was meant by manipulation. In recent years, however, the question of the meaning and scope of manipulation has become a subject of sharp controversy.

Norman S. Poser, *Stock Market Manipulation and Corporate Control Transactions*, 40 U. Miami L. Rev. 671, 672 (1986) (footnotes omitted).

403. Jerrold E. Salzman, *Manipulation vs Exploitation*, at p. 1, Conference on Market Manipulation: Law, Economics, and Public Policy sponsored by the Center for Study of Futures and Options Markets and the American Bar Association, Washington, DC (Nov. 8–9, 1990).

6

THE BATTLE OVER OTC DERIVATIVES

6:1 THE SWAPS AND OTC DERIVATIVES MARKETS ARE BORN

A long-running debate whether over-the-counter (OTC) derivatives, such as swaps, should be subject to regulation by the Commodity Futures Trading Commission (CFTC) began in the 1980s.[1] The swaps market was just then developing, and it was unclear whether swaps were a form of futures contract that was subject to regulation under the Commodity Exchange Act of 1936.[2] If such regulation had been applied, the swaps market would have died an early death. This was because futures contracts could only be traded on regulated exchanges known as "contract markets," which would have been impractical at the time for swaps.[3]

The CFTC decided in favor of allowing the swaps market to develop by issuing a policy statement in 1989, declaring that OTC swaps were not subject to the exchange-trading requirement. The CFTC set several restrictions on this interpretation, including requirements that the swaps not be exchange traded or cleared by a clearinghouse, that their terms not be standardized or subject to offset, and that only commercial entities could be counterparties to the swaps.[4] There were concerns, however, whether that interpretation was binding on the courts, since the CFTC had no exemption authority from Commodity Exchange Act jurisdiction.[5]

Also of concern was a decision by a federal judge in New York that OTC energy contracts traded by institutions (such as BP North America Petroleum) in the Brent oil market were subject to the antimanipulation provisions of the Commodity Exchange Act, as well as the antitrust laws.[6] The court noted that some 95 percent of the trading in the Brent oil market was for hedging or speculation that did not require the actual delivery of the oil. The plaintiff claimed that defendants were selling oil in the Brent market at below market prices in order to gain tax advantages, a process that was called "tax spinning." That trading involved wash sales that the court held could be manipulative when entered into for the purpose of artificially depressing prices. The trading on the Brent market was also held by the court to be futures contracts that were subject to CFTC jurisdiction, which meant that this was an illegal exchange since it was not registered with the CFTC as a contract market.

---

1. A swap contract involves an exchange of payment flows or values. For example, Party A with a fixed rate loan could swap those payments for Party B's floating interest rate obligations. Such exchanges are usually arranged by a swap dealer. *See*, Thrifty Oil Co. v. Bank of Am. Nat'l Trust & Sav. Ass'n, 322 F.3d 1039, 1042-1043 (9th Cir. 2002) (describing swap contracts).

2. *See*, Mark D. Young & William L. Stein, *Swap Transactions Under the Commodity Exchange Act: Is Congressional Action Needed*? 76 Geo. L. J. 1917 (1988) (discussing the need to resolve regulatory uncertainty over the swaps market).

3. *See*, Jerry W. Markham, *"Confederate Bonds," "General Custer," and the Regulation of Derivative Financial Instruments*, 25 Seton Hall L. Rev. 1 (1994) (describing concerns over swaps regulation).

4. *Statement Concerning Swap Transactions*, 54 Fed. Reg. 30694 (July 21, 1989).

5. *See*, Jerry W. Markham, *Merging the SEC and CFTC: A Clash of Cultures*, 78 U. Cinn. L. Rev. 537, 575 (2009) (discussing that uncertainty).

6. Transnor (Bermuda) Ltd. v. BP North America Petroleum, Comm. Fut. L. Rep. (CCH) ¶ 24,829 (S.D.N.Y. 1990).

That ruling effectively prevented U.S. institutional traders from participating in the Brent market.[7] The CFTC issued an interpretation that the judge's ruling was wrong and the CFTC declared that institutional traders participating in the Brent oil market were exempt from regulation under the Commodity Exchange Act.[8] It was again unclear whether the CFTC had the authority to overturn a judicial decision and declare a market to be exempt from regulation under the Commodity Exchange Act.[9]

In order to provide regulatory certainty for the OTC energy and swaps markets, Congress included a provision in the Futures Trading Practices Act of 1992 that allowed the CFTC to exempt OTC derivatives from regulation when the parties were sophisticated institutional traders.[10] The CFTC quickly adopted exemptions for swaps and OTC energy derivatives.[11] That energy market exemption applied to institutional trading in contracts for the purchase and sale of crude oil, condensates, natural gas, natural gas liquids, or their derivatives when used primarily as an energy source.[12] The OTC energy exemption explicitly did not exempt such transactions from the antimanipulation provisions of the Commodity Exchange Act.[13] The swap exemption more broadly covered all swap products. It too explicitly concluded that even exempt swaps would be subject to the statute's antimanipulation provisions.[14]

Critics of financial innovation warned that the burgeoning swaps market could turn into a "financial Jurassic Park."[15] That prediction seemed to have been fulfilled when an unexpected increase in interest rates by the Federal Reserve Board (the Fed) in 1994 caused massive losses in OTC derivatives and mortgaged-backed securities.[16] Those losses were decried in Congress

---

7. *See*, Eric C. Bettelheim & Jerry W. Markham, *The Transnor Decision and Its Aftermath*, 8 OIL & GAS L. & TAX. REV. 76 (1991) (describing the effects of this case).

8. CFTC, *Statutory Interpretation Concerning Forward Transactions*, COMM. FUT. L. REP. (CCH) ¶ 24,925 (1990).

9. *See*, Eric C. Bettelheim & Jerry W. Markham, *More on Transnor*, 8 OIL & GAS L. & TAX. REV. 223 (1991) (describing the CFTC interpretation and concerns).

10. Pub. L. No. 102-546, 106 Stat. 3590.

11. *See* William T. Maitland & Jerry W. Markham, *CFTC Rules to Provide Legal Certainty for OTC Products*, FUT. INDUST. MAG., Nov.-Dec., 1992, at 20 (describing that action).

12. The exemption allowed trading by offset in such contracts as long as there was at least a putative delivery obligation. CFTC, *Exemption for Certain Contracts Involving Energy Products*, 58 Fed. Reg. 21286 (April 20, 1993).

13. *Id.* at 21294.

14. 17 C.F.R. § 35.2.

15. Henry T.C. Hu, *Hedging Expectations: "Derivative Reality" and the Law and Finance of the Corporate Objective*, 73 TEX. L. REV. 985, 989-990 (1995).

16. The following are examples of those losses:

> Macy's defaulted on a swap contract that involved some $83 million in interest payments; a unit of Metallgesellschaft A.G. lost some $1.37 billion from mismatched derivative transactions; Kashima Oil in Japan lost some $1.5 billion in currency transactions; Gibson Greetings Inc. lost some $19 million from derivative trading; Kidder Peabody lost some $350 million in "phantom" derivative trades; a New York municipal bond fund failed to disclose that some 40 percent of its assets were invested in derivatives; Procter & Gamble lost over $150 million from derivative trading; Orange County in California lost $140 million; David Askin's Granite Hedge Fund had losses of an estimated $600 million from "market neutral" derivatives; City College of Chicago claimed that it was misled in the purchase of $100 million in derivative obligations; Cargill's hedge funds lost some $100 million from mortgage-backed securities; Piper Capital Management had difficulty valuing its derivatives and lost some $700 million from derivative transactions; HYM Financial Inc. in New Jersey lost all of its capital from derivatives; Dell Computer lost some $26 million from derivative-based transactions; Air Products took a loss of $69 mil-

with calamitous warnings that the "multi-trillion dollar derivatives activities" of the ten largest banks were creating a "pyramidal house of cards"[17] that "could swamp our economy in a sea of red ink."[18] Those losses were also the subject of several reports by regulators, including the CFTC, the General Accounting Office, the Comptroller of the Currency, the International Monetary Fund, the minority staff of a House Committee, English regulators, and others.[19] Those concerns did not stop the growth of OTC derivatives.

6:2 THE CFMA AND THE ENRON LOOPHOLE

The OTC derivative losses from the 1994 interest rate rise soon faded from memory, but concerns continued over the lack of regulation of OTC derivatives. The Securities and Exchange Commission (SEC) and the CFTC had long been in competition over the regulation of securities-based derivatives, with the CFTC winning most of their jurisdictional battles. Undiscouraged by those setbacks, the SEC tried to impose some regulation on OTC derivatives by creating a special "broker-dealer lite" registration category for swaps and other OTC derivative dealers.[20]

The CFTC responded to the jurisdictional threat from the SEC's broker-dealer lite program with a proposal to study OTC derivatives to determine whether additional regulation was needed. The CFTC also claimed that the near failure of Long Term Capital Management, a systemically important giant hedge fund, in 1998 justified such regulation because that hedge fund was speculating in OTC derivatives. The industry, and other regulators, believed that the proposed study was actually an effort to lay the groundwork for the CFTC to impose such regulation. The Treasury Department, the Fed, and the SEC objected to the CFTC's action, and Congress stepped in and ordered the CFTC to desist from such action.[21] This proved to be a very controversial debate. Brooksley Born, the CFTC chair, was much vilified at the time for her efforts to regulate OTC derivatives but became a heroine for reformists after OTC derivatives were blamed for furthering the financial crisis in 2008. Her opponents, Robert Rubin and Lawrence Summers at Treasury and Alan Greenspan at the Federal Reserve Board, were then larger-than-life figures, but their reputations suffered considerably after the financial crisis because of their involvement in efforts to curb financial market risk taking.

Congress also directed the Presidential Working Group for Financial Markets (PWG), which had been created to coordinate regulation of derivatives after the stock market crash of 1987,

---

> lion on derivative contracts; an employee investment fund of Atlantic Richfield Company lost $22 million in derivative trades; several mutual funds were compensated by their advisers or brokers for millions of dollars in losses suffered from derivatives transactions; and Mead Corporation lost more than $12 million from derivatives trading.

Jerry W. Markham, *"Confederate Bonds," "General Custer," and the Regulation of Derivative Financial Instruments*, 25 Seton Hall L. Rev. 1, 28-31 (1994).

17. 140 Cong. Rec. H73-01, S5837 (1994) (remarks of Rep. Leach).

18. 140 Cong. Rec. S5828-04, S5837 (1994) (remarks of Rep. Dorgan).

19. Jerry W. Markham, *"Confederate Bonds," "General Custer," and the Regulation of Derivative Financial Instruments*, 25 Seton Hall L. Rev. 1, 33-40 (1994).

20. That registration category did not become popular until it morphed into the SEC's consolidated supervised entity (CSE) program that allowed large broker-dealers like Lehman Brothers, Bear Stearns, Merrill Lynch, Morgan Stanley, and Goldman Sachs to have reduced capital requirements. The CSE program nearly destroyed Wall Street during the financial crisis in 2008 after the risk models of those firms failed. *See,* Jerry W. Markham, *Merging the SEC and CFTC: A Clash of Cultures*, 78 U. Cinn. L. Rev. 537, 569-581 (2009) (describing that program and its failures).

21. *Id.* at 580-581 (describing that fight). *See also*, Jeff Madrick, Age of Greed 240 (2011) (describing the opposition of the Fed and Treasury heads to this proposal).

to conduct a study on the issue, and it recommended that OTC derivatives be exempted from regulation.[22] The Treasury Department later noted that the reason for the PWG recommendation was that institutional investors did not need regulation by the CFTC because such investors are sophisticated enough to protect their own interests. The Treasury Department also contended that CFTC regulation was unnecessary because "most OTC financial instruments (*e.g.*, interest rate swaps) were not susceptible to manipulation."[23]

In any event, the CFTC changed its views on OTC regulation after a new chair came on board and the agency began deregulating derivatives trading by professional and commercial traders. Congress endorsed that effort with the enactment of the Commodity Futures Modernization Act of 2000 (CFMA).[24] That legislation exempted OTC derivatives from regulation when the parties to the transactions were sophisticated counterparties. The exempted institutions included banks, investment bankers, pension funds, large businesses, and high net-worth individuals. "The primary justifications for recommending exclusion for such transactions were a determination that most OTC financial derivatives were not susceptible to manipulation and that the counterparties in such transactions do not need the same protections as smaller, unsophisticated market participants who rely on intermediaries to conduct their transactions."[25]

The CFMA created exemptions and exclusions from most regulation for electronic trading facilities used by institutional traders. These facilities were called "exempt commercial markets" (ECMs).[26] The ECM exclusion was often referred to as the "Enron loophole" because that provision was inserted into the CFMA at the last minute through the lobbying efforts of the Enron Corp., which was seeking to protect its popular electronic trading platform, EnronOnline, from regulation.[27]

At the height of its glory as the twentieth century ended, the Enron Corp. billed itself as the world's leading energy company. Enron owned pipelines and electrical generation facilities and even branched out into water production facilities around the world.[28] The company was noted for its innovative trading operations, which included a "gas bank" for natural gas purchases[29] as well as EnronOnline.[30] EnronOnline was awarded the *Financial Times*'s "Boldest Successful Business Investment Decision" award.

---

22. President's Working Group on Financial Markets, *Over-the-Counter Derivatives Markets and the Commodity Exchange Act* (1999).

23. Department of the Treasury, Blueprint for a Modernized Financial Regulatory Structure 47 (2008).

24. Pub. L. No. 106-544, 114 Stat. 2763 (2000).

25. U.S. Department of the Treasury, Blueprint for a Modernized Financial Regulatory Structure 47 (2008).

26. *See*, *Hearing Before the CFTC to Examine Trading on Regulated Exchanges and Exempt Commercial Markets*, 110th Cong. 1 (2007) (statement of Terry S. Arbit, CFTC general counsel).

27. Eric Lipton, *Gramm and the Enron Loophole*, New York Times, Nov. 17, 2008.

28. *See*, Jerry W. Markham, A Financial History of Modern U.S. Corporate Scandals, From Enron to Reform (2006) (describing the rise and fall of Enron).

29. *Id.* at 55-56.

30. The CFTC described EnronOnline (EOL) as follows:

> 1) an Enron trader activated a product on his or her server and made a two-way market for that product by posting a bid and an offer that Enron was willing to honor as a counterparty; 2) EOL displayed that bid and offer over its web site; 3) an EOL customer submitted an order to Enron by either hitting the bid or lifting an offer by clicking on the respective price displayed on-screen; 4) the order went back to the Enron server and was checked for volume, price and credit; and 5) a confirmation was then sent to the Enron trader and to the customer via the internet.

CFTC v. Enron Corp., 2004 U.S. Dist. LEXIS 28794, at *4 (S.D. Tex. 2004).

EnronOnline eventually traded over 2,000 different commodity contracts in fifteen different currencies. Products traded by Enron included U.S.-delivered natural gas and crude oil, weather derivatives, lumber, Argentine natural gas, and Dutch aluminum. EnronOnline executed 548,000 transactions in 2000, with a total notional amount of $336 billion. Before Enron's demise, EnronOnline traded a total of $880 billion in energy contracts, which constituted nearly 25 percent of all energy derivative contracts in the United States and earned nearly $3 billion for Enron. At its peak, EnronOnline's daily trading volume reached about $2.8 billion per day. This made it a serious competitor to the $13 billion per day in energy contracts traded on NYMEX, then the leading derivatives exchange for energy products.[31]

Enron shocked the nation when it declared bankruptcy in October 2001. It was then revealed that its executives had massively cooked the company's books in order to manipulate the price of Enron's shares. Enron drew more headlines after the disclosure of its manipulation of prices on the California wholesale electricity market in 2000–2001. That was a period during which California was experiencing electricity shortages that resulted in disruptive statewide electrical blackouts and brownouts. Those problems occurred after California restructured its wholesale electricity market.[32]

Enron was able to exploit that restructuring because it had been carried out in an incredibly inept manner by the California state government. "That the traders sought to take advantage and make money out of the political and regulatory debacle in California is clear. But that they were not the fundamental reason for the crisis is also clear. The causes reside in the way the power marketing structure was designed in the face of shifting supply and demand."[33] Among other

---

31. Jerry W. Markham, A Financial History of the United States from Enron-Era Scandals to the Subprime Crisis (2004-2006) 199 (2011).

32. That restructuring was described by one court as follows:

> In 1996, California created two new non-governmental entities to orchestrate the transmission and sale of electricity: the [the California Independent System Operator] ("CAISO") and the California Power Exchange ("CalPX"), both of which were California non-profit, public-benefit corporations. Until it ceased operation in 2001, CalPX was a crucial hub of the electricity generation market, overseeing an auction system for the sale and purchase of electricity on a non-discriminatory basis to meet the electricity loads of CalPX customers, called load-serving entities ("LSEs"), that provide electricity to retail, end-use customers. CalPX's auctions ran on a day-ahead and same-day basis. CalPX would determine, on an hourly basis, a single 'market clearing price which all electricity wholesalers would be paid based on short-term supply and demand bids submitted by all CalPX participants ("spot market"). In addition, CalPX operated a block forward market by matching supply and demand bids for long-term electricity contracts ("term market").
>
> Responsibility for the efficient functioning of the high-voltage transmission grid fell to CAISO and, to that end, it ran the spot market for electricity. During the time period in question in this case, if consumer demands were not met by scheduled supplies into CalPX or other sources, CAISO was required to procure additional electricity to serve consumers' requirements and maintain the stability of the grid. To facilitate this, CAISO purchased reserve capacity from wholesalers. This reserve capacity was left idle until CAISO required additional generation of power. If CAISO required additional generation of power, it issued an order to the wholesaler to generate such power out of the reserve capacity; if not, the reserve capacity was left ungenerated. The CAISO-operated market was called the "real time" or "imbalance market."

United States v. Reliant Energy Services Inc., 420 F. Supp. 2d 1043, 1045-1046 (N.D. Cal. 2006) (citation omitted).

33. Daniel Yergin, The Quest 393 (2011).

things, the wholesale electricity market was deregulated while retail prices were kept artificially low by the state in order to placate consumers.[34]

Enron made hundreds of millions of dollars in profits by manipulating the California electricity market through transactions it variously dubbed "Fat Boy," "Get Shorty," "Death Star," "Russian Roulette," "Ping Pong," and "Donkey."[35] Fat Boy was a strategy through which Enron withheld previously agreed-to deliveries of electricity so it could sell it at a higher price on the spot market. To execute this strategy, "the company would overschedule its load, supply only enough power to cover the inflated schedule, and thus leave extra supply in the market."[36] The utility created by California to operate its restructured electricity market, the Independent System Operator (ISO), would pay Enron for the electricity at a higher spot rate.

Under the Get Shorty strategy, Enron traders would fabricate and sell "emergency back-up power (known as ancillary services) to the ISO, receive payment, then cancel the schedules and cover their commitments by purchasing through a cheaper market closer to the time of delivery. "Under the 'Death Star' strategy, Enron allegedly sought to be paid 'for moving energy to relieve congestion without actually moving any energy or relieving any congestion.'"[37]

Outrage quickly grew when these and other transactions, like "hockey-stick bidding," were made public.[38] In exchange for leniency, three Enron traders pleaded guilty to obstruction of justice for engaging in such gaming transactions. It also turned out that Enron was not the only energy company seeking to exploit that dysfunctional market. Although EnronOnline was the largest electronic energy trading platform at the time of its demise, it had been widely copied by other competing energy trading firms, including Dynegy, which operated DynegyDirect. Other competitors included Mirant, Sempra Energy, Reliant Energy, El Paso, and Williams Cos.

The California electricity market was subject to regulation by the Federal Energy Regulatory Commission (FERC), an independent federal agency that is responsible for regulating the interstate transmission of natural gas, oil, and electricity.[39] FERC had embarked on a program of deregulation of the energy markets before the California energy crisis.[40] That effort included the use of "market-based tariffs" as a substitute for the fixed price tariffs traditionally used in utility

34. *See*, James L. Sweeeny, The California Electricity Crisis (2002) (describing the flaws in the deregulation of the California electricity market).

35. *See*, Jerry W. Markham & Lawrence H. Hunt Jr., *The California Energy Crisis: Enron's Gaming of Governor Gray's Imperfect Market,* 24 Fut. & Derv. L. Rep. 1 (2004) (describing this crisis).

36. Lockyer v. FERC, 383 F.3d 1006, 1015, n. 8 (9th Cr. 2004), *cert. denied, sub. nom.*, California ex rel. Brown, 551 U.S. 1140 (2007).

37. *Id.*

38. *Id.* at n. 7 ("Hockey-stick bidding is a fraudelent practice whereby an extremely high price is demanded for a small portion of a product in light of known inelastic demand [as was the case for energy in California during the energy crisis]").

39.FERC's mission is to "[a]ssist consumers in obtaining reliable, efficient and sustainable energy services at a reasonable cost through appropriate regulatory and market means." http://www.ferc.gov/about/about.asp (accessed May 28, 2011). FERC is the successor to the Federal Power Commission (FPC), which was created in 1920 to control federal hydroelectric projects. FPC powers were gradually expanded to cover most aspects of electrical power generation. Transportation of crude oil through pipelines and natural gas production were also added to its brief. The FPC was replaced and reorganized as FERC in 1977. FERC then began deregulating electricity and natural gas utilities. http://www.ferc.gov/students/whatisferc/history.htm (accessed June 14, 2011). *See generally*, Joseph T. Kelliher, *Market Manipulation, Market Power, and the Authority of the Federal Energy Regulatory Commission*, 26 Energy L. J. 1 (2005).

40. As a result of a natural gas shortage in the 1970s, the Natural Gas Policy Act of 1978 (Pub. L. 95-621, 92 Stat. 3351) ordered that more market-based competition be introduced into the energy distribution process as a substitute for price controls. *See*, Jerry W. Markham, A Financial History of Modern U.S. Corporate Scandals: From Enron to Reform (2006) (describing that change in process).

regulation.[41] As FERC discovered during the California energy crisis, markets fluctuate and are not always driven by rational motives, and self-interest will exploit market flaws.

FERC exercised jurisdiction under the Federal Power Act over wholesale electricity sales into the California market. The California Public Utility Commission (CPUC) retained jurisdiction over all retail sales of electricity in California.[42] The CPUC claimed that several energy companies (Duke Energy, Dynegy, Mirant, Reliant, and AES/Williams) had not been running their California plants at anywhere near full capacity during the electricity crisis in California in 2000–2001 in order to boost prices for the benefit of their trading operations. The CPUC report concluded that, had those plants operated at capacity, most of the blackouts and service interruptions in California during that crisis could have been avoided,[43] a claim that was disputed by FERC.[44]

The FERC staff conducted its own investigation into the causes of the California energy crisis. It concluded that EnronOnline had been used to manipulate California electricity prices. The FERC staff found that the trading strategies employed by EnronOnline violated the antigaming provisions of FERC-approved tariffs for the California electricity market. EnronOnline provided informational advantages to Enron, and it was able to "manipulate thinly traded physical markets to profit in financial markets," allowing it to earn over $500 million in 2000 and 2001.[45] EnronOnline was "a primary driver of wash trading, which created a false sense of liquidity, which can cause artificial volatility and distorted prices. Electricity prices in California's spot markets were affected by economic withholding and inflated price bidding, in violation of tariff anti-gaming provisions."[46]

The FERC staff further found that, while "supply-demand imbalance, flawed market design and inconsistent rules made possible significant market manipulation . . . , [w]ithout underlying market dysfunction, attempts to manipulate the market would not be successful."[47] The Supreme Court later expressed agreement with that assessment.[48] The FERC study found that, while the energy companies took advantage of the flawed energy market, their role only accounted for some $3 billion of the $50 billion in inflated energy prices during the crisis.[49]

FERC's views on the causes of the California electricity crisis resulted in conflicts with the California attorney general, who wanted to blame only the traders. He later crowed that "[d]espite legal roadblocks and hurdles thrown up by FERC, the [California] Attorney General recovered more than $3.3 billion from power companies, including more than $2.5 billion in consumer benefits."[50]

---

41. *See*, California ex rel. Lockyer v. FERC, 383 F.3d 1006, 1012 (9th Cr. 2004), *cert. denied, sub. nom.*, California ex rel. Brown, 551 U.S. 1140 (2007) (describing this change).

42. United States v. Reliant Energy Services Inc., 420 F. Supp. 2d 1043, 1045-1046 (N.D. Cal. 2006) (citation omitted).

43. *See*, CPUC, *Report on Wholesale Electric Generation Investigation* (Sept. 2002) (describing those conclusions).

44. Daniel Weintraub, *Feds Say Generators Didn't Cause the Blackouts*, SACRAMENTO BEE, April 3, 2008, at B7.

45. FERC Staff Report, *Final Report on Price Manipulation in Western Markets: Fact-Finding Investigation of Potential Manipulation of Electric and Natural Gas Prices (Findings at a Glance)*, Doc. No. PAO2-2-000 (March 26, 2003), http://www.ferc.gov/legal/maj-ord-reg/land-docs/PART-I-3-26-03.pdf (accessed May 15, 2011).

46. *Id.*

47. *Id.*

48. Morgan Stanley Capital Group Inc. v. Public Utility District No. 1, 554 U.S. 527, 539-540 (2008) (citations omitted).

49. Daniel Weintraub, *Feds Say Generators Didn't Cause the Blackouts*, SACRAMENTO BEE, April 3, 2008, at B7.

50. State of California Office of the Attorney General, Energy Unit, http://ag.ca.gov/cfs/energy.php (accessed May 22, 2011).

Natural gas prices also rose to extraordinary levels during the California electricity crisis and facilitated increased electricity prices. "Markets for natural gas and electricity in California are inextricably linked, and dysfunctions in each fed off one another. Spot gas prices drove electricity prices, and manipulation of price indices apparently drove, at least in part, dysfunctions in the natural gas market."[51] The increases in natural gas prices were found by FERC to have been the "result of dysfunctions in the natural gas market [that] stemmed from efforts to manipulate price indices compiled by trade organizations, including reporting of false data and wash trading."[52]

These wash trades were also called "round-trip" trades. They involved offsetting purchases and sales by the same traders. Those trades were used to boost trading volumes, so that it would appear to other market participants that the round-trip traders were large traders with liquidity that could handle large trades for market participants.[53] Traders were also using round-trip trades to set artificial prices that could be used to justify charging more favorable prices on actual contracts. These wash trades were reported to industry publications such as *Inside FERC's Gas Market Report*, the *Gas Daily*, and *Natural Gas Intelligence*. The FERC staff found that such "false reporting became epidemic."[54]

FERC brought a number of actions against traders involved in exploiting the energy markets during the California electricity crisis under its power to regulate natural gas and electricity. FERC issued two "show cause" orders covering more than sixty energy companies for participating in gaming practices and anomalous market behavior that allegedly violated tariffs under FERC's jurisdiction.[55] Large settlements were obtained in those proceedings.[56] In total, El Paso, Williams, Dynegy, Duke, Mirant, and Enron agreed to pay more than $4 billion to settle consumer and utility claims in California.[57]

The Enron bankruptcy estate agreed to pay $47.4 million in cash and allowed an $875 million claim in bankruptcy on behalf of public utilities and consumers in California. Enron also agreed to pay a $600 million penalty to California and other affected by the electricity crisis.[58] FERC

51. FERC Staff Report, *Final Report on Price Manipulation in Western Markets: Fact-Finding Investigation of Potential Manipulation of Electric and Natural Gas Prices (Findings at a Glance)*, Doc. No. PAO2-2-000 (March 26, 2003), http://www.ferc.gov/legal/maj-ord-reg/land-docs/PART-I-3-26-03.pdf (accessed May 15, 2011).

52. *Id.* at ES-1.

53. California ex rel. Lockyer v. FERC, 383 F.3d 1006, 1015, n. 6 (9th Cr. 2004), *cert. denied, sub. nom.*, California ex rel. Brown, 551 U.S. 1140 (2007) ("Round-trip trades are a mechanism for market manipulation through which an entity attempts to inflate transaction volume through the continuous and frequent sale of a particular commodity. The trades create the appearance of increased revenue and demand, but in actuality produce no net income.").

54. FERC Staff Report, *Final Report on Price Manipulation in Western Markets: Fact-Finding Investigation of Potential Manipulation of Electric and Natural Gas Prices (Findings at a Glance)*, Doc. No. PAO2-2-000 at ES-6 (March 26, 2003), http://www.ferc.gov/legal/maj-ord-reg/land-docs/PART-I-3-26-03.pdf (accessed May 15, 2011).

55. Show Cause Orders re Reliant and Enron. In re American Electric Power Service Corp. et al., 103 FERC ¶ 61,345 (2003), *reh'g denied*, 106 FERC ¶ 61,020 (2004), and In re Enron Power Marketing Inc. et al., 103 FERC ¶ 61,346 (2003)

56. Amita Sharma, *Sempra Energy Reaches Settlement in Energy Crisis Lawsuits*, April 28, 2010, http://www.kpbs.org/news/2010/apr/28/sempra-energy-reaches-settlement-energy-crisis-law/ (accessed May 18, 2011).

57. Edison International, *California Parties Settle With Enron*, http:/www.edison.com/pressroom/pr.asp?bu=&year=O&id=5859.

58. Jad Mouawad, *Settlement Reached with Enron*, New York Times, July 15, 2005, http://www.nytimes.com/2005/07/16/business/16enron.html (accessed May 20, 2011). The value of the bankruptcy claim was

additionally ordered Enron to return $32.5 million in profits from trading abuses.[59] FERC directed an administrative law judge to determine whether Enron should disgorge profits because of its market behavior between January 16, 1997, and June 25, 2003.[60]

Sempra Energy agreed to pay a total of $700 million to settle claims brought on behalf of California consumers, CPUC, and other California regulators.[61] This settlement concerned claims that Sempra had overcharged the state in long-term contracts entered into during the middle of the California electricity crisis.[62] Sempra agreed to pay $7.2 million to settle gaming charges and other anomalous market behavior claims brought by FERC.[63] Mirant paid $458 million to settle FERC and other claims arising from the California energy crisis.[64] Coral Power agreed to pay $7.7 million to settle FERC claims that stemmed from gaming practices.[65] Coral also agreed to pay $4 million to settle FERC charges over its inadequate response to FERC information requests related to the Western energy crisis.[66] Dynegy paid $3 million to settle FERC gaming charges, which included congestion and double selling charges.[67] In a separate action, FERC approved a $281 million settlement between Dynegy and California relating to refund claims.[68] In 2003, the FERC accepted an offer by Powerex to settle gaming charges in exchange for a $1.3 million payment.[69]

A FERC administrative law judge found that the El Paso Corp. had withheld supplies of natural gas to California in order to affect prices. El Paso paid $1.69 billion to settle the FERC proceedings.[70] Duke Energy North America LLC paid $2.5 million to settle FERC charges of "economic"

estimated to be about twenty cents on the dollar. *Id. See also,* Chad Gilbert, *Enron OKs $1.5 Billion Settlement with States*, SACRAMENTO BEE, July 16, 2005.

59. *FERC, Order on Initial Decision and Consolidating Dockets*, 108 FERC ¶ 61,071 (July 22, 2004). FERC found that Enron had manipulated the market by entering into a services agreement with the El Paso Electric Company that allowed Enron to control El Paso's electric market desk and its generation capability without informing FERC. *Id.* at 2.

60. *Id.* FERC staff testified in front of an administrative law judge that the profits earned by Enron between 1997 and 2003 that it should disgorge amounted to $1.8 billion. *See* www.ferc.gov/industries/electric/indus-act/wec/rev-chron.asp.

61. Eric Wolf, *Sempra to Pay $400 Million in Settlement from 2000-02 Energy Crisis*, NORTH COUNTY TIMES, April 20, 2010, http://www.nctimes.com/app/blogs/wp/?p=8957. Class actions over the trading practices by the energy firms during the California electricity crisis were also allowed to proceed. In re Western States Wholesale Natural Gas Antitrust Litigation, 2008 U.S. Dist. LEXIS (D. Nev.).

62. FERC Presentation on Western Crisis, http://www.ferc.gov/industries/electric/indus-act/wec/rev-chron.asp; *see also*, FERC News Release, Commission Issues Sweeping Show Cause Orders to Companies Alleged to Have Gamed Western Energy Markets, June 25, 2003. This settlement followed a FERC decision that changed the manner of calculating the refund due by the companies involved from $1.8 billion (as calculated by an administrative law judge) to $3 billion. *See San Diego Gas & Elec. Co. v. Sellers of Energy and Ancillary Services,* 93 FERC ¶ 61,121, at 61,349-50, 61,366 (2000) (November 1 Order); *see also*, Sempra Energy 2008 Financial Report, 148-149 (describing this settlement).

63. *FERC Order Approving Sempra Contested Settlement*, 108 FERC ¶ 61,114 (Aug. 2, 2004).

64. *See* FERC News Release, Commission Approves Settlement Valued at $500 Million Between Mirant, California Parties and FERC Staff, Docket Numbers EL00-95-000 *et al.* and EL00-98-000 *et al.* (April 13, 2005), http://www.ferc.gov/media/news-releases/2005/2005-2/04-13-05-mirant.asp#skipnav.

65. *FERC Order Approving Coral Settlement*, 108 FERC ¶ 61,115 (August 2, 2004).

66. Monica Perin, *Coral Energy settles with FERC*, HOUSTON BUSINESS JOURNAL, Friday, March 4, 2005, http://www.bizjournals.com/houston/stories/2005/02/28/daily73.html#ixzz1Mor3mYfM.

67. *FERC Order Approving Dynegy Power Marketing Inc. Contested Settlement*, 108 FERC ¶ 61,145 (August 5, 2004).

68. *FERC Order on Settlement Agreement*, 109 FERC ¶ 61,071 (October 25, 2004).

69. *FERC Order Approving Powerex Corp. Contested Settlement*, 106 FERC ¶ 61,304 (March 26, 2004).

70. In re El Paso Corp. et al., 105 FERC ¶ 61,201 (2004). That was not the end of El Paso's regulatory

and "physical" withholding of natural gas supplies to the California market, as well as "wash" trading in which the company bought and sold from itself.[71] FERC later approved a $207 million settlement with Duke that settled other FERC claims, state claims, and class actions over Duke's activities in the Western energy market during the California crisis.[72]

Reliant Resources Inc. and related entities agreed to pay California customers a total of $13.8 million to settle charges that it withheld electric power from California over a two-day period in order to mitigate losses in an existing forward position.[73] A Reliant trader was also accused of aiding BP Energy to manipulate electricity prices for purposes of improving BP Energy's revenues through mark-to-market accounting increases in position values. Reliant agreed to pay up to $50 million to settle charges over its involvement in that affair and for other charges relating to alleged economic and physical withholding.[74] BP Energy entered into a settlement with FERC pursuant to which the company agreed to donate $3 million to energy assistance programs for low-income homes in California and Arizona.[75]

FERC also charged that Reliant engaged in "churning" or "burst" trading—that is, "the repeated buying and selling of substantial quantities of physical spot gas in a short period of time."[76] The use of the term "churning" used by FERC in attacking that trading was a bit of a misnomer, at least to commodity and securities traders. In those markets, churning is the excessive trading of a customer account controlled by a broker in order to generate excessive commissions without regard to the customer's interests. Rapid in-and-out trading, called "scalping," was also common in commodity markets and was not considered manipulative.[77]

6:3 THE CFTC SHIFTS STRATEGIES

The CFTC was also a participant in the regulatory fracas over the trading of the energy companies during the California electricity crisis. In *CFTC v. Enron Corp.*,[78] a district court entered a consent order of permanent injunction and imposed a $35 million civil monetary penalty on the bankrupt Enron. The CFTC charged that Enron engaged in manipulative activities on its electronic trading platform through rigged trading that involved buying an enormous amount of natural gas in a period of fifteen minutes. That "buying spree" drove prices up, but the Enron traders then

---

problems. The company was also involved in an accounting scandal involving its overstatement of oil and natural gas reserves that required it to restate five years of earnings and to take a $1.7 billion charge to equity for 2003 and 2004. JERRY W. MARKHAM, A FINANCIAL HISTORY OF THE UNITED STATES FROM ENRON-ERA SCANDALS TO THE SUBPRIME CRISIS (2004-2006) 204 (2011). The company decided in 2011 to split off its drilling unit from its pipeline operations because of inconsistencies in the business models for those operations. Daniel Gilbert & Gina Chon, *El Paso Planning to Split in Two*, WALL STREET JOURNAL, May 25, 2011, at B7.

71. In re Duke Energy North America LLC et al., 105 FERC ¶ 61,307 (2003).

72. In re Duke Energy et al., 109 FERC ¶ 61,257 (2004).

73. In re Reliant Resources Inc., FERC Doc. PAO2-2-001 (2003).

74. In re Reliant Resources Inc., FERC Doc. Nos. PAO2-2-001, ELO3-59-000, & IN03-10-000 (Oct. 2, 2003).

75. In re Fact-Finding Investigation into Possible Manipulation of Electric and Natural Gas Prices, Doc. Nos. PA02-2-011 & EL03-60-000 FERC (July 18, 2003).

76. FERC Staff Report, *Final Report on Price Manipulation in Western Markets: Fact-Finding Investigation of Potential Manipulation of Electric and Natural Gas Prices (Findings at a Glance)*, Doc. No. PAO2-2-000 at II-2, II-3 (March 26, 2003), http://www.ferc.gov/legal/maj-ord-reg/land-docs/PART-I-3-26-03.pdf (accessed May 15, 2011).

77. *See*, Jerry W. Markham & Lawrence H. Hunt Jr., *The California Energy Crisis: Enron's Gaming of Governor Gray's Imperfect Market,* 24 FUT. & DERV. L. REP. 6 (2004) (criticizing this claim by FERC).

78. CFTC v. Enron Corp., COMM. FUT. L. REP. (CCH) ¶ 29,811 (S.D. Tex. 2004).

quickly unwound the position, causing prices to drop.[79] One Enron trader agreed to cover the trading losses of another Enron trader (about $80,000) in order to induce him to participate in this scheme.[80] The district court held that these activities would support a CFTC claim for actual or attempted manipulation.[81]

The CFTC also claimed that EnronOnline was an illegal futures exchange because it was not registered with the CFTC as a "contract market." Alternatively, the CFTC claimed that EnronOnline should have notified the agency that the platform was exempt from registration under the CFMA, which it did not do.[82]

The CFTC charged other energy-trading firms with having engaged in manipulative trading. However, a CFTC commissioner publicly declared that many of the strategies at issue in the California energy crisis were not actionable as an actual manipulation of commodity futures prices under the Commodity Exchange Act. Instead, the commissioner stated that such trading was a "regulatory arbitrage in the classic sense" and was the result of the inept deregulation of the California electricity market.[83]

That statement would seem to have signaled that the CFTC had washed its hands of the issue, but that was hardly the case. The CFTC filed manipulation charges against numerous energy companies, but, as the CFTC commissioner noted, instead of charging actual price manipulation, the CFTC took a different approach. It sued a large number of large energy companies under the theory of "attempted" manipulation through "false reports" on trades intended to skew prices on energy indices. "That is, the manipulation, or attempt at manipulation, was carried out through false reporting, which itself is a separate violation of the Act."[84] The Commodity Exchange Act thus prohibits "false or misleading or knowingly inaccurate reports concerning crop or market information or conditions that affect or tend to affect the price of any commodity in interstate commerce."[85]

---

79. CFTC v. Enron Corp., 2004 U.S. Dist. LEXIS 28794, at *4 (S.D. Tex. 2004).

80. *Id.*

81. *Id.*

82. CFTC v. Enron Corp., Complaint, ¶¶ 32-35 (S.D. Tex. March 12, 2003).

83. The CFTC commissioner stated,

> With regard to energy, many trading strategies that have been discussed in the press would not satisfy a legal or economic definition of manipulation. One of the lesser known aspects of the recent problems in the market for electricity is the fact that inconsistent regulatory treatment led to strategic behavior by certain companies and utilities participating in them. In California, for example, methods mandated for price aggregation and artificial transmission constraints ignored market reality and forced separation of the day-ahead energy market from real-time transmission supply and demand. This led to opportunities for arbitraging price differences ostensibly created by regulation.
>
> Indeed, many strategies employed in California were regulatory arbitrage in the classic sense. We're talking buy low, sell high—buy the low price-capped power in California, sell the power back via a loophole allowing out-of-state power to be priced without caps; buy the low priced power in the day-ahead market, taking the risk that you can then sell the high priced power in the real-time market characterized by regulatory incentives that gave rise to distortions in supply. While the cash power markets are outside the jurisdiction of the CFTC, it seems these activities would not likely satisfy any standard for an actionable case of manipulation, much less meet our standard for manipulation.

Sharon Brown-Hruska, *Market Manipulation in the Energy Markets*, 23 FUT. & DERV. L. REP. 1, 4 (2003).

84. *Id.* These attempted manipulation cases are described in COMM. FUT. L. REP. (CCH) ¶ 30,598 (C.F.T.C. 2007) (list of CFTC settlements in these energy market cases).

85. 7 U.S.C. § 13(a)(2).

Attempted manipulation had been charged in other cases, but those claims were almost always a throwaway for the real charges of actual manipulation, and charges of false reports were rarely brought. This shift in manipulation theory was already under way at the CFTC before the Enron bankruptcy as a result of the attempted manipulation claims in the Abrams orange juice case that is discussed in Chapter 4. However, attempted manipulation and false report charges became the centerpiece of CFTC manipulation actions as the Enron affair unfolded and criticism grew over the CFTC's inability to deal with price manipulations. This new approach proved to be highly lucrative for the CFTC in terms of the publicity generated by settlements with the energy trading firms, which proved to be huge cash cows that could be milked as easily by the CFTC as they were by the California authorities and FERC.

The CFTC's new approach ostensibly was intended to make its staff's evidentiary burden lighter in manipulation cases. In actuality, the strategic value of this shift was to induce settlements that could be publicized in the press. Settlement on attempted manipulation grounds was desirable to defendants because such a claim was of but little use to plaintiffs' counsel in private class action claims that usually follow the filing of CFTC administrative proceedings or injunctive actions. In order to obtain damages, class action plaintiffs must bear the burden of proving the elements of an artificial price and that the defendant had the ability to, and did, influence prices. Savvy defense lawyers could use those hurdles to negotiate a settlement of attempted manipulation with the CFTC that neither admitted nor denied the charges. The defense lawyers would then use the lack of CFTC support for actual manipulation to negotiate a lower class action settlement amount with the class action lawyers.

Between 2002 and 2009, the CFTC brought actions against forty-two energy firms and thirty-one individuals under this shift in theory.[86] Those firms included some of the largest energy companies in the world, many of which had also been charged by FERC with improper market behavior. The CFTC imposed over $445 million in fines in settlements from those actions.[87] The CFTC claimed in those cases, which were variously filed as administrative proceedings and injunctive actions in federal court, that false reports of energy trades were given to private publications in order to affect price indexes compiled by those publications.[88]

---

86. The CFTC also settled a few cases of actual manipulation by consent. *See*, In the Matter of Avista Energy Inc., COMM. FUT. L. REP. (CCH) ¶ 28,623 (C.F.T.C. 2001) (electricity futures); In the Matter of Eisler, COMM. FUT. L. REP. (CCH) ¶ 29,664 (C.F.T.C. 2004) (PSE Technology Index option contract).

87. Michael S. Sackeim, *Energy Prosecutions: Is the CFTC Out of Gas?* 29 FUT. & DERV. L. REP. 13 (2009). *See also*, CFTC Division of Enforcement, *CFTC Energy Market Enforcement Results*, COMM. FUT. L. REP. (CCH) ¶ 30,598 (Aug. 2, 2007) (listing thirty-eight cases in which more than $300 million in civil penalties were assessed). Not all of the CFTC fines were collected. The *Wall Street Journal* reported in July 2011 that since 2005, the SEC and CFTC had announced settlements totaling $12.3 billion in penalties but had failed to collect $4.5 billion of that amount. The CFTC had not collected about 75 percent of the fines it imposed in settlements during that period. Jean Eaglesham, *Chasing Fraud, Then Chasing Cash*, WALL STREET JOURNAL, July 8, 2011, at C1.

88. If "everyone's doing it" was a cognizable defense, it would have been a good one indeed for these CFTC charges. *See*, In the Matter of Dynegy Marketing & Trade, COMM. FUT. L. REP. (CCH) ¶ 29,634 (C.F.T.C. 2002) (false reports to affect natural gas price indexes); In the Matter of El Paso Merchant Energy, L.P., COMM. FUT. L. REP. (CCH) ¶ 29,431 (C.F.T.C. 2003) (false reports of nonexistent natural gas prices in order to affect index); In the Matter of WD Energy Services Inc., COMM. FUT. L. REP. (CCH) ¶ 29,544 (C.F.T.C. 2003) (false reports of natural gas prices in order to affect index); In the Matter of Enserco Energy Inc., COMM. FUT. L. REP. (CCH) ¶ 29,554 (C.F.T.C. 2003) (false reports of natural gas prices in order to affect index); In the Matter of Duke Energy Trading & Marketing LLC, COMM. FUT. L. REP. (CCH) ¶ 29,583 (C.F.T.C. 2003) (false reports of natural gas prices in order to affect index); In the Matter of CMS Marketing Services & Trading Co., COMM. FUT. L. REP. (CCH) ¶ 29,634 (C.F.T.C. 2003) (false reports and attempted manipulation of natural gas prices); In the Matter of Reliant Energy Services, COMM. FUT. L. REP. (CCH) ¶ 29,639 (C.F.T.C. 2003) (attempted

Charges of attempted manipulation and false reporting by the CFTC survived various motions to dismiss or for summary judgment in the federal courts.[89] For example, in *CFTC v. Enron Corp.*,[90] a district court denied a motion to dismiss a case brought by the CFTC against Hunter Shively, a trader for EnronOnline. Shively was charged with actual and attempted manipulation after engaging in a fifteen-minute buying spree in Henry Hub natural gas spot market contracts through EnronOnline. Shively sought to "bid up" prices and agreed to cover any losses among traders who assisted that operation. The court noted that, historically, manipulation required a purchase of long futures contracts in excess of deliverable supplies or the purchase of the entire cash supply, or a combination of both. However, the court concluded that proof of control of the relevant cash market was no longer necessary to prove actual or attempted manipulation. Shively paid $300,000 to the CFTC to settle the case after the judge's decision.[91]

---

manipulation and non-bona fide transactions in electricity contracts); In the Matter of Cinergy Marketing & Trading LP, COMM. FUT. L. REP. (CCH) ¶ 29,911 (C.F.T.C. 2004) (false reports of natural gas prices in order to affect index compiled by private publications); In the Matter of Mirant Americas Energy Marketing LP, COMM. FUT. L. REP. (CCH) ¶ 29,925 (C.F.T.C. 2004) (false reports of prices in order to affect index); In the Matter of Aquila Merchant Services Inc., COMM. FUT. L. REP. (CCH) ¶ 29,668 (C.F.T.C. 2004) (false reports of natural gas prices to benefit cash prices); In the Matter of Calpine Energy Services LP, COMM. FUT. L. REP. (CCH) ¶ 29,669 (C.F.T.C. 2004) (false reports of natural gas prices); In the Matter of Entergy-Koch Trading, COMM. FUT. L. REP. (CCH) ¶ 29,670 (C.F.T.C. 2004) (false reports of natural gas prices in order to affect index prices); In the Matter of e prime Inc., COMM. FUT. L. REP. (CCH) ¶ 29,671 (C.F.T.C. 2004) (false reports of natural gas prices in order to affect index); In the Matter of Oneok Energy Marketing & Trading Co. LP, COMM. FUT. L. REP. (CCH) ¶ 29,673 (C.F.T.C. 2004) (false reports of natural gas trades that did not occur in order to affect index); In the Matter of Western Gas Resources Inc., COMM. FUT. L. REP. (CCH) ¶ 29,794 (C.F.T.C. 2004) (false reports of natural gas prices in order to affect NYMEX futures contract prices); In the Matter of Coral Energy Resources LP, COMM. FUT. L. REP. (CCH) ¶ 29,815 (C.F.T.C. 2004) (false reports of natural gas prices in order to affect index); CFTC v. American Electric Power Co. Inc., COMM. FUT. L. REP. (CCH) ¶ 30,014 (S.D. Ohio 2005) (false reports of natural gas prices in order to affect index); CFTC v. Foley, COMM. FUT. L. REP. (CCH) ¶ 30,333 (S.D. Ohio 2006) (supervisor directed false reports of natural gas prices in order to affect index); CFTC v. Atha, COMM. FUT. L. REP. (CCH) ¶¶ 30,374 & 30,375 (N.D. Ga. 2006) (false reports of natural gas prices in order to affect index); In the Matter of Dominion Resources, COMM. FUT. L. REP. (CCH) ¶ 30,331 (C.F.T.C. 2006) (false reports of natural gas prices in order to affect index); CFTC v. NRG Energy Inc., COMM. FUT. L. REP. (CCH) ¶ 30,433 (D. Minn. 2007) (false reports of natural gas prices in order to affect index); CFTC v. Reed, COMM. FUT. L. REP. (CCH) ¶ 30,481 (D. Colo. 2007) (false reports of natural gas prices in order to affect index); CFTC v. Bradley, COMM. FUT. L. REP. (CCH) ¶¶ 30,573 & 30,542 (N.D. Ok. 2007 (false reports of natural gas prices in order to affect index); In the Matter of Marathon Petroleum Company LLC, COMM. FUT. L. REP. (CCH) ¶ 30,591 (C.F.T.C. 2007) (attempted manipulation of Texas intermediate crude oil by selling at below market prices); CFTC v. Atha, COMM. FUT. L. REP. (CCH) ¶ 30,731 (N.D. Ga. 2007) (false reports of natural gas prices in order to affect index); CFTC v. Richmond, COMM. FUT. L. REP. (CCH) ¶ 30,460 (D. Colo. 2007) (false reports of natural gas prices in order to affect index); CFTC v. Energy Transfer Partners LP, COMM. FUT. L. REP. (CCH) ¶ 30,803 (N.D. Tex. 2008) (false reports of natural gas prices in order to affect index); CFTC v. Whitney, COMM. FUT. L. REP. (CCH) ¶ 30,814 (S.D. Tex. 2008) (false reports of natural gas prices in order to affect index).

89. *See, e.g.*, CFTC v. Jonson, 408 F. Supp. 2d 259 (S.D. Tex. 2005) (motion to dismiss manipulation claims by false reporting denied).

90. CFTC v. Enron Corp., 2004 U.S. Dist. LEXIS 28794 (S.D. Tex. 2004).

91. Tom Fowler, *A Former Enron Natural Gas Trader Will Pay $300,000 to Settle A Claim by Regulators That He Manipulated Natural Gas Prices in 2001*, HOUSTON CHRONICLE, July 21, 2004, at 3. Shively later became global co-head of UBS AG's commodities business before that large international bank nearly cratered during the financial crisis in 2008. Saijel Kishan, *UBS's Commodities Co-Head Quits to Join Hedge Fund*, Bloomberg Wire Service, http://www.bloomberg.com/apps/news?pid=newsarchive&sid=aypAJ8Fhk i1I&refer=home (accessed Feb. 23. 2012).

In *CFTC v. Bradley*,[92] the district court denied a motion for summary judgment on a claim of attempted manipulation by making false reports to industry publications that reported on transactions in natural gas prices.[93] The district court found a genuine issue of material fact as to whether the defendant's conduct met the specific intent standard for manipulation. In *CFTC v. Reed*,[94] a district court held that the CFTC had jurisdiction over manipulation in cash markets, as well as futures contracts in natural gas. The court further held that the false report prohibition in the Commodity Exchange Act was not unconstitutionally overbroad or void for vagueness. False reporting claims were also allowed to proceed by a federal district in *In re Natural Gas Commodity Litigation*,[95] a private class action lawsuit involving the natural gas market.

The CFTC was less successful when its new theories were subjected to the test of actual combat in a trial. In *CFTC v. Dizona*,[96] the CFTC charged that Anthony Dizona, a trader on the West trading desk of Coral Energy Resources LP., attempted to manipulate natural gas prices on eight occasions between October 2001 and June 2002 by making false reports to private industry trade publications such as *Inside FERC Gas Market Report* and *Natural Gas Intelligence.*[97] The CFTC charged that Dizona had acted with five other traders, who had settled the charges brought against them before trial. The evidence showed that the volume of trading reported by the Coral traders was often far in excess of the amount actually traded in the market—in one instance, 2,000 percent more.[98] An audio recording admitted into evidence revealed that:

---

92. CFTC v. Bradley, Comm. Fut. L. Rep. (CCH) ¶ 30,289 (N.D. Ok. 2006).

93. *See also*, CFTC v. Bradley, Comm. Fut. L. Rep. (CCH) ¶ 30,453 (N.D. Ok. 2007) (motion seeking bifurcated trial denied). Consent injunctions were later entered in this case. CFTC v. Bradley, Comm. Fut. L. Rep. (CCH) ¶¶ 30,573 & 30,542 (N.D. Ok. 2007).

94. CFTC v. Reed, Comm. Fut. L. Rep. (CCH) ¶ 30,547 (D. Colo. 2007)

95. In re Natural Gas Commodity Litigation, 337 F Supp. 2d 498 (S.D. N.Y. 2004).

96. CFTC v. Dizon, 594 F.3d 408 (5th Cir. 2010).

97. Dizona traders had previously settled with the CFTC without admitting or denying the charges. The CFTC asserted in that case,

> During the relevant period, natural gas traders reported natural gas market information to reporting firms like Natural Gas Intelligence ("*NGI*") and *Inside FERC.* These reporting firms compile their price indexes using price and volume information taken from actual, fixed price, physical, natural gas trades executed between two counterparties. Accordingly, these reporting firms sought from natural gas traders specific market information, i.e., price and volume data, derived from fixed price, physical, natural gas trades the traders actually executed. Natural gas traders submitted price and volume data to various reporting firms so that they would use their market information in compiling their indexes. Natural gas traders generally knew that these reporting firms sought to compile their indexes using price and volume data derived from fixed price, physical, natural gas trades.
>
> These reporting firms' price indexes are widely used by natural gas market participants for various purposes, including the pricing and settlement of natural gas transactions in interstate commerce. Moreover, natural gas futures and options traders refer to the indexes for price discovery and for assessing price risks. For instance, an increase in prices at a natural gas trading hub signals either stronger demand or weakened supply, and futures traders take account of both price movements and changes in the supply/demand balance when conducting their futures trading.
>
> Consequently, because market participants use the natural gas price indexes in the natural gas spot, over-the-counter derivatives, futures, and options markets, the price and volume data reported by natural gas traders to reporting firms is market information that affects or tends to affect the price of natural gas in interstate commerce, and could affect or tend to affect the natural gas futures and options contracts traded on the NYMEX.

In the Matter of Coral Energy Resources, LP, Comm. Fut. L. Rep. (CCH) ¶ 29,815 (C.F.T.C. 2004).

98. 594 F.3d at 412, n. 1.

> Dizona talked to Carol Taylor, a trader in Canada, asking where she wants the price, and she responded "low." Dizona then laughed and asked if "a dollar fifty would be great for you?" He further stated, "Let me test our book and if, if, if I can report it low for you I will." Taylor responded, "That would be great because we don't have enough to even report this month unfortunately." To which Dizona responded, "You can make it up, can't you?" Taylor said, "We can, but we don't feel right about that." Dizona then said, "Oh, you crazy Canadians." At one point, Dizona said he would help her and be her "immoral person," apparently by reporting a low trade. He also referred to "Houston," which was where he was located, as doing the "dirty work for [her]."[99]

The jury found for the CFTC on the attempted manipulation charges, but rejected the false report charges. The district court judge then set aside the jury verdict on the attempted manipulation charges, and the Fifth Circuit Court of Appeals affirmed. The Court of Appeals held that Dizona's statements on the audio recordings were "incriminating but too vague to sufficiently support the jury's finding that he attempted to manipulate the price of natural gas on eight occasions." Further, an expert witness's finding of a general biased reporting at Dizona's trading desk was insufficient to demonstrate that Dizona made the actual false entries into the spreadsheets that were then reported to the trade publications. "With this evidence alone, the Commission cannot show that Dizona attempted to manipulate the market price of natural gas."[100]

The CFTC lost another case that went to trial under the new attempted manipulation and false reporting theories. That case, *CFTC v. Delay*,[101] involved a claim by the CFTC that a trader had falsely reported inflated cash feeder cattle prices to the U.S. Department of Agriculture in order to influence its index of cattle prices. That index was used to price the value of the Chicago Mercantile Exchange's feeder cattle futures contract that the defendant was trading. The defendant's inflated cash feeder cattle prices benefited his futures contracts. This was a relatively simple manipulation case, but both the CFTC and the defendant Delay agreed that such complex issues were beyond the credence of a jury and both agreed to a bench trial.[102] This underscored a historical problem with manipulation claims, *viz*, markets and trading strategies are complex and it is often difficult to separate the legitimate from the illegitimate. Although the federal judge in Nebraska found that Delay's conduct was "highly suspicious," he also found that the defendant had provided legitimate reasons for the abnormally high cash feeder cattle prices. The case was then dismissed.

6:4 THE JUSTICE DEPARTMENT INTERVENES

One of the key items on the to-do list when the George W. Bush administration entered office was the development of a coherent energy policy. That effort was spearheaded by Vice President Richard Cheney, who headed a group of cabinet heads and senior officials serving on the National Energy Policy Development Group (NEPDG). Among other things, the NEPDG noted that "America in the year 2001 faces the most serious energy shortage since the oil embargoes of the 1970s," and it referred pointedly to the then ongoing electricity crisis in California.[103] The report sought a

99. 594 F.3d at 413.

100. 594 F.3d at 418.

101. CFTC v. Delay, 2006 WL 3359076 (D. Neb. 2006).

102. "A jury was picked, and one day of evidence was presented. Sensing that the glazed eyes of the jurors did not bode well for a rational outcome, the plaintiff and the defendant wisely agreed to narrow the claims and waive a jury." *Id.* at n. 1.

103. Report of the National Energy Policy Development Group, *Reliable, Affordable, and Environmentally Sound Energy for America's Future* viii (May 16, 2001).

comprehensive long-term and integrated energy, environmental, and economic policy. However, its efforts were bogged down by claims that the NEPDG violated the Federal Advisory Committee Act[104] by closing its proceedings to the public, an issue that reached the Supreme Court[105] before being dismissed several years after the group's report was issued.[106] The result was that public attention was diverted from the policy issues that were causing higher energy prices to claims of manipulation by the CFTC, FERC, and the Justice Department and the demonizing of speculators by members of Congress.

Enticed by the large settlements being obtained by the CFTC from the energy firms, the Justice Department started its own crusade against those companies and their employees. Various Enron traders were targeted for prosecution for their role in the gaming transactions that exploited the dysfunctional California energy market. One Enron trader, Jeffrey Richter, pleaded guilty to making false statements to the government and to engaging in fraudulent "Load Shift" and "Get Shorty" trades. Another Enron trader, John Forney, pleaded guilty to a criminal charge in connection with his "Ricochet" and "Death Star" trades. Still another Enron trader, Timothy Belden, pleaded guilty to criminal charges. He had been prominently portrayed in a best-selling book on the Enron scandal, which seemed to have sealed his fate.[107]

The use of audio recordings of trader conversations became common in government prosecutions because most trading desks recorded trader conversations in order to verify the accuracy of trades and resolve order disputes with customers. Instead of a defensive tool, however, these recordings became a feast for prosecutors as they listened into the casual conversations of traders discussing how they might exploit market inefficiencies. Several of the tapes were posted on government websites for general viewing in the wake of the Enron trading scandal.[108] Audio recordings of Enron traders exploiting the California energy market became famous and even found their way into the *Congressional Record*, where it was noted that "the release of the so-called 'Grandma Millie' tapes of foul-mouthed Enron traders in Portland boasting of illegal trading schemes spurred widespread condemnation and pressure on Congress to investigate other energy companies."[109] The reference to Grandma Millie was made by an Enron trader joking about trading profits that Enron traders "stole from those poor grandmothers in California," including "Grandma Millie."[110]

Guilty pleas to criminal charges were also entered by several El Paso Corp. traders and a Reliant trader for submitting false natural gas trading data to privately owned publications.[111] Three other El Paso traders were found guilty after a trial of false reporting and were sentenced to prison terms ranging from eleven to fourteen years.[112] However, a jury acquitted one trader of charges that he had falsified trading data while acting as a trader at Duke Energy

---

104. 5 U.S.C. § Appx. 2.

105. Cheney v. U.S. Dist. Ct., 542 U.S. 367 (2004).

106. In re Cheney, 406 F.3d 723 (D.C. Cir. 2005).

107. Bethany McLean & Peter Elkind, The Smartest Guys in the Room: The Amazing Rise and Scandalous Fall of Enron 264-279 (2003).

108. *See, e.g.*, State of California Office of the Attorney General, Energy Unit, http://ag.ca.gov/cfs/energy.php (accessed May 22, 2011).

109. Cong. Rec. S-15659 (July 15, 2004).

110. Jerry W. Markham, A Financial History of the United States from Enron-Era Scandals to the Subprime Crisis (2004-2006) 134 (2011).

111. U.S. Attorney's Office, S.D. Tex. *El Paso Merchant Energy Traders Sentenced to Prison* (Dec. 19, 2009), http://www.fbi.gov/houston/press-releases/2009/ho121709a.htm (accessed May 23, 2011).

112. *El Paso Gas Traders Slapped With Long Prison Terms*, http://blog.chron.com/newswatchenergy/2009/12/el-paso-gas-traders-slapped-with-long-prison-terms/ (accessed May 22, 2011).

through round-trip trades that allowed him to inflate company profits. Some criminal charges brought against two other Duke traders resulted in acquittals, and the remaining charges were dismissed.[113]

Michelle Valencia, a trader at Dynegy, was indicted for false reporting under the Commodity Exchange Act. She was accused of submitting monthly false trading reports between December 1999 through May 2001 to *Inside FERC's Gas Market Report* and to *Natural Gas Intelligence*. Those were widely read publications in the natural gas industry that published at the first of each month a natural gas price index for physical gas transactions at various natural gas locations ("hubs") in the United States and Canada.[114]

The Valencia case made its way up to the Fifth Circuit Court of Appeals before trial on the issue of whether the false reporting charge was unconstitutionally vague or overbroad. The district court had found the term to be overly vague, but the Fifth Circuit ruled that it could be read in a way that was not overly broad.[115] Nevertheless, after a four-week trial, Valencia was not convicted on any of the Commodity Exchange Act false reporting charges. Instead, the jury found her guilty on seven counts of wire fraud for the same conduct, which were upheld on appeal.[116] Valencia was tried with another trader who was found guilty of one count of wire fraud, but the jury also hung on Commodity Exchange Act false reporting charges.

So the false reporting charges turned into a lot of smoke, but no fire, at least in that case. Nevertheless, piling on the energy companies involved in the California energy crisis became a blood sport for regulators and prosecutors after the Enron trading scandals. Reliant Resources Inc. was among those hit by multiple attacks. It settled a claim with the SEC that its round-trip energy trades had falsely increased gross revenues presented to shareholders by $8 billion.[117] That was not considered harmless error even though the opposite side of the trades showed losses that offset those "revenues" and, therefore, resulted in no reporting of false profits. A unit of Reliant settled a claim brought by the CFTC over that trading.[118] Reliant also agreed to pay up to $50

113. Jerry W. Markham, A Financial History of the United States from Enron-Era Scandals to the Subprime Crisis (2004-2006) 204 (2011).

114. United States v. Valencia, 2006 WL 3716657 (S.D. Tex.), *aff'd*, 600 F.3d 389 (5th Cir.), *cert. denied*, --- U.S. ---, 131 S. Ct. 285 (2010).

115. United States v. Valencia, 394 F.3d 352 (5th Cir. 2004), *cert. denied*, 544 U.S. 1034 (2005). The Court of Appeals stated:

> Although a natural reading of § 13(a)(2) [of the Commodity Exchange Act] is consistent with the district court's determination that the reporting prong of the statute is overbroad and criminalizes innocent conduct, Supreme Court precedent mandates that the statute be read narrowly in order to prevent that outcome. Accordingly, we hold the knowledge requirement of the reporting prong of § 13(a)(2) applies to the false or misleading character of the reports, as well as to delivery and inaccuracy.

394 F.3d at 356-357. *See also*, *CFTC v. Reed*, Comm. Fut. L. Rep. (CCH) ¶ 30,547 (D. Colo. Bankruptcy, 2007) (false reporting prohibition in Section 9(a)(2) of the Commodity Exchange Act not void for vagueness or overly broad). A court held long before the creation of the CFTC that the term "manipulate" was not void for vagueness merely because it was not defined in the Commodity Exchange Act. Bartlett Frazier Co. v. Hyde, 65 F.2d 350, 354 (C. A. 7 1933), *cert. denied*, 290 U.S. 654 (1934).

116. United States v. Valencia, 2006 WL 3716657 (S.D. Tex.), *aff'd*, 600 F.3d 389 (5th Cir.), *cert. denied*, --- U.S. ---, 131 S. Ct. 285 (2010).

117. In the Matter of Reliant Resources Inc., Securities Exchange Act Release No. 34-47828 (S.E.C. May 12, 2003). Reliant was not the only energy company attacked by the SEC for its energy trading accounting activities. *See*, In the Matter of Dynegy Inc., Securities Exchange Act Release No. 34-46537 (S.E.C. Sept. 24, 2002) (settlement by consent).

118. In the Matter of Reliant Energy Services, Comm. Fut. L. Rep. (CCH) ¶ 29,639 (C.F.T.C. 2003).

million to settle charges brought by FERC over its withholding of energy from the California electricity market. That was then the largest-ever FERC settlement.[119] Reliant paid another $445 million to settle claims with the attorney generals of various western states over the California electricity crisis.[120]

More striking, the Justice Department indicted Reliant Energy and four of its traders for manipulative activity in the California electricity market during 2000 in violation of the antimanipulation provisions of the Commodity Exchange Act. The Reliant defendants were accused of shutting down four of the five Reliant California generating plants in order to reduce supplies and increase prices. By doing so, Reliant was able to convert a multimillion dollar loss on electricity contracts into large profits. Attorney General John Ashcroft personally announced the indictment of those defendants.[121] Their conviction seemed assured because Reliant had kept tape recordings of the traders' conversations in which they had discussed shutting down the plants in order to profit from their trading in the California electricity market.[122]

A federal district court allowed the Reliant case to go forward, even though there had been only one other criminal prosecution under the false reports prohibition in the sixty-five-year history of the Commodity Exchange Act.[123] The CFTC and its predecessor, the Commodity Exchange Authority, had also brought only a few such cases administratively before the CFTC began its assault on the energy traders.[124] The district court further rejected claims that the false reports charge was overly broad and constitutionally vague, that the Commodity Exchange Act did not

119. Jerry W. Markham, A Financial History of Modern U.S. Corporate Scandals: From Enron to Reform 137 (2006). *See also*, In re Reliant Resources Inc. et al., 102 FERC ¶ 61,108 (2003).

120. Oregon Dept. of Justice, *AG Announces $445 Million Agreement With Reliant Energy Inc. of Houston*, http://www.doj.state.or.us/releases/2005/rel081505.shtml (accessed May 23, 2011).

121. U.S. Dept. of Justice, *Reliant Energy Services Inc. and Four of Its Officers Charged with Criminal Manipulation of California Electricity Market* (April 8, 2004), http://www.fbi.gov/news/pressrel/press-releases/reliant-energy-services-inc.-and-four-of-its-officers-charged-with-criminal-manipulation-of-california-electricity-market (accessed May 23, 2011).

122. *See*, Jerry W. Markham, A Financial History of the United States from Enron-Era Scandals to the Subprime Crisis (2004-2006) 201 (2011) (describing this case).

123. The district court stated:

> If commodities price manipulation were sufficiently harmful to society to require a criminal prohibition, it seems strange that it would take the government this long to get around to enforcing the statute. Surely, if there is such a thing as criminal market manipulation, the California energy crisis in the early 21st century cannot be the first instance of such conduct. Perhaps, the government has been able to deal with market manipulation through other criminal laws. If so, one wonders what a prosecution under the CEA adds to the government's law enforcement arsenal? But the absence of prior prosecutions is not enough to support dismissal of the indictment.

United States v. Reliant Energy Services Inc., 420 F. Supp. 2d 1043, 1054 (N.D. Cal. 2006).

124. For example, in 1946, the Commodity Exchange Authority had found that false reports in telegrams were used to manipulate commodity prices. *In re McGuigan*, 5 Ag. Dec. 249 (1946). A few years later, in 1951, the District of Columbia Court of Appeals upheld a finding by the secretary of agriculture in a Commodity Exchange Authority case that false reports involving lard were used in an attempted price manipulation. *Moore v. Brannan*, 191 F.2d 775 (D.C. Cir.), *cert. denied*, 342 U.S. 860 (1951). Similarly, in another 1950s case, the Commodity Exchange Authority found false information had been disseminated concerning soybean shipments and supplies. *In re Landon Butler*, 14 Ag. Dec. 429 (1955). In still another 1955 decision, the Commodity Exchange Authority found false statements were made concerning delivery intentions. *In re Winn & Lovett Grocery Co.*, 14 Ag. Dec. 561 (1955). In *United Egg Producers v. Bauer Int'l Corp.*, F. Supp. 1375 (S.D.N.Y. 1970), a district court found false reports had been made concerning egg imports.

apply to the cash market transactions of Reliant, and that FERC had exclusive jurisdiction over the California electricity market.[125]

Nevertheless, the district court issued jury instructions and made an evidentiary ruling that made it very difficult for the government to prove its case. The Ninth Circuit upheld that evidentiary ruling, in part, and remanded for further consideration.[126] The district court's rulings allowed expert witnesses called by the defense to testify that the defendants' trading activities were "objectively reasonable" and within market rules.[127] This convinced the prosecutors that, after more than three years of pretrial skirmishing, they should settle what was becoming an increasingly shaky case.

The Reliant settlement with the Justice Department imposed a relatively inconsequential $22 million fine on Reliant. An even more unusual feature in this settlement was the grant of a deferred prosecution agreement to the defendants after an indictment. Such agreements suspend the bringing of criminal charges for a specified period, and the charges are dropped altogether if the defendant does not commit another crime during that period. Deferred prosecution agreements were usually limited to corporate defendants. Here, however, the individual defendants were included as well. They were given no jail time even though the attorney general had claimed in his press conference announcing the indictment that they had committed very serious crimes.[128]

6:5 THE BP CASE

The Justice Department's vision of a gravy train of publicity and fines from Commodity Exchange Act manipulation charges was renewed when it bought a joint action with the CFTC against BP Products of North America Inc. (BP). BP was a unit of one of the largest energy companies in the world.[129] The government charged that BP traders manipulated the propane market for residential and commercial heating in the Northeast in February 2004 and that it attempted to manipulate that market in April 2003. This manipulation case was somewhat unique in that there were no related commodity futures trading on a regulated exchange.

The CFTC charged that BP and its employees, by their own admission, controlled the cash market in propane "at will," allowing BP to dictate prices and reap large trading profits. Among other things, it was claimed that BP's trading bench had sold propane at an inflated price, obtained a dominant position in the cash commodity, and withheld supplies in order to force the shorts to pay artificial prices.[130]

BP agreed to settle with the CFTC by paying $125 million in fines and $53 million in restitution to propane consumers. This was the largest settlement for a manipulation case in the CFTC's his-

---

125. United States v. Reliant Energy Services Inc., 420 F. Supp. 2d 1043 (N.D. Cal. 2006).

126. United States v. Reliant Energy Services Inc., 2006 U.S. App. LEXIS 16995 (9th Cir. 2006).

127. United States v. Reliant Energy Services Inc., 2006 U.S. Dist. LEXIS 18822 (N.D. Cal. 2007).

128. Pamela A. MacLean, *Reliant's Hard-Ball Defense Plan Prevails*, NAT'L L. J., April 5, 2007. That leniency should be contrasted with the fate of other traders. The Fifth Circuit affirmed the sentencing and plea agreement of another Reliant trader who had pleaded guilty to a single count of false reporting under the Commodity Exchange Act and was given a sentence of more than four and a half years. United States v. Futch, 278 Fed. Appx. 387 (5th Cir. 2008), *cert. denied*, 555 U.S. 1102 (2009). Fourteen- and eleven-year sentences were given to the El Paso traders. Michelle Valencia, the Dynegy trader convicted of wire fraud for false reporting, was given a sentence of more than four and a half years; the district court refused to deviate from sentencing guidelines although she was a caregiver for a daughter with a physical disability. The district court found that the child was conceived while Valencia was awaiting sentencing and that Valencia had the opportunity, but failed, to abort the child. United States v. Valencia, 600 F.3d 389, 433 (5th Cir.), *cert. denied*, --- U.S. ---, 131 S. Ct. 285 (2010).

129. *CFTC v. BP Products North America Inc.*, 2007 WL 3407430 (N.D. Ill. 2007).

130. *Id.* The CFTC charged that BP traders

tory. BP also agreed to establish a compliance and ethics program and to hire a corporate "monitor" to oversee its trading activities and to "cooperate" in future investigations. The Department of Justice simultaneously announced that BP America Inc. agreed to enter into a deferred prosecution agreement based upon the same conduct that was the subject of the CFTC complaint."[131] BP agreed to pay the Justice Department a $100 million criminal penalty, plus $25 million into a consumer fraud fund. This meant that BP had to pay a total of $303 million to settle the CFTC and Justice Department charges.[132]

Four BP traders were indicted for their role in the activity. Those charges proved a disaster for the Justice Department. The district court hearing the case, in *United States v. Radley*,[133] dismissed the indictments against those individuals. The court found that the conduct charged was not manipulative because it involved only actual bids and offers that created legally enforceable obligations. The district court also rejected a claim that the defendants had engaged in manipulation by withholding product from the market. The district court stated that, "[a]bsent a contract obligation or statutorily imposed position restriction, neither of which was present in this case, a party is never required to sell or purchase anything. To refuse to do so is not misleading or fraudulent, regardless of the motivation."[134] The district court went further and stated that "[a]cting in a manner that shifts the price of a commodity in a favorable direction is the business of profit-making enterprises, and if it is done without fraud or misrepresentation, it does not clearly violate the CEA."[135]

> conspired to manipulate the February 2004 propane market for propane transported in the TEPPCO pipeline system (hereinafter referred to as "TET" propane). As a result, the price of TET propane was artificial and inflated from February 12, 2004 through March 2, 2004. . . . In accordance with the plan, the employees used the financial resources of BP to buy contracts for substantially all of the February 2004 TET propane supply to become the dominant owner, or "long-holder," of TET propane. The employees, at specific times thereafter, withheld supply from the market while continuing to purchase contracts to own more than the supply of TET propane in the TEPPCO system. BP's dominant ownership position, continued purchases of said propane subsequent to obtaining such a position, and withholding of supply at specific times thereafter, all distorted and made artificial the price of TET propane during February 2004. As a result of the employees' conduct, by the end of February 2004, BP acquired ownership of substantially all of the available supply of February 2004 TET propane in the United States. The employees executing the plan thus cornered the market for February 2004 TET propane, distorted and made artificial the price of February 2004 TET propane, and sold a portion of the supply at an artificial and inflated price.

Id.

131. CFTC Press Release No. 5405-07, *BP Agrees to Pay a Total of $303 Million in Sanctions to Settle Charges of Manipulation and Attempted Manipulation in the Propane Market* (Oct. 25, 2007), http://www.cftc.gov/pressroom/pressreleases/pr5405-07.html (accessed May 23, 2011).

132. That massive payout did not buy BP any peace from the government. Political pressure from the Obama administration required BP to forgo dividends and establish a $20 billion fund for damages caused by the giant Gulf oil spill during the summer of 2010, in addition to the more than $3 billion spent on cleanup. Jonathan Weisman & Guy Chazan, *BP Agrees to $20 Billion Fund*, WALL STREET JOURNAL, June 17, 2010. A subsequent investigation found that substantial amounts of funds paid by BP to communities for cleanup efforts had been spent on things other than cleanup, including Tasers, new SUVs, personal computers, and iPads. Michael Kunzelman, *Gulf Coast States Spent Millions in BP Grants; But Review Finds Not All Expenses Related to Oil Spill*, BOSTON GLOBE, April 12, 2011, at 6. BP also ran into more problems with a venture in Russia. Gregory L. White, *BP-Rosenfet Deal "Dead" for Now,* WALL STREET JOURNAL, May 24, 2011.

133. 659 F. Supp. 2d 803 (S.D. Tex. 2009), *aff'd*, 632 F.3d 177 (5th Cir. 2011).

134. 659 F. Supp. 2d at 815-816 (footnote omitted).

135. 659 F. Supp. 2d at 815-816 (footnote omitted).

Equally damaging was the court's holding in *Radley* that the Enron loophole in the CFMA excluded the transactions at issue from the Commodity Exchange Act.[136] The district court held that the Enron loophole exempted contracts by "eligible contract participants" that are individually negotiated and not executed on a "trading facility."[137] That was the case for the contracts at issue. The district court also found the manipulation charges unconstitutionally void for vagueness.[138]

The Fifth Circuit Court of Appeals affirmed the dismissal of the indictment.[139] The Fifth Circuit noted that the trading in TET propane futures did not occur on an exchange; rather it was conducted on an electronic trading platform called "Chalkboard." The indictment charged that defendants were manipulating the prices of TET propane on Chalkboard.[140] The defendants used "stacked bids" that were designed "to trick other market participants into believing that demand for the commodity was strong and came from more than one source."[141] The Fifth Circuit held that the defendants' challenged activities were exempted from the Commodity Exchange Act. A wire fraud charge was also rejected.[142]

The alleged BP manipulation was blamed in Congress on the "Enron loophole,"[143] and derivatives experts claimed that the decision in *Radley* would make prosecution of commodity manipulation "virtually impossible."[144] In that regard, Professor Frank Partnoy at the University of San Diego School of Law contended that, "if the government can't prosecute, it will never know exactly how much manipulation really goes on. 'Anyone who's actually engaging in manipulative trading will be thrilled to read this opinion.'"[145]

---

136. 7 U.S.C. § 2(g).

137. 659 F. Supp. 2d at 812. *See generally*, Michael S. Sackeim, *False Reporting of OTC Energy Transactions*, 13 REV. OF SEC. & COMM. REG. 149 (2004) (describing application of this section to false reports involving over-the-counter commodity trades). *Compare*, CFTC v. Johnson, 408 F. Supp. 2d 259 (S.D. Tex. 2005) (exception did not apply to fictitious reports); United States v. Futch, 279 Fed. App. 387 (5th Cir. 2008), *cert. denied*, 555 U.S. 1102 (2009) (same).

138. 659 F. Supp. 2d at 812.

139. United Sates v. Radley, 632 F.3d 177 (5th Cir. 2011).

140. The indictment charged,

> Beginning in early February 2004, the Appellees began purchasing a large number of futures contracts for delivery at the end of that month—*i.e.*, taking a "long position" in February TET propane. They did so through the Chalkboard system, placing multiple bids at different prices and quantities. They also entered agreements to sell February TET propane at the the [Oil Price Information Service] average price. Because of Appellees' ambitious (and risky) buying campaign, the price of futures skyrocketed from 61 cents per gallon on February 9, 2004 to a high of 94 cents on February 27, 2004, the last trading day before delivery on February 29. After the February contracts came due, the price of propane futures plummeted. On March 1, the price of March TET propane fell almost 25 cents per gallon to settle at 61.75 cents.
>
> BP made money from Appellees' activity in two ways. First, some of the people who sold futures contracts (the "shorts") did not actually have any propane to sell ("naked shorts"); in order to fulfill their obligation, they needed to repurchase TET propane at the high price prevailing after Appellees' buying campaign was underway, often from Appellees themselves. Second, Appellees' contracts to sell at future OPIS prices generated profits because the OPIS price increased with Appellees' voracious demand.

632 F.3d at 179-180.

141. 632 F.3d at 180. The Oil Price Information Service (OPIS) reported the average daily price of trading on Chalkboard. 632 F.3d at 179.

142. 632 F.3d at 185.

143. Jeremy Grant, *BP Suspends Three Traders*, FINANCIAL TIMES (LONDON), July 13, 2006.

144. Daniel Newhauser, *Lost in the "Enron Loophole*," http://www.law.com/jsp/law/LawArticleFriendly.jsp?id=1202437871928 (accessed May 25, 2011).

145. *Id.*

6:6 FALSE REPORTS TO EXCHANGES

The CFTC reached into its regulatory grab bag to find still another provision in the Commodity Exchange Act that it could use to attack manipulative false reports. Section 9(a)(4) of the Commodity Exchange Act[146] makes it illegal for any person willfully to falsify, conceal, or cover up by any trick, scheme, or artifice any material fact to a registered contract market. The CFTC applied this provision to attack traders misrepresenting their positions to exchanges in order to avoid exchange actions or to conceal their trading from the market.[147] The CFTC sought to create this new approach and theory through its usual modus operandi, consent settlements.

In one such case, *In the Matter of Eisler*,[148] the CFTC charged that the chair of NYMEX used his position on a NYMEX settlement price committee to set inflated settlement prices of options on index futures contracts in order to benefit his personal trading account. In finding a violation of Section 9(a)(4) of the CEA, the CFTC consent order analyzed the respondent's activities and found that they met all four of the traditional elements of manipulation required by Section 9(a)(2). He was thus found to have had the ability to influence market prices, he specifically intended to do so, artificial prices existed, and he caused those artificial prices.

From the *Eisler* opinion, one might think that Section 9(a)(4) was simply a subset of the more broadly based manipulation cases traditionally brought under the general antimanipulation provisions of Section 9(a)(2) of the Commodity Exchange Act. This is because both sections prohibit false reports to the market and both require proof of the elements of manipulation. That did not prove to be the case. Subsequent section 9(a)(4) claims made by the CFTC threw still another twist into manipulation charges. Through that back door, the CFTC once again sought to reduce its burden in proving actual manipulation of prices.

In *In the Matter of EMF Financial Products LLC*,[149] the CFTC, through a consent order, held that the respondent, EMF, violated Section 9(a)(4) by falsely providing information about its positions and financing to the Chicago Board of Trade (CBOT). The CBOT was concerned with the size of the EMF's position in the September 2005 ten-year U.S. Treasury note futures contract and a large long position in the underlying cheapest-to-deliver Treasuries (CTD) on the September futures contract.[150] Interestingly, unlike the *Eisler* case, the CFTC made no find-

---

146. 7 U.S.C. § 13(a)(4) (2006).

147. The CFTC also applied Section 9(a)(4) of the Commodity Exchange Act in a non-manipulation context in order to address false statements made by commodity pool operators and forex dealers to the National Futures Association, the industry self-regulatory body. Several consent orders or default injunctions were entered on the basis of such charges. *See, e. g.*, CFTC v. Kim, 2011 U.S. Dist. LEXIS 49197 (S.D.N.Y.); CFTC v. Napoletano, 2009 U.S. Dist. LEXIS 46719 (S.D.N.Y.); CFTC v. Nations Invs., LLC, 2008 U.S. Dist. LEXIS 82970 (S.D. Fl.); CFTC v. Lake Dow Capital, LLC, 2007 U.S. Dist. LEXIS 99469 (N.D. Ga.); and In the Matter of Belsky, 2008 CFTC LEXIS 104 (C.F.T.C.);

148. In the Matter of Eisler, COMM. FUT. L. REP. (CCH) ¶ 29,664 (C.F.T.C. 2004).

149. 2009 CFTC LEXIS 79.

150. The CFTC found that

> EMF misrepresented the size of its cash position in the CTD and failed to disclose its large position in the CTD in the repurchase ("repo") market. EMF also failed to disclose that EMF was financing its large long position in the CTD through a repo financing mechanism known as General Collateral Financing ("GCF"), which made those notes unavailable to market participants. Accordingly, EMF withheld from the CBOT information concerning its position and control of up to $11.9 billion of the CTD at the same time that it held the large long futures position.

Id.

ings of any traditional elements of attempted or actual manipulation such as intent to create an artificial price.[151]

In *In the Matter of Vitol Inc.*,[152] the CFTC, in another administrative consent order, found that the respondents withheld information from NYMEX in 2007 that would have required their futures trading positions to be aggregated as related accounts. As a result of that deception, the trading positions of respondents were treated as separate for purposes of NYMEX position and accountability rules. Those exchange restrictions are directed at limiting the ability of speculators to manipulate the markets whether acting alone or in concert with others. Once again, the elements of manipulation were not addressed. In still another such case, *In the Matter of Morgan Stanley Capital Group Inc.*,[153] the CFTC, in an administrative consent order, found a violation of Section 9(a)(4). There, the respondent, a futures commission merchant, failed to report a block trade of a customer to NYMEX until after the close of trading on February 6, 2009. That delay concealed the trade from NYMEX and violated a NYMEX rule requiring reports of block trades within five minutes of execution. Similar charges were brought and settled by consent in *In the Matter of UBS Securities LLC*.[154]

A district court in *CFTC v. Amaranth Advisors LLC*[155] considered a Section 9(a)(4) claim that was filed along with a Section 9(a)(2) manipulation charge. The defendants were accused of covering up their manipulative activities by submitting a false letter to NYMEX. The court noted that this was the first time that a federal court had considered the scope of Section 9(a)(4). The court held that such a claim sounded in fraud and must be pleaded with particularity, a burden that the CFTC met in this case. The court also equated Section 9(a)(4) with 18 U.S.C. 1001, which prohibits false statements to government officials and contains no requirement of manipulative intent. This suggested that the court was of the view that the elements of a Section 9(a)(4) claim need not include the elements of a Section 9(a)(2) manipulation charge. The court in *Amaranth*[156] later entered a consent injunction that enjoined the defendant from violations of both Section 9(a)(2) and 9(a)(4).[157]

6:7 RIGGED TRADE MANIPULATIONS AND SECTION 4(C)

Rigged trades often involve the manipulation of one contract that serves as a price setter for another market or contracts that are not traded directly in the market. The CFTC added such rigged trades to its revamped approach to manipulation. Like false reports and attempted manipulation, such cases were historically rare. Rigged trading cases were traditionally brought under Section 4c of the Commodity Exchange Act, which proscribes practices deemed abusive, such as wash trades and fictitious transactions.[158]

---

151. In the Matter of Morgan Stanley Capital Group Inc., COMM. FUT. L. REP. (CCH) ¶ 31,564 (C.F.T.C. 2010).

152. 2010 CFTC LEXIS 54 (C.F.T.C.).

153. *See also*, In the Matter of Daniels, 2011 CFTC LEXIS 9 (C.F.T.C.) (consent order making similar findings).

154. In the Matter of UBS Securities LLC, 2010 CFTC LEXIS 27. *See also*, In the Matter of McCormick, 2010 CFTC LEXIS 61 (consent order in which respondent floor broker submitted false trading cards that were used to conceal his trading losses from the Chicago Mercantile Exchange).

155. 554 F. Supp. 2d 523, 535 (S.D.N.Y. 2008).

156. 2009 U.S. Dist. LEXIS 101406 (S.D.N.Y.).

157. Amaranth settled a class action claim over this conduct for $77.1 million. *Amaranth's $77.1 Million Manipulation Settlement Approved*, Bloomberg, Dec. 20, 2011, http://www.bloomberg.com/news/2011-12-20/amaranth-s-77-1-million-manipulation-settlement-approved-1-.html (accessed March 22, 2012).

158. 7 U.S.C. § 6c. This provision is discussed in Chapter 4.

One rigged trading case, *In the Matter of Avista Energy Inc.*,[159] involved a pre-Enron manipulation of the electricity market. The CFTC found that the respondent used rigged trades to manipulate the settlement prices of electricity futures contracts traded on the NYMEX on four days during the period April through July 1998. The manipulation was conducted in order to increase the respondent's gain on its over-the-counter options positions, the value of which was based on the settlement prices on the NYMEX. Due to the illiquidity of the market for the electricity futures contracts, the respondent was able to raise and lower settlement prices through large orders at the close of trading.[160] The CFTC also stated in that case that the test for attempted manipulation and actual manipulation "is a flexible one." Section 4c violations were also found because the trades were not competitively executed.

Another respondent refused to settle charges related to the *Avista* case and went to trial before a CFTC administrative law judge, who found violations. That decision was reviewed by the CFTC and affirmed by the Second Circuit Court of Appeals. That case gave the CFTC its first-ever victory in a contested manipulation case. However, that win did not come until some twelve years after the trading in question. In that case, *In the Matter of DiPlacido*,[161] the CFTC charged a floor broker on the NYMEX with improperly executing the Avista trades. The respondent DiPlacido had sought an "ugly" close and traded through the orders of other market participants in order to achieve an artificial price. The CFTC noted that this was the first time that it "considered a manipulation case based on trading floor practices in an adjudicated decision."[162] Only two of the CFTC commissioners and an acting chair participated in this decision.

---

159. *In the Matter of Avista Energy Inc.*, COMM. FUT. L. REP. (CCH) ¶ 28,623 (C.F.T.C. 2001).

160. Specifically, the CFTC charged that

> Avista Energy entered into cash-settled over-the-counter ("OTC") derivatives contracts, whose value at expiration was based on the daily settlement price of one of the Western U.S. electricity futures contracts on the expiration day of options trading (the "Options Expiration Day"). Through this manipulative scheme, Avista Energy was able to realize or increase its net gain on these option contracts that were in or near the money.
>
> Avista Energy was able to create artificial settlement prices in NYMEX PV and/or COB electricity futures contracts through the manner in which it placed large orders for NYMEX Western U.S. electricity futures contracts on the Options Expiration Days in April, May, July, and August 1998. Specifically, Avista Energy's Traders engaged in these manipulative practices: (a) selling May and June 1998 NYMEX PV electricity futures contracts at prices less than the prevailing bids during the close on the April and May 1998 Options Expiration Days; (b) purchasing August and September 1998 NYMEX PV electricity futures contracts at prices higher than the prevailing offers during the close on the July and August 1998 Options Expiration Days; and (c) purchasing August 1998 NYMEX COB electricity futures contracts at prices higher than the prevailing offers during the close on the July 1998 Options Expiration Day. In addition, Avista Energy's Traders supported one of the manipulations through non-competitive trading.

COMM. FUT. L. REP. (CCH) ¶ 28,623.

161. In the Matter of DiPlacido, COMM. FUT. L. REP. ¶ 30,970 (C.F.T.C. 2008), *aff'd sub nom.*, DiPlacido v. CFTC, No. 08-5559-ag, 2009 U.S. App. LEXIS 22692 (2d Cir. 2009), *cert denied*, 2010 U.S. LEXIS 2461 (2010).

162. COMM. FUT. L. REP. ¶ 30,970. The CFTC noted that the previous

> manipulation cases the Commission has decided were based on allegations of manipulation involving traditional market "corners" or "squeezes," through which the alleged manipulator unlawfully creates artificial prices on the futures market through control of the cash market, or by obtaining futures contracts requiring delivery of commodities greater than available supply. The trade practice based manipulation at issue in this case is based on the manipulation theory

The CFTC's decision in *DiPlacido* used the traditional four-part manipulation test to find that the respondent had engaged in an actual manipulation in violation of the Commodity Exchange Act even though there was no showing of market power or control of the cash market on his part. Rather, the CFTC believed that it was sufficient to show that DiPlacido had merely the "ability to influence" prices. That showing was made because DiPlacido's trading volume was a significant percentage of the average trading volume on the exchange in this illiquid contract. It was further found that DiPlacido's trades established artificial prices in violating bids and offers of other traders by offering at lower than prevailing bids or bidding at higher than prevailing offers on the trading floor.[163]

The CFTC ruled in *DiPlacido* that a trader executing large orders on the same side of an illiquid market during the close has a duty to execute those orders so as to minimize their effect on price. "Bidding at higher than prevailing prices or offering at lower than prevailing prices self-evidently maximizes price impact in derogation of that duty."[164] This holding sought to create a duty on floor traders to maintain a fair and orderly market that is akin to the duty placed on specialists and other market makers in the securities industry, but never previously imposed on futures traders.[165] The CFTC also found attempted manipulation and a violation of Section 4(c) from DiPlacido's trading.[166] The CFTC imposed a twenty-year trading ban on DiPlacido and ordered him to pay a civil penalty of $1 million. Other individual settling respondents were given only modest sanctions, and Avista was subject only to a civil penalty.[167] The obvious message from this case was settle or be destroyed.

The Second Circuit affirmed the CFTC's decision in *DiPlacido* in an unpublished opinion, rejecting among other claims that the respondent had not been given fair notice of the CFTC's shift in manipulation theories.[168] The CFTC's finding of intent was also upheld because of his violating bids and offers and because taped conversations had evidenced the signaling of manipulative intent. In addition, the CFTC had relied on evidence that artificial prices were a "reasonably probable consequence" of DiPlacido's large trades during the close of an illiquid market.[169]

The district court in *In re Natural Gas Commodity Litigation*[170] also provided support for rigged trading manipulation charges. The court held that allegations of wash trading of nonexchange-

---

> adopted by the Judicial Officer of the U.S. Department of Agriculture in In re Henner, 30 Agric. Dec. 1151 (1971), a case brought by the Commission's predecessor agency, the Commodity Exchange Authority.

Id.

163. *Id.*

164. Comm. Fut. L. Rep. ¶ 30,970.

165. *See*, Jerry W. Markham, *Manipulation of Commodity Futures Prices: The Unprosecutable Crime*, 8 Yale J. on Reg. 281, 363-369 (1991) (advocating adoption of fair and orderly market requirements in futures industry).

166. Comm. Fut. L. Rep. ¶ 30,970.

167. *See*, In the Matter of DiPlacido, Comm. Fut. L. Rep. ¶ 29,153 (C.F.T.C. 2002) (respondent agreed to pay civil penalty of $155,000 and submitted to a twenty-four-month trading prohibition); In the Matter of Taylor, Comm. Fut. L. Rep. ¶ 29,594 (C.F.T.C. 2003) (respondent agreed to pay a $155,000 civil money penalty and submitted to thirty-month trading ban). *See also*, In the Matter of Avista Energy Inc., Comm. Fut. L. Rep. (CCH) ¶ 28,623 (C.F.T.C. 2001) (corporate respondent agreed to pay a civil penalty of $2.1 million and faced no trading bar); In the Matter of Johns, Comm. Fut. L. Rep. (CCH) ¶ 28,628 (C.F.T.C. 2001) (corporate trader agreed to a $50,000 penalty and twelve-month trading ban); In the Matter of Griswold, 2001 WL 951376 (C.F.T.C. 2003) (corporate trader agreed to a $110,000 penalty and eighteen-month trading ban).

168. DiPlacido v. CFTC, 2009 U.S. App. LEXIS 22692 (2d Cir. 2009), *cert denied*, 2010 U.S. LEXIS 2461 (2010).

169. *Id.*

170. In re Natural Gas Commodity Litigation, 337 F Supp. 2d 498 (S.D. N.Y. 2004).

traded instruments would allow a private right of action for manipulation. That was the case even if such trades would not support a private right of action under Section 4(c) of the Commodity Exchange Act.[171]

In *In the Matter of Moore Capital Management LP*,[172] the CFTC found, by consent, a failure to supervise a trader "attempting" to manipulate the settlement prices of platinum and palladium futures contracts on NYMEX during the period of November 2007 through May 2008. The trader was "banging the close" by market-on-close orders executed in the last ten seconds of daily trading on the floor in order to push up prices. The sizes of the trades were relatively large in those illiquid markets.[173] A federal district court, however, dismissed a private action involving the activities at issue in the *Moore Capital* case, holding that the allegations in the CFTC complaint did not establish manipulative intent because those claims had been settled by consent and were improperly included in the plaintiffs' pleadings. The fact that certain emails had been deleted by the defendants also failed to establish manipulative intent.[174]

The CFTC continued its efforts to make law through consent proceedings. In *In the Matter of Marathon Petroleum Company LLC*,[175] the CFTC, in a consent order, found that respondent's trader deliberately traded through the prevailing market price during a thirty-minute price settlement period on the NYMEX. That trading was in futures but was done in order to depress cash prices for West Texas intermediate crude oil. The respondent also agreed to sell West Texas intermediate crude oil at prices deemed by the CFTC to be lower than necessary.

In the Matter of Shell Trading US Co.,[176] the CFTC settled by consent an administrative proceeding involving prearranged trading in NYMEX crude oil futures. The CFTC found only Section 4(c) violations and did not charge manipulation. Apparently, this omission was due to the fact that, while "the traders prearranged the trade by agreeing on the quantity and the settlement month, and agreeing to take the opposite positions of the trade[,] [t]here was no prearrangement as to price." Similar charges were settled in *In the Matter of Cantor Fitzgerald & Co.*,[177] where an "employee of Cantor simultaneously entered orders with certain floor brokers from two different floor brokerage operations, on behalf of the same customer, to buy and sell New York Mercantile Exchange ("NYMEX") Reformulated Gasoline Blendstock for Oxygen Blending ("RB gasoline") futures contracts for the same quantity, price and contract month. In each instance, the employee prearranged to have these identical orders executed opposite each other."

A nonenergy market of concern was the Chicago Mercantile Exchange (CME) spot cheese market. A report by the Government Accountability Office (GAO) in 2007 found that few trades occurred on the CME in spot cheese and that a small number of traders were making those trades. The GAO believed that this made the market susceptible to manipulation but noted that the CFTC had not

---

171. 337 F. Supp. 2d at 510.

172. In the Matter of Moore Capital Management, LP, COMM. FUT. L. REP. (CCH) ¶ 31,567 (C.F.T.C. 2010).

173. *See also*, In the Matter of Pia, 2011 CFTC LEXIS 45 (2011) (same charges).

174. In re Platinum and Palladium Commodities Litigation, — F. Supp. 2d —, 2011 WL 4048780 (S.D.N.Y. 2011). In In re Rough Rice Commodity Litigation, 2012 WL 473091 (N.D. Ill.), a district court rejected the use of CFTC findings in a consent order in In the Matter of Taylor, 2011 WL 281741 (C.F.T.C.). It also rejected an effort to turn a position limit violation into a manipulation claim, holding that no artificial price was shown.

175. In the Matter of Marathon Petroleum Company LLC, COMM. FUT. L. REP. (CCH) ¶ 30,591 (C.F.T.C. 2007).

176. In the Matter of Shell Trading US Co., 2006 CFTC LEXIS 2 (C.F.T.C. 2006).

177. In the Matter of Cantor Fitzgerald & Co., 2011 WL 639922 (C.F.T.C.).

brought any cases making such charges.[178] Thereafter, in *In the Matter of Dairy Farmers of America Inc.*,[179] the CFTC charged attempted manipulation by a dairy farm marketing cooperative in a case that was settled by consent in 2008. It was found that the Dairy Farmers of America (DFA) cooperative attempted to manipulate the Class III milk futures contract on the CME. This was done through the purchase of a correlated commodity, block cheddar cheese, on the CME's spot call market. A $12 million civil penalty was imposed as well as speculative trading suspensions.[180]

In *Anderson v. Dairy Farmers of America Inc.*,[181] a district court denied summary judgment in a private action that sought damages over the activities at issue in the CFTC proceeding.[182] The court held that, in order to establish that an artificial price existed for the purposes of a CEA manipulation claim, "a plaintiff need not establish fraud, misrepresentation, or a violation of exchange rules on the part of the defendant."[183] Rather, the court believed that the proper analysis was to determine "whether the specific facts of a case support a finding that the commodity price was determined by forces other than legitimate forces of supply and demand and whether a defendant intended to cause that artificial price."[184] The court held there was an issue of fact over whether the price of cheese and Class III milk reflected factors other than legitimate market forces of supply and demand, and whether the DFA intended to cause artificial prices.[185] A more practical approach was taken by the GAO, which recommended that consideration be given to eliminating cheese prices from the formula for determining minimum federal milk pricing. Alternatively, it suggested better monitoring of price reporting.[186]

6:8 FERC ENTERS THE MANIPULATION ARENA

In order to address what it perceived to be market flaws, to protect and maintain the competitive natural gas market, and "to continue its light-handed regulation of the gas sales within its

---

178. GAO, *Spot Cheese Market, Market Oversight Has Increased, But Concerns Remain Over Potential Manipulation*, 2-4 (June 2007).

179. In the Matter of Dairy Farmers of America Inc., Comm. Fut. L. Rep. (CCH) ¶ 30,962.

180. A similar case was brought by the Commodity Exchange Authority in 1947 and is discussed in Chapter 3. In re Zenith-Godley Co., 6 Agric. Dec. 900 (1947).

181. Anderson v. Dairy Farmers of America Inc., 2010 U.S. Dist. LEXIS 104191(D. Minn.).

182. The court noted that

> the CME Cheese Spot Call is a thinly traded market, which during the relevant time period opened for only fifteen minutes a day and comprised only 2% of the sales of cheese in the United States. Yet, the price at which cheese traded on the CME Cheese Spot Call effectively set the price for cheese purchases nationwide. From May 21 to June 23, 2004, DFA purchased 323 loads of cheddar cheese blocks at $1.80 per pound. DFA was the sole purchaser of cheese on the CME Spot Call during that period. Plaintiffs allege that DFA's cheese purchases prevented cheese prices from dipping below $1.80 and that DFA was able to liquidate its long Class III milk futures contracts at a profit during the relevant time period. In addition, the price of cheese plummeted after DFA ceased purchasing cheese, indicating that DFA's purchases of cheese—allegedly without commercial need for the cheese—prevented the "determination of [cheese] prices by free competition alone."

Anderson v. Dairy Farmers of America Inc., 2010 U.S. Dist. LEXIS 104191(D. Minn.).

183. *Id.*

184. *Id.*

185. *See also*, In re Dairy Farmers of America Inc., 767 F. Supp. 2d 880 (N.D. Ill. 2011) (antitrust claims over DFA's trading). *See generally*, Ice Cream Liquidation Inc. v. Land O'Lakes Inc., 253 F. Supp. 2d 262 (D. Conn. 2003) (antitrust claims that cream and butter prices manipulated by trading on the CME).

186. GAO, *Spot Cheese Market, Market Oversight Has Increased, But Concerns Remain Over Potential Manipulation* (June 2007).

jurisdiction,"[187] FERC adopted a number of antimanipulation prohibitions in the wake of the Enron-era energy trading scandals. FERC Order 644, which was adopted in November 2003, established a Code of Conduct that prohibited pipelines and sellers of natural gas for resale at negotiated rates from engaging in actions that were without a legitimate business purpose. Also prohibited were actions that were "intended to or foreseeably could manipulate market prices, market conditions, or market rules for natural gas."[188] Prohibited activities included wash trades and collusion for the purpose of market manipulation.[189] The FERC order also required sellers reporting transaction data to provide accurate and factual data that was not "knowingly" false or misleading.[190] These prohibitions were designed to sweep up the Enron-era prohibitions that FERC had already found to be in violation of its tariff schedules.

In addition, in "reaction to the clear evidence of manipulation by Enron and others in the Western electricity markets in 2000 and 2001" that cost consumers billions,[191] Congress passed new legislation. A provision in the Energy Policy Act of 2005 (EPAct)[192] gave FERC power to attack the manipulation of energy prices. That legislation also added civil penalty authority to make its sanctions bite.[193] Congress couched that new antimanipulation statute in the terms of the antimanipulation authority given to the SEC in Section 10(b) of the Securities Exchange Act of 1934 (34 Act).[194] It chose deliberately not to use the antimanipulation language in the Commodity Exchange Act that had so long frustrated the CFTC.[195]

---

187. FERC http://www.ferc.gov/whats-new/comm-meet/021606/G-1.pdf.

188. 18 CFR § 284.288(a), (d) and (e) and § 284.403(a), (d) and (e) (2005).

189. The FERC Code of Conduct stated:

> Any person making natural gas sales for resale in interstate commerce . . . is prohibited from engaging in actions or transactions that are without a legitimate business purpose and that are intended to or foreseeably could manipulate market prices, market conditions, or market rules for natural gas. Prohibited actions and transactions include but are not limited to: (1) Pre-arranged offsetting trades of the same product among the same parties, which involve no economic risk and no net change in beneficial ownership (sometimes called wash trades); and (2) Collusion with another party for the purpose of manipulating market prices, market conditions, or market rules for natural gas.

18 C.F.R. 284.403(a).

190. 18 C.F.R. § 284.288(b) and § 284.403(b). *See*, In re NRG Energy Inc., 118 FERC 61,025 (Jan. 18, 2007) ($500,000 civil penalty imposed by consent for self-reported violation of Market Behavior Rules involving misrepresenting the availability of a unit that was used to ensure system reliability as a part of a market power analysis).

191. Letter from Senator Maria Cantwell et al. to the Federal Trade Commission, April 8, 2008, http://cantwell.senate.gov/news/record.cfm?id=295769 (accessed June 22, 2011). *See generally*, Mark N. Cooper, *The Failure of Federal Authorities to Protect American Energy Consumers from Market Power and Other Abusive Practices*, 19 Loy. Consumer L. Rev. 315 (2007) (criticizing lack of federal regulation of energy traders).

192. Pub. L. No. 109-58, § 1283, 119 Stat. 594 (2005).

193. 15 U.S.C. § § 717t-1 & 3414(b)(6); 16 U.S.C. §§ 823b, 825o-1, & 1824(e).

194. 15 U.S.C. § 78j(b). The FERC antimanipulation provision states:

> It shall be unlawful for any entity . . . , directly or indirectly, to use or employ, in connection with the purchase or sale of electric energy or the purchase or sale of transmission services subject to the jurisdiction of the Commission, any manipulative or deceptive device or contrivance (as those terms are used in section [10b of the 34 Act] . . .), in contravention of such rules and regulations as the Commission may prescribe as necessary or appropriate in the public interest or for the protection of electric ratepayers.

16 U.S.C. § 824v(a). *See generally*, Catherine Krupka & Athena Velie, *There's a New Sheriff in Town: Energy Derivatives and FERC*, Fut. Indust. Mag. 19 (July–August 2007) (discussing this legislation).

195. 7 U.S.C. § 13(a)(2).

FERC adopted a rule to implement this authority[196] that included the prohibitory language in SEC Rule 10b-5 adopted by the SEC under Section 10(b) of the 34 Act.[197] FERC noted there was a substantial body of precedent under the SEC rule that would guide the interpretation of the FERC rule.[198] It also asserted that the new FERC rule was not intended to expand its existing jurisdiction. Rather, only entities engaging in manipulation "in connection with" a transaction already subject to FERC jurisdiction would be subject to the new antimanipulation authority. Fraud and manipulation in a first or retail sale would not be subject to the prohibition.[199] However, FERC asserted that the application of the new rule would not be limited to just traditional manipulation. It was also intended, in FERC's view, to permit the commission "to police all forms of fraud and manipulation that affect natural gas and electric energy transactions and activities the Commission is charged with protecting."[200]

FERC stated that the elements required to prove manipulation under its new rule would be the same as those under SEC Rule 10b-5. Specifically, FERC acknowledged that in SEC actions under Section 10(b) it must be shown that the defendant "(1) Made a material misrepresentation or a material omission as to which he had a duty to speak, or used a fraudulent device; (2) with scienter; and (3) in connection with the purchase or sale of securities."[201] FERC concluded, however, that it need not "show reliance, loss causation or damages because 'the Commission's duty is to enforce the remedial and preventive terms of the statute in the public interest, and not merely to police those whose plain violations have already caused demonstrable loss or injury.'"[202] This was an effort to avoid having to prove an artificial price and its cause. FERC recognized that limitation by adopting a scienter requirement of "knowing or intentional misconduct," including "recklessness," as applied by the courts under Rule 10b-5.[203] "The final rule is not intended to regulate negligent practices or corporate mismanagement, but rather to deter or punish fraud in wholesale energy markets."[204]

FERC did choose to "clarify that the new rule creates no new affirmative duty of disclosure."[205] "Absent a tariff requirement or Commission directive mandating disclosure, there is no violation of the final rule simply because an entity chooses not to disclose all non-public information in its possession."[206] Nevertheless, FERC asserted that voluntary submission of false information could result in liability under the new rule.[207]

The new FERC antimanipulation authority in EPAct has a limitation not found in the 34 Act. The EPAct expressly denied the availability of a private right of action under the new FERC antimanipulation authority.[208] This raised some interesting policy issues since the SEC had long

196. 18 C.F.R. § 1c.1.

197. 17 C.F.R. § 240.10b-5.

198. *Prohibition of Energy Market Manipulation*, 71 Fed. Reg. 4244, 4266 (Jan. 26, 2006).

199. 71 Fed. Reg. at 4247-48. However, the court in the Enron bankruptcy proceeding held that claims that Enron's manipulation and gaming of the California electricity violated state antitrust law were preempted by the Federal Power Act and the filed rate doctrine. In re Enron Corp., Case. No. 01 B 16034 (AJG) (S.D.N.Y. Bkrptcy, July 6, 2005) (unpublished opinion).

200. 71 Fed. Reg. at 4249.

201. 71 Fed. Reg. at 4253 (footnotes and citations omitted).

202. 71 Fed. Reg. at 4253 (footnotes and citations omitted).

203. 71 Fed. Reg. at 4253-4254.

204. 71 Fed. Reg. at 4246.

205. 71 Fed. Reg. at 4251 ("Nothing in the final rule requires disclosure of sensitive information that would only function to weaken an entity's bargaining position in arm's-length, bilateral negotiations.").

206. *Id.*

207. 71 Fed. Reg. at 4252.

208. 16 U.S.C. § 824v(b).

claimed that class action and individual litigants acted as "private attorney generals" in enforcing the federal securities laws and were an important adjunct to the SEC's limited resources.[209]

FERC began using the new antimanipulation rule to sanction companies using multiple bids of affiliates to defeat pro rata allocations and FERC open-access transportation policy.[210] In 2009, FERC collected over $38 million in civil penalties and a similar amount in illegal profit disgorgements from such actions.[211] Derivatives also became involved in the application of the new EPAct antimanipulation authority as a defense to a private antitrust action. In *Simon v. Keyspan Corp.*,[212] a plaintiff charged that the defendant Keyspan Corp., a provider of wholesale electricity and electricity-generating capacity in New York, violated the antitrust laws by engaging in a swap and hedging transaction with Morgan Stanley Capital Group Inc.

The swap and hedging agreement fixed the otherwise floating rate for electricity received by Keyspan. Morgan Stanley, in turn, entered into a separate hedge that protected it from losses on the contract with Keyspan. Morgan Stanley earned a built-in fifty-cent differential between the two contracts. The defendant claimed this arrangement lessened Keyspan's ability to compete for lower electricity charges. FERC investigated this conduct to determine if it constituted manipulation under its new EPAct authority. FERC concluded that there had been no unlawful withholding of electricity under this arrangement. Although Keyspan had previously entered into an antitrust decree with the Justice Department over the issue, the district court dismissed the antitrust claim under the filed rate doctrine because of FERC's action, as well as on standing grounds.[213]

The new FERC antimanipulation authority in the EPAct immediately raised a jurisdictional issue with the CFTC over whether the two agencies would share authority to attack energy price manipulations involving futures trading over which the CFTC had traditionally exercised exclusive jurisdiction.[214] The EPAct directed FERC and the CFTC to enter into a memorandum of understanding (MOU) to ensure that "information requests to markets within the respective jurisdiction of each agency are properly coordinated to minimize duplicative information requests" and to address "the treatment of proprietary trading information."[215] According to the MOU negotiated

209. Amanda M. Rose, *Reforming Securities Litigation Reform: Restructuring the Relationship Between Public and Private Enforcement of Rule 10b-5*, 108 COLUM. L. REV. 1301 (2008) (describing the private attorney general concept and its defects).

210. *See*, In the Matter of Jefferson Energy Trading LLC, 126 FERC ¶ 61,040 (Jan. 15, 2009); In the Matter of National Fuel Marketing Co. LLC, 135 FERC ¶ 61,011 (April 7, 2011); In the Matter of Klabzuba Oil & Gas FLP, 126 FERC ¶ 61,040 (Jan. 15, 2009); In the Matter of ONEOK Inc., 126 FERC ¶ 61,040 (Jan. 15, 2009); In the Matter of Tenaska Marketing Ventures, 126 FERC ¶ 61,040 (Jan. 15, 2009). FERC had also attacked a number of practices that it thought undermined its market-based rate approach, including "flipping," prohibited "buy, sell transactions," and "shipper must have title" requirements. *See, e.g.*, In the Matter of BP Energy Co., 121 FERC ¶ 61,088 (Oct. 25, 2007) (consent to sanction for such violations); In the Matter of ONEOK Inc., 126 FERC ¶ 61,040 (Jan. 15, 2009). For a description of the FERC investigative process and the factors it considers in assessing civil penalties, including self-reporting of violations, see FERC Office of Enforcement, *Report on Enforcement*, Doc. No. AD07-13-000 (Nov. 14, 2007).

211. Theodore A. Gebhard and James F. Mongoven, *Prohibiting Fraud and Deception in Wholesale Petroleum Markets: The New Federal Trade Commission Market Manipulation Rule*, 31 ENERGY L. J. 125, 132 (2010).

212. Simon v. Keyspan Corp., 2011 U.S. Dist. LEXIS 29252 (S.D.N.Y. 2011).

213. In a consent decree with the Justice Department over this conduct, Morgan Stanley agreed to pay $4.8 million, which was about 20 percent of its profits from the transaction. Noting the novelty of the government's action, a federal district court approved the settlement. *Court Clears Consent Decree in Antitrust Suit Against Morgan Stanley*, 44 SEC. REG. & L. REP. (BNA) 1565 (Aug. 20, 2012).

214. 7 U.S.C. § 2(a)(1)(A) (2006) ("The Commission shall have exclusive jurisdiction . . . with respect to . . . [commodity] 'option[s]' . . . and transactions involving contracts of sale of a commodity for future delivery.")

215. Pub. L. No. 109-58, § 1283, §§ 316 & 1281.

between FERC and CFTC, each agency agreed to refer to the other potential violations that are within the jurisdiction of the other agency. FERC was also given access to information from commodity exchanges it might need in connection with its investigations.[216]

What this really meant was double jeopardy from agency regulatory actions.[217] In simultaneous actions filed by the CFTC and FERC, Energy Transfer Partners LP was charged in federal court with attempted manipulation by the CFTC under the Commodity Exchange Act.[218] Energy Transfer Partners was also simultaneously charged administratively with violating the FERC's new manipulation authority under the EPAct.[219] FERC went beyond the attempted manipulation claims made by the CFTC and claimed an actual market power manipulation.[220] Energy Transfer Partners agreed to pay $10 million to settle the CFTC action and $30 million to settle with FERC.[221]

---

216. CFTC, MOU Between CFTC and FERC, http://www.cftc.gov/files/opa/opacftcfercmou.pdf (accessed May 30, 2011).

217. *See* Allan Horwich, *Warnings to the Unwary: Multi-Jurisdictional Federal Enforcement of Manipulation and Deception in the Energy Markets After the Energy Policy Act of 2005*, 27 Energy L.J. 363 (2006) (describing overlapping jurisdiction). Section 720 of the Dodd-Frank Wall Street Reform and Consumer Protection Act of 2010 also required a MOU between the CFTC and FERC. Pub. L. No. 111-203, 124 Stat. 1376 (2010).

218. CFTC v. Energy Transfer Partners LP, CIV. No. 07 CV1301-K (N.D. Tex. 2007). The CFTC's complaint charged that

> from September 2005 to early December 2005, the defendants (1) attempted to manipulate the price of natural gas for delivery at the HSC by selling on the Intercontinental Exchange (ICE) massive quantities of natural gas at HSC [Houston Ship Channel] to place downward pressure on natural gas prices at HSC; and (2) by reporting those transactions to *Inside FERC Gas Market Reports* (Inside FERC), attempted to manipulate the index price of natural gas at HSC that was calculated and disseminated by *Inside FERC* in its October and December 2005 monthly subscriptions.
>
> The complaint further alleged that the defendants engaged in this scheme in an attempt to benefit their financial basis swap positions tied to the *Inside FERC* October and December 2005 HSC natural gas index prices. The vast majority of the physical HSC natural gas transactions and the financial basis swaps at issue in the complaint were executed on ICE.

Energy Transfer Partners, L.P. and Three of Its Subsidiaries to Pay a $10 Million Penalty to Settle CFTC Action Alleging Attempted Manipulation of Natural Gas Prices, CFTC Press Release No. 5471-08 (March 17, 2008).

219. In the Matter of Energy Transfer Partners LP, Doc. No. IN06-3-002 (F.E.R.C. 2007).

220. The FERC show cause order alleged that

> [Energy Transfer Partners ("ETP")] dominated sales of fixed-price gas at HSC [Houston Ship Channel], often comprising 80 percent or more of total sales. ETP reported its fixed price sales at HSC to [FERC] and thus was able to use its domination of the market to virtually set the FERC HSC index. In spite of ETP's sales activity at HSC, it was consistently a net buyer of monthly gas priced at the IFERC HSC index, and thus was positioned to benefit from the lower prices it caused in the months it manipulated fixed-price sales at HSC. . . .
>
> At the same time, ETP had entered into . . . basis swaps to leverage its benefit from suppressing monthly physical prices at HSC. . . . [Thus,] ETP profited if the difference between prices at HSC and the NYMEX Contract widened, i.e., the price at HSC became lower relative to the higher priced NYMEX Contract. . . . Because ETP had the power to suppress price at HSC, this was not really a bet at all, but a manipulation that was spectacularly successful in October 2005—ETP realized more than $40,000,000 in unjust profits—and highly profitable in eight other months from January 2004 through December 2005.

Id.

221. Hershey v. Energy Transfer Partners LP, 610 F.3d 239, 244 (5th Cir. 2010).

A class action that sought to piggyback on the CFTC and FERC actions did not meet with similar success. In *In re Energy Transfer Partners Natural Gas Litigation*,[222] a district court dismissed the class action. The district court held that plaintiffs failed to allege that defendants intended to manipulate futures prices on NYMEX (or the physical commodity underlying NYMEX futures contracts) when they sold massive amounts of physical natural gas to aid their swap positions on the then unregulated InterContinental Exchange (ICE).[223] The prices for the physical transactions were reported to various trade papers that published the prices.

The plaintiffs in this class action argued there was a correlation between the NYMEX contracts and the defendants' trading in swaps and natural gas, but the court rejected that claim. This decision was affirmed on appeal to the Fifth Circuit Court of Appeals.[224] The Fifth Circuit held that the plaintiffs failed to sufficiently allege that defendants specifically intended to manipulate NYMEX natural gas futures products: "there must be a purpose to create prices not responsive to the forces of supply and demand."[225]

The role of ICE in the *Energy Transfer Partners* case renewed concerns over the Enron loophole in the CFMA that excluded swaps traded on "exempt commercial markets" (ECMs) from CFTC regulation.[226] ICE, which succeeded EnronOnline as the leading electronic market after the failure

---

222. 2009 WL 2633781 (S.D. TEX. 2009).

223. As the Fifth Circuit noted in this litigation,

> The Henry Hub is not the exclusive delivery point for all natural gas in the United States. Defendants' purchases and sales represent the bulk of the trades involving natural gas delivered through the HSC, a major conduit of natural gas to the Texas market. Because the price of delivery can vary among hubs, many large traders in natural gas commodities arbitrage—a practice of taking advantage of the price differential among markets. . . . Defendants here used natural gas futures "basis swaps" to accomplish this arbitrage. A swap is a pure financial instrument, based on the difference between two fluctuating values. In the natural gas basis swaps here, the value of the swap is the difference between the settlement price of the NYMEX natural gas futures contract for a given contract month and that of the monthly index at the HSC for that same month. Put simply, the wider the gap between prices at the Henry Hub and the HSC, the more money Defendants stood to make from their basis swaps.

Hershey v. Energy Transfer Partners, L.P., 610 F.3d 239, 242-243 (5th Cir. 2010) (citation omitted).

224. Hershey v. Energy Transfer Partners LP, 610 F.3d 239 (5th Cir. 2010).

225. 610 F.3d at 246. The Fifth Circuit further ruled,

> Plaintiffs attempt to tie Defendants' manipulation of the HSC prices to the price of Henry Hub natural gas and NYMEX futures contracts by arguing that Defendants knew or should have known that their manipulation of natural gas prices at HSC would result in the artificial suppression of the prices of NYMEX natural gas futures contracts. In other words, Plaintiffs argue that Defendants were aware that the correlation between the natural gas hubs would cause the Henry Hub price to sink if they flooded the HSC. Directing a similar argument to the underlying commodity, Plaintiffs contend that because Defendants submitted artificially low HSC price information for publication, the depression of Henry Hub spot prices was "intentional and inevitable." Plaintiffs' argument is without merit: intentionality and inevitability are not legally equivalent.

610 F.3d at 248.

226. A CFTC general counsel has noted,

> Exempt Commercial Markets are electronic trading facilities that restrict trading to principal-to-principal transactions between "eligible commercial entities." The term "eligible commercial entities," like the name "Exempt Commercial Markets," connotes a purely commercial market-

of Enron, was such an exempt market. The growth of electronic trading, coupled with its exempt regulatory status, made it a popular venue for hedge funds and other professional traders. ICE also provided opportunities for regulatory arbitrage that traders were quick to exploit.

The actions against *Energy Transfer Partners* were coordinated between FERC and the CFTC. However, a subsequent case involving a large hedge fund resulted in a jurisdictional conflict between those two agencies. Amaranth, which had hired several former Enron traders, had made massive profits from trading the long side of the natural gas market in the wake of Hurricanes Katrina and Rita. Amaranth changed its natural gas outlook in 2006 and went massively short in the January 2007 NYMEX natural gas futures contract. That trading initially proved successful, but its large size caught the eye of the CFTC and NYMEX.[227] Under pressure from the CFTC, NYMEX forced Amaranth to reduce its futures positions, but Amaranth avoided the effect of that order by shifting into unregulated natural gas swaps on ICE.

That regulatory arbitrage backfired badly on Amaranth and its lead trader, Brian Hunter. They not only lost more than $6 billion in a single week from their natural gas trading,[228] but were also subjected to overlapping regulatory actions by both the CFTC and FERC.[229] The FERC proceed-

---

> place among entities that can make or take delivery of the underlying commodity. But that also is not quite right. Under the statutory definitions of the CFMA, pooled investment vehicles such as hedge funds qualify as "eligible commercial entities," and their participation on certain Exempt Commercial Markets has become both active and significant.

Terry S. Arbit, CFTC General Counsel, Testimony at the Hearing Before the CFTC to Examine Trading on Regulated Exchanges and Exempt Commercial Markets 1 (Sept. 18, 2007), http://www.cftc.gov/stellent/groups/public/@newsroom/documents/speechandtestimony/opaarbit_091807.pdf. (accessed April 26, 2008).

227. A senate staff subcommittee report later asserted that

> Amaranth bought and sold thousands of natural gas contracts on a daily basis, and tens of thousands of contracts on certain days. It accumulated tens of thousands of natural gas holdings, or "positions," on both NYMEX and ICE. . . . Amaranth held as many as 100,000 natural gas contracts in a single month, representing 1 trillion cubic feet of natural gas, or 5% of the natural gas used in the entire United States in a year. At times Amaranth controlled 40% of all of the outstanding contracts on NYMEX for natural gas in the winter season (October 2006 through March 2007), including as much as 75 percent of the outstanding contracts to deliver natural gas in November 2006.
>
> Amaranth's large positions and trades caused significant price movements in key natural gas futures prices and price relationships. For example, Amaranth's purchases of contracts to deliver natural gas in the winter months, in conjunction with Amaranth's sales of natural gas contracts for delivery in the summer months, drove winter prices far above summer prices. These differences between winter and summer prices, called "price spreads," were far higher in 2006 than in previous years—until the collapse of Amaranth, when the price spreads returned to more normal levels. On several specific dates, Amaranth's massive trades were responsible for large jumps in the price differences between the futures contracts for March and April 2007. Traders interviewed by the Subcommittee said that during the spring and summer of 2006 the differences between winter and summer prices were "clearly out-of-whack," at "ridiculous" levels, and unjustified by supply or demand.

U.S. Senate Permanent Subcommittee on Investigations of the Committee on Homeland Security and Governmental Affairs, Staff Report: *Excessive Speculation in the Natural Gas Market* 2-3 (2007).

228. *See*, Ann Davis, *Moving the Market: Ex-Amaranth Trader Fights Regulator*, Wall Street Journal, July 25, 2007, at C2 (describing that loss).

229. *See*, CFTC v. Amaranth Advisors LLC, 523 F. Supp. 2d 328 (S.D.N.Y. 2007) (describing these actions).

ing charged that Amaranth and Hunter manipulated the price of the NYMEX natural gas futures contract. FERC charged that respondents engaged in extensive sales during the final thirty minutes of trading on three dates in 2006 with the intention of causing artificial settlement prices for the futures contracts. Those settlement prices, in turn, artificially affected the prices of transactions over which FERC had jurisdiction.[230] The CFTC charged that the defendants attempted to manipulate those same NYMEX contracts "by deliberately waiting to sell a substantial number of those contracts in the final minutes before the close of trading."[231]

As the Southern District of New York noted in the action brought by the CFTC, "Amaranth is being pursued by two federal regulatory agencies in two separate proceedings in two different jurisdictions, based on the same alleged conduct."[232] However, the district court refused to stay the FERC proceeding. The court rejected defendants' claim that the CFTC had exclusive jurisdiction over manipulation claims related to futures trading.[233] The district court for the District of Columbia, in a separate proceeding brought by Hunter, also declined to enjoin the FERC proceeding, and that decision was affirmed on appeal.[234]

The Amaranth defendants filed other motions to challenge these actions. Proving that nothing about manipulation is uncomplicated, a district court judge in the Southern District of New York noted the existence of a division of authority among the courts on the degree of particularity required to plead a manipulation claim under the CEA.[235] The district court held that CEA manipulation charges need not be pleaded with particularity under the Federal Rules of Civil Procedure, unless the charges involve fraud.[236] The district court found that the CFTC adequately pleaded

230. In re Hunter, 2010 FERC LEXIS 82 (F.E.R.C.).

231. CFTC v. Amaranth Advisors LLC, 554 F. Supp. 2d 523, 525 (S.D.N.Y. 2007).

232. CFTC v. Amaranth Advisors LLC, 523 F. Supp. 2d 328, 331-32 (S.D.N.Y. 2007).

233. 523 F. Supp. 2d at 338. The district court did state that

> Amaranth's concern in having to defend itself in two separate actions for the violations of the two Acts based on the same underlying conduct does not justify a stay of the FERC proceeding, but the concern is understandable. Accordingly, I urge FERC to work with the CFTC and Amaranth to coordinate their efforts in the two proceedings, to maximize efficiency and minimize duplication.

532 F. Supp. 2d at 338-339. NYMEX had also protested before Congress that FERC's expansive interpretation of its new antimanipulation authority under the EPAct was intruding on the CFTC's exclusive jurisdiction over futures trading. *See*, Testimony of Dr. James Newsome, CEO New York Mercantile Exchange Inc., Before the Subcommittee on General Farm Commodities and Risk Management, United States House of Representatives, *reprinted*, Comm. Fut. L. Rep. (CCH) ¶ 30,640 (Sep. 26, 2007).

234. Hunter v. FERC, 527 F. Supp. 2d 9 & 12 (D.D.C. 2007), *aff'd*, 2009 U.S. App. LEXIS 23417 (D.C. Cir. 2009) (*per curiam*). This was not the only case of regulatory overlap in prosecuting manipulation of energy prices. In *SEC v. Lee*, 720 F. Supp. 2d 305 (S.D.N.Y. 2010), a federal district court denied a motion to dismiss multiple actions brought by the Securities and Exchange Commission, the CFTC, the Chicago Mercantile Exchange (as successor to the New York Mercantile Exchange), and the Bank of Montreal (BMO) against an alleged fraudulent scheme perpetrated by a BMO trader, his supervisor, and third-party brokerage firms between 2003 and 2007. The fraud involved the inflation of the trader's book on energy derivatives by mismarking their value.

235. CFTC v. Amaranth Advisors LLC, 554 F. Supp. 2d 523 (S.D.N.Y. 2007).

236. *Compare*, CFTC v. Enron Corp., 2004 U.S. Dist. LEXIS 28794 at *3 (S.D. Tex. 2004) (manipulation claims under Section 9(a)(2) of the Commodity Exchange Act need not be pleaded with particularity); Premium Plus Partners LP v. Davis, 2005 U.S. Dist. LEXIS 6158, at *15 (N.D. Ill. 2005) (heightened pleading requirements did not apply to manipulation claim under Commodity Exchange Act); and *CFTC v. Reed*, Comm. Fut. L. Rep. (CCH) ¶ 30,547 (D. Colo. 2007) (unclear whether particularity is required but pleading was particular), *with*, In re Amaranth Natural Gas Commodities Litigation, 587 F. Supp. 2d 513

an attempted manipulation claim.[237] The district court later denied summary judgment motions on a manipulation claim because of a dispute of facts over whether the requisite intent standard was met. [238] The district court also held in *CFTC v. Amaranth Advisors LLC*[239] that proof of intent of attempted manipulation under the CEA could be inferred from text messages. There, the defendant's trader stated that he needed a contract to "get smashed." The trader further disclosed that he was willing to sell contracts near the close of trading, which he knew would affect the settlement price.

The Amaranth defendants later settled the CFTC charges, without admitting or denying the claims, by agreeing to a permanent injunction from future violations of the Commodity Exchange Act, and they agreed to pay a civil penalty of $5.5 million.[240] Amaranth also settled with FERC by agreeing to pay $7.5 million of the $291 million sought by FERC when it brought the action.[241] Brian Hunter refused to settle and was hit with a $30 million civil penalty by FERC after it found that Hunter "sold significant numbers of futures contracts during the settlement periods of the at-issue months with the intent to depress prices and financially benefit his significant derivative positions held on other platforms."[242] The CFTC joined with Hunter on appeal in contending that FERC did not have jurisdiction to impose such a fine.[243] The District of Columbia Court of Appeals ruled on March 15, 2013 that FERC did not have jurisdiction to bring such an action.[244]

Amaranth's troubles continued with the certification of a class action seeking damages for its trading.[245] The district court in that action granted a prejudgment attachment of Amaranth's (much depleted) assets in order to prevent those assets from being returned to Amaranth's investors.[246]

(S.D.N.Y. 2008) (a plaintiff alleging market manipulation that sounds in fraud must plead with particularity the nature, purpose, and effect of the fraudulent conduct and the roles of the defendants); *In re Natural Gas Commodity Litig.*, 358 F. Supp. 2d 336, 343 (S.D.N.Y. 2005) (particularity required in pleading manipulation claim under the Commodity Exchange Act); Hershey v. Energy Transfer Partners LP, 610 F.3d 239 (5th Cir. 2010) (plaintiffs must allege that defendants specifically intended to manipulate underlying contract price and allegations that defendants knew or should have known that their manipulative actions would depress natural gas futures prices failed to state claim under Commodity Exchange Act); In re Crude Oil Commodity Litigation, Comm. Fut. L. Rep. (CCH) ¶ 30,541 (S.D.N.Y. 2007) (manipulation claim not pleaded with sufficient particularity).

237. The new FERC antimanipulation authority raised a host of other procedural issues. *See*, William Scherman, John Shepherd, & Jason Fleischer, *The New FERC Enforcement: Due Process Issues in the Post-EPACT 2005 Enforcement Cases*, 31 Energy L.J. 55 (2010); Charles J. Engel III & Brandon E. Reavis, *FERC's Market Manipulation Investigatory and Enforcement Process*, Fin. Fraud L. Rep. 53 (Jan. 2010).

238. CFTC v. Hunter, 2012 WL 297838 (S.D.N.Y.).

239. CFTC v. Amaranth Advisors LLC, 554 F. Supp. 2d 523 (S.D.N.Y. 2007).

240. CFTC v. Amaranth Advisors LLC, 2009 U.S. Dist. LEXIS 101406 (S.D.N.Y.).

241. *Compare*, *Energy Regulator Seeks $291 Million From Traders and Failed Fund*, New York Times, July 27, 2007, http://www.nytimes.com/2007/07/27/business/27ferc.html?_r=0 (accessed on March 4, 2013), *with*, FERC, *Order Approving Uncontested Settlement* (F.E.R.C. Aug. 12, 2009), http://www.ferc.gov/enforcement/market-manipulation/amaranth.pdf (accessed May 31, 2011) (stating that Amaranth's depleted financial condition did not permit a higher penalty).

242. FERC, *FERC Orders $30 Million Fine Against Former Amaranth Trader* (F.E.R.C. April 11, 2011), http://www.ferc.gov/media/news-releases/2011/2011-2/04-21-11-G-1.pdf (accessed May 31, 2011).

243. *U.S. Regulators Square Off on Who Can Sanction* Trader Reuters, Feb. 7, 2013, available at http://www.reuters.com/article/2013/02/06/usa-ferc-hunter-idUSL1N0B69HH20130206 (visited on Feb. 7, 2013.

244. Hunter v. FERC, 2013 U.S. App. LEXIS 5167 (D.C. Cir. 2013).

245. In re Amaranth Natural Gas Commodities Litig., 269 F.R.D. 366 (S.D.N.Y. 2010).

246. In re Amaranth Natural Gas Commodities Litig., Comm. Fut. L. Rep. (CCH) ¶ 31,568 (S.D.N.Y. 2010).

6:9 THE FEDERAL TRADE COMMISSION ENTERS THE MANIPULATION ARENA

Crude oil prices began to rise in 2002, "as increases in global oil consumption progressively absorbed most of the remainder of the world's buffer of excess capacity."[247] In 2003, the price of crude oil increased to more than $30 a barrel from what was considered the "normal" $20 per barrel that the Organization of Petroleum Exporting Countries (OPEC) had targeted for some time.[248] That increase was attributed in part to actions by the federal government in filling the strategic petroleum reserve (SPR). The government had previously deferred purchases when prices were high, but in the aftermath of 9/11 the government began making purchases for the SPR without consideration of price. During a one-month period "crude oil prices caused by SPR deposits spiked the U.S. spot price of home heating oil by 13 percent, jet fuel by 10 percent, and diesel fuel by 8 percent, imposing on U.S. consumers additional crude oil costs of between $500 million and $1 billion."[249]

In any event, by 2005 the OPEC target price of $20 per barrel was an "artifact of history."[250] Gasoline prices hit a record $1.75 for regular gasoline in March 2004[251] and rose to over $2 per gallon a few months later.[252] A poll conducted in April 2005 found that 58 percent of Americans were experiencing financial hardship as the result of increased gasoline prices, which were then averaging $2.22 per gallon of regular gas.[253] Things got worse. Crude oil prices doubled to $60 per barrel in August 2005.[254] These "soaring" prices were discounted by the Federal Reserve Board as mere "headline" inflation that was not having an appreciable effect on "core" inflation, which excludes price increases for consumer goods in measuring the rate of inflation.[255] Nevertheless,

247. ALAN GREENSPAN, THE AGE OF TURBULENCE 437 (2007). Energy prices had fallen sharply in the fourth quarter of 2001 due to increased production and favorable weather, but that only caused OPEC to announce that it was cutting production by 1.5 million barrels a day in order to increase prices. JERRY W. MARKHAM, A FINANCIAL HISTORY OF MODERN U.S. CORPORATE SCANDALS: FROM ENRON TO REFORM 523 (2006).

248. Interagency Task Force on Commodity Markets, *Interim Report on Crude Oil* 7 (July 2008).

249. *U.S. Strategic Petroleum Reserve: Recent Policy Has Increased Costs to Consumers But Not Overall U.S. Energy Security: Report by the Minority Staff of the Senate Permanent Subcommittee on Investigations of the Committee on Governmental Affairs*, 108th Cong., 1st Sess. 2 (2003).

250. DANIEL YERGIN, THE QUEST 163 (2011).

251.http://money.cnn.com/2004/03/30/news/economy/gas_prices/ (accessed June 16, 2011).

252. http://money.cnn.com/2004/05/18/pf/autos/gas_prices/ (accessed June 16, 2011). However, when adjusted for inflation, this price spike had less effect than the Jimmy Carter–era price increases in 1979-1981. http://www1.eere.energy.gov/vehiclesandfuels/facts/2005/fcvt_fotw364.html (accessed June 16, 2011).

253. CNNU.S., *Gas Prices a "Hardship" for Many*, http://articles.cnn.com/2005-04-04/us/gas.poll_1_gas-prices-hardship-fuel-efficient-model?_s=PM:US (accessed June 30, 2011).

254. Dan Strumpf & Liam Pleven, *Traders Accused in Oil-Price Plot*, WALL STREET JOURNAL, May 25, 2011.

255. In retrospect, this Fed report provides no comfort for its economic prediction capabilities. It also cheerfully stated in a report submitted in February 2006, not long before the wheels came off the economy,

> The economic expansion remained firmly entrenched in 2005, although the growth of real GDP late in the year was apparently restrained by the effects of the hurricanes and by sharp drops in some volatile categories of spending. In the labor market, payroll employment rose moderately for a second year in a row, and the unemployment rate declined further. As in 2004, headline inflation was boosted appreciably by soaring energy prices; however, core inflation remained subdued. In 2005, financial market conditions were once again supportive of growth, with long-term market interest rates low and credit spreads and risk premiums narrow.

Federal Reserve, Monetary Policy Report submitted to the Congress on February 15, 2006, pursuant to section 2B of the Federal Reserve Act, § 2 *Economic and Financial Developments in 2005 and Early 2006.*

those energy prices became a political football in Congress and the press, and the blame was laid on speculators.[256]

In 2006, Congress added the Federal Trade Commission (FTC) to the list of agencies tasked with attacking commodity price manipulations. The FTC had entered the antimanipulation picture in July 2005 when Congress directed that agency to investigate complaints of gasoline price gouging.[257] Specifically, the FTC was asked to investigate whether "the price of gasoline is being artificially manipulated by reducing refinery capacity or by any other form of market manipulation or price gouging practices."[258] That legislation brought manipulation regulation full circle, since, as described in Chapter 1, it had been the FTC's investigation of the grain trade after World War I that set the stage for the legislation that evolved into the Commodity Exchange Act.

Unwilling to await the FTC's report, twenty-one senators proposed legislation in September 2005 that sought to grant the FTC power to "protect consumers from price-gouging during energy emergencies" and that "would institute new protections for American consumers from manipulation of oil and gasoline markets."[259] The gasoline price rice was heightened by Hurricanes Katrina and Rita, which "tore a large hole in the world supply. Prices of gasoline, diesel fuel, and home heating oil soared."[260] Those price increases continued into 2006. Crude oil traded at $70 per barrel on April 17, 2006, and then increased to over $75 per barrel, causing protests when gasoline prices jumped to more than $3 per gallon.[261] In the Atlanta area, gas was being sold at over $6 per gallon.[262] This price run-up set off shock waves through the economy and resulted in a call for a windfall profits tax on the oil companies.[263]

---

256. Even Saudi Arabia was blaming the speculators for the high prices. Evin G. Hall, *Saudis Often Warned U.S. About Oil Speculators, Cables Show*, Kansas City Star, May 25, 2011, http://www.kansascity.com/2011/05/25/2903397/saudis-often-warned-us-about-oil.html#ixzz1NfmWsk7W.

257. That directive was included in the EPAct, the same legislation that gave FERC its new antimanipulation powers. Energy Policy Act of 2005, Pub. L. No. 109-58, § 1809, 119 Stat. 594 (2005).

258. *Id.* The FTC's 2006 fiscal year appropriations legislation also directed it to investigate possible price gouging of gasoline sales after Hurricane Katrina. Science, State, Justice, Commerce, and Related Agencies Appropriations Act, 2006, Pub. L. No. 109-108, § 632, 119 Stat. 2290 (2005).

259. 151 Cong. Rec. S10238 (Sept. 20, 2005) (remarks of Senator Cantwell). That legislative proposal was modeled after the EPAct provisions granting FERC antimanipulation authority in the electricity and natural gas markets. *Id.*

260. Alan Greenspan, The Age of Turbulence 437 (2007). The FTC reported,

> As recently as January 2002, the average retail price of regular grade conventional gasoline in the United States was about $1.10 per gallon, including taxes. It rose to nearly $2.00 per gallon by May 2004 and to about $2.50 per gallon by August 2005. Then, at the end of the summer of 2005, Hurricanes Katrina and Rita hit major portions of the Gulf Coast region. Gasoline prices rose more than 45 cents per gallon in the week following Katrina. Moreover, the ranges of prices following the hurricanes were substantially larger than the ranges that prevailed in more normal times—not only between different cities and regions, but also between individual stations within a city. The huge and rapid price increases observed within particular regions and at some individual stations led to allegations of price gouging.

Federal Trade Commission, *Investigation of Gasoline Price Manipulation and Post-Katrina Gasoline Price Increases* ii *(Executive Summary)* (Spring 2006).

261. Jerry W. Markham, A Financial History of the United States from the Subprime Crisis to the Great Recession (2006–2009) 207 (2011).

262. 151 Cong. Rec. S10238 (Sept. 20, 2005) (remarks of Senator Kohl).

263. Federal Trade Commission, *Investigation of Gasoline Price Manipulation and Post-Katrina Gasoline Price Increases* vi *(Executive Summary)* (Spring 2006).

The FTC issued its gasoline investigation report in the spring of 2006. The FTC noted that manipulation was an undefined term in the Commodity Exchange Act and that the "courts and others have struggled to define the term."[264] However, even by broadly defining the term, the FTC's massive investigation of the industry could find no manipulation by refiners.[265] In addition, very little retail price gouging could be found.[266] The findings in the FTC's gasoline price report that manipulation was not causing high prices did not deter Congress from enacting more antimanipulation legislation. It included in the Energy Independence and Security Act (EISA Act), which was signed into law on December 19, 2007, provisions that gave the FTC new authority to police "market manipulation" and "false reporting" in the petroleum industry.[267]

It was claimed in Congress that this was "a consumer-friendly bill because we have protected consumers by making market manipulation of oil markets a Federal crime."[268] However, the need for the bill was less than obvious and not well reasoned. As the Senate sponsor of this legislation stated, "I know we have heard stories. I know there are lots of issues about speculation. But by giving the FTC new authority to issue fines per violation, we are giving consumers more protection."[269]

Section 811 of EISA was modeled after Section 10(b) of the 34 Act. It prohibited anyone, in connection with wholesale purchases or sales of crude oil, gasoline, or petroleum distillates, to use any "manipulative or deceptive device or contrivance, in contravention of such rules and regulations as the Federal Trade Commission may prescribe as necessary or appropriate in the public interest or for the protection of United States citizens." Section 812 of EISA prohibited anyone from reporting information to a federal agency related to the wholesale price of crude oil, gasoline, or petroleum distillates (1) that the person "knew, or reasonably should have known," to be false or misleading; (2) that was required to be reported to such federal agency; and (3) as to which "the person intended the false or misleading data to affect data compiled . . . for statistical or analytical purposes" with respect to the market for such products.[270]

After the enactment of that legislation, the FTC requested public comments in a concept release seeking a proposed definition of manipulation, which it formulated as follows:

> Market manipulation shall mean knowingly using or employing, directly or indirectly, a manipulative or deceptive device or contrivance—in connection with the purchase or sale

---

264. *Id.* at ii.

265. *Id.* at vi.

266. *Id.* at x. The FTC's report gave a homily on the defects of price controls, noting that, while such controls had been occasionally invoked,

> A general consensus has emerged . . . that in most markets competition is more effective than any form of price control in ensuring that consumers get the full benefits of innovation and productive and distributive efficiencies. Numerous formerly regulated industries have been substantially deregulated. Consumers are best protected when markets are kept free and open. These benefits to consumers depend, of course, on law enforcement agencies that can keep markets competitive and free from distortion and manipulation.

Id. at 185, n. 3.

267. Pub. L. 110-140, 121 Stat. 1492, Title VIII, Subtitle B, *codified at* 42 U.S.C. §§ 17301-17305. *See*, Malyshev, Panhuys & Dorn, *FTC Joins Others Agencies in Policing Oil Industry "Market Manipulation" and "False Reporting,"* 4 Fut. & Derv. L. Rep. 1 (2008) (discussing this legislation).

268. 153 Cong. Rec. S15421-01, 2007 WL 4354222, U.S. Sen., Proceedings and Debates of the 110th Cong., 1st Sess., Dec. 13, 2007 (remarks of Sen. Cantwell).

269. *Id.*

270. *Id.*

> of crude oil, gasoline, or petroleum distillates at wholesale—for the purpose or with the effect of increasing the market price thereof relative to costs.[271]

This proposed definition was somewhat unhelpful because it failed to define the term "manipulative device or contrivance." The proposal was also overly broad in that it would apply to every market transaction since every trade has some "effect" on the market price, even if only an infinitesimal one.

The FTC sought further comment on whether various market scenarios would constitute manipulation, such as withholding supplies from market, as had been done in the California electricity crisis.[272] The FTC also sought comment on whether its new antimanipulation authority "may subject market participants to similar overlapping agency oversight, and create the potential for market participants to be subject to differing standards of conduct and multiple levels of liability."[273] It also sought comment on how it should determine what constitutes an artificial price.[274]

After reviewing public comments on its concept release, the FTC proposed an antimanipulation rule. The FTC decided in this proposal to follow FERC's lead and "adopt largely the language and structure of SEC Rule 10b-5" as its own manipulation standard.[275] The FTC also refused to cede any jurisdiction to the CFTC, stating that its proposed rule proscribes all manipulative or deceptive conduct in wholesale markets. The FTC did state that it would not "improperly intrude upon the jurisdiction of the CFTC or any other agency [including FERC] whose authority may overlap in whole or in part with respect to such activities."[276] The FTC also declined to promulgate "any specific conduct obligations, such as a duty to supply, provide access, or disclose."[277]

The FTC's proposed rule did not require a showing of price effect in order to establish a violation. This was because the FTC recognized the practical difficulty of making such a showing. Remarkably, the FTC stated that "requiring a showing of price effects raises an unnecessary risk of regulatory error. Prices of commodity products such as petroleum are inherently volatile and are a function of many factors. The Commission's experience in investigating petroleum pricing anomalies demonstrates the difficulty of identifying price changes that result directly from any

271. *Prohibitions on Market Manipulation and False Information in Subtitle B of the Energy Independence and Security Act of 2007*, 73 Fed. Reg. 25614, 25620 (May 7, 2008).

272. 73 Fed. Reg. 25623.

273. 73 Fed. Reg. at 25621. The FTC also sought comment on whether various practices might violate its new authority, including making false reports to private publications on transactions in thinly traded markets. *Id.*

274. 73 Fed. Reg. at 25622.

275. *Prohibitions on Market Manipulation and False Information in Subtitle B of Title VIII of the Energy Independence and Security Act of 2007*, 73 Fed. Reg. 48317, 48322 (Aug. 19, 2008). The FTC's justification for this measure was as follows:

> Following the example of SEC Rule 10b-5, the Commission believes that its proposed Rule would contribute to well-functioning marketplaces. Markets function best when market participants can presume that the best available information relevant to their decision-making is not distorted. Manipulative or deceptive conduct distorts the marketplace signals that guide resource allocation. When market participants react to distorted market price signals, short-term purchase and sale decisions may be altered and long-term capital investments may be adversely influenced. Finally, if manipulative or deceptive conduct recurs, it may increase the cost of doing business if market participants are required to invest in defensive measures.

Id. at 48323 (footnotes omitted)

276. 73 Fed. Reg. at 48324.

277. 73 Fed. Reg. at 48327.

specific act or conduct."[278] This signaled that the FTC was conceding that it would face a formidable obstacle if it was required to prove whether any particular act was actually manipulative. Instead, the FTC held the view that "[p]roof of an overt manipulative or deceptive act together with proof of requisite intent provide sufficient safeguards against both regulatory overreach and judicial error."[279] This was the definition used by the CFTC in its attempted manipulation cases.

After considering public comments, the FTC revised its proposed antimanipulation rule to "better focus it on wholesale petroleum markets, which differ significantly from securities markets."[280] The revised rule added language "to sharpen its focus on fraudulent and deceptive conduct and to reduce potential adverse effects on legitimate business conduct."[281] This was done by adding an explicit scienter standard of "knowingly." The FTC stated that its definition of "knowingly" was derived from the "extreme recklessness" standard articulated by the Seventh and District of Columbia Circuit Courts of Appeals in decisions delineating the appropriate scienter standard under SEC Rule 10b-5.[282] The FTC also recognized the overbreadth of its originally proposed definition of manipulation and limited its reach to an activity that "distorts or tends to distort market conditions."[283]

The FTC asserted that its revised proposed rule would not impose an affirmative duty to disclose information. The revised proposed rule would apply if a covered entity was required to or voluntarily provided information, but failed "to disclose a material fact, thereby making the information provided misleading."[284] In proposing its revised rule, the FTC repeated its prior concern that it not be shouldered with the burden of showing that prohibited conduct had a price effect. The rationale for this exclusion was stated to be that "there is no economic justification for fraudulent or deceptive conduct in any market," whatever its effects.[285]

The FTC also asserted that imposing the evidentiary burden on it of proving price effect "would introduce an unnecessary risk that conduct detrimental to the integrity of the market would escape successful challenge."[286] It further observed that "[o]vercoming the practical problems associated with identifying and proving a specific price effect from fraudulent or deceptive conduct in wholesale petroleum markets may not be possible in many, if not most, cases"[287]—a lesson the CFTC had learned after many years of hard experience.

The FTC adopted its antimanipulation rule in August 2009.[288] The FTC stated that, while it was modeled after SEC Rule 10b-5, the FTC rule was tailored to account for the significant differences

---

278. 73 Fed. Reg. at 48329-30 (footnote omitted).

279. 73 Fed. Reg. at 48330, n. 144.

280. *Prohibitions on Market Manipulation in Subtitle B of Title VIII of the Energy Independence and Security Act of 2007*, 74 Fed. Reg. 18304, 18310 (April 22, 2009).

281. 74 Fed. Reg. at 18310, *citing* SEC v. Steadman, 967 F.2d 6436, 641-42 (D.C. Cir. 1992) *and* Sundstrand Corp. v. Sun Chemical Corp., 553 F.2d 1033, 1045 (7th Cir. 1977), *cert. denied*, 434 U.S. 875 (1977). This emphasis on SEC-type disclosure fraud standards raised concerns that the FTC rule (and that of FERC) would not reach market power manipulations that were based on economic power and not fraud. *See*, Craig Pirrong, *Energy Market Manipulation: Definition, Diagnosis, and Deterrence*, 31 ENERGY L. J. 1 (2010).

282. 74 Fed. Reg. at 18312-18313.

283. 74 Fed. Reg. at 18321.

284. *Id.*

285. 74 Fed. Reg. at 18322 (footnote omitted).

286. *Id.*

287. *Id.* (citation omitted).

288. *Prohibitions on Market Manipulation*, 74 Fed. Reg. 40686 (Nov. 4, 2009). That rule prohibited

> any person, directly or indirectly, in connection with the purchase or sale of crude oil, gasoline, or petroleum distillates at wholesale, from (a) knowingly engaging in any act, practice, or course

between wholesale petroleum markets and securities markets. In the former, market participants are sophisticated and experienced commercial entities that are able to engage in a substantial amount of self-protection, while securities market participants are often significantly less sophisticated in dealing with information gaps.[289] That claim, however, overlooks the fact that sophisticated financial institutions now largely dominate the securities markets.[290]

The FTC eschewed market power and excessive speculation and manipulation concerns in favor of an antifraud standard.[291] The FTC's final rule defined "knowingly" to mean "that the person knew or must have known that his or her conduct was fraudulent or deceptive" but adhered to a scienter standard of "extreme recklessness."[292] The FTC tried, however, to depart from that standard, as applied in the securities industry ("an extreme departure from the standards of ordinary care"), by changing the formula to "either knew or must have known that his or her conduct created a danger of misleading buyers or sellers."[293]

The FTC did admit to some limits on its jurisdiction. It stated that the newly adopted antimanipulation rule would not ordinarily be applied to renewable fuels, such as ethanol. Yet the rule would apply even to those fuels if there was "a sufficient nexus" between conduct involving those products and wholesale petroleum markets. The FTC also would not apply the rule to components of ethanol like corn and sugar.[294] The FTC continued to refuse to concede exclusive jurisdiction to the CFTC over futures manipulations.[295] However, it did later enter into a memorandum of understanding with the CFTC in which both agencies agreed to share information in the exercise of their respective jurisdictions.[296]

The FTC noted that EISA does not create an express private right of action for its new antimanipulation authority. The agency stated that it remained for Congress or the courts to decide whether there should be an implied private right of action for violations of its rule.[297] In light of the history behind the implied private right of action regarding Rule 10b-5 actions as discussed in Chapter 3, plaintiffs may have some difficulty in persuading the courts to engraft such a right onto EISA.

> of business—including the making of any untrue statement of material fact—that operates or would operate as a fraud or deceit upon any person, or (b) intentionally failing to state a material fact that under the circumstances renders a statement made by such person misleading, provided that such omission distorts or is likely to distort market conditions for any such product.

16 C.F.R. § 317.3. *See*, Theodore A. Gebhard & James F. Mongoven, *Prohibiting Fraud and Deception in Wholesale Petroleum Markets: The New Federal Trade Commission Market Manipulation Rule*, 31 Energy L. J. 125, 133 (2010) (describing the rule's elements).

289. 74 Fed. Reg. at 40690.

290. *See*, III Jerry W. Markham, A Financial History of the United States From the Age of Derivatives to the New Millennium 181-182 (2002) (describing the growth of institutional traders).

291. *Id.* at n. 53.

292. 74 Fed. Reg. at 40691. The FTC noted, *Id.*, that the Supreme Court has reserved judgment on the extreme recklessness standard. *See*, Tellabs Inc. v. Makor Issues & Rights Ltd., 551 U.S. 308, 319, n. 3 (2007).

293. 74 Fed. Reg. at 40692 (citations and footnotes omitted).

294. 74 Fed. Reg. at 40695.

295. 74 Fed. Reg. at 40691.

296. *Memorandum of Understanding Between the Commodity Futures Trading Commission (CFTC) and the Federal Trade Commission (FTC) Regarding Information Sharing in Areas of Common Regulatory Interest* (April 6, 2011), http://www.ftc.gov/os/2011/04/110412ftccftc-mou.pdf (accessed June 21, 2011).

297. 74 F.R. at 18312 (describing concern of commentators that the adoption of Rule 10b-5 language may lead courts to find an implied right of action, as was done for that rule).

The FTC also sought to define the extent to which its rule would preempt state laws. Its new Rule 317.4 states that the FTC did not intend that its antimanipulation rule would "preempt the laws of any state or local government, except to the extent that any such law conflicts with" the CFTC Rule.[298] That preemption was intended to be a narrow one because the FTC preemption rule goes on to state that state law would not conflict if "it affords equal or greater protection from the prohibited practices" in the FTC antimanipulation rule.[299]

6:10 CLOSING THE ENRON LOOPHOLE

The failure of the Enron Corp. and its gaming of the California electricity market focused congressional attention on the Enron loophole in the CFMA.[300] Those critics renewed their assault on that exemption as gasoline prices rose. In defense of his agency's failure to take action against Enron before its collapse, CFTC chair James Newsome testified before Congress that the "CFTC does not regulate trading of energy products on spot (cash) markets or forward markets, which are excluded from our jurisdiction by the CEA."[301] An acting CFTC chair later contradicted that claim. He testified before Congress that the CFTC had retained fraud and manipulation jurisdiction over ECMs under the CFMA.[302]

In the event, Senator Diane Feinstein introduced amendments to the Energy Policy Act of 2003 that sought to require comprehensive CFTC regulation of OTC electricity and natural gas derivatives contracts.[303] That effort was voted down 56 to 41 in the Senate.[304] The Feinstein proposal was also rejected as an amendment to the CFTC's reauthorization legislation in 2005.[305] "Renouncing proposals to extend its authority to OTC commodity markets, CFTC Chair Reuben Jeffery stated in March 2006 that 'the CFTC has no interest, ability or desire to regulate over-the-counter commodities markets' and is not looking to expand its oversight authority into those areas either."[306]

---

298. 16 C.F.R. § 317.4.

299. *Id.*

300. As one article also noted:

> Almost immediately, the CFMA's exemption of energy derivatives from regulatory oversight became a contested issue, as lawmakers questioned whether regulation—of energy trading or of non-bank traders in general—could have prevented Enron's failure. Critics attacked the current regulatory scheme and blamed most, if not all, of Enron's wrongdoings on "huge loopholes" in the CFMA (i.e., the energy exemptions) that had "improperly catered to the interests of Enron and the energy industry."

Alexia Brunet & Meredith Shafe, *Beyond Enron: Regulation in Energy Derivatives Trading*, 27 NW. J. INT'L L. & BUS. 665, 685-686 (2007) (footnotes omitted).

301. *Impact of Enron Bankruptcy on Energy Markets*, Testimony of James E. Newsome Before the Subcommittee on Energy and Air Quality of the Committee on Energy and Commerce, U.S. House of Representatives (February 13, 2002).

302. Testimony of Acting CFTC Chair Walter Lukken Before the House Subcommittee on Oversight and Investigations of the Committee on Energy and Commerce, 110th Cong., 1st Sess. at 193 (Dec. 12, 2007).

303. Alexia Brunet & Meredith Shafe, *Beyond Enron: Regulation in Energy Derivatives Trading*, 27 NW. J. INT'L L. & BUS. 687 (2007).

304. *Id.* at 689.

305. *Id.* at 700.

306. *Id.* at 701 (footnote omitted).

Senator Feinstein, nevertheless, continued to push for such legislation over the opposition of the CFTC. In April 2006, Feinstein introduced another bill, the Oil and Gas Traders Oversight Act,[307] which sought "to increase transparency and accountability in the energy markets so that the federal government can determine if speculation or manipulation is occurring in the oil, gas, and electricity markets."[308] That bill would have allowed the CFTC to impose record-keeping and reporting requirements on OTC energy traders, but it too was not passed. Opponents argued that "the CFTC has demonstrated that it has adequate authority and the ability to police the false reporting and attempted manipulation of energy prices, under CEA . . . [through the] collection of fines over the past five years in excess of $300 million."[309]

The Senate Permanent Subcommittee on Investigations began investigating the energy markets in 2001, while the Enron scandal was unfolding. Five years later, in June 2006, that subcommittee issued a bipartisan staff report, which decried the increased crude oil and natural gas prices.[310] The staff report concluded that "traditional forces of supply and demand cannot fully account for these increases."[311] The staff report found that increased demand from China and the instability of supply from producing countries had built a "risk premium" into prices. Nevertheless, the energy market had boomed only after traders poured billions into the markets in order to speculate or hedge against price changes.

The staff report stated that speculators in the form of "large financial institutions, hedge funds, pension funds, and other investment funds have been pouring billions of dollars into the energy commodities markets—perhaps as much as $60 billion in the regulated U.S. oil futures market alone—to try to take advantage of price changes or to hedge against them."[312] The staff report claimed that these "speculators" had made "tens and perhaps hundreds of millions of dollars in profits trading in energy commodities."[313]

The staff report found "substantial evidence" from the reports of several analysts that these speculators had "significantly increased prices" and that the "speculative purchases of oil futures have added as much as $20–$25 per barrel to the current price of crude oil." The staff report claimed that this price increase had provided an incentive for oil companies to increase inven-

---

307. S. 2642, 109th Cong. (April 206).

308. United States Senate, Office of Senator Feinstein, http://feinstein.senate.gov/06releases/r-ieca-ltr926.htm (accessed June 26, 2011).

309. Alexia Brunet & Meredith Shafe, *Beyond Enron: Regulation in Energy Derivatives Trading*, 27 NW. J. INT'L L. & BUS. 665, 704 (2007).

310. The report found,

> Over the past 6 years, crude oil, gasoline, and natural gas prices have risen significantly. Crude oil has risen from a range of $25-$30 per barrel in 2000, to a range of $60-$75 per barrel in 2006. High crude oil prices are a major reason for the record or near-record highs of the prices of a variety of petroleum products, including gasoline, heating oil, diesel fuel, and jet fuel. The average price for a gallon of regular unleaded gasoline has jumped from $1.46 per gallon in 2000 to $2.36 per gallon over the past 12 months, with peaks at $3.14 per gallon in September 2005, and $2.93 per gallon in May 2006. Rising crude oil prices have helped push up natural gas prices as well: the price of natural gas has risen from $2-$3 per million BTU (British Thermal Unit) in 2000 to a typical range of $6-$8 per million BTU during the past year.

U.S. Senate Permanent Subcommittee on Investigations of the Committee on Homeland Security and Governmental Affairs, Staff Report*: The Role of Market Speculation in Rising Oil and Gas Prices: A Need to Put the Cop Back on the Beat*, S. Prt. No. 109-65, 109th Congress, 2nd Sess. 1 (June 27, 2006).

311. *Id.*

312. *Id.* at 2.

313. *Id.*

tories in order to capture future price premiums. It based that conclusion on its finding that U.S. oil inventories were then at an eight-year high and that oil inventories in the thirty-four member nations of the Organization for Economic Cooperation and Development (OECD) were at a twenty-year high.[314]

The subcommittee's staff report recommended that Congress "eliminate the 'Enron Loophole' that currently limits CFTC oversight of key U.S. energy commodity markets and put the CFTC back on the beat policing these markets."[315] It further recommended "Large Trader Reports," such as those used to identify the trading of large traders in the futures markets,[316] be required for traders in over-the-counter derivatives in energy products, both here and abroad.[317] The staff also recommended that the CFTC conduct hearings to determine if electronic energy exchanges, such as ICE, should be required to publish daily trading data.[318]

In mid-2007, the Senate Permanent Subcommittee on Investigations issued another staff report.[319] It focused on Amaranth's trading and losses. The report found that "from early 2006 until its September collapse, Amaranth dominated trading in the U.S. natural gas financial markets."[320] The subcommittee staff found that "[p]urchasers of natural gas during the summer of 2006 for delivery in the following winter months paid inflated prices due to Amaranth's large-scale speculative trading."[321] The subcommittee staff believed that the Enron loophole was preventing the CFTC from acting effectively to prevent such manipulation and price distortions.[322]

Thereafter, in October 2007, the Government Accountability Office (GAO) submitted a report to Congress on the CFTC's market oversight abilities in the energy derivatives market.[323] The report noted that OTC trading in exempt commercial markets (ECMs) had grown substantially after the enactment of the Enron loophole in the CFMA.[324] It also observed several new trends that were affecting the energy markets, including fundamental factors, an influx of new traders such as hedge funds, and increased investment in commodity index funds.[325] The GAO concluded that the effects on prices of any one of those factors were unclear.[326] Nevertheless, the GAO report recommended that Congress should consider whether the current regulatory structure for energy derivatives traded in ECMs was adequate for ensuring fair trading and accurate pricing of energy commodities.[327]

The CFTC was brought under further pressure from Congress in its reauthorization hearings. Those hearings had been started in 2005, but were delayed for three years over the Feinstein

314. *Id.* at 3.

315. *Id.* at 7.

316. 17 C.F.R. Parts 16-18.

317. U.S. Senate Permanent Subcommittee on Investigations of the Committee on Homeland Security and Governmental Affairs, Staff Report: *The Role of Market Speculation in Rising Oil and Gas Prices: A Need to Put the Cop Back on the Beat*, S. Prt. No. 109-65, 109th Congress, 2nd Sess. 7 (June 27, 2006).

318. *Id.*

319. U.S. Senate Permanent Subcommittee on Investigations of the Committee on Homeland Security and Governmental Affairs, Staff Report: *Excessive Speculation in the Natural Gas Market* (2007).

320. *Id.* at 2.

321. *Id.* at 3.

322. *Id.* at 7.

323. GAO, *Commodity Futures Trading Commission: Trends in Energy Derivatives Markets Raise Questions About CFTC's Oversight* (Oct. 19, 2007).

324. *Id.* at 2

325. *Id.* at 1.

326. *Id.* at 4

327. *Id.* at 6.

amendments and other issues.[328] Giving way to pressure, the CFTC conducted its own hearings in September 2007 on the need for closing the Enron loophole.[329] The CFTC, thereafter, issued a report recommending legislation to narrow the Enron loophole.[330] The CFTC report noted that the Enron loophole had served as an "incubator for new concepts to see if they take hold in the marketplace" and provided healthy competition to the regulated exchanges.[331] Nevertheless, the CFTC asked Congress for more regulatory authority over high-volume exempt commercial markets, such as ICE.[332] The CFTC asserted that, when an ECM grows to the extent that it serves the same price discovery functions as a regulated exchange, such as NYMEX, it should be subject to comparable regulation. This would mean, among other things, that like regulated contract markets, high-volume ECMs would have to exercise self-regulatory responsibilities in order to prevent price manipulations.[333] The CFTC also sought authority to increase civil penalties for manipulation violations.[334]

Crude oil prices rose by 57 percent in 2007 and continued to increase in the first half of 2008. "The CFTC determined in 2008 that Wall Street speculators were increasing their positions in energy markets to capitalize off of political unrest in heavy oil-producing nations."[335] On January 2, 2008, as a stunt, a trader on the NYMEX floor bid crude oil up several cents and pushed it through $100 per barrel for the first time in history.[336] More than two years later, the CFTC brought a case against ConAgra Trade Group Inc. over that caper. Rather than charging manipulation, the CFTC asserted that this conduct violated Section 4(c) of the Commodity Exchange Act because it caused a non–bona fide price to be reported to NYMEX. The individual trader engaging in this conduct was not charged, but ConAgra agreed to pay $12 million to settle the CFTC's charges over this bit of silliness.[337]

NYMEX took down that price print after other traders complained, but that did not stop the advance of crude oil prices. Crude oil closed on NYMEX for the first time at over $100 per barrel on February 20, 2008, and moved to over $110 per barrel on March 14, 2008.[338] Congress responded to those price increases by enacting the CFTC Reauthorization Act of 2008.[339] That legislation significantly expanded the CFTC's regulatory authority over the ECMs that were op-

328. Alexia Brunet & Meredith Shafe, *Beyond Enron: Regulation in Energy Derivatives Trading*, 27 NW. J. INT'L L. & BUS. 665, 697 (2007).

329. *See*, 72 Fed. Reg. 5214 (Sept. 18, 2007) (announcing the holding and scope of that hearing).

330. CFTC, *Report on the Oversight of Trading on Regulated Futures Exchanges and Exempt Commercial Markets* (Oct. 2007).

331. *Id.* at 132.

332. *Id.* at 132-133.

333. Testimony of Acting CFTC Chairman Walter Lukken Before the House Subcommittee on Oversight and Investigations of the Committee on Energy and Commerce, 110th Cong., 1st Sess. 11 (Dec. 12, 2007).

334. Tina Seeley & Matthew Leising, *$1 Million Fines Sought for Futures Violations; Agency Requests Greater Penalty in Manipulation Cases*, HOUSTON CHRONICLE, Oct. 25, 2007, at Bus. 3.

335. Rep. Leonard Boswell (D-Iowa), http://www.boswellforcongress.com/news/boswell-wants-hearings-gas-prices (accessed Aug. 22, 2011).

336. CFTC, *CFTC Sanctions ConAgra Trade Group Inc. $12 Million for Causing a Non-Bona Fide Price to Be Reported in the NYMEX Crude Oil Futures Contract*, CFTC News Release No. 5873-10 (Aug. 16, 2010), http://www.cftc.gov/PressRoom/PressReleases/pr5873-10.html (accessed July 2, 2011).

337. In the Matter of ConAgra Trade Group, Inc., 2010 CFTC LEXIS 49 (C.F.T.C. Aug. 16, 2010).

338. JERRY W. MARKHAM, A FINANCIAL HISTORY OF THE UNITED STATES FROM THE SUBPRIME CRISIS TO THE GREAT RECESSION (2006–2009) 474, 493 (2011).

339. The CFTC Reauthorization Act of 2008 was enacted as Title XIII of the Food, Conservation, and Energy Act of 2008 on June 18, 2008, Pub. L. No. 110-246 (2008). That legislation was passed twice (due to some clerical issues) over the veto of President George W. Bush. JERRY W. MARKHAM, A FINANCIAL HISTORY OF THE UNITED STATES FROM ENRON-ERA SCANDALS TO THE SUBPRIME CRISIS (2004–2006) 210 (2011).

erating under the Enron loophole. The new act created a new regulatory category for ECMs that trade "significant price discovery contracts" (SPDCs). This was a special provision directed at ICE for its hosting of the Amaranth trading.[340]

The CFTC Reauthorization Act of 2008 allowed the CFTC to adopt rules regulating SPDCs and market participants through expanded reporting requirements. Markets trading SPDCs were required to adopt "core principles" such as those used by regulated exchanges. Included among those principles were, as requested by the CFTC, obligations to prevent manipulation. Large traders were also required to report their SPDC transactions, as well as their regulated trades.[341] The CFTC was given expanded authority over fraud involving principal-to-principal transactions, including previously exempt OTC energy contracts.[342]

Some congressional critics contended that the CFTC Reauthorization Act of 2008 did not go far enough because it did not regulate trading on foreign exchanges through terminals located in the United States. The Prevent Unfair Manipulation of Prices Act (PUMP Act) was introduced in Congress to close that remnant of the Enron loophole by regulating such foreign transactions. It also sought to further regulate speculative trading in OTC energy swaps, "which experts estimate could lower the cost of oil by $20 to $30 a barrel"—crude oil was then trading around $100 per barrel.[343] The average price of a gallon of gasoline rose to $4 in June 2008. Crude oil prices continued to climb, reaching a record price of $145.80 per barrel on the NYMEX on July 11, 2008.[344]

Congress held more than forty hearings on the rise of energy prices in the first six months of 2008, and numerous bills were introduced to attack speculators.[345] Hearings were also held in the summer of 2008 to consider legislation to bar speculation in crude oil.[346] A *Wall Street Journal* editorial noted that Congress had previously barred speculative trading in only one commodity, onions.[347] However, the *Journal* editorial pointed out that a subsequent economic study concluded that futures trading had actually helped stabilize onion prices before the ban.

Bill O'Reilly, the populist Fox News commentator, later called oil speculators "crooks" and wanted to increase their margin requirements to 50 percent. However, another Fox news commentator John Stossel pointed out to O'Reilly that government efforts to control speculation usually fail. Pulling out an onion he just happened to in his pocket, Stossel noted that Congress had tried to stop volatility in onion prices by banning futures trading in that commodity in 1958. Onion prices became more volatile after that ban.[348]

---

340. *See*, JERRY W. MARKHAM, A FINANCIAL HISTORY OF THE UNITED STATES FROM ENRON-ERA SCANDALS TO THE SUBPRIME CRISIS (2004–2006) 210-211 (2011) (the amendments relating to the Enron exception might be best referred to as the "ICE amendments").

341. JERRY W. MARKHAM, A FINANCIAL HISTORY OF THE UNITED STATES FROM ENRON-ERA SCANDALS TO THE SUBPRIME CRISIS (2004–2006) 211 (2011).

342. 7 U.S.C. § 6b.

343. *Pump Act Would End Speculation On The Oil Futures Market*, http:// www.newreviewsite.com/articles/PUMP-ACT-WOULD-END-SPECULATION-ON-THE-OIL-FUTURES -MARKET/307 (accessed June 26, 2011). *See also*, Alexia Brunet & Meredith Shafe, *Beyond Enron: Regulation in Energy Derivatives Trading*, 27 NW. J. INT'L L. & BUS. 704 (2007) (describing the Pump Act).

344. JERRY W. MARKHAM, A FINANCIAL HISTORY OF THE UNITED STATES FROM THE SUBPRIME CRISIS TO THE GREAT RECESSION (2006–2009) 516 (2011).

345. JERRY W. MARKHAM, A FINANCIAL HISTORY OF THE UNITED STATES FROM ENRON-ERA SCANDALS TO THE SUBPRIME CRISIS (2004–2006) 212 (2011).

346. *Id.* at 207.

347. *The Onion Ringer*, WALL STREET JOURNAL, July 8, 2008, at A20.

348. Bill O'Reilly Battles John Stossel Over the Price of Oil, http://www.youtube.com/watch?v=ClgDcxKQdfM (accessed on March 4, 2013).

Hysteria over gasoline prices continued. The *New York Times* claimed that "[h]igh oil prices have helped bring down the American economy and to devastate Detroit."[349] Gasoline prices also played a key role in the then ongoing congressional campaigns.[350] As gasoline prices continued to rise, the CFTC took a number of steps to deflect criticism that it was incapable of preventing or detecting price manipulations. Among other things, the agency entered into an information-sharing agreement with the Financial Services Authority (FSA) in the United Kingdom. Pursuant to that agreement, the FSA agreed to share information on trading in crude oil contracts traded on ICE Futures Europe (the successor to the International Petroleum Exchange of London) that were linked to the settlement price of NYMEX crude oil contracts.[351] The CFTC also commenced a nationwide crude oil investigation. Although it normally conducts its investigations in confidence the CFTC took the "extraordinary step of disclosing this investigation because of today's unprecedented market conditions."[352]

An interagency task force was formed in 2008 to investigate and determine what was driving up crude oil prices. That task force was chaired by the CFTC and included representatives from the Departments of Energy, Agriculture, and Treasury, the Federal Reserve Board, the FTC, and the SEC.[353] The task force's findings did not support claims that gas prices were being driven by speculative manipulators. Rather, the task force's interim report, which was released in July 2008, concluded that increases in oil prices between 2003 and 2008 were largely the result of fundamentals of supply and demand, rather than speculation.[354]

---

349. Floyd Norris, *Sense and Reality on Energy*, New York Times, Aug. 29, 2008, at C1.

350. Kirk Johnson & Monica Davey, Voters to Congressional Candidates: 'Energy Is the No. 1 Issue,' New York Times, Aug. 22, 2008, at A12.

351. CFTC Press Release 5503-08 (May 29, 2008), http://www.cftc.gov/PressRoom/ PressReleases/ pr5503-08.html (accessed June 24, 2011). The CFTC also released a report by its chief economist on developments in trading in the U.S. crude oil futures market. The report concluded that increased hedging by swap dealers that began in 2004 had actually enhanced liquidity in the back months—that is, those with the longest deferred delivery date. CFTC Office of Chief Economist, *Market Growth Trader Participation and Pricing in Energy Futures Markets*, Com. Fut. L. Rep. (CCH) ¶ 30,451 (CFTC 2007).

352. CFTC Press Release 5503-08 (May 29, 2008), http://www.cftc.gov/PressRoom/ PressReleases/ pr5503-08.html (accessed June 24, 2011).

353. Interagency Task Force on Commodity Markets, *Interim Report on Crude Oil* (July 2008).

354. The report stated:

> The Task Force's preliminary assessment is that current oil prices and the increase in oil prices between January 2003 and June 2008 are largely due to fundamental supply and demand factors. During this same period, activity on the crude oil futures market—as measured by the number of contracts outstanding, trading activity, and the number of traders—has increased significantly. While these increases broadly coincided with the run-up in crude oil prices, the Task Force's preliminary analysis to date does not support the proposition that speculative activity has systematically driven changes in oil prices.
>
> The world economy has expanded at its fastest pace in decades, and that strong growth has translated into substantial increases in the demand for oil, particularly from emerging market countries. On the supply side, the production of oil has responded sluggishly, compounded by production shortfalls associated with geopolitical unrest in countries with large oil reserves. As it is very difficult to rely on substitutes for oil in the short term, very large price increases have occurred as the market balances supply and demand.
>
> If a group of market participants has systematically driven prices, detailed daily position data should show that that group's position changes preceded price changes. The Task Force's preliminary analysis, based on the evidence available to date, suggests that changes in futures market participation by speculators have not systematically preceded price changes. On the contrary, most speculative traders typically alter their positions following price changes, suggesting that they are responding to new information—just as one would expect in an efficiently operating market.

The size of the crude oil futures market was found to have grown significantly during that period, but the agencies preparing the report could not find support for the proposition that speculative activity had systematically driven changes in oil prices. Indeed, the task force discovered that speculators had been net short during some of the larger price increases in crude oil. The task force also concluded that the reason for the price increases was an imbalance between supply and demand.[355]

Crude oil prices dropped by some 80 percent between July and December 2008, but then began to accelerate again.[356] Those renewed price increases were occurring as the Obama administration entered office. The new administration soon began an attack on "speculators" as responsible for those price gains. Despite the findings of its interagency task force in 2008 that fundamentals and not speculation were driving prices, the CFTC's new chair, Gary Gensler, announced in July 2009 that the agency would hold hearings to determine if the recent price increases were due to speculation.[357] A *Wall Street Journal* editorial then charged that the hearings were being held to steer blame away from the ongoing price run-up in commodities that the paper blamed on "the Federal Reserve's easy money and the Obama Administration's spending and debt party."[358] The editorial asserted that the Obama administration was engaging in the "age-old scapegoating" of speculators "that our superstitious ancestors would have recognized."[359]

The *Wall Street Journal* also reported that the CFTC planned to issue a new report that would blame speculators as playing a significant role in causing the price volatility in crude oil.[360] A CFTC commissioner, Bart Chilton, was reported as claiming that the earlier interagency task force's findings had been based on "deeply flawed data."[361] However, crude oil prices dropped over the next few months, closing at $77.50 per barrel on October 10, 2008.[362] That turnaround occurred while the then ongoing financial crisis was reaching its peak. Congressional attention then shifted to credit default swaps.

Id. at 3.

355. *Id.* at 4.

356. *The Politics of "Speculation,"* WALL STREET JOURNAL, July 29, 2009, at A14.

357. Sarah N. Lynch, *CFTC Chief Seeks Curbs on Oil Trade; Data Rift?* WALL STREET JOURNAL, July 29, 2009, at C1. Another target was the exchange-traded funds, such as the U.S. Oil Fund and U.S. Natural Gas Fund. The U.S. Natural Gas fund accounts for as much as 30 percent of the gas futures market. Carolyn Cui, *Oil, Gas ETF Backer Aims to Defend Funds*, WALL STREET JOURNAL, Aug. 3, 2009, at C1.

358. *Id.*

359. *The Politics of "Speculation,"* WALL STREET JOURNAL, July 29, 2009, at A14. The editorial further argued,

> Truth is, we need more speculators, not less. They're the people who can help prices find the right level, because there is no "right" level other than the one the market gives us. And that's why, in turn, excessive speculation is nothing more—or less—than a convenient fiction for when prices don't move the way politicians would like.

360. Ianthe Jeanne Dugan & Alistair MacDonald, *Traders Blamed for Oil Spike—CFTC Will Pin '08 Price Surge on Speculators, in a Reversal From Bush Findings*, WALL STREET JOURNAL, July 28, 2009, at A1.

361. Sarah N. Lynch, *CFTC Chief Seeks Curbs on Oil Trade; Data Rift?* WALL STREET JOURNAL, July 29, 2009, at C1.

362. JERRY W. MARKHAM, A FINANCIAL HISTORY OF THE UNITED STATES FROM THE SUBPRIME CRISIS TO THE GREAT RECESSION (2006–2009) 567 (2011).

7

THE DODD-FRANK ACT

7:1 THE CREDIT DEFAULT SWAPS MARKET

The Commodity Futures Modernization Act of 2000 (CFMA) authorized the Securities and Exchange Commission (SEC) to apply the antifraud provisions of Section 10(b) of the Securities Exchange Act of 1934 (34 Act) to security-based swaps. This was done in a somewhat convoluted manner in order to apply only Section 10(b) and not other provisions in the securities laws to those security-based swaps.[1] The SEC made little use of that provision before the financial crisis of 2008, but became active in pursuing such cases when credit default swaps became the target of criticism.[2] The growth of the over-the-counter (OTC) derivatives market raised concerns over their safety even before the financial crisis, but those concerns were largely ignored.[3] The failure, and

---

1. The SEC's jurisdiction over security-based swaps was sharply limited under the CFMA. *See,* CSX Corp. v. Children's Inv. Fund Mgmt. (UK) LLP, 654 F.3d 276, 288-290 (2d Cir. 2008) (Winter J. concurring and describing limited jurisdiction of SEC for security-based swaps under CFMA). However, as described below, the Dodd-Frank Act, which was adopted in 2010, greatly expanded both SEC and CFTC jurisdiction over swaps. *See generally, Further Definition of "Swap," "Security-Based Swap," and "Security-Based Swap Agreement"; Mixed Swaps; Security-Based Swap Agreement Recordkeeping,* 77 Fed. Reg. 48208 (Aug. 13, 2012) (defining security-based swaps under Dodd-Frank). As the Second Circuit noted:

> In December 2000, Congress enacted the CFMA to, among other things, clarify the status of swap agreements under the securities laws. CFMA § 2, 114 Stat. at 2763A-366. Sections 302 and 303 of the CMFA define "swap agreements" and then expressly exclude them from the definition of "securities," but amend section 10(b) to reach swap agreements.

Caiola v. Citibank, N.A., 295 F.3d 312, 327(2d Cir. 2002). *See also,* SEC v. Rorech, 673 F. Supp. 2d 217 (S.D.N.Y. 2009) (describing this provision and the definition of credit default swaps that was adopted from the Gramm-Leach-Bliley Act, Pub. L. No. 106-102, § 206B, 113 Stat. 1338 (1999); In the Matter of Perry, 2009 WL 2163550 (S.E.C.) (consent order finding that respondent controlled more than 5 percent of an issuer's stock through equity swaps and that this subjected the respondent to SEC reporting requirements for such beneficial ownership).

2. One court defined credit default swaps as

> a common type of credit derivative in which the protection buyer makes a fixed payment to the protection seller in return for a payment that is contingent upon a "credit event"—such as a bankruptcy—occurring to the company that issued the security (the "reference entity") or the security itself (the "reference obligation"). The contingent payment is often made against delivery of a "deliverable obligation"—usually the reference obligation or other security issued by the reference entity—by the protection buyer to the protection seller. This delivery is known as the "physical settlement."

Deutsche Bank AG v. Ambac Credit Products LLC, 2006 U.S. Dist. LEXIS 45322 (S.D.N.Y. 2006).

3. As Warren Buffett famously and prophetically stated in his annual report to shareholders in 2002,

> The derivatives genie is now well out of the bottle, and these instruments will almost certainly multiply in variety and number until some event makes their toxicity clear. Knowledge of how

the government bailout of several systemically important financial institutions during that crisis, were claimed to be "due to bad derivatives bets" made under the cover of the Enron loophole.[4]

The growth of the credit default swaps market had been phenomenal. The notional amount of outstanding credit default swaps in 2000 was $900 billion.[5] That figure increased to $62 trillion by 2008.[6] Although it was estimated that 80 percent of the credit default swap market was speculative in nature,[7] credit default swaps also performed a hedging function. Among other things, they were used to enhance the creditworthiness of subprime mortgage securitizations that were bundled into collateralized debt obligations (CDOs).[8] As a result of such credit enhancements, the credit rating agencies gave the upper tranches of CDOs (called "super seniors") triple AAA ratings. This was the same credit rating that was given to U.S. government debt before it lost that rating in 2011. Because of their perceived safety, many financial institutions invested in super seniors. For the same reason, the banking regulators gave those instruments special capital treatment, encouraging banks to keep such investment on their books while selling off more risky lower-classed tranches of the CDOs.[9]

That safety proved elusive after many CDOs were downgraded by the credit ratings agencies during the financial crisis in 2008. A credit downgrade at the American International Group Inc. (AIG) in September 2008 raised systemic concerns over whether AIG would default on its $500

> dangerous they are has already permeated the electricity and gas businesses, in which the eruption of major troubles caused the use of derivatives to diminish dramatically. Elsewhere, however, the derivatives business continues to expand unchecked. Central banks and governments have so far found no effective way to control, or even monitor, the risks posed by these contracts. . . . I believe Berkshire should be a fortress of financial strength—for the sake of our owners, creditors, policyholders and employees. We try to be alert to any sort of megacatastrophe risk, and that posture may make us unduly apprehensive about the burgeoning quantities of long-term derivatives contracts and the massive amount of uncollateralized receivables that are growing alongside. In our view, however, derivatives are financial weapons of mass destruction, carrying dangers that, while now latent, are potentially lethal.

Berkshire Hathaway Inc., 2002 Annual Report 15 (2002), http://www.berkshirehathaway.com/2002ar/2002ar.pdf (accessed July 5, 2010).

4. *See*, Lynn A. Stout, *Derivatives and the Legal Origin of the 2008 Credit Crisis*, 1 Harv. Bus. L. Rev. 1 (2011) (blaming the financial crisis on the Enron loophole in the CFMA and stating that "traditional legal restraints on OTC speculation were systematically dismantled during the 1980s and 1990s, culminating in 2000 with the enactment of the CFMA. That legislation set the stage for the 2008 crises by legalizing, for the first time in U.S. history, speculative OTC trading in derivatives"). For a contrarian view, *see*, Jerry W. Markham, *Regulating Credit Default Swaps in the Wake of the Subprime Crisis*, Working Paper Presented at the International Monetary Fund Seminar on Current Developments in Monetary and Financial Law, Washington, DC (Dec. 2, 2009) (hereinafter "*Regulating Credit Default Swaps*"). *See also,* Jerry W. Markham, *Glass Steagall vs. Gramm-Leach-Bliley: A Test Match for the Bankers*, 12 U. Penn. L. & Bus. J. 1081 (2010) (also exonerating the deregulation measures for banks in the Financial Modernization Act of 1999, Publ. L. No. 106-102, 113 Stat. 1338 (the "Gram-Leach-Bliley Act") as the cause of the financial crisis).

5. Nat'l Ass'n of Professional Ins. Agents, *Congress Exempted Credit Default Swaps From State Gaming Laws in 2000*, http://www.pianet.com/NewsCenter/BizPolitics/10-15-08-7.htm (accessed July 3, 2011).

6. *See* International Swap and Derivatives Association Inc., Market Survey (2009), http://www.isda.org/statistics/pdf/ISDA-Market-Survey-historical-data.pdf (accessed July 1, 2011).

7. *See* Arthur D. Postal, *Credit Default Swaps Belong Under Supervision of States*, P&C Nat'l Underwriter, Feb. 23, 2009, http://www.property-casualty.com/Issues/2009/7/Pages/Credit-Default-Swaps-Belong-Under-Supervision-Of-States.aspx (accessed November 12, 2009).

8. *See* UBS AG, Shareholder Report on UBS's Write-Downs § 4.22 (2008) (describing the role of credit default swaps in subprime CDO securitizations).

9. Jerry W. Markham, *Glass Steagall vs. Gramm-Leach-Bliley: A Test Match for the Bankers*, 12 U. Penn. L. & Bus. J. 1081 (2010).

billion CDS portfolio. The failure of Lehman Brothers created a market panic. Lehman's collapse raised concerns that credit default swaps written on its debt obligations could generate claims of up to $400 billion. However, after offsetting claims were netted, the actual exposure was only $5.2 billion.[10]

In any event, the federal government decided that the failure of AIG in the wake of the Lehman Brothers failure could destroy the entire financial system. The government mounted a $183 billion rescue of AIG.[11] The failure of AIG was blamed on losses from its credit default business. AIG was one of the larger issuers of subprime credit default swaps.[12] It failed after receiving massive collateral calls on its subprime exposures that were triggered by the sharp decline in the value of subprime mortgages and after AIG's credit rating was cut.[13]

Ben Bernanke, the chair of the Federal Reserve Board (the Fed), turned AIG and the CDS market into a pariah when he declared in congressional testimony that nothing had made him angrier than the AIG failure, which he attributed to AIG's exploitation of "a huge gap in the regulatory system."[14] He asserted that AIG's credit default operation was nothing more than a hedge fund attached to a large and stable insurance company that "made huge numbers of irresponsible bets, [and] took huge losses. There was no regulatory oversight because there was a gap in the system."[15] Bernanke stated that the government was forced to expend billions of dollars to save AIG because its failure would have been "disastrous for the economy."[16]

The Treasury Department proposed legislation in June 2009 to impose margin requirements for OTC derivatives and to otherwise broaden SEC and Commodity Futures Trading Commission (CFTC) regulation of those instruments.[17] This proposal sought to achieve that goal by repealing the Enron loophole for swaps.[18] SEC chair Christopher Cox also sought authority from Congress

10. *See* Mary Williams Walsh, *Tracking Firm Says Bets Placed on Lehman Have Been Quietly Settled*, New York Times, Oct. 23, 2008, at A20 (describing that resolution).

11. 6 International Monetary Fund, Current Developments in Monetary and Financial Law 301-302 (2012).

12. *See*, Roddy Boyd, Fatal Risk (2011) (describing AIG's rise and fall).

13. Jerry W. Markham, *Glass Steagall vs. Gramm-Leach-Bliley: A Test Match for the Bankers*, 12 U. Penn. L. & Bus. J. 1081, 1129 (2010).

14. David Wessel, In Fed We Trust, 194 (2009).

15. *Id.*

16. *Id.* A report by the Troubled Asset Relief Program (TARP) inspector general (the TARP Cop) Neil Barofsky issued in November 2009 charged that the Fed's takeover of AIG had been badly flawed in paying Goldman Sachs and other large investment banks in full to settle their credit default swaps with AIG. *AIG and Systemic Risk*, Wall Street Journal, Nov. 20, at A26. The Financial Inquiry Commission that was appointed by Congress to ascertain the causes of the crisis split badly on what actually caused the financial crisis, but the Democratic majority found that

> AIG was so interconnected with many large commercial banks, investment banks, and other financial institutions through counterparty credit relationships on credit default swaps and other activities such as securities lending that its potential failure created systemic risk. The government concluded AIG was too big to fail and committed more than $180 billion to its rescue. Without the bailout, AIG's default and collapse could have brought down its counterparties, causing cascading losses and collapses throughout the financial system.

Financial Inquiry Commission, The Financial Crisis Inquiry Report 352 (2011).

17. *See* U.S. Department of the Treasury, Financial Regulatory Reform: A New Foundation: Rebuilding Financial Supervision and Regulation (2009), http://www.house.gov/apps/list/hearing/financialsvcs_dem/testimony_-_treasury.pdf.

18. *See* Edmund L. Andrews, *Unresolved Questions After Hearing with Geithner*, New York Times, July 11, 2009, at B3.

to regulate the credit default swap market after the AIG failure. He stated that the market lacked transparency and was susceptible to fraud and manipulation.[19]

These proposals floated about in Congress for about a year, but became bogged down in fights over the scope and application of such regulation, as well as concerns over other aspects of the Obama administration's proposals for financial services regulation. That logjam was broken by the highly publicized case filed by the SEC against Goldman Sachs over a credit default swap that allowed hedge fund manager John Paulson to make $1 billion in profits from credit default swaps.[20] The filing of that case touched off a populist crusade against such instruments.[21] President Obama joined the fray by announcing, just after the case was filed, that he would veto the pending financial services legislation if it did not regulate OTC derivatives.[22]

7:2 THE SEC'S ANTIMANIPULATION ROLE AFTER DODD-FRANK

The CFTC Reauthorization Act of 2008 failed to close the Enron loophole for credit default swaps, but that oversight was corrected under the Dodd-Frank Wall Street Reform and Consumer Protection Act of 2010.[23] The Dodd-Frank Act, which was signed into law on July 21, 2010, regulated the previously unregulated swaps market.[24] Most swaps will now be exchange traded and cleared through a regulated central counterparty.[25] Dodd-Frank also allowed regulators to impose capital and margin requirements on swap dealers and major swap participants,[26] but not end-users.[27] It requires standardized swaps to be cleared through a central counterparty or clearinghouse.[28] Following the approach taken with the Federal Energy Regulatory Commission (FERC) and the Federal Trade Commission (FTC), described in Chapter 6, Dodd-Frank also expanded the CFTC's antimanipulation authority to conform to that of the SEC[29] and authorized the CFTC to attack abusive trading practices.[30]

The Dodd-Frank Act amended the federal securities laws and repealed a residue of the Enron loophole, in order to authorize the SEC substantively to regulate securities-based swaps and security-based swap dealers.[31] Dodd-Frank gave the SEC broad and exclusive jurisdiction over "security-based swaps," while the CFTC was given jurisdiction over other swaps, and joint jurisdiction was declared for the SEC and CFTC over "mixed swaps."[32] The SEC was authorized by

19. Christopher Cox, *Swapping Secrecy for Transparency*, New York Times, Oct. 19, 2009, at WK12.

20. SEC v. Goldman Sachs & Co. 10 CV 3229 (S.D.N.Y. April 15, 2010).

21. *See*, Jerry W. Markham, *SEC v. Goldman Sachs & Co.: Serious Fraud or Just More Banker Bashing*? 30 Fut. & Derv. L. Rep. 7, 8 (2010) (discussing the politics of the case and its weaknesses).

22. Damian Paletta & Victoria McGrane, *SEC v. Goldman Sachs: Fraud Allegations Further Inflame Fight Over Financial Regulation*, Wall Street Journal, April 17, 2010 at A5.

23. Pub. L. No. 111-203, 124 Stat. 1376 (2010).

24. *See*, Kristin N. Johnson, *Things Fall Apart: Regulating the Credit Default Swap Commons*, 82 U. Colo. L. Rev. 167 (2011) (describing that legislation).

25. Dodd-Frank §§ 762 & 763.

26. Dodd-Frank §§ 747 & 753.

27. Dodd-Frank §§ 731 & 764.

28. Dodd-Frank §§ 723. Commercial entities were exempted from the clearinghouse requirement. Dodd-Frank § 723.

29. Dodd-Frank § 753.

30. Dodd-Frank § 747.

31. Dodd-Frank § 762.

32. Dodd-Frank § 712. To delineate the regulatory roles of the SEC and CFTC over swaps, Dodd-Frank defines the term "swap" (§ 721) and then defines smaller subsets of that—the "securities-based swap" (a swap on a narrow-based index of securities or on the single issuer) (Dodd-Frank § 761) and the "mixed swap" (basically any other swap that has a financial basis such as interest rates, currencies, quantitative

Dodd-Frank to apply its existing antimanipulation powers to swap transactions that fall within its new jurisdiction.[33]

In another sweeping grant of antimanipulation authority, Section 763(g) of the Dodd Frank Act authorized the SEC to adopt rules that are reasonably designed to prevent fraudulent, deceptive, or manipulative practices in connection with security-based swaps.[34] Interestingly, that power was to be exercised under Section 9 of the 34 Act,[35] rather than Section 10(b) in that statute. As described in Chapter 3, the burden of proof for proving manipulation is heavier under Section 9 than it is for Section 10(b).

In November 2010 the SEC proposed under that provision a new rule, Rule 9j-1, which sought to incorporate the prohibitions of Section 10(b) of the 34 Act *and* those in Section 17(a) of the 33 Act into its definition of fraud and manipulation under this new power.[36] The proposed rule would apply to "any person," which the SEC stated would include issuers, broker-dealers, security-based swap dealers, major security-based swap participants, persons associated with a security-based swap dealer or major security-based swap participant, security-based swap counterparties, and any other individuals or entities. The SEC noted that there would be no exceptions to the proposed rule's applicability, including no exceptions for end-users of security-based swaps.[37]

The proposed rule sought to extend its prohibitions to the exercise of any right or performance of any obligation under a security-based swap, or the avoidance of such exercise or performance. Because some security-based swaps require ongoing payments, deliveries, and collateral postings between the parties throughout the term of the security-based swap, the SEC proposed to make "explicit the liability of persons that engage in misconduct to trigger, avoid, or affect the value of such ongoing payments or deliveries."[38]

The proposed rule would also apply to, among other things, fraudulent conduct in connection with a security-based swap that affects the value of cash flow, payments, or deliveries, such as by triggering the obligation of a counterparty to make a large payment or to post additional collateral; conduct that triggers the exercise of a right or performance of an obligation or affects the payments to be made; or actions taken in order to avoid having to make a large payment, post additional collateral, or perform another obligation under a security-based swap.[39]

---

measures, or the occurrence of a change associated with a potential financial, economic, or commercial event) (Dodd-Frank § 761).

33. 15 U.S.C.§ 78(j)(b).

34. Dodd-Frank § 763(g). Section 763(g) added a new subparagraph (j) to Section 9 to make it unlawful for

> any person, directly or indirectly, by the use of any means or instrumentality of interstate commerce or of the mails, or of any facility of any national securities exchange, to effect any transaction in, or to induce or attempt to induce the purchase or sale of, any security-based swap, in connection with which such person engages in any fraudulent, deceptive, or manipulative act or practice, makes any fictitious quotation, or engages in any transaction, practice, or course of business which operates as a fraud or deceit upon any person.

15 U.S.C. § 78i(j).

35. 15 U.S.C. § 78i (heading).

36. *Prohibition Against Fraud, Manipulation, and Deception in Connection With Security-Based Swaps*, 75 Fed. Reg. 68560 (Nov. 10, 2008).

37. 75 Fed. Reg. at 68562.

38. *Id.*

39. 75 Fed. Reg. at 68563.

The SEC stated that the prohibitions in the proposed rule that were modeled after Rule 10b-5 would require scienter to establish a violation (i.e., "knowing" or "recklessly"), while the prohibitions taken from Sections 17(a)(2) and (a)(3) of the 33 Act would not require such a showing. Negligence, the SEC asserted, would be sufficient for Section 17(a)–type violations. The proposed rule also varied the language somewhat that it borrowed from Rule 10b-5. The proposed rule thus includes "manipulative" conduct, a term that is not used in Rule 10b-5, but is found in Section 10(b).[40]

Through this rule, the SEC was essentially seeking to amend Section 9 by substituting the language in that statute for that found in the Rule 10b-5 prohibition and Section 17(a). The SEC was clearly hoping that, in doing so, it would rid itself of the more troubling requirements in Section 9 that were inserted by Congress when it was originally enacted.

The proposed rule would apply to a person "directly" or "indirectly" engaging in prohibited conduct. The SEC asserted that this means that a person may be liable "whether the person engages in the misconduct alone or through others."[41] As described above, Section 9(f) of the Exchange Act provides for a private right of action only for violations of Sections 9(a), (b) and (c), and not for violations of Section 9(j) where the new Dodd-Frank authority was added. Although proposed in 2010, this rule proposal had not been adopted at the time this book was in final production (July 2013).

7:3 HIGH-FREQUENCY TRADING

A market phenomenon in the twentieth century was the growth of electronic markets that gave rise to algorithmic trading, which in turn generated rapid-fire orders to take advantage of the most transient market inefficiencies.[42] The rapidity of this trading gave rise to its label "high-frequency trading." High-frequency trading has been driving trading volumes on both the stock and commodity markets in the twenty-first century.[43] By 2009, more than two-thirds of stock-market volume was attributable to "high-frequency traders, who can buy or sell in less than 400 microseconds, or nearly a thousand times faster than you can blink your eye."[44] Illustrative of the desire for speed in executing orders was a decision by high-frequency traders to build a 3,000-mile-long fiber optic cable between New York and London in order to reduce latency—that is, to increase transmission speed—by 5.2 milliseconds at a cost of $300 million.[45] The Chicago Board Options Exchange and the OneChicago single stock futures exchange moved their electronic trading platforms to New Jersey in order to reduce latency of orders entered in the New York area.[46]

---

40. 75 Fed. Reg. at 68563.

41. 75. Fed. Reg. at 68564. That assertion was made, however, before the Supreme Court's decision in *Janus Capital Group Inc. v. First Derivative Traders*, 564 U.S. ---, --- (2011).

42. *See*, Jerry W. Markham & Daniel J. Harty, *For Whom the Bell Tolls: The Demise of Exchange Trading Floors and the Growth of ECNs*, 33 Iowa J. Corp. L. 865 (2008) (describing growth of this trading).

43. Dennis K. Berman, *The Game: Saving the Stock Market Only to Destroy It*, Wall Street Journal, Aug. 24, 2010, at C1.

44. Jason Zweig, *The Intelligent Investor: Staying Calm in a World of Dark Pools, Dark Doings*, Wall Street Journal, Oct. 24, 2009, at B1.

45. Matthew Philips, *Stock Trading Is About to Get 5.2 Milliseconds Faster*, March 29, 2012. Bloomberg, http://www.businessweek.com/articles/2012-03-29/trading-at-the-speed-of-light (accessed April 4, 2012).

46. CBOE Moving Flagship Exchange Platform to New Jersey, Traders Magazine.com, April 5, 2012, http://www.tradersmagazine.com/news/cboe-moving-flagship-options-exchange-platform-nj-109923-1.html?ET=tradersmagazine:e1371:54248a:&st=email&utm_source=editorial&utm_medium=email&utm_campaign=tm_xtra_040512 (accessed April 19, 2012).

High-frequency trading also gave rise to trading practices that raised regulatory concerns.[47] A report by the United Nations Conference on Trade and Development found a correlation in short-term movements in securities and commodities that was attributed to high-frequency trading.[48] Other economic reports also argued that the "financialization" of commodity markets by high-frequency and index traders was causing a correlation of prices that varied from fundamental factors affecting those commodities.[49]

The SEC became concerned as the volume of high-frequency trading increased. It dusted off a provision in the Market Reform Act of 1990,[50] which added Section 13(h) to the 34 Act after the stock market crash of 1987.[51] That amendment authorized the SEC to create a reporting system that would allow the agency to monitor trading activity of large traders. The SEC had proposed such a large trader reporting system in 1991. The proposal would have required reports on positions traded in excess of 10,000 shares or $4 million in any twenty-four-hour period.[52] The SEC stated in this proposal that its present system of "electronic blue sheets" was inadequate for trade reconstruction in this environment.[53]

---

47. *See, e.g.*, Graham Bowley, *Clamping Down on Rapid Trades*, New York Times, Oct. 9, 2011, at A1.

48. Maria Kolesnikova, *High-Frequency Trades Seen Boosting Commodity-Stocks Link*, Bloomberg, http://www.bloomberg.com/news/2012-03-26/high-frequency-trades-seen-boosting-commodity-stocks-link.html (accessed March 28, 2012).

49. Gregory Meyer, *Challenge to Conventional Wisdom on Speculators*, Financial Times (London), Aug. 30, 2011.

50. Pub. L. No. 101-432, 104 Stat. 963 (1990).

51. 15 U.S.C. § 78m(h).

52. *Large Trader Reporting System*, 56 Fed. Reg. 42550 (Aug. 28, 1991). In proposing that requirement in 1991, the SEC stated:

> During the past decade, the securities markets have experienced a fundamental change in the predominant type of market participant and the manner in which such participants conduct business. Market information and communication systems have become global in nature and have increased the scope and velocity at which information is disseminated to investors. As a result, securities are now traded rapidly in a global securities market. During this period of change, the securities markets also have experienced a significant increase in activity and volatility. Further, in today's securities market many small individual investors have relinquished direct management of their investments to professional investment managers. Accordingly, large institutional investors such as public and private pension or retirement funds, mutual funds, insurance companies, foundations, hedge funds and investment managers have grown extraordinarily in number and size, and have become a predominant type of market participant. Investor demands for returns greater than market averages have caused institutional investors and investment managers to develop complex and innovative relationships, products, and trading strategies. These new investment relationships, products and strategies have led to increased specialization in investment management and linked capital markets around the world. These developments enable institutional investors to trade large amounts of securities and commodities with stunning swiftness to minimize risk or to profit from small differences in valuation.

56 Fed. Reg. at 42550 (footnote omitted).

53. 56 Fed. Reg. at 42550. The SEC elsewhere noted:

> For several decades, the Commission requested . . . [trader] information by mailing questionnaire forms (known as "blue sheets" because of the color on which the forms were printed) to broker-dealers to be manually completed and mailed back to the Commission. In the late 1980s, as the volume of trading and securities transactions dramatically increased, the Commission and the securities self-regulatory organizations ("SROs") worked together to develop and implement a system with a universal electronic format, commonly known as the "electronic blue sheet" or "EBS" system, to replace the manual process.

The SEC reproposed this rule in 1994. The revised proposal would have doubled the level of trading that would require reporting and expanded the reach of the reports to index arbitrage and program traders.[54] This rule proposal was not adopted. Instead, the SEC adopted Rule 17a-25[55] under Section 17 of the 34 Act,[56] which gave the SEC power to impose record-keeping requirements on broker-dealers and other industry participants. Rule 17a-25 requires brokers-dealers to submit electronically to the SEC, upon request, information on customer and firm securities trading.[57]

Electronic trading also raised problems with market crashes. An algorithmic error on February 3, 2010, on NYMEX caused a sharp increase in price and volume in crude oil futures contracts.[58] Such minicrashes became common on electronic trading platforms.[59] Embarrassingly, an initial public offering by BATS Global Markets Inc. had to be canceled on March 23, 2012, as the result of a computer error that caused its share price to plunge from $16 per share to a few cents. The price of Apple shares also plunged briefly as a result of the error. BATS was one of the largest electronic securities markets and this failure in its computer raised further questions on the reliability of electronic trading.[60] The initial public offering by Facebook in May 2012 was also marred by a computer glitch on NASDAQ, requiring the offering to be suspended for thirty minutes on the opening.[61] Still another computer problem disrupted trading in the stock of the Kraft Foods Group Inc. on October 3, 2012, causing a phenomenal spread of $7 per share in bid and ask prices for a brief period.[62]

SEC chair Mary Schapiro blamed a lack of uniformity in exchange rules for furthering problems with electronic trading and urged the exchanges to build a trading data center so that future events could be more easily tracked.[63] The SEC also proposed rules that would automatically stop trading through dynamically placed bands around stock prices. Such price limits were long used

---

> The universal EBS format permits the Commission and the SROs to conduct timely and thorough surveillance and enforcement inquiries. Firms generally use software to scan their account records and download the appropriate information into the standard EBS format, and then transmit the data to the Securities Industry Automation Corporation ("SIAC"). In turn, SIAC routes the file electronically to the Commission's mainframe computer.

SEC, Securities Exchange Act Release No. 44494, 75 S.E.C. Docket 748, 2001 WL 745633(June 29, 2001).

54. *Large Trader Reporting System*, 59 Fed. Reg. 7917 (Feb. 9, 1994).

55. 17 C.F.R. § 240.17a-25.

56. 15 U.S.C. § 78q.

57. SEC, Securities Exchange Act Release No. 44494, 75 S.E.C. Docket 748, 2001 WL 745633 (June 29, 2001).

58. Jenny Strasburg & Sarah N. Lynch, *Infinium Is Focus of CME*, Wall Street Journal, Aug. 26, 2010, at C3.

59. *The Fast and Furious*, The Economist, Feb. 25, 2012.

60. Tom Lauricella, Scott Patterson & David Benoit, *Trading Firm IPO Fizzles in Seconds*, Wall Street Journal, March 23, 2012, at A1.

61. Jenny Strasburg, Jacob Bunge & Gina Chon, *Nasdaq's Facebook Problem*, Wall Street Journal, May 21, 2012, at A1.

62. Alexander Scaggs & Matt Jarzemsky, *Kraft Hit by Trading Glitch*, Wall Street Journal, October 4, 2012, at C4.

63. Jerry W. Markham, A Financial History of the United States From the Subprime Crisis to the Great Recession (2006-2009) 690 (2011). Schapiro was seeking to restore the reputation of the SEC after the Enron-era financial scandals and a disturbing lack of involvement during the financial crisis in 2008 and its failure to uncover the massive Madoff Ponzi scheme. Among the activist rules adopted by the SEC under Schapiro was one that requires municipal bond underwriters to pay the issuer a fair and reasonable price for their bonds. That rule raises the issue of what is fair and reasonable. Mary Williams Walsh, *Tighter Rules Are Issued on Municipal Bond Deals*, New York Times, May 5, 2012, at B1. Indeed, that is why markets exist—to determine what is a fair and reasonable price.

in the futures industry but drew criticism from the Chicago Mercantile Exchange (CME) when the SEC proposed them for stocks.

The SEC also proposed a rule in April 2010 that sought to track high-frequency traders by assigning them codes and requiring them to report their trading to the agency when requested.[64] Not long afterward, high-frequency electronic traders were thought to have triggered a "flash crash" on May 6, 2010, that caused a 1,000-point drop in the Dow Jones Industrial Average in the course of a few minutes.[65] The SEC mounted an intensive investigation of the flash crash and issued a report in September 2010, which found that it was triggered by a large mutual fund complex that entered an automated algorithmic order to sell 75,000 E-Mini futures contracts valued at over $4 billion in order to hedge an existing position. The algorithm dictated an execution rate of 9 percent of trading volume without regard to time or price. High-frequency traders responded and drove prices down in the E-Mini futures contract, touching off a stock-market-wide downturn.[66]

In the wake of the flash crash and at the request of the SEC, the exchanges agreed to adopt circuit breakers to interrupt trading when such a sharp downturn begins. Trading was halted on exchanges in various products 265 times during a one-year period after such restrictions were imposed.[67] The trading restrictions adopted in June 2012 required "limit-up" and "limit-down" trading halts for individual stocks like those used in the commodity futures markets. Market-wide circuit breakers were also broadened.[68]

Another computer glitch disrupted U.S. stock markets on August 1, 2012. The problem was caused by computer problems at a brokerage firm, Knight Capital Group Inc., a high-frequency trader. That firm lost some $440 million as a result of that breakdown.[69] A flash crash occurred in crude oil futures trading on September 17, 2012, with crude oil prices dropping by $3 per barrel in less than a minute near the close of trading. The CFTC began an investigation to determine whether high-frequency traders had caused that price break.[70] That was not the first such problem on NYMEX. An algorithmic error occurred on February 3, 2010, at NYMEX, causing a sharp increase in price and volume on the close of the sweet crude futures contract.[71] The NYSE experienced a trading glitch on November 12, 2012 that affected trading in some 200 stocks during the day and required the exchange to set the closing prices for those stocks.[72] The number of computing problems on electronic trading platforms continued to increase, raising further concerns.[73]

---

64. Fawn Johnson, *SEC Plans Trader ID System: Agency Is Trying to Get Its Arms Around "High Frequency" Transactions*, Wall Street Journal, April 15, 2010.

65. Jerry W. Markham, A Financial History of the U.S. From the Subprime Crisis to the Great Recession (2006-2009) 690 (2011). *See also,* Tom Lauricella & Scott Patterson, *Legacy of the Flash Crash: Enduring Worries of Repeat*, Wall Street Journal, Aug. 6, 2010, at A1.

66. Report of the Staffs of the CFTC & SEC to the Joint Advisory Committee on Emerging Regulatory Issues, *Findings Regarding the Market Events on May 6, 2010* (Sept. 30, 2010).

67. Nathaniel Popper, *BATS Flaw, Not So Rare, Data Shows*, New York Times, March 29, 2012, at B1.

68. SEC, *SEC Approves Proposals to Address Extraordinary Volatility in Individual Stocks and Broader Stock Market*, http://www.sec.gov/news/press/2012/2012-107.htm (accessed June 21, 2012).

69. Jenny Strasburg, Tom Lauricella & Scott Patterson, *Electronic Trading Glitches Hit Market*, Wall Street Journal, Aug. 2, 2012, at A1.

70. Jerry A. DiColo & Carolyn Cui, *Crude Oil's Fall Leaves Trail of Queries*, Wall Street Journal, Sept. 18 at C4.

71. Jenny Strasburg & Sarah N. Lynch, *Infinium Is Focus of CME*, Wall Street Journal, Aug. 26, 2010, at C3.

72. Chris Dieterich and Jacob Bunge, *Outage at the Big Board Muddles Day's Trading*, Wall Street Journal, Nov. 13, 2012 at C4.

73. Nathaniel Popper, *In New Year, Errors Mount on High-Speed Exchanges*, New York Times, Jan. 11, 2013 at B1.

The SEC subsequently began an examination of "kill switches"—that is, algorithms used by broker-dealers engaged in high-frequency trading to cancel orders that unexpectedly run amok.[74] The SEC later proposed the adoption of a new Regulation Systems Compliance and Integrity (SCI) that will require electronic trading platforms to determine whether their systems have sufficient capacity, integrity, reliability and security to handle their trading volumes and to promote a fair and orderly market.[75]

The SEC also turned to Section 13(h) of the 34 Act[76] after the flash crash to adopt a large trader reporting system like the one used by the CFTC.[77] Large traders under the new SEC rule 13h-1[78] will be given identifier numbers that will require their trades to be reported to the SEC by their broker-dealers.[79] A large trader was defined as a person whose transactions in National Market System securities equal or exceed 2 million shares or $20 million during any calendar day, or 20 million shares or $200 million during any calendar month.

The Dodd-Frank Act required the SEC to hire an independent consultant to report on the effect of high-frequency trading and other technological advances on the market.[80] Dodd-Frank also required the SEC and the CFTC to conduct a joint study on the feasibility of requiring the derivatives industry to adopt computer-readable algorithmic descriptions for complex and standardized financial derivatives in order to better calculate net exposures to such instruments and to define regulated contracts.[81] The Financial Industry Regulatory Authority (FINRA), the securities industry self-regulatory body, was requiring high-frequency traders to disclose their proprietary algorithms as a part of an investigation into improper trading activities.[82]

This was an indication of the course that future regulation was likely to take: computer vs. computer. The Dodd-Frank Act further opened that door with a provision requiring the SEC and CFTC to conduct a study on the feasibility of requiring the derivatives industry to have standardized computer-readable algorithmic descriptions of derivative products.[83] A CFTC commissioner also sought a budget shift from more staff to technology that would allow more effective surveillance and regulation.[84]

Other electronic trading activities such as "stub quotes" and "naked access" also came under regulatory scrutiny. Stub quotes were price quotations by market makers well away from current market prices. These off-market quotes were used to fulfill exchange market maker obligations. The NYSE and NASDAQ curbed stub quotes by requiring quotes to be within current market ranges.[85] Naked access (sometimes referred to as "sponsored access") involved a practice by

74. *SEC Reviewing Technology at Brokerages Following Glitches*, Reuters, Sept. 27, 2012, http://in.reuters.com/article/2012/09/26/sec-technology-review-idINL1E8KQFE020120926 (accessed September 27, 2012).

75. SEC, Regulation SCI (Systems Compliance and Integrity), 78 Fed. Reg. 18083 (March 8, 2013).

76. 15 U.S.C. § 78m(h).

77. SEC, Securities Exchange Act Release No. 64976, 2011 SEC LEXIS 2573 (July 27, 2011).

78. 17 C.F.R. 240.13h-1.

79. 15 U.S.C. § 78m(h).

80. Dodd-Frank § 967.

81. *Id.* at § 719.

82. Sarah Lynch & Jonathan Spicer, *Exclusive: Regulators Seek Trading Secrets*, Reuters, http://www.reuters.com/article/2011/09/01/us-financial-regulation-algos-idUSTRE7806J420110901 (accessed March 28, 2012).

83. Dodd-Frank Act § 719(b).

84. Jamila Trindle, *CFTC Commissioner Criticizes Agency's Spending*, MarketWatch, http://www.marketwatch.com/story/cftc-commissioner-criticizes-agencys-spending-2011-07-06-1643290 (accessed March 12, 2012).

85. Geoffrey Poitras & Simon Fraser, Handbook of Research on Stock Market Globalization (eds.) ch. 12 (2012).

some broker-dealers that allowed high-frequency traders to access an exchange's trading facilities without broker-dealer intermediation or supervision. The SEC adopted a rule in 2010 that restricted direct access arrangements.[86] The rule prohibits broker-dealers from providing customers with "unfiltered" or "naked" access to an electronic exchange or to an electronic order matching service, which are called Alternative Trading Systems (ATS). It also requires brokers-dealers to adopt risk management and supervisory controls to prevent order errors and ensure compliance with credit restrictions and exposure to customer defaults.[87]

"Flash trades" were another high-frequency trading concern. These are orders that are canceled immediately upon communication or withdrawn if not executed immediately after communication.[88] Such flash orders, sometimes referred to as "quote stuffing,"[89] were specifically authorized by the SEC in Rule 602 of its Regulation NMS (National Market System).[90] SEC Rule 602 thus allowed exchanges to exclude such orders from consolidated quotation data because of their ephemeral nature. However, electronic traders began using flash orders for a variety of purposes and in large amounts. Among other things, the SEC noted that "[f]or those seeking liquidity, the flash mechanism may attract additional liquidity from market participants who are not willing to display their trading interest publicly."[91]

The SEC also noted that some large institutional traders were reluctant to display their own quotations publicly because they do not want to disclose their trading plans to other market participants, but are willing to respond to flash orders on an order-by-order basis. Flash orders also helped reduce the transaction costs of those institutional investors.[92]

The SEC sought public comment in September 2009 on whether its exception from quotation reports should be continued for flash orders. Among other things, the SEC was concerned with the fact that flash orders provided professional short-term traders an advantage over long-term investors.[93] The SEC also discovered that some firms were entering ninety orders for every one executed.[94] The SEC, however, deferred a decision on that issue. Instead, the agency issued a concept release in January 2010 that launched a broad-based review of the current equity market structure to determine whether the agency's rules had kept pace with the growth of electronic trading, including the role of flash orders and "pinging" orders that seek to flush out other traders.[95]

Another concern was "dark pools," which are anonymous trading platforms for stock listed on public markets.[96] Orders placed through an exchange are visible to the public and all other market participants, but an order or an indication of interest entered on a dark pool is revealed only to other dark pool participants. This gives dark pool participants access to information unavailable to the public.

---

86. Tara Bhupathi, *Technology's Latest Market Manipulator? High Frequency Trading: The Strategies, Tools, Risks, and Responses*, 11 N.C.J.L. & Tech. 377, 392-393 (2010).

87. 17 C.F.R. § 240.15c3-5.

88. 74 Fed. Reg. 48632 (Sept. 23, 2009).

89. Tom Lauricella & Jenny Strasburg, *SEC Probes Cancelled Trades*, Wall Street Journal, Sept. 2, 2010, at A1.

90. 17 C.F.R. § 242.602(a)(1)(i)(A).

91. 74 Fed. Reg. 48632, 48638 (Sept. 23, 2009). Securities Exchange Act Release No. 34-60684, 74 Fed. Reg. 48632 (Sept. 23, 2009).

92. 74 Fed. Reg. 48632, 48638, n. 56.

93. 74 Fed. Reg. at 48638.

94. S.*E.C. to Study Rapid-Fire Orders*, New York Times, Sept. 8, 2010, at B9. *See generally*, David D. Gruberg, *Decent Exposure: The SEC's Lack of Authority and Restraint in Proposing to Eliminate Flash Trading*, 65 U. Miami L. Rev. 263 (2010-2011) (criticizing SEC effort to limit flash trades).

95. SEC, *Concept Release on Equity Market Structure*, 75 Fed. Reg. 3594 (Jan. 21, 2010).

96. Austin J. Sandler, *The Invisible Power of Machines: Revisiting the Proposed Flash Order Ban in the Wake of the Flash Crash*, 2011 Duke L. & Tech Rev. 3, n. 18.

"As a result, dark pool participants are able to have their orders filled, while those on publicly displayed markets go unfilled, even though dark pools use the information from publicly displayed markets to price the dark pool transactions. When dark pools share information about their trading interest with other dark pools, they can function like private networks that exclude the public investor."[97]

The SEC proposed rules to limit such exclusions by dark pools.[98] The agency also accused an electronic dark pool operator of improperly sharing trading information with a high-frequency trading affiliate.[99] Another SEC case, which was settled, involved claims that an electronic trading platform had misrepresented the manner in which it filled customer orders.[100] In still another dark pool case in October 2012, the SEC accused a pool of using an affiliate to trade ahead of customer orders. The dark pool paid $1.2 million to settle those charges.[101] The dark pools were, in any event, pulling trading volume away from the New York Stock Exchange (NYSE) as high-frequency traders sought to avoid regulatory scrutiny.[102]

In March 2012, the SEC began investigating whether the securities exchanges were favoring large traders over smaller ones in trading in securities with multiple listings.[103] The SEC was also investigating whether high-frequency traders were colluding to manipulate markets,[104] and it was probing the relationships of high-frequency traders with the electronic exchanges on which they traded.[105] Some traders were claiming that outmoded SEC regulations were encouraging high-frequency trading abuses.[106] In the meantime, high frequency trading was slowing in the U.S. as profits dropped. Profits in 2012 from such trading were projected to be down by 35 percent over the prior year.[107] High frequency traders continued their efforts to forestall regulation that would curb their activities.[108] However, this trading continued to raise concerns after it was reported in March 2013 that the CFTC was investigating to determine whether high frequency traders were engaging in wash sales.[109]

Some of the trading abuses on electronic platforms were familiar ones. The SEC discovered that wash and matched trades were being executed on MarketXT in order to increase payments from vendors of trade data.[110] A related abuse was "trade shredding," which involved splitting

97. SEC Fact Sheet, *Strengthening the Regulation of Dark Pools* (Oct. 21, 2009), http://www.sec.gov/news/press/2009/2009-223-fs.htm (accessed April 21, 2012).

98. *Id.*

99. Scott Patterson & Jenny Strasburg, *Traders Navigate a Murky New World*, WALL STREET JOURNAL, April 9, 2012.

100. Scott Patterson & Jenny Strasburg, *Source's Cover Blown by SEC*, WALL STREET JOURNAL, April 25, 2012 at A1.

101. Jenny Strasburg & Scott Patterson, *'Dark Pool,' SEC Settle*, WALL STREET JOURNAL, Oct. 4, 2012, at C1.

102. Jacob Bunge, *Trading Shift Pinches NYSE Profit*, WALL STREET JOURNAL, May 1, 2012, at C7.

103. Hal Weltzman, Kara Scannell & Telis Demos, *SEC Investigates US Exchanges Operators' Use of Multiple Markets*, FINANCIAL TIMES (LONDON), March 12, 2012, at 1.

104. Scott Patterson & Jean Eaglesham, *SEC Probes Rapid Trading*, WALL STREET JOURNAL, March 23, 2012, at A1.

105. Jean Eaglesham, Jenny Strasburg & Scott Patterson, *SEC Probes Ties to High-Speed Traders*, WALL STREET JOURNAL, April 4, 2012, at C1.

106. Scott Patterson, *Traders See SEC Speed Trap*, WALL STREET JOURNAL, May 9, 2012, at C2.

107. Nathaniel Popper, *High-Speed Trading No Longer Hurtling Forward*, NEW YORK TIMES, Oct. 15, 2012 at C1.

108. Jenny Strasburg and Scott Patterson, *High-Speed Traders Race to Fend Off Regulations*, WALL STREET JOURNAL, Dec. 28, 2012, at A1.

109. Scott Patterson, Jenny Strasburg & Jamila Trindle, *"Wash Trades" Scrutinized*, WALL STREET JOURNAL, March 18, 2013, at C1.

110. Securities Exchange Act Release No. 34-51163 (SEC Feb. 9, 2005). *See also*, Amanat v. SEC, 2008

orders in order to increase revenues from the market data vendors. In another case, respondents were found to have used an electronic platform to engage in wash trades for tax purposes. Still another case involved a failure by an electronic trading platform to provide equal access to market information by subscribers.[111]

Europe was taking a different approach. On September 26, 2012, the Economics and Monetary Affairs Committee of the European Parliament unanimously voted its approval (45–0) of legislation that would restrict high-frequency traders (HFT) in the European Union. The proposed legislation would require HFT orders to be posted for at least one half second, which would considerably reduce the speed of HFT. That committee also sought controls that would curb commodity price speculation by position limits like those used in the United States. It also sought to restrict bank proprietary trading and to push derivative trading in bonds and commodities onto electronic trading platforms that would be separate from the equity exchanges.[112] Germany was simultaneously considering preemptive action against HFTs. The government there enacted a legislative proposal that requires HFTs to register with the German Federal Supervisory Authority. This legislation will assess fees against HFTs that trade "excessively," and they could also be required to disclose their fees algorithms to the government.[113] Canada and Australia were imposing restrictions and fees on HFTs. Canada was also curbing dark pools.[114]

7:4 NEW CFTC ANTIMANIPULATION POWERS UNDER DODD-FRANK

Crude oil and gasoline were not the only commodities to experience sharp price increases before the financial crisis. Corn prices set a new record in June 2007, rising to $7.87 per bushel.[115] Wheat and soybean prices also rose after flooding in the Midwest. Wheat prices surged in early 2008; rice futures prices more than doubled between November 2007 and April 2008; oats saw substantial price increases during the 2007–2008 crop year, and the soybean complex (beans, meal, and oil) reached record highs on March 3, 2008. "Soybeans for May 2008 delivery were $9.40 per bushel in early September 2007, peaked at $15.60 on March 3, 2008, and declined to roughly $13.00 per bushel in May 2008."[116]

"Cotton futures and option prices rose in late 2007 and early 2008, but began a steady increase in February 2008 and spiked in the first week of March 2008."[117] The CFTC staff investigated trading in the Cotton No. 2 futures and option contracts during the week of March 3, 2008, which was when open outcry trading in that contract on the Intercontinental Exchange (ICE) was discon-

---

WL 723890 (3rd Cir. 2008) (court affirms SEC order finding that respondent entered a massive amount of matched orders and wash sales in order to qualify for rebates from NASDAQ).

111. Jerry W. Markham & Daniel J. Harty, *For Whom the Bell Tolls: The Demise of Exchange Trading Floors and the Growth of ECNs*, 33 Iowa J. Corp. L. 865, 924 (2008).

112. Huw Jones, *EU Lawmakers Back Curbs on High Frequency Share Trade*, Reuters, September 26, 2012, http://www.reuters.com/article/2012/09/26/us-eu-mifid-idUSBRE88P1A920120926 (accessed September 27, 2012).

113. Christopher Lawton & Andreas Kissler, *Germany to Tap Brakes on High-Speed Trading*, Wall Street Journal, Sept. 26, 2012, at C1.

114. *See*, Nathaniel Popper, *Beyond Wall St., Curbs on High-Speed Trades Proceed*, New York Times, Sept. 26, 2012.

115. Steven Rattner, *The Great Corn Con*, New York Times, June 24, 2011, at A19.

116. *CFTC Staff Report on Cotton Futures and Option Market Activity During the Week of March 3, 2008*, 10, n. 18 (Jan. 4, 2010).

117. *Id.* at 1.

tinued in favor of electronic trading. The CFTC staff could find no evidence of manipulation.[118] Nevertheless, these price increases and continuing concerns over gasoline prices led to a provision in the Dodd-Frank Act that gave the CFTC additional antimanipulation authority. That legislation failed to stop the rise in cotton prices.

The CFTC fined a Merrill Lynch commodity trading unit $350,000 for exceeding speculative limits on Cotton No. 2 futures trading on ICE in January 2011, but this too had no effect on cotton prices.[119]Cotton prices rose again in March 2012 after India stopped all cotton exports over supply concerns.[120]Fundamentals did reassert themselves a few months later, and cotton prices plunged after the government reported record supplies on hand and India lifted its export ban. Cotton prices jumped 30 percent in June 2012, giving rise to claims that a short squeeze was under way. However, the buying pressure appeared to be coming from China.[121] Proving that fundamentals drive markets, another commodity price explosion was under way in corn in August 2012 as a severe drought cut crop estimates dramatically.[122] The results of this volatility were widespread, including breaking of cotton contracts and a wave of lawsuits.[123]

Section 753 of the Dodd-Frank Act prohibits any "manipulative or deceptive device or contrivance" in violation of CFTC rules adopted within one year of the enactment of that legislation.[124] This "fraud based"[125] provision was intended to create "a strong bright line" as to what constitutes manipulation.[126] Dodd-Frank also amended Section 22 of the CEA to expand available private rights of action by persons who sustain damages "in connection with" the purchase or sale of a futures or swap contract.[127] The amendment allows damages suffered as a result of a manipulation of the price of any futures contract or swap or the price of the commodity underlying such contract or swap. A private right of action was also allowed for damages caused by "any manipulative device or contrivance" that is identified in CFTC rule 180.1.

This amendment meant that the CFTC joined FERC, the FTC, and the SEC as the agencies having the same authority to attack the same practices in commodity price manipulations within the scope of their exclusive and overlapping jurisdictions.[128] Section 753 in Dodd-Frank also added a "special provision" for manipulation by "false reporting." That provision provides a "good faith mistake" exception to this prohibition. This would include mistakenly transmitting, in good faith, false or misleading or inaccurate information to a price reporting service.

118. *Id.* at 5.

119. CFTC, *CFTC Orders Merrill Lynch Commodities, Inc. to Pay $350,000 Civil Penalty for Violating Cotton Futures Speculative Position Limits*, CFTC Press Release No. PR6154-11 (Dec. 7, 2011), http://www.cftc.gov/PressRoom/PressReleases/pr6154-11 (accessed October 9, 2012).

120. Debiprasad Nayak, *India Halts Cotton Exports*, Wall Street Journal, March 5, 2012, at C4.

121. Alexander Wexler, *Cotton Picking on Shorts*, Wall Street Journal, June 20, 2012, at C4.

122. *What's News*, Wall Street Journal, Aug. 11–12, 2012, at A1.

123. Michael Rothfeld & Carolyn Cui, *Plague of Broken Contracts Frays Cotton Market*, Wall Street Journal, Aug. 31, 2012, at A1.

124. Dodd-Frank §§ 753, *codified* at 7 U.S.C. 9(c). This limitation set a deadline of July 21, 2011, for those rules. *Id.*

125. 156 Cong. Rec. S5924 (July 15, 2010) (remarks of Sen. Reed)

126. 156 Cong. Rec. S3348 (May 6, 2010) (remarks of Sen. Cantwell).

127. Dodd-Frank § 753(c).

128. According to Senator Cantwell, this "manipulative or deceptive device or contrivance" provision was added to give the CFTC the same authority previously granted to FERC and which allowed FERC to sanction Amaranth and Energy Trading Partners. 156 Cong. Rec. S3348 (May 6, 2010). The CFTC has also acknowledged this new power is "similar" to that of the SEC, FERC, and FTC. *Prohibition of Market Manipulation*, 75 Fed. Reg. 67,657 (Nov. 3, 2010).

Despite the historical shortcomings of the CFTC's preexisting antimanipulation authority in Section 9(a)(2) of the CEA, Section 753 in Dodd-Frank left that authority intact.[129] Section 753 was thus intended to supplement, rather than supplant, the "existing anti-manipulation authority for other types of manipulative conduct. Nor does it negate or undermine any of the case law that has developed construing the CEA's existing anti-manipulation provisions."[130]

Section 753 borrowed the "manipulative or deceptive device or contrivance" language from Section 10(b) of the 34 Act. Material included in the *Congressional Record* by its Senate sponsor, Maria Cantwell (D-WA), stated that Section 753 addresses "fraud based manipulation, including manipulation by false reporting."[131] Cantwell stated that the "language in this amendment is patterned after the law that the SEC uses to go after fraud and manipulation; that there can be no manipulative devices or contrivances. It is a strong and clear legal standard that allows regulators to successfully go after reckless and manipulative behavior."[132]

The CFTC has also asserted that this new authority was a "broad, catch-all provision reaching fraud in all its forms—that is, intentional or reckless conduct that deceives or defrauds market participants."[133] The CFTC urged that the new authority "be given a broad, remedial reading, embracing the use or employment, or attempted use or employment, of any manipulative or deceptive contrivance for the purpose of impairing, obstructing, or defeating the integrity of the markets subject to the jurisdiction of the Commission."[134]

The CFTC proposed a new rule, Rule 180.1, to implement its authority under Section 753.[135] The CFTC stated that its proposed rule was "modeled on SEC Rule 10b-5, with modification to reflect the CFTC's distinct regulatory mission and responsibilities."[136] Proposed Rule 180.1 sought to prohibit and make it unlawful to "intentionally or recklessly" (i) "employ any manipulative device, scheme, or artifice to defraud;" (ii) "make any untrue or misleading statement of a material fact or to omit to state a material fact; or (iii) engage in any act, practice, or course of business, which operates or would operate as a fraud or deceit upon any person." The CFTC also added a provision not found in Rule 10b-5, *viz*, to "knowingly or recklessly deliver" a "false or misleading or inaccurate report concerning crop or market information or conditions that affect or tend to affect the price of any commodity."[137]

The CFTC set forth its views on the appropriate scienter standard for violations of proposed Rule 180.1. The CFTC asserted that Rule 180.1 is directed at "fraud and fraud-based manipulative devices and contrivances employed intentionally or recklessly, regardless of whether the conduct in question was intended to create or did create an artificial price."[138] That provision sought to read out the most difficult elements of proof under the CFTC's old manipulation authority—that is, the intent to create, and creation of, an artificial price.

---

129. 7 U.S.C. § 13(a)(2).

130. Cong. Rec. S5924 (July 15, 2010). *See also,* Statement of Senator Lincoln on Section 753 (Senator Cantwell's amendment "will supplement the CFTC's existing standards . . .") 156 Cong. Rec. S3349 (May 6, 2010).

131. 156 Cong. Rec. S5924 (July 15, 2010).

132. 156 Cong. Rec. S3348 (May 6, 2010) (remarks of Sen. Cantwell).

133. *Prohibition of Market Manipulation,* 75 Fed. Reg. 67657, 67659 (Nov. 3, 2010).

134. 75 Fed. Reg. at 67659.

135. *Prohibition of Market Manipulation,* 75 Fed. Reg. 67657 (Nov. 3, 2010).

136. 75 Fed. Reg. at 67659.

137. 75 Fed. Reg. at 67659.

138. CFTC Office of Public Affairs, *Q & A—Anti-Manipulation and Anti-Fraud Final Rules* (2011), http://www.cftc.gov/ucm/groups/public/@newsroom/documents/file/amaf_qa_final.pdf (accessed August 10, 2011).

The CFTC stated that scienter "in this context refers to a mental state embracing intent to deceive, manipulate or defraud, and it includes recklessness."[139] "[O]nly intentional or reckless conduct," not just "negligent conduct, even gross negligence," will satisfy this scienter requirement.[140] The CFTC stated that judicial precedent under Rule 10b-5 should "guide, but not control," the interpretation of the scienter standard under its new proposed rule.

The CFTC sought "sufficient leeway" to permit application of the scienter standard to Rule 180.1 in a way "that comports with the purposes of the CEA and the functioning of the markets regulated by the CFTC." This meant to the CFTC that its proposed scienter standard would be "tailored to the facts and circumstances of each case."[141] In other words, it means whatever the CFTC might want it to mean in any particular case.[142]

The CFTC also addressed the "in connection with" requirement contained in the statutory language adopted by Dodd-Frank from Section 10(b) of the 34 Act by stating that the CFTC would be "guided" by securities law precedent. That standard would "be satisfied whenever misstatements . . . are made in a manner reasonably calculated to influence market participants."[143] This actually seems to be another scienter requirement, as opposed to a jurisdictional requirement of "in connection with" that the Supreme Court established under Rule 10b-5 (discussed in Chapter 5).

The CFTC asserted that "the common law elements of fraud, reliance, loss causation, and damages, are not required to establish a violation" of Rule 180.1 in the context of a CFTC enforcement action."[144] Rather, the CFTC believed that "[r]eliance, loss causation and damages are elements of private claims."[145] The CFTC stated that this distinction is necessary "because the government's duty is to enforce the remedial and preventative terms of the statute in the public interest, and not merely to police those whose plain violations have already caused demonstrable loss or injury."[146] Dodd-Frank, however, injected damages and reliance in CFTC actions by allowing restitution in CFTC enforcement actions only to customers who have sustained losses proximately caused by violations and only in the amount of such losses.[147]

The CFTC addressed the materiality standard and again turned to Rule 10b-5 precedent for guidance. It approved the Supreme Court's standards for misrepresentations and omissions under Section 10(b) of the 34 Act.[148] The CFTC asserted that statements of optimism (or "puffery") alone are not material.[149] The CFTC also noted that Dodd-Frank included a provision in its new antimanipulation authority that no CFTC rule "shall require any person to disclose to another person nonpublic information that may be material to the market price, rate, or level of the commodity transaction, except as necessary to make any statement made to the other person in or in connection with the transaction not misleading in any material respect."[150] This provision preserved the historical rejection of the application of the SEC's insider trading concept to the securities markets.

---

139. 75 Fed. Reg. at 67659 (footnotes omitted).

140. 75 Fed. Reg. at 67659 (footnotes omitted).

141. 75 Fed. Reg. at 67659.

142. This attitude was consistent with an ongoing effort in Congress that sought to make criminal prosecutions easier, but threatened to sweep up innocuous and unintentional conduct as well. *See*, Gary Fields & John R. Emshwiller, *As Federal Crime List Grows, Threshold of Guilt Declines*, WALL STREET JOURNAL, Sept. 27, 2011, at A1 (describing this process).

143. 75 Fed. Reg. at 67659-60 (footnote omitted).

144. 75 Fed. Reg. at 67659-60 (footnote omitted).

145. 75 Fed. Reg. at 67660 (footnote omitted).

146. 75 Fed. Reg. at 67660 (footnote omitted).

147. Dodd-Frank § 744.

148. 75 Fed. Reg. at 67660.

149. 75 Fed. Reg. at 67660.

150. 75 Fed. Reg. at 67660, n. 32.

The CFTC sought to prohibit attempted manipulation under its proposed Rule 180.1.[151] The CFTC stated that this would require showing only the "(1) the requisite intent and (2) an overt act in furtherance of that intent."[152] This attempted manipulation standard seemed unnecessary and redundant, however, in light of the CFTC's effort to eliminate reliance, loss causation, and damages from its burden of proof for even actual violations.

The CFTC proposed another new rule, Rule 180.2, that "mirrors" its prior manipulation and attempted manipulation statutory authority under the Commodity Exchange Act.[153] However, the CFTC sought some wiggle room to expand the old precedents under that provision, stating that it proposed to "continue interpreting the prohibition on price manipulation and attempted price manipulation to encompass every effort to influence the price of a swap, commodity, or commodity futures contract that is intended to interfere with the legitimate forces of supply and demand in the marketplace."[154] The CFTC stated that it "reaffirms this broad reading of the term 'manipulation' . . . while also recognizing that manipulation cases are fact-intensive and that the law in this area will continue to evolve largely on a case-by-case basis."[155]

The CFTC then sought to vastly ease the prior manipulation standards imposed under the old Commodity Exchange Act provisions. It attempted to remove the requirement of an artificial price under its old standards, which had bogged commodity manipulation cases down into duels between experts on whether prices were artificial. The CFTC based that claim on an old CEA case, *In the Matter of Henner*,[156] which the CFTC had successfully relied on in the *DiPlacido* case to win its first-ever contested manipulation case under the Commodity Exchange Act.[157]

The CFTC stated that the CEA cases established a "conclusive presumption" of manipulation when a party enters orders above the existing market price and that further proof of an artificial price is unnecessary. "Cases of this nature, where distorted prices foreseeably follow from the device employed by the manipulator, do not require detailed economic analysis of the effect on prices."[158] The CFTC noted that economic analysis might in some cases be appropriate for determining whether the conduct "actually caused an artificial price. The Commission stresses, however, that an illegal effect on price can often be conclusively presumed from the nature of the conduct in question and other factual circumstances not requiring expert economic analysis."[159]

The CFTC then proceeded to rewrite the old CEA manipulation law even further to the point that it would become a completely new standard. The CFTC "emphasiz[ed]" that, "consistent with the weight of existing precedent, . . . the conduct giving rise to a manipulation charge need not itself be fraudulent or otherwise illegal." The CFTC asserted that this claim was supported by *DiPlacido*, an unpublished Second Circuit opinion, the "landmark" *Henner* decision, and *In the Matter of Zenith-Godley*.[160] The CFTC stated that the conduct

151. 75 Fed. Reg. at 67660.

152. 75 Fed. Reg. at 67660 (footnote omitted).

153. 75 Fed. Reg. at 67660.

154. 75 Fed. Reg. at 67660 (footnote omitted).

155. 75 Fed. Reg. at 67660.

156. 30 Ag. Dec. 1151 (C.E.A. 1971).

157. In the Matter of DiPlacido, Comm. Fut. L. Rep. ¶ 30, 970 (C.F.T.C. 2008), *aff'd sub nom.*, DiPlacido v. CFTC, No. 08-5559-ag, 2009 U.S. App. LEXIS 22692 (2d Cir. 2009), *cert denied*, 2010 U.S. LEXIS 2461 (2010).

158. 75 Fed. Reg. at 67661.

159. 75 Fed. Reg. at 67661.

160. In re Zenith Godley, 6 Ag. Dec. 900 (C.E.A. 1947). The *Zenith-Godley* case hardly supported a

in those cases was not found to be "intrinsically fraudulent or otherwise illegal apart from violating the CEA."[161]

After reviewing comments on its proposed rule, the CFTC adopted Rule 180.1,[162] with a minor exception, as proposed.[163] In adopting the rule, however, the CFTC stated that it was providing clarification and interpretative guidance for the benefit of commentators.[164] It stated that Rule 180.1 was patterned after SEC Rule 10b-5, except that Rule 180.1 additionally bars attempted violations as well as actual ones. The CFTC also did not include a "purchaser or seller" requirement in Rule 180.1.[165] The CFTC further asserted that to "account for the differences between the securities markets and the derivatives markets, the Commission will be guided, but not controlled, by the substantial body of judicial precedent applying the comparable language of SEC Rule 10b-5."[166] This again seemed to signal that the CFTC would pick or reject those cases and requirements applied in Rule 10b-5 cases whenever necessary to aid its cause in any particular case. That hardly gives notice to traders as to what conduct is legal or illegal. They are left to guess at what the CFTC, or the courts, might selectively determine is prohibited conduct.[167]

The CFTC declined to adopt a broad SEC insider trading prohibition into Rule 180.1 because of the prohibition in Dodd-Frank against such claims.[168] The CFTC, therefore, conceded that "it is not a violation of final Rule 180.1 to withhold information that a market participant lawfully possesses about market conditions . . . either in an anonymous market setting or in bilateral negotiations."[169] Nevertheless, the CFTC stated that disclosure of material nonpublic information is required when necessary to make any statement made to the other person in or in connection with the transaction not misleading.

The CFTC adopted the misappropriation theory for nonpublic information. It stated that Rule 180.1 "prohibits trading on the basis of material nonpublic information in breach of a pre-existing duty (established by another law or rule, agreement, understanding, or some other source) and trading on the basis of material nonpublic information that was obtained through fraud or deception."[170] The CFTC declined to adopt a fraud-on-the-market theory for private actions under Rule 180.1. The CFTC posited that its own actions would be unaffected by such

---

claim of innocent conduct. In that case, the Dairyman's League Cooperative Association of New York was found to have manipulated spot butter prices in order to increase fluid milk prices, which were set on the basis of Grade A butter prices. The respondents bought 97 percent of the butter sold on the exchange during a five-day period and increased the price of butter by 1.5 cents. After the League stopped its trading, prices dropped by 10 cents. The trading substantially increased price differences between Chicago and New York butter, causing butter to be sent to New York from Chicago.

161. 75 Fed. Reg. at 67661.

162. 17 C.F.R. § 180.1

163. 76 Fed. Reg. 41398 (July 14, 2011).

164. 76 Fed. Reg. at 41399.

165. 76 Fed. Reg. at 41399, n. 6.

166. 76 Fed. Reg. at 41399.

167. In *Stoller v. CFTC*, 834 F.2d 262 (1987), the Second Circuit reversed a CFTC finding of violations under Section 4(c) for wash trades used by a trader to move back to the end of the delivery line (oldest longs are the first to receive delivery notices and so the trader "refreshed" his position with wash trades). The CFTC had shifted its definition of a wash sale and conceded at oral argument that a sale immediately followed by a buy would not be a prohibited wash sale, because there would be market risk no matter how brief the exposure to the market. The court was unable to accept that "subtle and refined" distinction between a prohibited wash sale and bona fide trading and reversed the case. 834 F.2d at 267.

168. 76 Fed. Reg. at 41402. *See*, Dodd-Frank § 753.

169. 76 Fed. Reg. at 41402.

170. CFTC Office of Public Affairs, *Q & A—Anti-Manipulation and Anti-Fraud Final Rules* (2011).

a requirement because, in the CFTC's view, it was not required to prove reliance in its own enforcement actions.[171]

The CFTC's adopting release reiterated its prior assertion that it was unnecessary for the government to prove price or market effect to establish a violation of Rule 180.1.[172] As for scienter, the CFTC stated that it would define recklessness as conduct that "'departs so far from the standards of ordinary care that it is very difficult to believe the actor was not aware of what he or she was doing.' Proof of knowledge, however, is not required."[173] The CFTC declined to take a position on the "collective knowledge" theory of liability that had split the circuit courts—that is, that the conduct of one corporate agent can be combined with another corporate agent's state of mind in order to hold a corporation liable for fraud.[174] The CFTC also stated that the "in connection with" language of its rule would be broadly interpreted in the same manner as the federal securities laws. That broad interpretation would apply to cross-market manipulation cases.[175] Finally, the CFTC declined to adopt a new economics-based definition of manipulation.[176]

With respect to Rule 180.2, the CFTC stated that it would continue to apply its traditional four-part test for manipulation, including the requirement that a person act with the required specific intent. "In other words, recklessness will not suffice under final Rule 180.2 as it will under final Rule 180.1. The Commission finds this level of intent necessary to ensure that legitimate conduct is not captured by final Rule 180.2, which covers non-fraud based manipulation."[177] The CFTC backed down a bit from its language in the proposing release that an artificial price may be "conclusively presumed" in some cases, stating that this did not mean that an artificial price may be conclusively presumed in all cases.[178] The CFTC also interpreted the "indirectly" language in Rule 180.2 to include cases in which an individual uses a third party, such as an executing broker, to conduct a manipulation.[179]

7:5 "SPOOFING"

Section 747 of the Dodd-Frank Act amended Section 4(c) of the Commodity Exchange Act[180] by expanding its prohibitions to include other "disruptive" trading such as "spoofing," which involves bidding or offering with the intent to cancel the bid or offer before execution.[181] Another prohibition

---

171. 76 Fed. Reg. at 41403.
172. 76 Fed. Reg. at 41403.
173. 76 Fed. Reg. at 41404 (footnotes and citations omitted).
174. 76 Fed. Reg. at 41405. *See generally*, Patricia S. Abril & Ann Morales Olazabal, *The Locus of Corporate Scienter*, 2006 Colum. Bus. L. Rev. 81 (discussing this concept); Michael J. Kaufman & John M. Wunderlich, *The Core Operations Inference in Private Securities Fraud Litigation* (July 14, 2011). Available at SSRN: http://ssrn.com/abstract=1885650 (same).
175. 76 Fed. Reg. at 41406.
176. *Id.*
177. 76 Fed. Reg. at 41407.
178. 76 Fed. Reg. at 41408.
179. 76 Fed. Reg. at 41408.
180. 7 U.S.C. § 6c.
181. As was noted on the Senate floor,

> The Dodd-Lincoln bill strengthens existing law to target specific market abuses that have arisen in recent years. These abuses are outlawed as disruptive practices in section 747 of the underlying bill.

Cong Rec. S3349 (May 6, 2010) (remarks of Sen. Lincoln).

was directed at violating existing bids and offers of other traders. In addition, under Section 747, the CFTC now has the authority to prohibit "any other trading practice that is disruptive of fair and equitable trading." The CFTC had asked for the authority to regulate these types of practice in a joint report with the SEC on harmonization of regulation.[182]

The CFTC sought public comment on what approach it should take in adopting rules to implement this new Section 4(c) authority.[183] The agency sought comment on nineteen questions concerning the scope of this authority. Among other things, the CFTC sought comment on how it should distinguish between orderly and disorderly trading; whether brokers should have an obligation to ensure that customer orders are not disruptive; how it should distinguish "spoofing" from other, legitimate trading activity; and what other practices should be classified as disruptive.[184] It questioned whether orders (as well as executed trades) should be included as disruptive practices.

The CFTC was particularly concerned with manipulative activity during the closing period on exchanges when settlement prices were set because those prices are used to price cash market or other positions.[185] Dodd-Frank prohibited any practice that "demonstrates intentional or reckless disregard for the orderly execution of transactions during the closing period." The legislative history and earlier bill versions suggest that this is the equivalent of "marking the close," otherwise referred to as "banging the close" or "painting the tape."[186]

Painting the tape has also been the subject of concern by the SEC in the securities markets.[187] Indeed, the issue was raised in the hearings that led to the enactment of the 34 Act. A witness there thus complained of manipulations involving "buying at the close every day enough to take all the stock that was offered and close it an eighth higher each day, and as they manipulated the stock up they had their employees and high-pressure men out through the country distributing stock on the strength of the quotations that were made on these legitimate exchanges."[188]

"Marking the close" has also been the subject of judicial decisions in the securities industry.[189] In *United States v. Georgiou*,[190] a district court noted that "marking the close . . . is a form of market manipulation that involve[s] attempting to influence the closing price of a publicly trade[d] share by executing purchase or sale orders at or near the close of normal trading hours. Such activity can artificially inflate or depress the closing price for that security and can affect the price of the

---

182. *A Joint Report of the SEC and the CFTC on Harmonization of Regulation* 92 (Oct. 16, 2009).

183. CFTC, *Advance Notice of Proposed Rulemaking; Request for Comments, Antidisruptive Practices Authority Contained in the Dodd-Frank Wall Street Reform and Consumer Protection Act*, 75 Fed. Reg. 67301 (Nov. 2, 2010). The CFTC staff also held a roundtable discussion on December 2, 2010, seeking input on how it should implement this new authority. http://www.cftc.gov/ucm/groups/public/@swaps/documents/dfsubmission/dfsubmission24_120210-transcri.pdf.

184. 75 Fed. Reg. at 67301.

185. *See, e.g.*, In the Matter of DiPlacido, COMM. FUT. L. REP. ¶ 30, 970 (C.F.T.C. 2008), *aff'd sub nom.*, DiPlacido v. CFTC, 2009 U.S. App. LEXIS 22692 (2d Cir. 2009), *cert denied*, 2010 U.S. LEXIS 2461 (2010).

186. *See*, Senate Engrossed Version, 156 Cong. Rec. S4239-02 (May 20, 2010).

187. *See, e.g.*, SEC v. Masri, 523 F. Supp. 2d 361, 367 (S.D.N.Y. 2007); SEC v. Drexel Burnham Lambert Inc., SEC Litig. Rel. No. 11859, 1988 SEC LEXIS 1865 (S.D.N.Y.); SEC v. Jefferies, SEC Litig. Rel. No. 2314, 1987 SEC LEXIS 2314 (S.D.N.Y.).

188. *Stock Exchange Practices: Hearing Before the Senate Committee on Banking and Currency on S. Res. 84 and S. Res. 56, and S. Res. 97*, 73d Cong., 1st Sess. 7019 (1934).

189. *See generally, e.g.*, SEC v. Kwak, 2008 WL 410427 (D. Conn. 2008) (manipulation through matching trades and marking the close). In *SEC v. Wilson*, 2009 WL 2381954 (D. Conn. 2009), the SEC was ordered to pay attorney fees when it failed to prove manipulation violations involving wash trades and marking the close.

190. United States v. Georgiou, 742 F. Supp. 2d 613, 624 (E.D. Pa. 2010).

market on close orders, which are orders submitted to purchase shares at or near as possible to the closing price."[191]

The securities exchanges, has long struggled with this problem, having rules regulating trading in the closing period that are designed to suppress such disruptive trading, especially activities that affect market-on-close orders. New York Stock Exchange Rule 123C, for example, regulated the entry, modifications, and cancellations of market-on-close and limit-on-close orders. NYSE ARCA Equities, an electronic trading platform, uses a Dutch auction to set the closing price at a level that will result in the most executions.[192]

---

191. *See also*, United States v. Gilbert, 1981 WL 1662 (S.D.N.Y. 1981) (convictions for "painting the tape" in violation of Sections 9 and 10(b) of the 34 Act upheld); SEC v. Schiffer, 1998 WL 307375 (S.D.N.Y. 1998) (marking-the-close in order to increase the price of a stock in violation of Sections 9 and 10(b) of the 34 Act and Section 17(a) of the 33 Act); T.H.C. Inc. v. Fortune Petroleum Corp., 1999 WL 182593 (S.D.N.Y.) (marking the close allegations sufficiently pleaded under Section 10(b) of the 34 Act); Black v. Finantra Capital Inc., 418 F.3d 203 (2d Cir. 2005) (jury verdict upheld in finding Section 10(b) violations in a scheme that involved marking the close); SEC v. Parnes, 2001 WL 1658275 (S.D.N.Y.) (complaint failed adequately to plead violations of Section 10(b) of the 34 Act upheld and Section 17(a) of the 33 Act because it did not specify which individual defendants engaged in marking-the-close); Nanopierce Technologies Inc. v. Southridge Capital Management LLC, 2002 WL 31819207 (S.D.N.Y.) (painting the tape allegations adequately pleaded under Section 10(b)); Compudyne Corp. v. Shane, 453 F. Supp. 2d 807, 823 (S.D.N.Y. 2006) (pleadings sufficient under Section 10(b) where it was alleged that defendants manipulated the price of ITIS stock by "dumping a large volume of stock on the market," by employing "pre-arranged sales" and "short sales," by "covering short positions," and by "painting the tape."); Jag Media Holdings Inc. v. A.G. Edwards & Sons Inc., 387 F. Supp. 2d 691, 696 (S.D. Tex. 2004) (plaintiffs claimed that "[t]his manipulation was achieved through the use of various trading techniques such as matched trades, washed trades, 'painting the tape' and selling counterfeit shares (*i.e.*, 'naked short sales')" in death spiral short-selling scheme but allegations inadequate to establish Section 10(b) claim); SEC v. Lauer, 2008 WL 4372896 (S.D.N.Y. 2008) (collateral estoppel found on claims of the "following manipulative trading practices: (1) they dominated and controlled the markets for these securities by preventing the natural operation of supply and demand; (2) they prevented a competitive market from developing for these securities; (3) they marked the close; (4) they engaged in economically irrational trading; (5) they engaged in matched trades; and (6) they failed to disclose their control"). *Compare*, *Pension Committee v. Bank of America Securities LLC*, 592 F. Supp. 2d 608, 627 (S.D. N.Y. 2009) (defendant not on notice of painting the tape scheme by Lauer); Internet Law Library Inc. v. Southridge Capital Management LLC, 223 F. Supp. 2d 474, 480 (S.D.N.Y. 2002) (defendants were alleged to have made use of a multitude of manipulative techniques in a "death spiral" downward manipulation scheme including "painting the tape," "hitting the bids," and "dumping" large amounts of stock on the market, with an eye toward artificially affecting the price of the stock). *But see* limitation of this decision in *ATSI Communications Inc. v. Shaar Fund Ltd.*, 493 F.3d 87, 106 (2d Cir. 2007). In *SEC v. Competitive Technologies Inc.*, 2005 WL 1719725 (D. Conn. 2005), the court held that allegations were sufficient for alleging violations of Section 9 and 10(b) of the 34 Act that involved "several techniques that served to create a misleading appearance of active trading and increased demand for the stock. The defendants placed late-day orders to raise the reported closing price of the stock (*i.e.*, 'marking the close'), placed successive, small-amount buy orders in increasing prices to simulate increased demand (*i.e.*, 'painting the tape'), and arranged identical buy and sell orders and other buy orders, to simulate active trading and to offset the impact of other sales of the stock (*i.e.*, 'matching orders')." *See also*, SEC v. Kwak, 2008 WL 410427 (D. Conn. 2008) (jury verdict upheld on claims defendants manipulated the stock of Competitive Technologies Inc. "by 'matching trades' in violation of section 9(a)(1) [of the 34 Act] and by 'marking the close' in violation of section 9(a)(2)' of that statute). *But see*, SEC v. Wilson, 2009 WL 2381954 (D. Conn. 2009) (jury finds for one defendant); SEC v. Zico Investment Holdings, SEC Litigation Release No. 11763 (S.D.N.Y. 1988) (consent injunction to charges that stock was manipulated downward in order to aid a takeover attempt; trades were made through a London account on a U.S. exchange at the close of trading over a four-day period).

192. NYSE ARCA Equities, http://www.nyse.com/equities/nysearcaequities/1157623605155.html (accessed May 3, 2012). BATS uses a similar approach. If there are inadequate orders to set a viable price, BATS uses the last execution price for eligible trades. BATS, US Equities Auction Process, http://www. batstrading. com/resources/membership/BATS_Auction_Process.pdf (accessed May 5, 2012).

FINRA Rule 6140 stated that "[n]o member shall offer that a transaction or transactions to buy or sell a designated security will influence the closing transaction in that security." Traders may be sanctioned for violations of those rules. For example, the National Association of Securities Dealers (NASD), FINRA's predecessor, sanctioned a trader for manipulative market-on-close sell orders at artificially low prices. Those orders allowed the respondent to purchase stock from his customer at the artificially low price established by his last trade.[193]

The CFTC also sought public comment on whether rules should be adopted under the new Section 747 Dodd-Frank authority that would regulate algorithmic trading. The CFTC noted that electronic trading system algorithms preclude order executions other than at the best available price. However, it expressed concern with whether a trader in an illiquid market should be allowed to "buy the board" and then enter a bid at a higher price. The CFTC asked whether it should require electronic trading systems to adopt algorithmic rules to prevent disruptive trading practices.[194] The CFTC further queried whether executing brokers should be responsible for trader activity and whether special supervisory requirements should be imposed.[195] CFTC chair Gary Gensler stated separately that there is no assurance trading algorithms are well designed by traders but that the role of the government has never included regulating trading strategies.[196]

The CFTC asked a number of questions on how "spoofing" should be defined. Should it include a larger than needed order that was entered to insure execution but was expected to be canceled in part? Does it include multiple orders that are canceled in order to move prices or give a false appearance of liquidity?

Spoofing was initially a manipulative Internet practice[197] that involved fraud schemes that altered or falsified the source of emails.[198] "[A]n unscrupulous user may, for example, create a posting that is seemingly authored by a public company officer in order to manipulate the company's stock. Ostensibly, an investor may recognize the named author of a particular posting and trust the information contained therein as accurate; however, the author of the posting may not actually be the purported company official but rather an impostor attempting to manipulate the stock price."[199] Consistent with that Internet-age definition is *SEC v. Dorozhko*,[200] in which the defendant was charged with hacking into a company's computer system to acquire and trade on

193. FINRA News Release, *NASD Suspends and Sanctions Trader for Marking the Close; Issues Cautionary Note Prior to Russell 2000 Rebalance* (June 26, 2002). *See also*, *Regulators Examining Market-Close Stock Surges*, NEW YORK TIMES, Oct. 24, 2008 (investigations of trading near the close while the market was evidencing unusual volatility).

194. 75 Fed. Reg. at 67301.

195. 75 Fed. Reg. at 67301.

196. Tom Steinert-Threlkeld, Gensler: Regulators Can't Assume Algos Are Designed Well, Securities Technology Monitor, March 29, 2012, http://www.securitiestechnologymonitor.com/news/cftc-to-consider-automated-processes-concept-release-30276-1.html?utm_source=dlvr.it& utm_medium=facebook (accessed April 19, 2012).

197. The term "spoofing" seems to have originated as the name of a card game invented by an English comedian, Arthur Roberts, in the 1880s. The term came to mean a hoax or the gentle mocking of someone. WEBSTER'S NEW UNIVERSAL UNABRIDGED DICTIONARY 1843 (1996).

198. *See*, Wendler & Erza P.C. v. Am. Int'l Group, 521 F.3d 790, 791 (7th Cir. 20) ("'Spoofing' means taking steps that make a message appear to originate from an address other than its actual source"); United States v. Vosburgh, 602 F.3d 512, 525 (4th Cir. 2010), *cert. denied*,—U.S.—(2011) (same). This may include schemes that make it "appear that one is using a specific router when in fact one is secretly using a different router . . . or 'Internet hijacking.'" United States v. Latham, 379 Fed. Appx. 570, 571 (9th Cir. 2010) (unpublished opinion).

199. Nancy Toross, *Double-Click on This: Keeping Pace With On-Line Market Manipulation*, 32 LOY. L.A.L. REV. 1399, 1418-1419 (1999) (footnotes omitted).

200. 606 F. Supp. 2d 321, 325 (S.D.N.Y. 2008).

inside information. The defendant concealed his identity by spoofing—that is, routing his attack through an IP address in the Netherlands that was not the actual user. The district court dismissed the charges, finding no duty to disclose on the part of the hacker, and no manipulation. The Second Circuit reversed, holding that a defendant may commit fraud by misrepresenting himself to gain access to nonpublic information.[201]

In 2000 the NASD (now FINRA) gave "spoofing" a somewhat different definition in an investigation of a practice in which orders are placed and then canceled before execution in order to attract market interest.[202] In *In the Matter of Yoshikawa*,[203] the SEC upheld NASD sanctions imposed on a trader for "fraudulently entering orders designed to improve the price of certain securities and then rapidly placing larger orders on the opposite side of the market from that of his initial order in order to take advantage of the price change he had caused." The SEC also noted that it had settled several cases involving similar conduct, a practice it called "auto-execution manipulation."[204]

More recently, FINRA sanctioned a firm for entering legitimate limit orders and numerous non–bona fide orders in order to attract market interest to its legitimate orders. Securities regulators were also looking at "layering," which involves sending out a large number of orders and wash trading in order to make a market look liquid.[205] That investigation grew after it was discovered that a day trading firm, Swift Trade Inc., had created a global network of traders that were layering securities. The Financial Services Authority in London fined Swift $13 million for such abusive trading. FINRA also planned an action against the firm.[206]

In another case that was settled by consent, the SEC defined layering as follows:

> Layering concerns the use of non-bona fide orders, or orders that the trader does not intend to have executed, to induce others to buy or sell the security at a price not representative of actual supply and demand. More specifically, a trader places a buy (or sell) order that is intended to be executed, and then immediately enters numerous non-bona fide sell (or buy) orders for the purpose of attracting interest to the bona fide order. These non-bona fide orders are not intended to be executed. The nature of these orders is to induce, or trick, other market participants to execute against the initial, bona fide order. Immediately after the execution against the bona fide order, the trader cancels the open, non-bona fide orders, and repeats this strategy on the opposite side of the market to close out the position.[207]

---

201. SEC v. Dorozhko, 574 F.3d 42 (2d Cir. 2009).

202. John Connor, *No Joke: NASD Plans Crackdown on 'Spoofing,' Placing and Canceling a Quote to Spark a Move*, Wall Street Journal, Feb. 28, 2000, at C9.

203. In the Matter of Yoshikawa, 2006 SEC LEXIS 948, n. 36 (S.E.C. 2006).

204. *See also, Securities Trader Accused of 'Spoofing' Agrees to Nearly $350K FINRA Settlement*, 43 Sec. Reg. & L. Rep. (BNA) 1741 (Aug. 22, 2011) (FINRA settlement for trader entering numerous orders in one account to push up the national best bid or offer. He canceled those orders after executing an order on the opposite side of the market at that more favorable price for another account).

205. Tom Steinert-Threlkeld, *Regulators Finishing Probes on "Layering," "Spoofing" of Trades*, Securities Technology Monitor, May 24, 2012, http://www.tradersmagazine.com/news/layering-spoofing-trades-equities-110033-1.html.

206. Scott Patterson, *Regulators Target Day-Trading Firm*, Wall Street Journal, July 31, 2012, at A1.

207. In the Matter of Hold Brothers On-Line Investment Services, LLC, 2012 SEC LEXIS 3029 (S.E.C.). *See also*, Scott Patterson, *Day-Trading Titan Fined*, Wall Street Journal, Dec. 19, 2012, at C4 (SEC imposes fines for layering); In the Matter of Biremis Corp. Fed. Sec. L. Rep. (CCH) ¶ 80,222 (S.E.C. 2013) SEC administrative proceeding settlement for layering).

In still another case that was settled by consent, the SEC charged a spoofing manipulation of the National Best Bid or Offer (NBBO) market maker stock quotes. The SEC found violations of its limit order display rule,[208] which required NASDAQ market makers to display public customer limit orders that were priced better than the market maker's NBBO quote or that constituted an increase in the size of the market maker's quote. The respondent placed several buy limit orders on an electronic trading platform, which became the new NBBO. The respondent then almost immediately placed opposing orders through another account and then quickly canceled the first orders, sticking the market makers with execution of the second set of orders at an artificially high price. It was a petty scheme, bringing in profits of about $18,000.[209]

In the event, the CFTC decided to change course on its approach to Section 747 of Dodd-Frank. Instead of adopting a rule to implement its provisions, the CFTC issued a proposed interpretive order intended to provide market participants with guidance concerning the types of trading, conduct, and practices prohibited by its new disruptive trading practices authority.[210] The CFTC interpreted Section 747 of Dodd-Frank to prohibit a trader from buying or selling a contract at other than the best available price. The CFTC opined that this was a "per se offense, that is, the Commission is not required to show that a person violating bids or offers did so with any intent to disrupt fair and equitable trading."[211] The CFTC stated that this interpretation would not apply to automatically executed orders in an electronic trading system over which the trader has no control. Further, it does not create a "best execution" requirement, like that in the securities industry, for trades made across multiple platforms.[212] It would also not apply to orders that "buy the board.[213]

The CFTC further interpreted Section 747's prohibitions to include trading activities that demonstrate "intentional or reckless disregard for the orderly execution of transactions during the closing period."[214] The House version of Section 747 of Dodd-Frank had only referred to intentional acts for orderly executions during the closing period, but the Senate version widened the standard to include reckless disregard.[215] The CFTC stated that the "inclusion of a scienter requirement means that accidental, or even negligent, trading conduct and practices will not suffice . . . ; rather a market participant must at least act recklessly."[216] The CFTC interpreted the "closing period" to be the period when the daily settlement price is determined by the rules of the trading facility. The CFTC said that violations during the closing period will "include executed orders as well as any bids and offers submitted by individuals for the purposes of disrupting fair and equitable trading."[217]

---

208. 17 C.F.R. § 24011Ac1-4.

209. In the Matter of Frazee, 2003 SEC LEXIS 632 (S.E.C.).

210. CFTC, *Proposed Interpretive Order, Antidisruptive Practices Authority*, 76 Fed. Reg. 14943 (2011). The CFTC withdrew its prior notice of proposed rules under Section 747 of Dodd-Frank. 76 Fed. Reg. 14826 (March 18, 2011).

211. 76 Fed. Reg. at 14945-46. Section 4(c) had previously required "knowing" participation in a prohibited transaction, like a wash or fictitious trade. *See Reddy v. CFTC*, 191 F.3d 109, 119 (2d Cir. 1999). As also noted in *CFTC v. Savage*, 611 F.2d 270, 284 (9th Cir. 1979), "section 4c requires knowledge, as defined for purposes of section 4b [7 U.S.C. § 6b, the CEA antifraud provision that requires reckless conduct]. One cannot have an 'accommodation' sale or a 'fictitious' transaction if one in fact believes he is bargaining faithfully and intends to effect a bona fide trade."

212. 76 Fed. Reg. at 14946. For a discussion of the SEC's best execution requirement, *see* 23A Jerry W. Markham & Thomas Lee Hazen, Broker-Dealer Operations Under Securities and Commodity Laws § 9:2 (2011).

213. 66 Fed. Reg. at 14946.

214. 7 U.S.C. § 6c(a)(5)(B).

215. *See* Senate Engrossed Version, 156 Cong. Rec. S4239-02 (May 20, 2010).

216. 76 Fed. Reg. at 14946.

217. 76 Fed. Reg. at 14946.

The CFTC signaled that it would be taking a new approach to trade practices in *In the Matter of Ecoval Dairy Trade Inc.*,[218] a case that was brought before the effective date of Dodd-Frank. That case involved an attempted manipulation brought under the CFTC's traditional manipulation authority that was settled by consent. The CFTC charged that the respondent traded on an electronic exchange, Globex, with the intent to "push" the prices of nonfat dry milk futures contracts higher. The firm was seeking to establish a large short position in those same futures contracts with the hope that the market would then sell off and allow a profit. The CFTC charged that Ecoval attempted to manipulate futures prices higher by (1) executing trades by 'lifting' offers, and then immediately bidding a higher price than just paid in the trade; (2) placing both bids and offers above prevailing market prices across multiple contract months in order to establish higher price ranges in the market; (3) consistently placing bids above the opening price or the prevailing price across multiple contracts; and (4) bidding, and then quickly cancelling the bids, without the intent to have the bids filled." The Ecoval trader was trying to entice other traders to trade at prices more favorable to his strategy.

Dodd-Frank has other implications for trade practices. In a startling change in regulatory philosophy, Dodd-Frank adopted the concept of an "orderly market" for trading in futures markets. The SEC had employed this concept for years, but had rejected it for use in the futures markets. The SEC used the fair and orderly market standard to impose market-making obligations on specialists and NASDAQ market makers.[219] Because of the historical time and place advantage given to specialists, the SEC required them to maintain an orderly market in the securities in which they specialized.[220] This included buying into downturns for their own account and selling into rallies.[221] Similar obligations were extended to market makers on NASDAQ.[222] These obligations were not always met. Market makers and specialists performed poorly during the stock market crash of 1987.[223] The SEC also sanctioned the National Association of Securities Dealers (NASD) and caused its reorganization after the discovery of widespread collusion among NASDAQ market makers in setting bid and ask prices.[224]

The emergency powers provision in the Commodity Exchange Act did contain language that allowed the CFTC to direct an exchange during a market emergency to take such action as the CFTC might believe necessary "to maintain or restore *orderly* trading in, or liquidation of, any futures contract."[225] However, that power was rarely used.[226] Dodd-Frank broadened the use of the orderly

---

218. In the Matter of Ecoval Dairy Trade Inc., 2011 CFTC LEXIS 44 (2011)

219. 76 Fed. Reg. 14946. The 34 Act grants the SEC the authority to adopt regulations necessary "to maintain fair and orderly markets." 15 U.S.C. § 78k(b).

220. 17 C.F.R. § 240.11b-1.

221. Jerry W. Markham, *Manipulation of Commodity Futures Prices: The Unprosecutable Crime*, 8 YALE J. ON REG. 281, 363 (1991).

222. Both specialists and NASDAQ market makers have been found to breach these obligations. *See*, 23A JERRY W. MARKHAM & THOMAS LEE HAZEN, BROKER-DEALER OPERATIONS UNDER SECURITIES AND COMMODITY LAWS ch. 9 (2011) (discussing cases and describing obligations).

223. *See* Jerry W. Markham & Rita M. Stephanz, *The Stock Market Crash of 1987: The United States Looks at New Recommendations*, 76 GEO. L. J. 1993 (1988) (describing those failures).

224. *See*, Jerry W. Markham & Daniel J. Harty, *For Whom the Bell Tolls: The Demise of Exchange Trading Floors and the Growth of ECNs*, 33 J. CORP. L. 865, 900-901 (2008) (describing that scandal and other problems with specialists)

225. 7 U.S.C. § 12a(9) (emphasis supplied).

226. Some twenty years ago this author advocated a fair and orderly market requirement like that of the SEC for the futures markets, stating that such a requirement reflects a social judgment that large traders should not be permitted to abuse these markets by causing disruptions affecting consumers and the economy in general. It also reflects the difficulty and frustration of attempting to prove purposeful conduct and artificial-

trading concept to include authority for the CFTFC to prohibit trading activities that demonstrate "intentional or reckless disregard for the orderly execution of transactions during the closing period."[227]

The CFTC stated in its interpretation that it intended to use this securities market concept to assess whether orders entered during the closing period are disruptive in assessing violations of Section 747 of Dodd-Frank.[228] The CFTC asserted that "[c]oncepts applicable to the securities markets are useful in analyzing commodity markets because of similarities between the two areas."[229] The CFTC did state that, "absent an intentional or reckless disregard for the orderly execution of transactions during the closing period," a person would not be liable for executing an order that had a substantial effect on the settlement price.[230]

The CFTC broadly asserted that, in its view, "an orderly market may be characterized by, among other things, parameters such as a rational relationship between consecutive prices, a strong correlation between price changes and the volume of trades, levels of volatility that do not materially reduce liquidity, accurate relationships between the price of a derivative and the underlying such as a physical commodity or financial instrument, and reasonable spreads between contracts for near months and for remote months."[231] The CFTC stated that participants in the commodity and securities markets are already familiar with these assessments of orderliness in connection with issues of market manipulation and risk mitigation.[232]

The CFTC further addressed spoofing in its interpretation, stating that it occurs when a trader intends to cancel a bid or offer before execution. The CFTC characterized such conduct as something more than reckless behavior, thereby adopting a specific intent requirement. Accidental or negligent conduct would not be a violation.[233] Consequently, order changes would not be spoofing if they were "part of a legitimate, good-faith attempt to consummate a trade."[234] This would include the good-faith cancellation of partially filled orders. However, "if a person's intent when placing a bid or offer was to cancel the entire bid or offer prior to execution, regardless of whether such bid or offer was subsequently filled, that conduct may violate" the spoofing prohibition.[235]

The CFTC stated that spoofing would also include: "(i) Submitting or cancelling bids or offers to overload the quotation system of a registered entity; (ii) submitting or cancelling bids or offers to delay another person's execution of trades; and (iii) submitting or cancelling multiple bids or offers to create an appearance of false market depth."[236] The spoofing prohibition would not include requests for quotes and other authorized pretrade communica-

---

ity of prices. Jerry W. Markham, *Manipulation of Commodity Futures Prices: The Unprosecutable Crime*, 8 YALE J. ON REG. 281, 363-365 (1991).

227. 7 U.S.C. § 6c(a)(5)(B).

228. 76 Fed. Reg. at 14946.

229. 76 Fed. Reg. at 14946, n. 43 (citations omitted). In *Hammond v. Smith Barney, Harris Upham & Co.*, COMM. FUT. L. REP. (CCH) ¶ 24,617 (C.F.T.C. 1990), the CFTC had earlier stated that, when concepts under the Commodity Exchange Act are directly comparable to concepts underlying provisions of the securities laws, the CFTC will generally give significant weight to the views of the courts that have interpreted the relevant securities statutes. Nevertheless, it noted that there may be a divergence of the two industries on many issues.

230. 76 Fed. Reg. at 14947, n. 45.

231. 76 Fed. Reg. at 14946-19497.

232. 76 Fed. Reg. at 14946-19497.

233. 76 Fed. Reg. at 14947, n. 50.

234. 76 Fed. Reg. at 14947.

235. 76 Fed. Reg. at 19497.

236. 76 Fed. Reg. at 19497 (footnote omitted).

tions.[237] Nevertheless, the prohibition would apply to bids and offers in preopening periods and during trading halts.[238]

The CFTC had to go pretty far afield to find precedent for this interpretation. It cited a case brought by FINRA in the securities industry,[239] which was settled by consent, as its support.[240] There, a high-frequency trader entered numerous layered, non–bona fide market-moving orders to generate selling or buying interest in specific stocks. This prompted other market participants to enter orders that were executed against limit orders previously entered by the respondent. Once those limit orders were filled, the respondent canceled its spoof orders. The CFTC also stated that because a spoofing "violation does not require a pattern of activity, even a single instance of trading activity can be disruptive of fair and equitable trading."[241]

7:6 THE CFTC BECOMES AN ANTISPECULATION AGENCY

The CFTC had been supportive of speculation as adding liquidity and enhancing price discovery before Dodd-Frank. It had also been generally known as a hands-off regulator. The CFTC underwent a culture change under its new chair, Gary Gensler, a former partner at Goldman Sachs and a former supporter of deregulation under the CFMA while in the Treasury Department. As a member of the Obama administration, Gensler quickly did a volte-face and became a strident advocate for controlling speculation.[242]

Under Gensler, the CFTC stepped up its surveillance of high-frequency traders.[243] The CFTC created a new enforcement "squad" for swaps and abusive and manipulative trading by high-frequency trading.[244] Gensler additionally sought to regulate "direct access" by requiring greater supervision of the activities of such traders.[245] The CFTC appointed an advisory committee in March 2012 to help it define high-frequency trading and to advise on what regulation was needed for such trading.[246]

The CFTC filed a case in May 2011 charging Arcadia Petroleum Ltd., a Swiss company, and its traders, with manipulating crude oil prices. The case was filed in the midst of rising concern over gasoline prices, making the agency look aggressive. However, the activity at issue involved the alleged manipulation of prices down, as well as up, which meant that its trading had not contributed to increased energy prices in any meaningful way, and the company stoutly denied the charges.[247]

---

237. 76 Fed. Reg. at 19497.

238. 76 Fed. Reg. at 19497.

239. The futures industry has its own SRO, the National Futures Association (NFA).

240. Trillium Brokerage Services LLC, Letter of Acceptance, Waiver and Consent, No. 2007007678201 (FINRA, Sept. 12, 2010).

241. 76 Fed. Reg. at 19497.

242. Deborah Solomon, *Dodd-Frank: A Year Later: Commodity Cop Getting Grief From All Sides*, Wall Street Journal, July 19, 2011, at C1.

243. Scott Patterson, *CFTC Targets Rapid Trades*, Wall Street Journal, March 15, 2012.

244. Kara Scannell & Gregory Meyer, *Swaps Squad to Oversee $300tn US Market*, Financial Times (London), March 20, 2012, at 21.

245. *Gensler Predicts CFTC Will Take Up Concept Release on Direct Access Users*, 44 Sec. Reg. & L. Rep. (BNA) 292 (Feb. 6, 2012).

246. Telis Demos, *US Regulator Convenes Panel on HFT*, Financial Times (London), March 16, 2012.

247. Graham Bowley, *U.S. Suit Sees Manipulation of Oil Trades*, New York Times, May 25, 2011, at A1; Dan Strumpf, *Global Finance: Firm in CFTC Case Defends Trades*, Wall Street Journal, May 26, 2011, at C3.

The CFTC appeared to be using its campaign against banging-the-close transactions as a political tool to deflect criticism for its regulatory shortcomings. After MF Global Holdings Ltd. spectacularly declared bankruptcy in 2011, the CFTC discovered that there was a $1.2 billion shortfall in customer funds. In addition to suppressing manipulation, a prime mission of the CFTC is to protect customer funds, but the agency could not account for the shortfall even after months of investigation. The CFTC came under much criticism in the press and in Congress. Instead of taking effective action on that issue, the CFTC charged a broker at MG Global with banging the close on twelve occasions in the palladium and platinum futures contracts traded on NYMEX from June 2006 to May 2008. That case was filed in March 2012, almost six years after that trading began.[248] The charges in the MF Global case had nothing to do with the shortfall in customer funds and had only short-term effects, but the case made the news because it involved MF Global.

More spectacularly, the Commodity Exchange Act false reporting manipulation provisions were used by the CFTC under Gensler as the basis for an investigation into claims that large banks had manipulated the popular and widely used London interbank offered rate (Libor) interest rate index during the financial crisis. That interest rate setting mechanism serves as a global guide for the setting of interest rates for everything from commercial loans to credit cards. Angela Knight, the CEO of British Bankers' Association, called the Libor rate "the world's most important number" because it set interest rates on loans valued at $300 trillion.[249] The Libor rate is set by participating banks that provide their unsecured borrowing costs to Thomson Reuters, which publishes the rate.[250]

The CFTC and Department of Justice entered into a $453 million settlement with Barclays PLC in June 2012. The bank was charged with false reports and attempting to manipulate the Libor and Euribor (euro zone) rates in violation of the Commodity Exchange Act. Barclays was charged with providing artificial quotes (usually about one basis point = .0001 percent) to the compilers of those indexes during the financial crisis. The CFTC found that "throughout the global financial crisis in late August 2007 through early 2009, as a result of instructions from Barclays' senior management, the Bank routinely made artificially low Libor submissions to protect Barclays' reputation from negative market and media perceptions concerning Barclays' financial condition."[251] The chair of Barclays, Marcus Agius, resigned in the wake of criticism over this activity.

The bank was alleged to have taken this action in order to aid its trading positions and to conceal from the market that Barclays was paying higher rates in order to attract funds. Barclays also thought that other banks were submitting artificially low rates in order to aid their derivatives positions. Barclays believed it had to follow this practice and to be at least in the upper range in order to suppress concerns that its financial condition was at risk as reflected by its paying interest rates higher than its peers. By lowering the rate, however, Barclays was giving up income on its loans that were tied to Libor. In 2008, Barclays had some $500 billion in outstanding retail and commercial loans, but it is unclear how much of that was tied to Libor and how much the lower rates benefited its derivative positions.

---

248. Tatyana Shumsky & Jamila Trindle, *CFTC Charges Ex-Broker at MF Global*, WALL STREET JOURNAL, May 18, 2011.

249. David Enrich & Max Colchester, WALL STREET JOURNAL, Sept. 11, 2012, at A1; Brooke Masters, *Total Overhaul for "Broken" Libor*, FINANCIAL TIMES (LONDON), Sept. 28, 2012, at 1.

250. Brooke Masters & Caroline Binham, *Regulators Consider Overhaul of LIBOR*, FINANCIAL TIMES (LONDON), March 6, 2012, at 1.

251. *CFTC Orders Barclays to Pay $200 Million Penalty for Attempted Manipulation of and False Reporting concerning LIBOR and Euribor Benchmark Interest Rates*, CFTC Press Release No. PR6289-12 (June 27, 2012).

UBS AG and other institutions suspended or fired more than a dozen senior traders as a result of those investigations.[252] On December 19, 2012, UBS AG agreed to pay regulatory authorities in the U.S., U.K., and Switzerland a total of $1.5 billion to settle charges over its role in the Libor rate manipulation scandal. A UBS Japanese subsidiary pled guilty to a criminal charge in the U.S. for its role in that manipulation, and two traders in that unit were indicted.[253] Three individuals at other firms were arrested in London as a part of the Libor rate manipulation inquiry there.[254] The Royal Bank of Scotland agreed to pay $612 million to settle charges in the U.S. over its Libor rate manipulations. It also pleaded guilty to a criminal charge for this conduct.[255]

A fight broke out between criminal investigators in the United States and those in London over who would assume jurisdiction over a trader who was the center of the LIBOR rate fixing.[256] Regulatory authorities in the U.S. also expanded their investigations into Euribor rate manipulations,[257] and European regulators were seeking changes in that index, which they concluded had "significant weaknesses."[258] Deutsche Bank suspended five traders for their manipulation of the Euribor rate. [259] It was also reported that Deutsche Bank AG had made profits of over $654 million from trading on Libor fluctuations in 2008.[260]

The CFTC investigation of the Libor manipulation was followed by a flood of private actions seeking damages for the reduced interest rates resulting from the banks' collusion.[261] A Federal District Court dismissed antitrust charges over the LIBOR manipulation, but allowed Commodity Exchange Act claims to go forward.[262] A wolf pack of thirty state attorney generals was also investigating the manipulation of the LIBOR rate.[263]

The Libor investigation broadened to include regulators from the United Kingdom, Japan, Canada, and other countries.[264] The probe widened further in 2013 after banks in Singapore reported that their traders had colluded to manipulate rates in the offshore foreign-exchange market.[265] Japanese regulators were also investigating whether traders had manipulated its Tokyo interbank

252. Harry Wilson, *Canada Latest to Join Libor Inquiry*, Telegraph (UK), Feb. 16, 2012.

253. David Enrich and Jean Eaglesham, *UBS Admits Rigging Rates in 'Epic' Plot*, Wall Street Journal, Dec. 20, 2012, at A1.

254. David Enrich, *Libor Dragnet Snares Three Men in U.K.*, Wall Street Journal, Dec. 12, 2012, at C3.

255. Caroline Binham, Kara Scannell & Ben McLannahan, *Interest Rate Fixing Scandal Shakes Three Continents*, Financial Times (London) Feb. 7, 2013 at 1.

256. David Enrich Evan Perez, *U.S. and U.K. in Tussle Over Trader*, Wall Street Journal March 14, 2013 at C1.

257. David Enrich, *Banking Industry Squirms Over European Rate Probe*, Wall Street Journal, Dec. 10, 2012, at A1.

258. David Enrich and Geoffrey T. Smith, *Regulators Push for Euribor Overhaul*, Wall Street Journal, Jan. 12-13, 2013, at B2.

259. Caroline Binham, Kara Scannell & Ben McLannahan, *Interest Rate Fixing Scandal Shakes Three Continents*, Financial Times (London) Feb. 7, 2013 at 1.

260. Jean Eaglesham, *Bank Made Huge Bet, and Profit on Libor*, Wall Street Journal, Jan. 10, 2013, at A1.

261. Jean Eaglesham, *Suits Mount in Rate Scandal*, Wall Street Journal, Aug. 27, 2012, at A1.

262. Jean Eaglesham, *Libor Cases Antitrust Claims Against Banks are Dismissed*, Wall Street Journal, March 30–31, 2013, at B4.

263. Jean Eaglesham, *Ruling in Rate Probe Doesn't Slow Cases*, Wall Street Journal, April 4, 2013, at C1.

264. Brooke Masters & Kara Scannell, *Criminal Route Eyed in Libor Inquiry*, Financial Times (London), Sept. 8, 2011, at 1.

265. Rachel Armstrong, *Exclusive – Bank Probes Find Manipulation in Singapore's Offshore FX Market*, Reuters Jan. 28, 2013 available at http://uk.reuters.com/article/2013/01/28/uk-singapore-probe-ndfs-idUKBRE90R06J20130128 (accessed on Jan. 29, 2013).

offered rate (Tibor) index.[266] English regulatory authorities announced that they would be undertaking a complete revamp of how Libor is computed, but it was later sold to the NYSE.[267] The Economic and Monetary Affairs Committee of the European Parliament proposed legislation that would impose a minimum prison sentence of five years for manipulating Libor.[268]

It appeared that regulators at the Federal Reserve Bank of New York were aware of, and indifferent to, the fact that the banks were understating borrowing costs in their Libor reporting as early as 2007. The same was true at the Bank of England. It was also clear in 2007 that there was a disconnect between Libor and the normal spread of that rate over the Fed funds rate.[269]

On April 16, 2008, the *Wall Street Journal* published a front-page story questioning the veracity of the index and whether the banks were sending false signals to the rate setters.[270] On May 30, 2008 the *Wall Street Journal* reported that Libor rates were being reported as lower than actual rates.[271] In June 2008, the then head of the New York Fed and later Treasury secretary, Timothy Geithner, wrote to the head of the Bank of England, Mervyn King, asking that the Libor rate problem be fixed and that action be taken to prevent manipulation. Geithner made that inquiry after being told in May 2008 by a senior official at the Federal Reserve Board Bank of New York of her concerns that the LIBOR rate was being manipulated.[272] Barclays personnel had also advised the New York Fed in April 2008 that the bank was misrepresenting its Libor rate postings in order to avoid drawing attention to its higher funding costs. In October 2008, a Barclays employee stated to a New York Fed official that the Libor rate-setting mechanism was "rubbish."[273] No action was taken by the Fed or anyone else until the CFTC filed its case in June 2012.[274]

There was some irony in this episode. During the period Barclays and other banks were trying to depress interest rates, the Federal Reserve Board and other central banks were also massively manipulating interest rates downward in order to prevent a collapse of the global economy. The Fed Funds rate was raised by the Fed to 5.25 percent in June 2009, before the Fed began cutting that rate beginning in September 2007 to zero and then to 25 basis points in December 2008, where it remained for more than four years.[275] Fed chair Ben Bernanke testified in 2009, with respect to the Fed's efforts to aid the banking system during the financial crisis,

> In fulfilling its traditional lending function, the Federal Reserve enhances the stability of our financial system, increases the willingness of financial institutions to extend credit, and helps

266. Caroline Binham, Kara Scannell & Ben McLannahan, *Interest Rate Fixing Scandal Shakes Three Continents*, FIN. TIMES (LONDON) Feb. 7, 2013 at 1.

267. Brooke Masters, *Total Overhaul for "Broken" Libor*, FINANCIAL TIMES (LONDON), Sept. 28, 2012, at 1.

268. Charlie Dunmore, EU Lawmakers Back Jail for Interest Rate Riggers, Reuters, Oct. 9, 2012, http://af.reuters.com/article/energyOilNews/idAFL6E8L990S20121009 (accessed October 10, 2012).

269. JERRY W. MARKHAM, A FINANCIAL HISTORY OF THE U.S. FROM THE SUBPRIME CRISIS TO THE GREAT RECESSION (2006-2009) 461 (2011).

270. Carrick Mollenkamp, *Libor Fog: Bankers Cast Doubt on Key Rate Amid Crisis*, WALL STREET JOURNAL, April 16, 2008, at A1.

271. Carrick Mollenkamp & Laurence Norman, *International Finance: Under Watch, Libor Rises—Rate Hits 2.68% Ahead of Report on System Accuracy*, WALL STREET JOURNAL, May 30, 2008, at C2.

272. Shahien Nasiripour, *Geithner was Told of LIBOR Fears in 2008*, FINANCIAL TIMES (LONDON), Dec. 19, 2012 at 2.

273. Damian Paletta, Jon Hilsenrath & Dana Cimilluca, *Libor Talks Go Back to Early '08*, WALL STREET JOURNAL, July 14, 2012 at B2.

274. Dana Cimilluca & Damian Paletta, *Libor Scandal Ensnares Fed, BOE*, WALL STREET JOURNAL, July 18, 2012 at C1.

275. Federal Reserve Board. *Open Market Operations*, http://www.federalreserve.gov/monetarypolicy/openmarket.htm (accessed August 23, 2012).

> to ease conditions in interbank lending markets, reducing the overall cost of capital to banks. In addition, some interest rates, including the rates on some adjustable-rate mortgages, are tied contractually to key interbank rates, such as the London interbank offered rate (Libor). To the extent that the provision of ample liquidity to banks reduces Libor, other borrowers will also see their payments decline.[276]

Barclays had other manipulation problems. FERC issued an order requiring Barclays to show cause why it should not have to pay $470 million to settle charges that it manipulated electricity prices in the United States. Barclays traders were engaged in a "loss leader" scheme that involved selling electricity at a loss in order to benefit related swaps positions.[277] Barclays lost some $4 million from its trading in the physical electricity market but made $35 million on its swaps as a result of that activity. [278] The $470 million penalty sought by FERC was more than it had collected in fines in all its history.

FERC was also demanding a much smaller fine of $1.6 million from Deutsche Bank AG for allegedly manipulating California electricity prices. One Deutsche Bank trader had helped design the software used by the California market operator where the trading took place. In a separate proceeding, FERC suspended the trading privileges of an energy trading operation at JPMorgan Chase & Co. and was demanding a massive fine.[279]

It was reported in March 2013 that the CFTC was conducting an investigation into the gold price fixing in London to determine whether it was being manipulated. That gold price fix is done daily and is determined by five large banks: Barclays, Deutsche Bank, HSBC Holdings PLC, Bank of Nova Scotia and Société Générale. The silver price fixing in London was also being examined. It is set by Deutsche Bank, HSBC Holdings PLC, and Bank of Nova Scotia.[280]

The CFTC was also on the attack against a relatively new entrant to the commodity derivatives market, *viz*, "commodity index traders (including pension and endowment funds) that seek exposure to commodities through passive long-term investment in commodity indexes."[281] The volume of futures trading had increased by 500 percent in the ten-year period between 1998 and 2008, and a portion of that increase was due to index traders.[282] These traders typically engage in these investments as part of a portfolio diversification theory.

Among the large index funds were the Goldman Sachs Commodity Index (GSCI) and the Dow Jones-AIG Commodity Index (DJ-AIG). The index traders came under scrutiny because of concerns that their trading was increasing the demand side of commodity pricing, particularly

276. Ben S. Bernanke, *Federal Reserve Programs to Strengthen Credit Markets and the Economy*, Before the Committee on Financial Services, U.S. House of Representatives, Washington, DC (Feb. 10, 2009), http://www.federalreserve.gov/newsevents/testimony/bernanke20090210a.htm (accessed August 23, 2012).

277. *Power Market Watchdog Seeks Barclays Fine*, Reuters, Nov. 1, 2012, available at http://www.reuters.com/article/2012/11/01/us-barclays-ferc-idUSBRE89U1QV20121101 (accessed on Nov. 1, 2012).

278. Ben Protess and Michael J de la Merced, *An Energy Regulator vs. Wall St.*, New York Times, Nov. 2, 2012, at B1.

279. Ryan Tracy, *Clashes Coming on Energy Trades*, Wall Street Journal, Nov. 19, 2012, at C1.

280. Katy Burne, Matt Day & Tatyana Shumsky, *U.S. Probes Gold Pricing*, Wall Street Journal, March 14, 2013 at A1.

281. CFTC Staff Report, *Commodity Swap Dealers & Index Traders With Commission Recommendations*, 1 (Sept. 2008). The CFTC has described index traders as "those that are [generally] seeking a more general exposure to commodity prices, typically in a long-only, unleveraged, and passively-managed manner using a standardized commodity index." CFTC, *Commission Actions in Response to the Comprehensive Review of the Commitments of Traders Reporting Program* 10 (2006).

282. Jerry W. Markham, A Financial History of the U.S. From Enron Era Scandals to The Subprime Crisis (2004-2006) 209 (2011).

oil. However, a CFTC staff report found that the trading by index traders in NYMEX crude oil futures actually declined during the period under study (December 31, 2007, to June 30, 2008). The necessity of rolling over these long-term positions as contract markets expired increased volume, but seemed to be handled smoothly.[283] CFTC commissioner Bart Chilton had been particularly critical of index traders in energy futures, which he called "massive passives."[284] Chilton dissented from the CFTC staff report on index traders, asserting the data on which the report was based was inconclusive and incomplete.[285]

The Senate Permanent Subcommittee on Investigations of the Committee on Homeland Security and Governmental Affairs issued a report on "excessive speculation" in the wheat market that blamed increased prices on index traders.[286] The report noted that wheat prices had risen from about $3 per bushel in mid-2006 to $11 a bushel in early 2008 and then fell to $3.50 per bushel at the end of 2008.[287] The report charged that "index traders, who buy wheat futures contracts and hold them without regard to the fundamentals of supply and demand in the cash market for wheat, have created a significant additional demand for wheat futures contracts that has as much as doubled the overall demand for wheat contracts."[288] The report claimed that this additional demand had created a disparity between cash and futures prices in wheat and resulted in "turmoil" in the market.[289] The staff report recommended ending CFTC waivers and exemptions from position limits for index traders and imposing even more restrictive position limits if necessary in order to discourage index traders.[290]

CFTC commissioner Chilton was also given support in his concerns over index trading by the report of the Senate's Permanent Subcommittee on Investigations that blamed index traders for fueling a rise in the wheat market. The chair of that subcommittee, Carl Levin (D-MI), criticized the CFTC for allowing those traders to trade under hedge limit exceptions, rather than speculative limits.[291] The subcommittee report recommended that "the CFTC phase out waivers and exemptions from position limits that were granted to index traders purchasing wheat futures contracts to help offset their sales of speculative financial instruments tied to commodity indexes."[292]

The head of the Chicago Mercantile Exchange came to the defense of the index traders and swap dealers, stating that they "are not engaged in traditional speculative activity, *i.e.*, trying to beat the market. . . . Index funds aggregate the buying and selling decisions of many thousands of investors, most of whom are doing what they have been taught for decades to do: diversify-

---

283. CFTC Staff Report, *Commodity Swap Dealers & Index Traders With Commission Recommendations*, 4 (Sept. 2008).

284. Kara Scannell, *CFTC's Energy-Industry Gadfly Gets His Way*, Wall Street Journal, June 12, 2010, at B1.

285. CFTC Staff Report, *Commodity Swap Dealers & Index Traders With Commission Recommendations*, 60-62 (Sept. 2008).

286. *Excessive Speculation in the Wheat Market*, Majority and Minority Staff Report of the Senate Permanent Subcommittee on Investigations of the Committee on Homeland Security and Governmental Affairs (June 24, 2009).

287. *Id.* at 9.

288. *Id.* at 12.

289. *Id.* at 3.

290. *Id.* at 14.

291. Bill Tomson, *Panel Faults Wheat Speculators*, Wall Street Journal, June 24, 2009, at C14. Wheat and soybean prices had risen sharply in 2007 after heavy rains caused widespread crop damage. Jerry W. Markham, A Financial History of the U.S. From Enron Era Scandals to The Subprime Crisis (2004-2006) 212 (2011).

292. Senate Permanent Subcommittee on Investigations, Majority and Minority Staff Report, *Excessive Speculation in the Wheat Market* 2 (June 24, 2009).

ing their investment portfolios and hedging inflation risks to their investment returns in order to maximize their retirement savings and their individual wealth."[293]

CFTC commissioner Chilton further claimed that silver prices were manipulated in 2008 as prices soared, but no enforcement actions from the CFTC were immediately forthcoming.[294] A columnist in the *New York Times* in March 2011 cited claims of a conspiracy to silence a whistleblower, Andrew Maguire, involving the trading activity in silver. The reporter noted that in "the past six months, the value of the precious metal has increased nearly 80 percent, to more than $34 an ounce from around $19 an ounce. In the last month alone, its price has increased nearly 23 percent. This kind of price action in the silver market is reminiscent of the fortune-busting, roller-coaster ride enjoyed by the Hunt Brothers, Nelson Bunker and William Herbert, back in 1970s and early 1980s when they tried unsuccessfully to corner the market."[295]

The CFTC investigation of this trading in silver dragged on for four years and involved an examination of more than 100,000 documents.[296] The silver investigation was reported as having been closed in 2012 by the CFTC without bringing any charges.[297] A class action lawsuit charged that JPMorgan Chase and HSBC Bank manipulated the price of silver downward in 2008. It was further claimed that those two banks caused a massive silver price rise in 2010 when they covered their short positions. HSBC entered into a settlement of those claims.[298] One class action claimed that JPMorgan and HSBC were using electronic trading to manipulate the price of silver downward through financial instruments in the form of an exchange-traded fund (ETF) backed by silver bars that were traded on the New York Stock Exchange's commodity unit, Arca (NYSE-Arca).[299] The several class actions over this conduct were consolidated in the federal district court

293. Statement of Craig S. Donohue Chief Executive Officer of CME Group Inc. Before the CFTC Hearing on Energy Position Limits and Hedge Exemptions (July 28, 2009), http://www.cftc.gov/ucm/groups/public/@newsroom/documents/file/hearing072809_dohohue.pdf (accessed August 25, 2011).

294. Susan Pulliam & Carolyn Cui, *Silver-Market Probe: Act Now, CFTC Is Urged*, WALL STREET JOURNAL, OCT. 27, 2010, at C1. *Compare*, Carolyn Cui, *CFTC Relents and Probes Silver Market: Persistent Complaints of Foul Play Draw The Still-Skeptical Agency to Investigate*, WALL STREET JOURNAL, Sept. 25, 2008, at C1 (claims that banks were manipulating silver prices downward).

295. William D. Cohan, *A Conspiracy With a Silver Lining*, NEW YORK TIMES, March 2, 2011, http://opinionator.blogs.nytimes.com/2011/03/02/a-conspiracy-with-a-silver-lining/ (accessed March 5, 2012).

296. Andrew Hickley, *CFTC Silver Manipulation Probe Continues*, GFS News, Nov. 7, 2011, http://www.gfsnews.com/article/3509/1/CFTC_silver_manipulation_probe_continues

297. Jack Farchy & and Gregory Meyer, *US Set to Drop 4-Year Probe Into Silver Price*, FINANCIAL TIMES (LONDON), Aug. 6, 2012, at 1.

298. Gregory Meyer, *HSBC Dropped From Silver Price Suppression Lawsuit*, FINANCIAL TIMES (LONDON) Sept. 14, 2011.

299. Silver bars were deliverable on these ETF contracts on the London Bullion Market Association or against the silver futures contract traded on the COMEX and GLOBEX platforms of the CME Group Inc. The complaint charged,

> Defendants had a strong incentive to suppress downward the price of silver as measured by the NYSE-Arca and CME/COMEX instruments. For example, Defendants could pledge their silver to the ETFs in exchange for ETF shares, sell their shares to other market participants, drive down the prices of silver through trades on NYSE-Arca and CME/COMEX, buy back their ETF shares from investors at lower prices, and return their (now lower priced) silver ETF shares in exchange for the silver bars initially pledged against those shares, the real value of which remained the same, and only notionally appears lower because of Defendants' suppression.

Kensik v. JP Morgan Chase & Co. ¶¶ 2, 15 (N.D. Ill.), http://www.gata.org/files/SilverManipulationLawsuit-NIllinois-12-07-2010.pdf (accessed March 5, 2012).

in New York.[300] A consolidated class action claim further charged a market power manipulation by JPMorgan Chase, but it was dismissed.[301]

7:7 MARGIN REQUIREMENTS AND MANIPULATION

Margin requirements have long been viewed as a way for the government to curb speculation. As described in earlier chapters, the government changed its views on margin requirements for futures, initially viewing position limits as a more effective regulatory tool for limiting speculation. The government changed that view but was unable to convince Congress that such authority was needed. The SEC had long been the advocate of high margin requirements as a tool for curbing speculation under the 34 Act. The Federal Reserve Board initially aided that effort with high margin requirements.

In 1979, the New York Fed conducted a study on stock margins and concluded that changes in margins may not reduce stock market volatility.[302] In 1982 the Fed advised Congress that it was reviewing existing policy over margin requirements.[303] The Fed's study was completed two years later. It concluded that the goals of Congress in setting margin requirements in the 1930s were largely irrelevant to modern markets.[304] The Federal Reserve study "cast significant doubt on the need to retain high initial margins to prevent excessive fluctuations of stock prices" because trading on margin no longer had a significant effect on stock prices. Over the prior half century, the "amplitude of fluctuations in stock prices had not differed greatly from that recorded before the imposition of federal margin regulations, with the exception of the late 1920s."[305]

Fed chair Paul Volcker advised Congress in the transmission of that report that margins on financial futures should be more closely aligned with the underlying securities. However, he also suggested that stock margins be lowered to achieve that parity. The Fed believed that stock margins should be based on the actual loan value of particular securities and not an arbitrary percentage that had been used in the past as a speculative curb. Volcker further advised that authority for setting margins should be given to self-regulatory organizations (SROs), such as the New York Stock Exchange and the National Association of Securities Dealers Inc. (now FINRA). This proposed revamping of margin requirements would be overseen by a council of federal agencies with a veto power over SRO set margins. This regulatory council would be composed of the SEC and CFTC and a tiebreaker body that would be either the Fed or the Treasury.[306]

That proposal was not adopted and, as described in Chapter 5, efforts to impose higher margins on stock index futures after the stock market crash of 1987 were beaten back. The only significant effort on the convergence of stock and futures occurred in connection with the

---

300. In re Commodity Exchange Inc., Silver Futures and Options Trading Litigation, 775 F. Supp. 2d 1382 (S.D.N.Y. 2011).

301. In re Commodity Exchange Inc., Silver Futures and Options Trading Litigation, 1:11-md-02213-RPP (S.D.N.Y. 2011, http://www.scribd.com/doc/65207178/11-09-12-FINAL-Consolidated-Class-Action-Complaint (accessed March 5, 2012).

302. FEDERAL RESERVE BANK OF NEW YORK STAFF STUDY: SECURITIES CREDIT REGULATIONS OF THE BOARD OF GOVERNORS OF THE FEDERAL RESERVE SYSTEM, Ch. II at 28 (Dec. 1984).

303. Jerry W. Markham, *Federal Regulation of Margin in the Commodity Futures Industry: History and Theory*, 64 TEMP. L. REV. 59, 97 (1991).

304. A STUDY BY THE STAFF OF THE BOARD OF GOVERNORS OF THE FEDERAL RESERVE: A REVIEW AND EVALUATION OF FEDERAL MARGIN REGULATIONS (Dec. 1984).

305. FEDERAL RESERVE BANK OF NEW YORK STAFF STUDY: SECURITIES CREDIT REGULATIONS OF THE BOARD OF GOVERNORS OF THE FEDERAL RESERVE SYSTEM, Ch. II at 28 (Dec. 1984).

306. Jerry W. Markham, *Federal Regulation of Margin in the Commodity Futures Industry: History and Theory*, 64 TEMP. L. REV. 59, 97 (1991).

trading of single stock futures. Before the enactment of the Commodity Futures Modernization Act of 2000, futures trading was not permitted on single stocks because of concerns by the SEC over manipulation. A compromise was reached in the CFMA, which allowed single stock futures to be jointly regulated by the SEC and CFTC.[307] Most futures contracts have initial margins of less than 5 percent of the notional amount of the contract. However, the SEC mandated a margin of 20 percent for single stock futures. The result was to discourage trading in single stock futures in the United States. Instead, the largest single stock futures exchange was located in South Africa.[308]

A strange phenomenon in the margin area was also being observed after the financial crisis in 2008. Historically, the commodity exchanges had staunchly resisted government pressures to increase margin requirements or to pressure speculators to lighten their positions in order to dampen speculation and push down prices by relieving that demand pressure. That attitude changed in the wake of the Dodd-Frank Act. For example, ICE announced in February 2011 that it was placing traders holding cotton positions in the delivery month under special scrutiny. In addition, the exchange said traders would be required to prove that they had an economic need for the cotton under contract. This action came in the wake of a 19 percent increase in cotton and much criticism of speculators.[309]

As the price of silver jumped, the CME made some extraordinary margin increases in that commodity, which seemed to be directed at dampening speculation instead of contract performance concerns, the historical basis for setting futures margins. Traders charged that a series of margin increases by the CME in silver futures in 2011 "helped snuff out silver's record-breaking rally. CME raised silver margins by a total of 84% between April 26 and May 5, which market participants said triggered a 27% decline from April 29 to May 6 in silver prices as investors who lacked adequate funds were forced out of the market."[310] The CME also raised margins on gold later in the year as the price of that metal exploded. Gold prices continued to rally, but then began to fall after announcement of another margin increase.[311]

The CME defended its actions on the grounds that the margin increases were needed to ensure contract performance in the face of high market volatility.[312] However, the size and intensity of those increases raised concerns that the increases were a political response to pressure from regulators and members of Congress.[313] This seemed odd in light of the CME's history of resisting such political pressure, but some monumental changes had occurred that had changed the perspective of the CME. Historically, exchanges were member-owned institutions that were fiercely protective of their members' interests. This caused the exchanges to resist government intervention in market pricing and regulation. However, like other exchanges, the CME had demutualized as a result of competition from electronic markets that raised demands for capital, which was obtained

---

307. Customer Margin Rules Relating to Security Futures, 2001 SEC LEXIS 1969 (Sept. 26, 2001).

308. Lawrence Hunt Jr., *The Paulson Report Is a Non-Starter*, 67 FIN. WORLD WIDE 53 (July 2008).

309. Carolyn Cui & Leslie Josephs, *A Cotton Market Targets Speculators*, WALL STREET JOURNAL, Feb. 4, 2011 at C1.

310. Tatyana Shumsky, *CME Group: Comex Gold Margins Raised to Protect Investors*, WALL STREET JOURNAL, Aug. 11, 2011.

311. Liam Pleven & Tatyana Shumsky, *Gold Sinks 5.6 % as Rally Hits Wall*, WALL STREET JOURNAL, Aug. 25, 2011, at C1; *Tarnished Gold*, FINANCIAL TIMES (LONDON), Aug. 26, 2011, at 1.

312. Tatyana Shumsky, *CME Group: Comex Gold Margins Raised to Protect Investors*, WALL STREET JOURNAL, Aug. 11, 2011.

313. *See, e.g.*, Jonathan Leff & Robert Gibbons, *Analysis: Commodity Price Margins: Art, Science or Politics?* (May 12, 2011), http://www.reuters.com/article/2011/05/12/us-exchange-margin-idUSTRE74B0N320110512 (accessed August 25, 2011).

by going public.[314] As a public company, the CME became much more susceptible to political pressures.[315]

Margin was also addressed in Section 731 of the Dodd-Frank Act, which extended margin requirements to the newly regulated swaps and to the OTC derivatives market. Section 731 requires the CFTC to adopt initial and variation margin requirements for nonbank swap dealers and major swap participants. Dodd-Frank further authorized bank prudential regulators to set initial and variation margin requirements for banks that act as swap dealers. The prudential bank regulator is to act jointly with the CFTC and SEC in setting margin requirements for uncleared swaps.

This margin authority was added in the wake of the massive governmental bailout of the American International Group (AIG). That company had a large book of credit default swaps that provided protection from credit events on triple-A rated subprime collateralized debt obligations. The irony of adding the Dodd-Frank margin authority for swaps is that AIG's problems were due to collateral calls—read margin calls—on those positions by Goldman Sachs and others. AIG could not meet those calls and had to be rescued by government bailout funds. It was thus demands for increased margins that were at the center of the crisis.

The CFTC proposed rules to implement Section 731 in April 2011.[316] The proposed rules would not impose margin requirements on nonfinancial end users of swaps and would allow covered swap dealers to set their margin requirements based on approved internal or industry risk models. Bank regulators would allow only the use of approved models. That same approach had been used by swap dealers before Dodd-Frank in risk measurement assessment for collateral requirements imposed on their counterparties.

The CFTC proposed an alternative approach that would allow margin requirements for uncleared swaps to track those imposed on related cleared swap products, if an appropriate risk model was not available.[317] The CFTC proposals raised concerns that margins on uncleared swaps could significantly increase the costs of trading in those instruments.[318] Bank regulators took a different alternative approach, using percentages of notional amounts as the basis for their alternative margin calculation.

The CFTC expanded its enforcement program to include electronic exchange-based charges. In *In the Matter of Noble Americas Corp.*,[319] the CFTC found by consent that the respondent had engaged in wash sales through transactions on Globex, the CME's electronic exchange. In *CFTC v. Rhazi*,[320] the district court entered an injunction against a rogue trader engaged in a prearranged

---

314. *See generally,* Jake Keaveny, *In Defense of Market Self-Regulation: An Analysis of the History of Futures Regulation and the Trend Toward Demutualization*, 70 BROOKLYN L. REV. 1419 (2005) (describing this change).

315. Nevertheless, the CME reduced margins on crude oil futures contracts on August 25, 2011, after a decline in volatility. Dan Strumpf, *CME Cuts Margin on Crude-Oil Futures*, WALL STREET JOURNAL, Aug. 25, 2011.

316. *Margin Requirements for Uncleared Swaps for Swap Dealers and Major Swap Participants,* 76 Fed. Reg. 23732 (April 28, 2011).

317. 76 Fed. Reg. at 23737-38.

318. Sutherland Asbill & Brennan LLP, Proposed Margin Requirements for Uncleared Swaps Could Significantly Increase the Costs Associated with Over-the-Counter Swap Transactions and May Apply to Some End-Users (April 13, 2011), http://www.sutherland.com/files/News/2cdb2ea6-c430-4bf8-8d0b-ebacea475c78/Presentation/NewsAttachment/861e46c3-ba13-48e2-9eb7-21a18db2dac2/ProposedMargin RequirementsforUnclearedSwapsApril2011.pdf) (accessed August 27, 2011).

319. In the Matter of Noble Americas Corp., 2010 WL 1803817 (C.F.T.C.). *See also,* In the Matter of Pinemore LP, 2010 WL 332377 (C.F.T.C.).

320. CFTC v. Rhazi, Comm. Fut. L. Rep. (CCH) ¶ 32,016 (S.D.N.Y. 2011).

trading scheme between his personal accounts and those of his employer. The defendant was a trader based in London at the foreign affiliate of a U.S. bank, which was the target of the fraud. The trading was conducted on Globex. In *In the Matter of Enskilda Futures Ltd.*,[321] the CFTC found by consent that an offshore broker accepted numerous wash sale orders that were executed on Globex. The CFTC found that the futures commission merchant (FCM) failed to supervise the entry of those orders.[322]

In *CFTC v. Optiver Holding BV*,[323] the CFTC brought charges of attempted manipulation of energy futures contracts through Globex. The CFTC charged that defendants used a computer program they called the "Hammer" to carry out their manipulation. The defendants had stated that they wanted to "really bully" the market and to move the market during its close, as well as making up a "fairy story" to cover up their manipulation.[324] The CFTC also transcribed and posted on its website some attention-getting quotes in taped conversations of Optiver traders as a means to hype the CFTC's case.[325]

The CFTC filed the *Optiver* case with a blast of publicity in 2008,[326] but it provided no evidence of any serious effect the scheme might have had on the rise in energy prices. The amount at issue was a comparatively paltry profit of some $1 million from trading on both sides of the market and was not indicative of a long side manipulation that would drive up energy prices. The defendants profited in relatively small amounts whether prices went up or down. The CFTC also acknowledged that NYMEX had previously discovered and shut down the trading scheme. Optiver settled the CFTC charges in April 2012 by agreeing to pay $14 million.[327]

In *CFTC v. Parnon Energy Inc.*,[328] the CFTC charged that in 2008 the defendants had engaged in a cross-market manipulation scheme involving the accumulation and sell-off of a large position in physical crude oil in order to manipulate futures prices on the New York Mercantile Exchange (NYMEX) and on ICE. The defendants were claimed to have made in excess of $50 million from that trading.

In *In the Matter of Lui*,[329] the CFTC, by consent, imposed sanctions against a respondent for prearranging trades on the Globex electronic trading platform at the Chicago Mercantile Exchange. The respondent was trading several of his customer accounts against each other, resulting in profits for the customers on one side of the trades and losses to customers on the other. The CFTC also brought a case against the Royal Bank of Canada (RBC) in April 2012,

321. In the Matter of Enskilda Futures Ltd., Comm. Fut. L. Rep. (CCH) ¶ 32,062 (C.F.T.C. 2011).

322. *See also,* In the Matter of Noble Americas Corp., 2010 WL 1803817 (C.F.T.C.) (CFTC by consent finds that the respondent had engaged in wash sales through transactions on Globex).

323. CFTC v. Optiver Holding BV, 08-Civ 6560 (S.D.N.Y. July 24, 2008). *See*, Statement of Acting CFTC Chairman Walter L. Luken, July 24, 2008, reprinted at http://www.cftc.gov/ucm/groups/public/@newsroom/documents/pressrelease/lukkenoptiverstatement072408.pdf (accessed June 24, 2011) (heralding the filing of this case).

324. *CFTC Case Background Information*, CFTC Press Release 5521-08, July 24, 2008, CFTC v. Optiver US, LLC, et al., http://www.cftc.gov/ucm/groups/public/@newsroom/ documents/file/ enfoptiverbackground.pdf (accessed June 24, 2011).

325. http://www.cftc.gov/ucm/groups/ public/@lrenforcementactions/ documents/file/enfoptivertranscripts exhibita.pdf (accessed June 24, 2011).

326. Statement of Acting Chairman Walter L. Lukken (As Prepared for Delivery), July 24, 2008, http://www.cftc.gov/ucm/groups/public/@newsroom/documents/pressrelease/lukkenoptiverstatement072408.pdf (accessed June 24, 2011).

327. Jerry A. DiColo, Dan Strumpf & Jamila Trindle, *Target on Manipulation, But It's Tough to Hit*, Wall Street Journal, April 20, 2012, at C1.

328. CFTC v. Parnon Energy Inc. (S.D.N.Y. 2011).

329. In the Matter of Lui, Comm. Fut. L. Rep. (CCH) ¶ 30,491 (C.F.T.C. 2007).

which charged that it had engaged in massive wash sales for tax purposes through OneChicago, an electronic futures exchange that is partly owned by the CME.[330] RBC vowed to fight those charges.

7:8 POSITION LIMITS

CFTC chair Gary Gensler sought to impose speculative position limits on energy traders after the agency was accused of failing to curb prices oil prices that rose to $145 per barrel.[331] Although CFTC staff members had concluded that it did not have the data needed to justify such limits,[332] the CFTC proposed them anyway. The proposed limits sought to restrict the size of positions that could be held by speculators in crude oil options and futures contracts on the NYMEX.[333] However, the CFTC withdrew that proposed speculative limit rule for the NYMEX energy contracts after the passage of Dodd-Frank.[334] That action was taken in response to Section 737 of the Dodd-Frank Act, which broadened the CFTC's power to adopt position limits for futures and swaps for the purposes of curbing "excessive speculation" and deterring "market manipulation."[335] Section 737 allowed the CFTC to impose a broad range of position limits on traditional exchange-traded futures and options. It also applied to swaps that are "economically equivalent" to futures or options contracts on physical commodities.

In addition, Section 737 required the CFTC to establish aggregate position limits for any "group or class of trader" for contracts based on the same underlying commodity across exchanges, swap execution facilities, foreign boards of trade, and over-the-counter (OTC) swaps that perform a significant price discovery function. Dodd-Frank required that position limits on energy and metals commodities be adopted by January 2011, and on agricultural commodities by April 2011. Those deadlines were not met because the CFTC's proposals implementing Section 737 proved to be highly controversial.

The CFTC first publicly considered proposed rules to implement the Section 737 position limits at a meeting held on December 16, 2010. Apparently because of dissent among the commission members, the chair, Gary Gensler, abruptly adjourned the meeting without holding a vote on the proposed rules.[336] On January 13, 2011, the CFTC again met and this time voted to approve the publication of proposed rules to impose position limits on twenty-eight commodity futures and option contracts and on "economically equivalent" swaps. The CFTC proposal sought to impose position limits on "spot" months—that is, the contract delivery month that is approaching expiration—which would limit holdings to 25 percent of available deliverable supplies on certain commodities.[337] The CFTC advised that nonspot month limits would be imposed in a second phase implementing this rule making.

---

330. Jean Eaglesham, Jamila Trindle & Caroline Van Hasselt, *CFTC Deals Out Royal Pain*, Wall Street Journal, April 3, 2012, at C1.

331. Sarah N. Lynch, *CFTC Chief Seeks Curbs on Oil Trade*, Wall Street Journal, July 29, 2009, at C1.

332. Sarah N. Lynch, *CFTC Staff Divided on Oil Limits*, Wall Street Journal, May 14, 2010, at C7.

333. *Federal Speculative Position Limits for Referenced Energy Contracts and Associated Regulations*, 75 Fed. Reg. 4144 (Jan. 26, 2010).

334. 75 Fed. Reg. 50950 (Aug. 18, 2011).

335. 7 U.S.C. § 6a(a)(3).

336. Jeffrey Sparshot, *Global Finance: CFTC Vote on Trading Curbs Stalls*, Wall Street Journal, Dec. 17, 2010, at C3.

337. *Position Limits for Derivatives*, 76 Fed. Reg. 4752 (Jan. 26, 2011). The CFTC had set conditional spot position limits on natural gas in February 2010. Brian Scheld, *Coal Trader*, http://plattsenergyweektv.com/story.aspx?storyid=163115&catid=293 (accessed August 23, 2011).

This rule proposal was the resurrection of an earlier CFTC proposal that was shouted down by the industry in 1978. As described in Chapter 4, the 1978 proposal was called "Charlie's rule," after CFTC staff member Charles Robinson, who propounded the idea.[338] The proposal would have required the futures exchanges to limit positions of traders in maturing futures contracts to no more than 25 percent of the open interest in that future unless the exchange affirmatively determined that the position was not a threat to orderly trading.

The 1978 proposal was highly controversial and was not adopted because of uncertainty over what was expected of the exchanges under its provisions.[339] The CFTC vote on the publication of its 2011 Dodd-Frank position limit proposals was equally controversial. One commissioner dissented, and two other expressed reservations over whether the proposals should actually be adopted. Of particular interest was a statement by Democratic commissioner Michael Dunn, who voted in favor of the proposed rules "in order to gather more information." He stated that the "CFTC staff has been unable to find any reliable economic analysis to support either the contention that excessive speculation is affecting the markets [the CFTC] regulate[s] or that position limits will prevent excessive speculation." The commissioner was concerned that, in the absence of any concrete economic evidence, position limits would be "a cure for a disease that does not exist or at worst, a placebo for one that does."[340]

Concerned over the CFTC's dithering, several Democratic members of Congress introduced legislation in September 2011 that would have established speculative position limits that would limit the size of any one speculator to 5 percent of the oil futures market.[341] That seemed to have turned the tide. The new position limits were approved by the CFTC in a 3–2 vote on October 18, 2011, with both Republican commissioners dissenting. Over 15,000 comments were received on the proposals.

The *Wall Street Journal* characterized the rule as an effort to "curb bets" on commodities and that it "raises the bar on betting."[342] The *New York Times* reported that CFTC chair Gary Gensler viewed the rule as the "nation's best hope for reining in speculative commodities trading."[343] Two industry groups challenged the new position limit rules in court. Interestingly, again underscoring the conflation of the securities and commodity industries, it was a securities industry trade group, the Securities Industry and Financial Markets Association (SIFMA), and the International Swaps and Derivatives Association Inc. (ISDA), the OTC swaps dealers association, that challenged the rule, rather than the commodity futures exchanges. Their lawsuit claimed that the CFTC's new position limit rules would impair liquidity and increase price volatility and that the CFTC had not conducted an adequate cost-benefit analysis of the rule as required by statute.[344] The lawsuit was

338. *See*, Jerry W. Markham, *Manipulation of Commodity Futures Prices—The Unprosecutable Crime*, 8 Yale J. on Reg. 281, 370 (1991) (describing the CFTC rule proposal that was published at 43 Fed. Reg. 15438 (Apr. 13, 1978)).

339. *Id.* at 371.

340. Michael V. Dunn, *Opening Statement, Public Meeting on Proposed Rules Under Dodd-Frank Act*, http://www.cftc.gov/PressRoom/SpeechesTestimony/dunnstatement011311.html (accessed August 23, 2011).

341. *Lawmakers Introduce Senate Bills to Limit Positions in Oil to 5% of Market*, 43 Sec. Reg. & L. Rep. (BNA) 1971 (Sept. 26, 2011).

342. Scott Patterson & Jamila Trindle, *CFTC Raises Bar on Betting*, Wall Street Journal, Oct. 19, 2010, at C3.

343. Ben Protess, *Commodity Panel Moves to Rein in Speculative Trading*, New York Times, Oct. 18, 2010, at B5.

344. CFTC commissioner Scott O'Malia expressed skepticism about the proposed position limit rules at the January 13, 2011, CFTC meeting. Although he supported their publication to gather information, he too was concerned that the CFTC lacked proper data to formulate effective position limits. Scott D. O'Malia,

lent support by the two CFTC Republican commissioners who expressed concern with the lack of data needed to set appropriate position limits during the debate on those rules in 2011.[345] The CFTC later loosened those position limits, but the federal district court ruled in favor of ISDA and SIFMA and struck the new CFTC position limits on September 28, 2012. The court held that CFTC had misread the provisions of the Dodd-Frank Act.[346]

The CFTC commissioners were also advised by staff that the agency did not have the authority to limit speculative trading under its emergency powers in the Commodity Exchange Act.[347] The CFTC did, however, bring a high-profile case against Citigroup, on September 21, 2012, fining it $525,000 for violating speculative limits in wheat.[348] In another action brought by the CFTC, JPMorgan Chase agreed to pay $600,000 to settle charges that the bank violated speculative limits in the No. 2 cotton futures contract. The CFTC also settled speculative limit violations brought against a Chinese firm that was trading cotton and soybean futures. An Australian firm settled charges that it violated speculative limits in wheat and cotton.[349]

The CFTC was also seeking to expand its reporting requirements to attack speculation. The CFTC proposed rules that would allow it to collect certain ownership, control, and related information for all trading accounts active on futures exchanges in the United States. The CFTC stated that better surveillance tools were needed in light of dramatic changes on the commodity futures markets, which were now being driven by electronic traders, who were supplanting the traditional exchange floors.[350] The CFTC noted with respect to trading on designated contract markets (DCMs),

> Between 2000 and 2009, electronic trading grew from approximately 9 percent to approximately 81 percent of volume on all U.S. DCMs. Over the same time period, the number of actively-traded futures and options contracts listed on U.S. exchanges increased more than seven fold, from approximately 266 contracts in 2000 to approximately 1,866 contracts in 2009. Most importantly, total DCM futures and options trading volume rose from approximately 594.5 million contracts in 2000 to approximately 2.78 billion in 2009, an increase of over 368%. . . .
>
> Whereas the Commission once monitored trading via on-site surveillance of open-outcry pits, today surveillance is primarily electronic and data-driven. Paradoxically, while electronic trading has conferred important informational advantages, including improved audit trails,

---

Statement, Prior to Notice of Proposed Rulemaking: Position Limits for Derivatives, http://www.cftc.gov/PressRoom/Speeches Testimony/omaliastatement011311.html (accessed August 23, 2011). Commissioner Jill Sommers in dissent argued that the position limits should be postponed until the CFTC was able to collect the information needed to set proper limits. She stated that "we should conduct a complete analysis of the swap market data before we determine the appropriate formula to propose. We have not done that." Jill E. Sommers, *Opening Statement, Open Meeting on the Ninth Series of Proposed Rulemakings under the Dodd-Frank Act*, Jan. 13, 2011, http://www.cftc.gov/PressRoom/Speeches Testimony/sommersstatement011311.html (accessed August 23, 2011).

345. *Lawmakers Ask CFTC to Consider Rule to Limit Commodity Index Funds*, 44 Sec. Reg. & L. Rep. (BNA) 688 (April 2, 2012); *Senate Bill Would Require CFTC to Ensure Hedgers Hold the Majority of Energy Futures*, 44 Sec. Reg. & L. Rep. (BNA) 686 (April 2, 2012).

346. International Swaps & Derivatives Ass'n v. United States Commodity Futures Trading Commission, 2012 U.S. Dist. LEXIS 139788 (D. D.C.).

347. 7 U.S.C. § 12a(9).

348. CFTC Press Release No. PR6358-12 (Sept. 21, 2012).

349. *CFTC Nets $3M in Spec Limits Cases*, 44 Sec. Reg. & L. Rep. (BNA) 1847 (Oct. 1, 2012)

350. Account Ownership and Control Report, 75 Fed. Reg. 41775, 41777 (C.F.T.C. July 19, 2010) (footnote omitted).

> the concomitant increases in trading volumes, products offered, and trader dispersion and anonymity have created equally important regulatory challenges. Foremost among these is scale. Effective surveillance of millions of daily records—for example, an average of approximately 2.9 million trades per day in December 2009—requires automated systems capable of intelligently searching for patterns and anomalies buried deep within the data. Crucially, it also requires comprehensive data streams with sufficient reference points to uncover relationships where none appear to exist and to analyze information based on desired criteria.

The CFTC further noted that the integration between traditionally regulated contract markets and OTC trading facilities required improved surveillance methods in order to ensure that trading in one market is not used to distort prices in other markets or to facilitate abusive trading practices across markets.[351] That proposal remained pending into 2013.

7:9 SHORT SELLING AND OTHER TRADING RESTRICTIONS

Reducing speculative demand and restricting short selling has long been a popular political response to concerns over price volatility, but such restrictions have proved to be no panacea over the years. James Edward Meeker conducted a survey of speculative trading restrictions imposed by governments throughout history and he found that they were generally ineffective.[352] The Dutch government banned short sales in the stock of the Dutch East India Company (Verenigde Oost-Indische Compagnie) in 1610.[353] That ban was largely ignored, but the Dutch government tried again in 1689 with a tax on short sale profits.[354] That too proved to be ineffective. Holland discovered that "no statute can destroy the irresistible laws of economics" and abandoned such efforts.[355]

In 1733, Sir John Barnard's Act prohibited short sales in England, but it proved to be unenforceable and was repealed in 1860.[356] England prohibited short sales in bank stocks in 1866 through the Leeman's Act.[357] As described below, although that law proved unworkable, the SEC took such an approach during the financial crisis in 2008. A French royal decree in 1724 prohibited short sales and "term" dealings." Another royal decree in 1785 prohibited short sales and futures trading, but those proscriptions were largely ignored. Napoleon prohibited short selling in France in 1802 by making such transactions unenforceable gambling contracts. That law proved to be unenforceable and was repealed in 1885.[358]

Germany banned speculation in futures contracts with its bourse law in 1896 that prohibited short selling. That legislation was enacted in response to a coffee corner, price volatility in sugar and grain prices, and, of particular concern, futures contracts for wheat and flour.[359] The German law was strengthened in 1900.[360] The result of that legislation was that "the market became highly

---

351. *Id.*

352. James Edward Meeker, Short Selling (1932).

353. I Jerry W. Markham, A Financial History of the United States, From Christopher Columbus to the Robber Barons (1492-1900) 94-95 (2002).

354. James J. Angel & Douglas M. McCabe, *The Business Ethics of Short Selling and Naked Short Selling*, 85 J. Bus. Ethics 239 (Spring 2008).

355. James Edward Meeker, Short Selling 13 (1932).

356. *Id.*

357. *Id.*

358. *Id.* at 218-221.

359. Birl E. Schultz, The Securities Market and How It Works 214 (1946).

360. The following provision was then added to the German Civil Code:

susceptible to unfavorable developments and rumors; and, in the absence of all steadying influence, any adverse factors were accompanied by fluctuations such as had rarely been witnessed in former times."[361] "German capital was diverted to the financial centers of other countries."[362]

"Foreign brokers, seeing a new field of activity opened to them in Germany, flocked to Berlin and established agencies for the sale of stocks in London, Paris, Amsterdam and New York. Seventy such offices were opened in Berlin within one year after the law was passed, and did a flourishing business."[363] That legislation stopped derivatives trading on German exchanges for almost 100 years. U.S. brokerage markets exploited that market, until the German courts began treating even U.S. futures transactions as gambling contracts.[364] In the 1990s, Germany legalized derivatives, and Eurex, a German exchange, soon surpassed the U.S. exchanges as the largest futures exchange in the world.[365] However, Germany did not lose its fixation with short sales. The government there imposed controls on such trading during and after the Financial Crisis in 2008. In 2012, German prosecutors indicted two former Porsche executives for engaging in massive stock market manipulation of the stock of Volkswagen AG. Porsche's trading squeezed short traders and caused them billions of dollars in losses. A federal judge had previously dismissed a civil lawsuit in the U.S. over that trading.[366]

The United States has a long history with short sales. The New York legislature prohibited short sale transactions in 1812; the statute made contracts for the sale of stock void unless the seller owned the shares at the time of the agreement to sell. This New York law was much criticized and repealed in 1858.[367]

An industrial commission was created by President William McKinley in 1898 to study the condition of labor and capital.[368] It initially recommended federal legislation to prohibit short sales.[369] However, that commission issued a report in 1901 on the distribution of farm products that supported speculation in the futures markets.[370] It even concluded that short selling favorably

---

> If a contract for the future delivery of commodities or securities has been closed with the intention that the difference between the price agreed on and the Stock Exchange or market price at the time of delivery shall be paid by the loser to the winner, such contract is to be considered as a wager. This shall also apply if only one of the contracting parties intends that the difference should be paid and the other party knows or should know such intention.

G. Plochman, *The German Bourse Law*, 187 North American Rev. 742, 743 (May 1908).

361. *Id.* at 746.

362. *Id.* at 747.

363. State of New York, *Report of Governor Hughes Committee on Speculation in Securities and Commodities* 22 (June 7, 1909). For an extended discussion of the effects of this German law that was considered during congressional hearings in the United States in the 1930s on stock manipulations, see *Stock Exchange Practices: Hearing Before the Senate Committee on Banking and Currency on S. Res. 84, S. Res. 56 and S. Res. 97*, 73d Cong., 1st Sess. 7159-7165 (1934). It was reported that the German law only facilitated price manipulations. *Id.* at 7163.

364. William P. Rogers & Jerry W. Markham, *The Application of West German Statutes to United States Commodity Futures Contracts: An Unnecessary Clash of Policies*, 19 Geo. J.L. & Policy in Int'l Bus. 273 (1987).

365. III Jerry W. Markham, A Financial History of History of the United States, From the Age of Derivatives to the New Millennium (1970-2001) 271 (2002).

366. Mellissa Eddy and Nicholas Kulish, *Ex-Porsche Officials Charged in VW Bid*, New York Times, Dec. 4, 2012, at B1.

367. James Edward Meeker, Short Selling 231-232 (1932).

368. *The Industrial Commission*, New York Times, Sept. 7, 1898.

369. II Jerry W. Markham, A Financial History of the United States, From J.P. Morgan to the Institutional Investor (1900-1970) 4-5 (2002).

370. VI *Report of the Industrial Commission on the Distribution of Farm Products* (1901).

affected farmers when the shorts covered their positions, which had the effect of increasing prices. Conversely, long speculators would depress prices when they sold out their positions.[371]

Those conclusions did not sway President Theodore Roosevelt, who advised Congress in 1908 (after the Panic of 1907) that it was desirable that "there should be measures taken to prevent at least the grosser forms of gambling in securities and commodities, such as making large sales of what men do not possess and 'cornering' the market. . . . There is no moral difference between gambling at cards or in lotteries or on the race track and gambling in the stock market. One method is just as pernicious to the body politic as the other in kind, and in degree the evil worked is far greater."[372] The president, recognizing the difficulty in dealing with speculation, recommended that Congress study "both the successes and failures" of the prohibitions imposed by Germany on speculation "so as to do nothing harmful."[373]

The House congressional committee, the Pujo Committee (named after its chair, Representative Arsene Pujo [D-La]), which was created in the wake of the stock market's Panic of 1907, concluded that short selling was no more harmful than buying stocks, but recommended that brokers be prohibited from lending stock to customers to fulfill short sale delivery requirements,[374] a practice that remains common in the industry today. The Pujo Committee was concerned by the testimony of an NYSE official who testified that short selling would be legitimate and desirable for a trader to engage in while a "panic was raging over the country and it was desirable to protect interests which could not be sold."[375]

Although the public generally believed that short traders artificially depressed prices, the massive study of the grain trade by the Federal Trade Commission in the 1920s found that existing evidence did not support that claim.[376] The FTC stated that it was harder to manipulate prices on the short side. Nevertheless, the concentration of "more or less incompetent traders in the long side of the market, the temptation, apart from the possibility of cornering or squeezing the market, to manipulate on the short side may be greater for the professional trader than to manipulate on the long side."[377]

NYSE rules prohibited "bear raids," but no violations were found even in the wake of the stock market crash of 1929.[378] Nevertheless, short selling was briefly prohibited on the NYSE for two

---

371. *Id.* at 189-190. The report of the Industrial Commission stated:

> The professional speculator is in the market not for the purpose of depressing or raising prices. He is as ready to make money on a rise as on a fall in prices. In either case he will try to ascertain what the probable tendency of the market is before he embarks in any undertaking. No speculator or clique of speculators in their senses would undertake to try to depress prices in the face of a rising market. Such attempts are made at times by "bear rings" after they have already sold in anticipation of a falling market and think that by bold manipulation they may for a time create a panic in the face of an opposite tendency of the market and get out before a reaction sets in. But the repeated failures both of bull and bear cliques have not only served to teach speculators a lesson and thus to diminish the number of such ventures, but are also the best proof that the "bear" is by no means the only factor in the market.

Id. at 190.

372. 42 Cong. Rec. 1347, 1349 (Jan. 1, 1908) (message from the president).

373. *Id. See also*, § 1:3 (describing the German legislation).

374. *Report of the Committee Appointed Pursuant to House Resolutions 429 and 504 to Investigate the Concentration of Control of Money and Credit*, H. Rep. No. 1593, 62d Cong., 3d Sess. 52 (1913).

375. *Id.* at 53.

376. VII Federal Trade Commission, Report on the Grain Trade 244 (1923).

377. *Id.* at 9.

378. James Edward Meeker, Short Selling 17 (1932).

days during the Great Depression, September 21 and 22, 1931. Interestingly, Canada undertook an extensive examination of short selling in 1931 through its "Stamp Commission," which found futures trading to be beneficial and refused to recommend restrictions on short sales.[379]

The federal securities laws that were enacted in the 1930s allowed the SEC to regulate short sales. As described in Chapter 2, the SEC had tried to dampen the effect of short sales in the securities markets with the adoption of its tick test rule (Rule 10a-1) after a market decline in 1937.[380] That rule allowed short sales only after an uptick in the price of the stock being shorted. The SEC sought to achieve three objectives through that rule: "(i) allowing relatively unrestricted short selling in an advancing market; (ii) preventing short selling at successively lower prices, thus eliminating short selling as a tool for driving the market down; and (iii) preventing short sellers from accelerating a declining market by exhausting all remaining bids at one price level, causing successively lower prices to be established by long sellers."[381]

This rule reflected a buy side bias at the SEC, which prefers markets to go up rather than down. In contrast, the commodity futures industry views markets as being two-sided and considers short speculators as important to the price discovery process as the longs. As a Treasury Department report noted in 2008,

> A short sale in the securities context is usually depicted as a risky bet that stock prices will decline. Moreover, some observers contend that heavy short-selling deliberately to drive down the price of a stock may constitute manipulation. In contrast, short selling in the futures context is generally viewed as a necessary and critical component of liquidity in the futures markets. Although the risk profile of short selling is similar in both the futures and securities contexts (price declines mean profitability for the short, while price increases mean unlimited potential losses), the SEC imposes extensive restrictions on the practice while the CFTC imposes few.[382]

After a broad study of the securities markets in 1962, the SEC recommended additional regulation of short sales in order "to relieve the added pressure that short selling may create during a severe decline in the general market or a declining price trend in a particular security."[383] The SEC apparently took no action on that recommendation. It did conduct a study of the tick test rule in 1976, concluding that the rule was outdated by changes in market structure. "[P]ractices like the traditional 'bear raid' are now much more difficult to engage in, since any attempt at such an effort under today's market and regulatory conditions is likely to be detected and stopped."[384]

The SEC adopted a new Regulation SHO in 2004 that imposed order marking requirements for short sales.[385] That regulation also created a pilot program pursuant to which the SEC could exclude designated securities from the operation of the tick test of Rule 10a-1 and any short sale

---

379. *Id.* at 15.

380. 17 C.F.R. § 240.10a-1.

381. *Short Sales*, 69 Fed. Reg. 48008, 48009 (Aug. 6, 2004). *See generally*, Jonathon R. Macey, Mark Mitchell, & Jeffrey Netter, *Restrictions on Short Sales: An Analysis of the Uptick Rule and Its Role in View of the October 1987 Stock Market Crash*, 74 Cornell L. Rev. 799 (1989) (describing this SEC rule).

382. Department of the Treasury, *Blueprint for a Modernized Financial Regulatory Structure* 117 (March 2008). *See also*, David C. Worley, *The Regulation of Short Sales: The Long and Short of It*, 55 Brooklyn L. Rev. 1255 (1990) (describing criticism of SEC tick test).

383. *Report of the Special Study of the Securities Markets of the Securities Exchange Commission*, H. Doc. No. 95, pt. 2, 88th Cong., 1st Sess. 293 (1963).

384. *Short Sales of Securities*, Exchange Act Release No. 13,091 [1976 Transfer Binder] Fed. Sec. L. Rep. (CCH) ¶ 80,837 (Dec. 21, 1976).

385. *Short Sales*, 69 Fed. Reg. 48008 (Aug. 6, 2004).

price test rule of any exchange or NASDAQ.[386] On July 3, 2007, the SEC eliminated Rule 10a-1 and added Rule 201 under Regulation SHO that provided that there shall be no price test for short selling in any security.[387] This rule change came not long before the onset of the financial crisis that peaked in 2008. That event led to claims by financial services firms that their stock was facing unwarranted attacks from short sellers. It was claimed that predatory shorts were destroying public confidence in those firms, which included Lehman Brothers, Citigroup Bear Stearns, AIG, Fannie Mae, and Freddie Mac.[388] Jamie Dimon, the CEO at JPMorgan Chase, claimed that such short selling "is even worse than insider trading" and that it is a "deliberate and malicious destruction of value and people's lives."[389]

The SEC received more than 5,000 complaints about "naked short sales during an eighteen-month period starting January 1, 2007. . . ." These were short traders who sold without having first located securities for borrowing to cover their short position.[390] Interestingly, the Seventh Circuit had previously ruled in *Sullivan & Long Inc. v. Scattered Corp.*[391] that naked short selling was not an undesirable practice even when the short sold more stock than was outstanding. The court applied some reasoning based on the thought of the Chicago school of law and economics:

> The plaintiffs complain that the defendant prevented them from profiting from their purchases by flooding the market with successive waves of short sales, thus keeping the market price from fluctuating upward from time to time ("capping the price," they call it). Such upturns would have enabled them either to buy in at a higher price than the short-sale price and thus make a profit, if they had bought from Scattered, or to sell at a profit stock that they already owned. But "flooding" a market with short sales is not a rational formula for keeping the price falling. On the other side of each such sale is a buyer who thinks the market price will rise. If he is right, the short seller will lose money, and the more shares he has sold short, the more money he will lose.[392]

---

386. *Short Sales*, 69 Fed. Reg. 48008, 48009 (Aug. 6, 2004).

387. *Regulation SHO and Rule 10a-1*, 72 Fed. Reg. 36348 (July 3, 2007).

388. Jerry W. Markham, A Financial History of the U.S. From the Subprime Crisis to the Great Recession (2006-2009) 511 (2011).

389. Jenny Anderson, *S.E.C. Unveils Measures to Limit Short Selling*, New York Times, July 16, 2008, at C1.

390. Jerry W. Markham, A Financial History of the U.S. From the Subprime Crisis to the Great Recession (2006-2009) 511-512 (2011). *See generally*, Alexis B. Stokes, *In Pursuit of the Naked Short*, 5 N.Y.U. J. L. & Bus. 1 (2009).

391. Sullivan & Long Inc. v. Scattered Corp., 47 F.3d 857 (7th Cir.), *cert. denied*, 516 U.S. 818 (1995).

392. 47 F.3d at 862. The court further stated:

> The plaintiffs analogize Scattered's plan to the scam in the movie *The Producers*. The "defendants" in that movie sold shares in a play to investors. They sold more than 100 percent of the shares, confident that the play—"Springtime for Hitler"—would be a flop, so that the investors would not ask for their share of the profits (there would be no profits). The play was a success, so the scam was exposed and they were sent to jail. Where the analogy fails is that while investors reasonably believe that the promoter will not sell more shares than exist, since he would then be defrauding the investors, a buyer of stock does not have a basis for equal confidence that the number of shares of a stock that is being sold short does not exceed the total number of shares in existence, since the seller is not trying to raise money for a venture. If even one share of a stock is sold short, there will be more shares actually or potentially for sale than there are shares in existence—since by definition the short seller does not own the share or shares that he is selling short—unless the short seller has borrowed stock in order to be able to make delivery if the buyer wants delivery.

47 F.3d at 863.

Ignoring that case and the long history of unsuccessful efforts to control markets by restricting short selling, the SEC attacked "naked shorts" in the press and in enforcement actions.[393] On July 15, 2008, the SEC issued a temporary emergency order prohibiting naked short selling in the stocks of nineteen major financial companies, including Fannie Mae, Freddie Mac, Lehman Brothers, Merrill Lynch, and Morgan Stanley. This rule required brokers handling short sales to have borrowed securities in their possession before conducting a short sale.[394] The Dow Jones Industrial Average jumped by 276.74 points on that news.[395]

The stocks of Fannie Mae, Freddie Mac, and Lehman Brothers Holdings also appeared, briefly, to have stabilized. However, Lehman Brothers failed on September 14, 2008, setting off a global financial crisis. On September 18, 2008, the SEC imposed a temporary ban on all short selling on the stocks of 799 financial services firms.[396] That ban was easily avoided through single stock futures and other derivatives.[397] The ban was also widely criticized, and the SEC chair, Christopher Cox, claimed that the agency had ordered the ban only after intensive pressure from the Fed and Treasury.[398]

The SEC took this action under the emergency powers granted by Section 12(k) of the 34 Act,[399] which was added to the statute by the Market Reform Act of 1990.[400] As described in Chapter 5, that authority was added by Congress after the stock market crash of 1987. The SEC stated that its suspension of short sales was necessary because it was "concerned about the possible unnecessary or artificial price movements based on unfounded rumors regarding the stability of financial institutions and other issuers exacerbated by 'naked' short selling." The SEC's concern over short selling was no longer limited to the financial institutions that were the subject of the earlier July emergency order restricting naked short sales on certain financial institutions. "In addition, we have become concerned that some persons may take advantage of issuers that have become temporarily weakened by current market conditions to engage in inappropriate short selling in the securities of such issuers."[401]

The SEC attacked rumormongers who were purportedly circulating sensational rumors designed to aid short traders by driving down the price of particular stocks.[402] The SEC also adopted an "interim final temporary rule" requiring hedge funds and other large institutional investors to

---

393. *See generally*, Kevin A. Crisp, *Giving Investors Short Shrift: How Short Sale Constraints Decrease Market Efficiency and a Modest Proposal for Letting More Shorts Go Naked*, 8 J. Bus. & Sec. L.135 (2008).

394. Jenny Anderson, *S.E.C. Unveils Measures to Limit Short-Selling*, New York Times, July 16, 2008, at C1.

395. Jenny Anderson, *Shares Revive Amid Confusing Signs From S.E.C.*, New York Times, July 17, 2008, at C1.

396. Vikas Bajaj & Graham Browley, *S.E.C. Temporarily Blocks Short Sales of Financial Stocks*, New York Times, Sept. 20, 2008.

397. However, the SEC did bring a few enforcement actions over violations of its short sale restrictions. *See*, In the Matter of Lightspeed LLC, 2009 WL 2528415 (S.E.C.); In the Matter of Goldman Sachs Execution & Clearing LP, 2010 WL 1782448 (S.E.C.).

398. *Traders Group Faults SEC Over Decision on Short Selling Ban*, 41 Sec. Reg. & L. Rep. (BNA) 85 (Jan. 19. 2009).

399. 15 U.S.C. § 78l(k).

400. Pub. L. No. 101-432, 104 Stat. 963 (1990).

401. *Emergency Order Pursuant to Section 12(K)(2) of the Securities Exchange Act of 1934 Taking Temporary Action to Respond to Market Developments*, 73 Fed. Reg. 54875 (Sept. 23, 2008).

402. Jerry W. Markham, A Financial History of the U.S. From the Subprime Crisis to the Great Recession (2006-2009) 510 (2011).

disclose their short positions on a daily basis.[403] The SEC agreed to delay publication of those reports so that traders' exiting positions would not be exposed to attacks by other traders.[404] A "naked" short selling antifraud rule was also adopted.[405]

The short sale restrictions imposed during the financial crisis were generally viewed as ineffective.[406] Nevertheless, the new SEC chair, Mary Schapiro, advocated a return to the tick test when she assumed office.[407] The SEC first amended Regulation SHO in 2009 in order to prevent future naked short sales by requiring prompt buy-ins where there is a failure to deliver.[408] The SEC further amended Regulation SHO in 2010 to impose a modified tick test in the form of a circuit breaker–type short sale restriction. Under that amendment, exchanges and other trading centers must prohibit short sales at a price that is less than or equal to the national best bid where a security falls more than 10 percent in value from its last closing price.[409]

Section 417 of the Dodd-Frank Act also required the SEC to conduct a study on short selling and directed the SEC to consider creating a pilot program in which public companies would agree to have their trades marked "short," "market-maker short," "buy," "buy to cover," or "long." Those trades would then be reported in real time in the pilot program. The SEC sought comments on that study and pilot program in May 2011, but took no immediate action.[410]

France, Italy, Spain, and Belgium were also concerned with speculative attacks on their banks and banned or restricted short selling in the securities of those institutions.[411] However, OneChicago, a U.S. exchange trading single stock futures, advertised that these bans could be circumvented by short positions on that exchange.[412] Short sale regulatory concerns continued in Europe after a financial crisis in Greece in 2010. "Greek Prime Minister George Papandreou blamed his country's problems on speculators in the spring of 2010, an accusation echoed by his Italian counterpart,

---

403. *Disclosure of Short Sales and Short Positions by Institutional Investment Managers*, 73 Fed. Reg. 61678 (Oct. 17, 2008).

404. A Utah law was also passed that allowed its corporations to collect a $10,000 per day fee from broker-dealers that fail to notify the Utah securities commission that short sales would not be delivered on time. Jed Horowitz & Carol S. Redmond, *Securities Industry Weighs Suit Over New Utah Short-Sale Law*, Wall Street Journal, May 30, 2006, at C5.

405. *"Naked" Short Selling Antifraud Rule*, 73 Fed. Reg. 61666 (Oct. 17, 2008).

406. *See*, Robert Battalio, Hamid Mehran & Paul Schultz, Federal Reserve Bank of New York Staff Report, *Market Declines: Is Banning Short Selling the Solution?* (Sept. 2011) (reviewing effects of short selling). *See also*, Floyd Norris, *Questioning the Benefit of Curbing Short Sales*, New York Times, Dec. 16, 2011, at B1, B6 (discussing effects of short selling).

407. *SEC Depression-Era Uptick Rule Said Irrelevant to Modern Marketplace*, 41 Sec. Reg. & L. Rep. (BNA) 413 (March 9, 2009).

408. *Amendments to Regulation SHO*, 74 Fed. Reg. 38266 (July 31, 2009).

409. *Amendments to Regulation SHO,* 2010 WL 675942 (Feb. 26, 2010).

410. *Short Sale Reporting Study Required by Dodd-Frank Act Section 417(a)(2)*, 76 Fed. Reg. 26787 (May 9, 2011).

411. *Europe Short Bans Extended,* Wall Street Journal, Aug. 26, 2011, at C3. After Italy imposed restrictions on short sales, the market in the affected securities immediately dropped further. *Italian Securities Regulator Adopts Temporary Rules to Curb Market Speculation*, 43 Sec. Reg. & L. Rep. (CCH) 1490 (July 18, 2011).The EU Parliament approved a ban on naked short sales of sovereign debt credit default swaps. *EU Lawmakers OK Ban on Naked Selling of Sovereign Debt Credit Default Swaps*, 43 Sec. Reg. & L. Rep. (CCH) 1437 (July 11, 2011). The Financial Services Agency in Japan had also acted to sanction Barclays Capital for violating its short sale restrictions. Kana Inagaki and Hiroyuki Kachi, *Japan Raps Barclay Capital*, Wall Street Journal, Sept 30, 2011.

412. OneChicago, *Europe's Short-Selling Ban*, http://www.onechicago.com/?p=8607 (accessed August 26, 2011).

Silvio Berlusconi, this summer. The view seems to be that their fiscal troubles are the result of insidious outside 'manipulation,' not years of wasteful spending and antigrowth policies."[413]

In May 2010, forgetting its past, Germany banned naked short sales on euro zone bonds and certain financial institutions.[414] German regulatory authorities also sent out a directive to firms engaging in high frequency trading, which ordered them to take actions to prevent manipulative trading practices such as "spoofing" and "layering."[415]

France, Spain, Italy, and Belgium imposed temporary short sale restrictions on bank stocks in August 2011.[416] The European Parliament voted on July 5, 2011, to support legislation that would prohibit naked short sales through synthetic credit default swaps on sovereign debt and other trading. In May 2011, European finance ministers agreed to a more narrow limitation on short sales of shares of sovereign debt.[417] The short sale bans in Europe were later adjudged to have had no positive effects.[418] Nevertheless, on April 2, 2013, Italy banned short sales in the stock of Monte del Paschi di Siena SpA, Italy's third largest bank, which was facing severe financial difficulties.

7:10 PROPRIETARY TRADING AND THE VOLCKER RULE

Another limitation on speculation arrived in the form of the so-called Volcker Rule, named after its chief proponent, Paul Volcker, the former Fed chair. He had advocated a return of the Glass-Steagall restrictions on investment banking activities by commercial banks.[419] The Glass-Steagall Act prohibited banks from engaging in equity underwritings, but that restriction had been gutted over the years by the courts and bank regulators and was repealed by the Gramm-Leach-Bliley Act in 1999.[420]

After the failure of several large banks and massive losses by others during the financial crisis of 2008, claims were made that the removal of the Glass-Steagall restrictions was a precipitating factor in causing those losses. That was actually not the case because commercial banks were already heavily involved in the subprime mortgage market, which was the underlying cause of the financial crisis, before the passage of the Gramm-Leach-Bliley Act.[421] Nevertheless, Volcker, who was appointed as a member of the newly elected President Obama's Economic Recovery Advisory Board, urged that commercial banks be again removed from investment banking activities and prohibited from owning or trading "risky" securities.[422] However, the risky securities

413. *Short on Solutions*, WALL STREET JOURNAL, Aug. 16, 2011, at A12.

414. Charles Forelle & Patrick McGroarty, *Market Tumult: Taking the Naked Ban to a New Level*, WALL STREET JOURNAL, May 20, 2010 at C2.

415. BaFin, *BaFin Publishes Information on the Prevention of Market Manipulation in an Automated Trading Environment*, available at http://www.bafin.de/SharedDocs/Veroeffentlichungen/EN/Meldung/2012/meldung _121218_layering_en.html (accessed on April 1, 2013).

416. *Short on Solutions*, WALL STREET JOURNAL, Aug. 16, 2011, at A12. Great Britain and the Czech Republic sued the European Union in European Court of Justice over the adoption of short sale restrictions. Yeganeh Torbati, *Osborne Files Suit Over EU Short-Selling Rules—FT*, Reuters, http://www.reuters.com/article/2012/05/31/osborne-european-union-idUSL5E8GVHBH20120531 (accessed June 3, 2010).

417. *Financial Briefing Book*, WALL STREET JOURNAL, May 18, 2011, at C2.

418. Nina Mehta, *Shorting Bans Do Little to Help Europe Banks, Instinet Says*, Bloomberg, http://www.bloomberg.com/news/2011-10-03/short-sale-bans-doing-little-to-help-europe-banks-instinet-says.html (accessed March 23, 2012).

419. Banking Act of 1933, ch. 89, 48 Stat. 162. For a description of Volcker's role in the passage of the provisions in Dodd-Frank that restrict proprietary trading, *see*, WILLIAM L. SILBER, VOLCKER 273-296 (2012).

420. Pub. L. No. 106-102, 113 Stat. 1338.

421. *See*, Jerry W. Markham, *The Subprime Crisis: A Test Match for the Bankers*, 12 U. PENN. L & BUS. J. 1081 (2010) (discussing those claims).

422. Jerry W. Markham, *The Subprime Crisis: A Test Match for the Bankers*, 12 U. PENN. L & BUS. J. 1081, 1107 (2010).

of concern were actually triple-A rated tranches of collateralized debt obligations securitizing subprime mortgages.[423]

The Dodd-Frank Act adopted a modified version of the Volcker rule. Proprietary trading was restricted, but hedging activities, brokered trades, and market making were exempted from that restriction.[424] The passage of that provision was intended to be a safety and soundness measure, rather than an attempt to limit speculation. Nevertheless, it acted as a curb on speculation because that bar removed some large trading operations from the markets.

The Dodd-Frank restrictions on proprietary trading were to be implemented by the Office of the Comptroller of the Currency, the Federal Deposit Insurance Corporation, the Fed, SEC, and CFTC, with input from the Dodd-Frank–created super council of regulators—the Financial Stability Oversight Council.[425] Those regulators proposed joint rules for defining prohibited proprietary trades.[426] Those rule proposals were sharply criticized by the affected banks, which mounted a massive lobbying campaign to water down the rules.

Among the strongest critics of the Volcker rule was the CEO of JPMorgan Chase, Jamie Dimon, who had become a Wall Street rock star after leading JPMorgan safely through the financial crisis in 2008. The pushback by the banks on the Volcker rule was having effect until JPMorgan stunned the market on May 10, 2012, by announcing a $2 billion trading loss, which quickly grew to more than $5 billion. The losses were attributed to mistakes in hedging exposure to European debt, but it turned out that the trades were directional bets on an index of investment-grade corporate debt. The trading had proved profitable for a while, but caused massive losses when the market did not perform as expected. Dimon then found himself pilloried in the press and before Congress for his criticism of the Volcker rule.[427]

7:11 OIL PRICES AGAIN

Energy prices became a prime focus of Congress after the California electricity crisis and as energy prices rose rapidly. The result was new antimanipulation authority for FERC and the Federal Trade Commission (FTC). However, that legislation did not end the rise in commodity prices. Crude oil prices resumed their rise from $76.01 per barrel on the NYMEX on July 16, 2010 (just before the signing of Dodd-Frank), to $112.29 per barrel on April 22, 2011,[428] an increase fueled by Middle East unrest and the revolution in Libya.[429] Gas prices at the pump jumped in April to an average of $3.684 per gallon for regular gasoline, a seasonal high.[430]

---

423. See, Jerry W. Markham, *Regulating Credit Default Swaps in the Wake of the Subprime Crisis*, Chapter 9 in International Monetary Fund, *Restoring Financial Stability: The Legal Response: Current Developments in Monetary and Financial Law*, Volume 6 (IMF: Washington, D.C. 2012) (describing those investments).

424. The Dodd-Frank Wall Street Reform and Consumer Protection Act of 2010, § 619.

425. *Public Input for the Study Regarding the Implementation of the Prohibitions on Proprietary Trading and Certain Relationships With Hedge Funds and Private Equity Fund*, 75 Fed. Reg. 61758 (Oct. 6, 2010).

426. *See*, *Prohibitions and Restrictions on Proprietary Trading and Certain Interests in, and Relationships With, Hedge Funds and Covered Funds*, 77 Fed. Reg. 8332 (Feb. 14, 2012) (describing this joint rule-making process).

427. Jessica Silver-Greenberg & Nelson D. Schwartz, *Discord at Key JPMorgan Unit Is Blamed in Bank's Huge Loss*, New York Times, May 20, 2012, at A1.

428. NYMEX, Crude Oil Price History, http://www.nyse.tv/crude-oil-price-history.htm (accessed August 20, 2011).

429. Jerry A. DiColo, *Next Problem for Oil: Nigerian Elections*, Wall Street Journal, April 4, 2011, at C3.

430. Ben Lefebvre, *Corporate News: The Week Ahead: Rising Gas Prices Cut Two Ways*, Wall Street Journal, April 11, 2011, at B2.

The CFTC released data showing that 95 percent of crude oil futures trading in U.S. markets was due to "day trading." Such trading involves traders taking short-term in-and-out positions to profit from brief market price changes, up or down. "Scalpers" have long traded on the floors of U.S. commodity exchanges, seeking to profit from such quick in-and-out trades.[431] This is also a popular technique for high-frequency traders that trade on the basis of computer algorithms.

Only a little over 5 percent on crude oil trading on NYMEX was due to changes in overnight positions, which generally are for hedging or for speculators expressing a longer-term view on oil prices.[432] This played into the Obama administration's desire to turn the political focus away from the fundamental supply and demand factors driving oil prices by blaming speculators for the price increases. Copying a page from the battered playbook of the George W. Bush administration, which had launched the ill-advised Enron Task Force to deflect criticism of its regulatory policies, President Obama created a Justice Department–led intergovernmental task force that was to focus on "the role of traders and speculators" in the oil price surge.[433] That effort produced nothing but a few meetings over the next year.[434]

The oil companies predictably came under attack once again as a result of the large profits they made in times of soaring crude oil prices.[435] The FTC announced in June 2011 that it was conducting a sweeping investigation of the oil market to ascertain whether it was being manipulated.[436] "FTC Chairman Jon Leibowitz said the agency's investigation will focus on determining 'whether certain oil producers, refiners, transporters . . . or financial traders' have engaged or are engaging in practices that have lessened or may lessen competition—or have engaged in manipulation—in the production, refining, transportation, distribution, or wholesale supply of crude oil or petroleum products."[437] That investigation proved to be a vain quest for glory. In September 2011, Leibowitz reported that the FTC had found that fundamental supply and demand factors were driving gasoline prices, not speculators. That was a hard pill to swallow as gasoline prices reached near all-time seasonal highs over the Labor Day weekend.[438]

Members of Congress, immune to such technicalities as supply and demand, were seeking additional legislation to limit commodity speculation.[439] Senators Bernard Sanders (Socialist-VT) and Bill Nelson

---

431. *See,* Dupont v. United States, 300 U.S. 150, 152 (1937) (a scalping broker is one "who makes his profit in fractional movements on the exchange, buying and selling with great rapidity, thus often purchasing and selling the same amount of the commodity at the same price within a few moments or hours.").

432. Gregory Meyer, *CFTC Data Reveal Day Traders' Role in Volatile Oil Markets*, FINANCIAL TIMES (LONDON), July 6, 2011, at 21.

433. Carol E. Lee, *U.S. News: White House's Task Force to Probe Oil, Gas Markets*, WALL STREET JOURNAL, April 22, 2011, at A5.

434. Helene Cooper, *As Gas Prices Cast Cloud, Obama Calls for Scrutiny on Market*, NEW YORK TIMES, April 18, 2012, at A19.

435. An inadvertent email disclosure revealed that Chevron had made $360 million in profits from its energy trading operations in the first two quarters of 2011. Brian Baskin, *Chevron's Email "Oops" Reveals Energy Giant's Sway Over Markets*, WALL STREET JOURNAL, July 16-17, 2011, at B1.

436. Tennille Tracy & Jerry A. DiColo, *FTC Launches Oil-Trade Probe*, WALL STREET JOURNAL, June 21, 2011, at C3.

437. Courant.com, *Blumenthal Applauds FTC Decision to Probe Petroleum Industry*, http://articles.courant.com/2011-06-20/business/hc-ftc-investigates-petroleum-industr20110620_1_crude-oil-independent-connecticut-petroleum-association-energy-markets (accessed Aug. 19, 2011).

438. Jamila Trindle, *Speculation's Part in Pump Prices Minimized*, WALL STREET JOURNAL, Sept. 2, 2011, at C3.

439. Ianthe Jeanne Dugan & Liam Pleven, *Senators Aim to Tighten Rules on Oil*, WALL STREET JOURNAL, June 20, 2011, at C3. Although other commodity prices were soaring, those increases were receiving little attention in the United States Jon Hilsenrath, *Fed Plays Down Inflation: Speeches Signal U.S. to Keep Credit Cheap as Others Tighten*, WALL STREET JOURNAL, April 12, 2011, at A1 (oil prices

(D-FL) introduced legislation in June 2011 that would have sharply limited the size of positions that speculators could take on in the markets.[440] Nelson introduced the Anti-Excessive Speculation Act of 2011. It sought to cap speculation to 20 percent of energy trading, a reduction from what he claimed was an existing level of 50 percent. Nelson charged that speculators were adding 25 percent to the cost of a barrel of oil.[441] That legislative effort was renewed in 2012 as the presidential campaign began to heat up. Sanders and sixty Democratic members of Congress introduced legislation in March 2012 that would have forced the CFTC to impose position limits on oil futures trading.[442]

The Democratic members of a congressional staff committee claimed in a May 2011 report that speculation in the oil markets had inflated prices by 30 percent.[443] That report recommended that congressional focus should be "on countering the growing impact of excessive speculation, rather than pursuing the oil industry's priorities of increasing domestic drilling or repealing safety measures put in place after the devastating BP oil spill [in the Gulf of Mexico in 2010]."[444]

An incredible number of hearings were held in Congress over rising energy prices.[445] Attacks on speculators also included a *Wall Street Journal* op-ed piece by consumer advocate Ralph Nader,

---

up 70 percent and other commodity prices up 40 percent over prior summer). *See also*, Javier Bias & Emiko Terazono, *Food Commodity Prices Soar as US Crop Forecast Cut*, FINANCIAL TIMES (LONDON), Aug. 12, 2011, at 1 (U.S. food prices continued to increase as the result of draught conditions and high temperatures).

440. Ianthe Jeanne Dugan & Liam Pleven, *Senators Aim to Tighten Rules on Oil*, WALL STREET JOURNAL, June 20, 2011, at C3.

441. Gretchen Morgenson, *Speculators Get a Break in a New Rule*, NEW YORK TIMES, Sept. 25, 2011, at B1-B2.

442. *Lawmakers Tell CFTC to Enact Position Limits Immediately*, 44 SEC. REG. & L. REP. (BNA) 544 (March 12, 2012); *U.S. Senators Press for Position Limits in Oil Markets*, Reuters, http://www.reuters.com/article/2012/03/21/usa-oil-limits-idUSL1E8ELNOC20120321 (accessed March 22, 2012).

443. David Sheppard & Ayesha Rascoe, *House Democrats Urge Limits on Oil Speculators*, http://www.reuters.com/article/2011/05/23/us-oil-speculation-idUSTRE74M4HN20110523 (accessed August 24, 2011).

444. Democratic Staff of the Committee on Oversight and Government Reform, U.S. House of Representatives, *Real Help for American Consumers: Who's Profiting at the Pump?* 3 (May 23, 2011).

445. *See, e.g., Retail Gas Prices (Part I): Consumer Effects*, Hearing Before the Task Force on Competition Policy and Antitrust Laws of the Committee on the Judiciary, House of Representatives, 110 Cong., 2d Sess., Serial No. 110-102, May 7, 2008; *Rising Diesel Fuel Costs in the Trucking Industry*, Hearing Before the Subcommittee on Highways and Transit of the Committee on Transportation and Infrastructure, House of Representatives, 110th Congress, 2d Sess. Serial No. 110-124, May 6, 2008; *Retail Gas Prices (Part II): Competition in the Oil Industry*, Hearing Before the Task Force on Competition Policy and Antitrust Laws of the Committee on the Judiciary, House of Representatives, 110th Congress, 2d Sess., Serial No. 110-180, May 22, 2008; *Sustainable, Energy-Efficient Transportation Infrastructure*, Hearing Before the Subcommittee on Technology and Innovation Committee on Science and Technology, House of Representatives, 110th Cong., 2d Sess., Serial No. 110-110, June 24, 2008; *Hearing to Review the Source of Dramatic Movements in the Commodity Markets (Agriculture and Energy): A Change in Market Fundamentals or Influence of Institutional Investors?* Hearing Before the Subcommittee on General Farm Commodities and Risk Management of the Committee on Agriculture, House of Representatives, 110th Cong., 2d Sess., Serial No. 110-37, May 15, 2008; *Implications of a Weaker Dollar for Oil Prices and the U.S. Economy*, Hearing Before the Committee on Financial Services, U.S. House of Representatives, 110th Cong., 2d Sess., Serial No. 110-131, July 24, 2008; *Oil and Gas Development: Exemptions from Health and Environmental Protections*, Hearing Before the Committee on Oversight and Government Reform, House of Representatives, 110th Cong., 1st Sess., October 31, 2007; *Energy Speculation: Is Greater Regulation Necessary to Stop Price Manipulation?* Hearing Before the Subcommittee on Oversight and Investigations of the Committee on Energy and Commerce, House of Representatives, 110th Cong., 1st Sess., Serial No. 110-78, December 12, 2007; *Member Proposals on Energy Tax Incentives*, Hearing Before the Subcommittee on Select Revenue Measures of the Committee on Way and Means, U.S. House of Representatives, 110th Cong., 1st Sess., Serial No. 110-32, April 24, 2007; *Hearing on Energy and Tax Policy*, Hearing Before the Subcommittee on Select Revenue Measures of Committee on Ways and Means, U.S. House of Representatives, 110th Cong., 1st Sess., Serial

No. 110-31, April 19, 2007; *Hearing to Review Reauthorization of the Commodity Exchange Act*, Hearing before the Subcommittee on General Farm Commodities and Risk Management of the Committee on Agriculture, House of Representatives, 110th Cong., 1st Sess., Serial No. 110-27, September 26, 2007; *Hearing to Review Reauthorization of the Commodity Futures Trading Commission*, Hearing Before the Subcommittee on General Farm and Risk Management of the Committee on Agriculture, House of Representatives, 110th Cong., 2d Sess., Serial No. 110-32, October 24, 2007; *Hearings to Review Legislation Amending the Commodity Exchange Act*, Hearings Before the Committee on Agriculture, House of Representatives, 110th Cong., 2d Sess., Serial No. 110-40, July 9, 10, 11, 2008; *Hearing to Review Trading in Energy Markets*, Hearing Before the Committee on Agriculture, House of Representatives, 110th Cong., 2d Sess., Serial No. 110-38, June 24, 2008; *Hot Fuels: Big Oil's Double Standard for Measuring Gasoline,* Hearing Before the Subcommittee on Domestic Policy of the Committee on Oversight and Government Reform, House of Representatives, 110th Cong., 1st Sess., Serial No. 110-195, June 8, 2007; *Energy Speculation: Is Greater Regulation Necessary to Stop Price Manipulation (Part II)*, Hearing Before the Subcommittee on Oversight and Investigations of the Committee on Energy and Commerce, House of Representatives, 110th Cong., 2d Sess., Serial No. 110-128, June 23, 2008; *Hearing on Economics of Dependence on Foreign Oil: Rising Gasoline Prices*, Hearing Before the Subcommittee on Health of the Committee on Energy and Commerce, House of Representatives, 110th Cong., 2d Sess., Serial No. 110-132, June 24, 2008; *Hearing on Plugging Into Energy Independence with 150 MPG Vehicles*, Hearing Before the Select Committee on Energy Independence and Global Warming, House of Representatives, 110th Cong., 1st Sess., July 12, 2007; *Oil Shock: Potential for Crisis*, Hearing Before the Select Committee on Energy Independence and Global Warming, House of Representatives, 110th Cong., 1st Sess., Serial No. 110-19, November 7, 2007; *Blowing in the Wind: Renewable Energy as the Answer to an Economy Adrift*, Hearing Before the Committee on Energy Independence and Global Warming, House of Representatives, 110th Cong., 2d Sess., Serial No. 110-27, March 6, 2008; *Pumping Up Prices: The Strategic Petroleum Reserve and Record Gas Prices*, Hearing Before the Select Committee on Energy Independence and Global Warming, House of Representatives, 110th Cong., 2d Sess., Serial No. 110-34, April 24, 2008; *Drilling for Answers: Oil Company Profits, Runaway Prices and the Pursuit of Alternatives*, Hearing Before the Select Committee on Energy Independence and Global Warming, House of Representatives, 110th Cong., 2d Sess., Serial No. 110-30, April 1, 2008; *The Future of Oil*, Hearing before the Select Committee on Energy Independence and Global Warming, House of Representatives, 110th Cong., 2d Sess., Serial No. 110-39, June 11, 2008; *Oversight of the Bush Administration's Energy Policy*, Hearing Before the Select Committee on Energy Independence and Global Warming, House of Representatives, 110th Cong., 2d Sess., Serial No. 110-38, May 22, 2008; *Immediate Relief From High Oil Prices: Deploying the Strategic Petroleum Reserves*, Hearing Before the Select Committee on Energy Independence on Global Warming, House of Representative, 110th Cong., 2d Sess., Serial No. 110-44, July 23, 2008; *Investing in the Future: R&D Needs to Meet America's Energy and Climate Challenges*, Hearing Before the Select Committee on Energy Independence and Global Warming, House of Representatives, 110th Cong., 2d Sess., Serial No. 110-48, September 10, 2008; *Hearing on Renewing America's Future: Energy Visions of Tomorrow, Today*, Hearing before the Select Committee on Energy Independence and Global Warming, House of Representatives, 110th Cong., 2d Sess., Serial No. 110-47, July 31, 2008; *What's Cooking with Gas: The Role of Natural Gas in Energy Independence and Global Warming Solutions*, Hearing Before the Select Committee on Energy Independence and Global Warming, House of Representatives, 110th Cong., 2d Sess., Serial No. 110-46, July 30, 2008; *Innovation, Jobs, and Energy Independence: Reinvigorating the Domestic Auto Industry*, Hearing before the Select Committee on Energy Independence and Global Warming, House of Representatives, 110th Cong., 2d Sess., Serial No. 110-51, December 9, 2008; *$4 Gasoline and Fuel Economy: Auto Industry at a Crossroads,* Hearing Before the Select Committee on Energy Independence and Global Warming, House of Representatives, 110th Cong., 2d Sess., Serial No. 110-42, June 26, 2008; *Geopolitics of Oil*, Hearing Before the Committee on Energy and Natural Resources, U.S. Senate, 110th Cong., 1st Sess., S. Hrg. 110-6, January 10, 2007; *Oil and Gas Royalty Management at DOI*, Hearing Before the Committee on Energy and Natural Resources, U.S. Senate, 110th Cong., 1st Sess. on Issues Relating to Oil and Gas Royalty Management at the Department of the Interior, S. Hrg. 110-7, January 18, 2007; *Excessive Speculation in the Natural Gas Market*, Hearing Before the Permanent Subcommittee on Homeland Security and Governmental Affairs, U.S. Senate, 110th Cong., 1st Sess., S. Hrg. 110-235, June 25 and July 9, 2007; *Energy Efficiency Promotion Act of 2007*, Hearing Before the Committee on Energy and Natural Resources, U.S. Senate, 110th Cong., 1st Sess. on S. 1115 to Promote the Efficient Use of Oil, Natural Gas, and Electricity, Reduce Oil Consumption, and Heighten

Energy Efficiency Standards for Consumer Products and Industrial Equipment, and for Other Purposes, S. Hrg. 110-85, April 23, 2007; *Short-Term Energy Outlook: Summer 2007*, Hearing Before the Committee on Energy and Natural Resources, U.S. Senate, 110th Cong., 1st Sess. to Receive Testimony on the Outlook and Gasoline for the Summer Driving Season, S. Hrg. 110-99; *Current Energy Legislation*, Hearing Before the Subcommittee on Energy of the Committee on Energy and Natural Resources, U.S. Senate, 110th Cong., 1st Sess., S. 645, S. 838, S. 1089, S. 1203, H.R. 85, H.R. 1126, S. Hrg. 110-12, May 22, 2007; *The Impact of Rising Gas Prices on America's Small Business*, Hearing Before the Committee on Small Business and Entrepreneurship, U.S. Senate, 110th Cong., 1st Sess., S. Hrg. 110-210, June 14, 2007; *Is Market Concentration in the U.S. Petroleum Industry Harming Consumers?* Hearing Before the Joint Economic Committee, Congress of the United States, 110th Cong., 1st Sess., S. Hrg. 110-202, May 23, 2007; *Clean Coal, Oil and Gas Development: New Energy Opportunities Through Carbon Capture and Storage*, Hearing Before a Subcommittee of the Committee on Appropriations, U.S. Senate, 110th Cong., 1st Sess., Special Hearing, 110-265, August 13, 2007; *Oil Inventory Policies*, Hearing Before the Committee on Energy and Natural Resources, U.S. Senate, 110th Cong., 2d Sess. to Receive Testimony on U.S. Oil Inventory Policies, Including the Strategic Petroleum Reserve Policies, Hearing on S. 110-358, February 26, 2008; *Energy Market Effects on Recently Passed RFS,* Hearing Before the Committee on Energy and Natural Resources, U.S. Senate, 110th Cong., 2d Sess. to Receive Testimony on the Energy Market Effects on the Recently-Passed Renewable Fuel Standard, S. Hrg. 110-362, February 7, 2008; *Oversight of the Oil, Gas, and Mineral Revenue Programs Managed by the Department of the Interior,* Hearing Before a Subcommittee of the Committee on Appropriations, U.S. Senate, 110th Cong., 2d Sess. Special Hearing, 110-386, February 26, 2008; *High Price of Commodities: 2008*, Hearings Before the Committee on Homeland Security and Governmental Affairs, U.S. Senate, 110th Cong., 2d Sess., S. Hearing. 110-705, May 7, 2008, *Fuel Subsidies: Is There an Impact on Food Supply and Prices,* May 20, 2008, *Financial Speculation in Commodity Markets: Are Institutional Investors and Hedge Funds Contributing to Food and Energy Inflation?* June 24, 2008, *Ending Excessive Speculation in Commodity Markets: Legislative Options, Role, Responsibilities, and Resources: Needs of the Commodity Futures Trading Commission for Oversight of Energy Market and Oil Futures Contracts,* Joint Hearing Before the Committee on Agriculture, Nutrition, and Forestry and the Subcommittee on Financial Services and General Government of the Committee on Appropriations, U.S. Senate, 2d Session, Special Hearing, 110-731, June 17, 2008; *Energy Security: An American Imperative*, Hearing Before the Committee on Homeland Security and Governmental Affairs, U.S. Senate, 110th Cong., 2d Sess., S. Hearing 110-1023, July 22, 2008; *Oil Bubble or New Reality: How Will Skyrocketing Oil Prices Affect the U.S. Economy*? Hearing Before the Joint Economic Committee, Congress of the United States, 110th Cong., 2d Sess., S. Hearing 110-, June 25, 2008; *Renewable Electricity*, Hearing Before the Committee on Energy and Natural Resources, U.S. Senate, 110th Cong., 2d Sess. to Examine the Challenges and Regional Solutions to Developing Transmission for Renewable Electricity Resources, S. Hearing 110-538, June 17, 2008; *Future Energy Needs*, Hearing before the Committee on Energy and Natural Resources, U.S. Senate, 110th Cong., 2d Sess. to Receive Testimony on the Challenges to Meeting Future Energy Needs and to Developing the Technologies for Meeting Increased Global Energy Demand in the Context of the Need to Address Global Climate Change, S. Hearing, 110-541, June 25, 2008; *Electricity Generation*, Hearing Before the Committee on Energy and Natural Resources, U.S. Senate, 110th Cong., 2d Sess. to Consider the Value and Examine the Progress of Electricity Generation from Concentrating Solar Power, S. Hrg. 110-570, July 2, 2008; *Energy Information Administration's Forecasts for Oil and Gasoline Prices*, Hearing Before a Subcommittee of the Committee on Appropriations, U.S. Senate, 110th Cong., 2d Sess. Special Hearing, on 110-768, June 25, 2008; *Food Feed, and Fuel Production: Today and Tomorrow*, Field Hearing Before the Committee on Agriculture, Nutrition, and Forestry, U.S. Senate, 110th Cong., 2d Sess., Senate Hearing on S110-699, August 18, 2008; *Workshop on Oil Prices*, Workshop Before the Committee on Energy and Natural Resources, U.S. Senate, 110th Cong., 2d Sess. on Why Oil and Transportation Fuel Prices and This Winter's Expected Fuel Prices Will Be So High, and What Can Be Done to Address these Situations, S. Hrg. 110-602, July 17, 2008; *Transforming Forest Waste to Biofuels and the Renewable Fuels Standard,* Field Hearing Before the Committee on Agriculture, Nutrition, and Forestry, U.S. Senate, 110th Cong., 2d Sess., S. Hrg. 110-700, August 18, 2008; *Summit on Energy*, Hearing Before the Committee on Energy and Natural Resources, U.S. Senate, 110th Cong., 2d Sess. to Consider How We Achieve a More Secure, Reliable, Sustainable and Affordable Energy Future for the American People, S. Hrg. 110-654, September 12, 2008; *Vehicles Powered by the Electric Grid,* Hearing Before the Committee on Energy and Natural Resources, U.S. Senate, 110th Cong., 2d Sess. to Receive Testimony Regarding the Current State of Vehicles Powered

who advocated a special tax on speculators.[446] A bill was introduced in Congress to impose a tax on the Wall Street "gambling casino" in order to "both raise needed revenue for the Treasury and rein in speculation on Wall Street."[447] In February 2013, Massachusetts secretary of state William Galvin wrote to the Department of Energy and CFTC and asked them to curb speculation in oil prices in order to tamp down a recent rise in gas prices.[448]

Attacks against oil speculators went global after French president Nicolas Sarkozy delivered a speech in June 2011, in which he harshly decried inflated prices and urged that commodity price speculators be treated in the same fashion as the mafia. He stated that "[w]e should extend regulation to all products exchanged on the commodity derivatives markets, to all players involved and to all the tools used in the process. . . . Because price manipulation there is. On the stock markets, such manipulation is criminal, in both senses of the word. Why would we accept it on the commodity markets?"[449] Sarkozy claimed that 85 percent of buy side traders in the U.S. markets were "financial players" who, he claimed, were improperly speculating.[450]

Michael Barnier, the European Union (EU) internal-market commissioner, was seeking rules to limit speculation, "a bit like the Americans."[451] The European Union thereafter proposed actions to monitor wholesale energy markets for manipulation and trading abuses. That monitoring was to be conducted by a team of regulators based in Slovenia.[452] However, that proposal was

---

by the Electric Grid and the Prospects for Wider Deployment in the Near Future, S. Hrg. 110-671, September 16, 2008; *Speculative Investment in Energy Markets*, Hearing Before the Subcommittee on Energy of the Committee on Energy and Natural Resources, U.S. Senate, 2d Session to Receive Testimony on Recent Analyses of the Role of Speculative Investment in Energy Markets, S. Hrg. 110-670, September 16, 2008; *Oil, Oligarchs, and Opportunity: Energy from Central Asia to Europe,* Hearing Before the Committee on Foreign Relations, U.S. Senate, 110th Cong., 2d Sess., S. Hrg. 110-668, June 12, 2008; *High Diesel Fuel Prices,* Hearing Before the Committee on Energy and Natural Resources, U.S. Senate, 110th Cong., 2d Sess. to Examine Why Diesel Fuel Prices Have Been So High and What Can Be Done to Address the Situation, S. Hrg. 110-680, September 23, 2008.

446. Ralph Nader, *Time for a Tax on Speculation*, Wall Street Journal, Nov. 2, 2011, at A17.

447. *Wall Street Trading Could Generate Taxes,* Politico, http://www.politico.com/news/stories/1011/65140.html#ixzz1prUJr2Hi (accessed March 22, 2012).

448. Ira Kator, *Battle Heats Up Over Oil Costs*, Boston Herald, Feb. 22, 2013.

449. Address by Nicolas Sarkozy to the European Commission Conference on Commodities and Raw Materials, Brussels (June 14, 2011). Sarkozy also stated,

> The first oil crisis hit nearly forty years ago. That was in 1973 and a stunned world watched as the price of oil rose from 3 to 18 dollars a barrel. This morning, it stood at 119 dollars the barrel. . . . In oil, the financial markets are 35 times larger than the physical market. They trade in financial volume, 35 times the value of the physical quantity of oil. And they tell me that speculation is not a problem! 35 times!

450. Rudy Ruitenberg, *Agricultural Futures Markets Need Global Regulation, France's Sarkozy Says* (June 16, 2011), http://www.bloomberg.com/news/2011-06-16/agriculture-markets-require-global-governance-and-regulation-sarkozy-says.html (accessed August 25, 2011).

451. *EU's Barnier Eyes Commodity Speculation Controls* (May 24, 2011), http://www.reuters.com/article/2011/05/24/us-eu-markets-idUSTRE74N66G20110524 (accessed August 24, 2011).

452. Pete Harrison, *EU Moves to Clamp Down on Energy Insider Trading*, http://uk.reuters.com/article/2011/06/29/uk-eu-energy-trading-idUKTRE75S4QP20110629 (accessed August 24, 2011). The new European Securities and Markets Authority was seeking to address short selling concerns. Mark Scott, *In Europe, Securities Overseer Spreads Gospel of Streamlined Regulation,* New York Times, Dec. 27, 2011, at B6. The European Commission was also considering the issuance of market forecast reports as a way of limiting speculation. Caitriona Murphy, *EU Price Forecasts to Ease Volatility Worries*, Irish Independent, Aug. 30, 2011, www.independent.ie/farming/news-features/eu-price-forecasts-to-ease-volatility-worries-2860761.html (accessed March 27, 2012).

dropped in June 2012, after oil prices declined sharply.[453] The European Union did try to define and outline market activities that are deemed manipulative, including false or misleading pricing signals. A "non-exhaustive" list of suspicious activities that regulators should focus on included traders responsible for a significant percentage of daily trading volume that leads to a significant price change, trades concentrated in a short time period that lead to a price change that is later reversed, wash trades, fictitious trades, spoofing, and banging the close.[454]

Prosecutors in Italy took market manipulation claims to a new level in November 2012. They sought judicial permission to prosecute employees of two credit rating agencies, Standard & Poor's and Fitch, for market manipulation in connection with their downgrading of Italy's credit rating.[455]

The United Nations Conference on Trade and Development issued a report arguing that financial investments in commodities need to be controlled because speculation was accounting for 20 percent of their price.[456] A report sponsored by the Food and Agriculture Organization of the United Nations in 2011 contained the following statement attacking speculation:

> Throughout history, speculation has been strictly circumscribed or prohibited because of its market distorting effects and its disruption to the social order. For a variety of reasons, speculation and modern-day speculators have gained increasing respectability, particularly in the United States of America. An overabundance of food and dwindling numbers of agriculturalists have banished the millennial-old concerns of hoarding and shortages in the richer nations. Also, owing to the enormous profitability of commodity linked products, banks and other traders have waged a successful public relations campaign, surmounting criticism traditionally associated with speculative activities. The creed of free market orthodoxy, defining agricultural markets as just another set of institutional arrangements to be gainfully exploited, has also stifled any debate over the morality of food profiteering and the effects upon the poor. Finally, aided by an admiring "celebrity conscious" media, speculators have ascended to a savvy venerable class, able to amass fortunes at the push of a button.[457]

Critics also charged that the trading of "paper barrels" on NYMEX had caused the "financialization" of the crude oil market and fostered unwanted speculation in oil prices. Increased oil prices also furthered the weakening of the dollar, which was affected by oil prices. "So as the 'price' of the dollar went down against other currencies, particularly the euro, the price of oil went up."[458]

The Institute of International Finance (IIF) could find no evidence that speculators were causing price explosions. That global group opposed efforts by regulators to limit commodity speculation. "'Officials or people that want to argue for possible regulation of commodities

---

453. Carolyn Cui, *Regulators Back Off Tougher Curbs on Oil*, WALL STREET JOURNAL, June 21, 2012, at C1.

454. European Commission Directive 2003/124/EC, Articles 4 & 5.

455. Eric Sylvers, *Italy Calls for Downgrade Trial*, FINANCIAL TIMES (London), Nov. 13, 2013, at 13.

456. *UN Agency Urges Controls on Financial Investors in Commodity Markets*, http://online.wsj.com/article/BT-CO-20110605-702087.html?mod=dist_smartbrief (accessed August 22, 2011). A financial crisis in Greece was also claimed to be raising the specter of another crisis in the United States and elsewhere because of possible liabilities from credit default swaps on Greek sovereign debt. Louise Story, *Derivatives Cloud the Possible Fallout from a Greek Default,* NEW YORK TIMES, JUNE 23, 2011 at B1.

457. Food and Agriculture Organization of the United Nations (ed. Adam Prakash), *Safeguarding Food Security in Volatile Global Markets* (2011) at p. 265 (citations omitted), http://www.fao.org/docrep/013/i2107e/i2107e13.pdf. (accessed September 14, 2011).

458. DANIEL YERGIN, THE QUEST 165 (2011).

should do more analysis, more homework to really prove the case that financial investments do have an impact on price,' said Hung Tran of the IIF."[459] "[E]xtensive research has produced a near-consensus among academic experts that speculation has not been a key driver of recent oil price fluctuations."[460] In any event, blaming the speculators for price increases was achieving nothing.[461]

The political dimension of the oil price increases reached new global heights after President Obama announced on June 23, 2011, that the United States and twenty-seven other nations were releasing crude oil from their strategic reserves. That action was taken in an effort to push down gasoline prices and replace supplies lost as a result of the ongoing conflict in Libya.[462] That announcement was accompanied by more claims of manipulation because crude oil prices dropped before the public release announcing the drawdown. The CFTC then began an investigation to determine whether the announcement had been leaked in advance to traders in oil futures.[463] In the event, the drawdown did little to ease consumer costs because crude oil prices bounced back within a week of that announcement from $90 to $95 per barrel.[464]

Senator Bernard of Vermont, a self-described socialist, tried to whip up more animosity toward speculators and the always unpopular "Wall Street" financiers in August 2011 by leaking confidential CFTC large trader reports to the press.[465] Those reports disclosed the names of traders in the crude oil market during the historic price run-up in 2008.[466] Large investment banks such as Goldman Sachs and Morgan Stanley were the largest traders, with combined positions almost twice that of the energy companies. However, it appeared that the banks were overall net short the market, which undercut claims that they were seeking to drive the market upward. Hedge funds and pension funds were also significant investors in oil in 2008.[467] The CFTC reported that increased commodity prices at the end of 2010 had attracted a number of investors cum speculators such as hedge and mutual funds in numbers exceeding those drawn into the markets by the price run-up in 2008.[468]

---

459. Christopher Doering, *Global Bank Group Slams New Commodity Oversight*, Reuters, http://uk.reuters.com/article/2011/09/12/uk-financial-regulation-g-idUKTRE78B5B120110912 (accessed March 23, 2012).

460. Tim Worstall, *Futures Speculation Doesn't Increase Spot Oil Prices*, April 22, 2012 (citation omitted), http://www.forbes.com/sites/timworstall/2012/04/22/futures-speculation-doesnt-increase-spot-oil-prices/ (accessed April 23, 2012).

461. Gillian Tett, *Beware Whacking Speculators for Price Swings*, Financial Times (London), Sept. 8, 2011.

462. *Oil Release Shocks Markets*, Financial Times (London), June 24, 2011, at 1.

463. Jerry A. DiColo, *Oil Trades Before IEA Move Draw CFTC Eye*, Wall Street Journal, June 25-26, 2011, at C14.

464. David Bird & Dan Strumpf, *One Week Later, Oil Back Near $95*, Wall Street Journal, June 30, 2011, at C14.

465. Nicole Gaudiano, *Sanders' Data Release Concerns Futures Traders*, Gannett News Service, Aug. 19, 2011.

466. Industry representatives expressed alarm that this leak could drive trading off of U.S. markets because traders view their positions to be highly proprietary and do not want competitors to have that knowledge. Sarah N. Lynch, *U.S. Senator's Leak of Oil Trading Information Sparks Concern* (Aug. 19, 2011), http://www.calgaryherald.com/business/senator+leak+trading+information+sparks+concern/5276858/story.html#ixzz1W8vuocn7 (accessed August 26, 2011). *See also*, Ianthe Jeanne Dugan & Liam Plevin, *Debate Heats Up Over Commodities Holdings*, Wall Street Journal, Aug. 31, 2011, at C1; *Bernie Sanders Confidential*, Wall Street Journal, Sept. 1, 2011, at A16 (discussing this controversy).

467. Ianthe Jeanne Dugan & Liam Pleven, *As Oil Spiked, Many Traded*, Wall Street Journal, Aug. 18, 2011, at C1.

468. Carolyn Cui & Susan Pulliam, *Investors Pile Into Commodities*, Wall Street Journal, Dec. 8, 2010, at C1.

In any event, commodity prices continued to increase in 2011. Fed chair Ben Bernanke could propose no solution to the economic downturn in his address in Jackson Hole, Wyoming, in late August 2011. Commodity prices rose after his remarks.[469] The corn crop was also reported to be smaller than expected, placing more pressure on prices.[470] Wheat prices rose to $8.17 per bushel on May 18, 2011, nearly doubling over the prior year.[471] Wheat prices reached almost $9 per bushel in 2011 before falling back to $6.50 per bushel in early 2012.[472] Within a few months, however, fundamentals began reasserting themselves and pushed down oil and other commodity prices. Concerns were then raised that the bull market that began in 1999 for gold, oil, and other commodities was ending.[473] Predictions were also made that, through increased production, the United States could rid itself of dependence on foreign oil by 2035.[474] Nevertheless, calls continued in Congress for limits on speculators.[475]

Increased gasoline and crude oil prices in 2012 again focused attention on speculators and became a subject of the then ongoing presidential campaign. Despite all the new crude oil regulators with antimanipulation powers, West Texas Intermediate crude oil was trading at $106.50 a barrel on March 2, 2012. President Obama warned on March 6 that there was no "silver bullet" to cut prices.[476] Nevertheless, CFTC commissioner Bart Chilton was claiming in March 2012 that speculators were driving up the price of fuel for the trucking and airline industries.[477]

Rising crude oil prices raised more concern as Iran threatened to disrupt supplies, but speculators continued to receive blame for elevated price levels. Senator Bob Casey (D-PA) asked the CFTC to curb speculation in the oil markets. "'Consumers shouldn't be forced to pay higher prices at the pump because of speculative bets on Wall Street,' Casey wrote in a letter to CFTC Chairman Gary Gensler. 'Nearly two years ago Congress gave the CFTC the tools to crackdown on speculation in the oil market, and with sky high prices at the pump it's time they used it.'"[478]

There was concern expressed by the Mitt Romney presidential campaign over energy price fundamentals. The Obama administration was under fire from Romney for refusing drilling permits in the Gulf of Mexico after the BP oil spill in 2010. The administration was also receiving criticism for refusing to allow the building of an extension of the Keystone oil pipeline system from Canada, and efforts to promote "green" energy turned into scandal after the bankruptcy

---

469. Reuters, *Oil Rises as Irene Targets US East Coast*, Aug. 26, 2011, http://www.cnbc.com/id/44280980 (accessed August 29, 2011).

470. Gregory Meyer, *Lower US Corn Harvest Forecasts Raise Fears Over Higher Food Prices*, Financial Times (London), Aug. 29, 2011, at 1.

471. *Mideast Nations Pressured by Wheat-Price Rise: WSJ*, http://articles.marketwatch.com/2011-05-19/markets/30964044_1_wheat-futures-prices-wheat-futures-wheat-prices (accessed March 5, 2012).

472. Liam Pleven, Margret Coker & Benoit Faucon, *Iran Buying More Wheat, Fearing More Curbs*, Wall Street Journal, March 27, 2012, at C1.

473. Liam Pleven, *A Rare Speed Bump in Commodities' Long Run*, Wall Street Journal, May 14, 2012, at C1; David Bird, *Look Out Below, Analysts Say, as Oil Trips Below $90*, Wall Street Journal, May 14, 2012, at C9.

474. Angel Gonzalez, *Expanded Oil Drilling Helps U.S. Wean Itself From Mideast*, Wall Street Journal, June 27, 2012, at A1.

475. *Senators Urge Regulators to Act On Speculative Trading Limits*, Dow Jones Newswire, http://online.wsj.com/article/BT-CO-20120516-716461.html (accessed May 20, 2012).

476. Keityh Johnson, *With Gas Prices Rising, Obama Feels Heat*, Wall Street Journal, March 7, 2012, at A4.

477. Kaja Whitehouse, *Oil Speculation Costing Airline, Trucking Industries $39 Billion a Year: CFTC Commissioner*, New York Post, March 8, 2012.

478. Vicki Needham, *Dem Sen. Casey Calls on CFTC to Act Against Oil Speculators*, The Hill, March 4, 2012, http://thehill.com/blogs/e2-wire/e2-wire/214003-dem-sen-casey-calls-on-cftc-to-act-against-oil-speculators (accessed March 5, 2012).

of Solyndra, a California solar panel manufacturer that had been given $535 million in federal loan guarantees.[479] In response, the Obama administration announced that it was considering another drawdown on the country's strategic petroleum reserve in August 2012 even though the last drawdown had failed to lower prices for more than a few days.[480] In all events, high gasoline prices continued into 2013, with no real governmental effort to increase supplies. As described in Chapter 8, however, new extraction methods were driving natural gas prices down sharply. Natural gas prices fell from $7.12 per million BTUs in 2007 to under $2 in 2012 because supplies were increased.

479. Coral Davenport, *Obama vs. Romney—Energy: Fuel for the Fire*, THE NAT. J., Aug. 23, 2012.
480. *Oil Prices Above $96 Amid Broader Market Gains*, ASSOCIATED PRESS, Aug. 21, 2012.

8

CHALLENGES FOR THE NEW MANIPULATION STANDARDS

8:1 STATUTORY INTERPRETATION OF BORROWED LANGUAGE

The enactment of new financial services legislation is often followed by years, even decades, of prolonged and complex litigation in which the courts define the terms of the statute and set the limits of its reach. These cases begin in the federal district courts and then wind their way through the Circuit Court of Appeals and perhaps to the Supreme Court, a process that takes years. As new issues periodically occur, that review procedure will begin anew. Some issues never reach as far as the Supreme Court, and the district and circuit courts may disagree on their application, at least until the Supreme Court does act.

Congress circumvented this extended judicial review process for the new antimanipulative powers that it gave the Federal Energy Regulatory Commission (FERC), the Federal Trade Commission (FTC) and the Commodity Futures Trading Commission (CFTC). This feat was accomplished by borrowing language from Section 10(b) of the Securities Exchange Act of 1934 (34 Act), which had already been interpreted by thousands of judicial decisions.[1] By choosing not to write on a clean slate, Congress invoked a familiar canon of statutory construction, which posits that language borrowed by the legislature from one statute to be inserted into another should generally be given the same meaning in both statutes.[2]

An analysis of the legislative history of those amendments evidences that Congress intended to borrow the language from Section 10(b) in order to adopt its attending jurisprudence. The Energy Policy Act of 2005 (EPAct)[3] that gave FERC its new manipulation authority was clearly borrowed from Section 10(b) of the 34 Act.[4] The chair of FERC testified before Congress that the EPAct

---

1. 15 U.S.C. § 78j(b).

2. 2A Sutherland, Statutory Construction § 52.02 (N. Singer 4th ed. 1984). "The 'general rule that adoption of the wording of a statute from another legislative jurisdiction carries with it the previous judicial interpretations of the wording . . . is a presumption of legislative intention . . . which varies in strength with the similarity of the language, the established character of the decisions in the jurisdiction from which the language was adopted and the presence or lack of other indicia of intention.'" Yates v. United States, 354 U.S. 298, 309 (1957) (citation omitted). As the Congressional Research Service has also noted,

> In appropriate circumstances, courts will assume that "adoption of the wording of a statute from another legislative jurisdiction carries with it the previous judicial interpretations of the wording." . . . For the presumption to operate, the previous judicial interpretations must have been "known and settled."

Congressional Research Service, *Report for Congress, Statutory Interpretation: General Principles and Recent Trends*, at CRS-5 (Aug. 31, 2010) (citations omitted).

3. Pub. L. No. 109-58, § 1283, 119 Stat. 594 (2005).

4. *Energy Speculation: Is Greater Regulation Necessary to Stop Price Manipulation?* Testimony of the Honorable Joseph T. Kelliher Chairman FERC Before the House Subcommittee on Oversight and Investi-

directed that FERC "adopt the statutory model in section 10(b) of the Securities Exchange Act of 1934, rather than the anti-manipulation provision administered by the CFTC."[5] The FERC, therefore, modeled its antimanipulation rule "closely on Securities Exchange Commission rules implementing section 10(b). We believe this approach makes germane the substantial body of precedent with respect to the 1934 Act."[6]

The Energy Independence and Security Act (EISA), which gave the FTC its new authority to police "market manipulation,"[7] was also clearly borrowed from Section 10(b).[8] Its Senate sponsor, Maria Cantwell (D-WA), asserted that "the new authority granted to the FTC is modeled on the anti-manipulation authorities utilized by other agencies such as the Securities and Exchange Commission and the Federal Energy Regulatory Commission."[9] In promulgating its new anti-manipulation rule, the FTC stated that it would "adopt largely the language and structure of SEC Rule 10b-5" as its own manipulation standard.[10] In adopting the rule, the FTC further stated that it was "[f]ollowing the example of SEC Rule 10b-5."[11]

The CFTC's new antimanipulation authority under Section 753 of the Dodd-Frank Act Wall Street Reform and Consumer Protection Act of 2010 was also borrowed from the same source. Senator Cantwell, its Senate sponsor, asserted on the Senate floor that the "language in this amendment is patterned after the law that the SEC uses to go after fraud and manipulation; that there can be no manipulative devices or contrivances. It is a strong and clear legal standard that allows regulators to successfully go after reckless and manipulative behavior."[12]

Senator Cantwell was certainly aware of the canon of statutory construction on language borrowed from another statute. During the debates on Section 753 of the Dodd-Frank Act, Cantwell stated on the Senate floor that this language was borrowed in part because "Federal case law is clear that when the Congress uses language identical to that used in another statute, Congress intended for the courts and the Commission to interpret the new authority in a similar manner, and Congress has made sure that its intention is clear."[13]

Senator Cantwell, in earlier debates over this provision, also specifically referenced the case law on the borrowing of statutory language. She stated that "a substantial body of case law has developed over the last half century around section 10(b). This will provide certainty in how this legislation will be interpreted and applied by the Courts and the CFTC."[14]

---

gations Committee on Energy and Commerce (Dec. 12, 2007). *See also*, J. Michel Marcoux, *Canaries in the Coal Mine: Facts from Securities Fraud Private Civil Actions Can Identify Intent to Manipulate Energy Markets*, 29 ENERGY L.J. 141-156 (2008) (discussing that borrowing).

5. *Energy Speculation: Is Greater Regulation Necessary to Stop Price Manipulation?* Testimony of the Honorable Joseph T. Kelliher Chairman FERC Before the House Subcommittee on Oversight and Investigations Committee on Energy and Commerce (Dec. 12, 2007).

6. *Id.*

7. Pub. L. 110-140, 121 Stat. 1492, Title VIII, Subtitle B, *codified at* 42 U.S.C. §§ 17301-17305. *See*, Peter Malyshev, Vincent Van Panhuys & Melissa Dorn, *FTC Joins Other Agencies in Policing Oil Industry "Market Manipulation" and "False Reporting,"* 4 FUT. & DERV. L. REP. 1 (2008) (discussing this legislation).

8. *Prohibitions on Market Manipulation and False Information in Subtitle B of Title VIII of the Energy Independence and Security Act of 2007*, 73 Fed. Reg. 48317, 48322 (Aug. 19, 2008).

9. Letter from Senator Maria Cantwell et al. to the Federal Trade Commission, April 8, 2008, http://cantwell.senate.gov/news/record.cfm?id=295769 (accessed June 22, 2011).

10. *Prohibitions on Market Manipulation and False Information in Subtitle B of Title VIII of the Energy Independence and Security Act of 2007*, 73 Fed. Reg. 48317, 48322 (Aug. 19, 2008).

11. *Id.*

12. 156 Cong. Rec. S3348 (May 6, 2010) (remarks of Sen. Cantwell).

13. 156 Cong. Rec. S3348 (May 6, 2010).

14. 155 Cong. Rec. S9557 (Sept. 17, 2009).

Consequently, it seems clear that cases brought under the borrowed Section 10(b) language in CFTC, FERC, and FTC will be bound, not just guided, by the precedent developed over the years that has interpreted and limited its scope and application. As described in Chapter 7, the law under Section 10(b) of the 34 Act was well known and settled on a broad number of issues by the Supreme Court at the time the language from that statute was added to the powers of the CFTC, FTC and FERC. That precedent includes numerous interpretations by the Supreme Court on nearly every element of liability under Section 10(b) of the 34 Act.

In *Ernst & Ernst v. Hochfelder*,[15] the Supreme Court held that the use of the word "manipulative" in Section 10(b) is "virtually a term of art when used in connection with securities markets." This comment invokes another canon of statutory construction that must be considered in the context of borrowed language. In a famous article on statutory construction, professor and later Supreme Court justice Felix Frankfurter noted that "[w]ords of art bring their art with them. They bear the meaning of their habitat whether it be a phrase of technical significance in the scientific or business world, or whether it be loaded with the recondite connotations of feudalism."[16] As the Supreme Court has also held, "[w]here Congress borrows terms of art," the Court presumes that Congress "knows and adopts the cluster of ideas that were attached to each borrowed word . . . and the meaning its use will convey to the judicial mind unless otherwise instructed."[17]

Under this canon of statutory construction, the treatment of "manipulation" as a "virtual" term of art by the Supreme Court would be applicable to the new antimanipulation powers given to the CFTC, FTC, and FERC. The Supreme Court in *Santa Fe v. Green*,[18] as it did in *Hochfelder*, narrowly defined manipulation to refer "generally to practices, such as wash sales, matched orders, or rigged prices, that are intended to mislead investors by artificially affecting market activity."[19]

The CFTC, FERC, and FTC initially were enthusiastic in adopting the borrowing concept for their new Section 10(b) authority, but now seem to be having second thoughts. As described in Chapters 6 and 7, the FERC, FTC, and CFTC gave lip service to the limitations of Section 10(b) of the 34 Act when adopting rules to implement their new antimanipulation powers that were borrowed from that statute. However, each agency reserved the right to reject anything associated with Section 10(b) that it believed should not be applied to its particular industry. The agencies contended that the Section 10(b) case law would be used as a "guide," rather than binding precedent.

This basically means that the agencies will claim leeway to pick and choose among Rule 10b-5 jurisprudence in a way that will reduce their evidentiary burdens. Such cherry-picking is inconsistent with both the canons on statutory construction and with the congressional goal to achieve uniformity in manipulation standards by borrowing the Section 10(b) language. Congress believed that the language, as applied by the courts in Section 10(b) cases under the 34 Act, was the best time-tested means for attacking manipulation, whatever its burdens. The agencies may not like some of the judicially imposed restrictions on the reach of Section 10(b). Nevertheless, since its language was specifically borrowed by Congress with the intent that Section 10(b) judicial precedent apply, it is doubtful that the agencies will be able to interpret that language away.

It is unlikely on other grounds that the courts will give much deference to these agencies' interpretative efforts to expand their jurisdiction and relieve their evidentiary burdens. The so-called *Chevron* analysis,[20] which is used by the Supreme Court to determine instances when courts

15. Ernst & Ernst v. Hochfelder, 425 U.S. 185, 199 (1976).
16. Felix Frankfurter, *Some Reflections on the Reading of Statutes*, 47 COLUM. L. REV. 527, 537 (1947).
17. Morissette v. United States, 342 U.S. 246, 263 (1952).
18. Santa Fe v. Green, 430 U.S. 462 (1977).
19. 430 U.S. at 476-477.
20. Chevron U.S.A. Inc. v. NRDC, 467 U.S. 837 (1984).

should defer to agency expertise, does not grant judicial deference when the agency's interpretation concerns a matter that is dealt with commonly by the courts. None of the agencies exercising the new antimanipulative powers granted by Dodd-Frank, except the SEC, have any significant experience or expertise in dealing with the Section 10(b) language. As for the SEC, the Supreme Court has repeatedly "disagreed with the SEC's broad view of Section 10(b) or Rule 10b-5."[21] The Supreme Court has on several occasions also declined to grant deference to the SEC on its interpretations of Section 10(b) of the 34 Act.[22]

Consequently, interpretations by FERC, FTC, and CFTC that seek to avoid precedent borrowed from Section 10(b) cases under the 34 Act will likely be given little deference by the courts. There is also another reason why the borrowed language should be given the same universal treatment. The fact that the jurisdictions of CFTC, SEC, FERC, and FTC are overlapping is further reason for requiring uniformity in applying this standard.[23] It would be unfair, and constitutionally suspect, for a trader to be faced with multiple actions from multiple regulators over the same conduct with the same charging language, but which has different meanings under each regulatory scheme that uses language commonly borrowed from a single source. The *Amaranth* case described in Chapter 6 suggests that such overlap and disparity are likely unless the courts keep close check on inconsistent or overly expansive agency interpretations, which they have so far failed to do in earlier cases.

The Private Securities Litigation Reform Act of 1995 (PSLRA) raises further borrowing issues. As described in Chapter 5, PSLRA heightened the burden for pleading a claim under Rule 10b-5 for private plaintiffs by requiring particularized pleadings that evidence the basis of the fraud claim. The pleadings must also establish a "strong inference" of scienter as a condition for bringing a class action under Rule 10b-5.[24] There appears to be no private right of action for litigants under the FERC and FTC antimanipulative provisions but there are private rights of action under the Commodity Exchange Act, although they are limited in scope. Those limitations would seem to weigh in favor of borrowing the limits set for Section 10(b) cases by the PSLRA.

"The line between the permissible filling in of statutory gaps and the impermissible adding of statutory content may be indistinct in some instances, and statutory context, congressional purpose, and overriding presumptions may tip the scales."[25] Here, Congress appeared to be seeking to bor-

21. Janus Capital Group Inc. v. First Derivative Traders, 564 U.S. ---, n. 8 (2011) (citations omitted).

22. The Supreme Court noted in Janus Capital Group Inc. v. First Derivative Traders, 564 U.S. ---, n. 8 (2011), that it had

> previously expressed skepticism over the degree to which the SEC should receive deference regarding the private right of action. See Piper v. Chris-Craft Industries, Inc., 430 U. S. 1, 41, n. 27 (1977) (noting that the SEC's presumed expertise "is of limited value" when analyzing "whether a cause of action should be implied by judicial interpretation in favor of a particular class of litigants"). This also is not the first time this Court has disagreed with the SEC's broad view of § 10(b) or Rule 10b-5. See, e.g., Central Bank of Denver, N. A. v. First Interstate Bank of Denver, N. A., 511 U. S. 164, 188-191 (1994); Dirks v. SEC, 463 U. S. 646, 666, n. 27 (1983); Ernst & Ernst v. Hochfelder, 425 U. S. 185, 207 (1976); Blue Chip Stamps v. Manor Drug Stores, 421 U. S. 723, 746, n. 10 (1975).

23. According to Senator Cantwell, this "manipulative or deceptive device or contrivance" provision was added to give the CFTC the same authority previously granted to FERC and which allowed FERC to sanction Amaranth and Energy Trading Partners. 156 Cong. Rec. S3348 (May 6, 2010). The CFTC has also acknowledged this new power is "similar" to that of the SEC, FERC, and FTC. *Prohibition of Market Manipulation*, 75 Fed. Reg. 67,657 (Nov. 3, 2010).

24. Pub. L. No. 104-67, 109 Stat. 737 (1995).

25. Congressional Research Service, *Report for Congress, Statutory Interpretation: General Principles*

row the whole of the law of manipulation under Section 10(b). Consequently, it may be argued that the PSLRA limitations may follow the language that was borrowed from Section 10(b). As the First Circuit has noted, "when Congress borrows language from one statute and incorporates it into a second statute, the language of the two acts should be interpreted the same way. . . . What is more, when borrowing of this sort occurs, the borrowed phrases do not shed their skins like so many reinvigorated reptiles. Rather, 'if a word is obviously transplanted from another legal source, whether the common law or other legislation, it brings the old soil with it.'"[26]

8:2 THE SCIENTER ISSUE

Senator Maria Cantwell stated in the floor debates on the Dodd-Frank Act amendments to the Commodity Exchange Act that the Section 10(b) language was "a different easier-to-prove manipulation standard" that the SEC "has employed successfully for over 75 years." Senator Cantwell further asserted that the amendment was needed because, under current law, it was very difficult for the CFTC to prove manipulation.[27] In actuality, what constitutes manipulation under Section 10(b) of the 34 Act may not vary all that much from a manipulation under the old Commodity Exchange Act authority.

This effort to lighten the burden of proving manipulation by borrowing language from Section 10(b) may have been fruitless. The courts and agencies, heretofore, have found little distinction between the elements needed to prove manipulation under the Commodity Exchange Act and Section 10(b) of the 34 Act. A joint report issued in 1984 by the Federal Reserve Board, CFTC, and SEC (the "Joint Report") addressed the issue of defining manipulation under both the federal securities laws and the Commodity Exchange Act.

The Joint Report found that neither the 34 Act nor the Commodity Exchange Act provides a "comprehensive definition of manipulation, and definitions from other sources are of a general nature."[28] The Joint Report concluded that, while the test for manipulation must be a practical one, it was "generally agreed that all manipulations" under both the 34 Act and the Commodity Exchange Act, regardless of type, have in common four elements: "(1) manipulative act, (2) intent, (3) causation, and (4) artificial price."[29]

Those are essentially the same elements traditionally applied by the courts in Commodity Exchange Act cases. The Seventh Circuit Court of Appeals thus noted in *Frey v. CFTC* that courts generally require four elements to prove manipulation under the Commodity Exchange Act: (1) the ability to influence prices; (2) intent; (3) existence of an artificial price; and (4) causation of the artificial price.[30]

The perceived difference in scienter requirements between the Commodity Exchange Act and those in Section 10(b) of the 34 Act was a critical factor in the adoption of the language from Section 10(b) for use by CFTC, FERC, and FTC. The sponsors of the legislation thus sought the addition of Section 10(b) manipulation authority to the statutes administered by CFTC, FERC, and FTC in order to lower their burden of proof in proving that the manipulator acted with the requisite intent or scienter. Those sponsors believed that the scienter barrier in the old Commodity Exchange Act was too high and that it had frustrated successful prosecutions.

---

and Recent Trends, at CRS-5 (Aug. 31, 2008) (citations omitted).

26. Greenwood Trust v. Commonwealth of Mass., 971 F.2d 818, 827 (1st Cir. 1992), *cert. denied*, 506 U.S. 1052 (1993) (citations omitted).

27. 155 Cong. Rec. S9557 (Sept. 17, 2009).

28. *A Study of the Effects on the Economy of Trading in Futures and Options Pursuant to Section 23(a) of the Commodity Exchange Act as Amended* VII-2 (Dec. 1984) (footnote omitted).

29. *Id.* at VII-3.

30. Frey v. CFTC, 931 F.2d 1171, 1175 (7th Cir. 1991).

As Senate sponsor Maria Cantwell asserted in the debates on the Dodd-Frank Section 753 amendment to the Commodity Exchange Act, the CFTC had found it very difficult to establish manipulation claims because it had "to prove that someone had specific intent to manipulate, and that is a very difficult standard to prove. Most individuals don't write an e-mail, for example, saying they intend to manipulate prices, but that is currently what the law requires the Commodity Futures Trading Commission to prove: 'specific intent' to manipulate."[31] Senator Cantwell believed that the "reckless" intent standard under Section 10(b) would be easier to prove than the specific intent test under the Commodity Exchange Act.[32]

Actually, the distinction between the two scienter standards is so nuanced that it probably will make little difference in the overwhelming majority of cases. The Fed, SEC, and CFTC concluded in their 1984 Joint Report that, under both the 34 Act and the Commodity Exchange Act, the "essence of a manipulative act is that it is capable of causing an artificial price" and that the intent "has as its purpose the creation of an artificial price."[33] This evidences that even the regulators recognize that the basis for manipulation under both statutory schemes is a specific manipulative intent to create an artificial price. As the Supreme Court also held, Section 10(b) is directed at "intentional or willful conduct designed to deceive or defraud."[34]

It may be argued that the extreme recklessness standard, nevertheless, waters down the old Commodity Exchange Act specific intent requirement. Even if that were true, the difference would be so slight as to have little if any effect in real world applications. This is because, as described in Chapter 5, the extreme reckless standard is a high one that closely approximates a specific intent test, if it is not one itself.

Scienter requirements for trading market violations are in all events problematic. To illustrate, posit the following examples of human conduct for purposes of measuring various intent standards:

(1) Party A driving a Mack truck approaches a busy intersection at high speed. Party A increases his speed even further as he drives through the traffic light while it is still red and, with eyes open, tries to, and does, hit a car coming through the intersection.

(2) Party B is driving the same model Mack truck and approaches the same busy intersection at high speed when the light is already red. Party B decides not to stop. Instead, she closes her eyes and speeds up to go through the intersection against the light. Party B does not deliberately try to hit a car in the busy intersection, but knows that there is a substantial likelihood that this will be the result of her actions and that proves to be the case.

(3) Party C is driving a family car at the speed limit and reaches the busy intersection just as the light changes to red. Thinking that he can clear the intersection before any opposing cars accelerate after their light turns green and enter the intersection, and intending and expecting no harm to anyone, Party C speeds up and hits another car in the intersection.

(4) Party D, driving a pickup truck at the speed limit, reaches to pick up an object he has dropped on the floor of his truck and does not see the green light change to red. He strikes another car in the intersection.

31. Cong. Rec. S3348 (May 6, 2010).

32. 155 Cong. Rec. S9557 (Sept. 17, 2009).

33. *A Study of the Effects on the Economy of Trading in Futures and Options Pursuant to Section 23(a) of the Commodity Exchange Act as Amended* VII-3 (Dec. 1984).

34. Ernst & Ernst v. Hochfelder, 425 U.S. 185, 199 (1976).

The results in all four scenarios are the same. All four parties ran the red light and hit another automobile. Party A would be guilty of the specific intentional act of trying to cause a wreck and endanger life. Party B engaged in an intentional act, but one of a slightly lesser degree, which may be described as extreme or gross recklessness—that is, a wanton disregard for the rules of the road. The conduct of Parties A and B will be treated as very serious crimes and both will be punished severely. Party B may draw a lesser sentence, but her conduct was so reckless that it will still constitute a serious felony. There may be some distinction in the degree of punishment, but the intent of both drivers was on a level that everyone will agree is criminal and deserving of severe punishment.

The intent of both Party A and Party B is essentially the same. They deliberately engaged in conduct that was intended to cause, or was indifferent to, the predictable consequences of their actions. Party C and Party D are different cases. They did not intend to hit anyone, but their conduct was such that there was a possibility that their lack of care, simple negligence, would lead to an accident. Consequently, Parties C and D will not face the same serious criminal charges as Parties A and B even though the results of their actions were the same as those in the case of Parties A and B.

These distinctions are value judgments that are taught to every first-year law student in tort classes and are for the most part readily understandable in the context of ordinary mishaps or intentional misconduct that causes physical or monetary damages.[35] However, the value judgments associated with trading in the commodity and securities markets are much more complex than ordinary automobile accidents. Automobile drivers are penalized for speeding, but fast-moving markets mean that traders must operate at high speeds, milliseconds in the case of high-frequency traders, and must take sometimes enormous risks in order to profit. The rules of the road for automobiles are designed to prevent risk taking and are, for the most part, well known by auto drivers. This is not the case for traders operating in complex, ever-changing financial markets where there are few red lights for guidance.

The purpose of the rules of the road is to sharply restrict risk taking by automobile drivers. Society seeks to discourage risk taking with automobiles because the injuries or deaths that follow are a burden on society. Not all risks can be obviated by traffic regulations, but speed limits, lane change rules, and other restrictions seek to have all drivers proceed in the same fashion, within a range of speeds and with the same restrictions on their driving practices. In contrast, the success of traders in financial markets is based on the amount of risk they incur, and traders have many styles that adopt varying levels of risk and defy one-size-fits-all regulation.

The willingness to accept risk is at the very heart of a market. The immutable rule of Wall Street is "no risk, no gain" or, less prosaically, "no guts, no glory." In contrast, the amount of risk taken in driving automobiles will measure the number and severity of injuries. The more risk, the higher the death and casualty count. In trading markets, risk taking will determine the amount of the trader's profits and losses. The greater the risk, the greater the reward; conversely, no risk, no reward.

There is economic value in limiting driving fatalities and injuries through risk reduction, but that is not so much the case with financial markets. The stock and commodity markets are made more efficient by speculators who take risks in order to exploit market inefficiencies. Bad traders making bad decisions will lose, but will add liquidity and aid price discovery by, if nothing more, demonstrating that the price they are trading at is not an efficient one. Bad drivers do not offer comparable value.

In exposing market flaws, the market can be corrected by the speculator and the pricing of stocks and commodities rendered more efficient. In taking advantage of the weaknesses of other

35. One could still argue over the comparable negligence and punishment of Parties C and D.

traders, the speculator exposes that market prices are being supported by unknowledgeable or misinformed traders or by traders that have no market power to support a price at a particular level. In doing so, the speculator identifies market inefficiencies.

Risk taking by speculators provides valuable liquidity to the market, providing for ready access to and exit from markets and permitting greater opportunity for commercial firms to hedge their risks.[36] Risky driving practices provide no such benefits.

Prohibiting "excessive speculation" is an effort to prevent excessive risk taking. There is, however, no way to measure the point where risk taking becomes excessive. There are no speed limits in financial markets, nor should there be, because the market allocates fines in the form of trading losses limiting market liquidity.

For these reasons, risk taking in financial markets is not a good fit for the scienter standards that govern automobiles or other regulations involving human behavior in one-on-one situations. Even an extremely reckless trader falls outside the regulatory model that addresses automobile driving and other dangerous activities. Extreme risk in financial markets is rewarded with large gains and is punished with large losses. Extreme risk takers challenge market assumptions that may be stale or just wrong. Requiring all traders to trade in the same manner, at the same speed, and with the same risk exposure will remove innovation, dampen the use of greater market insights by successful traders, and lessen the value of skill in trading. Those limitations will result in more inefficient markets.

Scienter standards adopted from criminal or tort law are a very poor measure for determining the existence of manipulation for another reason. Under such tests, traders engaged in the same activity with differing states of mind will have the same market effects, but one may be considered a felon while the other is not. Such distinctions may work for regulating the bad behavior of automobile drivers but do not fit well in trading markets where risk taking is accepted, and needed, and where there are few stop signs or other rules of the road to guide traders.

8:3 THE OPEN-MARKET VERSUS CLOSED-MARKET DEBATE

The conflicts that arise in applying a tort-based scienter test to manipulative market trading have given rise to an unresolved debate in the courts over whether "open-market" trades can constitute manipulation. An open-market trade is a bona fide transaction that is conducted with manipulative intent. An open-market transaction "involves real parties and real economic risk,"[37] while a closed-market trade is a non–bona fide transaction, say a wash trade.

---

36. The Supreme Court has noted,

> The advent of speculation in futures markets produced well-recognized benefits for producers and processors of agricultural commodities. A farmer who takes a "short" position in the futures market is protected against a price decline; a processor who takes a "long" position is protected against a price increase. Such "hedging" is facilitated by the availability of speculators willing to assume the market risk that the hedging farmer or processor wants to avoid. The speculators' participation in the market substantially enlarges the number of potential buyers and sellers of executory contracts and therefore makes it easier for farmers and processors to make firm commitments for future delivery at a fixed price. The liquidity of a futures contract, upon which hedging depends, is directly related to the amount of speculation that takes place. . . . Those who seek financial gain by taking positions in the futures market generally are called "speculators" or "investors"; without their participation, futures markets "simply would not exist."

Merrill Lynch, Pierce, Fenner & Smith Inc. v. Curran, 456 U.S. 353, 358-359 (1982) (footnotes omitted).

37. David L. Kornblau, Allison Lurton & Jonathan M. Sperling, *Market Manipulation and Algorithmic Trad-*

The debate over whether open-market trades should be treated as manipulative when the requisite intent is present turns on the concept of fraud that is the basis for liability under Section 10(b) of the 34 Act. The antimanipulation prohibition in Section 10(b) is often distinguished from the old Commodity Exchange Act antimanipulation authority as being "fraud"-based.[38] That description is not helpful. The Supreme Court has repeatedly held that Section 10(b) does not incorporate common-law fraud into the 34 Act.[39] This leaves open to interpretation what constitutes fraud under that statute.

A plaintiff must plead and prove the existence of one of four kinds of manipulative or deceptive fraudulent devices forbidden by Section 10(b) and SEC Rule 10b-5: "(1) 'any device, scheme, or artifice to defraud'; (2) 'any untrue statement of a material fact'; (3) the omission of 'a material fact necessary in order to make the statements made . . . not misleading'; or (4) any other 'act, practice, or course of business' that 'operates . . . as a fraud or deceit.'"[40]

In contrast, the historical antimanipulation authority in the Commodity Exchange Act before the passage of Dodd-Frank covers what is stated to be "non-fraud"-based manipulation.[41] These distinctions are not certain in scope, and fraud-based manipulation, in any event, has its own limits and raises issues of what constitutes fraud, particularly in the context of open-market trades. The SEC has claimed "that open-market activities amount to market manipulation if the trader's 'sole intent' in placing an order is to move the price of a stock. In other words, the SEC considers manipulation to occur when, absent manipulative intent, the trader would not have made the bid or offer."[42]

---

ing: The Next Wave of Regulatory Enforcement? 44 Sec. Reg. & L. Re. (BNA) 369, 370 (Feb. 20, 2012).

38. *See, e.g.*, Cong. Rec. S5924 (July 15, 2010) (remarks of Sen. Cantwell); 156 Cong. Rec. S5902 (July 15, 2010) (remarks of Sen. Lincoln).

39. *See, e.g.*, Stoneridge Investment Partners LLC v. Scientific-Atlanta Inc., 552 U. S. 148, 162 (2008).

40. The Wharf (Holdings) Ltd. v. United Int'l Holdings Inc., 532 U.S. 588, 593 (2001) (quoting from Rule 10b-5).

41. 76 Fed. Reg. 41398, 41407 (July 14, 2011).

42. David L. Kornblau, Allison Lurton & Jonathan M. Sperling, *Market Manipulation and Algorithmic Trading: The Next Wave of Regulatory Enforcement*? 44 Sec. Reg. & L. Re. (BNA) 369, 370 (Feb. 20, 2012). *Compare*, *In the Matter of Setteducati*, 2003 WL 22570689 (S.E.C.), where the SEC, in dismissing a manipulation claim, found that bid quotations were not shown to have been unreflective of market forces. The SEC stated that, in determining the existence of manipulation, it will generally seek to determine whether the trading and surrounding circumstances present an effort to interfere with the free forces of supply and demand. That determination almost always requires inferences drawn from a mass of factual detail, including patterns of behavior, and apparent irregularities in trading data. The SEC said that it has identified various (nonexclusive) "earmarks" of manipulation in its cases, such as a rampant price surge dictated by the firm that controls the securities market, little investor interest, and abundant supply in the absence of any known prospects for the issue or favorable developments affecting it. This analysis seems to be focusing on market power manipulations such as those brought under the Commodity Exchange Act. *See also*, *In the Matter of Fertman*, 51 S.E.C. 943, 948-949 (1994), where the SEC similarly stated,

> Many of the classic factors from which we have inferred manipulative activity in the past are present in this case. These include a rapid surge in a security's prices that is driven by control of the security's supply and that occurs despite scant investor interest in the security and in the absence of any known prospects for or favorable developments affecting the issuer. Further, the trading pattern here was characteristic of a manipulation, as many of the purchases and sales among the Accounts and the trading account of the WBFI branch office were made in large blocks of substantially identical size, at substantially the same time. This trading, effected at increasing prices, both raised the prices of the stocks and created the illusion of a demand for them.

(footnotes and citations omitted). *See also*, Wright v. SEC, 112 F.2d 89 (2d Cir. 1940) (orders were not shown to be matched orders).

This claim was given some credence by the District of Columbia Court of Appeals in *Markowski v. SEC*.[43] There, the court reviewed a SEC administrative decision involving an open-market manipulation claim. The respondents were found by the SEC to have engaged in manipulation in violation of Section 10(b) of the 34 Act by supporting a stock's price. The respondents argued that they could not have engaged in manipulation because their bids and trades were "real" in that they involved real customers, real transactions, and real money. The Court of Appeals observed that the traders' activities were unlike classic manipulation schemes that use fraudulent devices such as "wash sales" or "matched sales," which are closed-market trades.[44]

The court in *Markowski* noted that this claim raised "interesting questions." In the absence of fictitious trades, it could be difficult to "separate a 'manipulative' investor from one who is simply overenthusiastic, a true believer in the object of investment. Both may amass huge inventories and place high bids, even though there are scant objective data supporting the implicit estimate of the stock's value."[45] In such circumstances, legality would "depend entirely on whether the investor's intent was 'an investment purpose' or 'solely to affect the price of [the] security.'"[46] The court in *Markowski* also noted the debate among commentators over the circumstances under which liability for manipulation should be imposed where open-market trades are involved.[47] The court concluded, however, that it could not find the SEC's interpretation to be unreasonable in

43. *Markowski v. SEC*, 274 F.3d 525 (D.C. Cir. 2001), *cert. denied*, 537 U.S. 819 (2002).

44. *See generally*, In the Matter of James J. Pasztor, Securities Exchange Act Release No. 42008, 70 S.E.C. Docket 1979, 1999 WL 820621 (1999) (failure to supervise for allowing matched orders and wash trades); In the Matter of Caito, Securities Exchange Act Release No. 42181, 71 S.E.C. Docket 402, 1999 WL 1068471 (1999) (manipulation by dominating and controlling market through bid and ask quotations at artificial levels, by reducing the float to prevent price declines, and by selling stocks under a guaranteed profit arrangement with another broker). *Compare*, In the Matter of Blake, Securities Exchange Act Release No. 52036 (July 14, 2005) (manipulation found by consent where defendant made purchases at increasing prices).

45. 274 F.3d at 528.

46. 274 F.3d at 528.

47. The Court stated:

> Given the typical ambiguity of intent, commentators have suggested that imposing liability may chill investors from transactions that actually contribute to the efficiency of securities markets. Daniel R. Fischel & David J. Ross, "Should the Law Prohibit 'Manipulation' in Financial Markets?" 105 Harv. L. Rev. 503, 523 (1991) (expressing concerns about the manipulation doctrine's overdeterrence effects); see also Mulheren, 938 F.2d at 368 (expressing misgivings about basing 10b-5 violations purely on whether or not a "transaction is effected for an investment purpose").
>
> Commentators have also suggested that where manipulative behavior is solely defined in terms of the actor's purpose, it may well be self-deterring as a general matter, so that any need for an external sanction is slight. Purely "trade-based" manipulation schemes, in which the manipulator simply buys a security in order to induce higher prices and then sells to take advantage of the price change, are likely to fail. First, it is difficult unilaterally to cause price to rise. Second, it is even more difficult to sell subsequently at a price high enough to cover both purchase costs *and* transaction costs. For one thing, if the actor's purchases are such as to give the market a material upward thrust, his later sales may equivalently drive it down. See Fischel & Ross, *supra*, at 512-19. But see Steve Thel, "$850,000 in Six Minutes—The Mechanics of Securities Manipulation," 79 Cornell L. Rev. 219 (1994) (suggesting that manipulators may profit from very small, short-lived price changes).

274 F.3d at 528. *See generally*, Matthijs Nelemans, *Redefining Trade-Based Market Manipulation*, 42 VAL. U.L. REV. 1169 (2008) (discussing trade-based manipulations).

light of what appears to be the determination of Congress that manipulation can be illegal solely because of the actor's purpose.[48]

The Second Circuit Court of Appeals has been a bit more skeptical of open-market manipulation claims and has sown much confusion where this issue has been raised. In *United States v. Mulheren*,[49] the government charged that the defendant made a large purchase of shares of Gulf & Western Industries Inc. at $45 per share in order to raise the market price of the stock to that level as a favor to an infamous insider trader, Ivan Boesky. Boesky wanted to sell a block of his stock back to Gulf & Western at that price and needed a print on the New York Stock Exchange tape to justify the price.

The government's theory of the case in *Mulheren* was that "when an investor, who is neither a fiduciary nor an insider, engages in securities transactions in *the open market* with the sole intent to affect the price of the security, the transaction is manipulative and violates Rule 10b-5."[50] The government further argued that unlawful manipulation will occur "even though the investor has not acted for the 'purpose of inducing the purchase or sale of such security by others,' an element the government would have had to prove had it chosen to proceed under the manipulation statute, §9(a)(2) [of the 34 Act]."[51] As described in Chapter 3, the SEC long ago sought to avoid the higher burdens imposed under Section 9 in favor of what it thought were the lesser burdens of Section 10(b).

The Second Circuit had misgivings about the government's theory, but it assumed, without deciding the issue, that a trader could be convicted under Rule 10b-5 where the purpose of his transaction is solely to affect the price of a security.[52] Even with that assumption, however, the court found that the government failed to establish manipulative intent. That is, the government could not prove that the defendant's buying at a price higher than what was necessary was an effort to raise the price to a level sought by another trader instead of an independent investment decision. The court noted that the defendant lost $64,000 on the trade, which was inconsistent with a common hallmark of a manipulation—that is, profits to the manipulator.[53] Moreover, "[n]one of the traditional badges of manipulation are present in this case," such as "fictitious accounts, matched orders, wash sales, dissemination of false literature."[54]

In *United States v. Regan*,[55] which was decided shortly before *Mulheren*, the Second Circuit applied Section 10(b) more broadly in affirming the conviction of a Drexel Burnham Lambert

48. 274 F.3d at 529.

49. United States v. Mulheren, 938 F.2d 364 (2d Cir. 1991).

50. 938 F.2d at 368 (emphasis added).

51. *Id.*

52. *Id.*

53. 938 F.2d at 370.

54. *Id.* As the Second Circuit held in an earlier case, "[s]o long as the investor's motive in buying or selling a security is not to create an artificial demand for, or supply of, the security, illegal market manipulation is not established." Chris-Craft Industries Inc. v. Piper Aircraft Corp. 480 F.2d 341, 383 (2d Cir.), *cert. denied, sub nom.*, First Boston Corp. v. Chris-Craft Industries, 414 U.S. 341, 383 (1973) (citing Section 9(a)(2) of the 34 Act). *See also*, In re Pet Quarters Inc. Securities Litigation, Fed Sec. L. Rep. (CCH) ¶ 93,809 (E.D. Ark. 2006) (complaint charging "death spiral" scheme in which short sellers loan money to a target and then drive its price down through short sales dismissed because of insufficient allegations of intent).

55. United States v. Regan, 937 F.2d 823, 829 (2d Cir. 1991), *amended on other grounds*, 946 F.2d 188 (2d Cir. 1991), *cert. denied sub nom.*, Zarechi v. United States, 504 U.S. 940 (1992). *See also*, Collier v. Akys Ltd., Fed Sec. L. Rep. (CCH) ¶ 93,847 (2d Cir. 2006) (unpublished opinion) (manipulation claim involving claim that defendant hedge funds made misrepresentations and omissions to inflate stock price so that it would "take off" and hurt short traders not found to have pleaded loss causation in a manipulation claim under Section 10(b)).

trader. Drexel Burnham was the underwriter for a convertible bond offering. Two defendants, one a trader at Drexel and the other at a hedge fund, thought the price of the stock into which the bond could be converted was being "levitated" by the issuer in order to make the offering more attractive and at a lower interest rate. The defendants sought to counter that activity by arranging the sale of 40,000 shares of the issuer's stock to a third-party broker-dealer at an artificially low price. The defendants did not disclose to the broker-dealer that the hedge fund owned the securities or Drexel's involvement in the transaction and the underwriting.

The Second Circuit found that this behavior "artificially depressed" the market price and fit "comfortably within this full range of wrongful acts" proscribed by Section 10(b). "Failure to disclose that market prices are being artificially depressed operates as a deceit on the market place and is an omission of a material fact."[56] This holding may have elements of acceptance of open-market manipulation. However, the trade could also be viewed as a closed-market transaction since its placement appears to have a non–bona fide trade.

These decisions led to much confusion in the lower courts. In *Nanopierce Technologies Inc. v. Southridge Capital Management LLC*,[57] a federal district court judge took note of the fact that "the law of the Second Circuit on so-called open-market manipulation—where the alleged manipulator has made otherwise legitimate trades, yet with the subjective intent to affect the stock price thereby—is not yet fully settled."[58]

In *In re College Bound Consolidated Litigation*,[59] a district court judge in New York declined to decide the issue left open by *Mulheren* whether open market trades conducted at the close of trading in order to inflate a stock price could be manipulative. Instead, the district court found that plaintiffs had not pleaded the necessary elements of an open-market manipulation scheme, even if such trading was deemed to be illegal. The court identified the elements of an open-market manipulation claim outlined in *Mulheren* as: "(1) profit or personal gain to the alleged manipulator; (2) deceptive intent; (3) market domination; and (4) economic reasonableness of the alleged manipulation."[60] Actually, those elements sound more like the elements of a market power manipulation under the Commodity Exchange Act.

Subsequently, in *ATSI Communications Inc. v. The Shaar Fund Ltd.*,[61] the Second Circuit reviewed the manipulation standards set by the various circuit courts and noted that existing case law requires "a showing that an alleged manipulator engaged in market activity aimed at deceiv-

---

56. 937 F.2d at 829. In an earlier decision, *SEC v. Management Dynamics Inc.*, 515 F.2d 801 (2d Cir. 1975), the Second Circuit had simply labeled manipulation as a per se violation of Rule 10b-5: "The promulgation of false and misleading quotations or manipulations of the market violate the antifraud provisions." 515 F.2d at 810.

57. Nanopierce Technologies Inc. v. Southridge Capital Management LLC, 2002 WL 31819207 (S.D.N.Y.).

58. Id. at p. *7 *citing* United States v. Mulheren, 938 F.2d 364 (2d Cir. 1991).

59. In re College Bound Consolidated Litigation, 1995 U.S. Dist. LEXIS 10684 (S.D.N.Y.).

60. In re College Bound Consolidated Litigation, 1995 U.S. Dist. LEXIS 10684 *15 (S.D.N.Y.) (quotation marks omitted). Another judge in the Southern District of New York also noted that "the law of the Second Circuit on so-called open-market manipulation—where the alleged manipulator has made otherwise legitimate trades, yet with the subjective intent to affect the stock price thereby—is not yet fully settled." Nanopierce Techs. Inc. v. Southridge Capital Management LLC, 2002 U.S. 24049 at 21 (S.D.N.Y. 2002). Muddying the waters even further was a statement by a district court in *In re Belch Securities Litigation*, 928 F. Supp. 1279, 1298 (S.D.N.Y. 1996), that "the absence of allegations of market dominance and price movement are not fatal to" a claim of market manipulation, for although "these may be classic attributes of market manipulation, they are not requisites."

61. ATSI Communications Inc. v. The Shaar Fund Ltd., 493 F.3d 87 (2d Cir. 2007).

ing investors as to how other market participants have valued a security."[62] The courts look to see "whether trading activity sends a false pricing signal to the market."[63]

The Second Circuit then went on in that case to make a rather startling assertion that Section 10(b) "seeks a market where 'competing judgments of buyers and sellers as to the fair price of the security brings about a situation where the market price reflects as nearly as possible *a just price*.'"[64] As described in Chapter 1, the concept of a "just price" was a medieval view of how markets should work that has long been abandoned by modern market-based economies.

The Second Circuit in *ATSI Communications* leavened that pronouncement by concluding that short selling in large volume to the distress of other market participants is not itself actionable. To be actionable as a manipulative act, short selling of securities must be willfully combined with something more to create a false impression of how market participants value a security.[65] The court even defended short selling, noting that it provided liquidity and aided price efficiency. "In essence, taking a short position is no different than taking a long position."[66]

The Second Circuit in *ATSI Communications* also asserted that a "market manipulation claim . . . cannot be based solely upon misrepresentations or omissions. There must be some market activity, such as 'wash sales, matched orders, or rigged prices.'"[67] The court held that "a claim for market manipulation is a claim for fraud" that requires pleading the following elements: "(1) manipulative acts; (2) damage (3) caused by reliance on an assumption of an efficient market free of manipulation; (4) scienter; (5) in connection with the purchase or sale of securities; (6) furthered by the defendant's use of the mails or any facility of a national securities exchange."[68]

In *SEC v. Masri*,[69] a judge in the Southern District of New York addressed the open-market issue a few months after the Second Circuit's decision in *ATSI Communications*, but the district court in *Masri* did not cite *ATSI*. The district court in *Masri* expressed its view that manipulation could be carried out through open-market transactions that are otherwise legitimate but are done with the subjective intent to affect the stock price. Nevertheless, the court in *Masri* concluded that the issue whether otherwise legitimate transactions are illegal if done with manipulative intent remains unresolved by the courts and was a matter of uncertainty in the decisions addressing that concern. The district court did catalogue some practices that have been found to be manipulative. They included such things as unauthorized stock placements, stock parking, secret sales without disclosing the real party in interest, guaranteeing profits to encourage short selling, fraudulently low appraisals, painting the tape, and matched orders.[70]

In *Dodona I LLC v. Goldman Sachs & Co.*,[71] the district court dismissed a market manipulation claim involving synthetic collateralized debt obligations on the basis of the decision in *ATSI*

62. 493 F.3d at 100-101.
63. 493 F.3d at 100.
64. 493 F.3d at 100-101 (emphasis added).
65. 493 F.3d at 101 (citations omitted).
66. 493 F.3d at 101.
67. 493 F.3d. 87, 101 (2d Cir. 2007) (citations omitted).
68. 493 F.3d at 101.
69. *SEC v. Masri*, 523 F. Supp. 2d 361, 367 (S.D.N.Y. 2007)
70. See also, Stephen J. Choi & A.C. Pritchard, *Should Issuers Be on the Hook for Laddering? An Empirical Analysis of the IPO Market Manipulation Litigation*, 73 U. CINN. L. REV. 179 (2004) (describing widespread abuses in initial public offerings). *See also*, Unites States v. Russo, 74 F.3d 1383 (2d Cir. 1996), *cert. denied*, 519 U.S. 927 (1996) (Rule 10b-5 violated by manipulation scheme involving short selling and parking of stock to maintain the price of a security); Edward J. Mawod & Co. v. SEC, 591 F.2d 588 (10th Cir. 1979) (manipulation involving wash sales, rigged trades, and "float" trades).
71. Dodona I LLC v. Goldman Sachs & Co., 2012 WL 935815 (S.D.N.Y.).

Communications. The district court stated that a "claim for market manipulation cannot be based on a misrepresentation or omission alone, but must involve a manipulative market activity." The court found that the claims in the case before it sounded more like fraud by misrepresentation or omission rather than market manipulation and, therefore, dismissed the manipulation claims.[72]

Adding to this confusion, in *Wilson v. Merrill Lynch & Co. Inc.*,[73] the Second Circuit cited the manipulation standards in the *ATSI Communications* case, but held that a manipulation claim would be defeated by disclosures of the defendant's activities. There, the broker was placing artificial bids to keep an auction rate securities auction from failing, but it had disclosed publicly on its website that it might engage in such activity.

In *GFL Advantage Fund Ltd. v. Colkitt*,[74] the Third Circuit rejected a claim of manipulation under Rule 10b-5 where a lender was selling securities short to push the price of a stock downward in order to profit from a loan arrangement. The loan required a payoff in the securities being manipulated. The downward manipulation required the borrower to exchange more shares to retire the same amount of debt. The Third Circuit held that this was a legitimate trading strategy. The defendant was found to be responding to market forces and had not intended to manipulate prices even though the short sales may have had the effect of pushing prices down. Selling short would not alone be enough to establish a violation.[75]

The Third Circuit in *GFL Advantage Fund* agreed with the *Markowski* court that it might be difficult to "distinguish between legitimate trading strategies intended to anticipate and respond to prevailing market forces and those designed to manipulate prices and deceive purchasers and sellers."[76] The Third Circuit stated that a claim under Section 10(b) must "establish that the alleged manipulator injected 'inaccurate information' into the market or created a false impression of market activity."[77] "Such a construction permits courts to differentiate between legitimate trading activities that permissibly may influence prices, such as short sales, and 'ingenious devices that might be used to manipulate securities prices,' . . . such as wash sales and matched orders."[78]

The old antimanipulation authority under the Commodity Exchange Act has also raised the issue of open- versus closed-market transactions. In *United States v. Radley*,[79] which is described in Chapter 6, the Fifth Circuit held that the defendants could dissemble to others concerning their trading positions because there was no obligation "to disclose their strategy to even the most informal of inquiries from other parties."[80] There the defendants were making open-market "stacked bids" in order to affect prices, but the trades being made were actual open-market transactions. "While weaving its damned-if-you-do-damned-if-you-don't web, the indictment demonstrates that Appellees' bids were bona fide and that other market participants freely chose which bids to accept and which to reject. Unless they were somehow illusory, which was not the case, Appellees' bids were part of their transactions in February TET propane futures."[81]

---

72. In Alki Partners LP Vatas Holding GMbh, 769 F. Supp. 2d 478 (S.D.N.Y. 2011), a district court dismissed manipulation claims that were based on an efficient market theory. The pleadings also failed to plead scienter accurately.

73. Wilson v. Merrill Lynch & Co. Inc., 671 F.3d 120 (2d Cir. 2011). *Accord*: Anschutz Corp. v. Merrill Lynch & Co. Inc., 2012 U.S. App. LEXIS 17006 (2d Cir. 2012).

74. GFL Advantage Fund Ltd. v. Colkitt, 272 F.3d 189 (3d Cir. 2001), *cert. denied*, 536 U.S. 923 (2002).

75. 272 F.3d at 204.

76. 272 F.3d at 205.

77. 272 F.3d at 205.

78. 272 F.3d at 205.

79. United Sates v. Radley, 632 F.3d 177 (5th Cir. 2011).

80. 632 F.3d at 184.

81. 632 F.3d at 183-184. The district court in *Radley* also concluded,

In *CFTC v. Delay*,[82] a federal district court held that, while the defendant had profited from his trading, they were lawful profits from actual trading. "Simply stated, it is not a violation of the statute to report feeder cattle sales to the USDA with the intention of moving the CME index up or down—rather, to be unlawful, the reported sales must be sham or nonexistent transactions, or the reports must be knowingly false or misleading. In this case, it turns out that the sales were real and the reports were true."

In contrast, in *CFTC v. Amaranth Advisors LLC*,[83] the district court rejected a claim that the CFTC must allege an unlawful fraudulent act in order to prove manipulation. Rather, the court believed that even open-market activities conducted with the intent of artificially affecting the price of a commodity, and not for any legitimate economic reason, could constitute proof of attempted market manipulation.

The *Amaranth* transactions involved "marking the close," which the court ruled could be manipulative if conducted with the requisite intent even though they were open-market trades. The district court noted the decisions in *Masri* and *ATSI Communications* on open-market trades under the 34 Act, but held that this issue was not relevant to an attempted manipulation claim under the Commodity Exchange Act.

The CFTC embraced the approach of including open-market operations as manipulation in adopting Rule 180.2. As described in Chapter 7, that rule was intended to encapsulate the old, pre–Dodd-Frank Commodity Exchange Act antimanipulation authority and distinguish it from the new Section 10(b) authority added by Dodd-Frank. In the course of adopting that rule, the CFTC "emphasiz[ed]" that, "consistent with the weight of existing precedent, . . . the conduct giving rise to a manipulation charge need not itself be fraudulent or otherwise illegal."[84]

The CFTC asserted that this claim was supported by *DiPlacido*, an unpublished Second Circuit opinion,[85] the "landmark" *Henner* decision, and *In the Matter of Zenith-Godley*, another CEA.[86] The CFTC stated that the conduct in those cases was not found to be "intrinsically fraudulent or otherwise illegal apart from violating the CEA."[87]

In the event, the issue of open-market trades as manipulation under both the old Commodity Exchange Act and Section 10(b)'s language remains open for the Supreme Court to finally resolve. The open-market versus closed-market trade issue raises important market efficiency concerns for the Supreme Court to consider. Aggressive traders will become timid if they are punished when their market strategy turns out wrong and prices are affected adversely or when they take advantage of other market participants and make large profits. It is only when a trader acts intentionally to cheat or defraud someone through manipulative devices such as wash trades that sanctions should

---

> The superseding indictment does not allege a single lie or misrepresentation. The "best bids," even if they were higher than any others, were actually bids, and when they were accepted, defendants actually went through with the transactions. Other counterparties may have assumed that the "stacked bids" came from multiple parties, but defendants did not perpetuate or cause this misconception. Since defendants were willing and able to follow through on all of the bids, they were not misleading.

United States v. Radley, 659 F. Supp. 2d 803, 815 (S.D. Tex. 2009) (footnote omitted).

82. CFTC v. Delay, 2006 WL 3359076 (D. Neb. 2006).

83. CFTC v. Amaranth Advisors LLC, 554 F. Supp. 2d 523 (S.D.N.Y. 2007)

84. *Prohibition of Market Manipulation*, 75 Fed. Reg. 67657, 67661 (Nov. 3, 2010).

85. In the Matter of DiPlacido, COMM. FUT. L. REP. ¶ 30, 970 (C.F.T.C. 2008), *aff'd sub nom.*, DiPlacido v. CFTC, No. 08-5559-ag, 2009 U.S. App. LEXIS 22692 (2d Cir. 2009), *cert denied*, 2010 U.S. LEXIS 2461 (2010).

86. In re Zenith Godley, 6 AG. DEC. 900 (C.E.A. 1947).

87. 75 Fed. Reg. at 67661.

be brought to bear. A continuing concern is the use of trades, even "real" trades in an illiquid market, that are manipulated to benefit the trader's position in another market or under a contract that references prices on the illiquid market. This misconduct could be attacked by prohibiting the trader from trading in the illiquid market when such trading will affect other pricing for his benefit and to the detriment of others.

In all events, a clear line is needed on what conduct is prohibited so that uncertainty will not unduly hamper aggressive price discovery and market efficiency. Traders should not have to obtain a legal opinion before engaging in a novel strategy or a strategy in which they seek to outwit other market participants. Sports analogies have lost favor in some academic circles, but they might prove useful in understanding the role of traders and market competition and why their trading practices, even if intentionally deceptive, may add value to the market.

Professor Thomas A. Hieronymus noted many years ago that, in reality, "[f]utures trading is a contact sport played by competitive people who place a high value on winning. A futures market is not a scholarly seminar in which learned men debate what is, and arrive at, an equilibrium price; it is a game in which businessmen compete, with money at hazard, to establish a market price that works. Competition is sometimes a vicious business but it works well."[88]

Picking up on Professor Hieronymus's theme that trading markets have traditionally been a contact sport brings us to football. The European version of football (soccer to most Americans) has rules against player contact. As a result, the sport is extremely boring to many ardent American football buffs, who are unimpressed by soccer players falling to the ground and clutching their knee at every hint of contact. In contrast, American football is a contact sport with collision at its heart. It provides a good metaphor on how competitive markets should work.

Football was nearly banned in the United States early in its history because the uncontrolled violence it engendered resulted in many serious injuries and several deaths. Defenders of the game helped save it by pointing to its value to society in building character. The game was also saved by adopting rule changes that allowed for violent contact but without the attending mayhem that had threatened the sport's continuance.[89]

Today, football games are played under a set of rules that apply fixed penalties for each infraction, without changing the character of the game. Players know what conduct is prohibited, and they train to avoid it.[90] Rules preserve the competition in football, while banning conduct that can cause serious injury through actions that opposing players cannot protect against. At the same time, those rules do not prohibit hard contact and do not level the playing field for all players.

Success in football depends on skill, size, speed, agility, acumen, and risk taking, as well as much luck. There are no handicaps, as in golf, for small, slow, and unskilled football players and there is no equalization of abilities on the playing field. A large player is free to smash a smaller player in head-to-head contact. It is up to the smaller player to protect himself; that is not the duty of the larger player. Fast running backs are not required to slow down in order to allow larger, slower defenders to catch up with them. In addition, a football team must play well or it may lose. If you are wrong in football, you lose. If someone is smarter, bigger, quicker, or just luckier, you lose. If someone has a better game plan, you lose, no tears.[91]

---

88. THOMAS HIERONYMUS, ECONOMICS OF FUTURES TRADING FOR COMMERCIAL AND PERSONAL PROFIT 327-328 (1977).

89. *See*, JOHN J. MILLER, THE BIG SCRUM (2011) (describing those events).

90. Modern technology is also doing much to ensure that the rules are evenly and correctly applied by the referee through televised replays.

91. One professor has advocated adoption of a football model for capital markets that would, like the National Football League, separate gambling from the actual play of the game. This would be accomplished

Financial markets similarly need a defined set of rules that can be evenly applied, while also recognizing that trading is a contact sport that must allow for fierce competition. Trading may not be a blood sport, but when one speculator gains, a trader on the other side of the market loses real money; it is a zero sum game.[92] Every speculator intends to damage his counterpart, because the speculator gains only when the counterparty loses. The long speculator is seeking to buy something from the counterparty at a price less than what the speculator believes is its actual market value. Loss to the counterparty is intended, and skill and deception are needed to inflict that damage. Deception, at least in the form of nondisclosure, is necessary because if the speculator's reasons for trading are disclosed his advantage is lost.

Tort law punishes those who intentionally cause damage by fraud in contractual relations. In the famous case of *Pasley v. Freeman*,[93] a party who misrepresented the creditworthiness of a third party that the plaintiff was contracting with was found guilty of deceit. The tort of fraud and deceit will occur where a party intentionally misrepresents a fact to the counterparty in a contract.[94] Once again, however, that tort model does not make a good fit for trading in active markets.

In football (and most other sports except golf), deception is a key part of play. The quarterback "sneak," the "statute of liberty," and the "play action pass" are all designed to deceive opponents and are heartily cheered by fans. The game of volleyball involves plays called by the setter to deceive the opposite side as to where the ball will be struck. Hockey players try to deceive the defender in making passes and seeking to score. The baseball pitcher is admired, and rewarded financially, when he successfully conceals and mixes his pitches to fool hitters.[95] Deception also plays deeply in the art of war. As Sun Tzu noted in the fourth century BC, "all warfare is based on deception."[96]

Such deceptive tactics are at the heart of most sport competitions and are deeply imbued and encouraged in American culture. Yet regulators seek to penalize deception, even in benign forms,

---

by replacing the "expectations" market (the stock market) with the "real" market (the production of things). *See*, Roger L. Martin, Fixing the Game: Bubbles, Crashes and What Capitalism Can Learn From the NFL (2011) Under this model, executives would be compensated through a metric that is not based on the company's stock price—that is, return on equity.

This "real market" proposal is a rejection of theories that propound that executive compensation should be aligned with shareholder interests. That is, compensation would reward executives when the company's stock price increased. That was done in prior years through grants of stock options, but that model led to massive price manipulations in the Enron-era scandals when executives inflated earnings in order to pump up their stock price. Of course, return on equity is a metric that can be, and was, manipulated as easily as the stock market.

This NFL model presumably would leave the trading ("expectations") markets as the Las Vegas of capitalism. The proponent of this model, however, seeks to punish speculators by taxing their gains "to all of our benefit." *Id.* at 218. In short, this NFL model is simply another populist attack on speculation. However, if the NFL model was faithfully followed, then gamblers cum speculators would be pretty much left alone by the government. Gambling is now available not only in Vegas but on riverboats and Indian reservations across the nation with but little or no government interference. The Internet now makes gambling, even if illegal, available to everyone everywhere. This seems ironic since speculation has been condemned and regulated because it was viewed as gambling.

92. The hedger may not actually sustain an overall loss from its commercial activities, but the hedge position in futures contracts in isolation will show a gain or loss.

93. Pasley v. Freeman, 3 T.R. 51 (1789).

94. See Derry v. Peek, LR 14 App Cas 337 (1888).

95. Players even "steal" bases in baseball.

96. Sun Tzu, The Art of War (fourth century BC). Winston Churchill also famously remarked to Joseph Stalin, "In wartime truth is so precious that she should always be attended by a bodyguard of lies." Ben Macintyre, Double Cross 3 (2012).

when exercised in equally competitive trading markets. This is because regulators want a golf competition model for the markets they regulate, not football.

Traders in financial markets often enter into trades in order to mislead and deceive other market participants about the trader's true trading intentions. Traders, by necessity, try to mask their trading by entering orders that will deceive other traders. Traders may send flash orders they do not intend to be executed in order to discover the trading interests of other traders and to lure them into the market. As described in Chapter 7, those orders are seeking liquidity, and market liquidity is a good thing. If the market knows the trader's strategy in advance, however, other participants will act to thwart the trader and profit from that knowledge.

"Deceptive" conduct is normal and has existed in trading markets for centuries. Nathan Rothschild was known and admired for his trading acumen in the 1820s. One of Rothschild's better-known stratagems was that, when he wanted to acquire a large long position in the "funds," he would first enter sell orders for those securities. The sell orders would give rise to a rumor that Rothschild was bearing the market, causing a selloff. Rothschild would then buy up the securities at a now cheaper price.[97] Was that practice a manipulation or just astute trading? Rothschild can hardly be condemned for trading on the gullibility of other traders who were themselves seeking to profit from what they thought was their own information advantage.

Such practices continued in modern markets in this century. Cantor Fitzgerald, a prime dealer in U.S. government securities, allowed traders to conceal their trading plans through various deceptive tactics. "[I]f Merrill Lynch wanted to sell 200 million U.S. Treasury bonds, they . . . might put up a bid for bonds to convince competitors there was a big buyer out there, only to sell in the bond futures pits of Chicago."[98] This avoided the drop in price that would have occurred had the market thought Merrill Lynch was dumping a large position in a market lacking strength. Was this fraud or manipulation or just an astute trading strategy?

A professor of finance and economics at the New York University Stern Business School and a former trader noted,

> Speculators and market makers can both disguise their intentions like secret agents. At financial institutions, speculators call themselves proprietary traders to sound respectable and often pursue mixed strategies to mask their behavior. They deal with customers when it suits their purpose, serving as ready buyers while accumulating a speculative position. They misrepresent themselves as low-risk market makers to reduce their capital requirements.[99]

Paul Tudor Jones, a large hedge fund operator, was reported to have stated that he often used his market power to move market prices. In 1987, he pushed up silver prices, giving rise to concerns that there was a disruption in supplies in the market. The result was even higher prices on which he profited. Jones was quoted as saying that he could "go into any market at just the right moment, by giving it a little gas on the upside, I can create the illusion of a bull market. But, unless the market is really sound, the price is going to come right down.' . . . but a short term advantage was all that he needed."[100] These unguarded remarks by Jones exemplify the mind-set of large traders, who seek to affect the market in ways by which they can profit. As shown in earlier chapters, Jones's stratagem was no different from the ploys of the grain traders of the nineteenth century and those that followed. Is such trading illegal manipulation or is it instinctive market behavior?

97. John Francis, Chronicles and Characters of the Stock Exchange 303-304 (1844).
98. Tom Barbash, On Top of the World: Cantor Fitzgerald, Howard Lutnick, & 9/11 92-93 (2003).
99. William L. Silber, Volcker 289 (2012).
100. Jeff madrick, Age of Greed 263 (2011).

Where is the line to be drawn on what is permissible? Where does a football play change from artful deception to an illegal block in the back.

A trader in pork bellies on the Chicago Mercantile Exchange openly boasted to the *Wall Street Journal* that he had placed both buy and sell orders on Globex, the CME electronic exchange, in order to "create some interest" in this once popular, but now moribund, market.[101] Those orders gave the false impression that there was liquidity on both sides of the market. That conduct was intended to influence the market for the trader's personal gain, but is it illegal? The trader stood ready to buy and sell at those prices. His capital was at risk and his intention was to profit by jump-starting the market.

A Norwegian court dismissed market manipulation claims against Svend Egil Larsen and Peder Veiby, who were charged with manipulating the prices of various Norwegian stocks by reverse engineering the algorithmic code of an electronic trading platform called Timber Hill, which was owned by Interactive Brokers in the United States. The defendants had been able to determine how the algorithms on Timber Hill would react to various trading patterns. They were then able to influence the price of low-volume stocks through thousands of trades. The Norwegian court noted that the defendants' trades were made in the open market, and experts testified that their trading activities were a common practice that made the market more efficient.

Larsen boasted after his conviction that he had found another algorithm flaw at UBS platform, which failed to have a bottom limit on trades, allowing Larsen to buy stock cheap.[102] Should UBS be protected from its own programming defect? Is trading a gentleman's game that forsakes advantage and forgives the errors of opponents? Undoubtedly, the programming that these Norwegians were able to exploit has been corrected, resulting in a better trading platform in both instances.

Traders also often enter orders that are otherwise inconsistent with their outlook on the market in order to "feel" for the bottom or the top of a market. Scale-up and scale-down orders that are to be executed at ascending or descending prices are used for similar purposes.[103] Traders may also "gun the stops"—for example, sell down the market in order to touch off pending limit orders and thereby trigger additional buying or selling.[104] This has been a common practice in markets for years.

Traders seek to exploit market flaws. That is how they profit. Traders seek to take advantage of those with less knowledge or skill. Like Paul Tudor Jones, large traders seek to move market prices in their favor by stealth and design. Traders seek to take advantage of the weakness and ignorance of others and force their opponent to lose money for the benefit of the trader that they are themselves seeking to damage. That is what trading is all about. Are all of those traders deliberately trying to run a red light or are they are simply acting on their belief that there is a market flaw to exploit that will allow them to profit?

---

101. Carolyn Cui & Theopolis Waters, *Pork Bellies Now "Nontrading Places,"* WALL STREET JOURNAL, Dec. 28, 2010, at C1.

102. Michael Stothard, *Court Clears Norwegian Day-Trade Duo Who Outwitted Big US Broker*, FINANCIAL TIMES (LONDON) May 3, 2012, at 1. In another area, in the United States, a programmer who stole the source code for a high-frequency trading program from Goldman Sachs had his federal conviction reversed. United States v. Aleynikov, 2012 U.S. App. LEXIS 7439 (2d Cir.). He had been charged with violations of the National Stolen Property Act (18 U.S.C. § 2314) and the Economic Espionage Act of 1996 (18 U.S.C. § 1832). However, that same programmer was later indicted under New York State law for the same conduct by the Manhattan district attorney's office. Peter Lattman, *Ex-Goldman Programmer Again Faces Theft Charge*, NEW YORK TIMES, Aug. 10, 2012, at B1.

103. *See, e.g.*, SEC Litigation Release No. 1204 (June 24, 1958) (describing an indictment for manipulation that used, among other things, scale-up orders).

104. SEC Release No. 34-41527, 64 Fed. Reg. 33533, 33534, n. 9 (June 23, 1999).

The CFTC and SEC have rejected the contact sport model for regulating stocks and derivatives. Their approach is to seek a model closer to the game of golf. The rules of golf define the game as a noncontact sport which equalizes competition by handicaps. The SEC and now the CFTC seek to level the playing field by seeking to handicap the larger players. Their theory is that such handicaps will allow smaller players to compete equally. In fact, larger, faster traders will generally outcompete the smaller trader even with a handicap, but the handicap does come at the cost of less market efficiency.

As described in Chapter 5, the SEC sought to adopt this handicapping model for the stock markets through its doctrine of equal access to information, but the Supreme Court rejected that philosophy. The rejection of that model is also reflected in Supreme Court decisions that dismiss manipulation claims that are not accompanied by some bad conduct. Nevertheless, the SEC continues to cling to its equal-access-to-information doctrine through its high-profile insider trading cases, which seem not to have deterred anyone from engaging in such activity.

The SEC's first reaction to the growth of flash orders was to express concern over the advantage given by such trades to short-term professional traders over long-term investors. That short-term advantage should not trouble long-term investors, but the larger question is why the SEC seeks to equalize advantages in trading. Another example of this SEC philosophy of a handicap market system is found in the fine it imposed on the New York Stock Exchange (NYSE) on September 14, 2012. The NYSE was raising revenue from its largest customers, the high-frequency traders, by providing special access and customized information feeds. The sale of that data raised regulatory concerns at the SEC,[105] which fined the NYSE $5 million for providing data to large traders in advance of its disclosure to other market participants.[106]

The SEC's concern in that case was that the NYSE was providing unequal access to information. High-speed traders could pay for data streams from the NYSE that were more efficient than those made available to other market participants. The SEC's complaint against the NYSE charged among other things that

> [b]eginning in June 2008, one NYSE proprietary feed sent real-time depth-of-book market data, which included information about its current best-priced quotations and execution prices, to its subscribers before NYSE sent data to a Securities Information Processor (the "Network Processor") that made quotes and trades available for sale to the public on a consolidated basis. Another NYSE proprietary feed, during multiple intervals of high-volume trading during the first half of 2010, sent quote data to customers before NYSE sent it to the Network Processor. The disparities ranged from single-digit milliseconds to, on occasion, multiple seconds.[107]

This claim again demonstrates the SEC's effort to turn market competition into a golf match where everyone is equalized by a handicap. In reality, information is simply a commodity that should be available for sale just as is any other commodity. Consumers can buy an upgraded

105. Jenny Strasburg & Scott Patterson, *SEC Keeps Wary Eye on Exchanges,* Wall Street Journal, Sept. 17, 2012, at C1.

106. Jenny Strasburg & Scott Patterson, *NYSE Is Fined in Data Probe*, Wall Street Journal, Sept. 15, 2012, at A1.

107. In the Matter of New York Stock Exchange LLC, Securities Exchange Act Release No. 67857 (S.E.C. Sept. 14, 2012). In another action, Goldman Sachs agreed to pay $6.75 million to the options exchanges to settle charges over mismarking of market maker orders as customer orders. Customer orders are supposed to have priority over market maker trades, and that mismarking allowed the market makers to avoid that priority. Liz Moyer & Jacob Bunge, *Goldman Settles Trading Case*, Wall Street Journal, Oct. 9, 2012, at C2.

cable TV package that is denied to those not willing to pay that extra premium. If a large trader wants to pay more for better information, what is wrong with that? It is a better product, and the exchange should be allowed to profit from its sale. If other traders do not want to pay the premium for the information, then they can choose to trade in some other instrument or trade without the advantage of that information.

Such a pragmatic view of the market is beyond the ability of regulators or populist politicians. The SEC charges against the NYSE also contain another object lesson. The government acts only on an after-the-fact basis through highly publicized "I gotcha" cases. The government is incapable of dealing with markets in real time. The conduct at issue in the NYSE case occurred from 2008 to 2010, but the SEC's complaint was not filed until two years later.

This trader equality regulatory approach is not limited to asymmetrical access to information. As described in Chapter 7, the SEC has also expressed concern over practices that provide professional short-term traders an advantage over long-term investors. High frequency traders raise other asymmetrical advantage concerns. In December 2012, the CFTC's chief economist issued a report which claimed that high frequency traders made a profit of as much as $5.05 whenever their trades were matched with more traditional traders in S&P 500 Index futures contracts. This led CFTC commissioner Bart Chilton to charge that the high frequency traders were becoming the "new middleman in exchange trading, and they're taking some of the cream off the top." The Financial Stability Oversight Council, the super-regulatory council created by Dodd-Frank, was also examining high frequency trading to determine whether it posed a yet unknown threat to the financial system.[108]

8:4 ARTIFICIAL PRICE AND ATTEMPTED MANIPULATION

Another major obstacle in proving manipulation has been the element of proving an artificial price. As described in Chapter 6, the FTC and FERC have eschewed the necessity of proving that element in their enforcement cases under the new Section 10(b)–style antimanipulation authority. The CFTC has also sought to avoid this essential element of manipulation—artificial price—under its old Commodity Exchange Act antimanipulation authority by simply charging attempted, instead of actual, manipulation. Dodd-Frank included attempted manipulation in its Section 753 addition of Section 10(b) authority, so undoubtedly the CFTC will continue to favor such cases.

Troubling in all of these efforts by these agencies to reduce their evidentiary burden is that the regulators are signaling an intent to attack any market practice they deem undesirable and without any proof that it is actually harmful. This is further evidenced by government effort to charge only attempted manipulation. In the view of the government, such trading would only require proof of intent that the government will argue is present any time a trading practice it dislikes is discovered.

This end around the requirement for proving an artificial price seeks to undermine the need for showing this essential element of a manipulation claim. If there is no artificial price, there is no manipulation. The avoidance of proving an artificial price also ignores the admonition of the Supreme Court in *Ernst & Ernst v. Hochfelder*,[109] which held that Section 10(b) of the 34 Act is addressed to "intentional or willful conduct designed to deceive or defraud investors *by controlling or artificially affecting the price of securities.*"[110]

---

108. Nathaniel Popper and Christopher Leonard, *High-Speed Trades Hurt Investors, a Study Says*, New York Times, Dec. 4, 2012, at B1.

109. Ernst & Ernst v. Hochfelder, 425 U.S. 185 (1976).

110. Ernst & Ernst v. Hochfelder, 425 U.S. 185, 199 (1976) (emphasis supplied).

The essence of the fraud in a Section 10(b) manipulation case is the creation of an artificial price. The artificial price element cannot be decoupled from the essence of the crime of manipulation. The government should not be given a free ride to attack trading practices it does not like without some showing that the practices will actually cause an artificial price and that the putative respondent intended such a result.

Of course, this analysis begs the question of what is an artificial price, which leads back to the core problem in manipulation claims—that is, there is no definition of that term other than some allusions to a price that does not reflect the forces of supply and demand. The vagueness of that standard only sets the stage for extended and complicated litigation and a "battle of the economists" over whether the price was artificial. That exercise is a costly but necessary one if the present structure for manipulation remains. Traders must be protected from arbitrary governmental claims that are designed for publicity and not market efficiency.

As noted, the CFTC has sought to avoid this barrier through charges of "attempted" manipulation, which the CFTC claims does not require the proving of an artificial price. It can be rightfully argued that an attempt to manipulate the market should not be ignored simply because it failed. However, the danger is that the government will charge attempted manipulation solely as a means to attack a trading practice without any showing that the practice was inherently bad or actually manipulative. To guard against that prosecutorial abuse, the government should be required to show that the actor intended to cause, and would likely have caused, a severe market disruption by improper methods but for the intervention of some fortuitous event.

A similar analysis applies to the traditional element of manipulation claims that an actor must have the "ability" to create an artificial price in order to be guilty of a manipulation. An example may be helpful in understanding why this limitation is needed. Say that a trader enters a one-lot transaction at an artificially high or low price on a highly liquid exchange where thousands of trades are executed every minute during the trading day. The trader knew the order was set at a price that did not reflect market fundamentals, but so what? If an order is not material, it will not have the ability to have an actionable effect on the market.

Under the weight of much Supreme Court precedence, as described in Chapter 7, if it is not "material," there can be no violation of a Section 10(b)–type statute. The government seeks to avoid this limitation by claiming that even short-term price effects are material and are criminal. Economically, it can be said that every order affects the market, but that is like saying that the air stirred by a butterfly's wings in Africa gave rise to a wind that became a hurricane that devastated America's coast.

The causation elements will also play a critical role in Section 10(b)–based manipulation cases because they require the parties to sort out whether, and to what extent, extraneous factors caused the loss. The complexities of factoring the effects on the market of those outside events into the amount of damages caused by the defendant's misstatement may be mind-bogglingly complex.

The government seeks to avoid the burden of proving the reliance and causation elements required by the Supreme Court in private actions on the grounds that it is acting in the public interest. This too engenders issues similar to those raised in attempted manipulation claims, since no actual violation is alleged to have occurred. This gives the government a free ride in attacking practices it does not like, but which have not been shown to be actually manipulative or particularly harmful. If there is no reliance by anyone on conduct of the alleged manipulator or if there is no causation flowing from that trader's conduct, there is no harm and there should be no foul.

This does not mean that the government should have to wait until an investor is actually defrauded or the market distorted if it becomes aware of a not yet launched operation seeking such a result. In actuality, however, such cases are rarely, if ever, brought because the government is simply too slow-footed for such a preemptive strike. Nevertheless, assuming the existence of such an unlikely case, the issue becomes, how does the government prove that a manipulation is being planned? How does the government separate loose talk on a trading desk, which is unlikely to be carried out, from a well-planned scheme that is about to be put into operation with potentially highly adverse effects on the market?

Truth be told, traders are always discussing how to take advantage of markets by finding a flaw overlooked by others. That is what they do. Traders are constantly seeking out market defects or weaknesses they can exploit to their advantage. Traders are always on the lookout for an information advantage over other traders. Traders are not successful because they possess a crystal ball of future market direction. Rather, they look for weaknesses in others, market defects, advance information unknown to others, and even regulatory arbitrages that give them an advantage.

Without an advantage, real or perceived, the trader is simply a blindfolded gambler tossing dice and hoping for a random favorable result. Traders bring value to the market by exposing flaws based on superior information or trading skill. Traders should be permitted to do so in the absence of proof that they pose a genuine threat of a market disruption.

The elements of reliance and ability to affect prices required to prove manipulation resolve the tension in sorting out bad conduct from good conduct. Those elements should require a showing that a manipulative scheme would depend on the reliance of others in order to be successful and that it is the cause of a loss. When coupled with the intent and ability elements, this will ensure that loose talk among traders is not elevated to a crime that is unlikely ever to occur or that is simply an astute effort to take advantage of market flaws or the weakness of other traders.

8:5 MANIPULATION BY FALSE REPORTS

Charges of commodity price manipulation by false reports were a rarity until the energy crisis in California. As described in Chapter 6, the CFTC and the Justice Department then launched a broad-scale assault on energy traders who were reporting fictitious "round trip" trades to private publications. That effort was successful in obtaining uncontested settlements for large sums of money from several big energy firms, but was less effective when a case actually went to trial.[111] Congress reacted through Section 753 of the Dodd-Frank Act, which was a "Special Provision for Manipulation by False Reporting." That amendment stated:

> Unlawful manipulation . . . shall include, but not be limited to, delivering, or causing to be delivered for transmission through the mails or interstate commerce, by any means of communication whatsoever, a false or misleading or inaccurate report concerning crop or market information or conditions that affect or tend to affect the price of any commodity in interstate commerce, knowing, or acting in reckless disregard of the fact that such report is false, misleading or inaccurate.

It is unclear what this "special provision" was intended to accomplish beyond what was already in the Commodity Exchange Act. Perhaps, Congress was seeking to clarify its reach. The language used, however, is problematic in achieving such a goal, particularly with the inclusion of the language from Section 10(b) of the 34 Act into that same amendment.

The Supreme Court decisions in *Stoneridge Investment Partners LLC v. Scientific-Atlanta Inc.*[112] and later *Janus Capital Group Inc. v. First Derivative Traders*[113] placed severe limits on the liability

111. *See, e.g.*, CFTC v. Delay, 2006 WL 3359076 (D. Neb. 2006).
112. Stoneridge Investment Partners LLC v. Scientific-Atlanta Inc., 552 U.S. 148 (2008).
113. Janus Capital Group Inc. v. First Derivative Traders, 564 U.S. --- (2011).

of actors who do not actually publish a false report. Those cases narrowly limit false reporting liability under Section 10(b)–type language to those that actually "make" a misleading statement or omission directly to investors, rather than the person who "created" the false report.

The decisions in *Stoneridge* and *Janus Capital* raise some perplexing questions in manipulation cases under the new false reporting language added by Section 753. That prohibition applies to anyone who is "delivering or causing to be delivered" false reports. It is questionable whether, under the *Stoneridge* and *Janus Capital* analysis, false reports are attributable to the traders creating the statement because the trader was not "delivering" the false information to the market. Instead, the false reports that tend to affect market prices are created by the traders and given to and then delivered by independent market publications. They make the decision to publish and they do the actual publication of the false reports, not the traders.

Thus the "causing to be delivered" language added by Dodd-Frank for false reports may not help the government to overcome the limitations of *Stoneridge* and *Janus Capital.* The majority of the Supreme Court justices in *Janus Capital* stated that "the rule we adopt today: [is] that the maker of a statement is the entity with authority over the content of the statement and whether and how to communicate it. Without such authority, it is not 'necessary or inevitable' that any falsehood will be contained in the statement."[114] In the round-trip false trading reports brought by the CFTC, the publisher of the industry newsletter was the one with the requisite authority to decide whether to publish to the market and it was the one who caused the report to be delivered, not a trader with no authority over what was to be published.

It may be fairly argued that, under *Janus Capital*, the "delivery" of a false report is made only by the publisher of the statement. The term "make" that was addressed in *Janus Capital* is thus synonymous with the term "delivered" that is used in Section 753 of Dodd-Frank. The person that "creates" a speech is the "speechwriter." The person that "makes" or "delivers" the speech is the "speechmaker." The speechwriter and the speechmaker may be the same person, but liability under *Janus Capital* will lie only for that person's role as a speechmaker. A speechwriter who "creates" a false statement would have no liability if he does not "deliver" the speech to the audience that will be actually affected by the false statement. This is true even if the speechwriter benefits from the false statements made by the speechmaker.

The argument against indirect application is strengthened by the fact that, unlike the Section 753 false reporting amendment, Section 10(b) of the 34 Act applies to conduct that is "directly or indirectly" fraudulent. The Supreme Court in *Janus Capital* held even that broad language did not erase the line between the creator of a statement and the maker/deliverer of the statement.[115] Also, if the "delivered" language in Section 753 is read more broadly, then it would apply to every false statement by anyone to anyone about commodity prices. Surely, that was not the intent of Congress. Traders in financial markets engage in constant "chatter" in which they make misrepresentations to other traders, but is it a crime to merely make the statement when no trade occurs by the maker of the statement or its recipient? This would mean, for example, that traders chatting with each other and trying to mislead each other on their positions or trading strategy would be guilty of a crime. Taken to its extreme, this would mean that a trader emailing a false statement to himself would have committed a crime.

False reports used for rigged trading manipulations raise additional issues. The maker of those rigged trades is not making any direct misrepresentations to the market. Rather, the rigged trades used to carry out such a manipulation are reported to the public by the exchange, not by the trader.

114. 564 U.S. at ---.

115. 564 U.S. at ---, n. 11.

Does this indirect publication constitute a delivery? Or do *Stoneridge* and *Janus Capital* absolve the trader of liability because the "delivery" or the "making" of the statement was done by the exchange?

The prohibitions in Section 4(c) of the Commodity Exchange Act make it illegal for "any person to offer to enter into, enter into, or confirm the execution" of wash and other prohibited transactions.[116] That language applies to the person engaged in the trade as opposed to the maker or deliverer of the report that is addressed by Dodd-Frank Section 753. Numerous cases have been brought under Section 4(c) for abusive trading without running afoul of the more difficult manipulation standards in the Commodity Exchange Act.[117] There is no need to charge manipulation because Congress made adequate provision for attacking such practices through Section 4(c), but the false reporting provision did not address trading, only the delivery of false reports. In times past, it was thought that the role of markets was to sift out false and bad information through price discovery.

The anomalies raised by *Stoneridge* are apparent from *SEC v. Goldman Sachs & Co.*,[118] the SEC's sensational case that was filed against that high-profile investment bank in the wake of the financial crisis. There, the SEC charged that Goldman Sachs engaged in a fraudulent scheme to conceal the involvement of hedge fund manager John Paulson in the selection of collateralized debt obligations (CDOs) that were sold to foreign institutional investors by Goldman Sachs. The SEC charged that Goldman Sachs failed to disclose in its offering and marketing materials that Paulson was selecting CDOs that he thought would fail. Paulson was taking a short in the CDOs and profited by some $1 billion while the investors that purchased the CDOs from Goldman Sachs lost a comparable amount.

Paulson was the alleged architect and mastermind of the scheme and the one who benefited when the CDOs failed, but he was not charged by the SEC. Paulson escaped sanction because,

---

116. 7 U.S.C. § 6c.

117. *See, e.g.*, Wilson v. CFTC, 322 F.3d 555 (2d Cir. 2003) (wash trades); Reddy v. CFTC, 191 F.3d 109 (2d Cir. 1999) (wash trades); United States v. Ashman, 979 F.2d 469 (7th Cir. 1992), *cert. denied*, 510 U.S. 814 (1993) (fraudulent trading scheme); CFTC v. Doyle, Comm. Fut. L. Rep. (CCH) ¶ 30,577 (S.D.N.Y. 2007) (default order in case involving fraudulent order allocation scheme); CFTC v. Burtztyn, Comm. Fut. L. Rep. (CCH) ¶ 30,390 (S.D.N.Y. 2006) (prearranged transactions); In the Matter of Haveman, Comm. Fut. L. Rep. (CCH) ¶ 31,948 (C.F.T.C. 2011) (consent order for fictitious trading); In the Matter of Pinemore, Comm. Fut. L. Rep. (CCH) ¶ 31,517 (C.F.T.C. 2010) (consent order for wash trading); In the Matter of Mostyer, Comm. Fut. L. Rep. (CCH) ¶ 31,314 (C.F.T.C. 2009) (consent order for fictitious trading) In the Matter of Karkazis, Comm. Fut. L. Rep. (CCH) ¶ 30,407 (C.F.T.C. 2006) (consent order involving round-trip trades); In the Matter of Credit Lyonnais Ltd., Comm. Fut. L. Rep. (CCH) ¶ 30,125 (C.F.T.C. 2005) (consent order for noncompetitive trades); In the Matter of Amajaro Trading Ltd., Comm. Fut. L. Rep. (CCH) ¶ 30,089 (C.F.T.C. 2005) (consent order for fictitious trades); In the Matter of Hencorp Becstone Futures LLC, Comm. Fut. L. Rep. (CCH) ¶ 29,936 (C.F.T.C. 2004) (consent order for wash sales); In the Matter of Knauth, Comm. Fut. L. Rep. (CCH) ¶ 29,762 (C.F.T.C. 2004) (consent decree involving round-trip trades); In the Matter of Gorski, Comm. Fut. L. Rep. (CCH) ¶ 29,726 (C.F.T.C. 2004) (finding of violative trading); In the Matter of Harmon, Comm. Fut. L. Rep. (CCH) ¶ 29,660 (C.F.T.C. 2004) (consent order for wash trades); In the Matter of Gugliaro, Comm. Fut. L. Rep. (CCH) ¶ 29,597 (C.F.T.C. 2003) (consent order for violative trading); In the Matter of Schiller, Comm. Fut. L. Rep. (CCH) ¶ 29,477 (C.F.T.C. 2003) (consent order for fraudulent order allocation scheme); In the Matter of Gugliaro, Comm. Fut. L. Rep. (CCH) ¶ 29,260 (C.F.T.C. 2003) (consent order for trading ahead of customer orders); In the Matter of Garber, Comm. Fut. L. Rep. (CCH) ¶ 29,573 (C.F.T.C. 2003) (consent order for wash trading); In the Matter of Joyce, Comm. Fut. L. Rep. (CCH) ¶ 29,178 (C.F.T.C. 2002) (consent order for wash and round-trip trading); In the Matter of Gugliaro, Comm. Fut. L. Rep. (CCH) ¶ 28,935 (C.F.T.C. 1998) (fictitious trading scheme); In the Matter of DiFrancesco, Comm. Fut. L. Rep. (CCH) ¶ 29,115 (C.F.T.C. 2002) (consent order for trading ahead of customer orders); In the Matter of Mayer, Comm. Fut. L. Rep. (CCH) ¶ 27,259 (C.F.T.C. 2003) (noncompetitive trading)

118. SEC v. Goldman Sachs & Co. 10 CV 3229 (S.D.N.Y. April 15, 2010).

under the *Stoneridge* decision, he made no direct misrepresentations to the foreign investors. Goldman Sachs, which lost money in the transaction, was charged with liability for underwriting the CDOs that allowed Paulson to profit. This was because the offering documents prepared by Goldman Sachs did not disclose Paulson's role as the short in the transaction.[119]

In its complaint against Goldman Sachs, the SEC specifically equated the term "delivered" with the term "make" for purposes of charging Goldman Sachs with liability for making false reports.[120] Under the *Stoneridge* decision, it was Goldman Sachs, not Paulson, who was the "maker" of the false statements when, as charged in the SEC's complaint, a Goldman Sachs employee "delivered" the allegedly deceptive marketing materials to the foreign investors. Paulson was at the center of the alleged scheme, but he did not "make" or deliver any false statements to the investors. Rather, it was Goldman Sachs that "delivered" the false statements. Presumably, the same analysis will apply for determining false reporting liability under Section 753 of Dodd-Frank.

The special provision in Section 753 on false reporting may raise the issue of whether Congress was seeking to overturn *Stoneridge*. If that was the intent of Congress, that effort was conducted by stealth and deception because more straightforward efforts to overturn that decision failed. Senator Arlen Specter (D-PA) and Representative Maxine Waters (D-CA.) unsuccessfully sought enactment of amendments in the congressional debates on Dodd-Frank that would have directly overturned the *Stoneridge* decision.[121]

In view of that legislative history, it is doubtful that Congress intended to overturn the *Stoneridge* decision through the special provision for manipulation by false reporting in Section 753 of Dodd-Frank. If Congress intended to reverse the *Stoneridge* decision or make it inapplicable to Section 753, the lawmakers would have undoubtedly directly addressed such a highly controversial issue.

Further evidencing Congress's awareness of the limitations imposed by the *Stoneridge* decision is Section 929Z of the Dodd-Frank Act. Instead of overturning *Stoneridge*, Congress, as a compromise, included a provision in Section 929Z that directed the Government Accountability Office (GAO) to study and report "on the courts interpretation of the scope of liability for secondary actors under Federal securities laws after January 14, 2008."[122] That date was not chosen by accident. It was the day before the *Stoneridge* decision was handed down by the Supreme Court.

The GAO issued its report about a year after the passage of Dodd-Frank. The report reviewed the elements of Rule 10b-5 claims and recounted the arguments for and against a private right of action against secondary actors, without reaching any real conclusion on whether *Stoneridge* should be overturned by legislation.[123] The GAO report noted that the Supreme Court had rejected private right of action for aiding and abetting violations of Section 10(b) in the 34 Act in *Central Bank of Denver v. First Interstate Bank of Denver*.[124]

The GAO report further noted that, following that decision, Congress had not chosen to include a private right of action for aiding and abetting in the Private Securities Litigation Reform Act of

---

119. *See*, Jerry W. Markham, *SEC v. Goldman Sachs & Co.: Serious Fraud or Just More Banker Bashing*, 30 FUT. & DERV. L. REP. 7, 8 (2010) (discussing the omission of Paulson from the case).

120. SEC v. Goldman Sachs & Co., Complaint ¶ 55 (S.D.N.Y 2010).

121. Baker & McKenzie, *Dispute Resolution*, http://www.bakermckenzie.com/files/Publication/e2e15f25-4bba-41de-a7b5-2fccd65d82dd/Presentation/PublicationAttachment/4210bc60-14af-4ad7-afdc-3608a355e-d1b/al_dr_doddfrankactimplicationsfederalsecuritieslitigation_jul10.pdf (accessed May 7, 2012); Government Accountability Office, GAO-11-664 *Securities Fraud Liability of Secondary Actors* 37 (July 21, 2011).

122. Dodd-Frank § 929Z.

123. Government Accountability Office, GAO-11-664 *Securities Fraud Liability of Secondary Actors* 37-45 (July 21, 2011).

124. Central Bank of Denver v. First Interstate Bank of Denver, 511 U.S. 164 (1994).

1995, an issue that was debated in its passage. "Because Congress chose not to overturn *Central Bank* by creating a private aiding and abetting cause of action for securities fraud when enacting PSLRA,[125] the Court concluded that there still was no private aiding and abetting action under Rule 10b-5."[126] Similarly, because Congress declined to include provisions in the Dodd-Frank Act that would have overturned the decision in *Stoneridge Investment Partners*, that decision remains in force.[127]

The scienter standard in Dodd-Frank's Section 753 "special provision for manipulation by false reporting" raises more issues. Section 753 imposes liability for false reports for "knowing" violations or where a party is "acting in reckless disregard of the fact that such report is false, misleading or inaccurate."[128] The statute then provides a defense for "Good Faith Mistakes.–Mistakenly transmitting, in good faith, false or misleading or inaccurate information to a price reporting service would not be sufficient to violate" this prohibition. There is no comparable language for scienter in the part of Section 753 that added the antimanipulation authority borrowed from Section 10(b). Congress thus knew how to specify reckless conduct as the scienter requirement for false reports, but chose not to use that same language in the parallel "manipulative or deceptive device or contrivance" portion that is contained in the same section of the statute.

This is a little confusing. Did Congress intend to use the same intent test for both? As noted above, a common canon of statutory construction would apply the reckless intent standard to the language that was borrowed from Section 10(b) of the 34 Act. Since that canon of statutory construction was explicitly recognized in the floor debates, why add such a standard to the false reports provision? Presumably the concern was that, since the special reports provision was not borrowed, it was necessary to add language that would accomplish the same result—that is, using reckless conduct as the intent test for both. However, that same result could have been accomplished by simply making false reports a manipulative scheme or device under the borrowed language of Section 10(b).

By creating a separate provision for special reports containing the reckless standard without including that language in the borrowed Section 10(b) language, Congress ran afoul of another canon of statutory construction. "[W]here Congress includes particular language in one section of a statute but omits it in another . . . , it is generally presumed that Congress acts intentionally and purposely in the disparate inclusion or exclusion." "[N]egative implications raised by disparate provisions are strongest when the portions of a statute treated differently had already been joined together and were being considered simultaneously when the language raising the implication was inserted."[129]

---

125. As described in Chapter 5, the Supreme Court held in *Central Bank of Denver v. First Interstate Bank of Denver*, 511 U.S. 164 (1994), that there was no private right of action for aiding and abetting liability under Section 10(b) of the 34 Act. Congress declined to overturn that ruling when it enacted the Private Securities Litigation Reform Act of 1995, but did allow the SEC to bring such claims. *See*, Section 104 of the PSLRA, 109 Stat. 757, codified at 15 U.S.C. § 78t(e).

126. Government Accountability Office, GAO-11-664 *Securities Fraud Liability of Secondary Actors* 25 (July 21, 2011) (citation and footnote omitted).

127. The Dodd-Frank Act did make some changes in the scienter standard in aiding and abetting actions brought by the SEC, but that only further evidences a determination not to overturn either the *Central Bank* or *Stoneridge* decisions. *See*, Dodd-Frank § 929O (adding "recklessly" as the scienter standard).

128. Dodd-Frank § 753.

129. Congressional Research Service, *Report for Congress, Statutory Interpretation: General Principles and Recent Trends* CRS-14 (Aug. 31, 2010) (footnotes and citations omitted). *See also, Bates v. United States*, 522 U.S. 23, 29 (1997) (use of "intent to defraud" language in one provision and omitted in a parallel provision evidenced congressional intent not to include the requirement in the latter section).

That was the case for the false reporting and Section 10(b) language. The provisions were added at the same time, but the borrowed Section 10(b) language does not contain the reckless standard. Does this mean that there is a difference in scienter standards under the two provisions? Does this mean that the borrowed Section 10(b) language will be interpreted as imposing an "extreme recklessness" standard versus a mere "reckless" standard for false reports? If so, what is the difference?

The resolution of those issues is made difficult because their legislative history is sparse. Senator Blanche Lincoln (D-AR) stated on the floor in the debates over the Dodd-Frank Act that Section 753 addresses "fraud based manipulation, including manipulation by false reporting" and was intended to supplement the CFTC's existing antimanipulation authority for other types of manipulative conduct.[130] Senator Lincoln thus equated fraud-based manipulation with manipulation by false reports. She did not attempt to draw a distinction in the scienter standard between these two forms of manipulation.

Further confusion is sown by the good faith defense for false reports that is contained in Section 753—that is, there is no liability for a false report made to "a price reporting service" if the false report was a good faith mistake. Senator Lincoln stated in the floor debates that the "good faith mistake provision in Section 753 is an affirmative defense. The burden of proof is on the person asserting the good faith mistake defense to show that he or she did not know or act in reckless disregard of the fact that the report was false, misleading, or inaccurate."[131] This statement seems to make clear that the false report provision was intended to be "fraud based," which would argue in favor of a higher, not lessened, scienter standard.

The claims made by Senator Lincoln with respect to the good faith provision are problematic on other grounds. She argues that the false reports provision was intended to shift the burden of proof so that the government need only show that a report is false. Once it is shown that the report is false, at least according to Senator Lincoln, the burden would shift to the defendant to show that the false report was only a good faith mistake. This claim by Senator Lincoln appears to be an overstatement. The good faith defense by its terms applies only to false reports made to "a price reporting service." Does this mean there is absolute liability for false reports to other persons?

This claim by Senator Lincoln ignores the "reckless disregard" scienter standard in Section 753 for false reports. The prohibition on false reports and accompanying reckless scienter standard in Section 753 is contained in a clause that is separate from the good faith defense provision. The separate false report provision imposes the duty of proving scienter on the government, which is, of course, the standard for most, if not all, fraud-based claims.

Senator Lincoln's burden of proof claim would turn the normal burden of proving fraud on its head. There generally is no duty on the part of a defendant to prove innocence until the government has met its burden of showing that the defendant committed fraud, which includes proof of the required degree of scienter. This precept is basic to the American justice system. The government presents its evidence showing fraud and that evidence must be sufficient under the appropriate standard of proof to establish guilt. In criminal cases, the defendant's guilt must be established beyond a reasonable doubt; civil cases require a lesser standard, such as a preponderance or weight of the evidence standard. Only when that burden is met is the defendant required to offer evidence to rebut that of the government.

130. 156 Cong. Rec. S5924 (July 15, 2010). *See also*, Statement of Senator Lincoln on Section 753 ("Senator CANTWELL's amendment will supplement the CFTC's existing standards . . ."). 156 Cong. Rec. S3349 (May 6, 2010).

131. *Id.*

Under Senator Lincoln's assertion, the government would be relieved of the burden that the defendant acted with the required intent. Intent and fraud would be presumed once the government shows that a statement made by the defendant was inaccurate in any way. Even if the false statement was a completely innocent mistake, the government would have met its burden of proof for fraud, even for criminal fraud.

According to Senator Lincoln, the government would be relieved of the duty to prove that the defendant actually committed fraud. Instead, the burden would be on the defendant to prove his or her innocence, a rather startling change in roles in the American judicial system. A more reasonable interpretation of the good faith defense for false reports in Section 753 is that it is merely a way to encourage quick corrections for reports made to price reporting publications without fear of liability.

The good faith defense provision in Section 753 also raises more issues regarding the overall scope of the application of the false reports provision. It may be argued that the reference to a "price reporting service" in the good faith defense clause suggests that Congress expected that the false reports provision in Section 753 would apply to the creator of the false statement, rather than to just its maker that published the report.

It could be argued with equal or greater force that the good faith defense was added merely to give assurance that a person innocently passing on a false report is not viewed as committing fraud. The latter interpretation would be consistent with the *Stoneridge* opinion, which was a part of the law that was borrowed when Section 753 included the Section 10(b) language. To argue that this provision evidences that Congress was defining a deliverer of a false statement as the creator of the statement would also be inconsistent with the congressional determination not to overturn the *Stoneridge* case and instead to have the GAO study the issue. In all events, this language only serves to further muddy the waters in defining manipulation.

8:6 MINIMANIPULATIONS

Traditionally, the principal concern over commodity price manipulations was with the corner in which a party exercised market power to gain control over the cash commodity underlying the delivery obligation on a futures contract and held most of the long side of that futures contract as the delivery period approached. The manipulator then stood for delivery and the shorts were required to pay him any price demanded because there were no other available supplies at the terminal market to cover their short positions. The squeeze is a lesser variation of that conduct. Those manipulations had severe disruptive effects as the shorts scrambled to bring unneeded supplies to the terminal market to cover their positions. This manipulative conduct skewed price relationships with other markets, forcing consumers and processors in the affected area to pay inordinate, artificial prices.

Such massive market power manipulations are no longer of much concern, since most commodity futures and other derivatives now provide for a cash settlement of obligations, rather than actual delivery of the commodity underlying the contract. That change reduces or eliminates most of the adverse effects of a market power manipulation. In addition, most manipulations that threaten broad-scale disruption occur in markets with vast of supplies of cash commodities that no one party is likely to control.

A trader with market power can still bid up the futures market in order to aid contractual commitments tied to the derivative contract price. Such a manipulation provides profit opportunity when the trader can sell the related inventory at the higher price, but the profit will be reduced by any loss on the futures contracts when they are closed. In illiquid markets, the loss on the futures contract may be smaller in proportion to the gain on the related cash position. This is because only a few futures contracts will be needed to move the price and the loss on those futures will be small if the cash market position is proportionally larger.

Such a manipulation can be more easily conducted cheaply through false reports to industry price publications or by manipulating the close on the pricing date in an illiquid market. Such conduct is undesirable, and the counterparty in the cash market will have a legitimate claim for damages. However, these manipulations tend to be relatively small in terms of overall price effect and are usually short in duration.

Manipulative or abusive activities no longer need follow the principal types of manipulation that the Commodity Exchange Act sought to address. Most trading activity today involves large, active, high-speed traders who are seeking to profit from technical aberrations identified by algorithms. Some traders still possess and exercise market power in their trading, but they are generally trading on the basis of fundamental factors. Large traders also typically trade both sides of the market in order to capture profits. They do not seek to control either side of the market, long or short. Rather, they are seeking to capture the maximum profit from fundamental market moves through large positions in leveraged derivative trading, either short or long.

As noted in Chapter 6, Amaranth made large profits from trading the long side of the natural gas market in the wake of Hurricanes Katrina and Rita. Amaranth then changed its outlook and went massively short. That change in position caused Amaranth to sustain the unprecedented losses of some $6 billion that led to its demise. In all events, Amaranth made a poor case for claims that speculators needed to be attacked as manipulators because they were driving energy prices to artificial levels. Amaranth was short the market and would have benefited from a fall in prices. Instead, it was Amaranth that was driven and destroyed by market fundamentals that pushed prices up, not the other way round. Those fundamentals simply overwhelmed any ability on the part of Amaranth to influence prices, and those fundamentals later reasserted themselves and drove prices down sharply. Natural gas prices fell from $7.12 per million BTUs in 2007 to under $2 in 2012 as supplies increased.[132] Indeed, the availability of plentiful natural gas supplies was driving down prices in 2012 to the point that fear was raised over a bursting of the bubble in natural gas recovery companies.[133]

Amaranth was merely a distraction from the fundamentals that actually drive energy market prices. The recent fall in prices was due to expansion of natural gas supplies through exploitation of shale fields and the newly employed "fracking" technique.[134] Although that situation was a happy one for consumers, those low-cost sources are being threatened by an assault from both state and federal regulators who seek to restrict production from fracking because of yet unproven concerns over environmental damage.[135] It could also be fairly claimed that government regulations drive other energy prices higher by limiting supplies, such as crude oil, through drilling restrictions and by placing other restrictions on developing energy sources, such as nuclear power. Placing the political focus on speculators such as Amaranth only diverts public attention from those fundamental factors.

---

132. Liam Pleven, *The Case Against Commodities*, WALL STREET JOURNAL, Oct. 5, 2011, at C9; Dan Strumpf, Jerry A. DiColo, & David Bird, *Natural Gas Sinks Beneath $2 Levels*, WALL STREET JOURNAL, April 12, 2012, at C4.

133. Concerns were being raised over speculation in shale gas wells because falling prices could result in investment losses by drillers and operators. Ian Urbina, *Insiders Sound an Alarm Amid a Natural Gas Rush*, NEW YORK TIMES, June 26, 22011, at 1.

134. Liam Pleven, *The Case Against Commodities*, WALL STREET JOURNAL, Oct. 5, 2011, at C9; Dan Strumpf, Jerry A. DiColo, & David Bird, *Natural Gas Sinks Beneath $2 Levels*, WALL STREET JOURNAL, April 12, 2012, at C4.

135. Tennille Tracy, *Firms Given Time on Fracking*, WALL STREET JOURNAL, April 19, 2012, at A3.

In addition to false reports, the other form of minimanipulation of concern is so-called rigged trading. Such minimanipulations are typically short-term in duration and involve abusive trading practices, such as wash trades and matched orders. Historically, the parties engaging in such practices in the commodity futures markets were floor traders and floor brokers. Those traders used their time and place advantage to manipulate prices, as was charged in the *DiPlacido* case.[136] The trader there used his floor position to trade through other customer limit orders in order to assist customers to mark a related position favorably to such an artificial price.

These floor traders are now mostly anachronisms and are of diminishing concern. Most trading is now conducted electronically away from the exchange trading floor. Customer abuses associated with floor brokers and floor traders have declined sharply, and electronic trading has virtually eliminated the "trade through" of customer limit orders. [137] Trade throughs, referring to trades made higher than the lowest current offer or lower than the highest current bid at the time of execution, are prohibited by exchange rules.

Historically, the trade through prohibition did not apply on exchange trading floors in "fast" markets conditions—that is, a period in which prices fluctuate widely. That exception meant that floor traders could profit and customers be injured during periods of market volatility. Algorithms on electronic trading platforms now match orders automatically according to their priority of entry, reducing or eliminating concerns over the trade through problem.[138]

It has also been noted elsewhere,

> Many regulators report that customer abuses, in particular, have declined. However, new forms of trading lead to new types of abuses that require the attention of regulators. One of the more significant changes has been the regulators' allocation of resources away from floor activities towards order entry points, like the terminal operator's activities, short-term manipulations and other activities in illiquid markets, side-by-side trading products, and inter-market transactions.[139]

Algorithms also provide for more certainty in applying trading restrictions: "In electronic systems, the algorithm that matches orders or trades constitutes the trading and execution rules that govern the priority and manner of trading. This leaves no room for disputes as to the applicability of the trading rules contained in the system. . . . This eliminates disputes about the validity of, or uncertainty as to the legality of, that interest."[140]

That regulatory evolution evidences that technology can be used to thwart many of the former abuses. Nevertheless, trading abuses in the form of wash sales can also occur on an electronic exchange. In *In the Matter of Enskilda Futures Ltd.*,[141] for example, the CFTC found by consent that an offshore broker accepted numerous matching buy and sell orders from a non-U.S. hedge

---

136. In the Matter of DiPlacido, COMM. FUT. L. REP. ¶ 30,970 (C.F.T.C. 2008), *aff'd sub nom.*, DiPlacido v. CFTC, No. 08-5559-ag, 2009 U.S. App. LEXIS 22692 (2d Cir. 2009), *cert denied*, 2010 U.S. LEXIS 2461 (2010).

137. *See, e.g.*, Chicago Board of Trade, Chicago Board of Trade Rulebook 514.A.1 (prohibiting the "trade through" of an "existing bid or offer").

138. HANDBOOK OF RESEARCH ON STOCK MARKET GLOBALIZATION, Ch. 12 (2012).

139. Jerry W. Markham & Daniel J. Harty, *For Whom the Bell Tolls: The Demise of Exchange Trading Floors and the Growth of ECNs*, 33 IOWA J. CORP. L. 865, 928 (2008).

140. Andrea M. Corcoran, *The Uses of New Capital Markets: Electronic Commerce and the Rules of the Game in an International Marketplace*, 49 AM. U. L. REV. 581, 588 (2000).

141. In the Matter of Enskilda Futures Ltd., Comm. Fut. L. Rep. (CCH) ¶ 32,062 (C.F.T.C. 2011).

fund that were then executed through Globex, the CME's electronic trading platform.[142] Nevertheless, electronic algorithms could search for patterns in trades coming through FCMs that appear to be wash or other prohibited trades.

Electronic trading has also illuminated the once opaque foreign currency market where claims have been made that prices were being set non-competitively by large banks at disadvantageous prices.[143] "Algorithms can provide electronic records of exactly how and when a trade is transacted, allowing investors to check the price at which a bank bought or sold a currency on their behalf against the price quoted in the market. Some banks offer a time-stamp to the millisecond for each part of an order."[144]

On another front, the SEC announced in February 2013 that it had developed a software program that would detect anomalies in accounting statements of publicly traded companies and hedge fund results.[145] This technology should be extended to abusive trading practices. Computer algorithms could identify and reject such trades.

Actively traded markets are not generally much affected by minimanipulations because market power is usually required to move prices in those markets. Such markets are hard to manipulate and price distortions caused by speculators are usually short-lived. The real challenge is to referee illiquid markets where distortions are more easily carried out. The first step in effectively regulating illiquid markets to protect against abuse should be to identify such markets and advise the public and market participants that the market is an illiquid one.

This would include a warning that prices in illiquid markets may not reflect the fundamentals of supply and demand and may be distorted by even small trades. In such illiquid markets, rules that inhibit traders' ability to bang the close may be needed. If, for example, "chumming" is deemed undesirable it should be prohibited.[146] Spoofing quotes to raise other traders' interest or to seek price discovery should be more carefully examined to determine whether and when they should be restricted by algorithmic rules.

The tendency of the government to attack any practice that provides advantage emerged in the 2012 controversy over "hide-not-slide" orders. These are complex orders designed to free up "locked" markets. A locked market occurs where the bid and ask prices are the same, a once unusual occurrence because profits are made by market makers from the usual spread between the bid and ask. The SEC has prohibited trading in locked markets because matching orders can be used to generate fees through manipulative trading.

Electronic order-matching systems have removed many of the time and place advantages of the market makers, and locked markets are more common in a largely order-matching electronic system.[147] Market orders are displayed publicly and will slide to a lower or higher price in a

---

142. *See also*, In the Matter of Noble Americas Corp., 2010 WL 1803817 (C.F.T.C.) (CFTC by consent finds that the respondent had engaged in wash sales through transactions on Globex).

143. The Bank of New York Mellon was accused by the New York State Attorney General and by the U.S. Attorney in New York of cheating customers on foreign exchange fees. Eric Dash and Peter Lattman, *U.S. and New York Sue Bank of New York Mellon Over Exchange Fees*, New York Times, Oct. 5, 2011, at B3.

144. Nia Williams, *Smart New Models Shine Light Into Opaque FX World*, Reuters, Oct. 19, 2012, available at http://uk.reuters.com/article/2012/10/19/idUKL5E8LG58F20121019 (visited on Oct. 19, 2012).

145. Dina ElBoghdady, *SEC Developing New Fraud Detection Technology*, Washington Post, Feb. 15, 2013.

146. Chumming involves prearranged trades that seek to provide the illusion of liquidity in a new contract in order to attract the interest of other traders. *See*, In re Kansas City Board of Trade, Comm. Fut. L. Rep. (CCH) ¶ 22,809 (C.F.T.C. 1986) (sanctioning such conduct); *Report of the Special Study of the Options Market to the Securities and Exchange Commission* 171 (Dec. 22, 1978) (same). The term comes from a practice by fishermen of dumping large amounts of bait in the water to attract sharks or other predatory fish.

147. *See*, Scott Patterson & Jenny Strasburg, *For Superfast Stock Traders, A Way to Jump Ahead in Line*, Wall Street Journal, Sept. 19, 2012 at A1.

locked market, but that sliding order will be given priority at the original price when the market unlocks. The hide-not-slide order jumps that priority by not displaying the order at all in the locked market.

Although the SEC had once allowed this type of order, it began questioning in September 2012 whether it is manipulative after a whistleblower complained. In fact, such orders may actually be beneficial in returning liquidity to the once locked market. The SEC's action exemplifies the regulatory mentality that if someone has an advantage it must be bad and manipulative.[148] In any event, if the practice is deemed unfair, exchange algorithms can be modified to give priority to all traders on a first-in-time basis.

Another high frequency trader order under attack by the SEC was the "PL Select" order. This practice allowed high frequency traders to place a small order to sell at a set price, but that order could not be executed against a larger order, even one at a better price. Larger buy orders, such as those from a mutual fund, would pay more than the price offered by the PL Select order. The result was that smaller orders executed against the PL Select trade would receive more favorable prices than that paid by the large buy order trader.[149] Once again, to the extent such a practice is deemed abusive, such orders could be identified and rejected by a computer algorithm.

Concerns remain over minimanipulations even in more liquid markets in which a trader seeks to influence prices in, say, an option or futures contract in order to profit on a related cash or other correlated position held elsewhere on another exchange. The SEC observed this phenomenon when it conducted a special study of the options markets in 1978. That study found instances where the price of a stock was influenced in order to benefit an options position held on an exchange. "Capping" and "pegging" of stock prices were also used to protect or profit from related option positions.[150] Such minimanipulations were considered again in a 1984 joint study conducted by the SEC, CFTC, and the Fed. That study concluded, however, that such minimanipulators faced substantial risks from other traders and market forces.[151]

The CFTC is currently fixated on minimanipulations through "banging the close" transactions, which seek to set the closing or settlement price of a futures or other derivatives contract. That closing price often serves as the benchmark for the pricing of other transactions and for margin requirements. As described in Chapter 6, this type of activity gave the CFTC its only success in a contested manipulation case.[152] However, the practice remains widespread. The *Wall Street Journal* reported in a front-page article on December 6, 2012 that it had found that the practice of "marking-the-close," also called "portfolio pumping," was widespread. The *Journal* conducted an

148. The hide-not-slide order controversy was fueled by a former trader turned whistleblower. Another whistleblowing former trader complained that high-frequency traders were front-running exchange-traded funds. Congress's investigation of those traders will undoubtedly lead to more regulation. *See*, Scott Patterson, *Hill Peers Into Market's Fast Lane*, WALL STREET JOURNAL, Sept. 20, 2012, at C1.

149. Scott Patterson and Jean Eaglesham, *Exchanges Retreat on Trading Tool*, WALL STREET JOURNAL, Oct. 24, 2012, at C1.

150. *Report of the Special Study of the Options Markets to the Securities and Exchange Commission*, 96th Cong., 1st Sess. 173-182 (1978).

151. *A Study of the Effects on the Economy of Trading in Futures and Options Pursuant to Section 23(a) of the Commodity Exchange Act as Amended* VII-7 (Dec. 1984). More recently, the SEC found by consent that the respondent breached best execution requirements by manipulating time delays on cross-trades to the advantage of hedge fund customers. In the Matter of Shaw, Securities Exchange Release No. 34-73725 (S.E.C. 2011).

152. In the Matter of DiPlacido, COMM. FUT. L. REP. ¶ 30,970 (C.F.T.C. 2008), *aff'd sub nom.*, DiPlacido v. CFTC, No. 08-5559-ag, 2009 U.S. App. LEXIS 22692 (2d Cir. 2009), *cert denied*, 2010 U.S. LEXIS 2461 (2010).

analysis of trading in some 10,000 stocks going back to 2004. The *Journal's* study found that on the last trading day of each accounting quarter there was a steep jump in the number of stocks that beat the S&P market index by at least 5 percent and which then declined by more than 3 percent on the following trading day. The trades that boosted prices at the end of the quarter usually occurred late in the trading day in illiquid stocks and were blamed on hedge funds and other money managers, who were seeking to improve the quarterly net asset value ("NAV") of their portfolios reported quarterly to their investors. NAV is what attracts investors and determines much of the managers' fees.[153]

As described in Chapter 7, another problem is the manipulation of settlement prices to affect margin requirements. The gain or loss on a position from the prior day's settlement price will have to be paid as variation margin. As an administrative law judge at the CFTC noted,

> Setting a settlement price of a particular option contract at an artificial level above its "fair value" has a substantial impact on a trader's position. For traders who are long the market in a particular month, their account balance is valued at an artificially high level and gives the misleading appearance that their accounts earned money. For traders who are short the market for a particular month, their account is valued at too low a level and gives the misleading appearance that their accounts lost money. This apparent "loss" may trigger a margin call in which the trader is required to deposit additional margin money. If the account holder is unable to post the additional margin, one or more positions in the account will likely be liquidated—unfairly if the settlement price is artificial. As a matter of market integrity, therefore, it is important that the settlement price be set equal to the fair value at the close of trading so that neither the long nor the short is disadvantaged in any meaningful way.[154]

Rather than a complicated and prolonged manipulation case, a more effective means for dealing with such abuses is to shield the closing price from trading abuses. The closing price is, at the end of the day, just a snapshot at a single point in time of the price of a trade or trades made in the market. That price is obsolete immediately after it is set because the value of the commodity will continue to change even if there is no trade.

Commodity prices are not static; rather they change rapidly as new information enters the market. The advent of and popularity of electronic trading makes this clear because of the extension of trading hours from the few that were available on exchange floors to twenty hours or more. There is, therefore, nothing magic about the closing or settlement price. Indeed, the exchange's settlement price for margins may vary from the actual closing price. Both prices are simply prices at a given point in time. They are artificial and arbitrary prices that are selected from every twenty-four-hour period to set contract prices or exchange margins. The use of extended trading hours on electronic trading platforms also makes a closing price less relevant.

Nevertheless, by using such prices to set margins and contract settlements, traders are tempted to game the system by setting artificial closing or settlement prices. Indeed, "banging the close," "marking the close," and "painting the tape" have been a part of markets for decades. The exchanges have dealt with such practices by restricting the nature of market on close and other orders entered during the closing period. In the past, some commodity exchange committees set the settlement price, but that too led to abuses. In one action, which was settled by consent, the CFTC charged that the chair of the NYMEX used his position on a NYMEX settlement price committee to set

153. Jacob Zweig and Tom McGinty, *Fund Managers Lift Results With Timely Trading Sprees*, WALL STREET. JOURNAL, Dec. 6, 2012, at A1.

154. In the Matter of Eisler, 2004 CFTC LEXIS 9 (C.F.T.C.).

inflated settlement prices of options on index futures contracts. The respondent engaged in that activity in order to benefit his personal trading account by some $2 million on average between August 1, 1999, and May 12, 2000. Those inflated values allowed the respondent to avoid or substantively reduce margin calls on his trading account.[155]

Another example of practices that may be deemed abusive is "banging the beehive" in trading natural gas futures contracts on NYMEX. These orders are entered by high frequency traders just in advance of government's weekly natural gas inventory reports. The traders send in a flood of orders in order to destabilize the market at this critical time by touching off limit orders on one side or the other of the market. The high frequency traders then seek to profit from the large price swings induced by their trades.[156] There is, however, nothing new about this practice. The practice of "gunning-the stops" has long been used as a means of inducing market volatility by touching off "stop orders" that are placed as resting orders in order to automatically stop losses if the market drops or to sell stock if the market reaches an unexpectedly high level.

The solution to abuses in setting the closing or settlement price is to take the setting of that price out of the hands of the traders. With the advent of electronic trading, algorithms can be designed that could use an unpredictable time for setting a settlement price or that could use a variety of factors to set a settlement price. Computer algorithms could determine a daily settlement price randomly.

The real issue is what price exchanges should use in issuing margin calls. That value can be set by the exchanges without the use of a closing price that may be artificially manipulated. A possible solution for abuses connected with the closing price is to abandon the use of the closing price for setting prices on other positions and opt instead for the computer-generated settlement price for margins that will best protect the exchange from defaults and provide a more accurate measure for pricing contracts that use exchange-generated trades for their pricing. The CME Group took an important step in this direction when it took the setting of settlement prices in grain futures out of the hands of floor traders and substituted prices executed electronically. However, the affected floor traders then challenged that action in court.[157]

A needed step to regulating algorithmically is to identify practices deemed manipulative. Computer programs can then be built to reject or stymie such practices. Of course, traders will try to game the exchange's algorithms, just as did the Norwegian traders described above. Such attempts will require the exchange to stay one step ahead by constant adjustments of its algorithms and its surveillance systems.

A report by the International Organization of Securities Commissions (IOSCO) published in 2000 made a serious effort to identify practices that are widely recognized as manipulative:

- Engaging in a series of transactions that are reported on a public display facility to give the impression of activity or price movement in a security (*painting the tape)*;
- Improper transactions in which there is no genuine change in actual ownership of the security or derivative contract *(wash sales)*;
- Transactions where both buy and sell orders are entered at the same time, with the same price and quantity by different but colluding parties (*improper matched orders)*;

155. In the Matter of Eisler, Comm. Fut. L. Rep. (CCH) ¶ 29,664 (C.F.T.C. 2004).

156. Jerry A. Dicolo & Geoffrey Rogow, Gas Market Stung by Rapid Traders, Wall Street Journal, Oct. 16, 2012, available at http://online.wsj.com/article/SB10000872396390444657804578053153939092668.html?mod =WSJ_hps_sections_markets (visited on Oct. 17, 2012).

157. *Grain Traders Can Proceed on CME Price-Settlement Lawsuit — Judge*, Reuters, November 26, 2012, available at http://www.reuters.com/article/2012/11/26/court-cme-ruling-idUSL1E8MQ42A20121126 (visited on November 30, 2012).

- Increasing the bid for a security or derivative to increase its price *(advancing the bid)*;
- Buying activity at increasingly higher prices. Securities are sold in the market (often to retail customers) at the higher prices (*pumping and dumping)*;
- Buying or selling securities or derivatives contracts at the close of the market in an effort to alter the closing price of the security or derivatives contract *(marking the close)*;
- Securing such control of the bid or demand-side of both the derivative and the underlying asset that leads to a dominant position. This position can be exploited to manipulate the price of the derivative and/or the asset *(corner)*. As regards derivatives, in a corner, a market participant or group of participants accumulates a controlling position in an asset in the cash, derivative and other markets. The market participant or group of participants then requires those holding short positions to settle their obligations under the terms of their contracts, either by making delivery or by purchasing the asset from the manipulator or by offsetting in the derivatives market opposite the manipulator at prices distorted by the manipulator;
- Taking advantage of a shortage in an asset by controlling the demand-side and exploiting market congestion during such shortages in such a way as to create artificial prices *(squeeze)*; and
- Dissemination of false or misleading market information through media, including the Internet, or by any other means. The dissemination is done in order to move the price of a security, a derivative contract or the underlying asset in a direction that is favorable to the position held or a transaction planned by the person disseminating the information.[158]

The next step is to build computer programs that exclude orders associated with these practices. That is beyond this author's ability but should be well within the capabilities of programmers with basic market knowledge.

8:7 SURVEILLANCE BY COMPUTERS

A central part of the antimanipulation efforts by the CFTC and its predecessor, the Commodity Exchange Authority, over the years has been market surveillance that is carried out through large trader positions that disclose the owners of positions that may threaten the market. Those traders are contacted and asked what their intentions are in accumulating such a large position. The CFTC may "jawbone" the trader into reducing the position. As described in Chapter 4, CFTC may seek to discipline traders that exceed its speculative position limits, but such actions are usually taken only after the fact. The only preemptive enforcement action taken on the strength of such reports was the CFTC's soybean case against the Hunt family of Dallas, Texas.[159] However, the CFTC was unable to prevent the Hunts from taking delivery on those positions.

The CFTC surveillance system before Dodd-Frank had only limited access to swap positions of large traders. Even with access, however, it is questionable whether the CFTC can take any timely action on that information if its history with large trader futures reports is any example of what can be expected. Market power manipulation cases involved large positions that were readily apparent to the CFTC and the Commodity Exchange Authority, but that was no deterrent to manipulation. The CFTC surveillance system has also been of little, if any, use in dealing with minimanipulations.

CFTC chair Gary Gensler sought in the wake of Dodd-Frank to focus the efforts of his agency on increasing staff, at the expense of technology. However, that effort drew a protest from CFTC

---

158. OICU-IOSCO, *Investigating and Prosecuting Manipulation* 5-6 (May 2000) (footnotes omitted).
159. CFTC v. Hunt, 591 F.2d 1211, 1218-1219 (7th Cir.), *cert. denied*, 442 U.S. 921 (1979).

commissioner Scott O'Malia, who lamented that the CFTC's technology programs were inadequate for monitoring fast-moving markets and needed to be improved. O'Malia urged that the agency devote resources to developing a technology strategy for surveillance and oversight and a dedicated budget.[160] The history of the CFTC exemplifies why more surveillance will be ineffective. The government has had broad access to large trader reports for commodity futures since the 1920s, but they have served little purpose in stopping manipulations.

In a white paper issued in 2012, the International Organization of Securities Commissions asserted that securities regulators need to better monitor trading. The IOSCO report stated that "[c]urrent surveillance techniques, including the collection, storage and accessibility of data may be insufficient to capture in a timely manner all of the information necessary to monitor efficiently and effectively trading activity that occurs in the current highly automated and dispersed markets."[161] This report was undoubtedly a signal of the next regulatory attack on speculators—that is, increased market surveillance. IOSCO had also published "Principles for the Oversight of Screen-Based Trading Systems for Derivative Products" in 1990 that were used by several electronic exchanges to govern their operations.[162]

Illustrative of this new approach was a plan by the SEC to require a consolidated audit trail for equities and options that would capture customer and order event information for most orders in National Market System securities—the most actively traded securities—across all markets, from time of order inception through routing, cancellation, modification, or execution.[163] The SEC stated that this audit trail would significantly aid "efforts to detect and deter fraudulent and manipulative acts and practices in the marketplace."[164] This proposal generated much controversy because it was expected to cost several billions of dollars to report trading information in real time as the SEC had first proposed.

The SEC shrugged off those concerns and promised to move ahead on this proposal.[165] Thereafter, the SEC commissioners, in a 3–2 vote, decided in July 2012 to implement a widely expanded surveillance program that will require the exchanges and electronic trading platforms to develop a consolidated audit trail that will track all orders and their execution. The SEC also contracted with a private vendor to supply it with real-time trading data on the options exchanges.[166] The SEC additionally hired Tradeworx, a high-frequency trading firm, to design and build a "Midas" computer program that would supposedly allow the SEC to monitor high-speed trading in real time. According to the *New York Times*, this system would be "akin to an X-ray machine for the stock market."[167]

---

160. *O'Malia Calls CFTC's Current State of Technology "Unacceptable, Unsustainable,"* 44 Sec. Reg. & L. Rep. (BNA) 1473 (July 30, 2012).

161. The Board of the International Organization of Securities Commissions, *Technological Challenges to Effective Market Surveillance Issues and Regulatory Tools*, Consultation Report 29 (Aug. 2012).

162. *See*, III Jerry W. Markham, A Financial History of the United States, From the Age of Derivatives into the New Millennium (1970-2001) 271 (2002) (describing the use of those principals).

163. Alyse Gould, *Regulating High-Frequency Trading: Man V. Machine*, 12 J. High Tech. L. 273 (2011).

164. SEC, *Consolidated Audit Trail*, 75 Fed. Reg. 32556 (June 8, 2010).

165. Andrew Ackermen, *SEC Eases Reporting for Audits of Trading*, Wall Street Journal, Feb. 9, 2012, at C3. A new market surveillance system created for European Union markets did discover trading concerns on its first day of operation. *Redkite's "Quote Stuffing" Flag Triggered First Day of New Guidelines*, The Trade, May 4, 2102, http://www.thetradenews.com/news/Regions/Europe/Redkite%E2%80%99s_%E2%80%98quote_stuffing%E2%80%99_flag_triggered_first_day_of_new_guidelines.aspx (accessed May 7, 2012).

166. *SEC In Pact for Real-Time System on Order, Trade Data*, Bloomberg, July 20, 2012, http://www.bloomberg.com/news/2012-07-19/sec-in-pact-for-real-time-system-on-order-trade-data.html (accessed August 27, 2012).

167. Nathaniel Popper & Ben Protess, *To Regulate High Speed Traders, S.E.C. Turns to One of Them*, New York Times, Oct. 8, 2012, at B1.

This new audit trail requirement sounds exciting and "proactive," but the critical question is what the SEC will do with that data. The stock market is now dominated by high-frequency trading (HFT) that pulses the markets with algorithmically generated trades that are executed nearly at speeds beyond the capacity of a human being to follow. Even before the SEC adopted its new consolidated audit trail requirement, NASDAQ was producing some fifty gigabytes of trade data every day.[168] The government will sweep up this massive amount of data, but it is simply incapable of determining whether any one string of trades, or several, are manipulative or otherwise abusive. The government typically takes months, and more often years, to investigate particular trading activities before bringing a disciplinary action. More data to sift through will only lengthen that process.

The tension between demands for more regulation and advocates for free markets is raising another high-stakes battle over HFT. Economists disagree on the value of HFT, and the government has proved helpless in understanding it and its economic limitations. Therefore the government has been unable to decide whether HFT should be limited in some manner. The regulators are concerned that when something goes wrong with high-frequency trading, as something inevitably will, the government will be blamed for not preventing it. Unfortunately, the government has never been able to function in a preemptive capacity. It can only act with twenty-twenty hindsight. Predictably, this governmental inertia will mean that HFT will mature on its own and that traders will discover and exploit its flaws, which will then lead to more ineffective regulation. This is not to say that the government will not attempt to ferret out abusive practices associated with high-frequency trading. The *Financial Times* reported in March 2013 that the FBI had joined with the SEC to examine algorithmic traders and dark pools. Among other things, these government investigators were looking at "news aggregation," which means that a trader is broadly searching the web for information that can be aggregated and provide an informational advantage for the trader.[169]

In any event, it is likely that the data gathered from the SEC's new audit trail program will be useless in detecting or preventing manipulation. It will result mostly in increased costs to traders and the hiring of more bureaucrats to observe the collected data without any comprehension of what to look for in the form of manipulation. The SEC and FINRA's market watch programs are able to ferret out the more obvious cases of insider trading by investigating trading that occurs just before a market moving event. Uncovering complex manipulation and trading abuses will not be so easy and will continue to be done after the fact, involving years of investigation and complex litigation.

The SEC and CFTC may use their increased surveillance to intimidate traders and push them out of the securities markets into "dark pools" that pick their participants or into unregulated products (a shrinking universe after Dodd-Frank) or foreign markets. The regulated exchanges were supporting that effort as a means to curb this unwanted competition.[170] That is not a desirable goal and will only undercut market efficiency. Something else is needed.

As described in Chapter 7, Dodd-Frank took a seemingly bold stride in adopting the concept of a "fair and orderly" market that has long been employed in the securities industry. However,

---

168. Jonathan Spicer & Herbert Lash, *Who's Afraid of High-Frequency Trading*, Reuters, Dec. 2, 2009, http://www.reuters.com/article/2009/12/02/us-highfrequency-idUSN173583920091202 (accessed September 18, 2012).

169. Kara Scannell, *FBI Joins War Against Abuse of Fast Trading*, Financial Times (London), March 6, 2013, at 1.

170. Nathaniel Popper, *Exchanges Are Moving to Curb Private Trades*, New York Times, April 9, 2013, at B4.

the time for that reform has largely passed. The securities and futures industries are now mostly automated order-matching services that provide a lesser role for the specialists and market makers on which fair and orderly market obligations had been previously imposed. Indeed, the New York Stock Exchange (NYSE) has dropped the use of specialists in favor of something called "Designated Market Makers" that have reduced market making obligations The time and place advantage of those trading on exchange floors was the trade-off for imposing such obligations, but those advantages are disappearing. Similarly, the profit made by market makers on the spread between bid and ask quotes is increasingly more available to all traders electronically, and the ability of the market maker to profit from the spread is reduced.

As the SEC has noted:

> Traditionally, price discovery on the [New York Stock] Exchange took place almost exclusively on the Floor in the form of face-to-face interactions among brokers and specialists. These interactions have diminished as electronic trading has become more important on the Exchange.
>
> In addition, information that once was exclusive to the Floor, such as the most up-to-date quotes and last sale prices, is now widely available off the Floor through electronic means. At the same time, the Exchange believes that it is no longer the dominant trading market for many NYSE-listed securities, as competition from other market centers has increased.
>
> The increase in electronic executions on the Exchange as well as the increase in the use of smart routing engines by market participants of all types has reduced the advantages once enjoyed by Floor brokers and specialists. Indeed, NYSE has argued that the informational advantage has shifted "upstairs" where orders are now first "shopped" within a firm and then to others before being sent to the Floor for execution and, even then, orders are likely to be sent in pieces to multiple markets.[171]

In light of these changes, there is now an opportunity to rethink regulations designed to prevent market abuse. Algorithms are unbiased in their application of standards deemed necessary to make markets work efficiently. These standards are limitations on order entry, rather than a traffic light that speeding and reckless traders might run. Economics, not populist rhetoric, should control the development of those algorithmic rules.

Unfortunately, history has shown that the populist politicians cannot be deterred from their attacks on speculators, so manipulation claims and scandals will continue to dominate financial news in the future. In the unlikely event that serious attention will be focused on market abuses without the populist baggage, there is now an opportunity to deter and prevent abuses without the years of mostly unsuccessful litigation required for manipulation cases. The conversion to electronic trading from open outcry floor trading in both the commodity and securities markets provides such an opportunity.

The CFTC's enforcement program over the years has been largely focused on abuses by floor traders that involved exploitation of their time and place advantage on the floor. Those days are now largely history because the trading floor is a dying institution, being rapidly displaced by electronic trading platforms. Electronic trading platforms operate by rules dictated by algorithms, which can ensure rapid and equal access to the market without the distortion and inefficiency of

---

171. Notices, SEC, 73 Fed. Reg. 64379-80 (Oct. 24, 2008) (footnote omitted).

floor traders and specialists. As described above, those algorithmic rules have stopped "trade throughs" of customer orders that were an endemic problem on commodity exchange floors. Even more sophisticated algorithms can be used to address other market abuses. One obvious change of course would be to abandon efforts to measure whether prices are "artificial" or whether there was the intent to create such a price. Those elements lead nowhere except to lengthy, expensive, and often unsuccessful litigation. Instead, defined orders or patterns of trading should be restricted algorithmically if it is determined that they are not economically useful.

Congress seemed to have it right in adopting the prohibitions in Section 9 of the 34 Act[172] and Section 4(c) of the Commodity Exchange Act[173] against wash sales and other abusive practices. Those practices are universally considered abusive and are easily proved even where an intent requirement is included. Exchange algorithms could provide similar and more efficient relief from such practices by screening out same-source wash trades.

As described above, more efficient regulation could involve setting the settlement or closing prices on exchanges by algorithms to curb the practice of banging the close. If spoofing or other particular trading practices are deemed abusive, they can be monitored and blocked by an appropriate algorithm. Of course, as Google has learned, algorithms must be constantly adjusted to prevent circumvention of their access rules and abuses. New trading practices will constantly develop and, if abusive, can be restricted by exchange algorithms.

This approach would be an alternative to the present "fraud-based" and "market power" manipulation tests under the 34 Act and the Commodity Exchange Act. This technological approach would identify particular practices that are deemed abusive and focus on algorithms that directly deal with the practices of concern. Such trade practice rules should provide exact guidance to traders and limit practices that are abusive and likely to distort prices.

This prospect gives rise to the question of who should dictate the algorithms. Clearly, the onus should be on the regulator to show that a practice is actually abusive on grounds other than that it gives advantage to one trader over others. Government regulators are ill-suited for such a role. The government is always slow in reacting to market developments and rarely identifies an abusive trading practice until it has done much damage. There is a related danger that the government will overreach and impair market efficiency with unnecessary restrictions. The instinct of the government is also to ban anything that it does not understand or which might give one party an advantage over another, which is really what a market is all about.

The government is also loath to provide guidance on what might constitute an abuse, lest traders view the guidance as allowing any trading outside its scope. Government regulators would prefer to second-guess traders after the fact through splashy enforcement actions.

Still another danger is that government will use electronic trading–based regulations to try to control prices and impose costs and restrictions that will reduce market efficiency. As Henry David Thoreau famously stated, the "government never of itself furthered any enterprise, but by the alacrity with which it got out of its way."[174]

The alternative is for regulatory algorithms to be set by the electronic trading platforms or by self-regulatory bodies such as FINRA in the securities industry. FINRA has been active in responding to trading abuses. Its counterpart in the futures industry, the National Futures Association (NFA), has not assumed that role, leaving such oversight to the exchanges, which are now dominated by the Chicago Mercantile Exchange Group. Another source for such rules is the electronic trading platforms, but they are conflicted by their fee structures, which are driven by volume, and trad-

172. 15 U.S.C. § 78i.
173. 7 U.S.C. § 6c.
174. Henry David Thoreau, Civil Disobedience (1849).

ing restriction could reduce that volume and revenue stream. However, that conflict is offset to some extent by the exchanges' need to maintain a fair and orderly market, lest users turn to more efficient and fairer alternative markets. Unfortunately, there is no perfect solution for preventing trading abuses, but markets are not perfect under any circumstances.

8:8 POPULISM DOES NOT MAKE FOR EFFECTIVE REGULATION

Algorithms will provide a better market regulator than the host of regulatory agencies tasked with prosecuting manipulation. Dodd-Frank and other legislation designed to deter and punish manipulation will provide no panacea for halting volatile stock and commodity prices. Rather, that new legislation will only serve as a diversion from the fundamentals that drive prices and lead to volatility. Attacks on manipulators and excessive speculation are, at their core, a distraction from the root causes of unusually high or low prices for stocks or commodities.

Whenever prices increase sharply, consumers of a commodity protest the increased cost to their budget, while producers and stockholders are happy with a price rise. When prices decline, consumers are happy, but stockholders and producers of commodities are not. Politicians, and the public they represent, seek a quick cure that will make prices more to the liking of their consumer constituents through attacks on speculators.

This quest has been pursued for centuries without success. In extreme cases, as in medieval times, Germany in the nineteenth century, and the Soviet Union in the twentieth century, speculation was simply prohibited by the government. Those efforts failed miserably and only worsened economic conditions, sometimes catastrophically, as in the Soviet Union, where millions died of starvation and more millions were enslaved by a government-directed economy.

Price controls are another failed experiment in regulating prices. Those controls were deemed by governments to be necessary to control excessive speculation and manipulation. Although price controls continue to be imposed in times of war or perceived emergencies such as the inflationary period in the United States in the 1970s, it is generally recognized that price controls are ineffective and unworkable in a complex economy in which they can easily be avoided or evaded.

This lack of a ready lever to set or change prices leaves politicians exposed to the wrath of their constituents when rapid and adverse price changes occur. Politicians are then faced with the dilemma of dealing with the fundamentals driving prices or of assuaging the public hurt by adverse price changes. The response most often chosen is an attack on speculators through highly publicized congressional hearings and new legislation that imposes more regulation.

Members of Congress will also call for prosecution of any large traders in a market that is experiencing volatility. Federal regulators are generally happy to comply with those requests by bringing a high profile enforcement action. Those actions usually have nothing to do with the price changes, but the complexity of the charges and the belief that a wrongdoer has gotten its just deserts will divert the public from the real fundamentals affecting prices.

History shows that manipulation is often more of a political issue than a crime. Blaming speculators and manipulators for consumer price increases always provides good political cover for policy failures. Energy trading is now the principal focus of populist politicians who blame speculators and manipulators for high prices, but that is only a diversion from the broken energy policies that have prevailed since the 1970s.[175]

---

175. There is an observed economic phenomenon of "the striking correlation between energy prices and U.S. business cycles. Since 1973 every recession has been preceded by a rise in energy prices. Conversely, almost every energy price hike has been followed by a recession." Rajeev Dhawan & Karsten Jeske, *How Resilient Is the Modern Economy to Energy Price Shocks*? FED. RES. BD, RES. BANK OF ATLANTA ECON. REV. 21 (Third Quarter 2006).

The effort to achieve energy independence that began after World War II broke down in fights between producers and environmentalists over the effects of expanding energy resources. As a result, the building of hydroelectric dams, nuclear plants, oil pipelines, and oil refineries has all but ceased in this country, and drilling for oil and mining of coal have been sharply curbed. The massive BP oil spill in the Gulf of Mexico in 2010 and the earthquake and tsunami in Japan that destroyed some of its nuclear plants will ensure that energy supplies remain curbed, and in shortage, into the foreseeable future.

The California electricity crisis in 2000–2001 provided populists with plenty of fodder from Enron's gaming of the market, but the real culprit was a faulty plan by the government to deregulate only wholesale electricity prices. That failed effort was driven by the political desire to maintain low retail prices, even if wholesale prices increased dramatically. Something had to give when such price increases occurred. The result was rationing by necessity through rolling blackouts and brownouts.

Basic economics were simply ignored in the purely political endeavor to create a competitive market that shielded consumers from its effects. Instead of accepting the fact that the flaws in the government's politically designed electricity market made Enron's gaming possible, indeed encouraged them, regulators attacked the energy traders.

Congress took the same course and responded with more unneeded legislation granting antimanipulation powers to FERC. The CFTC joined the fray by attacking energy traders who were using round-trip trades to build their books and to briefly set prices. Those were hardly commendable practices, but not a cause of the high energy prices that riled consumers. The CFTC and other regulators extracted hundreds of millions of dollars in fines from the energy trading firms, but that only served as a tax on the shareholders of those companies. More importantly, those actions diverted attention from the true cause of the crisis, a fundamentally flawed market structure dictated by the government for political, not economic, reasons.

The rise in gasoline prices after Hurricanes Katrina and Rita led to more populist antimanipulation authority for the FTC, even though it could find little or no evidence of price manipulation. More energy price rises led to the reduction of the Enron loophole when the CFTC was reauthorized in 2008. Dodd-Frank sought to finish that job by granting even more antimanipulation powers to the CFTC. Of course, those legislative changes did nothing to change fundamentals: high gasoline prices continue.

Gasoline prices were a prominent factor in the presidential campaign in 2012, with speculators and manipulation blamed once again. President Obama went on the offensive by declaring that the government needed "more cops on the beat" at the CFTC to stop manipulation of oil prices. The president stated that "[w]e can't afford a situation where the speculators artificially manipulate markets by buying up oil, creating the perception of a shortage and driving prices higher, only to flip the oil for a quick profit."[176] He sought $52 million in additional spending for the CFTC even though there were already four agencies with antimanipulation powers, plus the Justice Department.

The president was doing what populist politicians always do by seeking to divert and distract the public's attention from market fundamentals to the villainous scapegoat "speculator," which is the political code word for a "manipulator." The president declared that increased domestic drilling would not affect gasoline prices because of the country's dependence on foreign oil, but he had no ready solution for that fundamental problem. Instead, he sought authority for the

176. Francesco Guerrera, *CME Chief Rebuts Obama*, Wall Street Journal, May 3, 2012, at C3.

government to increase margins on oil speculators.[177] He also wanted enhanced penalties for those found guilty of manipulation, seeking a penalty of up to $10 million for each day on which manipulation occurs.[178]

More alarming was a report issued in September 2012 by the United Nations Conference on Trade and Development that advocated direct government intervention in markets experiencing volatility "by buying or selling derivatives contracts with a view to averting price collapses or deflating price bubbles."[179] As described in Chapter 2, such an effort was tried and failed during the Great Depression in America. More sensible was a report on crude oil regulation issued by IOSCO in October 2012. IOSCO had previously expressed concern that the oil market could be manipulated by false price reports and was asked in 2010 by the Group of Twenty nations to report on whether the crude oil physical market needed additional regulation.[180] After a two-year investigation, IOSCO concluded that further regulation was not needed. However, after IOSCO issued that report, Total Oil Trading, a large oil trading operation, expressed concern that price benchmarks were not always being reported accurately, resulting in inaccurate oil prices.[181]

A group of House Democrats sought a tax on the trading of financial instruments in 2012 that they claimed would discourage speculation and provide revenue for the government.[182] Congressman John Larson (D-CT) joined the attack to create a smokescreen for flaws in the country's energy policies with a charge that "abusive" Wall Street oil speculation was "causing significant hardships for Americans at the pump."[183] Former congressman Joseph Kennedy II (D-MA) charged in an op-ed piece in the *New York Times* that "pure speculators" were driving up the price of oil by 40 percent and that gas prices could be reduced by $1 per gallon if speculators were removed from the market.[184]

These claims of speculator-caused inflation of gas prices were based on some apparently inscrutable formula, but missing from the equation was any analysis of how many dollars per gallon gasoline could be reduced if supplies were increased. The American consumer has not been told what the savings would be if government restrictions on oil exploration were removed. What would the price reduction be if new refineries could be built domestically and if nuclear and hydrologic energy were expanded?

The first step in assessing the cause of market disruptions or volatility should be to examine fundamentals affecting the particular market. For example, a run-up in energy price should be an occasion for reassessing fundamental supply and demand factors. As in the past, that inquiry will probably determine that the volatility is the result of a supply shortage or an increase in demand. That determination should then result in a political debate on resolving the hard choices between

177. Helene Cooper, *As Gas Prices Cast Cloud, Obama Calls for Scrutiny on Market*, NEW YORK TIMES, April 18, 2012, at A19.

178. Anna Fifield & Gregory Meyer, *Obama Push for Clampdown on Oil Market Abuse*, FINANCIAL TIMES (LONDON), April 18, 2012, at 13.

179. Reuters, *Volatile Commodities May Need Intervention—U.N.*, Sept. 12, 2012, http://in.reuters.com/article/2012/09/18/un-commodities-idINL5E8KEBUR20120918 (accessed September 24, 2012)

180. Sarah Kent, Carolyn Cui & Jamila Trindle, *Physical-Oil Oversight Won't Change*, WALL STREET JOURNAL, Oct. 4, 2012, at C3.

181. Javier Blas, *Total Arm Warns Over "Inaccurate" Benchmarks*, FINANCIAL TIMES (LONDON), Oct. 9, 2012, at 15.

182. The Floor Action Blog, *House Dems Propose Taxing Equity Trades to Fund New Federal Programs*, Sept. 17, 2012, http://thehill.com/blogs/floor-action/house/249893-house-dems-propose-taxing-equity-trades-to-fund-new-federal-programs (accessed September 18, 2012).

183. *Lawmakers Call for CFTC Action on Speculation*, 44 SEC. REG. & L. REP. (BNA) 792 (April 16, 2012).

184. Joseph P. Kennedy II, *The High Cost of Gambling on Oil*, NEW YORK TIMES, April 10, 2012.

increased production and the conflicting concerns over environmental protection. That debate should logically result in a reasoned choice of increasing supplies or accepting the pain that will be caused by market-generated conservation, which inevitably occurs as prices increase. Blaming energy price rises on manipulation and speculators only serves to divert attention and avoid dealing with those issues in a rational manner.

After resolving those issues, focus could be directed to examining whether traders improperly exploited the volatility caused by unstable fundamental factors. If so, the inquiry should shift to the individual trading practices in order to determine whether they are abusive and unnecessarily disruptive of price discovery. The fact that the trading was successful or aggressive should not control that inquiry. Rather, is there something about the practice that is inherently bad, such as a wash sale? The regulator should then consider two approaches in dealing with such practices. If the abuse is a familiar one that is already prohibited, then sanctions can be sought. If the practice is novel, rules can be proposed that will prohibit that activity.

These determinations should be made without regard to whether one type of trader has advantages over another. For example, the SEC sought public comment in September 2009 on whether its exception from quotation reports should be continued for flash orders. Among other things, the SEC was concerned with the fact that flash orders provided professional short-term traders an advantage over long-term investors.[185] However, the role of the SEC is not to prevent one class of trader from having an advantage over another. The market should make those decisions, not the government.

In any event, at the end of the day, federal antimanipulation legislation has simply not worked to prevent either manipulation or excessive speculation. The complex, lengthy, and often unsuccessful historical efforts to curb manipulations and "excessive speculation" all failed at great expense in time and government resources. It would, therefore, seem logical to give some thought to developing a new approach to the issue, such as exchange-generated algorithms to exclude trades that do not have economic value.

The alternative is that "excessive speculation" will continue to be condemned in Congress and by populist politicians everywhere, although no one has been able to define exactly what should be prohibited under that rubric. Rather, it is political cover for politicians unwilling to make the hard choices associated with fundamental economics.

There has been no want of trying by members of Congress, academics, lawyers, and others to achieve a definition of excessive speculation and manipulation, but none has emerged. Professor James Boyle wrote in 1920 that "[s]peculation in grain and future trading on the organized exchanges are fundamental market problems which interest every citizen. Unfortunately these questions are usually treated in a controversial manner, the discussions producing more heat than light."[186] This observation remains just as true now as it did then. Rising prices for consumer-related goods inevitably lead to populist attacks against speculators who are claimed to be manipulating the market.

Probably nothing can be done to correct the silly and never-ending game of blaming the speculator for adverse prices. Nevertheless, another approach is needed. History has shown that antimanipulation prohibitions and efforts to curb excessive speculation have been a near-complete failure. The May wheat manipulations in the 1920s and 1930s, the onion and egg manipulations that the Commodity Exchange Authority could not prevent, the Maine potato futures default that occurred just after the CFTC was created, the massive coffee market manipulation, the Hunt silver crisis, the stock market

185. 74 Fed. Reg. 48632, 48638 (Sept. 23, 2009).

186. James E. Boyle, Speculation and the Chicago Board of Trade (1920).

crash of 1987, Treasury market manipulations, the Enron-era trading scandals, Amaranth, and now the Libor rate manipulation, to name just a few, all proved that government regulation does not deter speculators and that the government is otherwise unable to prevent those scandals.

8:9 CONCLUSION

The effort to prevent speculators from exploiting and manipulating markets has spanned centuries but has not succeeded. Early efforts seeking to bar speculation by fiat met with little success. Economists came to realize that speculators provide valuable liquidity and price discovery in markets, but still market problems, real or perceived, are blamed on speculators. They are unpopular with the public and make good scapegoats for politicians. The blame game is not a harmless pastime that affects only speculators. It diverts needed attention from the real fundamental factors affecting market prices and causing price volatility.

Much has been written about punishing speculators for manipulating markets in order to create artificial prices, but populist politicians are engaged in an even less admirable enterprise. They preach that removing speculators from the market will reduce demand; by reducing demand, they argue, prices will decrease. No proof of such a claim has yet to come to light, but attacks on speculators continue.

The blame game merely diverts attention from the fundamental causes of market swings. The most blatant example is the energy market. As described earlier, a titanic struggle is being carried out in the energy markets between, on the one hand, the proponents of energy independence, who advocate increased drilling and other unpopular methods of increasing domestic energy supplies, and, on the other hand, the opponents of increased production, who favor environmental protection. Those environmental concerns are serious ones as demonstrated by the BP oil spill in the Gulf of Mexico and the problems with the nuclear plants in Japan after the tsunami. Those concerns should, however, be addressed directly by efforts to make extraction of oil and use of nuclear power more safe. That debate is not occurring and fundamentals are being ignored in the energy market. The result is that the market rations available supplies through increased prices that consumers protest, and the cycle continues.

Another unattractive aspect of the blame-the-speculator game is government overreaching. It is impossible to pick up a daily paper without encountering some sensational charges brought by the government against a financial institution. As demonstrated by former New York attorney general Eliot Spitzer, such cases can be used to gain fame and propel a prosecutor into high office, in his case the New York governorship. Such cases have in effect become a random tax on financial institutions.

Regulators often bring joint or multiple actions against the same financial institutions for the same conduct. They often scrap among themselves for the reward of the most publicity. One regulator will condone, or at least not condemn, conduct that another regulator will proclaim is blatantly manipulative and demand hundreds of millions of dollars as a sanction. The recent Libor manipulation case is a good example of such an occurrence. The New York Federal Reserve Bank, the principal regulator on such issues, was fully aware that the Libor rate was "rubbish" but only languidly sought to correct the mechanism. In contrast, the CFTC and the Justice Department sensationalized the flaws in the Libor rate-setting mechanism through their dramatic settlement with Barclays Bank, which occurred some four years after it was obvious to bank regulators that the rates were artificial.

A host of regulators are now attacking manipulation on multiple levels. Something better is needed. A proposal that surfaces periodically is consolidation of financial services regulation into a single regulator, but the multiple agencies now involved in that regulation are too adept at protecting their turf for such proposals to succeed. However, the recently announced merger between the Intercontinental Exchange (ICE) and the New York Stock Exchange has dramatically illustrated that the commodity and security markets are fully intertwined and could benefit from a single regulator. In the meantime, the bottom line will be that the addition of the new antimanipulation authority for the CFTC, FERC, and FTC will raise numerous and complex issues in their application that the courts will have to sort out over the coming decades.[187] It is doubtful that manipulation will be any easier to prove under that authority than that previously existing authority, but the lawyers will fatten on its intricacies.

It is also clear that manipulation charges will continue to draw headlines. For example, a front page article in the *New York Times* on July 21, 2013, charged that Goldman Sachs was running a giant shell game in aluminum by constantly moving customer supplies among a small group of warehouses near Detroit. The newspaper claimed that this activity increased storage fees and was causing a rise in aluminum costs. The article also charged that JPMorgan Chase was seeking to gain control of the copper market. The newspaper further claimed that financial services firms were buying power plants, pipelines, fleets of tankers and stockpiling commodities such as oil, wheat and cotton in order to profit at the expense of the consumer. That report immediately triggered a CFTC investigation.[188]

Competition authorities in the European Union were also charging that several large banks, including JPMorgan Chase, Goldman Sachs and Deutsche Bank, had blocked trading of credit default swaps on regulated exchanges in order to keep that lucrative business to themselves.[189] In July 2013, the CFTC and the new U.K. Financial Conduct Authority fined a HFT trading operation, Panther Energy Trading, LLC, for spoofing the CME Globex electronic market. The CFTC brought this action under its new Dodd-Frank powers.[190] It had earlier finalized its guidance on what would constitute disruptive trading practices under that new authority. Among other things, the CFTC stated that the violation of existing bids and offers did not require a showing of manipulative intent, but that at least reckless conduct must be shown to establish a violation of closing period disruptions (known as "banging the close." The CFTC further stated that a "spoofing violation will require the showing of specific intent, at a level above recklessness.[191] Manipulation claims thus continue to sow more and more confusion and evermore complexity.

187. For example, in *Commodity Exchange, Inc., Silver Futures and Options Trading Litigation*, 2012 WL 6700236 (S.D.N.Y.), a district court dismissed a case charging manipulation of silver prices because the complaint did not properly plead the elements of manipulation under the Commodity Exchange Act.

188. David Kocieniewski, *A Shuffle of Aluminum, But to Banks Pure Gold*, New York Times, July, 21, 2013, at A1.

189. Matthew Dalton, *Banks Face EU Swaps Case*, Wall Street Journal, July 2, 2013, at C3.

190. Scott Patterson & Jamila Trindle, *High-Speed Trader Pushed to Curb*, Wall Street Journal, July 23, 2013, at C3.

191. Antidisruptive Practices Authority, 78 Fed. Reg. 31890 (May 28, 2013).

INDEX

ABOUT THE AUTHOR

Jerry W. Markham is a professor of law at Florida International University College of Law in Miami. He previously served as professor of law at University of North Carolina at Chapel Hill and as adjunct professor of law at Georgetown Law School in Washington, DC. In addition to numerous law journal articles, Markham is the author of the three-volume *Financial History of the United States*, which was selected as a Choice Outstanding Academic Title in 2002. He has published a book on the Enron era scandals and a two-volume work on the financial crisis of 2008. Markham also authored a treatise and a history book on the law of commodity futures regulation, and he is the coauthor of a treatise on broker-dealer regulation and four casebooks on corporate law and banking regulation.

Before his move to academia, Professor Markham served as chief counsel in the Division of Enforcement, U.S. Commodity Futures Trading Commission; as secretary and counsel for Chicago Board Options Exchange, Inc.; and as an attorney in the Office of General Counsel at the Securities and Exchange Commission; and he was a partner with the international firm of Rogers & Wells (now Clifford Chance) in Washington, DC. Professor Markham has also served as a consultant and expert witness in several manipulation cases.

For Product Safety Concerns and Information please contact our EU
representative GPSR@taylorandfrancis.com
Taylor & Francis Verlag GmbH, Kaufingerstraße 24, 80331 München, Germany

www.ingramcontent.com/pod-product-compliance
Lightning Source LLC
LaVergne TN
LVHW080804011026
849160LV00015B/1525
* 9 7 8 0 7 6 5 6 3 6 7 4 4 *